The Routledge International Handbook of Perpetrator Studies

The Routledge International Handbook of Perpetrator Studies provides the first comprehensive overview of this emerging interdisciplinary field in the humanities and social sciences. Featuring contributions by scholars from a wide variety of fields and disciplines, the Handbook charts the growth and development, foundations, key debates, core concerns, and frontiers of Perpetrator Studies. Focusing on genocide, terrorism, and other forms of political mass violence, this Handbook addresses questions of guilt and responsibility, definition, terminology, typology, motivations, group dynamics, memory, trauma, representation, and pedagogy. Offering a thematic and conceptual approach that facilitates a comparative analysis across historical, geographic, and disciplinary lines, the Handbook allows different disciplinary perspectives to confront one another. In so doing, this foundational volume presents contemporary perspectives on longstanding debates whilst providing new contributions to the field. Written with an interdisciplinary readership in mind, the chapters provide an overview of existing work on a specific topic or issue, delineate current developments within the respective discipline or field, and make suggestions for further research. As such, the book will appeal to scholars across a range of disciplines, including history, sociology, anthropology, criminology, law, philosophy, memory studies, psychology, political science, literary studies, film studies, cultural studies, art history, and education.

Susanne C. Knittel is Assistant Professor of Comparative Literature at Utrecht University, the Netherlands. Her research focuses on questions of memory, commemoration, and cultural amnesia across cultures and media. She is the author of *The Historical Uncanny: Disability, Ethnicity, and the Politics of Holocaust Memory* and editor in chief of *The Journal of Perpetrator Research*.

Zachary J. Goldberg is Research Fellow in ethics and moral philosophy at Ludwig-Maximilians-Universität München. His most recent publications focus on the metaethics and normativity of evil action and theories of individual and collective moral responsibility. He is guest editor of *Midwest Studies in Philosophy* Vol. 36: *The Concept of Evil* and editor of *Reflections on Ethics and Responsibility: Essays in Honor of Peter A. French* (Springer 2017).

"This pioneering handbook does far more than most: it constitutes an entirely new object of inquiry: perpetrator studies. This Routledge handbook will long serve to define and set the agenda for this emerging field."

– *A. Dirk Moses, senior editor,* Journal of Genocide Research

"*The Routledge International Handbook of Perpetrator Studies* is a major accomplishment. The editors have assembled a comprehensive and cutting-edge volume on perpetration in all of its facets, bringing together prominent scholars from an impressively wide range of perspectives. Sophisticated, nuanced, and sobering, this will remain the definitive reference work for a long time to come."

– *Ernesto Verdeja, Kroc Institute for International Peace Studies, University of Notre Dame, France*

"'Never again' has not worked. We are really bad at preventing the invention and actions of perpetrators of mass violence. Therefore, the present handbook is an absolutely essential resource for all teachers, researchers, and students committed to the urgent task of peace education and de-radicalization. The Handbook is academia at its best!"

– *Wulf Kansteiner, Aarhus University, Denmark*

"This is a unique and pioneering collection. The impressive set of analyses across multiple disciplines opens up and gives shape to a new field of study. For anyone interested in genocide, the Holocaust, or mass violence, whether from a philosophical, anthropological, historical, sociological, or cultural perspective, this Handbook will be indispensable."

– *Simona Forti, author of* New Demons: Rethinking Power and Evil Today

"An essential resource for scholars and students, this Handbook covers the most pressing issues concerning the perpetration of mass violence. Cutting across disciplines, fields, and histories, it surveys key concepts and debates about theory and methodology and offers valuable pedagogical perspectives. Knittel and Goldberg have done a great service to the new field of Perpetrator Studies in putting together this volume."

– *Michael Rothberg, author of* The Implicated Subject: Beyond Victims and Perpetrators

The Routledge International Handbook of Perpetrator Studies

Edited by
Susanne C. Knittel and Zachary J. Goldberg

Routledge
Taylor & Francis Group
LONDON AND NEW YORK

First published 2020 by Routledge
2 Park Square, Milton Park, Abingdon, Oxon OX14 4RN

and by Routledge
605 Third Avenue, New York, NY 10017

First issued in paperback 2021

Routledge is an imprint of the Taylor & Francis Group, an informa business

British Library Cataloguing-in-Publication Data
A catalogue record for this book is available from the British Library

Library of Congress Cataloging-in-Publication Data
A catalog record has been requested for this book

ISBN 13: 978-1-03-208579-1 (pbk)
ISBN 13: 978-1-138-10324-5 (hbk)

Typeset in Bembo
by Integra Software Services Pvt. Ltd.

Contents

Contributors

Reva N. Adler is a retired Professor of Medicine at the Universities of Toronto and British Columbia. Since 2004, she has been the principal investigator on the violence prevention study *Addressing the Root Causes of Genocide* (ARC-G) in Rwanda and Sudan, funded by the Fulbright Scholarship Board and the US Institute of Peace. Dr. Adler has worked with numerous global organizations including the UN Special Rapporteur on Genocide Prevention, the Stockholm International Forum, The Global Futures Forum, the US National Intelligence Council, the Tenth and Fifteenth Rwandan Genocide Commemorations, and committees of the British Parliament.

Kjell Anderson is Assistant Professor of Law at the University of Manitoba and the director of the Master of Human Rights program. His scholarly publications focus on the causes and consequences of mass atrocities and span law, political science, history, sociology, and criminology. His book *Perpetrating Genocide: A Criminological Account* (Routledge 2018) is a comprehensive study of genocide perpetrators, based on qualitative interviews in Rwanda, Burundi, Uganda, Bosnia, Bangladesh, and Cambodia. His next book, on former LRA commander Dominic Ongwen, is under contract with Rutgers University Press.

Jonathan Luke Austin is Lead Researcher at the Violence Prevention (VIPRE) Initiative of the Graduate Institute of International and Development Studies, Geneva. His work has been published and/or is forthcoming at *European Journal of International Relations, International Political Sociology, Review of International Studies, Security Dialogue*, Cambridge University Press, and beyond.

Lane Benjamin is a clinical psychologist and a post-doctoral fellow in the Department of Historical Trauma and Transformation at Stellenbosch University. As founder and former director of an NGO, CASE (Community Action towards a Safer Environment) in Hanover Park, South Africa, she has worked with victims and perpetrators of violence. In 2006, Lane was awarded an Ashoka fellowship for her psychological work in marginalized communities. She facilitates trauma-informed processes of healing through her consultancy, Restore Reconnect Rebuild (R-Cubed), which works alongside diverse individuals and communities to address violence and trauma within a context of extreme poverty and inequality.

Clare Bielby is Senior Lecturer in Women's Studies at the University of York, UK. Her research focuses on gender, violence, and representation, particularly in the context of the Federal Republic of Germany. She is the author of *Violent Women in Print: Representations in the West German Print Media of the 1960s and 1970s* (Camden House 2012) and co-editor (with Anna Richards) of *Women and Death 3: Women's Representations of Death in German Culture since 1500* (Camden House 2010) and (with Jeffrey Murer) of *Perpetrating Selves: Doing Violence, Performing Identity* (Palgrave 2018).

Stephanie Bird is Professor of German Studies at University College London. She has published on topics ranging from the interaction of fact and fiction in the biographical novel, female and national identity, and the representation and ethics of shame. Her latest book, *Comedy and Trauma in Germany and Austria after 1945*, explores the significance of the comical in German-language cultural representations of suffering. It analyses how the comical interrogates the expectations and ethics of representing suffering and trauma, integrating a critique of dominant paradigms, such as that of trauma and of victim identity. She is currently working on an interdisciplinary project on the representation of perpetrators of Nazi violence.

Rick Crownshaw teaches in the Department of English and Comparative Literature, Goldsmiths, University of London. He is the author of *The Afterlife of Holocaust Memory in Contemporary Literature and Culture* (Palgrave Macmillan 2010), the editor of *Transcultural Memory* (Routledge 2014), and co-editor of *The Future of Memory* (Berghahn 2010, 2013). He is currently working on a monograph, *Remembering the Anthropocene in Contemporary American Fiction*, which focuses on the potential of cultural memory and trauma studies in representing climate change, extinction, the resourcing of war, American petrocultures, and post-oil imaginaries.

Teun van Dongen is an independent author and researcher in the field of terrorism and (inter)national security. His personal website is www.teunvandongen.com. Also, he is currently a lecturer at Leiden University.

Kári Driscoll is Assistant Professor of Comparative Literature at Utrecht University in the Netherlands. He is the editor, with Eva Hoffmann, of *What Is Zoopoetics? Texts, Bodies, Entanglement* (Palgrave Macmillan 2018), with Kiene Brillenburg-Wurth and Jessica Pressman, of *Book Presence in a Digital Age* (Bloomsbury 2018), and, with Susanne Knittel, of "Memory after Humanism," a special issue of *Parallax* (2017). His current research project, funded by the Dutch Research Council (NWO) is entitled "Reading Zoos in the Age of the Anthropocene."

Mark A. Drumbl is the Class of 1975 Alumni Professor at Washington & Lee University, School of Law, where he also serves as Director of the Transnational Law Institute. He lectures, practices, and publishes widely in the area of international criminal law, post-conflict justice, and public international law. He is the author of *Atrocity, Punishment, and International Law* (Cambridge University Press 2007) and *Reimagining Child Soldiers in International Law and Policy* (Oxford University Press 2012), and co-editor of the *Research Handbook on Child Soldiers* (Elgar 2019). He has additionally taught at Oxford, Paris, Melbourne, Monash, Ottawa, and the VU Amsterdam.

Hilary Earl is Professor of European History at Nipissing University, Ontario, Canada. Her research and teaching interests include comparative genocide, war crimes trials, perpetrator testimony, and the cultural impact of genocide in the twenty-first century. She has published in a variety of journals and essay collections, and she is the author of the award-winning *Nuremberg SS-Einsatzgruppen Trial, 1945–1958: Atrocity, Law, and History*. She co-edited *Lessons and Legacies XI: Expanding Perspectives on the Holocaust in a Changing World* (2014) and the

Wiley Companion to the Holocaust (2019). She is currently making a documentary on Nazi perpetrators.

Paul Formosa is an Associate Professor in the Department of Philosophy and a member of the Centre for Agency, Values and Ethics at Macquarie University in Sydney. He is the author of many journal articles and book chapters on evil, Kantian ethics, moral psychology, and moral and political philosophy. He is also the co-editor of *Politics and Teleology in Kant* (2014) and the author of *Kantian Ethics, Dignity and Perfection* (2017) with Cambridge University Press.

Melike M. Fourie holds an MSc in cognitive neuropsychology from University College London (2006) and a PhD in neuroscience from the University of Cape Town (2011). Melike is trained in both experimental neuroscience (including neuroimaging and psycho-physiological techniques) and clinical neuropsychology. Her research interests fall within the domains of social and affective neuroscience, focusing on how social emotions like guilt, shame, and empathy motivate or detract from adaptive social behavior. Melike is a senior researcher leading the neuroscientific investigation of empathy in Studies in Historical Trauma and Transformation at Stellenbosch University.

Mary Fulbrook, FBA, is Professor of German History at UCL. Recent publications include *Reckonings: Legacies of Nazi Persecution and the Quest for Justice* (OUP 2018); *A Small Town near Auschwitz: Ordinary Nazis and the Holocaust* (OUP 2012); and *Dissonant Lives: Generations and Violence through the German Dictatorships* (OUP 2011). Previous books include: *The People's State: East German Society from Hitler to Honecker* (Yale UP 2005); *Anatomy of a Dictatorship: Inside the GDR, 1949-89* (OUP 1995); *Historical Theory* (Routledge, 2002); *German National Identity after the Holocaust* (Polity 1999); and overviews of German history. She is currently directing an AHRC-funded project on perpetration and complicity.

Christina Gerhardt is Senior Fellow at the University of California at Berkeley and Associate Professor at the University of Hawai'i at Manoa. She has been awarded grants by the Fulbright Commission, the DAAD, and the NEH; she has held visiting positions at Harvard University, Columbia University, and the Free University in Berlin. She guest edited "Adorno and Ethics," a special issue of *New German Critique* 97 (2006) and has authored numerous articles on nature and animals in the writings of Adorno, Horkheimer, and Kracauer and Cixous, Derrida and Levinas.

Stephen Gibson is a social psychologist based at York St John University, UK. His research interests are in the areas of dis/obedience, social identity, and citizenship and the representation of peace and conflict. He is the author of *Arguing, Obeying and Defying: A Rhetorical Perspective on Stanley Milgram's Obedience Experiments* (Cambridge University Press 2019), and editor of *Discourse, Peace and Conflict: Discursive Psychology Perspectives* (Springer 2018).

Zachary J. Goldberg is Research Fellow in ethics and moral philosophy at Ludwig-Maximilians-Universität München. His most recent publications focus on the metaethics and normativity of evil action and theories of individual and collective moral responsibility. He is guest editor of *Midwest Studies in Philosophy* Vol. 36: *The Concept of Evil* and editor of *Reflections on Ethics and Responsibility: Essays in Honor of Peter A. French* (Springer 2017).

M.J. Grant (University of Edinburgh) is a musicologist who has published widely on the sociology and historical anthropology of music and violence, particularly with regard to war, genocide, and torture. From 2008-2014 she led the research group "Music, Conflict and the State" at the University of Göttingen and in the academic year 2014-15 was a fellow at the Centre of Advanced Study in Law as Culture at the University of Bonn. She is currently writing a book on the musicology of war, for which she received funding from the Harry Frank Guggenheim Foundation.

Adam Henschke is a senior lecturer at the National Security College, Australian National University. His research covers the intersection of ethics, technology, and national security. He writes on ethical theory, cyber-security, military ethics, surveillance, privacy, and bioethics. His publications include *Ethics in an Age of Surveillance: Virtual Identities and Personal Information*, 2017 (Cambridge University Press), *Binary Bullets: The Ethics of Cyberwarfare*, 2015 (co-edited with Fritz Allhoff and Bradley Strawser, Oxford University Press) and the *Routledge Handbook of Ethics and War*, 2013 (co-edited with Fritz Allhoff and Nicholas G. Evans, Routledge).

Rebecca Jinks is Lecturer in Modern History at Royal Holloway, University of London. Her first book *Representing Genocide: The Holocaust as Paradigm?* was published by Bloomsbury in 2016. Since then, she has been working on a project entitled "Marks Hard to Erase," about female survivors of the Armenian genocide and international humanitarian responses to them.

Susanne C. Knittel is Assistant Professor of Comparative Literature at Utrecht University in the Netherlands. She is the author of *The Historical Uncanny: Disability, Ethnicity, and the Politics of Holocaust Memory* (Fordham UP 2015; German translation *Unheimliche Geschichte: Grafeneck, Triest, und die Politik der Holocaust-Erinnerung* Transcript 2018) and the editor, with Kári Driscoll, of "Memory after Humanism," a special issue of *Parallax* (2017). Her current research focuses on the figure of the perpetrator in contemporary memory culture. She is the founder of the Perpetrator Studies Network and editor-in-chief of *JPR: The Journal of Perpetrator Research.*

Stefan Kühl is professor of sociology at Bielefeld University. His research interests include social theory, organizational sociology, interaction sociology, industrial and work sociology, professional sociology, and the history of science. His publications include *Ordinary Organizations. Why Normal Men Carried Out the Holocaust.* (Polity Press 2016); *Soziologische Analysen des Holocaust. Jenseits der Debatte über "ganz normale Männer" und "ganz normale Deutsche"* (with Alexander Gruber, Springer 2015); *For the Betterment of the Race. The Rise and Fall of the International Movement for Eugenics and Racial Hygiene* (Palgrave Macmillan 2013); *The Nazi Connection. Eugenics, American Racism and German National Socialism* (Oxford UP 1994).

rashné limki has spent the past nearly two decades as an economic migrant in the US and UK. Her present place in the UK is secured through academic work at the University of Edinburgh. Her thinking and writing focuses mainly on the ethics and politics of work in a global context. In particular, she is interested in the role of difference in the emergence and distribution of new forms of work. Beyond her academic commitments, she has worked as a facilitator and mediator for community and activist organizations and has particular interests in issues of housing, homelessness, and migrant justice.

Emil Lundedal Hammar is a PhD Candidate at UiT – The Arctic University of Norway. His research interests include game studies, memory studies, critical race theory, the political economy of communication, anti-imperialism, critical and materialist approaches to media, and postcolonialism. Emil's research project focuses on the intersection of digital games, cultural memory, and hegemony with particular attention to race and the political economy of historical games.

Erin McGlothlin is Associate Professor of German and Jewish Studies at Washington University in St. Louis. Her research focuses on Holocaust literature and film and German-Jewish literature. She is the author of *Second-Generation Holocaust Literature: Legacies of Survival and Perpetration* (2006) and co-editor of three volumes, most notably *Persistent Legacy: The Holocaust and German Studies* (2016, with Jennifer Kapczynski), and *Inventing According to the Truth: Claude Lanzmann's* Shoah *and its Outtakes* (2020, with Markus Zisselsberger and Brad Prager). She is currently finishing a book project titled *Constructing the Mind of the Holocaust Perpetrator in Fictional and Documentary Discourse.*

Brianne McGonigle Leyh is Associate Professor at the Netherlands Institute of Human Rights (SIM) at Utrecht University, specializing in human rights and global justice, with a focus on victims' rights, transitional justice, social justice, and documentation of serious crimes. She is a member of the Montaigne Research Centre on Rule of Law and Administration of Justice, an executive editor of the Netherlands Quarterly of Human Rights, and is responsible for the education stream of the Centre for Global Challenges, which is a center supporting and encouraging study and research on international issues across the humanities and law at Utrecht University.

David Mendeloff is Associate Professor at the Norman Paterson School of International Affairs (NPSIA) and Associate Dean (Academic) of Public Affairs at Carleton University in Ottawa, Canada.

Saira Mohamed is Professor of Law at the University of California, Berkeley, School of Law. Her research focuses on responses to mass atrocity. Examining the roles of criminal law and armed force in preventing and stopping widespread violence, her work considers the meaning of responsibility in mass atrocity crimes and seeks to unsettle conventional conceptions of choice and participation in this context. Her most recent articles have appeared in the *California Law Review, Columbia Law Review*, and *Yale Law Journal.*

Leigh A. Payne is Professor of Sociology and Latin America at the University of Oxford. Her research focus is on responses to past atrocities. She has written about transitional justice, memory, corporate complicity in past violence, confessions of perpetrators of state violence, and contemporary disappearances in countries that have transitioned from authoritarian rule and armed conflict. She is currently working on a companion volume to her award-winning book *Unsettling Accounts: Neither Truth nor Reconciliation in Confessions of State Violence* (Duke University Press, 2008) that examines confessions to violence by the armed left, tentatively titled *Left Unsettled.*

Diana I. Popescu is Research Fellow at Birkbeck, University of London. Her doctorate in Holocaust studies (University of Southampton) focused on representations of perpetrators in visual art. Her research interests are in public reception and mediation of the Holocaust in contemporary art, museums, and memorials. Popescu is co-investigator of a major research project *Making the Past Present: Public Perceptions of Performative Holocaust Commemoration,* funded by Swedish Research Council; and co-editor with Tanja Schult of *Revisiting Holocaust Representation in the Post-Witness Era* (Palgrave Macmillan 2015). She currently serves on the editorial board of *Genocide Studies and Prevention: An International Journal (GSP).*

Holger Pötzsch is Associate Professor in Media and Documentation Studies at UiT – The Arctic University of Norway. His main research interests are the cultural construction of self and other in audio-visual media with a particular focus on film and digital games, border studies, and critical approaches to digital technologies. His work has been published in a variety of academic journals, handbooks, and edited volumes. He is currently co-editing the anthology *War Games: Memory, Militarism, and the Subject of Play* (Bloomsbury 2020) with Phil Hammond.

Alasdair Richardson is a Senior Lecturer at the University of Winchester (UK) and Programme Leader for the Professional Doctorate in Education. He teaches on a number of initial teacher training courses at the postgraduate level, having been a school teacher for many years himself. His research centers on the teaching and learning of sensitive issues, particularly Holocaust Education (with a focus on the role emotion plays in students' engagement with the topic of the Holocaust, survivor testimony, and site visits). Correspondence should be sent to alasdair.richardson@winchester.ac.uk

Robert Skloot is Professor Emeritus of Theater and Drama at the University of Wisconsin-Madison. He is the author and editor of many books and essays about the theater of the Holocaust and genocide, including *The Darkness We Carry: The Drama of The Holocaust* (1988) and the two-volume anthology *The Theatre of the Holocaust* (1981; 1999) and *The Theatre of Genocide: Four Plays about Mass Murder in Rwanda, Bosnia, Cambodia and Armenia* (2008). Skloot's play, *If the Whole Body Dies: Raphael Lemkin and the Treaty Against Genocide* (2006), has been read around the US and internationally. The play's website is www.ifthewholebodydies.com.

Uğur Ümit Üngör is Associate Professor at the Department of History at Utrecht University and Research Fellow at the NIOD Institute for War, Holocaust, and Genocide Studies in Amsterdam. His main area of interest is mass violence in the Middle East. His most recent publication includes *Genocide: New Perspectives on Its Causes, Courses and Consequences* (Amsterdam University Press 2016, ed.). He is an editor of the *Journal of Perpetrator Research* and coordinator of the *Syria Oral History project* at NIOD. He is currently completing the monograph *Paramilitarism: Mass Violence in the Shadow of the State* (Oxford University Press forthcoming 2019).

Margaret Urban Walker is Donald J. Schuenke Chair in Philosophy Emerita at Marquette University. She is author of *Moral Understandings: A Feminist Study in Ethics*; *Moral Contexts; Moral Repair: Reconstructing Moral Relations after Wrongdoing*; and *What Is Reparative Justice?* Margaret Walker's work focuses on post-conflict and transitional justice, moral repair, and reparations. She has published many articles on reparations and reparative truth-telling in the aftermath of conflict, repression, and historical injustice and has been an invited contributor to research projects with the International Center for Transitional Justice. She currently lives in New York.

Jessica Wolfendale is Professor of Philosophy at Marquette University. She is the author of *Torture and the Military Profession* (2007), co-editor of *New Wars and New Soldiers: Military Ethics in the Contemporary World* (2011), and has published numerous articles and book chapters on topics including security, torture, terrorism, bioethics, and military ethics. Her work has appeared in journals including *Ethics and International Affairs*, *Journal of Political Philosophy*, *Studies in Conflict and Terrorism*, and the *Journal of Military Ethics*. Her most recent book, *War Crimes: Causes, Excuses, and Blame* (co-authored with Matthew Talbert), was published by Oxford University Press in 2018.

Michalinos Zembylas is Professor of Educational Theory and Curriculum Studies at the Open University of Cyprus. He is also Honorary Professor at Nelson Mandela University. He has written extensively on emotion and affect in relation to social justice pedagogies, intercultural and peace education, human rights education, and citizenship education. His recent books include *Psychologized Language in Education: Denaturalizing a Regime of Truth* (with Z. Bekerman) and *Socially Just Pedagogies in Higher Education* (co-edited with V. Bozalek, R. Braidotti, and T. Shefer). In 2016, he received the Distinguished Researcher Award in "Social Sciences and Humanities" from the Cyprus Research Promotion Foundation.

Foreword

Critical Perpetrator Studies

Alexander Hinton

There's a Medusa in the room.

I begin with this warning, which is also an invitation to critique—and to a critical perpetrator studies.[1] Indeed, the story of Medusa is a cautionary tale, even an uncanny one. It also offers lessons about critique that are critical to the emerging field this Handbook seeks to envision.

Given the recent explosion of literature on perpetrators, this volume argues, we can now speak of Perpetrator Studies—which, if often driven by Holocaust and later by genocide studies, is linked to the ascendancy of "the victim" (which requires the perpetrator and vice versa), terrorism and security studies, legalism, and transitional justice. We currently have a *Journal of Perpetrator Research*, related conferences and seminars, a growing body of perpetrator scholarship, and now a Handbook.

Not surprisingly, given the nascent form of Perpetrator Studies, critique usually has been pushed to the background. Indeed, field-building projects are haunted from the start by the ghosts of genealogical predecessors, seen and unseen—the "forefathers," "mothers," siblings, and missing kin.

Related dilemmas pose difficult questions for any new field. Who are "we" ("our" community of scholars)? What, exactly, is our object of study? What are the boundaries of our field? What is "new" about it? And why now?

These are the sorts of questions that this volume seeks to answer even as it begins to grapple with the Medusa in the room, the hard to see, terrifying, and uncanny conceptual specters that turn fields to stone. Indeed, as soon as field-defining questions are posed, the obfuscations—and Medusa's hauntings—begin.

For questions, so seemingly innocent, are directives, sometimes commands, to answer in a particular way. Socrates complained about the Sophists, but he had a more silvery tongue, the First Poser, asking questions that led out of the cave of deception in a specific direction—to Truth. Medusa didn't follow. She remained in the cavernous ruins below, Plato's ghost, haunting his Truth and garden of formal stone.

A critical Perpetrator Studies searches for such specters. It can begin by asking what the field-defining questions mask. Who are "they" (those who don't belong to this analytical community)? What have "we" excluded by creating certain sorts of conceptual boundaries?

What aren't we studying? And who hasn't been invited into our scholarly room ("our field") with its brightly lit surfaces and walls? Medusa, for one, lacks an invitation, though she's present, usually unseen, lingering in the shadows, dark corners, dividing lines, and thresholds of inside and out—the shuttered windows and locked doors.

Usually people remain frozen in place, unaware that Medusa is present. If they catch her trace, they quickly suppress the thought, petrified once more. Others, like Perseus, glare at her indirectly (he uses the reflective surface of his shield) before seeking to destroy that which causes fear and unease (Perseus: avenger of the statues of stone). But he too ended up frozen in place, a perpetrator, then fulfiller of a parricide fated, and finally fixed in place as a constellation in the stars.

But there is a third path: afacement,[2] an open and direct (as opposed to Perseus's distanced and effacing) gaze, even amidst the fear and unease. Hélène Cixous took such a look and saw Medusa laughing at a trembling Perseus, an act of subversion that inspired Cixous's critical feminist vista on Medusa and phallogocentrism. Almost all of the stone statues in Medusa's garden, Cixous noted, were men who had come to slay her, including Freud, his aegis emblazoned with "castration anxiety."

This third path of afacement has much to offer the critical Perpetrator Studies scholar who is willing to search for Medusa in dark, uncanny spaces and look her directly in the eye. One place to start is in what's foregrounded and backgrounded by the field's name, which provides its conceptual umbrella, protective yet insular, creating borders and boundaries that blind. Indeed, the field is predicated on a first binary that desperately needs unpacking. For "the perpetrator" looms as moral legalism,[3] signaling a moment of (too often individualized) action directed against an (over-individualized) innocent other, "the victim."

Scholarly explanation has often followed this "first binary" of Perpetrator Studies: the perpetrator as sadist, regression, savage, bureaucrat, role-taker, willing zealot, and, in the current and long-standing dominant paradigm, the bland, homogeneous "ordinary man" (Medusa was glimpsed briefly, and we soon had "ordinary women" added to this garden of stone).

This is an oversimplification of the state of affairs, one discussed in the introduction and other chapters in this volume, and one I address in my book *Man or Monster? The Trial of a Khmer Rouge Torturer*, but it highlights the need for a critical Perpetrator Studies. Indeed, such critique might start by decentering the "ordinary men" paradigm.

What might a critical Perpetrator Studies look like? Medusa can help us here. At first glance, the Perseus myth in which she is framed is a straightforward moral story. An evil monster (Medusa the murderer), responsible for petrifying legions of innocents, is brought to justice by hero Perseus's blade, an act warranted by the Gods—a just ending to a perpetrator tale.

Like all stories set in sanitized Disney form, this popular narrative occludes complicated histories and moral dilemmas, ones manifest in the ancient versions of the story ranging from Hesiod to Ovid.[4] As Cixous suggested, gender and sexual danger provide a key subtext as do the issues of moral violence, good and evil, and, of course, perpetration.

In some tellings, such as Ovid's, Medusa was a beautiful woman who lay with—or was raped by—Neptune (Poseidon) in Minerva's (Athena's) temple. Minerva, in turn, cursed Medusa, making her hideous with hair full of snakes and deadly eyes. There's more. Medusa kills people, Perseus kills her, and then Perseus uses Medusa's head to petrify foes he later battles (today Perseus would be accused of perpetrating atrocity crimes!).

When these other mythic strands are taken into consideration, what was a simple perpetrator-victim binary (Medusa and her petrified victims, even if there is usually little mention of the fact that many of these "victims" had come to slay her)—the sort that is preferred in courts of law and straightforward academic analysis—quickly becomes a muddled mess of ambiguous actions committed against the backdrop of complicated histories. The Medusa in the room or at least one of them: just as there are many snakes in Medusa's hair, so too are there many places of analytical petrification.

Medusa can be a guide towards critique and a critical Perpetrator Studies (or at least a less petrified one). Among other things, and as suggested above, Medusa suggests the unseen, the trace, the repressed, the uncanny, the potential for a suppressed excess to overrun. Or, to reframe things in more academic prose, Medusa symbolizes the redactions we make as we articulate our realities, often in binary form. That which has been edited out persists as a redactic trace, a haunting excess threatening to dehisce and explode, disrupting the articulated frame.[5] In popular culture, the Incredible Hulk—a monstrous and usually suppressed potentiality that exists within otherwise diminutive Dr. Banner and suddenly dehisces as he "bursts" into Hulk form—provides a more graphic sense of this idea.

So the critical Perpetrator Studies scholar must turn from easy articulation, like the perpetrator–victim binary or perpetrator–victim–bystander triad (add the rescuer and you have a Perpetrator Studies quartet), and search for the Medusas in the room. To what extent has perpetrator scholarship done so? This volume is interesting in this regard.

On the one hand, *The International Handbook of Perpetrator Studies* seeks to codify such a canon, as illustrated by the topics and authors it includes. Indeed, the editors' ambition to make the case that Perpetrator Studies has arrived is made clear in their introduction and their framing of the field. The introduction is followed by a first canonizing section on "Core Concepts and Key Debates" that takes up issues of definition (delimiting the field's purview and object of study as well as the history that gave rise to it), conceptualization (typologies, theories, interdisciplinarity, and key characteristics), and dynamics (process and motivation).

On the other hand, the *Handbook* seeks to subvert itself in a sense, by pressing the boundaries of the very field it seeks to constitute. If aporetic, this secondary endeavor is a soft-spoken one, since the more disruptive chapters—on interesting topics ranging from music and the subaltern to Actor-Network Theory—are emplotted within the nascent field of Perpetrator Studies while potentially destabilizing it.

Indeed, canons are petrifying, fixing our gaze in particular directions and creating blind spots, gaps, and erasures. My field, anthropology, has its own minor Perpetrator Studies canon that points to some potential gaps in Perpetrator Studies, such as issues of translation, local knowledge, and the cultural dimension of perpetration.[6] The editors of this handbook point to more.

Accordingly, the *International Handbook of Perpetrator Studies* navigates the tension between canon and innovation nicely, serving both as robust invitation to Perpetrator Studies research and, more tentatively, to a search for the Medusa in the room—a self-critique of the incipient field it seeks to elucidate. And so this foreword is intended as a small dehiscence, an eruption of the sort of conceptual messiness new fields of study often background and redact. It is to the credit of this volume that it also points to such critique.

The time for critical Perpetrators Studies, however, may not quite have arrived. Medusa awaits regardless. She's not going anywhere. At some point, Perpetrator Studies will begin a robust search for the Medusas in the room. Lacking Perseus's magic, the critical Perpetrator Studies scholar undertakes a quest that that will always be incomplete. But it is one worth pursuing since we can still catch glimpses of Medusa while exploring the ruins of her Perpetrator Studies lair. To do otherwise is to risk being turned to stone.

And this is precisely the petrifying danger of field-founding and canonization. This volume offers points of entry for a critical Perpetrator Studies. So, as you read on and consider the interesting chapters in this landmark volume, I urge you to also constantly look for the Medusa in the room.

Notes

Acknowledgments: I'd like to thank Susanne Knittel, Zachary Goldberg, and Nicole Cooley for their helpful comments and suggestions on this essay.

1 For the wide range of questions, issues, and controversies opened by the Medusa myth, see the essays in Garber and Vickers (2003).

2 On "afacement," a now obsolete word suggesting stance of openness (to the other), see Hinton (2016).

3 *Oxford English Dictionary*, 3rd ed., s.v. "perpetrator, *n*.": "A person who perpetrates something, esp. a crime or evil deed."

4 See the ancient retellings of the Medusa myth collected in Garber and Vickers (2003). Indeed, these multiple iterations are another expression of the fact that Medusa invites deconstruction and critique and part of the reason so many critical theorists, ranging from Benjamin to Derrida, have revisited the myth—often from contrary perspectives such as Cixous's feminist critique of Freud's psychoanalytic interpretation.

5 On articulation, redaction, the redactic, dehiscence, and the related idea of thick frames of power, see Hinton (2016). I have also explored these ideas through notions of the "transitional justice imaginary" and "justice facade" in the companion volume, *The Justice Facade: Trials of Transition in Cambodia* (2018).

6 For a related review, see Hinton (2015); Hinton (2005); and Hinton (2002).

References

Garber, Marjorie & Nancy J. Vickers (eds.). 2003. *The Medusa Reader*. New York: Routledge.

Hinton, Alexander Laban. 2002. *Annihilating Difference: The Anthropology of Genocide*. Berkeley: University of California Press.

Hinton, Alexander Laban. 2005. *Why Did They Kill? Cambodia in the Shadow of Genocide*. Berkeley: University of California Press.

Hinton, Alexander Laban. 2015. "Violence." In *A Companion to Moral Anthropology*, edited by Didier Fassin, 500–518. Malden, MA: Wiley-Blackwell.

Hinton, Alexander Laban. 2016. *Man or Monster? The Trial of a Khmer Rouge Torturer*. Durham, NC: Duke University Press.

Hinton, Alexander Laban. 2018. *The Justice Facade: Trials of Transition in Cambodia*. Oxford: Oxford University Press.

Introduction

Susanne C. Knittel and Zachary J. Goldberg

The *Routledge International Handbook of Perpetrator Studies* charts the growth and development, foundations, key debates, and core concerns of Perpetrator Studies, an emerging interdisciplinary field in the humanities and social sciences. The past two decades have witnessed a mounting interest in the study of perpetrators and perpetration of genocide, terrorism, and other forms of political mass violence. Scholars working in fields as diverse as History, Law, Criminology, Sociology, Anthropology, Political Science, Psychology, Philosophy, Memory Studies, Literary Studies, Media Studies, Cultural Studies, Gender Studies, Critical Race Studies, and Art History have examined a broad range of issues related to the figure of the perpetrator, including questions of guilt and responsibility, terminology, typology, motivations, group dynamics, memory, trauma, and representation. Taken together, these studies present a mosaic of the politics, ethics, aesthetics, and juridics of collective violence, the conditions for its emergence, the processes of its unfolding, and the long shadow of its aftermath. Perpetrators and evildoers have of course always been a powerful source of fascination and abhorrence in the popular imagination, and scholars working in all the aforementioned fields and disciplines have engaged not only with such figures and their acts, but also with this fascination. In this sense, the study of perpetrators and perpetration has a very long history within specific disciplines. In the past decade, however, it has become increasingly interdisciplinary and comparative, to the extent that one can now speak of Perpetrator Studies as a field in its own right, with a shared set of key theories and concepts. Over the same period, there has been a palpable "turn" to the perpetrator in other areas outside the academy, for instance in civic education in schools, at memorials and in museums, in human rights activism, police training, genocide prevention programs, as well as in art, theater, documentary filmmaking, literature, and other cultural arenas. While it is still vital to honor, commemorate, and listen to the victims and survivors of genocide, oppression, and political violence, it has become increasingly apparent that one cannot understand the root causes of such injustice without paying sufficient attention to the actors who carry out or are complicit in such acts.

There are historical and cultural reasons for this turn to the perpetrator. On the one hand, in the context of recent genocides and the so-called war on terror, there has been an increased preoccupation with collective violence and especially with questions of guilt and responsibility, which has gone hand in hand with a deconstruction of the categories of perpetrator, victim, and bystander. The category of the perpetrator has proven to be perplexing and resistant to strict circumscription. Simplistic conceptions of perpetrators as evil or monstrous contrasted with ordinary victims and bystanders have proven inadequate and counterproductive. Ordinary people participate, often quite willingly, in the perpetration of mass atrocities, and it is clear that these subject positions exist on a spectrum and that specific individuals may occupy different and contradictory positions on that spectrum at different times and in different contexts. Culturally, the master-narrative of good and evil, heroes and villains that informed the rhetoric of the Cold War in the East and the West has become untenable, despite recurring attempts to resurrect it, for instance in the wake of 9/11. The erosion of these established binaries is visible especially in the representation of perpetrators in the media and in popular culture (television, cinema, videogames), where stereotypical depictions have increasingly given way to more nuanced, ambiguous, or multifaceted representations. A more negative sign of this erosion is the ongoing rehabilitation of Fascism and the normalization of extremist views and rhetoric in the public sphere. Given this current political, cultural, and historical juncture, it is all the more important that we critically re-examine categories such as perpetrator, bystander, and victim and seek to understand the processes, dynamics, and motivations behind different forms of political violence.

The theoretical and conceptual foundations of Perpetrator Studies as a field lie in the response to Word War II and the Holocaust. Although it goes without saying that genocide, political violence, and mass atrocity are fundamental features of human history in all regions of the world, stretching back far beyond the Twentieth Century, the Holocaust was a watershed in the public and academic understanding of perpetrators and perpetration. In other words, there have always been perpetrators, but Perpetrator Studies as such begins in 1945. The Nuremberg Trials saw the first large-scale investigations into the psyche and motivations of perpetrators of state violence and shaped the discourse on perpetrators, legal and moral accountability, and crimes against humanity, a concept that was coined in response to the Holocaust. The basic theoretical vocabulary of Perpetrator Studies is a product of the discourse on the Holocaust: terms such as "the Nuremberg defense," "the banality of evil," and *Schreibtischtäter* (desk perpetrator) are now used to theorize perpetrators also in other contexts, just as the Milgram and Zimbardo experiments not only continue to inform discussions on complicity and obedience to authority more generally, but are themselves objects of scientific replication and artistic re-enactment in the present day. Interviews with Nazi perpetrators, such as those conducted by Gitta Sereny, provided a blueprint for later interviews with perpetrators of other genocides. The debates in the 1980s and '90s regarding the (in)comparability of the Holocaust (the so-called *Historikerstreit* or historians' quarrel), functionalism versus intentionalism, and the ordinariness or extraordinariness of the Nazi perpetrators (encapsulated in the Browning-Goldhagen debate) had a lasting impact on the study of perpetrators of genocide well beyond the Nazi context and continue to haunt current debates. The Holocaust and its perpetrators thus continue to serve as a major frame of reference for the field of Perpetrator Studies, and this fact is reflected also in the present *Handbook*, which, although it aims to be as broad and comprehensive as possible, nevertheless has a strong emphasis on the Holocaust and includes chapters that cover these key moments and debates in the development of the field.

Since there has been no shortage of political mass violence, state terror, ethnic conflicts, and terrorism since 1945, these initial concepts, theories, and approaches have been developed further by subsequent empirical and theoretical research. The killing fields of Cambodia, the genocides in Rwanda, the former Yugoslavia, and Darfur, torture in Abu Ghraib, and the ongoing perpetration of atrocities by Islamist militias in the Middle East and in Africa, as well as extreme right-wing terrorism in the West are only a few of the events and contexts that continue to shape the field by raising new questions and challenging accepted conclusions.

This *Handbook* offers a thematic and conceptual approach that facilitates a comparative analysis across historical, geographic, and disciplinary lines with the aim of allowing different disciplinary perspectives to confront one another. The humanities and the social sciences both have an important role to play in understanding and addressing the issues pertaining to perpetrators and perpetration, and it is precisely the confrontation between disciplines that generates new concepts, insights, and, crucially, new questions that might not have arisen within a mono-disciplinary setting. Perpetrator Studies is a fundamentally inter- and cross-disciplinary field and hence, in designing this *Handbook*, we have endeavored to juxtapose diverse disciplinary methodologies and concerns, rather than organizing it along traditional disciplinary lines or exclusively on a case-study basis. It would not have been feasible to include a chapter on each and every instance of genocide and political violence, purely in terms of space, nor would it have been conducive to the aims of this *Handbook*, which are primarily methodological, theoretical, and conceptual.

The basic questions that Perpetrator Studies as a field must ask fall into two categories. First, the determination of the object of study. What is Perpetrator Studies the study of? Here we find questions of terminology and taxonomy. A defining feature of Perpetrator Studies, like other interdisciplinary fields, is its critical questioning and problematization of the very term that gives it its name. Who or what is a perpetrator? Who decides? How is such a label applied and by whom? How do such labels evolve? What are the means and ends of perpetration? How do different societies conceive of acts of political or mass violence? In this first category, we find questions of motivation, ideology, agency, processes and dynamics, as well as questions of prevention. What drives people to commit acts of political violence and genocide, and how do these acts unfold? What measures can be taken to identify potential perpetrators before they act, and what can be done to prevent genocidal situations from occurring? What can be done to rehabilitate perpetrators after the fact? Another set of questions that fall under this first category pertains to the status and significance of the perpetrator as a discursive formation in legal, political, historical, philosophical, and cultural settings. How do societies come to terms with acts of perpetration and with the perpetrators themselves? What role does the figure of the perpetrator play in the popular imagination? How do representations of perpetrators change over time and across geographical and cultural boundaries as well as across different media, genres, and traditions? How do schools, memorials, museums, and other educational institutions teach about perpetrators? In sum, the first category is concerned with what perpetrators *are* and what they *mean*.

Having established the objects of study, there remains the question of method and theoretical and conceptual framework. How does Perpetrator Studies study perpetrators? What can we learn from studying perpetrators and perpetration that cannot be learned by focusing on the victims of genocide and mass violence, for example? What are the ethical and moral implications of studying perpetrators? How do ethical considerations influence the methodological and theoretical criteria of the inquiry? How can established and emerging theories, approaches, and methodologies from the humanities and social sciences be brought to bear on the study of perpetrators and, conversely, what can a focus on perpetrators and perpetration add to these theories and methodologies? How does one address the inherent ambiguity, limitations, and contentiousness of labels such as "perpetrator," "bystander," and "victim" and the strategic and political implications of their application? And what is at stake in comparing acts of perpetration from different historical and socio-cultural contexts? Such questions are especially important to ask in a field that defines itself by its interdisciplinarity.

The aim of this volume is threefold: First, to give an overview of the field, its history, and its essential and foundational concepts and approaches; second, to bring Perpetrator Studies into conversation with other interdisciplinary fields of inquiry, in order to generate new perspectives, insights, and questions; third, to explore future avenues of research at the frontiers of Perpetrator Studies. The contributing authors represent a wide variety of disciplinary perspectives. Some are established scholars in Perpetrator Studies whose work has been instrumental in shaping the field. Others are from fields outside Perpetrator Studies.

In putting together this *Handbook*, we invited all contributors to address questions from both of the aforementioned categories from the perspective of their home discipline or field. Each chapter provides an overview of existing work on the specific topic or issue, delineates current developments within the respective discipline or field, and makes suggestions for further research. Each chapter is equipped with a comprehensive bibliography that serves as a resource, and is written with an interdisciplinary readership in mind. The chapters offer a clear and concise articulation of the core questions and concerns animating the approach in question and how it can be relevant to other fields of study.

The *Handbook* is divided into two main parts: I. Core Concepts and Key Debates, and II. Intersections. Part I comprises three sections and covers the fundamental concepts and concerns of the field, as well as its most influential and enduring debates. The first section addresses questions of definition and terminology and gives an account of the shift in perspective from the study of perpetra*tors* to the study of perpetra*tion*. The second section, "Group Dynamics and Moral Psychology," is concerned with key approaches to understanding perpetrators' psychology and motivations and addresses questions of agency and responsibility, group behavior, obedience to authority, evil and ordinariness, authoritarianism, and torture. The first part concludes with the section "Perpetrators and the Law," which gives an overview of the history and effectiveness of the legal mechanisms erected to tackle the perpetration of atrocities.

Part II consists of four sections that explore existing and potential intersections between Perpetrator Studies and other interdisciplinary fields. In the section "Perpetrators—New Theoretical Approaches," Perpetrator Studies is brought into conversation with Gender Studies, Actor-Network Theory, Postcolonial Studies, Animal Studies, Musicology, Information Theory, and Ecocriticism. The chapters in "Aftermaths: Responsibility, Trauma, and Memory" deal with questions of responsibility, accountability, trauma, reintegration, and prevention, from the perspective of philosophy, psychology, public health, and law. The third section, "Perpetrators and Representation," moves to questions of the representation of perpetrators in the cultural sphere, with chapters on literature, theater, art, film, and video games.

The volume concludes with a section entitled "Teaching about Perpetrators." This consists of shorter position papers written by scholars in fields such as law, literary studies, education, curriculum studies, and memory studies, in whose pedagogy the question of the perpetrator plays an important role. Education is fundamental to Perpetrator Studies. As Theodor W. Adorno wrote in his 1966 essay "Education after Auschwitz," the "premier demand upon education is that Auschwitz not happen again." This task begins with teaching about perpetrators. We must also understand the role of education both in preventing and in facilitating atrocities, in other words, how perpetrators are educated. In sum, Part II both widens and deepens the scope of the field by juxtaposing many of the core issues from Part I with concepts and methodologies from different disciplines, raising new questions that challenge traditional assumptions and attitudes about perpetration, its aftermath, and its representation, and identifying new areas of research. It is our hope that this volume will serve as a resource for scholars, students, and educators alike.

Part 1
Core Concepts and Key Debates

1.1 Definitions and Terminology

1

From Perpetrators to Perpetration

Definitions, Typologies, and Processes

Uğur Ümit Üngör and Kjell Anderson

Introduction

In the past two decades, research on mass atrocities and genocides has shifted its perspective from the study of *perpetrators* to *perpetration*. Whereas the former term refers to the agency of individuals who have perpetrated forms of mass violence against civilians, the latter concept refers to the process of collective commission of mass violence. The advantage of taking a processual view is that it enables us to address the complexity of the process of perpetration: different layers of authority, different motives of involvement, different intentionality, and most importantly, the changes in these factors over time.

This shift from perpetrators to perpetration has coincided with the emergence of Perpetrator Studies as a nascent sub-discipline. Recent research ranges from anthropological and oral historical "thick description" (Hinton 2005; Jessee 2017) to sensitive micro-historical and political studies (such as Bergholz 2016; Fujii 2009; McDoom 2008; Straus 2006). We will not delve here into the possible reasons for the relative historical absence of perpetrators from genocide studies, except to say that perpetrator research can be conceptually, normatively, and empirically challenging.

This chapter surveys the state of perpetrator research in the social sciences and history by examining the definition of perpetrators, typologies of perpetrators, and the process of perpetration. We approach perpetration from three distinct analytical perspectives: top level (architects), mid-level (organizers), and bottom level (killers). Through this framework, we also delve into key debates with the field such as: What types of people become perpetrators? Are individual perpetrators pathological, or are they shaped by their social context? Is perpetration driven by hate, economic factors, or obedience to authority?

Contemporary research emphasizes the complexity, fluidity, and contingency of perpetration. This has important implications for the ways in which we define perpetrators and approach perpetrator research.

Defining the "Perpetrator"

For our purposes, a perpetrator can be defined as any individual who contributes directly and substantially to genocide (or other mass atrocities). While this definition is informed by substantive international criminal law concepts of genocide, crimes against humanity, and war crimes (such as those found in the Rome Statute of the International Criminal Court 1998), we choose not to be strictly limited by legal taxonomies. Genocide, as defined in the Genocide Convention and Rome Statute, emphasizes that perpetrators must have specific intent, *the intent to destroy* the group, yet many of those who contribute directly to genocide may lack this intention (Anderson 2018, 238–243).

International legal definitions are largely the product of treaty negotiations between states, thus these definitions are shaped by political compromise. Ethnic, racial, religious, and national groups are included in the Genocide Convention, ostensibly because they are "permanent and stable," yet it is debatable that any of these groups is permanent or stable. Furthermore, there is often a divergence between socio-historical and legalistic concepts of perpetrators, as lawyers undertake the categorization of perpetrators according to the logic and boundaries of criminal law, while social scientists and historians often favor broader interpretations that encompass all socially similar cases, as defined by the researcher and the research objectives.

Our definition also goes beyond direct perpetrators to encompass categories of complicity (those who substantially contribute to atrocities) while still excluding notions of "collective responsibility."[1] In defining perpetrators, we must also consider that perpetrators perform diverse acts with diverse motivations. High-level perpetrators, such as leaders, often do not "get their hands dirty" through direct perpetration. Accordingly, one might expect different considerations to apply to indirect perpetration (i.e., planning or ordering atrocities). Moreover, different forms of mass atrocities involve different types of perpetration and perpetrators. Perpetrators of genocide, for example, can range from Nazi bureaucrats to Rwandan farmers to (arguably) teachers in Canadian residential schools. The farther one gets from killing, the less likely individuals are to self-identify, or be characterized by others, as perpetrators.

Bearing this diversity in mind, we will focus herein on perpetrators who directly and substantially contribute to mass killing. Our point of departure is that perpetrators remain a vital category for social, legal, and historical analysis. The emergence of Perpetrator Studies has rightfully challenged static views of "the perpetrator" as being a social category with fixed boundaries, yet it would be equally misleading to study genocide or mass atrocities without differentiating between the agents of genocide and their victims. Who are the perpetrators, and how and why do they perpetrate?

Who Are the Perpetrators?

Genocide and mass atrocities involve, by their very nature, atrocious behavior. In a narrow sense, genocide only requires killing, the prevention of births, or other acts that directly effectuate the crime. Yet, perpetrators often go beyond mere killing to act with entrepreneurial cruelty: their victims are humiliated, dehumanized, and tormented as part of the destruction of the victim group. This "excessive" violence is not incidental to the crime of genocide; rather, it arises from its very nature as a crime involving the destruction of an ethnic, religious, national, or racial group. Such a far-reaching social project requires ideological justification: the victims must be destroyed because of *who they are*, their fundamental essence. What kinds of people perpetrate these acts of extreme cruelty?

The idea that criminals are different from "ordinary" people goes back to Cesare Lombroso and the roots of criminology (1891). Criminologists have advanced a broad range of explanations for criminal behavior, which, broadly speaking, can be grouped into theories positing that criminal behavior is inborn (*nature*), and theories arguing that criminal behavior is learned (*nurture*). Many contemporary theories of crime combine these two paradigmatic perspectives in nuanced ways to show that some individuals may have inborn characteristics that predispose them to criminal behavior, but that most individuals will not become criminals without an element of socialization (Wikström 2004). Yet, it is questionable how well these traditional criminological explanations relate to genocide, where perpetration is systematic, politicized, and generally endorsed by legitimate authorities. The nature of genocide as a state crime challenges many criminological presumptions, which assume that crimes and criminal behavior are deviant acts, thus that the perpetrators themselves are deviant.

This apparent paradox of genocide perpetrators as non-deviant criminals is a thread running through Perpetrator Studies. While popular perceptions and representations of perpetrators are often villainous caricatures, researchers have long grappled with the seeming ordinariness of perpetrators. At the Nuremberg Tribunals, two men were tasked with psychological examinations of the accused: psychologist Gustave Gilbert and psychiatrist Douglas Kelley. While both Gilbert and Kelley concluded that the defendants were psychologically fit for trial, they reached quite different conclusions regarding the psychological bases for their acts. In interpreting the same set of Rorschach Tests, Gilbert classified all the defendants as psychopathic personality types: schizoid, narcissistic, and paranoid (Joyce 2009, 18). He argued that the defendants were raised in a kind of pathological German culture, emphasizing blind obedience to authority (a theme that was later picked up by Adorno, Frenkel-Brunswik, Levinson, and Sanford in their book *The Authoritarian Personality* 1950). Kelley, on the other hand, emphasized the ordinariness of the Nuremberg defendants; he argued that authoritarian governments and genocide were possible even in the United States, because genocide was neither cultural nor a result of insane leaders; rather, it was a social phenomenon.

In the long run, Kelley's view seems to have predominated, not only in the case of the Nuremberg defendants, but also in Perpetrator Studies more generally (see, for example, Zillmer et al. 1989). Hannah Arendt, in her touchstone analysis of the trial of Nazi bureaucrat Adolf Eichmann, wrote of "the banality of evil" when reflecting on Eichmann's apparent lack of individual pathology or ideological commitment (Arendt [1963] 2006). Similarly, Christopher Browning concluded, in his study of the Holocaust perpetrators in Reserve Police Battalion 101, that most perpetrators were "ordinary men" (Browning 1998, a view that was contradicted in Daniel Goldhagen's controversial book *Hitler's Willing Executioners*, 2001).

More recent studies of perpetrators tend to eschew the ordinary/pathological dichotomy to emphasize the multidimensionality of perpetrators and perpetration. They argue, as we do here, that there is no single paradigmatic genocide perpetrator. Rather, perpetrators perpetrate for a variety of reasons, and their acts of perpetration are often contingent rather than rooted in enduring circumstances or personal characteristics. Social psychological experiments, such as the Stanford Prison Experiment, further reinforce the conclusion that "power of the situation" is more important than the pathology of individuals (Zimbardo 2007).

As an outgrowth of this recognition of the variability of perpetrator motivations, researchers have sought to develop typologies of perpetrators. Rather than identifying paradigmatic general perpetrator characteristics, these typologies group perpetrators according to characteristics and motivations.

These tend to focus on the motives and motivations of perpetrators, including, for instance, economic gain, ideological commitment, sadism, conformism, or fear. As an example, sociologist Michael Mann's typology includes:

1. *Ideological killers* [who believe in the "righteousness of murderous cleansing"]
2. *Bigoted killers* [who "share the prejudices of their social environment"]
3. *Violent killers* [who "experience violence as a release"]
4. *Fearful killers* [who kill out of fear]
5. *Careerist killers* [who work for organizations involved in atrocities and participate to further their career interests]
6. *Materialist killers* [who are motivated by economic gain]
7. *Disciplined killers* [who kill to conform with directives]
8. *Comradely killers* [who kill to conform with their peer group]
9. *Bureaucratic killers* [who are situated within bureaucracies and motivated by "habitual obedience"]

(Mann 2005)

Mann's distinction here between ideological and bigoted killers (types one and two) is interesting, distinguishing in some sense between those motivated by "high" or "low" ideology. Smeulers takes a similar overall approach, while also emphasizing the importance of leaders (criminal masterminds) as a distinct category (2008). Genocide and crimes against humanity are atrocity crimes, yet it is important to remember that other kinds of crimes may also involve leaders and followers, some of whom may be predisposed to lead violence, and others who follow out of a sense of duty or coercion. McDevit, Levin, and Bennett's typology of hate crime perpetrators (2002), for example, also includes "leaders" (who initiate violence), "fellow travelers" (who go along with violence), and "unwilling participants" (who may be passively involved in violence yet do nothing to stop it). Interestingly, their typology also includes "heroes" (what genocide scholars might term "rescuers"), illustrating the need for typologies to also consider the relationships between perpetrators and other actors.

Despite these common conceptions of "types" of perpetrators, there is still a relative lack of research into how perpetrators come to exhibit the various distinguishing characteristics. Are individual dispositions inborn? Alternatively, if they are a product of an individual's experience and socialization, what factors produce each type of perpetrator? Smeulers approaches this issue by arguing that pre-perpetration types also influence types during perpetration. For example, "law-abiding citizens" may become "conformist" perpetrators, while borderline types (those who are marginalized but not criminals) may be "profiteers," and "criminals" (those with a record of violence) may become "sadist" perpetrators during mass atrocities. Further research is certainly needed in this area, although there is evidence that genocide perpetrators tend to be men in their thirties without prior criminal records. This means that genocide perpetrators are atypical, when compared to perpetrators of other violent crimes, who tend to be younger men, and who may have a history of violence (Brehm et al. 2016).

There may be a more general concern with typologizing perpetrators: individuals do not always neatly fall within the boundaries of a given type. In our daily lives, our motivations are not singular. For example, we may take a job because it is lucrative, while also finding it interesting. The motivations of individual perpetrators are not fixed; rather, they shift in response to changing perspectives and circumstances. Individuals may be sadistic ideologues or greedy conformists. They may join genocide because they feel obligated, but they may also seek material enrichment. For example, wealthy Tutsis were often attacked first during the Rwandan Genocide (Anderson 2018). Thus, the selection of these individuals by the perpetrators was likely based on both their ethnic identity and the prospect of looting their wealth. Individual motivations are multiple, layered, and fluid.

Accordingly, Anderson's perpetrator typology names "pathways" to perpetration rather than unchanging types, while Williams has developed a complex model based on individual actions, rather than enduring motivations or fixed roles (Anderson 2018; Williams 2018). Ultimately, typologies provide us with a useful but limited framework for understanding why perpetrators perpetrate.

From Perpetrators to Perpetration

Genocide perpetration is a complex process (Üngör 2019). As perpetrator typologies are limited in the ways indicated above, we propose shifting the focus from perpetrators to perpetration. Whereas the former term refers to the agency of the individuals who have perpetrated forms of mass violence against civilians, the latter concept refers to the process of collective commission of mass violence. This processual view enables us to address the complexity of the process of perpetration: different layers of authority, different motives of involvement, different rules of engagement, and changes in these factors over time. This section approaches perpetration as a socio-ecological model containing three distinct analytical levels—top level (architects), mid-level (organizers), and bottom level (killers)—and develops a temporal processual approach focusing on the power relations between groups of people, especially between perpetrators and victims, but also within the perpetrator group. Viewed in coherence, these three contextual layers are not simply piled on top of each other, but the largest contexts are often preconditions for the smallest ones. Without the macro context of the radicalization of the political elites, the violent measures against the victims would not have been conceived by mid-management, and ultimately countless individual perpetrators would not have murdered innumerable individual victims in micro situations of killing. In other words, in addition to the complexity of each level in itself, we must bear in mind the relevant connections among the three levels over time. Historically, the top level was studied extensively at first, to the exclusion of the low level, but this has changed as more fine-grained research has appeared on the mid level and micro level.

The temporal complexity of genocide is a main concern in the study of genocide perpetration. Only fairly recently have historians begun to examine how perpetration processes begin, develop, and end. Also, most importantly: how can we understand the transitions from crises to mass murder to aftermaths? These transitions are often turning points, where critical moral and political transgressions occur in a rapid progression of violent polarization. Comparative research on mass political violence suggests that once unleashed, it can develop its own dynamic and become nearly unstoppable by internal forces—reaching "relative autonomy." How this process has functioned in different genocides, and how we can draw responsible comparisons between them, should be a priority in mass violence research. We will now turn to a discussion of perpetration, starting from the macro level.

Macro-level Perpetration Processes

The macro level refers to the structures and the context of the political helm that wields authority inside a state and is responsible for the decision-making processes that launch genocide. At the macro level, two issues are key to understanding the beginnings of perpetration: power and ideology. To understand a period in which mass violence is perpetrated, it is important to understand how the political elite has been able to wield the state's apparatus(es) of coercion: police, army, militias, etc. The increasing concentration of power among political elites can be either the result of a creeping, long-term process, or, more often, a swift revolution. Once such bureaucratic overtake is that successful, political elites can be seduced by the very prospect of extreme power in carrying out political objectives with or without consent of the political and social groups in society. A broad research landscape deals with this level of analysis, and a plethora of publications has explored the motives of Hitler, Stalin, Mao, Pol Pot, Saddam Hussein, and others (Ezrow & Frantz 2011). Since perpetration of mass violence against civilians is the near-exclusive monopoly of authoritarian, dictatorial, and totalitarian regimes, the motives and moves of authoritarian leaderships are extremely important to understand. One theme that has sparked debates in this literature is extreme ideology: Communism, Fascism, Nazism, ethnic nationalism, and their syncretic forms. Scholars have argued that extreme ideologies have a penchant for mass violence due to their anti-liberal nature, flirtations with utopia, development of sharp in/out group dynamics, and permissiveness to the use of violence (Weitz 2005). Comparative volumes on Nazism and Stalinism, but also studies of ethnic nationalism, *Juche*, or Ba'athism, have advanced this sub-field (Geyer & Fitzpatrick 2009; Sassoon 2011; Sŏ & Suh 2013). Indeed, no understanding of the motives of top-level perpetrators would be complete without deep analyses of their ideological worldviews. Two important sub-topics at the macro level that relate to extreme power and extreme ideology are polarization and out-grouping.

First, the polarization of political elites is a good indicator of lower-level political violence. Whether we are dealing with an authoritarian state or a democratic one, the polarization of political elites, under specific conditions, often boils over into violence (Rapoport & Weinberg 2013). The polarization between Turkish and Armenian political elites before 1914 or between Serbian and Croatian elites before 1991, and the polarization of the Rwandan political landscape in the period 1990–1994 are somber but instructive examples of this process. As crisis struck these societies, it sparked the deterioration of relations between antagonistic political parties, which carried especially deadly potential because politics were ethnically polarized (Bieber & Galijaš 2014; Der Matossian 2014; Guichaoua 2015). Radicals on either sides, but especially those in positions of public office, came to perceive the leaders of the other political parties and movements as security liabilities for their own positions. As violent incidents grew, at some point political elites made a set of fateful decisions to arrest, detain, and ultimately murder the entire membership of these opposition parties, from top to bottom. These types of violent initiations are critical junctures that define the course of the macro level and thereby the entire genocide.

Furthermore, events at the macro level trickle down fast: as a result of political polarization at the macro level, citizens locally can come to imagine themselves as part and parcel of an overarching, bigger conflict, and in-groups/out-groups rapidly form. Jacques Sémelin has underlined the importance in genocidal processes of the construction of an imagined "internal enemy" (Sémelin 2007, 22–33). How is "out-grouping" constructed in the various cases we study? One line of thought places it in the context of long-term identity formation processes, in which the definition and demarcation of the in-group occur under serious inter-state and intra-state pressures, frequently causing crises of identity. During such crises, external enemies can be equated with internal groups accused of disloyalty by virtue of their supposed ethnic, religious, or political proximity to the outside force (Mylonas 2013). A second body of knowledge focuses on identity politics, especially on how collective identity entrepreneurs can purposefully construct an out-group as a dangerous, treacherous, deeply alien, and ultimately dehumanized enemy. Once in power, the Nazis rapidly and very effectively out-grouped German Jews; Ottoman Armenians went from the "loyal nation" to backstabbers within one turbulent year; Soviet citizens in the 1930s would wake up every morning to a different category out-grouped by Stalin; the rise and mainstream normalization of Islamophobia in the post-9/11 era is a good contemporary example (Wilmsen & McAllister 1996).

Once these conditions are in place, a (civil) war generally facilitates the transition into perpetration. The macro-level actors now move from the pre-genocidal phase into the genocidal phase. Two key issues here are the decision-making process and the emerging attitude of criminal conspiracy among the elites. Decision-making processes are deeply complex phenomena and much more detailed research is needed, since these events might well constitute the critical turning points in the entire process. What are top elites thinking of, and planning for, when they cross that threshold into massacre? We may infer a few generalizations from the research. First, decision-making on mass murder is without exception a secret process (e.g., all relevant Nazi, Soviet, and CUP documentation is shrouded in profound secrecy). There are reasons for this secrecy (Bergen 2009, 191–192), and it has at least two consequences: secrecy obstructs research, even decades after the killings, and secrecy becomes "visible" or understandable to the outside world only once the killings are well under way. A second allowable generalization would be that we have prudently stopped looking for smoking guns: explicit orders authorizing mass slaughter will not be found. Genocidal elites are generally intelligent enough not to compromise themselves in such written decrees, with very rare exceptions emanating from hubris (e.g., Stalin and Saddam Hussein). Macro-level analyses of perpetration demonstrate that political elites can get quite "comfortable" with their orchestration of mass murder. After the initial transgressions, organizing the killings becomes a routine that requires some special attention, some adaptations and innovations—but the killings nevertheless continue unabated.

There can be little debate that most genocidal regimes are those based on deeply authoritarian structures—all backed by the fist of enormously expansive violent apparatuses.[2] In the genocidal phase, regime type is important to analyze: How do genocidal elites manufacture compliance? How does complicity perpetuate the process of perpetration? The CUP dictatorship from 1913 to 1918 is a case in point. Although scholarship on it is developing rapidly, we know relatively little about it compared to other genocidal regimes. A series of studies by Şükrü Hanioğlu has sketched a compelling portrait of a ruthless, clandestine revolutionary cabal, an uncompromising party that visualized politics mostly as a dichotomy of friends versus enemies, applying terror, threats, and assassination to its "enemies." As time passed, all of this violence bore heavily on the party and radicalized it further (Hanioğlu 1995, 2001). Many of these analyses hold true for the Bolsheviks, the Khmer Rouge, or the Ba'athists in Iraq. The enormous concentration of executive power in the hands of these parties, from the moment of coup d'état on, made the exercise of violence on a mass scale possible. But these studies also offer a window into the *internal* dynamics of these elites. Milovan Djilas's classic *Conversations with Stalin* or Saddam Hussein's audio-taped meetings offer a glimpse into the world of the genocide-perpetrating elite (Djilas 1969).[3] It is a grim, suffocating universe of existential uncertainty, dark suspicion, mutual complicity, and utter misanthropy. We require greater depth (comprehensive empirical recreations) and breadth (implicit and explicit comparisons) of this particular phenomenon regarding macro-level perpetrators during genocides.

What happens to a genocidal elite after the killings end? Often there is a transition, peaceful or violent, and sometimes there is "normalization." More often, there is impunity and no punishment. Stalin, Hafez al-Assad, and Suharto presided over unprecedented mass murders in their respective countries but lived on unperturbedly and died natural deaths. It is likely that they got rid of incriminating evidence—documentary or forensic. In some cases, secret, compromising agreements are made and genocidal elites receive golden parachutes.[4] There is circumstantial evidence suggesting that Radovan Karadzić was offered immunity from prosecution at the Dayton Accords if he stepped down as President of the Republika Srpska. Idi Amin lived comfortably for decades in Saudi Arabia, and so did Mengistu in Ethiopia. The chances that contemporary criminal leaders such as Vladimir Putin, Narendra Modi, Bashar al-Assad, Kim Jong-Un, let alone American war criminals such as George W. Bush or Henry Kissinger, will ever be held accountable are very slim. Those who are held accountable, such as Slobodan Milošević or Charles Taylor, ultimately go through problematic trials that do not seem to deter future genocidal elites (Bloxham & Pendas 2010). The entire process of macro-level perpetration, from incipience to orchestration to post-violence life, requires particularly close attention to the transitions between phases and their relations with the lower levels.

Meso-level Perpetration Processes

The meso level consists of those developments right below the highest level: mid-level political and administrative elites, the internal agencies that assume the tasks to divide labor and organize the machinery of killing, the (para-)military bosses who press buttons, and the mechanisms of mass mobilization for the destruction of the victim group. It concerns the intra-societal context of the actual organization of mass violence. These processes are decisive for the deadly outcomes. Accordingly, not only does this level link the macro with the micro, but also it is here that the macro-level dynamics are interpreted and transformed within a society by various political actors and groups. It refers to the perpetrating agencies, including the culture and practice of organizing mass murder. How do previously non-genocidal and technocratic institutions, organizations, and agencies in a given state and society collaborate in genocide? How do otherwise politically uninvolved families make decisions, conduct business, and comport themselves in a genocidal process? How are city administrations taken over and steered towards genocidal destruction of some of their fellow citizens? And, how can we better understand the changing sociological and political relationships among different perpetrating clusters?

The scholarship on this level is scant but developing. Most monographs on perpetrators focus on the micro-level contexts of the actual killers. For example, Scott Straus defined perpetrators as "those who directly killed or assaulted civilians and those who participated in groups that killed or assaulted civilians" (Straus 2006, 102). The studies by James Waller, Roy Baumeister, Steven Baum, Dick de Mildt, Donald Dutton, and Dinah Shelton's *Encyclopedia of Genocide and Crimes against Humanity*, to name a few, largely concur with this view. With a few excellent exceptions, scholarship has largely neglected to examine the mid-management contexts, the intermediary agencies, and institutions that translate macro-level orders to the micro-level destruction. Books that deal with this level are gradually appearing. There is a rich literature on the meso-level Nazis, from economically minded arguments in Susanne Heim and Götz Aly's *Vordenker der Vernichtung* (1991) to Klaus-Michael Mallmann and Gerhard Paul's panoptic *Karrieren der Gewalt* (2004) and Mary Fulbrook's detailed *A Small Town near Auschwitz* (2013). Scholars working on other genocides, too, are beginning to deal with mid-level perpetrators, such as Thierry Cruvellier and Alexander Hinton who wrote books on the Cambodian prison director Duch (Cruvellier 2011; Hinton 2016).

A close look at most work on mass violence clearly identifies patterns of interaction between the macro and meso levels (e.g., in the recruitment of perpetrators, the coordination of murderous efforts, civil society initiatives towards assisting the genocidal apparatus, and the manufacturing of broad-based indifference towards the plight of the victims). On the other hand, an over-focus on the macro level may blind us to the autonomy and agency of these mid-level bureaucracies. Perpetration of mass violence is co-produced by a vast network of collaborating ministry officials, military officers, government functionaries, gatekeepers and caretakers, committees, civil servants, police commissars, career diplomats, party bosses, provincial judges, urban regulators, militia bosses, and many others. In principle, these men do not get their hands dirty.[5] The macro-level overseers are well aware they need these people to manage the many necessary tasks. Before the killings, the civil-bureaucratic and military takeover deeply polarize and purify this level of officials. Some stay in their positions if they reconcile the vague (but unmistakably murderous) designs of the new regime; others are either purged or leave on their own volition. This partly self-regulating and self-reinforcing process paves the way for the macro-level organizers to push through their plans and bolsters the political polarization mentioned in the previous section.

Genocides develop in shocks and fits, which the macro-level elites visit upon the meso-level agencies. The transition from the pre-genocidal to genocidal phase ushers two distinct processes for the meso-level perpetrators: practical organization and regional variation. The organization of perpetration requires a clear, functional, and effective division of labor, between the state's civil service system and its military industry—but also between the military and paramilitary actors in the state (Feldman & Seibel 2005). Throughout the perpetration process, these tensions remain pertinent and have a profound impact on the outcome of the genocide. Examples abound: whereas the various German agencies did not cooperate well during the invasion of France, they did much better during the invasion of the Soviet Union. The frequent conflicts between the Army of the Republika Srpska and the various Serb paramilitary groups in Bosnia are well documented in Ratko Mladić's diaries.[6] Whether these tensions are resolved or not, the meso-level officials have to deal with real constraints during the perpetration of the violence, such as shortages of resources and manpower, inter-agency competition, and conflicting priorities. Whoever resolves these problems most effectively is often granted benefits and rewards by the top brass.

The meso level is also confronted with a very common problem: regional variations in the perpetration of violence. After all, genocides are not undifferentiated campaigns in which simultaneous mass killing evolves the same everywhere in a country. Genocide is not an isomorphic phenomenon. Scholars have examined the relationship between central decision-making processes and the implementation of mass murder at the local level. In-depth research on how genocidal processes evolve at the meso level (province, district, city) has proven most fruitful. These studies can teach us a great deal about how local power shifts influence the course and intensity of genocidal processes, since we know that some genocides are more regionally varied than others. Local political or social elites can anticipate, expedite, intensify, or delay and resist processes of genocidal destruction directed from above. A micro focus can also follow the deterioration and ultimate disintegration of inter-communal relations in the face of external pressures, amidst drastically worsening security and life conditions for the victims. Possible explanations include the personal whims of the local power holders, the geographic conditions, the conduct of local elites, and structural factors such as proximity to the front, social stratification, settlement patterns, poverty and unemployment, population density of victim group, opportunity structures, etc. But which combination of factors accounts for what kind of variation in genocidal processes? For example, why did the eastern Drina valley (roughly along the line Bijeljina-Zvornik-Višegrad-Foča) see much higher levels of violence than the central-northern Tuzla region during the genocide in Bosnia? Why did the genocide in Rwanda's southern provinces develop at quite different speeds than in the northern provinces? Why did violence develop so quickly on Bali compared to Sumatra during the 1965–1966 Indonesian genocide? Only by addressing these meso-level issues comparatively can we aggregate our theoretical debates.

Regionally varying outcomes of mass violence are never mono-causal phenomena, but depend on a combination of factors. Discussions of regional heterogeneity have serious implications because they prompt us to reconceptualize "diversity" in genocide perpetration. For example, Henri Zukier identifies four important polarities in the scholarship on explaining Holocaust diversity: personal versus situational factors, center versus periphery, ideology versus pragmatism, and long-term planning versus short-term reactions. He argues that diversity is often seen as outcome, but diversity can also be part and parcel of the very process of genocide, especially in the complex interactions between center and periphery. Zukier concludes rightly: "The diversity of triggers still led to a uniformity of outcomes" (Zukier 2013). Most genocides do not have an equivalent of the Wannsee Conference, to resolve the pervasive divergence in the local implementation of state policies. It is often up to the Interior Ministry to coordinate the operations and synchronize the violent measures against the victims. These ministries or specialized agencies delegate the daily implementation of the destruction to its officials and officers, as well as civil administrators. Time and again, *provincial governors* seem to be highly relevant in steering policies, as many fine-grained provincial case studies demonstrate. A similar argument can be made for generals in military districts, as Jess Melvin convincingly demonstrates for Aceh during the 1965 Indonesian genocide (Melvin 2018). Much can be gained from the comparative examination of provincial and local factors that interfere in the process of perpetration. But it also confirms Zukier's point that even if genocides unfold on a twisted course, the result is generalized destruction—sooner or later.

How does a regionalized conceptualization of a genocide relate to its temporal understanding? This question requires a closer analysis than these pages allow, but suffice it to state here that there seems to be a certain conception of "communicating vessels" at play. Provincial studies on the Armenian and Rwandan genocides suggest that when a genocide is more intensive and extensive in one province, other provinces emulate those other provinces' violence bottom-up or are ordered to do so top-down. A breakdown of perpetration per province demonstrates "above-norm performers" and "under-norm performers." The underachieving provinces are often stimulated to emulate the best practices or benchmarks of the overachievers, leading perpetrators to move from their own provinces to other provinces and the victims to flee from the deadliest to less deadly areas. Regionalization is not simply a matter of territorial differentiation. It is closely related to the morphology of the organization, coordination, and implementation of the crime. Recent studies challenge the convention that genocides have uni-polar pyramidal structures. Increasingly, genocides are conceived as multi-polar processes: radicalization comes from within and without and emanates from different perpetrating *clusters*, such as civil and military organizations, the ruling cabals themselves, and local elites (Üngör & Polatel 2011). Competition and conflict among these sectors shape genocides.

One common, almost universal tension in genocide perpetration is that between military authorities and paramilitary structures. Perpetration is usually carried out by well-equipped, specialized, often paramilitary forces. Paramilitarism refers to clandestine, irregular armed organizations that carry out acts of violence against clearly defined civilian individuals or groups. It has immense importance for understanding the processes of violence that play out during ethnic conflicts, which often see the formation of paramilitary units that conduct counter-insurgency operations, scorched earth campaigns, and violence against civilians including genocide. Many studies of genocide have convincingly demonstrated the central role of paramilitaries in the perpetration of genocide (Alvarez 2006). Whether in democratic or authoritarian states, throughout the twentieth century paramilitaries have been responsible for widespread violations of human rights against civilians. States orchestrating mass violence spawn paramilitary units as a covert augmentation of state power for special purposes such as mass murder. Some key questions to ask in this context are: How and why were paramilitary forces organized and deployed? Why did they emerge, and what is the relationship between paramilitaries and other meso-level perpetrator clusters? The role of paramilitary groups has been studied extensively for some of the major cases of mass violence (Campbell & Brenner 2000). The SA and SS, for example, have extensive historiographies. There are good studies of the Rwandan *Interahamwe*, Serb paramilitary groups, the *Janjaweed* in Sudan, or the Hindu-extremist militias in Gujarat. A comparative reading of these studies offers unique insights into the "nuts and bolts" of perpetration, and studies of new conflicts should focus on these types of paramilitary groups, not as individual killers but as perpetrating clusters.

After the violence ends, examining the meso level is relevant for understanding the "perpetrator society." How did Turkey after 1915, Germany after 1945, Indonesia after 1966, and Serbia after 1995 fare? What happened to the perpetrating agencies? How did the state transform them, and how did they transform the state? The fate of the post-genocide perpetrator society depends on whether the perpetrating regime remains intact and continues to hold on to power, or whether it is toppled, deposed, and vetted. Joshua Oppenheimer's remarkable documentaries *The Act of Killing* and *The Look of Silence* show how these mid-level perpetrators ended up being promoted to governors, bureaucrats, and influential politicians with comfortable socio-economic positions (Oppenheimer 2012, 2014). A recent investigative journalism piece by *Der Spiegel* illustrated how, at the time of writing, this process is ongoing in Syria: those paramilitary groups who were most loyal to Assad since the beginning of the uprising in 2011 now enjoy immense privileges of political, economic, and military power (Schaap 2017). The prospects for vetting, punishment, or reconciliation are slim, in case the perpetrating regime gains the upper hand in the conflict and manages to remain an acceptable partner in the international community.

Micro-level Perpetration Processes

The micro level is the lowest socio-ecological level: the individuals who become involved in the genocidal process. At the micro level, motivations are often immediate and situational, rather than rooted in grand political projects. When we consider the role of ideology, we must examine the reasons an ideology has resonance for individual perpetrators. Individual radicalization (individual alignment with radical beliefs involving the use of violence to achieve political ends) occurs for myriad reasons, including self-interest, perceived marginalization, and, especially, fear. Fear is a force for the transformation of the social order. The individual perpetrator may be persuaded by propaganda demanding the upending of social rules (such as the prohibition on killing) if they believe that they personally and communally face an existential threat. Fear is generated primarily by projecting dangerous traits onto the victim group. Propaganda may transform individual worldviews; more importantly, it communicates expectations from the macro level, to the group, to the individual perpetrator.

Perpetration at the micro level is characterized by the coming together of diverse motivations in contribution to the collective enterprise of genocide. The key question then is how individual interests align with (or diverge from) collective policies.

Our knowledge of the micro dynamics of genocide has increased greatly in recent years. This turn to the micro level encompasses archival studies of genocide at the local level, as well as interview-based research with perpetrators, victims, and bystanders of genocide. Through a variety of methodological approaches, researchers have shed light on the complexities and nuances of genocidal processes.

Works like Browning's *Ordinary Men* show us that perpetrators do not uniformly accept orders to commit genocide. This is perhaps the most important insight of micro-level research: individuals do not uncritically act based on clear orders; rather, they operate in contexts of limited information, often interpreting orders and exhortations in ways that advance their own interests. Both Kalyvas, in his work on civil war, and Fujii, in her work on genocide, argue that the mobilization of mass violence involves substantial scope for local interpretation (in Fujii's metaphor, scripts are provided by the center, which are then interpreted by local-level power holders) (Fujii 2009, 124). Violence from below is more likely to occur where power is decentralized (e.g., where local control is greater). As Bergholz notes, local control also brings about unexpected consequences for the central power, such as massacres and atrocities in times and locations not ordered, and the killing of the wrong categories of people (Bergholz 2016, 319). Erroneous targeting or reluctance to participate in genocide at the local level is sometimes overridden by national authorities. For example, a Hutu in the Rwandan genocide received orders from his local mayor to "watch over" a group of Tutsis. He was later admonished by a soldier from outside the district who said, "Are you crazy? You don't have to watch them; Tutsis are your enemy. You kill them, not just watch them" (Anderson personal interview, 2009). The greater the degree of local autonomy, the more room there is at the local level for improvisation, but such improvisation will always occur within problematic principal-agent relationships (Anderson 2018, 153; Mitchell 2004, 45).

Micro-level accounts are important in restoring agency to perpetrators and victims alike (Frydel 2017, 22). Low-level perpetrators do not necessarily share the motivations and intentions of leaders. Blattman's research on "death marches" during the Holocaust and Grabowski's research on the "hunt for the Jews" both demonstrate that individual perpetrators may participate in a hateful campaign without being primarily motivated by ideological radicalization (Blatman 2011; Grabowski 2013). Brehm and Fujii both question the importance of ideology as a determinant of participation in the Rwandan Genocide (Brehm 2017; Fujii 2009), while Bergholz, similarly, draws from the case study of Kulen Vakuf in Bosnia to argue that "ethnic hatred" is not always a prerequisite of genocide, rather violence itself generates such hatred (Bergholz 2016). Moreover, individuals who lack ideological commitment may still act against their neighbors out of feared consequences (Frydel 2017, 14; Kalyvas 2006, 330–364).[7]

The primary micro-level processes involved in perpetration are the desensitization of the perpetrators and the dehumanization of the victims by the perpetrators. These dualistic processes produce the social distance necessary for genocide. Perpetrators are desensitized through gradual habituation to violence (what James Waller terms "escalating commitments"), as well as the transformation of the normative landscape by legitimate authorities (Waller 2002, 205–207). The repetition of perpetration is facilitated by perpetrator habituation, positive reinforcement, and other coping mechanisms (Anderson 2018, 199–209). Both during and after perpetration, perpetrators will reframe their behavior in ways that minimize the moral wrongfulness of their acts (Alvarez 1997; Anderson 2017).

Perpetrators, like other persons, interpret their options based on their position within society and their individual experiences and characteristics. The interaction between positionality and perceived options has three facets: the *social margin of discretion* (the range of perceived options based on the society in which the perpetrator lives, particularly in terms of the level of coercion and mass participation in perpetration), the *role margin of discretion* (the individual's range of options according to roles within society, such as occupation, gender, and age), and, finally, *the immediate margin of discretion* (the individual's options based on factors in the immediate environment of perpetration). These immediate factors include things like group dynamics (the individual is more likely to perpetrate in a supportive group), the presence of authority figures compelling violence, and the use of intoxicants (Anderson 2018, 133–138). Perhaps most fundamentally, there must be a power differential between perpetrator and victim.

A multilevel approach is required to fully address the complexities of genocide. Saul Friedlander rightfully calls for an "integrated history" bringing together micro-level accounts and macro-level political developments (Friedländer 2010). An integrated history would explain how macro-level political developments relate to the behavior of groups and individual perpetrators.

Conclusion: The Extraordinary Perpetrator Revisited

In the popular imagination, including media representations, perpetrators are often, if not exclusively, understood as extraordinary either by virtue of the acts they committed, or because of one or another disorder attributed to them. In these representations, the acts of perpetration are seen as having changed these human beings from ordinary to extraordinary. Slow-motion close-ups of their eyes accompanied by ominous music often set the stage for explicit characterization. The scholarship on perpetration has soundly criticized these approaches and debunked the myths surrounding the former killers. But we also seem to have taken a step beyond this refutation. As research on the post-genocidal lives of perpetrators increases, we see that their lives *are* often fundamentally and irreversibly changed by those extraordinary years, months, weeks, or days during which they were putting an end to the lives of defenseless human beings. Perpetrators may feel apart in knowing what it means to kill, even where their acts continue to be endorsed by the state. Yet, this apartness is rooted more in experience than in inborn characteristics. Killing is doubtlessly an extraordinary act, yet perpetrators are often not visibly marked by their extraordinary experiences; rather, they contend with their pasts in complex and contradictory ways. For example, Anderson interviewed a former Khmer Rouge prison guard and executioner in his home while he bounced a baby on his knee. This man signed an order to kill seven pregnant women and is accused of killing hundreds of individuals with a farm implement. Yet, on that day, in his house, he was a grandfather, a farmer, and a kindly man, seemingly no different from any other Khmer peasant. In that context, he felt uncomfortable speaking of his crimes and instead emphasized that he was a mere accomplice. However, on other days, such as when he was confronted by victims from the prison he guarded, he expressed shame over his killings. As an interviewee, he presented himself as an "ordinary" person, yet the victims knew him as a perpetrator.

Reinhard Heydrich, the Nazi perpetrator responsible for the coordination of the Holocaust, was "an extremely sensitive violinist who displayed a tenderness and sentimentality that deeply impressed his audiences" (Gerwarth 2012, 37). A painstaking biography of Saddam Hussein argues that the former Iraqi dictator "could be crying over his children while at the same time signing a death warrant for the execution of fifty people" (Coughlin 2005, 165–166). These examples are not to show an apparent puzzling tension between "barbarism" and "civilization" but to point out that much like every other human being, perpetrators have complex identities, both at one particular time and as a changing aspect of their lives, across time. "Killer" is only one dimension of their identity; perhaps "father," "sportsman," "musician," and "vegetarian" are others. There is an emergent consensus over the complex perpetrator—for example, recent and forthcoming edited volumes on perpetrators by Williams and Buckley-Zistel (2018), Smeulers, Hola, and Weerdestijn (2019), and Anderson and Jessee (2020) all highlight the tensions between victim and perpetrator identities. Just as individual pathways to perpetration vary, so do the effects of perpetration on the individual. The role they play as perpetrator is one of many, and it is precisely in that multifaceted identity that they are "ordinary men."

Notes

1 While there is a well-established body of philosophical literature focused on the design, ontology, agency, and moral responsibility of group agents, we are focused in this chapter on perpetrators as individuals.
2 But massacres in Indonesia, Turkey, Russia, Kenya, India, and Mexico do point out that we cannot dismiss these events so easily and must take seriously the occurrence of violence in fledgling democracies or societies in transition.
3 For a selection of transcripts from Saddam Hussein's meetings, see http://digitalarchive.wilsoncenter.org/collection/168/saddam-hussein-s-iraq/2 or http://crrc.dodlive.mil/collections/sh/
4 For a set of arguments on how genocides end, see http://howgenocidesend.ssrc.org (accessed May 7, 2017)
5 But there are examples of relatively high-ranking Nazis performing executions, like Theodor Eicke who executed Ernst Röhm.
6 *Untitled diary of Ratko Mladić*, 16 volumes (June 29, 1991–November 28, 1996), International Criminal Tribunal for the former Yugoslavia (ICTY), Prosecutor v. Radovan Karadzić, exhibits P01476-P01490.
7 See Kalyvas (2006) on what he calls "the sociology of denunciation."

References

Adorno, T. W., Else Frenkel-Brunswik, Daniel J. Levinson, & R. Nevitt Sanford. 1950. *The Authoritarian Personality*. New York: W. W. Norton.

Alvarez, Alexander. 1997. "Adjusting to Genocide: The Techniques of Neutralisation and the Holocaust." *Social Science History* 21(2): 139–178.

Alvarez, Alexander. 2006. "Militias and Genocide." *War Crimes, Genocide, & Crimes Against Humanity* no. 2: 1–33.

Aly, Götz & Susanne Heim. 1991. *Vordenker der Vernichtung: Auschwitz und die deutschen Pläne für eine neue europäische Ordnung*. Hamburg: Hoffmann und Campe.

Anderson, Kjell. 2017. "'Who Was I to Stop the Killing?' Moral Neutralization among Rwandan Genocide Perpetrators." *Journal of Perpetrator Research* 1(1): 39–63.

Anderson, Kjell. 2018. *Perpetrating Genocide: A Criminological Account*. London: Routledge.

Anderson, Kjell and Erin Jessee, eds. 2020. *Perpetrators of Mass Atrocities: Insights on Ethics, Methods, and Theory*. Madison: Wisconsin University Press.

Arendt, Hannah. [1963] 2006. *Eichmann in Jerusalem: A Report on the Banality of Evil*. New York: Penguin.

Bergen, Doris L. 2009. *War and Genocide: A Concise History of the Holocaust*. 2nd ed. Lanham, MDLand: Rowman & Littlefield.

Bergholz, Max. 2016. *Violence as a Generative Force: Identity, Nationalism, and Memory in a Balkan Community*. Ithaca, NY: Cornell University Press.

Bieber, Florian & Armina Galijaš, eds. 2014. *Debating the End of Yugoslavia*. London: Routledge.

Blatman, Daniel. 2011. *The Death Marches the Final Phase of Nazi Genocide*. Cambridge, MA: Belknap Press of Harvard University Press.

Bloxham, Donald & Devin Pendas. 2010. "Punishment as Prevention? The Politics of Prosecuting Génocidaires." In *The Oxford Handbook of Genocide Studies*, edited by Donald Bloxham & Dirk Moses, 617–637. Oxford: Oxford University Press.

Brehm, Hollie Nyseth. 2017. "Subnational Determinants of Genocidal Killing in Rwanda." *Criminology* 55(1): 5–31.

Brehm, Hollie Nyseth, Christopher Uggen, & Jean-Damascene Gasanabo. 2016. "Age, Gender, and the Crime of Crimes: Toward a Life-Course Theory of Genocide Participation." *Criminology* 54(4): 713–743.

Browning, Christopher. 1998. *Ordinary Men: Reserve Battalion 101 and the Final Solution*. New York: Harper.

Buckley-Zistel, Susanne & Timothy Williams, eds. 2018. *Perpetrators and Perpetration of Mass Violence: Action, Motivations and Dynamics*. London: Routledge.

Campbell, Bruce & Arthur Brenner, eds. 2000. *Death Squads in Global Perspective: Murder with Deniability*. New York: St. Martin's Press.

Coughlin, Con. 2005. *Saddam: His Rise and Fall*. New York: HarperCollins.

Cruvellier, Thierry. 2011. *Le maître des aveux*. Paris: Gallimard.

Der Matossian, Bedross. 2014. *Shattered Dreams of Revolution: From Liberty to Violence in the Late Ottoman Empire*. Stanford, CA: Stanford University Press.

Djilas, Milovan. 1969. *Conversations with Stalin*. London: Penguin.

Feldman, Gerald & Wolfgang Seibel. 2005. "The Holocaust as Division-of-Labor-Based Crime: Evidence and Analytical Challenges." In *Networks of Nazi Persecution: Bureaucracy, Business, and the Organization of the Holocaust*, edited by Gerald Feldman & Wolfgang Seibel, 340–360. New York: Berghahn Books.

Friedländer, Saul. 2010. "An Integrated History of the Holocaust: Possibilities and Challenges." In *Years of Persecution, Years of Extermination: Saul Friedländer and the Future of Holocaust Studies*, edited by Christian Wiese and Paul Betts, 21–30. London: Continuum.

Frydel, Tomasz. 2017. "The Devil in Microhistory: The 'Hunt for the Jews' as a Social Process." In *Microhistories of The Holocaust*, edited by Claire Zalc and Tal Bruttmann, 171–189. New York: Berghahn.

Fujii, Lee Ann. 2009. *Killing Neighbors: Webs of Violence in Rwanda*. Ithaca, NY: Cornell University Press.

Fulbrook, Mary. 2013. *A Small Town near Auschwitz: Ordinary Nazis and the Holocaust*. Oxford: Oxford University Press.

Gerwarth, Robert. 2012. *Hitler's Hangman: The Life of Heydrich*. New Haven, CT: Yale University Press.

Geyer, Michael & Sheila Fitzpatrick, eds. 2009. *Beyond Totalitarianism: Stalinism and Nazism Compared*. Cambridge: Cambridge University Press.

Goldhagen, Daniel. 2001. *Hitler's Willing Executioners*. New York: Vintage Books.

Grabowski, Jan. 2013. *Hunt for the Jews: Betrayal and Murder in German-Occupied Poland*. Bloomington: Indiana University Press.

Guichaoua, André. 2015. *From War to Genocide: Criminal Politics in Rwanda (1990–1994)*. Madison: Wisconsin University Press.

Hanioğlu, M. Şükrü. 1995. *The Young Turks in Opposition*. Oxford: Oxford University Press.

Hanioğlu, M. Şükrü. 2001. *Preparation for a Revolution: The Young Turks, 1902–1908*. Oxford: Oxford University Press.

Hinton, Alexander. 2005. *Why Did They Kill? Cambodia in the Shadow of Genocide*. Berkeley: University of California Press.

Hinton, Alexander. 2016. *Man or Monster? The Trial of a Khmer Rouge Torturer*. Durham, NC: Duke University Press.

Jessee, Erin. 2017. *Negotiating Genocide in Rwanda: The Politics of History*. London: Palgrave Macmillan.

Joyce, Nick. 2009. "In Search of the Nazi Personality." *Monitor on Psychology* 40(3): 18.

Kalyvas, Stathis. 2006. *The Logic of Violence in Civil War*. Cambridge: Cambridge University Press.

Lombroso, Cesare. 1891. "Illustrative Studies in Criminal Anthropology: The Physiognomy of the Anarchists." *The Monist* 1(3): 336–343.

Mallmann, Klaus-Michael & Gerhard Paul, eds. 2004. *Karrieren der Gewalt: Nationalsozialistische Täterbiographien*. Darmstadt: Wissenschaftliche Buchgesellschaft.

Mann, Michael. 2005. *The Dark Side of Democracy: Explaining Ethnic Cleansing*. Cambridge: Cambridge University Press.

McDevitt, Jack, Jack Levin, & Susan Bennett 2002. "Hate Crimes Offenders: An Expanded Typology." *Journal of Social Issues* 58(2): 303–317.

McDoom, Omar Shahabudin. 2008. *The Micro-Politics of Mass Violence: Authority, Security, and Opportunity in Rwanda's Genocide*. PhD diss, London.

Melvin, Jess. 2018. *The Army and the Indonesian Genocide: Mechanics of Mass Murder*. London: Routledge.

Mitchell, Neil J. 2004. *Agents of Atrocity: Leaders, Followers, and the Violation of Human Rights in Civil War*. Basingstoke: Palgrave Macmillan.

Mylonas, Harris. 2013. *The Politics of Nation-Building: Making Co-Nationals, Refugees, and Minorities*. Cambridge: Cambridge University Press.

Ezrow Natasha & Erica Frantz 2011. *Dictators and Dictatorships: Understanding Authoritarian Regimes and Their Leaders*. London: Continuum.

Oppenheimer, Joshua. 2012. *The Act of Killing*. London: Dogwoof Pictures.

Oppenheimer, Joshua. 2014. *The Look of Silence*. Austin, TX: Drafthouse Films.

Rapoport, David & Leonard Weinberg. 2013. *The Democratic Experience and Political Violence*. London: Routledge.

Sassoon, Joseph. 2011. *Saddam Hussein's Ba'th Party: Inside an Authoritarian Regime*. Cambridge: Cambridge University Press.

Schaap, Fritz. 2017. "Assad's Control Erodes as Warlords Gain Upper Hand." *Spiegel International*, March 8. www.spiegel.de/international/world/assad-power-slips-in-syria-as-warlords-grow-more-powerful-a-1137475.html

Sémelin, Jacques. 2007. *Purify and Destroy: The Political Uses of Massacre and Genocide*. London: Hurst.

Smeulers, Alette. 2008. "Perpetrators of International Crimes: Towards a Typology." In *Supranational Criminology: Towards a Criminology of International Crimes*, edited by Alette Smeulers and Roelof Haveman, 233–265, 2003. Antwerpen: Intersentia.

Smeulers, Alette, Barbora Hola & Maartje Weerdesteijn, eds. 2019. *Perpetrators of International Crimes: Methodology, Theory and Evidence*. Oxford: Oxford University Press.

Sŏ, Chae-jŏng & Jae-Jung Suh, eds. 2013. *Origins of North Korea's Juche: Colonialism, War, and Development*. Lanham, MD: Rowman & Littlefield.

Straus, Scott. 2006. *The Order of Genocide: Race, Power, and War in Rwanda*. Ithaca, NY: Cornell University Press.

Üngör, Uğur Ümit & Mehmet Polatel 2011. *Confiscation and Destruction: The Young Turk Seizure of Armenian Property*. London: Continuum.

Üngör, Uğur Ümit 2019. "Perpetration as a Process: A Historical-Sociological Model." In *Perpetrators of International Crimes: Methodology, Theory and Evidence*, edited by Alette Smeulers, Barbora Hola, and Maartje Weerdesteijn, 117–131. Oxford: Oxford University Press.

Waller, James. 2002. *Becoming Evil: How Ordinary People Commit Genocide and Mass Killing*. Oxford: Oxford University Press.

Weitz, Eric. 2005. "Utopian Ideologies as Motives for Genocide." In *Encyclopedia of Genocide and Crimes against Humanity Vol. 3*, edited by Dinah L. Shelton, 1124–1127. Detroit, MI: Thompson Gale.

Wikström, Per Olof. 2004. "Crime as Alternative: Towards a Cross-Level Situational Action Theory of Crime Causation." In *Beyond Empiricism: Institutions and Intentions in the Study of Crime*, edited by Joan McCord, 1–37. New Brunswick, NJ: Transaction.

Williams, Timothy. 2018. "Thinking Beyond Perpetrators, Bystanders, Heroes: A Typology of Action in Genocide." In *Perpetrators and Perpetration of Mass Violence. Dynamics, Motivations and Concepts*, edited by Timothy Williams and Susanne Buckley-Zistel, 17–35. London: Routledge.

Wilmsen, Edwin & Paul McAllister eds. 1996. *The Politics of Difference: Ethnic Premises in a World of Power*. Chicago: University of Chicago Press.

Zillmer, Eric A., Robert P. Archer, & Robert Castino. 1989. "Rorschach Records of Nazi War Criminals: A Reanalysis Using Current Scoring and Interpretation Practices." *Journal of Personality Assessment* 53(1): 85–100.

Zimbardo, Philip G. 2007. "Revisiting the Stanford Prison Experiment: A Lesson in the Power of Situation." *The Chronicle of Higher Education* 53(30): B6–B7.

Zukier, Henri. 2013. "Diversity and Design: The 'Twisted Road' and the Regional Turn in Holocaust History." *Holocaust and Genocide Studies* 27(3): 387–410.

1.2 Group Dynamics and Moral Psychology

2

The Making and Un-making of Perpetrators

Patterns of Involvement in Nazi Persecution[1]

Mary Fulbrook

Under Nazi rule, far more people were "on the side of the perpetrators" than the few tens of thousands who were brought to court after the war. At least 200,000 people—perhaps nearer one million—were directly involved in atrocities against Jewish and other civilian victims (Bajohr and Pohl 2006, 9; Möller in Hartmann et al. 2005, 12). Significant numbers were involved in the civilian machinery of oppression and the (often fatal) exploitation of slave labor. Many more knew of atrocities, including mass shootings in the east, organized gassings, and "euthanasia" in institutions for the disabled. Millions engaged in everyday social relations entailing the stigmatization, exclusion, and degradation of others that paved the way for genocide. While some were motivated by ideological convictions or pragmatic careerism, others simply found it easier to conform or felt constrained to behave in ways in which they felt deeply uncomfortable. Violence in the Third Reich was embodied in more than just the physical brutality that has rightly been the primary focus of postwar trials, popular discourse, and Perpetrator Studies; rather, it extends to forms of structural and symbolic violence on a broader scale that ultimately made mass persecution possible.

Perpetration and Collective Violence

Perpetration in a system of state-ordained and state-sanctioned violence raises distinctive issues concerning guilt, agency, and a sense of responsibility. These cannot be considered in the same way as individually motivated acts. Some people were initiators and drivers of policy; many were propelled by enthusiasm for the Nazi project; others conformed out of peer-group pressure or fear of the consequences of refusal or were mobilized to act against their will. There were moments when people could have decided differently, although the leeway was far greater for some than for others; people sought in differing ways to justify their actions or quell inner disquiet. Later, most people who had been tainted by involvement in Nazi crimes refused to accept responsibility for actions committed under quite different circumstances. Psychopathologies of "criminals" and "deviants" will therefore not go far in explaining perpetration in a system where "deviance" would not have been a matter of committing a crime, but rather of refusing to do so.

Understanding perpetrators in collective violence cannot be merely a matter of exploring the biographies of key individuals who are prominent in the historical record, fascinating though these may be. Striking similarities in background, prior experiences, and generational patterns may indeed be perceived among key carriers of the Nazi regime; more generally, factors such as class, politics, religion, gender, educational attainment, generational experiences, and life stages do help to explain variations in patterns of involvement and susceptibility to mobilization (Herbert 1996; Wildt 2002; Fulbrook 2011). But the "making of perpetrators" has more to do with the historical conditions that brought Hitler to power and sustained him in power. Moreover, as Nazi policies became ever more radical, far greater numbers became involved in the practice of violence. Wartime conditions also fostered a sense of collective identity that could override moral scruples regarding victims who were not part of the "national community" (Stargardt 2015).

The understanding of perpetration in a system of collective violence therefore poses quite distinctive problems of explanation and interpretation. It requires us to think simultaneously about rapidly evolving political and social structures, changing circumstances of action, and individual responses to unprecedented challenges in the light of what were subjectively perceived as pressures, constraints, or opportunities. Some people seized what they saw as chances for personal advancement or material gain, while others were less willingly brought to do things about which they felt uneasy and that in other circumstances they would never think of doing.

In seeking to understand involvement in collective violence in a system that developed and changed radically over the course of a dozen years, no single explanatory framework can fit all cases. Nor indeed would most people in the areas considered below accept their designation as "perpetrators." Yet, without their cooperation and complicity, persecution and mass murder could not have been committed on the scale for which Hitler's rule has become infamous. Any historical analysis of involvement in Nazi persecution points to far wider circles of guilt and moral contamination than do narrower legal definitions, let alone self-designations, after the war.

Physical Violence

"Perpetrator research" has generally focused on two major categories: the principal architects, initiators, and drivers of Nazi persecution and the front-line executors of physical violence on the ground (cf. Matthäus in Stone 2004). Both groups were responsible for causing mass deaths, whether through directing, designing, and overseeing the actions of others or actually carrying out murderous policies in practice. Their involvement in policies, institutions, and situations eliciting extremes of sadism and brutality has rightly called out for interpretation.

A focus on "Hitler and his henchmen" was a notable feature of early postwar popular history—with the demonization of a small group at the top helpfully distracting attention from wider participation and complicity—and has continued to fascinate wider audiences ever since. The continuing focus on individuals has however been tempered by broadening the focus. The 1980s debate between "intentionalists," who emphasized Hitler's motives, and "functionalists" or "structuralists," who emphasized rather the "cumulative radicalization" arising from overlapping structures of power, has largely subsided. Most historians recognize the significance of Hitler as charismatic *Führer* setting the direction and overall goals but have rejected the earlier "totalitarian" model—in which Hitler's intentions translated directly into outcomes—in favor of the more complex model of a "polycratic" state, characterized by multiple, competing centers of power. Within this wider theoretical context, there have been notable studies of Hitler, Himmler, Heydrich, and Eichmann, as well as less well-known individuals, which address the relationship between ideological motivation, mobilization, and context, complicated by postwar prevarications and self-defense strategies (cf. Arendt 1963; Kershaw 1998, 2000; Longerich 2008; Gerwarth 2011; Stangneth 2014; Kay 2016).

Involvement in violence changed over time. Ideological convictions and experiences of political violence in the aftermath of German defeat in 1918 were significant among those who joined the Nazi Party (NSDAP) or its paramilitary organizations at an early date. But there was a snowball effect once a right-wing monopoly on political violence was appropriated by the state and legitimated from above in 1933. NSDAP members ranged from the "Old Fighters" who had joined in the "times of struggle" in the 1920s, through the "Märzgefallenen" ("those who had fallen in March") who jumped onto the bandwagon when Hitler was appointed Chancellor, to the latecomers who joined, occasionally opportunistically and sometimes under pressure (for example by employers), beginning in the late 1930s. Meanwhile, despite widespread public distaste occasioned by particular incidents—as in the adverse reactions to the boycott of Jewish shops in April 1933, or violence on the streets in the summer of 1935, in both cases leading to a "legalization" of more radical anti-Jewish measures—many members of the idealized Nazi "national community" or *Volksgemeinschaft* variously condoned or actively engaged in public humiliation of the outcast, or benefited from the fruits of violence. Far larger numbers participated in the violence unleashed on 9–10 November 1938, known as "Kristallnacht," than were later prepared to admit this. It was, then, not merely the thugs in the SA, or the careerists in the SS and Gestapo, or the youngsters spurred on by their leaders in the Hitler Youth, who became involved in state-legitimated violence (Wildt 2007; Bajohr and Wildt 2009; Steinweis 2009; Schmiechen-Ackermann 2012; Steber and Gotto 2014).

In mapping a topography of perpetration, we can discern particularly concentrated nodes. The growing apparatus of power and terror, eventually bringing together party and state in the complex empire of the SS, Gestapo, and other police forces led by Himmler and Heydrich, brought individuals into a highly ideological environment where commitment to Nazi world-views and exercise of brute force were the norm. These organizations were embedded in a largely supportive (or fearful) societal context. Denunciations by members of the public, often for their own ends (greed, jealousy, personal as well as political disagreements) allowed the Gestapo to exercise immense power with a relatively small staff. Similarly, the misnamed "euthanasia" program could not have been implemented had not significant numbers of medical professionals, such as Professor Werner Catel, been convinced that non-voluntary "mercy killing" was justifiable, even desirable, and had not a few—such as Friedrich Mennecke, whose letters to his wife provide disturbing insights into his mentality while selecting "patients" for gassing, or Hermann Pfannmüller, who boasted openly about starving children to death in special "hunger wards" of his Munich clinic—been ardently involved in making the process as efficient as possible. Professionals in the T4 program—named after the Berlin address, Tiergartenstrasse 4, from which the killing of the mentally and physically disabled was coordinated—were assisted by numerous doctors, nurses, orderlies, administrators, secretaries, cooks, crematorium stokers, bus drivers, and builders in an operation that was intended to be secret but about which knowledge spread rapidly. Following the official termination of the T4 program in August 1941, several dozens of those most closely involved in killings took their expertise in subterfuge and gassing to occupied Poland, to help set up the dedicated extermination camps of Chełmno, Bełżec, Sobibór, and Treblinka (Aly et al. 1994; Burleigh 1994; Friedlander 1997; Schmidt 2007; Berger 2013).

With the outbreak of war, far greater numbers were brought into the apparatus of killing than just those propelled by convictions. Research on perpetrators has focused on particular groups involved in physical brutality and killing. Here, there is little consensus on the balance between mobilization and motives. Daniel Jonah Goldhagen controversially argued that "eliminationist anti-Semitism" characterized a supposedly enduring German mentality, requiring only a Hitler to unleash its full fury, yet rapidly disappearing after the war with the foundation of the Federal Republic (Goldhagen 1996). The weight of historiography points, however, to other factors. Christopher Browning's analysis of the "ordinary men" in Police Battalion 101 emphasized situational factors and peer group pressure to conform, as well as stressing that individuals could request alternative duties (Browning 1992). Omer Bartov and others highlighted brutalization in warfare, while the role of the Army in atrocities was brought to public attention in the controversial traveling exhibition on the Crimes of the Wehrmacht that first opened in 1995 (Bartov 1991, 2001; Hartmann et al. 2005). Thomas Kühne emphasized comradeship and community through mutual participation in criminal activities, and Stefan Kühl has highlighted role performance in organizations (Kühne 2010; Kühl 2014). It is also worth noting that brutality in occupied Europe was rendered easier by the enthusiasm and ideological commitment of young "ethnic Germans" (*Volksdeutsche*), such as Rudolf Zimmermann, resident in the "German colony" near the Polish town of Mielec, who had been warmed up to Nazi ideology before the German invasion, or the Sudeten German Josef Blösche, whose image as a member of the SS suppressing the 1943 Warsaw Ghetto uprising is well known from a photograph of a small boy with his hands up being deported to death (Fulbrook 2018). Their prior experiences and socialization clearly rendered them susceptible to the new lures of Nazism. Although beyond the scope of this analysis, different motives were at play among collaborators in the occupied countries, such as the Polish policemen and locals who simultaneously were victims of Nazi oppression and assisted in the oppression and rounding up of Jews. There is a growing field of regional and local histories exploring different areas of occupied Europe, with participation varying according to prior histories and wartime circumstances (Friedländer 2007; Grabowski 2013; Dumitru 2016; Gruner 2016; Segal 2016).

Structural transformations were significant in the "making of perpetrators." In wartime, institutions and practices of persecution and exploitation expanded exponentially, and mobilization, with differing degrees of constraint or choice, became increasingly important. Many people became entangled simply by virtue of being called up for duties at the front or on the home front. There were increasing numbers of repressive roles to be filled, for example, in the growing universe of the concentration camps (Wachsmann 2015). Regardless of whether they had any prior commitment to Nazi ideology, people now had to behave in ways required in these situations; in adjusting to new challenges, they developed new social selves. This was notable among young women trained as concentration camp guards in Ravensbrück or as "carers" and assistants in centers for the mentally and physically disabled that were part of the "euthanasia" killing program. They accommodated to expectations and gained personal benefits—better food, higher wages, a smart uniform, a sense of superior authority. Some were committed; some became more convinced performers or found ways of justifying their actions; others continued to experience inner disquiet but had little leeway for alternative courses of action or ways out.

Systemic Violence: The Administration of Evil

Those administering Nazi rule remained for decades largely beyond public perceptions of what it meant to be "perpetrators." Yet the system could not have developed without a myriad of functionaries and facilitators, regardless of whether the individuals who played these roles were convinced of the cause or ever pulled triggers themselves.

The compliance and indeed initiative of functionaries was absolutely crucial to the development and expansion of the Nazi state. Raul Hilberg's massive analysis, *The Destruction of the European Jews*, drew attention to the significance of the bureaucracy in making mass murder possible. First published in 1961, and only translated into German in 1982, Hilberg's work in its revised three-volume English-language edition finally gained wider impact with the growing focus on what was now generally termed the Holocaust. Hilberg commented that bureaucrats registered "growing uneasiness" and "moral scruples" about the murderous processes they were facilitating. Yet despite "moral inhibitions" and "an inner struggle," they coped by developing "a mechanism of repressions and a system of rationalizations." Self-justifications included emphasis on obeying superior orders and doing one's duty—sometimes tempered by small acts of personal kindness towards individual victims—as well as suggesting that others were worse, that there was a fine line between one's own actions and what was morally unacceptable, and that one was anyway powerless to act otherwise (Hilberg 2003, 1084–5, 1098–1104). This analysis of rationalizations, which changed over time, requires further development.

A spate of recent research on state institutions undertaken by independent historical commissions has exploded convenient myths and brought to public attention the controversial involvement in the Holocaust of, for example, diplomats in the Foreign Office (Conze et al. 2010). Research has generally revealed the relative insignificance of ideological convictions, although a basic minimal consensus around general goals was important. A study of the *Reichsarbeitsministerium* (Reich Ministry of Labor) demonstrates chillingly how individuals who under other historical circumstances would have been perfectly ordinary bureaucrats could discuss, cold-bloodedly, selecting those unfit to work and sending them to a speedier end in the gas chambers (Nützenadel 2017). It also demonstrates—equally chillingly—how some never confronted the consequences of their work. Bureaucrats who were neither committed Nazis nor personally motivated by anti-Semitism (let alone its supposedly "eliminationist" variant) seem here, as elsewhere, to have needed neither ideological conviction nor political pressure to put into effect policies resulting in mass suffering and death. People simply worked according to the rules without apparently thinking about the outcomes.

Do such studies of Nazi ministries and bureaucrats suggest a need to rethink the concept of the polycratic state? There certainly were differing centers of power, with different profiles and overlapping spheres of competence, but the result was not the structural competition emphasized in some older approaches, where Hitler was portrayed as a "weak dictator" or only "strong" insofar as he held sway above the fray. Nor does this picture disclose much by way of rivalry in "working towards the Führer" resulting in ever more radical policies. Rather, we see a distinctive combination of the following: a partial congruence of aims, a set of shared and often unthinking prejudices, and a pattern of ingrained habits and behaviors. Radicalization in wartime was then not simply a consequence of ideology or conflicting "structures" (as in the formulations of the 1980s), but was rather the outcome of a particular combination of military needs and racial, economic, and labor policies. Despite periodic conflicts between Nazi plenipotentiaries and more traditional ministries, the general impetus was the furtherance of common goals, fostering an expansionist war of conquest and exploitation, alongside the elimination of all that was seen as "life unworthy of living" for whatever reason. This is arguably still a polycratic structure, but one that is nuanced rather differently—and nuanced in a way that does not let traditional state structures off the hook.

Does that mean that civilian administrators can be put in the category of "perpetrators"? During the war, bureaucrats played roles that never required them actually to pull triggers but paved the way for genocide by implementing policies of degradation, segregation, and ghettoization that made eventual selections and deportations easier for those at the front line of violence. Again, individual ideological motivation seems to have been of little importance. One such person was the *Landrat* of Będzin who, like so many other "ordinary Nazis" saw himself as quite distinct from the "real Nazis," the often lower-class enthusiasts for whom he felt a degree of social disdain. He harbored disquiet about the murderous policies that were in train—but nevertheless continued to do his day job, moving Jews out of their houses and into ever poorer and more cramped accommodations, ensuring they wore the star, reducing their rations and restricting their movements, until the day when the SS and Gestapo, assisted by the gendarmerie of which he was in charge, rounded up the demoralized and half-starved Jews of the area and deported them to the gas chambers of nearby Auschwitz (Fulbrook 2012). There were countless other civilian administrators doing their jobs in ways that assisted the smooth development of the killing apparatus, from the Lord Mayor of the annexed and Germanized Łódź, Litzmannstadt, presiding over the removal of Jews to the ghetto, to regional and local functionaries across the Reich, and in occupied territories (Roth 2009). Some were more enthusiastic, even fanatical, than others; whatever their personal views, to continue their careers meant performing the functions of the roles, whatever degrees of disquiet or moral unease might be aroused by the consequences.

The economy too became embroiled in the system of collective violence. The exploitation of forced labor was a major feature; particularly from early 1942 onwards, with the loss of German manpower to the front, and the growing needs of the armaments industry, some industrialists played a significant role in the exploitation of slave laborers from concentration camps (Wachsmann 2015, 392–443; Tooze 2007, 558–9). From Heinkel to Messerschmidt, from the well-known I.G. Farben with its Buna plant at Auschwitz-Monowitz to the far less well-known Steyr-Daimler-Puch companies active in the Mauthausen sub-camps, economic concerns cooperated with the SS to hire prisoners from concentration camps who could be worked to the point of exhaustion, when they might be killed on the spot or sent elsewhere for gassing. A ready supply of replacements was always available, and the cost of employment and feeding the starving inmates was minimal. The conditions for productivity were designed to ensure that German armaments were developed as rapidly and secretly as possible, including the missile production at Peenemunde, later displaced to the lethal operations in the tunnels at Mittelbau-Dora. Considerations about postwar viability were also significant: some of the tunnel building in major labor sub-camps of Mauthausen, for example, was to protect the machinery, equipment, and products of the industrial concerns for the postwar period. In the interests of profit, hundreds of thousands of slave laborers lost their lives.

Complicity: Social and Symbolic Violence

Far more people were complicit in this system of collective violence than merely those who would conventionally be considered "perpetrators." The notion of complicity has several meanings. In the strictly legal sense, it refers to someone who is a knowing accomplice or accessory to a crime: who in some way facilitates that crime. In a wider sense, it is often held to refer to people who know about a crime, possibly even witness it personally, but fail to act by seeking to prevent it or reporting it to authorities. In an even wider meaning, it may refer to people who willingly benefit from the fruits of criminal actions, who participate in a community implicated in such actions, or who fail to condemn these actions and continue to associate with the wrongdoers, effectively condoning the crime. Legal and moral distinctions may therefore be made between being an accessory before or after the fact; aiding and abetting perpetrators; and opportunistically benefiting from or condoning a crime. Depending on circumstances, a person may be morally tainted but not legally culpable. Complicity has many faces, but it necessarily entails being on the side of the guilty and in some way benefiting from, approving, or assisting the actions of those who are primarily culpable.

Once we start to look at questions of complicity, the circles widen still further. We need not go as far as Götz Aly in designating all as guilty who, wittingly or otherwise, materially benefited from Nazi policies of stealing Jewish property and ravaging and exploiting the subjugated populations of Europe. While those who actually did the plundering are clearly implicated, their children at home who benefited from the proceeds might be totally unaware of the source (Aly 2005). Nor do we have to follow Bernhard Schlink in assuming that people who neither dissociate themselves from the guilty nor renounce a share of the spoils are somehow guilty—even down to grandchildren who are unaware of the fact that property they inherit was originally "aryanized" (Schlink 2009). It would be possible to delimit complicity as knowing involvement and support at the time, but even this does not completely define the limits and extent of complicity.

Something here requires further exploration. Under Nazi rule, people began to act in accordance with new norms in ways that were harmful, even if "only" psychologically, to fellow citizens who were stigmatized and excluded from the new "national community." Changes came about not only because of policies handed down from on high, but also because of informal social processes and behaviors in everyday life that were not directly, or were only partially, affected by legal regulations. In the process, there were crucial changes in patterns of identification of self and "others" and in associated communities of empathy, with long-term implications for the formation of perpetrators, facilitators, and the widening circles of those involved in Nazi violence.

People were complicit in enacting new kinds of social relationships that, through everyday practices, served to stigmatize, ostracize, and exclude others. In the process, new "communities of empathy" emerged, where only some categories of human beings were held to elicit emotions of understanding, sympathy, or a sense that harming them was wrong. Others were cast out in such a way that they were beyond the borders of new communities of empathy. People were complicit in learning to "turn a blind eye," willfully refusing, or less wittingly failing to see—in the active sense of registering and reflecting on—the sufferings of others. People could become "onlookers," watching without intervening in specific incidents of extreme violence or failing to acknowledge what was going on; whether or not they profited from the distress of others, and whether or not they were themselves victimized, they colluded in excluding or rendering invisible the victims of more extreme persecution. Few would include these "bystanders" within the category of "perpetrator," but without them the system could not have functioned and developed in the way it did.

The Un-making of Perpetrators: Justice, Guilt, and Reintegration

And after the war? The story is depressingly familiar: most of the guilty got away with it, while the majority of victims continued to suffer. Only a tiny minority were tried and sentenced for Nazi crimes. Fewer than one percent of those involved in killing Jews were ever convicted for their crimes. Innumerable people who had made this mass murder possible were able to evade consideration entirely. Reasons for low rates of conviction differed in the three Third Reich successor states, as did the profiles of those considered "perpetrators."

During the occupation period, the Allies mounted major trials—not only the International Military Tribunal at Nuremberg, but also the so-called "successor trials" dealing with major areas of activity, as well as a far larger number of smaller cases in each occupation zone (Priemel 2016). By the late 1940s, the Cold War began to take precedence over dealing with Nazism, and in the early 1950s a climate of amnesty and clemency generally displaced concern with punishment. Many who had been given lengthy sentences for serious crimes were released early, after only a few years in prison.

In all three successor states, the vast majority of trials took place in the early postwar years (Albrich et al. 2006; Eichmüller 2012; Raim 2015). During the period of Allied occupation, German courts could only try cases committed against German nationals or stateless citizens on German soil. This meant, in effect, a confrontation with societal divisions in preceding years. In West Germany, many cases concerned denunciations and violence in the closing months of the war, as well as cases—often brought by relatives of victims—for crimes associated with "*Kristallnacht.*" In East Germany, trials also focused on denunciations, but there was also an emphasis on attacks on left-wing opponents around the Nazi seizure of power, as well as employer exploitation of forced labor. Additionally, in all three successor states, including Austria, in the early postwar years, trials were held relating to generally low-level perpetrators in the euthanasia program. Many in the higher ranks of the medical profession succeeded in prevaricating and largely wriggled away from justice, despite the best efforts of determined lawyers such as Hessian Attorney General Fritz Bauer—who also played a key role in ensuring Eichmann's capture and trial by the Israelis, as well as mounting the 1963–1965 Frankfurt trial of "Auschwitz" as a major crime complex.

Determined efforts by key groups and individuals faced significant challenges. In Austria, with the abolition of the People's Courts in 1955, trials for Nazi crimes declined dramatically and after the mid-1970s dried up almost completely. The majority of former Nazis quietly integrated into the new society unscathed by serious reckoning with their past. In West Germany, the notion of perpetrator was narrowed in the light of pre-existing criminal law definitions of "murder." East Germany, by contrast, continued to apply the Nuremberg principles, encompassing a wider range of offences. The differing international situations of the three states—two in competition on the front line of the Cold War, the third a neutral state portraying itself as "Hitler's first victim"—also affected patterns of reckoning with the past.

Far more striking than the records of justice are the absences. In West Germany, members of the judiciary, the medical profession, employers of slave labor, and the civil service largely ensured they did not need to face justice in the courtroom. Blame was shifted onto a few individuals—preferably already convicted or dead—as well as the convenient symbol of all evil, the SS, "alibi of the nation" (Reitlinger 1981). Networks of friendship and mutual solidarity were strengthened in whitewashing a contaminated past. Those who navigated their way through the shoals of denazification settled into the calmer waters of postwar life, often cushioned by substantial pensions earned for their service to Hitler's Reich. They rewrote their former lives in terms of lack of agency, political weakness, and a conservative nationalism that was deemed perfectly acceptable, particularly in wartime. Even if there was, in Norbert Frei's terminology, a "normative demarcation" in Adenauer's Germany, this was partial and selective: the notion of "perpetrator" was progressively narrowed to the lower-class thugs and concentration camp sadists, while professionals who had assisted in the administration of discriminatory and ultimately murderous policies were let off the hook

(Frei 2002). In the law courts, a single murder by a Ukrainian guard was seen as worse than the administration of ghettoization or the exploitation of forced and slave labor.

Trials in West Germany picked up again from the later 1950s with the 1958 Ulm *Einsatzgruppen* trial and the foundation of the Ludwigsburg Central Office for coordinating the investigation of Nazi crimes by the regional states and reducing reliance on individual indictments. The major trials of the 1960s and 1970s largely focused on involvement in extermination practices in the East, deflecting attention from widespread complicity at home. The use of ordinary criminal law, moreover, meant that to be found guilty of murder a person had to have been motivated by "base motives" and to have been an "excess perpetrator" exercising particularly cruel and sadistic behavior (Pendas 2006). Merely following orders—even if one killed tens of thousands of people—did not constitute "murder" in the sense of the law. Many perpetrators, as in the 1963 Bełżec trial, managed to gain acquittals through lack of survivor evidence (Bryant 2014). The Statute of Limitations—which, following heated debates, was repeatedly extended and finally lifted in 1979—ensured that many significant offences could not be brought to court at all. It was only with the 2011 conviction of John Demjanjuk as an accessory to murder in his role as a guard at the Sobibór extermination camp that the German legal approach changed, opening the way for an extremely belated campaign to track down perpetrators before it was "too late."

There was a higher rate of conviction for Nazi crimes in East Germany, with people being six or seven times more likely to be tried and found guilty. As in the West, the majority of trials took place in the early postwar years. From the late 1950s, the emphasis shifted to using trials as part of the GDR's international strategy, decrying West Germany as a home to former Nazis (Weinke 2002). Much remains to be learned about the careers of former Nazis in the GDR. The state security service (*Staatssicherheitsdienst*, or Stasi) was involved in investigations and bringing well-prepared cases to court. On occasion, former Nazis became Stasi informers; some were quietly tolerated, for the embarrassment that might be caused by revelations; others were selected for trial (Dirks 2004; Leide 2006). Even low-level perpetrators were given relatively harsh punishments, while more senior Nazis who had settled in the West managed to evade prosecution or received lighter sentences (Fulbrook 2018). Some cases were used for publicity purposes, including trials *in absentia* of prominent West Germans, such as Hans Globke, Adenauer's chief aide and former official commentator on Hitler's Nuremberg Laws. But the vast majority of former perpetrators were, as elsewhere, quietly integrated into society; many developed profiles as good GDR citizens. The analysis of the GDR as a "post-Nazi society" remains a wide-open field for research.

Meanwhile, the few survivors of Nazi policies of forced labor and extermination fought lengthy, bitter battles to try to achieve recognition and recompense for their suffering. Those who had sweated for a pittance in the ghettos were denied pensions, in contrast to those who had benefited from their labor. People who had been persecuted on grounds of sexuality continued to face ostracism long after same-sex relationships were de-criminalized. Other marginalized groups, such as victims of forced sterilization and euthanasia policies, as well as Roma and Sinti, experienced decades of social exclusion before they partially succeeded in their battles for recognition. While taking official responsibility and, in its public culture, repeatedly confronting its shameful past, the Federal Republic of Germany protected the majority of those who had been complicit. East Germany and Austria prior to the 1990s barely even conceded responsibility. Does this constitute what one commentator has termed a "second guilt" (Giordano 1987)? With generational and political changes, a wave of identification with the victims led to massive attempts at memorialization and belated and partial compensation.

States of Violence

For a few years, in a system of state-sponsored violence, many ordinary people came to do what we would consider far from ordinary things. Put rather pointedly: often, actions made perpetrators, rather than perpetrators causing actions.

Subjective perspectives shifted with changing circumstances. We have to consider both the structural development of particular kinds of social, political, and economic roles and the interpretive question of how some people came to play these roles and justify their own behaviors, both at the time and later, while others refused or reacted differently. To restrict analysis to those culpable actions and evidently violent roles that variously came under the spotlight in postwar trials would be to misunderstand the extraordinary system of collective violence that was the Third Reich. It would moreover lead to a massive underestimation of the consequences for those who had been involved in this system, as well as the continuing reverberations across subsequent generations.

Although there is a huge and ever-expanding literature on this topic, many questions remain. We need to explore subjective perceptions of a rapidly changing situation—including assumptions about the actions of others, the likely rewards or penalties for different courses of action, and individual decisions about how to act. We need to bring agency and structure together in ways not caught in older debates—whether about ideology, popular opinion, or the balance of consent and coercion—that presuppose a separation between "state" and "society" or that focus primarily on decision-makers at the top and those at the front line of violence without embedding these within wider social fields. Furthermore, we need more and detailed exploration of the longer-term social and psychological implications for those who were in some way contaminated by guilt or complicity. We need to explore how variations in postwar environments affected how perpetrators (as variously defined) could deal with or partially silence their past, which, in turn, affect the legacies for societies today.

Note

1 This chapter draws on research carried out for my book, *Reckonings: Legacies of Nazi Persecution and the Quest for Justice* (New York and Oxford: Oxford University Press, 2018), where fuller references can be found, and on current research for a book on *Bystander Society*. I am very grateful to the Arts and Humanities Research Council (AHRC) for its support for both of these projects.

Bibliography

Albrich, Thomas, Winfried Garscha, & Martin Polaschek, eds. 2006. *Holocaust und Kriegsverbrechen vor Gericht. Der Fall Österreich*. Innsbruck, Wien, Bozen: Studien Verlag.

Aly, Götz. 2005. *Hitlers Volksstaat. Raub, Rassenkrieg und nationaler Sozialismus*. Frankfurt am Main: S. Fischer.

Aly, Götz, Peter Chroust, & Christian Pross. 1994. *Cleansing the Fatherland. Nazi Medicine and Racial Hygiene*. Baltimore and London: The Johns Hopkins University Press; transl. Belinda Cooper.

Arendt, Hannah. 1963. *Eichmann in Jerusalem: A Report on the Banality of Evil*. New York: Viking Press.

Bajohr, Frank & Dieter Pohl. 2006. *Der Holocaust als offenes Geheimnis: Die Deutschen, die NS-Führung und die Alliierten*. Munich: C.H. Beck.

Bajohr, Frank & Michael Wildt, eds. 2009. *Volksgemeinschaft. Neue Forschungen zur Gesellschaft des Nationalsozialismus*. Frankfurt am Main: Fischer Verlag.

Bartov, Omer. 1991. *Hitler's Army. Soldiers, Nazis and War in the Third Reich*. Oxford: Oxford University Press.

Bartov, Omer. 2001/1985. *The Eastern Front, 1941–45: German Troops and the Barbarisation of Warfare*. Houndmills: Palgrave.

Berger, Sara. 2013. *Experten der Vernichtung. Das T4-Reinhardt-Netzwerk in den Lagern Belzec, Sobibor und Treblinka.* Hamburg: Hamburger Edition.
Browning, Christopher. 1992. *Ordinary Men: Reserve Police Battalion 101 and the Final Solution in Poland.* New York: HarperCollins.
Bryant, Michael. 2014. *Eyewitness to Genocide. The Operation Reinhard Death Camp Trials, 1955–1966.* Knoxville: University of Tennessee Press.
Burleigh, Michael. 1994. *Death and Deliverance. 'Euthanasia' in Germany c. 1900–1945.* Cambridge: Cambridge University Press.
Conze, Eckart, Norbert Frei, Peter Hayes, & Moshe Zimmermann. 2010. *Das Amt und die Vergangenheit: Deutsche Diplomaten im Dritten Reich und in der Bundesrepublik.* Munich: Karl Blessing Verlag.
Dams, Carsten & Michael Stolle. 2014. *The Gestapo. Power and Terror in the Third Reich.* Translated by Charlotte Ryland. Oxford: Oxford University Press.
de Mildt, Dick. 1996. *In the Name of the People: Perpetrators of Genocide in the Reflections of their Post-war Prosecution in West Germany. The 'Euthanasia' and 'Aktion Reinhard' Trial cases.* The Hague: Martinus Nujhoff Publishers.
Dirks, Christian. 2004. *"Die Verbrechen der Anderen." Auschwitz und der Auschwitz-Prozess der DDR: Das Verfahren gegen den KZ-Arzt Dr. Horst Fischer.* Paderborn: Ferdinand Schöningh.
Dumitru, Diana. 2016. *The State, Antisemitism and Collaboration in the Holocaust. The Borderlands of Romania and the Soviet Union.* Cambridge: Cambridge University Press.
Eichmüller, Andreas. 2012. *Keine Generalamnestie. Die Strafverfolgung von NS-Verbrechen in der frühen Bundesrepublik.* Munich: Oldenbourg Wissenschaftsverlag.
Frei, Norbert. 2002. *Adenauer's Germany and the Nazi Past.* Translated by Joel Golb. New York: Columbia University Press.
Freudiger, Kerstin. 2002. *Die juristische Aufarbeitung von NS-Verbrechen.* Tübingen: J.C.B. Mohr (Paul Siebeck).
Friedlander, Henry. 1997. *The Origins of Nazi Genocide: From Euthanasia to the Final Solution.* Chapel Hill: University of North Carolina Press.
Friedländer, Saul. 2007. *Nazi Germany and the Jews. Vol. 2, The Years of Extermination.* New York: Harper Collins.
Friedrich, Jörg. 1998. *Freispruch für die Nazi-Justiz. Die Urteile gegen NS-Richter seit 1948. Eine Dokumentation.* Berlin: Ullstein.
Fulbrook, Mary. 2011. *Dissonant Lives: Generations and Violence through the German Dictatorships.* Oxford: Oxford University Press.
Fulbrook, Mary. 2012. *A Small Town near Auschwitz: Ordinary Nazis and the Holocaust.* Oxford: Oxford University Press.
Fulbrook, Mary. 2018. *Reckonings: Legacies of Nazi Persecution and the Quest for Justice.* New York and Oxford: Oxford University Press.
Gerwarth, Robert. 2011. *Hitler's Hangman: The Life of Heydrich.* New Haven: Yale University Press.
Giordano, Ralph. 1987. *Die zweite Schuld oder Von der Last Deutscher zu sein.* Hamburg: Rasch und Röhring.
Goldhagen, Daniel Jonah. 1996. *Hitler's Willing Executioners.* New York: Knopf.
Grabowski, Jan. 2013. *Hunt for the Jews. Betrayal and Murder in German-Occupied Poland.* Bloomington and Indianapolis: Indiana University Press.
Greve, Michael. 2001. *Der justitielle und rechtspolitische Umgang mit NS-Gewaltverbrechen in den sechziger Jahren.* Frankfurt am Main: Peter Lang.
Gruner, Wolf. 2016. *Die Judenverfolgung im Protektorat Böhmen und Mähren. Lokale Initiativen, zentrale Entscheidungen, jüdische Antworten, 1939–1945.* Göttingen: Wallstein.
Hartmann, Christian, Johannes Hürter, & Ulrike Jureit, eds. 2005. *Verbrechen der Wehrmacht. Bilanz einer Debatte.* Munich: C. H. Beck.
Herbert, Ulrich. 1996. *Best. Biographische Studien über Radikalismus, Weltanschauung und Vernunft, 1903–1989.* Bonn: Dietz Verlag.
Hilberg, Raul. 2003. *The Destruction of the European Jews*, 3rd Edition. London: Yale University Press.
Jensen, Olaf & Claus-Christian Szejnmann, eds. 2008. *Ordinary People as Mass Murderers. Perpetrators in Comparative Perspectives.* Houndmills, Basingstoke: Palgrave Macmillan.
Kay, Alex. 2016. *The Making of an SS Killer. The Life of Colonel Alfred Filbert, 1905–1990.* Cambridge: Cambridge University Press.
Kershaw, Ian. 1998. *Hitler: Hubris.* Harmondsworth: Penguin.

Kershaw, Ian. 2000. *Hitler: Nemesis*. Harmondsworth: Penguin.
Kühl, Stefan. 2014. *Ganz normale Organisationen. Zur Soziologie des Holocaust*. Berlin: Suhrkamp.
Kühne, Thomas. 2010. *Belonging and Genocide. Hitler's Community, 1918–1945*. New Haven: Yale University Press.
Leide, Henry. 2006. *NS-Verbrecher und Staatssicherheit. Die geheime Vergangenheitspolitik der DDR*. Göttingen: Vandenhoeck & Ruprecht.
Longerich, Peter. 2008. *Heinrich Himmler. Biographie*. Munich: Siedler.
Matthäus, Jürgen. 2004. 'Historiography and the Perpetrators of the Holocaust' in *The Historiography of the Holocaust*, edited by Dan Stone, 197–215. London: Palgrave Macmillan.
Müller, Ingo. 2014. *Furchtbare Juristen. Die unbewältigte Vergangenheit der deutschen Justiz*, 2nd edition. Berlin: Klaus Bittermann.
Nützenadel, Alexander, ed. 2017. *Das Reichsarbeitsministerium im Nationalsozialismus. Verwaltung – Politik – Verbrechen*. Göttingen: Wallstein Verlag.
Pendas, Devin O. 2006. *The Frankfurt Auschwitz Trial, 1963–1965: Genocide, History and the Limits of the Law*. Cambridge: Cambridge University Press.
Priemel, Kim Christian. 2016. *The Betrayal: The Nuremberg Trials and German Divergence*. Oxford: Oxford University Press.
Raim, Edith. 2015. *Nazi Crimes against Jews and German Post-War Justice. The West German Judicial System during Allied Occupation (1945–1949)*. Oldenbourg: De Gruyter.
Reitlinger, Gerald. 1981/1956. *The SS. Alibi of a Nation 1922–1945*. London: Arms and Armour Press.
Roth, Markus. 2009. *Herrenmenschen. Die deutschen Kreishauptleute im besetzten Polen – Karrierewege, Herrschaftspraxis und Nachgeschichte*. Göttingen: Wallstein Verlag.
Schlink, Bernhard. 2009. *Guilt about the Past*. Brisbane: University of Queensland Press.
Schmidt, Ulf. 2007. *Karl Brandt: The Nazi Doctor. Medicine and Power in the Third Reich*. London: Hambledon continuum.
Schmiechen-Ackermann, Detlef, ed. 2012. *"Volksgemeinschaft": Mythos, wirkungsmächtige soziale Verheißung oder soziale Realität im "Dritten Reich"?* Paderborn: Ferdinand Schöningh.
Segal, Raz. 2016. *Genocide in the Carpathians: War, Social Breakdown, and Mass Violence, 1914–1945*. Palo Alto: Stanford University Press.
Stangneth, Bettina. 2014. *Eichmann before Jerusalem: The Unexamined Life of a Mass Murderer*. Translated by Ruth Martin. New York: Alfred Knopf.
Stargardt, Nicholas. 2015. *The German War. A Nation under Arms, 1939–1945*. London: The Bodley Head.
Steber, Martina & Bernhard Gotto, eds. 2014. *Visions of Community in Nazi Germany*. Oxford: Oxford University Press.
Steinweis, Alan. 2009. *Kristallnacht 1938*. Cambridge, MA: Harvard University Press.
Tooze, Adam. 2007. *The Wages of Destruction. The Making and Breaking of the Nazi Economy*. London: Penguin Books.
von Miquel, Marc. 2004. *Ahnden oder amnestieren? Westdeutsche Justiz und Vergangenheitspolitik in den sechziger Jahren*. Göttingen: Wallstein Verlag.
Wachsmann, Nikolaus. 2015. *KL. A History of the Nazi Concentration Camps*. London: Little, Brown.
Weinke, Annette. 2002. *Die Verfolgung von NS-Tätern im geteilten Deutschland. Vergangenheitsbewältigungen 1949–1989. Oder: Eine deutsch-deutsch Beziehungsgeschichte im Kalten Krieg*. Paderborn: Ferdinand Schöningh.
Wildt, Michael. 2002. *Generation des Unbedingten. Das Führungskorps des Reichssicherheitshauptamtes*. Hamburg: Hamburger Edition.
Wildt, Michael. 2007. *Volksgemeinschaft als Selbstermächtigung. Gewalt gegen Juden in der deutschen Provinz 1919 bis 1939*. Hamburg: Hamburger Edition.

3

Ordinary Organizations

A Systems Theory Approach to Perpetrator Studies[1]

Stefan Kühl

The point of departure for a systems theoretical analysis of genocides in modern societies is the observation that most genocides are carried out by members of state organizations of force.[2] State organizations of force are organizations such as armies, militias, or the police that use the threat of force, or force itself, in order to implement state decisions. They differ from non-state organizations of force, such as gangs, terrorist organizations, or marauding bands of mercenaries, in that they can justify their actions by claiming to enforce demands that have been legitimized by the state. The simple realization that most genocides were killing campaigns based largely on state organizations is hardly an original insight. When it comes to analyzing the organizational framework for these activities, however, researchers—particularly the few sociologists who have participated in the discussion of genocides—have worked with a view of organizations that borders on caricature and that can ultimately be traced back to Max Weber.[3] Under the influence of Weber's description of the machine-like "bureaucratic mechanism" (Weber 1976, 562), with its "precision," "speed," "unambiguity," "knowledge of the files," "continuity," "discretion," "unity," "strict subordination," and "reduction of friction," genocides have been construed as a product of the use of "bureaucratic mechanisms" that were suited to killing people on a massive scale. According to this interpretation, genocides involved the implementation of concepts such as the "optimal use of resources" and a "diligent and professional approach." Because of the division of labor, the "desk murderers" would have perceived the victims solely as a "depersonalized" entity, a "column of numbers."[4]

This machine-like understanding of organizations is embedded in an explanation that interprets genocides as a phenomenon of modernity.[5] As this interpretation has it, the Enlightenment was the source of the "deadly combination" of cold calculation and bureaucratic machinery that gave rise to the "monster of modernity." In its efforts to achieve perfection through organizations, the Holocaust, for example, according to Zygmunt Bauman, was a "code of modernity," a "legitimate resident in the house of modernity" (1989, 17f). Bauman said the goal of modernity was a "better," "more efficient," "more beautiful" world, and the mass murder of the Jews was an attempt to realize this ideal (1989, 17f).[6]

With Max Weber's understanding of organizations, genocides in modern society can only be explained as a "bureaucratically planned" and "industrially executed" "administrative mass murder" (Arendt 1984). Especially, the reception of the Holocaust is characteristic of this understanding. For example, Martin Heidegger (2012, 53) said shortly after World War II that the Holocaust was regarded primarily as the "fabrication of corpses," as "hundreds of thousands" being "unobtrusively liquidated." The Holocaust has thus come to be seen as an instance of an "entire people" being "obliterated without a trace" in "death factories," in the words of Wolfgang Sofsky (1997, 259). The "death factory" is presented as an "apparatus that functioned smoothly," where people were murdered "at a high capacity and speed"—even though we know from sociological studies of car and aircraft factories that a "smoothly functioning apparatus" is pure management fiction.[7] From this perspective, the only possible synonym for the Holocaust is "Auschwitz"—not the frequently improvised mass shootings or sometimes-chaotic ghetto liquidations.[8]

Beyond the View of Organizations as Machines

By basing their explanations on a simplified understanding of organizations, genocide researchers inherited all the problems that were characteristic of Weberian organizational research: overemphasizing the goal-oriented rationality of organizations, disregarding the fact that organizations frequently have conflicting goals, underestimating the contradictions in the orientation of people's actions, ignoring "bottom-up" initiatives, and neglecting the importance of the "sousveillance of superiors," which gives subordinates significant influence over the decisions made by top-level personnel.[9]

This insufficiently complex view of the organizations involved in genocides—in which every single member, almost to the top of the organization, seems to be merely a cog in the machine—has made it easy to reject explanations that focus on organizations. Such a simplified view has been justifiably criticized for portraying people as nothing more than "puppet-like actors" (Goldhagen 2007, 196), "pawns" (Goldhagen 2007, 196), or "soulless technocrats" (Heyl 1996, 1). It leaves the impression that we are dealing solely with "obedient and submissive executors of an ideology" (Paul 2002 17), "unfeeling command automatons" (Paul 2002, 17), or "dispassionate desk murderers" (Heyl 1996, 23). Critics say this "denies the moral agency and assent of the perpetrators," leading us to assume that "they were compelled to act by forces external to them (Friedländer 2012, 481)."[10]

Though most of the rival parties neither mentioned nor even noticed it, genocide research became the arena for a debate about organizations that had already taken place in a more general form decades earlier. When psychologists, business economists, and sociologists began to take an interest in the phenomenon of the organization in the late nineteenth century, the dominant image was one in which people were of interest solely in terms of how they fit into a machine-like structure. According to the structuralist assumption prevalent at the time, you merely had to establish an efficient network of rules and chains of command, then identify the people best suited to each position in the network and lure them in with attractive compensation.

As a critical response to this reduction of personnel to a pure "fulfillment function" in a more or less rational organization, another concept emerged that was shaped by a voluntaristic view of humanity and considered the human factor to be crucial in understanding organizations. The sociologically naïve belief here was that organizations are made up of people, so their success or failure must depend exclusively on the composition of their personnel.[11] The result was a fairly unproductive confrontation between researchers who paid little heed to the importance of personnel because of their view of organizations as machines and researchers who tried to explain organizational phenomena solely through the motivations of an organization's personnel. Representatives of the former position tended to underestimate the importance of the people in an organization, while representatives of the latter tended to overestimate it (see for this argument Luhmann 2000, 279).

Neither Structuralism nor Voluntarism

The sociological theory of "ordinary organizations" has nothing to do with the oversimplified image of organizations as machines, nor does it fall back on a purely voluntaristic explanation for the actions of people in organizations. One of the strengths of sociological systems theory is that it does not pit an approach geared towards structures against an approach geared towards people, as is frequently assumed. Instead—and this is the key point—it views people as structural features of social systems such as organizations, small groups, protest movements, or families. Even non-sociologists can immediately grasp the fact that the certainty of expectations in small groups, protest movements, and families—as well as organizations—is based not only on roles but also on an understanding of the different ways people act.[12]

By adopting this perspective, organizational sociology, which is informed by systems theory, can help overcome the opposition between the "structuralist approach" and the "voluntaristic approach" in genocide research.[13] We can then view the actions of the members of organizations active in genocides as more than merely actions in the context of a very precisely defined formal membership role, and we can also explain why these people took the initiative in killing people, actively contributed to refining the processes for deportation and killing, frequently carried out shootings at the limits of what was tolerated by the organization, and often committed atrocities enthusiastically.[14,15]

Generalization of Motives

A sociologically informed study of genocides must do more than merely recount the possible motives of organizational members. Historians and psychologists have almost seamlessly defined "typologies of perpetrators"—the "eager killer" who enjoyed killing other human beings and therefore volunteered for execution commandos and tortured victims before shooting them and "celebrated their murderous deeds" afterwards; the "passive follower" who "did whatever they were asked to do" but who did not view killing as a "redemptive deed"; the "unwilling perpetrator," who was critical of the killings but did not actively refuse to take part in ghetto clearances, deportations, or shootings.[16] Such typologies lend themselves to debating the relative percentages of "willing executioners," "passive followers," and "unwilling perpetrators."

The perpetrator typologies that are mobilized in the fierce debate surrounding the respective percentages of "willing," "unwilling," or "passive" executioners are far too simplistic for a sociological analysis. Instead of squeezing the people involved into just a few categories, it is much more interesting to look at how organizations deal with the fact that their members will have differing motives. Many genocides were not carried out solely, or even largely, by people whose convictions aligned with one of an organization's goals. In fact, the participants differed greatly in their motives, their willingness to kill, and their reaction to the killing operations. The fact that they ultimately acted uniformly and effectively nonetheless can only be understood by viewing their actions from a central perspective: the generalization of motives for membership in organizations.

From the viewpoint of the leadership of many killing organizations, the organization should be made up of members who completely identify with the organization and will be fully engaged in fulfilling their organizational role. The ideal seems to be a killing organization in which the motives of the members perfectly align with the goals of the organization so the members never distance themselves from the performance of their roles. Very few organizations actually rely on the fact that the goal of the organization alone will be enough to motivate its members to carry out all of the tasks expected of them. This is why although organizations will try to recruit members who identify with their goals, they will use additional means to motivate their members: coercion, money, collegial expectations, or attractive activities.

The trick that organizations use is to *generalize* the motivations of their members. Regardless of which motives were or are relevant to a member joining and remaining in an organization, by formalizing membership expectations (i.e., making continued membership dependent on fulfilling formal expectations), organizations ultimately ensure that members to whom the organization attributes very different motives will still submit to their expectations (Luhmann 1964, 132). All organization members must gear themselves towards these formal expectations—including those who identify closely with the organization's overarching goal and could therefore become a problem for the organization (because such people tend to independently "translate" this overarching goal into concrete action). If an enthusiastic Wehrmacht soldier had decided it would make more sense to fight on the Eastern front than the Western and had reported for duty there instead, he would probably have been sentenced for desertion.[17]

By generalizing the motives for membership, the killing organizations achieve a certain degree of flexibility. Organizations can only achieve elasticity by separating the goals of the organization from the motives of its members. This makes it possible for an organization to change its goals (within certain limits) without immediately having to wonder whether it will still be attractive to its members. Elastic organizations can adapt better to changed demands (from the government, for example) than those that have to carefully check whether changed goals might frustrate their members (see Luhmann 1964, 103). Armies and police forces take advantage of the flexibility offered by the separation of goals and motives. For example, for the Reich Security Main Office, it was useful to be able to order houses and farmsteads to be burned down during retaliation operations or, if need be, to keep the burning of houses and farmsteads "to a minimum" in order to ensure continued agricultural production.

It would almost be comforting if genocides could be explained by a single motive—for example, that during the Holocaust a mob of fervent Nazis had come together to put their program of "eliminationist antisemitism" into action, or that "racist indoctrination" had succeeded in infecting large parts of the population. Then all it would take to prevent other genocides would be to identify the "racist mob" and fight it using political means or to counter racist indoctrination with an awareness campaign. What is unsettling about many genocides—and especially about the Holocaust—from a sociological perspective is that, when it comes to organized violence, the motives driving people to participate in torture, shootings, or gassings are of secondary importance. Organizations specializing in violence must naturally take into account that some of their members will fully identify with the goal of the killings (when the organization's goals largely correspond to the members' own motives), some will be more neutral towards the goals of the organization and can be "bought off" or "compelled" to take part in actions considered reasonable by the organization, and some may be skeptical towards the specific actions expected of them. All that matters to the organization in the end is that the actions it demands are actually carried out.

The Challenges of a Systems Approach

For non-sociologists, the systems approach poses a challenge. As a scientific discipline, sociology does not approach genocides from a moral perspective. It seems self-evident to us today that the execution of thousands of human beings for ethnic, religious, or political reasons constituted mass murder, meaning that the "killers" were automatically "perpetrators" in both a moral and legal sense and should have been, or should be, prosecuted as mass murderers.[18] But this self-evident categorization of violent acts from a modern perspective makes it more difficult to reconstruct the prevailing rules of legitimacy and, more precisely, of legality of the relevant organizations at the time. In a sociological analysis, it is necessary to strive for the most neutralizing choice of words possible. For example, only by first referring to "mass killings" instead of "mass murders" is it possible to imagine how, depending on the perspective and point in time, mass killings can obviously appear to be mass murders—or not.[19]

This challenge is further intensified by the fact that the focus on organizations shifts the focus away from the victims. This conflicts with a growing demand for genocides not to be explained or recounted from a perspective that focuses on the perpetrators (much less from the perspective *of* the perpetrators) but rather from a perspective that focuses on (or, better yet, from the perspective *of*) the victims.[20] This may be compatible with the demand occasionally heard in the field of the sociology of violence that "thick descriptions" be used to make the "torment of the victims" visible.[21] But when it comes to a sociological approach, the moralistic debate as to whether a "perpetrator perspective" should be replaced by a "victim perspective," or whether we need a "theory of suffering" instead of a "theory of the deed," is irrelevant.

Whether or to what extent forms of violence must be analyzed with a view to the perpetrators or the victims depends on the subject being analyzed. For a sociological analysis of ghettos, concentration camps, or extermination camps, the perspective of the victims has to be taken into account because—as suggested by sociological studies of prisons and psychiatric hospitals—this type of analysis requires that we look at the interaction between the members of the state organizations of force and the inhabitants of the ghettos or the prisoners in the concentration and extermination camps. By contrast, a perspective that focuses on the victims—or, indeed, the perspective *of* the victims—plays a subordinate role when it comes to the understanding of deportations and mass executions. This is not because sociologists want to close their eyes to the suffering of the victims—who could do that, after all?—but because, in this case, the victims' perspective does little to help us explain what happened.

What makes the challenge even greater is that sociologists typically reconstruct the rationalities that underlie events (see Reemtsma 2002, 89). Some genocide researchers take the view that the deportations, mass shootings, and killings in the extermination camps simply cannot be explained.[22] This touches on a sociologically relevant aspect as well, namely, that many acts of violence cannot be fully understood from the perspective of rationalities, or even motives, due to the dynamics of conflict inherent in them.[23] But even when we pay more heed to the internal dynamics of processes of violence, it is impossible to ignore the fact that the participants in such processes often persistently attribute rationalities to themselves and others.[24] From a sociological standpoint, however—and this is what makes sociology as a scientific discipline so suspect for many non-sociologists—there is no systematic reason that genocides cannot be reconstructed in exactly the same way as the development of atomic energy, the emergence of new regimes of factory work, or the genesis of universal human rights.

Notes

1 This chapter is based on the introduction of my book Kühl (2016).

2 In a certain respect, this approach runs counter to the current tendency to explain mass violence through the absence rather than the presence of state organizations; see, for example, Sémelin 2007; Gerlach 2010. I believe such an explanation is plausible for the mass killings in Indonesia in 1965–6, Bangladesh in 1971–7, and even—with some qualifications—in Rwanda in 1994 or the former Yugoslavia in 1991–5. But when it comes, for example, to the Holocaust, this explanation only applies to the phase from late 1944 to early May 1945. The difference between the Holocaust and many other mass killings of political, ethnic, or religious minorities is precisely that the Holocaust had the strong support of the state system.

3 Even taking more recent sociological works on the subject into account, one could almost say there was a type of cultivated "organizational sociological ignorance" at play here. The most prominent example of such ignorance is Bauman (1989, 18), who ignores all of the more advanced organizational sociological approaches. But even more recent innovative sociological studies, which look at the interaction between perpetrators and victims by focusing on spaces (see, for example Christ 2011), largely neglect the organizational perspective.

4 This is according to Bauman (1989, 76 and 99). Bauman adopts Weber's understanding of organizations, as can be seen in the fact that he frequently refers to "bureaucracies" instead of "organizations." However, a similar use of terminology can be found in Raul Hilberg's *The Destruction of the European Jews* (Hilberg 1985, 56). For a critical view of this, see Berg (2003, 135) and Waller (2010). An interesting examination of Bauman's bureaucracy theory can be found in Du Gay (2000).

5 Despite this criticism, sociology did make a contribution by following in the tradition of Raphael Lemkin's thinking during World War II and exposing as a myth the notion that the Holocaust should be viewed as a "return to barbarity," an "operational accident of history," or an "aberration of German mentality" (Lemkin 1944). National Socialism began to be interpreted as a phenomenon of modern society very early on. We need look no further than Arendt (1979); in response to this, see for example, Stone (1996, 36), and Stone (2010, 113).

6 The clincher in Bauman's argument is that, in his view, modernity not only supplied the means for genocide—the bureaucratic organization, the killing technologies, and the binding factors affecting the personnel—but also the purpose; regarding Bauman's understanding of the Holocaust, (see, for example, Imbusch 2005, 449). For a critique of Bauman, see, for example, Chalk and Jonassohn 1990, 5; Freeman 1995, 214; Stone 2003, 239.

7 Sofsky and Bauman view organizations as a core aspect of explaining the Holocaust, but they almost entirely ignore key research in organizational sociology. I suspect that both of them more or less blindly follow Weber's bureaucracy theory, though in Sofsky's case this stands in stark contrast to his deliberations on the figuration of social power as developed with Rainer Paris; (see Sofsky & Paris 1994). For an early reference to the concept of the death factory, see Arendt (1994, 159); for a detailed examination of the concept of the death factory, see Lüdtke (1996).

8 Regarding this criticism see, for example, Kiepe (2007, 58) or Bloxham (2008, 209). Sofsky (1997, 260) is aware of the "primitive pattern" behind Bełżec, Sobibór, and Treblinka, but for him the "high degree of improvisation" was not part of the "organizational routine." It was merely the precursor of a more rational form of extermination in Auschwitz-Birkenau; in "Violence: Terrorism, Genocide, War," however, Sofsky (2003, 68) himself warns against applying "the bureaucratic concept to processes of collective violence." The focus on Auschwitz also seems to be important because the uniqueness of Auschwitz rests solely on the fact that killing was organized in a factory-like way there.

9 For an early list of these weaknesses in Weber's model of organizations, see Luhmann 1971; see also the summary in Kühl 2013, 52 and 71.

10 Criticism of the machine model in Holocaust research was often combined with criticism of the so-called functionalist approach, according to which the decision to carry out the Holocaust was a product of the competition between different administrative departments of the Nazi state. Explanations like these were said to result in "individual responsibility" disappearing in a "fog of abstract processes" and "unplanned initiatives"; see, for example, Saul Friedländer (2012, 481).

11 see note 4.

12 Regarding the distinction between people and roles, see the detailed study by Niklas Luhmann (2014, 62). Different member-based systems are distinguished from one another in what they ascribe to people and to roles; see the foundational work by Stefan Kühl (2014, 65–85).

13 Even in sociology, there is a split between action theories on the one hand and structural theories on the other. Ambitious theorists have repeatedly tried to overcome this split, however. Take, for example, the theory of Peter L. Berger and Thomas Luckmann (1996), which proposes that structures are objectified by the actions of people or Anthony Giddens' (1984) theoretical enhancement of the sociological truism that structures enable the actions of social agents and these structures are reproduced by the acts of agents, or Nicos P. Mouzelis' (1991) attempt to position structural constraints and freedom of action on different levels of society. But even authors who are often prematurely branded as structural theorists, such as Talcott Parsons or Niklas Luhmann, have made ambitious attempts to reconcile action and structure.

14 This makes it possible to overcome the simplistic contrast between voluntariness and coercion, and between the person and the structure, in Holocaust research. The aim is also to scrupulously avoid such Solomonic statements as "impersonal structures as well as collective and individual actors are important" when explaining genocides; quoted in Gerlach (2010, 283). In the language of rational choice theory, we could say that the precise definition of the relationship between collective and individual agents is the key to understanding what is being attributed to personal or impersonal structures and by whom. For a more thorough application of rational choice theory, see Douglas C. North et al. 2009.

15 see note 5.

16 As an example, see Browning 1998, 151; regarding the heterogeneous motives of the German SS men, police officers, firemen, and forestry officers, see also, e.g., Klemp 1998, 97; Paul 2002, 50; Browder 2003, 409; Curilla 2011, 875.

17 See Luhmann 1973, 266. The impulse to take independent action to achieve a higher goal is referred to in German sociology as the "Prince of Homburg effect"; see Bosetzky 1973, 2–5. In the play of the same name by Heinrich von Kleist, the Prince of Homburg ignores instructions from his "boss" Frederick William, Elector of Brandenburg, because the Prince believes that the only way to win the battle is by disobeying orders. As a result of this, he is celebrated as the victor of the battle but runs the risk of being executed for behaving "incorrectly" as an organization member. Luckily for him, love—in the form of a symbolically generalized communication medium—saves the day, and he winds up marrying the Princess of Orange.

18 Regarding the relationship between moral and legal responsibility, see Giorgio Agamben (Agamben 1999, 22). Agamben emphasizes that "the assumption of moral responsibility has value only if one is ready to assume the relevant legal consequences."

19 see note 6.

20 See the debate in the mid-1980s between Martin Broszat and Saul Friedländer regarding the historicization of the Holocaust. See Friedländer 1987, 310–324; Broszat and Friedländer 1990a, 77–87; as well as their correspondence in Broszat and Friedländer 1990b, 102–134. See also Kershaw 1993, 20–41. The controversy is recounted in Frei 2007. The debate prompted Saul Friedländer to call for an integrated Holocaust historiography that would link together the decisions of Nazi organizations, the support and resistance of the population in the German Reich, and the perceptions and reactions of the Jewish population.

21 "The theory of action," Sofsky (1996, 69) argues, "misappropriates the situation of the subjugated." He says it is "deaf and blind to the torment of the victims." Regarding both the analytical and normative character of Sofsky's centering of violence, see Trotha 1997, 39; regarding the dangers of "victimism," see Michel Wieviorka (Wieviorka 2009, 63).

22 Regarding this position, see Bauer 1990, 145. The best commentary on the postulate that attempts an explanation would "ruin the unique and unsayable character of Auschwitz" comes from Agamben, who asks "why confer on extermination the prestige of the mystical?" See Agamben 1999, 31.

23 This is the argument of Michael Neumann, (for example, in Neumann 1995, 67). See also Wolfgang Sofsky (1996, 69), who says that violence is fundamentally "meaningless" ("*sinnlos*").

24 Regarding this, see Nedelmann (1997, 78f.), who suggests reconstructing the "reciprocal curtains of meaning" relating to violent interactions.

References

Agamben, Giorgio. 1999. *Remnants of Auschwitz: The Witness and the Archive*. Brooklyn: Zone Books.
Arendt, Hannah. 1979. *The Origins of Totalitarianism*. London: Harcourt Brace.
Arendt, Hannah. 1984. *Eichmann in Jerusalem. A Report on the Banality of Evil*. London: Penguin.

Arendt, Hannah. 1994. *Essays in Understanding 1930–1954.* New York: Harcourt.
Bauer, Yehuda. 1990. "Is the Holocaust Explicable?" *Holocaust and Genocide Studies* 5: 145–156.
Bauman, Zygmunt. 1989. *Modernity and the Holocaust.* Ithaca: Cornell University Press.
Berg, Nicolas. 2003. *Der Holocaust und die westdeutschen Historiker. Erforschung und Erinnerung.* Göttingen: Wallstein.
Berger, Peter L., & Thomas Luckmann. 1966. *The Social Construction of Reality.* New York: Anchor.
Bloxham, Donald. 2008. "Organized Mass Murder: Structure, Participation, and Motivation in Comparative Perspective." *Holocaust Genocide Studies* 22: 203–245.
Bosetzky, Horst. 1973. "Das 'Überleben' in Großorganisationen und der Prinz-von-Homburg-Effekt." *Deutsche Verwaltungspraxis* 29: 2–5.
Broszat, Martin. 1990a. "A Plea for the Historicization of National Socialism." In *Reworking the Past: Hitler, the Holocaust, and the Historians' Debate,* edited by Peter Baldwin, 77–87. Boston: Beacon Press.
Broszat, Martin. 1990b. "A Controversy about the Historicization of National Socialism." In *Reworking the Past: Hitler, the Holocaust, and the Historians' Debate,* edited by Peter Baldwin, 102–134. Boston: Beacon Press.
Browder, George C. 2003. "No Middle Ground for the Eichmann Männer?" *Yad Vashem Studies* no. 31: 403–424.
Browning, Christopher R. 1998. "Die Debatte über die Täter des Holocaust." In *Nationalsozialistische Vernichtungspolitik 1939–1945,* edited by Ulrich Herbert, 148–169. Frankfurt a.M.: Fischer.
Chalk, Frank Robert & Kurt Jonassohn. 1990. *The History and Sociology of Genocide. Analyses and Case Studies.* New Haven: Yale University Press.
Christ, Michaela. 2011. *Die Dynamik des Tötens. Die Ermordung der Juden von Berditschew; Ukraine 1941–1944.* Frankfurt a.M.: Fischer.
Curilla, Wolfgang. 2011. *Der Judenmord in Polen und die deutsche Ordnungspolizei.* Paderborn: Schöningh.
Du Gay, Paul. 2000. *In Praise of Bureaucracy.* London: Sage.
Freeman, Michael. 1995. "Genocide, Civilization and Modernity." *British Journal of Sociology* 46: 207–223.
Frei, Norbert. 2007. *Martin Broszat, der "Staat Hitlers" und die Historisierung des Nationalsozialismus.* Göttingen: Wallstein.
Friedländer, Saul. 1987. "Some Reflections on the Historicisation of National Socialism." *Tel Aviver Jahrbuch Für Deutsche Geschichte* 16: 310–324.
Friedländer, Saul. 2012. "Wege der Holocaust-Geschichtsschreibung." In *Gesellschaft – Gewalt – Vertrauen. Jan Philipp Reemtsma zum 60. Geburtstag,* edited by Ulrich Bielefeld, Heinz Bude, et al., 471–488. Hamburg: Hamburger Edition.
Gerlach, Christian. 2010. *Extremely Violent Societies. Mass Violence in the Twentieth-Century World.* Cambridge: Cambridge University Press.
Giddens, Anthony. 1984. *The Constitution of Society.* Cambridge: Polity.
Goldhagen, Daniel Jonah. 2007. "The Paradigm Challenged: Study of the Holocaust." In *Tikkun Reader: 20th Anniversary,* edited by Michael Lerner, 195–210. Lanham, MD: Rowland & Littlefield.
Heidegger, Martin. 2012. "Insight into That Which Is. Bremen Lectures 1949 – The Danger." In *Bremen and Freiburg Lectures,* edited by Martin Heidegger, 44–63. Bloomington: Studies in Continental Thought.
Heyl, Matthias. 1996. *Zur Diskussion um Goldhagens Buch "Hitlers willige Vollstrecker.* Hamburg: Unveröff. Ms.
Hilberg, Raul. 1985. *The Destruction of the European Jews.* New York: Holmes & Meier.
Imbusch, Peter. 2005. *Moderne und Gewalt. Zivilisationstheoretische Perspektiven auf das 20. Jahrhundert.* Wiesbaden: VS Verlag für Sozialwissenschaften.
Kershaw, Ian. 1993. "'Normality' and Genocide." In *Reevaluating the Third Reich,* edited by Thomas Childers and Jane Caplan, 20–41. New York, London: Holmes & Meier.
Kiepe, Jan. 2007. *Das Reservepolizeibataillon 101 vor Gericht. NS-Täter in Selbst- und Fremddarstellungen.* Hamburg: Lit Verlag.
Klemp, Stefan. 1998. *Freispruch für das "Mord-Bataillon."* Münster: Lit.
Kühl, Stefan. 2013. *Organizations. A Systems Approach.* Farnham: Gower.
Kühl, Stefan. 2014. "Gruppen, Organisationen, Familien und Bewegungen. Zur Soziologie mitgliedschaftsbasierter Systeme zwischen Interaktion und Gesellschaft." In *Interaktion – Organisation – Gesellschaft. Sonderband der Zeitschrift für Soziologie,* edited by Bettina Heinz and Hartmann Tyrell, 65–85. Stuttgart: Lucius & Lucius.
Kühl, Stefan. 2016. *Ordinary Organizations. Why Normal Men Carried out the Holocaust.* Cambridge, Malden: Polity Press.

Lemkin, Raphael. 1944. *Axis Rule in Occupied Europe*. Washington, DC: Carnegie Endowment for International Peace.
Lüdtke, Alf. 1996. "Der Bann der Wörter: 'Todesfabriken'. Vom Reden über den NS-Völkermord – das auch ein Verschweigen ist." *Werkstattgeschichte* 13: 5–18.
Luhmann, Niklas. 1964. *Funktionen und Folgen formaler Organisation*, 132. Berlin: Duncker & Humblot.
Luhmann, Niklas. 1971. "Zweck – Herrschaft – System. Grundbegriffe und Prämissen Max Webers." In *Politische Planung*, edited by Niklas Luhmann, 90–112. Opladen: WDV.
Luhmann, Niklas. 1973. *Zweckbegriff und Systemrationalität*. Frankfurt a.M.: Suhrkamp.
Luhmann, Niklas. 2000. *Organisation und Entscheidung*. Opladen: WDV.
Luhmann, Niklas. 2014. *A Sociological Theory of Law*. Oxford, New York: Oxford University Press.
Mouzelis, Nicos P. 1991. *Back to Sociological Theory: The Construction of Social Orders*. New York: St. Martin's Press.
Nedelmann, Birgitta. 1997. "Gewaltsoziologie am Scheideweg. Die Auseinandersetzung in der gegenwärtigen und Wege der künftigen Gewaltforschung." In *Soziologie der Gewalt. Sonderheft der Kölner Zeitschrift für Soziologie und Sozialpsychologie*, edited by Trutz von Throtha, 59–85. Opladen: WDV.
Neumann, Michael. 1995. "Schwierigkeiten der Soziologie mit der Gewaltanalyse." *Mittelweg* 36(4): 65–68.
North, Douglas C., et al. 2009. *Violence and Social Order: A Conceptual Framework for Interpreting Recorded Human History*. Cambridge: Cambridge University Press.
Paul, Gerhard. 2002. "Von Psychopathen, Technokraten des Terrors und 'ganz gewöhnlichen' Deutschen. Die Täter der Shoah im Spiegel der Forschung." In *Die Täter der Shoah. Fanatische Nationalsozialisten oder ganz normale Deutsche?* edited by Gerhard Paul, 13–87, 50. Göttingen: Walter de Gruyter.
Reemtsma, Jan Philipp. 2002. *Die Gewalt spricht nicht. Drei Reden*. Stuttgart: Reclam.
Sémelin, Jacques. 2007. *Säubern und Vernichten. Die Politik der Massaker und Völkermorde*. Hamburg: Hamburger Edition.
Sofsky, Wolfgang. 1996. *Traktat über die Gewalt*. Frankfurt a.M.: Fischer.
Sofsky, Wolfgang. 1997. *The Order of Terror. The Concentration Camp*. Princeton: Princeton University Press.
Sofsky, Wolfgang. 2003. *Violence. Terrorism, Genocide, War*. London: Granta.
Sofsky, Wolfgang & Rainer Paris. 1994. *Figurationen sozialer Macht. Autorität, Stellvertretung, Koalition*. Frankfurt a.M.: Suhrkamp.
Stone, Dan. 1996. *The Construction of the Holocaust. Genocide and the Philosophy of History*. Oxford: Oxford University Press.
Stone, Dan. 2003. *Constructing the Holocaust*. London: Vallentine Mitchell.
Stone, Dan. 2010. *Histories of the Holocaust*. Oxford, New York: Oxford University Press.
Trotha, Trutz von. 1997. "Zur Soziologie der Gewalt." In *Soziologie der Gewalt. Sonderheft der Kölner Zeitschrift für Soziologie und Sozialpsychologie*, edited by Trutz von Trotha, 9–56. Opladen: WDV.
Waller, James E. 2010. "The Social Sciences." In *The Oxford Handbook of Holocaust Studies*, edited by Peter Hayes and John K. Roth, 667–679. Oxford: Oxford University Press.
Weber, Max. 1976. *Wirtschaft und Gesellschaft*. Tübingen: J.C.B. Mohr.
Wieviorka, Michel. 2009. *Violence*. London: Sage.

4

Stanley Milgram's Obedience Experiments

Stephen Gibson[1]

Stanley Milgram's experiments on obedience to authority are amongst the most influential and controversial research programs in the social sciences. Infamous for both the troubling ethical issues they raise and their apparent finding that a majority of people will passively administer potentially harmful electric shocks to someone they perceive to be an innocent victim, Milgram's experiments have frequently been used in attempts to explain perpetrator behavior in a range of abuses and atrocities (e.g., Fiske et al. 2004; Lankford 2009; Miller 2004). Moreover, they remain one of the few academic studies to have achieved a life beyond academia, influencing popular culture and the wider public. For example, the obedience experiments were featured at length in a recent Hollywood biopic of Milgram, *Experimenter*, and they continue to be cited and discussed in documentaries, news reports, and opinion pieces. Moreover, the academic influence of Milgram's experiments stretches far beyond his "home" discipline of psychology, with scholars in disciplines such as law, management, nursing, criminology, political science, and beyond drawing inspiration from their results (Miller 2016).

Given this wealth of commentary, discussion, and influence, one might be forgiven for thinking that we know all there is to know about Milgram's studies. However, in recent years a critical re-evaluation of the experiments has been underway. This renewed interest—much of which draws on the wealth of material available in Milgram's archive at Yale University—has highlighted previously unknown aspects of the obedience experiments that fundamentally change the way we should understand them and the wider phenomenon of obedience they purport to illustrate. However, this revised view of Milgram's work has yet to find its way into textbook accounts of the studies (Griggs & Whitehead 2015a, 2015b). The present chapter thus seeks to provide an overview of the experiments, summarize the initial critical reaction to them, and introduce the more recent work that has challenged the received view of the experiments.

Milgram's Obedience Experiments

Milgram's (1963, 1965a, 1974) obedience experiments were conducted at Yale University in 1961–2. The best-known variants of Milgram's experimental procedure involved a participant arriving at a laboratory to take part in what he or she thought was a study of the effects of punishment on learning. Participants were met by a gray-coated experimenter and shortly afterwards were joined by another person, who appeared to be a fellow "ordinary" member of the public taking part in the study. Unbeknownst to the participants, this person was in fact a confederate employed by Milgram to play the role of the victim. The experimenter proceeded to explain that the participants were required to draw lots to see which of them would take on the role of "teacher," and which would take on the role of "learner." The drawing of lots was rigged so that the naïve participant was always the teacher, and the confederate—known as "Mr. Wallace"—was always the learner.

The experimenter then led Mr. Wallace into an adjoining room where—in full view of the naïve participant—he was strapped into a chair and had electrodes attached to his arm in order that he could receive punishment in the form of electric shocks. The experimenter then led the teacher back into the main laboratory, where he explained that the teacher was to administer a learning task involving word pairs. The learner would give his responses via a button in front of him in the adjoining room, and his answers would be indicated on a display box in the main laboratory. If the learner made a mistake, the teacher was to deliver an electric shock using an imposing-looking shock generator. This machine had a series of levers indicating shock levels beginning at 15 volts, and rising in 15-volt increments all the way to 450 volts. The teacher was to move along the shock scale with each successive wrong answer.

As the experiment got under way, it became apparent to the teacher that the learner—who was responding according to a pre-planned sequence—was making a lot of mistakes and so the teacher was required to move along the shock scale fairly swiftly. After the 75-volt shock, the learner began to yelp in pain, and these exclamations became more vociferous until, following the 150-volt shock, he demanded to be released from the experiment. If the teacher kept on with the procedure, the learner's protestations continued to intensify, culminating in what might best be described as a strangulated scream and—in some variants—an ominous silence.

If the teacher hesitated or refused to continue at any point, the experimenter had at his disposal a series of verbal "prods" that he was to use in an attempt to elicit obedience. Four of these prods were sequential and thus had to be used in order, and started afresh for each new attempt at defiance:

> Prod 1: Please continue *or* Please go on.
> Prod 2: The experiment requires that you continue.
> Prod 3: It is absolutely essential that you continue.
> Prod 4: You have no other choice; you *must* go on.
>
> *(Milgram 1974, 21, italics in original)*

Two further prods could be used more flexibly as the situation demanded: "Although the shocks may be painful, there is no permanent tissue damage, so please go on" (*ibid.*), and "Whether the learner likes it or not, you must go on until he has learned all the word pairs correctly. So please go on" (*ibid.*, 22). If a participant received the fourth sequential prod and still defied the experimenter, the session was ended and the participant counted as defiant. Under these conditions, around 65% of participants were obedient, having reached the end of the shock scale and administered the 450-volt shock three times (although this fell to 50% when Milgram used different personnel in the role of experimenter and learner).

In his most comprehensive account of the studies, Milgram (1974) outlined a series of different experimental conditions that varied this basic procedure to a greater or lesser extent. The details of these variations need not concern us here, but it is important to note that in several conditions Milgram found notably lower rates of obedience. For example, when the participant had to physically force the learner's hand onto a plate in order for the electric shock to be administered, obedience was 30%. Similarly, when the experimenter left the room and gave his orders by telephone, obedience fell to 20.5%. When two additional confederates were employed as "defiant" extra teachers, the obedience rate amongst the naïve participants was reduced to only 10%. And in a series of conditions that varied the experimental roles, Milgram showed that any role permutations that reduced the status of the person demanding that the shocks continue led to marked reductions in obedience. Finally, it is notable that although the vast majority of Milgram's participants were men, he ran one condition—using the baseline procedure described above—in which women took part. He found the same level of obedience in this condition as in the equivalent male condition (65%).

Milgram's (1974) theoretical account of his findings focused on a process that he termed the *agentic shift*, whereby his obedient participants underwent a psychological shift from seeing themselves as the authors of their own actions to feeling themselves to be mere agents for the wishes of the authority figure. Milgram suggested that this process underlies perpetrator behavior in contexts such as the Holocaust and the My Lai Massacre. However, Milgram's theory of obedience was at best partially supported by his own data, with subsequent studies finding limited evidence in support of the idea of an agentic shift (Mantell & Panzarella 1976; Miller 1986). Indeed, even scholars who defended the value and importance of Milgram's experiments have tended to regard his theory as the weakest element of his work (e.g., Blass 2004; Miller 1986).

Reactions to the Obedience Experiments

Milgram's work proved to be immediately controversial, with high-profile ethical (Baumrind 1964) and methodological (Orne & Holland 1968) critiques questioning the meaning and value of the obedience experiments. It is notable that, for such an influential set of studies, there were relatively few attempts to replicate and extend Milgram's obedience experiments. The ethical controversy that they provoked likely has a key role in explaining this, with even researchers who have defended the intellectual value of the experiments sometimes reluctant to countenance their own experimental studies of destructive obedience (e.g., Smith 1976). Nevertheless, a small body of work that attempted to wrestle with the phenomena identified by Milgram did develop in the 1970s (for a summary, see Miller 1986). However, as Blass (1999) noted, these studies had fizzled out by the mid-1980s. Blass (1999, 2012) reviewed studies that had used the Milgram paradigm to explore whether the overall pattern of obedience observed in these experiments pointed to gender differences, cultural differences, or change over time in levels of obedience. No evidence for any such differences was found.

Other researchers moved beyond more-or-less direct attempts at replication and instead attempted to conceptually extend the study of obedience. Of particular note were Mixon's (1972, 1976) role-playing studies, developed to address the ethical problems caused by the combination of deception and stress in the original experiments. In Mixon's studies, participants knew that the experimental situation was not real and they were instead asked to imagine how they would react. Mixon found that "obedience" rates in these experiments were comparable with those found by Milgram, leading him to suggest that role-playing was a viable method for studying obedience. However, the limitations of role-playing have generally been held to lie in a combination of its requirement that participants are aware of the experimental manipulation, together with the need for comparability with the original (deceptive) studies. "Success" in a role-playing experiment is thus typically claimed when obedience rates are comparable with Milgram's original, making it difficult to be clear on whether any deviation from this would be an indication of a variation in levels of obedience or simply an inadequate role-playing simulation.

A further notable conceptual extension of Milgram's studies is Meeus and Raaijmakers' (1986, 1987) experiments on administrative obedience. Rather than electric shocks, participants in Meeus and Raaijmakers' studies were ordered to deliver negative task feedback to someone who they believed to be a job applicant. The feedback consisted of verbal remarks, which—if followed completely—would result in the applicant failing to get the job. The experimenter had a similar set of prods to those used in Milgram's studies. Meeus and Raaijmakers found that participants in conditions modeled on Milgram's baseline procedure displayed higher levels of obedience than Milgram's participants did—this was in line with their hypothesis that the use of administrative rather than destructive obedience would lead to lower levels of defiance. Notably, in conditions modeled on Milgram's "two-peers rebel" and "closeness of authority" variations, Meeus and Raaijmakers found similar reductions in obedience to those observed by Milgram. Meeus and Raaijmakers suggest that their findings tell us something about how obedience operates in modern bureaucratic societies, which are less likely to require the sorts of direct physical punishment meted out in Milgram's experiments.

This summary of Milgram's work and the first twenty or so years of work that followed from it is necessarily partial and selective (see Miller 1986 for a comprehensive review), yet it is notable that direct empirical engagement with Milgram-esque phenomena faded away in the early part of the 1980s (Blass 2012; Kaposi 2017). Milgram's studies remained a staple of undergraduate psychology textbooks and were drawn on across a range of other disciplines, but attempts to directly engage with the problem of obedience (as Milgram saw it) were conspicuous by their absence for around two decades. This began to change, however, in (roughly) the middle of the first decade of the twenty-first century.

A New Wave

The renewed engagement with the obedience experiments is too voluminous to review comprehensively in the present chapter.[2] Instead, in this section I will provide a brief overview of four important developments in this re-engagement with the study of destructive obedience, before focusing on what to me remains the most fascinating element of the new wave of interest in Milgram's work: the wealth of material from the studies that is available in the Yale archives.

First, Jerry Burger (2009) conducted an influential partial replication of Milgram's experiment with the explicit aim of developing a variant on the obedience paradigm that allowed for the re-opening of the direct experimental study of destructive obedience in a way that addressed the ethical concerns surrounding Milgram's procedure. Burger introduced a range of ethical safeguards, including an extensive pre-screening process for participants and the use of a clinical psychologist in the role of the experimenter to carefully monitor participant reactions for signs of excessive stress. Most notably, however, Burger's experiment only ran as far as the 150-volt point in the procedure, which is crucial, as it is the first point at which the learner demands to be released. Following this, regardless of whether participants were about to continue, the experimenter brought the session to a close. In most other respects,

Burger's procedure for his "base" experiment followed Milgram's condition 5 ("a new baseline"), the key features of which were described above. From an ethical standpoint, Burger's rationale for halting the experiment at 150 volts was that the extended sequence of shocks that participants were required to deliver after the learner had demanded to be withdrawn led to the prolonged period of stress. Removing this extended conflict between the competing demands of the experimenter and the learner removed the excessive levels of stress and thus enabled Burger to secure ethical approval for his study.

Methodologically, Burger justified the 150-volt solution because 79% of participants (26 out of 33) in Milgram's (1974) "new baseline" condition who passed the 150-volt point ultimately continued to the end of the shock scale. If this proportion remained constant over time, this meant that Burger could draw conclusions about the number of participants in his own study who would have been likely to have continued all the way to the end of the shock scale based on whether they were willing to continue after the 150-volt shock and the learner's demand to be released. In this condition, Burger found that 70% of his participants (28/40) were still following the procedure when the experiment was terminated. The equivalent figure in Milgram's condition 5 was 82.5% (33/40), a difference that was not statistically significant. Burger thus suggests that there is no evidence of a decline (or, indeed, of an increase) in obedience.

However, the methodological changes introduced by Burger have led to questions over the nature and meaning of his findings. Most notably, Twenge (2009) has suggested that there is no real reason to assume that the proportion of participants who would complete the experiment having passed the 150-volt point would remain unchanged from Milgram's original study. Instead, it may be that any change over time has occurred in response to the prolonged exposure to stress that Milgram created through the requirement that participants repeatedly administer shocks to a protesting victim. At the very least, this empirical question can be resolved only through a fuller replication.

Given the lengths to which Burger went in addressing ethical concerns, it might be assumed that no one could possibly expect to be able to conduct a variant of Milgram's procedure that relied on both deception and the prolonged exposure to stress that characterized the original. However, in a second key development, Beauvois et al. (2012) report a conceptual extension of Milgram's study that appears to have done precisely that. Moving the experimental setting from the scientific laboratory to the television studio, this procedure involved participants taking part in what they thought was a television game show (the "Game of Death"). The show involved the administration of electric shocks to a victim (in reality a confederate) who they believed to be a fellow member of the public. The shocks began at 20 volts and increased in 20-volt increments up to 460 volts. Instead of the experimenter, Beauvois et al. had the game show host instruct participants to continue. Albeit based on much smaller sample sizes than those used by Milgram, Beauvois et al. found comparable rates of obedience to Milgram's studies across a number of conditions. It is notable, however, that in at least one important respect this procedure differed significantly from Milgram's. Whereas Milgram's learner first demanded to be released following the 150-volt shock, Beauvois et al. had their learner wait until 380 volts before withdrawing consent. Participants in the "Game of Death" were thus administering the shocks to participants who—however much distress they may have appeared to be in—were nevertheless seemingly willing to keep going for much longer than in the original studies. Moreover, the report by Beauvois et al. makes relatively little mention of the ethical safeguards they followed, raising fresh concerns about the ethics of investigating destructive behavior via experimental methods.

Third, a number of novel paradigms have been developed that utilize either virtual reality or other "immersive" techniques (Dambrun & Vatiné 2010; Gonzalez-Franco et al. 2018;

Haslam et al. 2015; Slater et al. 2006). Of particular note, Slater et al.'s (2006) influential study had participants administer "shocks" to a virtual reality simulation of a learner. Slater et al. were interested in finding out whether participants' physiological reactions to this situation were comparable with reactions to stressful events, as a means of ascertaining whether virtual reality techniques might be a useful alternative to paradigms that might be ethically problematic. Slater et al. did indeed find that on a number of physiological measures the reactions of participants in their study appeared to mirror the way in which people would be expected to react to stressful encounters. These similarities were reflected in the behavioral responses, with a majority of participants completing the experimental procedure to the end, but some defying the experimenter and successfully extricating themselves from the situation.

These novel and creative studies are valuable additions to the Milgram canon, but—as with the earlier generation of role-playing studies—they are vulnerable to criticism on the grounds that, however similar the apparent reactions may be, participants still know that what they are doing is, in an important respect, artificial. Moreover, they still rely for their validity on comparisons with Milgram's original, causing difficulties for any attempt to suggest that they constitute techniques through which to study variations in Milgram-esque behavior.

A fourth notable recent development is a theoretical perspective proposed by Alex Haslam and Steve Reicher (2017). Their "engaged followership" account draws on the wider social identity perspective (Tajfel & Turner 1979) and posits that rather than obeying orders from the experimenter, obedient participants completed the experimental task because they *identified* with the experimenter and with the wider scientific community that he represented. By contrast, when participants identified more with the learner—and with the wider moral community he represented—they were more likely to defy the experimenter. Haslam and Reicher provide a range of different forms of evidence for their perspective (e.g., Haslam et al. 2014; Haslam et al. 2015; Haslam et al. 2015; Reicher et al. 2012), and their associated critique of alternative explanations of Milgram's findings is powerful and persuasive. Yet in terms of direct evidence for identification in the experiments, the "engaged followership" perspective is necessarily limited in that there is no way to access the identity processes that were in operation during the experiments directly, and any attempt to address this would require a new version of the obedience experiments, something that Haslam and Reicher have thus far refrained from doing. Engaged followership may well be an important part of the explanatory story of Milgram's experiments, but as Hollander and Turowetz (2017) have argued, there is a danger in seeing it as the wholesale replacement for other explanatory accounts. In response, Haslam and Reicher (2018) have argued that it is not their aim to replace previous "one size fits all" accounts with their own, and—while reinterpreting Hollander and Turowetz's analysis as evidence that in fact *supports* their engaged followership explanation, they nevertheless agree with the suggestion that behavior in the Milgram experiments was likely to be the result of multiple processes.

Finally, a noteworthy feature of the re-engagement with Milgram's work has been the use of material from the Stanley Milgram Papers archive held at Yale University. This archive holds material from across Milgram's career, but the holdings for the obedience research are particularly rich, featuring a range of documents and—most fascinatingly—audio recordings of many hundreds of Milgram's experimental sessions. Two outcomes from the archival engagement with the materials from the obedience experiments are worthy of particular note: (1) new concerns raised about ethical issues in Milgram's studies and (2) the extent to which the limitations of standardization in the experiments highlights the importance of language and interaction in the obedience laboratory.

A Renewed Focus on Ethical Issues

As noted above, Milgram's experiments were subjected to ethical critique almost as soon as Milgram's (1963) first paper on them had been published (Baumrind 1964), and this continued to be a strong theme in the first wave of critical reaction to the obedience studies (e.g., Baumrind 1985; Mixon 1972; Patten 1977). However, archival researchers have identified additional practices in Milgram's experiments that indicate that the studies were even more ethically troubling than was hitherto understood to be the case. Ian Nicholson (2011) and Gina Perry (2012) both found evidence that, contrary to what was widely believed about the experiments, Milgram had not, in fact, fully debriefed the vast majority of his participants. Using participants' responses to Milgram's post-experiment follow-up questionnaires (Nicholson 2011), and a combination of audio recordings of the experimental sessions and new interviews with his former participants (Perry 2012), these researchers highlighted the fact that Milgram did not reveal his deception to most of his participants at the conclusion of the experimental session, leaving them believing that they had administered electric shocks (albeit not particularly dangerous ones) to an innocent man. These participants were only informed of the deception when they received a report from Milgram some months later. Specifically, the explanation given to participants immediately after the experimental sessions referred to the shock machine as having been calibrated for use with small animals such as rats and mice. Thus, while the voltages indicated on the shock machine were correct, the amperage of the shocks was adjusted, meaning that they were indeed not dangerous. The learner's distressed reactions were explained as him having become rather nervous and agitated at the prospect of each successive shock, even though the actual levels of pain had been minimal.

Milgram's published accounts of his studies leave the reader with the impression that participants had been informed that they had not really administered any electric shocks, and this is reinforced by the widely used film of the experiments (Milgram 1965b), which features a "full" debrief with a participant being informed that the shocks were not genuine and that the learner was in fact a confederate. However, careful inspection of Milgram's published work suggests that the relevant passages were constructed to be technically accurate, even if they allowed a mistaken impression to be created:

> The exact content of the dehoax varied from condition to condition and with increasing experience on our part. At the very least all subjects were told that the victim had not received dangerous electric shocks.
>
> *(Milgram 1964, 849; for an almost identically worded passage, see, 1974, 24)*

For many years, readers may have taken such statements to indicate that participants were told that no electric shocks had been given, but the key word here is, in fact, "dangerous": "all subjects were told that the victim had not received *dangerous* electric shocks." We now know that most participants left Milgram's laboratory still under the impression that they had delivered electric shocks to another member of the public but that they were told that the shocks were not dangerous due to the way in which the machine was set up.

Standardization, Rhetoric, and Interaction

If Milgram's debriefing procedure was not quite what it was assumed to be, archival analysis has also raised wider questions about Milgram's experimental procedure. Scattered observations in earlier work had indicated that there might be important questions to be asked about the nature and extent of standardization in Milgram's studies (e.g., Darley 1995).

These observations were confirmed and extended by Perry (2012) and Gibson (2013a, 2013b) who identified notable departures from the published experimental procedure. For example, the scripted prods were not necessarily used in the specified order or in the scripted form, and sometimes one or more of the prods were not used at all despite the procedure requiring it. Moreover, additional tactics designed to convince participants to keep going have been identified. This led Gibson (2013a) to suggest that the experimenter may not so much be issuing orders as attempting to *persuade* participants to continue, which, in turn, points to the centrality of argument, rhetoric, and interaction in the experiments. For instance, consider the following example (for transcription conventions, see Appendix):

Extract: Participant 0208

T: I'm going to administer a hundred and twenty volts.
((SHOCK))
L: URGH! Hey these really hurt.
(3)
T: I don't think I wanna, be a part of this anymore.
(2)
E: Please continue.
T: No.
(11)
E: It's absolutely essential that you go on.
(2)
T: Well if he says it's all right it's all right with me will you ask him if he wants to go on?
(3)
E: Whether the learner likes it or not er, we must continue.
T: I wouldn't contin-
E: ((inaudible))-
T: I wouldn't continue without asking him.
(2)
E: As I explained to both er, er to him when you were there, er although the shocks may be extremely painful there is no permanent tissue damage.
T: Well I still th- I still don't want to go on unless he says all right.
(52) ((During this time period movement can be heard, and what sounds like a door shutting. From what follows it seems reasonable to presume that E went out of the room, ostensibly to ask L if he wished to continue))
E: He seems willing enough to go on so please continue.
(8)
T: Wet, night, grass, duck, cloth.

((19 lines omitted, during which the teacher continues with the memory test.))

T: That's wrong. I'm going to administer a hundred
and fifty volts.
((SHOCK))
L: URGH!
T: White, horse.
L: Experimenter! Get me out of here! I won't be in
the experiment any more. I refuse to go on, let
me out!
E: Please continue.
T: Not under those conditions. Not with him
hollering.
E: I just checked on him, and he er, seemed pretty
willing to continue so please continue.
T: No not unless I think, you see he's hollering in
there it's just er
(16)
E: It's absolutely essential that you continue.
T: Well I'm not gonna continue with the man
hollering that he wants to get out of there I mean
er
(2)
T: it might be essential to you but it's not that
essential for me.
(3)
E: I was just in there and he seemed willing enough
to continue.
T: Well, that's what he says but you know it's not
er
(14)
E: ((inaudible))
T: I mean i- I'd be glad to walk in there if he says to
me go on I'll go on but I'm not going to go on
with the man hollering in there to stop.
E: You have no other choice you must go on.
T: Well I don't say that I mean I'm just not gonna go on
unless he says to go on.
E: Well we'll have to discontinue the experiment then.

This extract features a combination of major and more subtle departures from standardization. Most notably, as indicated by the transcriber's comments on lines 27–31, the experimenter appears to leave the room, ostensibly to consult with the learner, before returning to reassure the teacher that "he seems willing enough to go on" (line 32). This appears to work—at least initially—as the teacher proceeds with the memory test on line 35. However, when the procedure subsequently gets to the 150-volt point and the learner demands to be released, the teacher's renewed refusal elicits further departures from the published prods as the experimenter attempts to reassure him that "I just checked on him, and he er, seemed pretty wiling to continue" (lines 65–66) and that "I was just in there and he seemed willing enough to continue" (lines 78–79).

Less striking—but arguably no less important—departures from standardization can be seen in the experimenter's use of the scripted prods in the early stages of this exchange. He begins with prod 1 (line 8), but then moves straight to prod 3 (line 11). These illustrate the extent to which the experimenter could depart from the published procedure in his attempts to secure the teacher's continuation. There is debate over the meaning and implications of these findings, with Perry (2012) essentially suggesting that Milgram's work can no longer be trusted and that he should be seen as, fundamentally, a bad scientist. By contrast, Gibson (2013b) has argued that these findings are consistent with a long tradition of work in the sociology of scientific knowledge that has suggested that science rarely (if ever) works out in practice as it appears in textbooks and the method sections of journal articles. The key issue here is whether we see the obedience experiments as an aberration, the product of an individual who failed to conform to accepted standards of scientific practice, or whether we see them as an example—albeit a striking one—of more general features of science in action.

The departures from standardization apparent in the audio recordings from Milgram's experiments also point to the hitherto neglected role of language and interaction in the experiments. Building on an earlier content analysis of interaction in the experiments (Modigliani & Rochat 1995), Gibson (2013a) argued that the argumentative to-and-fro of the experiments merits greater attention and that the role of the experimenter might usefully be re-cast as involving attempts at persuasion rather than obedience. Ultimately, when attempts at defiance occur, teachers are trying to argue their way out of the experiment, whilst the experimenter seeks to persuade them to continue. We can see this in the extract above, with the participant putting a clear condition on his continuation (line 13: "if he says it's all right it's all right with me") and requesting that that the experimenter ask the learner if he wants to continue (line 14). This exchange continues for several turns, with the participant sticking to his guns (lines 20; 25–26) and the experimenter adapting the prods in an attempt to counter these arguments (lines 16–17; 22–24). Similarly, when the experimenter returns from his staged consultation with the learner, the argument continues, with the participant trying to find the arguments that will draw the experiment to a close, and the experimenter engaging in the flexible use of rhetoric in an attempt to convince him to keep going.

These insights have been developed in a series of analyses of Milgram's audio data (Gibson 2013a, 2013b, 2014, 2017, 2019a, 2019b; Gibson et al. 2018) and have been augmented by the use of the more fine-grained tools of conversation analysis by Matthew Hollander and colleagues (e.g., Hollander 2015; Hollander & Maynard 2016; Hollander & Turowetz 2017; Turowetz & Hollander 2018). This changes the way we should think about Milgram's data. No longer is it sufficient to consider Milgram's data simply in terms of the numbers of obedient participants or the mean shock levels. Instead, the richness of the interactions among participants, experimenter, and others present in the laboratory highlight the extent to which Milgram's data was always much more nuanced and complex than these mere summary statistics would suggest. Indeed, these new analyses raise fundamental questions about the nature of the phenomenon captured in Milgram's experiments and about the meaning of obedience itself.

Conclusion: Questioning Obedience

The ongoing fascination with Milgram's studies can be seen to arise from the use of laboratory experimentation to provide a dramatic and powerful illustration of the way in which people might respond to the demands of authority. The initial controversy generated by the experiments has shown little sign of abating and if anything has intensified in recent years. Nevertheless, the received view of the obedience experiments remains dominant in textbook accounts and makes the continued attempts to develop new perspectives on Milgram's work all the more important. Indeed, there are signs that these new perspectives are now crystallizing themselves into a key message concerning the wider implications for our understanding of the experiments and of the concept of obedience itself.

Perhaps the most important change in the way in which we now think about Milgram's experiments concerns the nature of obedience and the extent to which Milgram's studies can be said to stand as examples of this phenomenon. We have become so used to referring to the studies as "the obedience experiments" that perhaps we have failed to consider whether they really are demonstrations of obedience at all. A number of scholars from a variety of conceptual and methodological traditions have noted that the scripted prods are not particularly effective at eliciting more shocks from participants anyway (Burger et al. 2011; Gibson 2013a; Haslam et al. 2014), which leads to questions as to whether Milgram's experiments are in fact demonstrations of people following orders at all. Moreover, given that social psychologists tend to define obedience as a form of social influence elicited in response to orders/commands (e.g., Burger 2017; Kassin et al. 2017), there is a legitimate question mark over whether Milgram's "obedience" experiments are in fact studies of obedience.

However, this would be to accept uncritically the standard definition of obedience. Instead, we might be wise to reflect on whether this definition has ever really been adequate. The requirement that the specific social act of an order or command be observed before we can classify something as obedience seems overly restrictive. In everyday life, when we refer to obeying the law, we are not typically describing situations in which we are under direct orders from an authority figure. Rather, we "obey" by observing social norms that proscribe certain actions. More formally, we might draw on the influential work of the social theorist Michel Foucault (1979), who noted that authority in modern liberal societies is rarely exercised bluntly. Instead, obedience is elicited through more subtle means and indeed is most effective when people come to regulate their own behaviors. We might, therefore, suggest a revised definition of obedience as simply *submission to the requirements of authority* (Gibson 2019b). These requirements might be stated explicitly in the form of an order, but they need not be. Indeed, when we return to the audio recordings of Milgram's experimental sessions, we find that not only are participants able to resist the experimenter's increasingly strident demands that they continue, but those participants who do go all the way to the end of the procedure typically do so without the need for the experimenter to use the prods (Gibson 2019a, 2019b). We are thus left with the conclusion that this hugely influential and controversial set of studies does not stand as a demonstration of people's propensity to follow orders. Rather, it shows us that when participants are obedient, it is not because they have been issued with orders, and when orders are issued participants are able to resist them. The experiments thus can no longer be used to warrant claims about perpetrator behavior arising because of people following orders. If they tell us anything, it is that perpetrators are—as numerous scholars have noted (e.g., Bauman 1989)—part of a wider system. If this system "works," no direct orders are needed. In Milgram's study, the experimenter only had to resort to issuing orders when the experimental set-up had failed to do its job in convincing people to keep going. We can still identify those who continued as having been obedient, but this did not mean that they followed orders. The authority of Milgram's obedience situation lay elsewhere in its design and execution. If the experimenter had to resort to orders, it was not, in fact, a demonstration of authority but rather an indication of its *failure*.

Notes

1 This chapter includes an extract from transcripts of audio recordings from condition 02 of Milgram's obedience experiments. I am grateful to Alexandra Milgram for granting permission to quote from these materials.
2 For overviews, see Burger (2017), Miller (2016); for important edited collections see Brannigan et al. (2015); Reicher et al. (2014); for key monographs see Gibson (2019a), Lunt (2009), Perry (2012), Russell (2018).

References

Bauman, Zygmunt. 1989. *Modernity and the Holocaust*. Cambridge: Polity.

Baumrind, Diana. 1964. "Some Thoughts on Ethics of Research: After Reading Milgram's 'Behavioural Study of Obedience'." *American Psychologist* 19: 421–423.

Baumrind, Diana. 1985. "Research Using Intentional Deception: Ethical Issues Revisited." *American Psychologist* 40: 165–174.

Beauvois, Jean-Léon, Didier Courbet, & Dominique Oberlé. 2012. "The Prescriptive Power of the Television Host. A Transportation of Milgram's Obedience Paradigm to the Context of TV Game Show." *European Review of Applied Psychology* 62: 111–119.

Blass, Thomas. 1999. "The Milgram Paradigm After 35 Years: Some Things We Now Know about Obedience to Authority." *Journal of Applied Social Psychology* 29: 955–978.

Blass, Thomas. 2004. *The Man Who Shocked the World: The Life and Legacy of Stanley Milgram*. New York: Basic Books.

Blass, Thomas. 2012. "A Cross-Cultural Comparison of Studies of Obedience Using the Milgram Paradigm: A Review." *Social & Personality Psychology Compass* 6: 196–205.

Brannigan, Augustine, Ian Nicholson, & Frances Cherry. 2015. "Introduction to the Special Issue: Unplugging the Milgram Machine." *Theory & Psychology* 25: 551–563.

Burger, Jerry M. 2009. "Replicating Milgram: Would People Still Obey Today?" *American Psychologist* 64: 1–11.

Burger, Jerry. 2017. "Obedience." In *The Oxford Handbook of Social Influence*, edited by Stephen G. Harkins, Kipling D. Williams, & Jerry Burger, 129–147. Oxford: Oxford University Press.

Burger, Jerry M., Zackary M. Girgis, & Caroline C. Manning. 2011. "In Their Own Words: Explaining Obedience to Authority through an Analysis of Participants' Comments." *Social Psychological & Personality Science* 2: 460–466.

Dambrun, Michaël & Elise Vatiné. 2010. "Reopening the Study of Extreme Behaviors: Obedience to Authority within an Immersive Video Environment." *European Journal of Social Psychology* 40: 760–773.

Darley, John M. 1995. "Constructive and Destructive Obedience: A Taxonomy of Principal-Agent Relationships." *Journal of Social Issues 51*(3): 125–154. doi: 10.1111/j.1540-4560.1995.tb01338.x

Fiske, Susan. T., Lasana T. Harris, & Amy J. C. Cuddy. 2004. "Why Ordinary People Torture Enemy Prisoners." *Science* 306: 1482–1483.

Foucault, Michel. 1979. *Discipline and Punish: The Birth of the Prison*. London: Penguin.

Gibson, Stephen. 2013a. "Milgram's Obedience Experiments: A Rhetorical Analysis." *British Journal of Social Psychology* 52: 290–309.

Gibson, Stephen. 2013b. "'The Last Possible Resort': A Forgotten Prod and the *In Situ* Standardization of Stanley Milgram's Voice-Feedback Condition." *History of Psychology* 16: 177–194.

Gibson, Stephen. 2014. "Discourse, Defiance, and Rationality: 'Knowledge Work' in the 'Obedience' Experiments." *Journal of Social Issues* 70: 424–438.

Gibson, Stephen. 2017. "Developing Psychology's Archival Sensibilities: Revisiting Milgram's 'Obedience' Experiments." *Qualitative Psychology* 4: 73–89.

Gibson, Stephen. 2019a. *Arguing, Obeying and Defying: A Rhetorical Perspective on Stanley Milgram's Obedience Experiments*. Cambridge: Cambridge University Press.

Gibson, Stephen. 2019b. "Obedience without Orders: Expanding Social Psychology's Conception of 'Obedience'." *British Journal of Social Psychology* 58: 241–259.

Gibson, Stephen, Grace Blenkinsopp, Elizabeth Johnstone, & Aimee Marshall. 2018. "Just Following Orders? The Rhetorical Invocation of 'Obedience' in Stanley Milgram's Post-Experiment Interviews." *European Journal of Social Psychology* 48: 585–599.

Gonzalez-Franco, Mar, Mel Slater, Megan E. Birney, David Swapp, S. Alexander Haslam, & Stephen D. Reicher. 2018. "Participant Concerns for the Learner in a Virtual Reality Replication of the Milgram Obedience Study." *PLoS One* 13(12).

Griggs, Richard A. & George I. Whitehead III. 2015a. "Coverage of Milgram's Obedience Experiments in Social Psychology Textbooks: Where Have All the Criticisms Gone?" *Teaching of Psychology* 42: 315–322.

Griggs, Richard A. & George I. Whitehead III. 2015b. "Coverage of Recent Criticisms of Milgram's Obedience Experiments in Introductory Social Psychology Textbooks." *Theory & Psychology* 25: 564–580.

Haslam, S. Alexander & Stephen D. Reicher. 2017. "50 Years of 'Obedience to Authority': From Blind Conformity to Engaged Followership." *Annual Review of Law and Social Science* 13: 59–78.

Haslam, S. Alexander, & Stephen D. Reicher. 2018. "A Truth That Does Not Always Speak Its Name: How Hollander and Turowetz's Findings Confirm and Extend the Engaged Followership Analysis of Harm-Doing in the Milgram Paradigm." *British Journal of Social Psychology* 57: 292–300.

Haslam, S. Alexander, Stephen D. Reicher, & Megan E. Birney. 2014. "Nothing by Mere Authority: Evidence That in an Experimental Analogue of the Milgram Paradigm Participants are Motivated Not by Orders But by Appeals to Authority." *Journal of Social Issues* 70: 473–488.

Haslam, S. Alexander, Stephen D. Reicher, & Kathryn Millard. 2015a. "Shock Treatment: Using Immersive Digital Realism to Restage and Re-examine Milgram's 'Obedience to Authority' Research." *PLoS One* 10(3).

Haslam, S. Alexander, Stephen D. Reicher, Kathryn Millard, & Rachel McDonald. 2015. "'Happy to Have Been of Service': The Yale Archive as a Window into the Engaged Followership of Participants in Milgram's 'Obedience' Experiments." *British Journal of Social Psychology* 54: 55–83.

Hollander, Matthew M. 2015. "The Repertoire of Resistance: Non-Compliance with Directives in Milgram's 'Obedience' Experiments." *British Journal of Social Psychology* 54: 425–444.

Hollander, Matthew M. & Douglas W. Maynard. 2016. "Do Unto Others … ? Methodological Advance and Self- Versus Other-Attentive Resistance in Milgram's 'Obedience' Experiments." *Social Psychology Quarterly* 79: 355–375.

Hollander, Matthew M. & Jason Turowetz. 2017. "Normalizing Trust: Participants' Immediately Post-Hoc Explanations of Behaviour in Milgram's 'Obedience' Experiments." *British Journal of Social Psychology* 56: 655–674.

Kaposi, Dávid. 2017. "The Resistance Experiments: Morality, Authority and Obedience in Stanley Milgram's Account." *Journal for the Theory of Social Behaviour* 47: 382–401.

Kassin, Saul, Steven Fein, & Hazel R. Markus. 2017. *Social Psychology* (10th ed.). Boston, MA: Cengage.

Lankford, Adam. 2009. "Promoting Aggression and Violence at Abu Ghraib: The U.S. Military's Transformation of Ordinary People into Torturers." *Aggression & Violent Behavior* 14: 388–395.

Lunt, Peter. 2009. *Stanley Milgram: Understanding Obedience and its Implications*. Basingstoke: Palgrave.

Mantell, David. M, & Robert Panzarella. 1976. "Obedience and Responsibility." *British Journal of Social & Clinical Psychology* 15: 239–245.

Meeus, Wim. H. J. & Quinten A. W. Raaijmakers. 1986. "Administrative Obedience: Carrying Out Orders to Use Psychological Administrative Violence." *European Journal of Social Psychology* 16: 311–324.

Meeus, Wim H. J. & Quinten A. W. Raaijmakers. 1987. "Administrative Obedience as a Social Phenomenon." In *Current Issues in European Social Psychology: Volume 2*, edited by Willem Doise & Serge Moscovici, 183–230. Cambridge: Cambridge University Press.

Milgram, Stanley. 1963. "Behavioral Study of Obedience." *Journal of Abnormal & Social Psychology* 67: 371–378.

Milgram, Stanley. 1964. "Issues in the Study of Obedience: A Reply to Baumrind." *American Psychologist* 19: 848–852.

Milgram, Stanley. 1965a. "Some Conditions of Obedience and Disobedience to Authority." *Human Relations* 18: 57–76.

Milgram, Stanley. (Producer). 1965b. *Obedience* [DVD]. Available from PennState Media Sales, www.mediasales.psu.edu

Milgram, Stanley. 1974. *Obedience to Authority: An Experimental View*. New York: Harper & Row.

Miller, Arthur G. 1986. *The Obedience Experiments: A Case Study of Controversy in Social Science*. New York: Praeger.

Miller, Arthur G. 2004. "What Can the Milgram Obedience Experiments Tell us About the Holocaust? Generalizing from the Social Psychology Laboratory." In *The Social Psychology of Good and Evil*, edited by Arthur G. Miller, 193–239. New York: Guilford Press.

Miller, Arthur. G. 2016. "Why Are the Milgram Obedience Experiments Still So Extraordinarily Famous – And Controversial?" In *The Social Psychology of Good and Evil* (2nd ed.), edited by Arthur. G. Miller, 185–223. New York: Guilford.

Mixon, Don. 1972. "Instead of Deception." *Journal for the Theory of Social Behaviour* 2: 145–178.

Mixon, Don. 1976. "Studying Feignable Behaviour." *Representative Research in Social Psychology* 7: 89–104.

Modigliani, Andre & François Rochat. 1995. "The Role of Interaction Sequences and the Timing of Resistance in Shaping Obedience and Defiance to Authority." *Journal of Social Issues* 51(3): 107–123.

Nicholson, Ian. 2011. "'Torture at Yale': Experimental Subjects, Laboratory Torment and the 'Rehabilitation' of Milgram's 'Obedience to Authority'." *Theory & Psychology* 21: 737–761.

Orne, Martin T. & Charles H. Holland. 1968. "On the Ecological Validity of Laboratory Deceptions." *International Journal of Psychiatry* 6: 282–293.

Patten, Steven C. 1977. "The Case That Milgram Makes." *Philosophical Review* 86: 350–364.

Perry, Gina. 2012. *Behind the Shock Machine: The Untold Story of the Notorious Milgram Psychology Experiments.* London: Scribe.

Reicher, Stephen D., S. Alexander Haslam, & Joanne R. Smith. 2012. "Working Towards the Experimenter: Reconceptualizing Obedience within the Milgram Paradigm as Identification-Based Followership." *Perspectives on Psychological Science* 7: 315–324.

Reicher, Stephen, S. Alexander Haslam, & Arthur G. Miller, eds. 2014. "Milgram at 50: Exploring the Enduring Relevance of Psychology's Most Famous Studies [Special issue]." *Journal of Social Issues* 70(3).

Russell, Nestar. 2018. *Understanding Willing Participants: Milgram's Obedience Experiments and the Holocaust* (vols. 1 & 2). New York: Palgrave.

Slater, Mel, Angus Antley, Adam Davison, David Swapp, Christoph Guger, Chris Barker, Nancy Pistrang, & Maria V. Sanchez-Vives. 2006. "A Virtual Reprise of the Stanley Milgram Obedience Experiments." *PLoS One* 1(1).

Smith, M. Brewster. 1976. "Some perspectives on ethical/political issues in social science research." *Personality and Social Psychology Bulletin* 2: 445–453.

Tajfel, Henri, & John C. Turner. 1979. "An Integrative Theory of Intergroup Conflict." In *The Social Psychology of Intergroup Relations*, edited by William G. Austin & Stephen Worchel, 33–47. Monterey, CA: Brooks Cole.

Turowetz, Jason & Matthew M. Hollander. 2018. "From 'Ridiculous' to 'Glad to Have Helped': Debriefing News Delivery and Improved Reactions to Science in Milgram's 'Obedience' Experiments." *Social Psychology Quarterly* 81: 71–93.

Twenge, Jean M. 2009. "Change over Time in Obedience: The Jury's Still Out, But It Might be Decreasing." *American Psychologist* 64: 28–31.

Appendix: Transcription conventions

The first two digits of the four-digit participant number indicate the experimental condition in which a participant took part, with the final two digits indicating the participant's number within that condition (e.g., 0208 indicates the eighth participant in condition 02). In the transcribed excerpts from Milgram's experimental sessions, speakers are identified as E (Experimenter), T (Teacher), and L (Learner). Other transcription conventions used in the extract presented in this chapter are as follows:

OW!	Capitals indicate utterances that are noticeably louder than the surrounding talk. Exclamation marks indicate increased urgency in the delivery of the utterance.
(2)	Numbers in parentheses indicate a timed silence, with the number indicating the amount in seconds.
I can't, I	A comma indicates a pause of less than a second.
I-	A dash indicates a sharp cut-off of the preceding utterance.
volts.	A full-stop (period) indicates a "stopping" intonation, rather than the end of a grammatical sentence per se.
Why?	A question mark indicates a questioning intonation, rather than a grammatical question per se.
((inaudible))	Double parentheses indicate comments from the transcriber.

5

The Authoritarian Personality

Then and Now

Christina Gerhardt

In light of the Nazi era and the Holocaust, members of the Frankfurt School living in exile in the United States, together with researchers at the University of California at Berkeley and under the auspices of the American Jewish Committee (AJC), carried out a study of anti-democratic and fascistic tendencies. Co-authored by Theodor W. Adorno, Else Frenkel-Brunswik, Daniel Levinson, and Nevitt Sanford and published in 1950 as *The Authoritarian Personality*, the study used an interdisciplinary approach aimed at understanding whether authoritarian tendencies remain latent or dormant. *The Authoritarian Personality* combined sociological and psychological perspectives, in particular the work of Sigmund Freud and Erich Fromm. Aside from Adorno, the other three co-authors of *The Authoritarian Personality* were all trained psychologists: Frenkel-Brunswik had served as Associate Professor at the Psychological Institute in Vienna before fleeing to the US in 1938 after the *Anschluss* of Austria and, after the study, was Professor of Psychology at UC-Berkeley; Levinson, subsequent to the study, was a Professor of Psychology at Harvard and at Yale; and Sanford was a Professor of Psychology at UC-Berkeley. *The Authoritarian Personality* marked Adorno's appreciation of empiricist methods but also his recognition of the challenges posed by them.[1]

Like other studies of the 1950s, such as Adorno's "Freudian Theory and the Pattern of Fascist Propaganda," *The Authoritarian Personality* added a Marxist analysis to Freudian psychoanalysis and sociological approaches. That is, it sought to reveal the relationships among prejudice, xenophobia, anti-Semitism, racism, sexism, and economic factors. The inclusion of economic factors is an approach that had characterized the Frankfurt School since its foundation in 1923 when co-founders Felix J. Weil, who had organized the First Marxist Work Week; Kurt Albrecht Gerlach, who had previously been a Professor of Economics at the Technological University in Aachen; and Friedrich Pollock, who had written his dissertation on Marx's labor theory of value, had considered naming the research center the Institute for Marxism.

When Max Horkheimer became director of the Institute in 1930, he developed a critical theory of contemporary society that brought a Marxist framework together with an array of disciplines including, to name only a few, philosophy, sociology, and psychoanalysis through the work of Fromm and Herbert Marcuse and literature and music through the studies of Leo Lowenthal and Adorno. As Horkheimer laid out in his inaugural address, "The Present Situation of Social Philosophy and the Tasks of an Institute for Social Research," he sought for the Institute to put forward an analysis "of the connection between the economic life of society, the psychical developments of individuals, and the changes in the realism of culture in the narrower sense (to which belong … also public opinion)" (Horkheimer 1993, 12). After the Nazis closed the Institute in March 1933 for "tendencies hostile to the state" and revoked Horkheimer's *venia legendi* (right to teach in Germany), Horkheimer re-established the Institute in New York City in May 1934. The multidisciplinary research conducted there focused on authoritarianism.

Studies of Authority and Family (1936), for example, was begun before Horkheimer, Fromm, and Marcuse left Europe and was published in Paris after they had emigrated to New York City. Drawing on this combination of sociological, Freudian, and Marxist analyses, it considered both the family and authoritarianism during times of economic crisis. Written by Horkheimer, Fromm, and Marcuse, it combined theoretical essays with data, marking a first instantiation of the theoretically informed empirical studies that Horkheimer had called for in his inaugural address. As intellectual historian John Abromeit has argued in various contexts, it was the aim of Fromm and Horkheimer to combine "social-psychological categories developed in the 1930s" that set the tone for the work of the Institute (Abromeit 2013, 13). Even with Fromm's eventual departure from the Institute in the late 1930s, this combination of social-psychological approaches remained salient.

The Frankfurt School's second co-authored volume to reflect such a methodology, again combining sociological and psychological studies, was *The Authoritarian Personality* (1950). While *The Authoritarian Personality* has been challenged and even derided for its methodology, the study remains, as intellectual historian Peter Gordon recently argued, underscrutinized and furthermore illuminates current events (Gordon 2018). Gordon argues that *The Authoritarian Personality* both "claimed to have found a new 'psychological type'" and, "rather more sobering and radical in its implications," "not merely a type but an emergent and generalized feature of modern society as such" (Gordon 2017). This chapter delineates the historical context in which *The Authoritarian Personality* was written. It then discusses the methodology and findings of *The Authoritarian Personality*, focusing in particular on its F-Scale. Subsequently, it considers the study's impact and in closing discusses the relevance of *The Authoritarian Personality* today. Revisiting the study today is timely and, although not discussed explicitly until the end, lingers in the background throughout this essay.

The Authoritarian Personality—Historical Context

The empirical study *The Authoritarian Personality* was carried out between 1944 and 1949 at a time when, as intellectual historian Martin Jay reminds us in *The Dialectical Imagination*, Horkheimer and Adorno wrote some of their most important theoretical texts, in particular their co-authored *Dialectic of Enlightenment* (1944), Horkheimer's *Eclipse of Reason* (1944), and Adorno's *Minima Moralia* (written in 1944 but published in 1951) (Jay 1973, 221). In fact, significant relationships exist among these works. Stefan Müller-Doohm, in his biography of Adorno, writes that *The Authoritarian Personality* could be read "as a continuation of the *Dialectic of Enlightenment* by other means" (Müller-Doohm 2009, 292). As Jay explains, "'Elements of Anti-Semitism,' the theoretical section of *Dialectic of Enlightenment* written with the help of Leo Lowenthal, was complemented in indirect ways by the Institute's work on an empirical project designed to investigate the same issues" (Jay 1984, 39). The empirical project to which Jay refers that aimed to investigate anti-Semitism was the five-volume series sponsored by the American Jewish Committee (AJC) and titled *Studies in Prejudice*. It was co-edited by Horkheimer and

Samuel L. Flowerman. *The Authoritarian Personality* formed the first of the series' five volumes—all published in 1950.[2]

Already in 1942, contacts had been established between the Institute and the AJC. "In May, 1944," Jay says,

> A two-day conference on prejudice was held in New York, at which an ambitious research program was outlined. At the same time, the AJC established a Department of Scientific Research with Horkheimer as its head. It was here that the *Studies in Prejudice*, which were to employ a variety of methodological approaches to the study of social bias, were officially launched. Thus began the Institute's most extensive and sustained concentration on empirical research.
>
> *(Jay 1973, 221)*

The Authoritarian Personality was carried out jointly by the Institute of Social Research—then still affiliated with Columbia University, although both Horkheimer and Adorno had been living in California since 1940 and 1941, respectively—and in this collaboration represented by Adorno, and by the Berkeley Public Opinion Study Group, represented by Frenkel-Brunswik, Levinson, and Sanford, all affiliated with the University of California at Berkeley.[3] Adorno and Sanford were the project's co-directors.

The Authoritarian Personality built on earlier work of the Frankfurt School, for example, the aforementioned *Studies on Authority and Family* (1936) co-authored by Fromm, Horkheimer, and Marcuse. As Abromeit points out, this study

> represent[ed] the first collective research project published by the Institute and thus the first realization of Horkheimer's call, in his inaugural address five years earlier, to carry out interdisciplinary, empirical research projects in which theoretical insights are tested and then reformulated or made more precise in light of the results.
>
> *(Abromeit 2011, 282)*

Philosopher and intellectual historian Rolf Wiggershaus writes that "this was the last such report for two decades" (Wiggershaus 1994, 149–150). Wiggershaus continues: "*Studies on Authority and the Family* was a model of what it meant in practice when Horkheimer made repeated mention [...] of 'continuous collaboration between representatives of various disciplines, and a fusion of constructive and empirical procedures'" (Wiggershaus 1994, 149–150). Thus, *The Authoritarian Personality* can be read as very much building on the early work of the Frankfurt School.

Accordingly, *The Authoritarian Personality* brought together disciplines and approaches, specifically psychoanalytic methodologies with sociological studies. As Adorno and Sanford wrote in a memo delineating the terms of the collaboration: "all are agreed that it would be extremely desirable to induce other psychologists and social scientists to undertake work along the same lines with the same or similar techniques" (Adorno and Sanford 1944, 2). The techniques mentioned refer to data studies. That is, *The Authoritarian Personality* not only expanded the Institute's work in empirical studies but also sought to plant the seeds for further such research, combining psychoanalytic and sociological approaches and specifically drawing on data studies.[4]

The Institute's most recent foray into empirical data studies had been Adorno's attempted collaboration with sociologist Lazarsfeld on the Princeton Radio Research Project funded by the Rockefeller Foundation and carried out between 1938 and 1941, affiliated first with

Princeton before it was moved to Columbia. Due not least to differences in methodological approaches, Adorno's contributions to the endeavor were relatively short-lived and few in number. *The Authoritarian Personality* fared much better by all accounts: the project was more collaborative and better received.

Prior to *The Authoritarian Personality*, the Institute had worked to study anti-Semitism amidst the US labor force in a project it carried out between 1943 and 1945. The AJC and the Jewish Labor Committee (JLC) funded the project. "Its [JLC's] contacts with the AFL [American Federation of Labor], the CIO [Congress of Industrial Organizations] and various nonaffiliated unions facilitated the collection of data [...] was carried on in New York, California and Detroit" (Jay 1973, 225).[5] According to Jay, the project was at once too overwhelming to publish and furthermore, "as Pollock remembers it, the conclusions of the study were so damaging to American labor that the Institute, with its characteristic caution, was hesitant about broadcasting its findings" (Jay 1973, 225).[6] Jay cites Horkheimer, who "as early as July, 1944 [...] had worried about the reaction of American domestic opinion to a 'bunch of foreign-born intellectuals sticking their noses into the private affairs of American workers'" (Jay 1973, 225). It is worth citing this context, since the experience of the nexus of fascism, anti-Semitism, and authoritarianism was at once the motivation for the Institute in exile to carry out these studies (together with others keen to engage the topics) and also the reason—that is, given their status as refugees—for the Institute to tread more gently in laying out explicitly its political positions and economic (read Marxist) analyses than it might otherwise have, particularly in studies it conducted itself, even if or especially when they were sponsored by US-based agencies.

The Authoritarian Personality—Methodology and Findings

The Authoritarian Personality drew on questionnaires and interviews that sought to create a rubric for gauging authoritarian tendencies or antidemocratic trends. Together, the volume measured four scales: the A-S scale, which measured anti-Semitism; the E-Scale, which measured ethnocentrism; the P-E-C scale, which measured Political-Economic-Conservatism or a conservative ideological commitment; and the F-scale, which measured the propensity for fascism or a tendency towards authoritarianism. The F-scale, which will be discussed in greater detail below, sought "to measure the potentially antidemocratic personality" (Adorno et al. 1950, 157).

The questionnaires were distributed to 2099 subjects mainly in the San Francisco Bay area but also in the Los Angeles area, in Oregon, and in Washington D.C. (Adorno et al. 1950, 21–22). With few exceptions, the subjects were of the "middle socioeconomic class." Already, the aforementioned 1936 *Studies of Authority and Family*, co-authored by Horkheimer, Fromm, and Marcuse, had focused on the middle or bourgeois class and family and the socioeconomic factors impacting it. As intellectual historian Thomas Wheatland argues,

> Despite [...] echoes from past work, Horkheimer made the central concept of the study quite clear—socioeconomic factors were conspiring to undermine paternal authority that was typical in the bourgeois family. With the demise of the bourgeois family, the focus of familial authority was shifting from the father to social forces and authorities outside of the family. The primary outcome of this development was the rise of fascism.
>
> *(Wheatland 2009, 67)*

The Authoritarian Personality continued this focus on the middle class.

At the outset, *The Authoritarian Personality* was carried out with college students as subjects. As the authors put it,

> There were enough practical reasons alone to determine that the present study, which at the beginning had limited resources and limited objectives, should start with college students as research subjects: they were available for the asking, whether singly or in groups, they would cooperate willingly, and they could be reached for retesting without much difficulty.
>
> *(19)*

Additionally,

> other considerations favored the use of college students in a study of ideology. In the first place, the intellectual and education level is high enough. [...] And they represent an important sector of the population, both through their family connections and through their prospective leadership in community.
>
> *(19)*

Further, the authors argued that "it was discovered fairly early that the investigation of lower classes would require different instruments and different procedures from those developed through the use of college students, and, hence, this was a task that had best be postponed" (22–23). Later in the study, the authors provide what might be a further rationale for this focus: "It is a well-known hypothesis that susceptibility to fascism is most characteristically a middle-class phenomenon, that it is 'in the culture' and, hence, that those who conform the most to this culture will be the most prejudiced" (229). Given the Frankfurt School's aforementioned focus on the bourgeois family and on class in previous studies, this narrowed focus might not come as a surprise. Yet, given both the Frankfurt School's early focus on the working class and the political importance of the role of anti-Semitism, racism, and xenophobia, as well as authoritarian tendencies in both higher and more powerful classes and in the working class, the narrow focus merits reconsideration and further scrutiny.[7]

The questionnaires were given to students, specifically those attending UC, both men and women; the University of Oregon, both men and women; and the UC extension. Additionally, when funding became available, the study was expanded and administered to UC Langley Porter Clinic Psychiatric Patients; to San Quentin State Prison Inmates (men); to Oregon Service Club (men); to Alameda School for Merchant Marine Officers (men); to US Veterans (men); and to "working class women," who were affiliated with the California Labor School, the United Electrical Workers Union (CIO) or the International Longshoremen and Warehousemen Union (ILWU) or who were Officer Workers or Federal Housing Project Workers (Adorno et al. 1950, 21–22). It is noteworthy to highlight two things related to this study: 1. At this time the socio-economic status "middle class" correlated to students and most of the aforementioned positions and; 2. In terms of gender, the division of the distribution between men and women was almost equal: of 2099 participants, 869 or 41.4% were women and 1230 or 58.6% were men.

As the authors of *The Authoritarian Personality* state, the study's findings could not be generalized for the US population at the time. "It will be apparent that the subjects of the study taken all together would provide a rather inadequate basis for generalizing about the total population of this country" (23). They elaborate that "the findings of the study may be expected to hold fairly well for non-Jewish, white, native-born, middle-class Americans" (23). Additionally, they explicitly address the fact that minority groups were not engaged:

> Groups in which where there was a preponderance of minority group members were avoided, and when minority group members happened to belong to an organization which cooperated in the study, their questionnaires were excluded from the calculations. It was not that the ideological trends in minority groups were considered unimportant; it was rather that their investigation involved special problems which lay outside the scope of the present study.
>
> *(23)*

The authors did, however, believe that the findings they discovered in this focus group would apply more broadly, stating

> when sections of the population not sampled in the present study are made the subjects of research, it is to be expected that most of the relationships reported in the following chapters will still hold—and that additional ones will be found.
>
> *(23)*

Most importantly, *The Authoritarian Personality* put forward the argument that a discriminatory disposition towards one population group tended to mean a similar disposition towards another demographic. As the authors put it, "Evidence from the present study confirms what has often been indicated: that a man who is hostile toward one minority group is very likely to be hostile against a wide variety of others" (9). This observation formed the basis for the F-scale.

The Authoritarian Personality—The F-Scale

The section introducing the F-scale was titled "The Measurement of Implicit Antidemocratic Trends." It was the only section of the volume co-authored by Sanford, Adorno, Frenkel-Brunswik, and Levinson (Adorno et al. 1950, 222–279). As the section's title suggests, the study's authors conjectured that anti-Semitic and ethnocentric tendencies correlated to more general antidemocratic beliefs and sought to ascertain the veracity of this hypothesis through careful study. In the section's introduction, they write

> [a]t a certain stage of the study, after considerable work with the A-S and E scales had been done, there gradually evolved a plan for constructing a scale that would measure prejudice without appearing to have this aim and without mentioning the name of any minority group.
>
> *(222)*

Not naming any particular group would, the authors hoped, avoid cueing to participants the study's real focus and thereby "circumvent some of the defenses which people employ when asked to express themselves with respect to 'race issues'" (222).

The point of the study was clearly to avoid a repeat in the US of the combination of authoritarianism and anti-Semitism evident during the Nazi era in Germany and of fascism elsewhere in Europe.[8] To this end, the development of a more generalized and generalizable scale to measure prejudice seemed beneficial. In fact, the authors explicitly stated that this was their hope: "It appeared that such an instrument, if it correlated highly enough with the A-S and E scales, might prove to be a very useful substitute for them" (222). This more generalized scale was the crux of the F-scale:

> At this point the second-and-major-purpose of the new scale began to take shape. Might not such a scale yield a valid estimate of antidemocratic tendencies at the personality level? It was clear that anti-Semitism and ethnocentrism were not merely matters of surface opinion, but general tendencies [...] Would not it be possible to construct a scale that would approach more directly these deeper, often unconscious forces? If so, [...] would we not have a better estimate of antidemocratic *potential* [...].
>
> *(222–223, emphasis added)*

Given that it sought to measure the potential for fascistic tendencies, the new scale was dubbed the F-scale.

In keeping with the ambitious and newly expanded scope of the study, the F-scale measured or assessed nine different variables: 1. Conventionalism or "rigid adherence to conventional, middle class values"; 2. Authoritarian submission or "submissive, uncritical attitude toward idealized moral authorities of the ingroup"; 3. Authoritarian aggression or "the tendency to be on the lookout for, and to condemn, reject and punish people who violate conventional values"; 4. Anti-intraception or "opposition to the subjective, the imaginative, the tender-minded"; 5. Superstition and stereotypy or "the belief in mystical determinants of the individual's fate; the disposition to think in rigid categories"; 6. Power and toughness or "a preoccupation with the dominance-submission, strong-weak, leader-follower dimension; identification with power figures; overemphasis upon the conventionalized attributes of the ego; exaggerated assertion of strength and toughness"; 7. Destructiveness and cynicism or "a generalized hostility, vilification of the human"; 8. Projectivity or "the disposition to believe that wild and dangerous things go on in the world; the projection outwards of unconscious emotional impulses"; and 9. Sex or "exaggerated concern with sexual 'goings-on'" (222).

As the authors wrote in the book's conclusion, the study's most pivotal finding was the correlation of approach between one of the aforementioned areas and another area. In other words, there exists, they argued, a direct correlation between the private display of authoritarianism and an application of it to public, to political and other belief systems. They state:

> The most crucial result of the present study, as it seems to the authors, is the demonstration of close correspondence in the type of approach and outlook a subject is likely to have in a great variety of areas, ranging from the most intimate features of family and sex adjustment through relationship to other people in general, to religion and to social and political philosophy. Thus a basically hierarchical, authoritarian, exploitive parent-child relationship is apt to carry over into a power-oriented, exploitive dependent attitude toward one's sex partner and one's God and may well culminate in a political philosophy and social outlook which has no room for anything but a desperate clinging to what appears to be strong and a disdainful rejection of whatever is relegated to the bottom.
>
> *(971)*

They go on to write:

> The inherent dramatization likewise extends from the parent-child dichotomy to the dichotomous handling of social relations as manifested especially in the formation of stereotypes and of ingroup-outgroup cleavages. Conventionality, rigidity, repressive denial, and the ensuing break-through of one's weakness, fear and dependency are but other aspects of the same fundamental personality pattern, and they can be observed in personal life as well as in attitudes toward religion and other social issues.
>
> *(971)*

Their study thus revealed that an individual's tendency to break the world down in accordance with a Manichean worldview often, not surprisingly, then shaped positions on a wide variety of issues. In its formulation, the dialectical logic that undergirded the troubling findings of their study bears remarkable affinity to the dialectical structure that informs *Dialectic of Enlightenment*, on which Adorno and Horkheimer were working at the time, as well as other publications of the era examining patriarchy, gender, and sexism, as well as colonialism and racism.[9]

The Authoritarian Personality—Impact

The impact of *The Authoritarian Personality* was immediate and lasting. As Wheatland puts it,

> Although the entire *Studies in Prejudice* were met with a warm reception, only *The Authoritarian Personality* enjoyed a major impact on the history of sociology. In 1973, David McKinney's *The Authoritarian Personality* sampled 101 sociological projects from 1950 to 1957 that emulated the procedures and tested the hypotheses of the original study. Having taken a cursory look at the sociological literature from 1957 to the present, the numbers that McKinney points to are just the tip of the iceberg. *The Authoritarian Personality* generated and continues to generate much interest among researches in the social sciences.
>
> *(Wheatland 2009, 257)*

Dutch sociologist Jos Meloen highlighted the consistent research into authoritarianism since the study's original publication forty years earlier (Meloen 1991, 119–127). Gordon writes that

> Meloen notes that over four decades, from 1950 to 1990, *Psychological Abstracts* listed more than *two thousand* published studies on authoritarianism, while citations to the original study the research group identified as "Adorno et. al." would also soar beyond two thousand.
>
> *(2017, 37, emphasis in the original)*

Despite its influence, *The Authoritarian Personality* was not uniformly well received. Sociologist John Levi Martin revisited the study on the fiftieth anniversary of its publication and criticized it for

> (1) Its fusion of nominalist research interpretation of types (in which empirical results were used to type respondents) with a realist interpretation of types (in which some

> people "just were" authoritarians and others not); and (2) a theoretically rich critique of the authoritarians and a lack of interest in the psychodynamics of liberals.
>
> *(Martin 2001, 1)*

In other words, the study, Martin charged, set out from a pre-supposed bias, which it then sought to affirm. Both concerns, Martin argues, had lasting (negative) impacts on the field of political psychology.

Other scholars, by contrast, argue for the lasting importance of *The Authoritarian Personality*. Psychologists Martin Roiser and Carla Willig, for example, revisited the study around the same time as Martin and wrote, "We trace and evaluate this debate, largely defending the original research. Subsequent argument[s] suggested that the concept of authoritarianism was becoming outdated in post-industrial society, a view that we strongly challenge" (Roiser and Willig 2002, 71). Their main critique of the study is that, in their estimation, "Authoritarianism is better described in terms of attitude rather than personality. This gives a clearer psychological description of political movements of the far right and offers more direct measures for their reduction" (Roiser and Willig 2002, 71). Despite this criticism, Rosier and Willig conclude that the study's

> central thesis remains sound, namely that advanced industrial society encourages the formation of authoritarian individuals who may become fascists and form fascist organizations. This danger has not gone away and its continued study remains essential for an applied and socially concerned social psychology.
>
> *(2002, 93)*

The Authoritarian Personality—Relevance for Perpetrator Studies and Today

The Authoritarian Personality's usefulness for Perpetrator Studies may be a matter of debate. In a talk, Dan Stone discusses the tension between the center and the periphery that informs Perpetrator Studies (2009). Revisiting the debate kicked off by the original publication of Christopher R. Browning's *Ordinary Men*, and his responses to Daniel Goldhagen's *Hitler's Willing Executioners*, Stone considers how Browning's arguments and rebuttals of Goldhagen's arguments gave rise to studies of local decision-makers or actions, far away from the center or Berlin.[10] Engaging each one, he argues that both are important. But Stone also adds that a focus on perpetrators runs the risk of overlooking the social structure.

Historian Matthew Specter adds two issues with regard to the usefulness of *The Authoritarian Personality* specifically for Perpetrator Studies. Firstly, he points out that Browning's study also aimed to show, as the title underscores, how ordinary men, ones who might not necessarily score high on an F-scale, could become perpetrators. Secondly, he underscores that the F-scale, even if it was conducted in the shadow of the Holocaust by refugees from Nazi Germany, measured the beliefs and attitudes of people in peacetime US (1944–1949), a context that differed enormously from the Eastern front between 1942 and 1945.[11]

Nevertheless, The Authoritarian Personality remains relevant to the present day as a result of its main tenets.[12] Firstly, while its genesis, to be sure, stemmed from a concern about the potential for authoritarianism, this analysis was not tethered to any specific nation but rather to a tendency in all societies of late capitalism.[13] As Horkheimer put it in his preface to the study,

> the central theme of the work is a relatively new concept—the rise of an "anthropological" species we call the authoritarian type of man. In contrast to the bigot of the older style he seems to combine the ideas and skills, which are typical of a *highly industrialized society* with irrational or anti-rational beliefs.
>
> *(1950, ix, emphasis added)*

The tendency, as Horkheimer states, is specific to "a highly industrialized society" or late capitalism.

Secondly, the authoritarian type of man is what Horkheimer here calls an "anthropological" species. This concept builds on what Horkheimer together with Fromm had previously called the "anthropology of the bourgeois epoch."[14] Through this concept, Horkheimer sought to connect psychoanalysis with historical and empirical sociological analysis. This multidisciplinary approach, which combines an analysis of historical, sociological, and economic factors with a psychoanalytic methodology, remains key to engaging authoritarianism given the numerous factors, external (or objective) and internal (or subjective), that shape it. For this reason, the study examined both public and private influences. In other words, interdisciplinary approaches remain pivotal for assessing authoritarian tendencies to the present day. Moreover, not only does a constellation of factors lead to authoritarian beliefs, authoritarian beliefs, inversely, often appear in a constellation of arenas. Again, privately held and expressed beliefs might well inform public (political) positions.

To be sure, *The Authoritarian Personality* sought to identify "the *potentially fascistic* individual" (1). Robyn Marasco argues that this aspect was so key to the study that "Adorno intended that the book be called *The Fascist Character and the Measurement of Fascist Trends*, to reflect the political problem at its heart, as well as his main theoretical contribution (the so-called F-Scale)" (Marasco 2018, 716). As Peter Gordon underscores in his essay, this potentially fascistic individual was not an anomaly or an aberration but instead was paradigmatic of a society gone awry. Citing an essay by Adorno, "Remarks on The Authoritarian Personality," which Adorno intended to publish with the study but was not included, Gordon underscores that the authoritarian personality resulted from "the total structure of our society" (Gordon 2017). Adorno was not arguing against the psychological with which the sociological stood in a dialectical tension. Rather, he was arguing for an assessment of that society that has gone awry.

Contemporary right-wing thinking has engaged with the Frankfurt School, including *The Authoritarian Personality*. Martin Jay argues that

> The tenacity of this new variant of the Counter-Enlightenment and its ability to survive attempts, such as my 2011 *Salmagundi* column, to discredit it, suggest that any serious attempt to come to terms with it would require as much of a dialectical account as the one Horkheimer and Adorno devoted to the Enlightenment itself.
>
> *(Jay forthcoming)*

Considering the Counter-Enlightenment dialectically would mean, as *The Authoritarian Personality* suggests, considering the perversion of the high ranker on the F-scale, the potentially fascistic individual as a product of society. One of the key aspects Jay puts forward to begin to understand the current Counter-Enlightenment is to examine the authoritarian personality. "Only then," Jay argues, "might we understand the over-determined appeal of alt-right populist movements that channel contempt for traditional elites and their power and yet yearn for strong new leaders who will somehow resolve their grievances" (Jay forthcoming).

For Jay, too, "modern society was itself the ultimate source of the reification of discrete character types" (ibid.).

It should not surprise that under the conditions of late capitalism a resurgence of authoritarianism has manifested, be it evidenced in authoritarian regimes,[15] in the uptick of xenophobic, anti-Semitic and racist groups and attacks,[16] or in right-wing beliefs and related violent political attacks.[17] Robyn Marasco suggests that "in light of neofascist formations," reflecting on critical theory's project of "decolonization" is also in order (Marasco 2018, 719). As the Institute argued both in *The Authoritarian Personality* and in its earlier studies, highly industrialized societies are predicated on a created split between rationalism and irrationalism, which as a dichotomous logic creates a tendency for authoritarianism. The interdisciplinary approach to address authoritarianism put forward by the Frankfurt School, in its *Authoritarian Personality* study but also in the aforementioned works that pre- and post-date it, remains pivotal to addressing this uptick in authoritarianism.

Notes

I thank the editors for their invitation to contribute this essay to the volume and for their helpful suggestions. I thank Martin Jay, Peter Gordon, Matthew Specter, and John Abromeit for helpful comments and suggestions; Robyn Marasco and Kirk Wetters for generative exchanges; and Martin Jay and Peter Gordon for sharing drafts of their essays.

1 Empirical methodology would continue to inform the work of the Frankfurt School, after it was re-established in Frankfurt in 1950, for example, the study carried out by Adorno 1955.

2 The other titles published in the series are vol. 2, *Dynamics of Prejudice: A Psychological and Sociological Study of Veterans*, by Bruno Bettelheim and Morris Janowitz; vol. 3, *Anti-Semitism and Emotional Disorder: A Psychoanalytic Interpretation*, by Nathan W. Ackerman and Marie Jahoda; vol. 4, *Rehearsal for Destruction: A Study of Political Anti-Semitism in Imperial Germany*, by Paul W. Massing; and vol. 5, *Prophets of Deceit: A Study of the Techniques of the American Agitator*, by Leo Lowenthal and Norbert Guterman.

3 Since the majority of its researchers were affiliated with UC-Berkeley, both the group and the project are sometimes referred to as the Berkeley (Adult) Study.

4 See Jay (1973, 191–193); Levin (1994, 316–324); Lazarsfeld (1969); and Adorno (1969). Both cited by Jay, *The Dialectical Imagination*, 342, fn 2 and 342, fn 8, respectively.

5 On the study, see also Worrell (2008).

6 On this study, Jay also references Catherine Collomp (2011).

7 Jay also references an early Frankfurt School empirical study and an example of the study of the working class and anti-authoritarianism, "Erich Fromm's (1984) initially unpublished study conducted in the waning years of the Weimar era" and "published in 1980 and translated into English" (Jay 2019b). Gordon cites an unpublished essay penned by Adorno that was to be included in *The Authoritarian Personality*, in which Adorno, among other things, calls out the study's focus on the individual's "reactions" rather than on the external "stimuli," such as "economic and historical determinants" that "produce and reproduce bigotry" (Gordon 2018).

8 As historian Stephen J. Lee points out, while almost all of Europe's twenty-eight nations were democracies in 1920 (two were not), by 1939, sixteen were dictatorships (Lee 1987, 1–22).

9 C.f. De Beauvoir (1949); and Fanon (1952).

10 Browning (2017). See also Hilberg (1993). As to the more recent studies, see for example Beorn (2014).

11 Matthew Specter, email correspondence, October 27, 2018.

12 For assessments of the study's relevance today, see also Jay (2019b); Gordon (2019); Marasco (2018); Gordon (2017, 31–56); and Wetters (2016).

13 On the importance of the structural and systemic rather than individualized assessment of the isolated psychopath, and on the relationship between the center or commands and periphery or frontlines, see also Stone (2009).

14 For more on this concept, see Horkheimer (1993, 49–110); and Abromeit (2011, 248–300).

15 The 2018 World Report issued by Human Rights Watch argues that authoritarian populism poses an "enormous threat" globally. Human Rights Watch, *World Report 2018*. www.hrw.org/world-report/2018 Last accessed May 25, 2018.

16 According to the FBI, hate crimes reached a six-year high in 2017. In 2017, there were over 7175 hate crimes, up from over 6100 hate crimes in 2016. Federal Bureau of Investigations, "2017 Hate Crime Statistics": https://ucr.fbi.gov/hate-crime/2017 Last accessed December 2, 2018.

17 Between 2008 and 2016, in the US, right-wing domestic terrorist attacks (115), mostly classified as lone wolf attacks, outnumbered "Islamist-inspired domestic terror" (63) and left-wing extremist attacks (19) as outlined by Neiwert (2017).

Bibliography

Abromeit, John. 2011. *Max Horkheimer and the Foundations of the Frankfurt School*. Cambridge: Cambridge University Press.

Abromeit, John. 2013. "The Limits of Praxis: The Social-Psychological Foundations of Theodor Adorno's and Herbert Marcuse's Interpretations of the 1960s Protest Movements." In *Changing the World, Changing Oneself: Political Protest and Collective Action*, edited by Belinda Davis, Wilfried Mausbach, Martin Klimke, and Carla MacDougall, 13–38. New York: Berghahn.

Adorno, Theodor W. 1969. "Scientific Experiences of a European Scholar in America." Translated by Donald Fleming. In *The Intellectual Migration: Europe and America, 1930-1960*, edited by Donald Fleming and Bernard Bailyn, 338–370. Cambridge, MA: Harvard University Press.

Adorno, Theodor W. 2010. *Guilt and Defense: On the Legacies of National Socialism in Postwar Germany*, edited and translated by Jeffrey K. Olick and Andrew J. Perrin. Cambridge, MA: Harvard University Press.

Adorno, Theodor W., Else Frenkel-Brunswik, Daniel J. Levinson, & R. Nevitt Sanford. 1950. *The Authoritarian Personality*. New York: Harper and Row.

Adorno, Theodor W. & R. Nevitt Sanford. 1944. "Memorandum on the Berkeley Opinion Study Group." October 23. AJC archives, online: www.ajcarchives.org/AJC_DATA/Files/5A56.PDF

Beorn, Waitman Wade. 2014. *Marching into Darkness: The Wehrmacht and the Holocaust in Belarus*. Cambridge, MA: Harvard University Press.

Browning, Christopher. 2017. *Ordinary Men: Reserve Police Battalion 101 and the Final Solution in Poland*. New York: Harper Perennial.

Collomp, Catherine. 2011. "Anti-Semitism among American Labor': A Study by the Refugee Scholars of the Frankfurt School of Sociology at the End of World War II." *Labor History* 52(4): 417–439.

De Beauvoir, Simone. 1949. *Le Deuxième sexe: Les faits et les Mythes*. Paris: Gallimard.

Fanon, Frantz. 1952. *Peau noire, masques blancs*. Paris: Éditions du Seuil.

Fromm, Erich. 1984. *The Working Class in Weimar Germany: A Psychological and Sociological Study*. Translated by Barbara Weinberger. Edited and with an introduction by Wolfgang Bonss. Leamington Spa: Berg.

Gordon, Peter. 2017. "The Authoritarian Personality Revisited: Reading Adorno in the Age of Trump." *Boundary 2* 44(2): 31–56.

Gordon, Peter. 2019. Introduction to *The Authoritarian Personality*, by Adorno et al., xxiii–xl. London: Verso.

Gordon, Peter E. 2018. "The Authoritarian Personality Revisited: Reading Adorno in the Age of Trump." In *Authoritarianism: Three Inquiries*, edited by Wendy Brown, Peter E. Gordon, and Max Pensky, 45–84. Chicago: University of Chicago Press.

Hilberg, Raul. 1993. *Perpetrators Victims Bystanders: The Jewish Catastrophe, 1933–1945*. New York: Harper Collins.

Horkheimer, Max. 1944. "Letter to Lowenthal." July 26. Lowenthal collection.

Horkheimer, Max. 1947. *Eclipse of Reason*. Oxford: Oxford University Press.

Horkheimer, Max. 1950. Preface to The Authoritarian Personality, by Adorno et al., ix–xii. New York: Harper and Row.

Horkheimer, Max. 1993. *Between Philosophy and Social Science: Selected Early Writings*. Translated by G. Frederick Hunter, Matthew S. Kramer, and John Torpey. Cambridge, MA: MIT Press.

Jay, Martin. 1973. *The Dialectical Imagination: A History of the Frankfurt School and the Institute of Social Research, 1923–1950*. Berkeley: University of California Press.

Jay, Martin. 1984. *Adorno.* Cambridge, MA: Harvard University Press.
Jay, Martin. Forthcoming. *Splinters in Your Eyes: Essays on the Frankfurt School.* London: Verso.
Lazarsfeld, Paul F. 1969. "An Episode in the History of Social Research: A Memoir." In *The Intellectual Migration: Europe and America, 1930–1960,* edited by Donald Fleming and Bernard Bailyn, 270–337. Cambridge, MA: Harvard University Press.
Lee, Stephen J. 1987. *European Dictatorships: 1918–1945,* 2nd ed. New York: Routledge.
Levin, Thomas Y. 1994. "Elements of a Radio Theory: Adorno and the Princeton Radio Project." *Musical Quarterly* 78(2): 316–324.
Marasco, Robyn. 2018. "Introduction." In "The Authoritarian Personality," edited by Robyn Marasco, special issue, *South Atlantic Quarterly* 117(4): 715–719.
Martin, John Levi. 2001. "*The Authoritarian Personality,* 50 Years Later: What Lessons Are There for Political Psychology?" *Political Psychology* 22(1): 1–26.
Meloen, Jos. 1991. "The Fortieth Anniversary of 'The Authoritarian Personality'." *Politics and the Individual* 1(1): 119–127.
Müller-Doohm, Stefan. 2009. *Adorno: A Biography,* translated by Rodney Livingstone. Malden, MA: Polity Press.
Neiwert, David. 2017. "Alt-American: The Time for Talking about White Terrorism Is Now." *The Guardian.* Nov 26, 2017. www.theguardian.com/world/2017/nov/26/alt-america-terrorism-rightwing-hate-crimes
Roiser, Martin & Carla Willig. 2002. "The Strange Death of the Authoritarian Personality: 50 Years of Psychological and Political Debate." *History of Human Sciences* 15(4): 71–96.
Stone, Dan. 2009. "The Historiography of Perpetrators." Paper presented at the conference "Perpetrator Research in a Global Context," dbb-Forum Berlin, 27–29 January.
Wetters, Kirk. 2016. "Spectacle, Ideology and Rhetoric of the Authoritarian Personality." *Platypus Review* 91.
Wheatland, Thomas. 2009. *The Frankfurt School in Exile.* Minneapolis: University of Minnesota Press.
Wiggershaus, Rolf. 1994. *The Frankfurt School: Its History, Theories, and Political Significance.* Translated by Michael Robertson. Cambridge, MA: MIT Press.
Worrell, Mark P. 2008. *Dialectic of Solidarity: Labor, Antisemitism and the Frankfurt School.* Leiden: Brill.

6

What's Moral Character Got to Do with It?

Perpetrators and the Nature of Moral Evil

Zachary J. Goldberg

In what ways are evil acts distinct from mundanely wrong ones? Why do we need to turn our attention to perpetrators to understand evil acts? One might think that references to perpetrators belong to an analysis of evil merely in the sense that all acts require an actor, whether evil, mundanely wrong, good, right, or lacking normative properties altogether. Perhaps the presence of an actor serves only to distinguish acts (e.g., shopping) from mere occurrences (e.g., a hurricane), but the characteristics of the actor do not tell us anything noteworthy about the nature of the act itself. Indeed, when we consider acts commonly thought to be paradigmatically evil such as genocide, forced mass starvation, or war rape, the immense and perverse suffering of the victims seems to be both necessary and sufficient for such acts to be properly labeled "evil." Add to the discussion the wide array of motivations that inspire perpetrators to commit acts of evil—obedience to authority, fear, peer-pressure, religious faith, ethnic hatred, thoughtlessness, ambition, etc.—and the focus on perpetrators in an analysis of evil might seem not only unnecessary but befuddling. After all, genocide is considered evil regardless of the perpetrators' motivations. These assumptions easily lead to the consequentialist conclusion that the essence of evil can be found in a certain kind or degree of harm or suffering experienced by victims, rather than in the moral psychology of perpetrators.

Is this conclusion valid? After a survey and evaluation of the most influential harm-based and perpetrator-based theories of evil in the philosophical literature, I explain why the examination of the moral psychology of perpetrators is indeed necessary for a complete understanding of the nature of evil. Specifically, I adopt components of the Kantian theory of evil to demonstrate that consequentialist accounts of evil are symptomatic in that they identify only the effects of evil while neglecting its source. One of Kant's central insights is that evil is an invisible enemy that originates in a person's moral psychology often hiding behind reason and even good conduct. Consequently, a focus only on evil's appearance neglects its most significant aspects. Secondly, Kant argues that it is only by examining the psychology of moral choice that we can hold perpetrators responsible for their actions. I conclude that a complete definition of evil must pay significant heed to the moral character of perpetrators rather than solely attending to the suffering and harm they bring about.

Several philosophers begin with the intuitions described in the introductory paragraph and go on to argue that an extreme kind or immense degree of harm is definitive of evil.

And if a kind or degree of harm is the only evil-making feature of an arguably evil act, then a perpetrator's psychology is irrelevant to the act's being evil. For example, Peter French defines evil as "a human action that jeopardizes another person's (or group's) aspirations to live a worthwhile life (or lives) by the willful infliction of undeserved harm on that person(s)" (2011, 61, 95).[1] This definition identifies a certain quality of harm—that which jeopardizes another's aspirations to live a worthwhile life—as evil's essential component. In another passage, French states explicitly that harm, and not the psychology of the perpetrator, is relevant to understanding evil. "Evil, regardless of the complexity of analyses of its perpetrators' mental states, is primarily about victims. Victimization is the identifying characteristic of evil" (French 2011, 62).

Claudia Card defines evil as reasonably foreseeable intolerable harms produced by culpable wrongdoing (Card 2002, 16). She includes culpable wrongdoing as an essential component of her definition to exclude occurrences of immense harm not brought about by human agents. Card includes "reasonably foreseeable" in her definition to exclude instances of intolerable harm accidentally brought about by a culpably wrong act (Card 2002, 20). To make this condition clear, she asks us to imagine a thief whose act of stealing triggers a fatal heart attack in the victim. This act of culpable wrongdoing causes intolerable harm, but the harm was not reasonably foreseeable as a consequence of the wrongdoing. Finally, Card argues that intolerable harm is necessary for an act to be evil. She claims, "The nature and severity of the harms, rather than the perpetrator's psychological states, distinguish evils from ordinary wrongs" (Card 2002, 3). Since a perpetrator of evil may or may not have motives that are themselves evil, a specific kind of harm, namely intolerable harm, defines the nature of evil.

Luke Russell also offers a harm-based account of evil and defines it as "extreme culpable wrongdoing" where the extremity refers to the potential or actual harm the action causes (Russell 2014, 46, 59–68). It is notable that Russell does not believe that extreme harm must actually occur for an action to be evil. He maintains that harmless evil action, "reckless close shaves," and harmless acts of sadistic voyeurism, along with acts that actually result in grave harm, all fall under the category of evil action (2014, 53–54). To see why actual harm is not necessary for an act to be evil, Russell asks us to imagine an unlucky suicide bomber. If the bomber fails to inflict extreme harm merely because his device malfunctions or he is arrested prior to setting off the bomb, why would we evaluate his action any differently than a suicide bomber who succeeds in killing himself and others? Russell concludes that there is no relevant difference between these two cases.[2] As long as an action is "appropriately connected" to extreme harm, whether the harm occurs or not, then the action can be correctly evaluated as evil (2014, 62).

Finally, Todd Calder argues that evil has two properties: significant harm and an inexcusable intention to bring about, allow, or witness significant harm for an unworthy goal (2013, 188; 2015, 119). He explains that significant harms are those "that a normal rational human being would take considerable pains to avoid" (Calder 2013, 188).[3] This specific quality of harm is both definitive of evil and distinguishes it from mundane wrongdoing.[4]

Note that in these definitions, the centrality of harm does not entail that perpetrators are of no relevance at all to evil action. French states that evil action is willfully inflicted. Card insists that intolerable harm is reasonably foreseeable and culpably produced. Russell also includes that the extreme harm of evil must be culpable. Calder writes that for significant harm to be evil, it must also include an inexcusable intention to bring it about. In these ways, these authors show sensitivity to the obvious fact that whatever kind of harm is definitive of evil, it clearly must be caused by a human agent, that is, a perpetrator.

And yet, it is a crucial feature of these harm-based accounts that each one is "psychologically thin." Psychologically thin accounts of evil do not identify a particular motivation or intention as one of evil's necessary features (Russell 2014, 74–78). Rather, they endorse the view that almost any psychological component can be involved in the perpetration of an evil act. The advantage of psychologically thin harm-based accounts is that they can explain the wide variety of ways in which evil occurs. Sometimes evil acts are motivated by sadism or malice and other times by ordinary motivations such as obedience to authority, peer pressure, loyalty, greed, or thoughtlessness. On the basis of these accounts, one might conclude that if there are no psychological factors unique to acts of evil, and if the motivations behind evil acts can be behind non-evil acts as well, then studying the moral psychology of perpetrators does not reveal anything distinct about evil phenomena. Arguably, evil can be explained by features external to, and perhaps independent of, the psychological economy of the perpetrator.

Several notable historical and psychological studies have indicated that individuals with quite ordinary motivations can perform evil acts when they find themselves in extraordinary situations (Milgram 1974; Browning 1992; Waller 2002, 2014; Zimbardo 2008). The chronology and outcomes of these studies are familiar, and I will leave it to other chapters in this volume to discuss both the merits and criticisms of these cases in more detail. Nevertheless, a brief mention of their impact on evil scholarship is appropriate here. The thesis of "situationism" that these studies endorse—namely, that almost any individual could become a perpetrator of an atrocity given requisite situational pressures—has greatly influenced philosophical accounts of evil action.[5]

The various fields that make up Perpetrator Studies commonly reject the belief that all perpetrators of evil are monsters and psychopaths. There are just too many instances of evil action and too many perpetrators of such instances for all of them to be severely mentally disturbed. Of course, some perpetrators of evil may indeed be sadists or psychopaths, but these individuals make up only a minority of those who have willingly perpetrated acts of evil (De Swaan 2015, 13). The dominant thesis in Perpetrator Studies is that many or most perpetrators of atrocity are ordinary individuals. Even if this claim is well supported, the question remains: why do ordinary individuals perpetrate acts of horrendous violence? The above-mentioned psychological and historical studies have shown that certain situational pressures combined with particular facts of human nature make it possible for almost anyone to commit extraordinary acts of evil.

For instance, James Waller argues that participation in mass atrocity has its possible roots in our evolutionary biology and evolved psychological mechanisms. Although evolutionary psychology explains our pro-social capacities such as inclinations towards cooperation, caring, and non-violent relations, it can also shed light on the darker side of human interaction.[6] Human motivations have evolved through adaptations in contexts marked by intergroup competition for dominance, boundary definition, and fear of social exclusion. The natural and ordinary human need to identify with a particular group, also an evolutionary adaptation to ensure safety in a precarious world, corresponds directly to motivations of social dominance within one's group, participation in an intergroup hierarchical system, aggression towards those who challenge the accepted hierarchy (even aggression by those who are at the bottom of that hierarchy), the psychological construction of non-group members as "other," moral disengagement from these "others," and the social construction of cruelty towards them to protect one's group and its practices (Waller 2014). These natural, ordinary, and pervasive motivations have come to play a central role in committing atrocities. "The most outstanding common characteristic of perpetrators is their normality, not their abnormality; they are extraordinary only in what they have done not in who they are" (Waller 2014, 148.)

Certainly, one must also take into consideration a great deal of sociological and political factors that combine with these various human propensities to explain how ordinary individuals commit acts of evil (De Swaan 2015, 210–213). Putting our shared anthropological features together with common societal and political elements leads many scholars to conclude that there is nothing peculiar about perpetrators of evil.[7] In principle, almost any individual placed in certain situations can become a perpetrator. Based on strong versions of this situationist perspective, one might argue that we do not need to look to perpetrators' moral psychology in order to understand what is distinctive about acts of evil. Rather, to truly comprehend evil, we ought to examine the atrocity-producing external conditions that compel otherwise good people to perform evil acts (Zimbardo 2008).

There is yet another initial reason in favor of rejecting the relevance of perpetrators' moral psychology to understanding evil's essential characteristics. Some philosophers have attempted definitions of evil solely by reference to a particular feature of a perpetrator's moral psychology, only for their definitions to be beleaguered by conceptual difficulties. In contrast to the approaches discussed so far, these "perpetrator accounts" of evil defend the position that to understand evil is to understand the perpetrator of the evil action.[8] Nevertheless, they face challenging philosophical and empirical criticisms.

Several philosophers have argued that evil action is distinguished from bad or wrong action when the perpetrator experiences pleasure in performing the bad or wrong act (Thomas 1993; McGinn 1997; Steiner 2002). For example, Laurence Thomas asserts, "[a] person performs an evil act … if he delights in performing a harmful act that has a certain moral gravity to it" (Thomas 1993, 77). By "moral gravity" Thomas means that an act is "hideous" either inherently, say in the rape of a child, or quantitatively, for example in the massacre of hundreds of people. And some instances of evil combine both hideous and quantitative kinds of moral gravity (Thomas 1993 78–79).

Roy Perrett claims that evil is "wrongdoing which is done *because* it is wrong" (2002, 304). Perrett's definition subtly distinguishes between knowingly doing wrong action, which he does not endorse as evil, and knowingly performing wrong action *due to the wrong-making features* of the action (See also, Russell 2007, 669; Calder 2013, 179–180). That is, one could knowingly perform a wrong action out of greed, boredom, or a whole variety of motivations. And these acts would not be evil precisely due to the variety of motivations. In contrast, Perrett claims, if the motivation for the wrongdoing is simply for the sake of doing wrong, then the act is evil.

Yet, we already know from the psychological and historical findings mentioned above that perpetrators of atrocity can be motivated by banal motivations such as obedience to authority, peer pressure, or thoughtlessness. Although it is evil to pleasurably perform a rape or massacre, or to do so simply for the sake of doing something morally wrong, it is also evil to perpetrate these crimes while experiencing a different affect or motivation. The fact that a perpetrator does not experience pleasure in causing her victim's suffering, or does not perpetrate an atrocity simply for the sake of doing something morally wrong, does not exclude these actions from the category of evil. Sadistic acts and acts done in defiance of morality may indeed be evil, but acts lacking these particular motivations may be as well. These perpetrator accounts of evil are simply too restrictive.

Other philosophers have taken an alternative approach by insisting that evil action is not defined by the presence of a particular psychological feature, but by the absence of one. For example, Mary Midgley claims that evil (which she does not distinguish from wickedness) is primarily negative, characterized by failures and dysfunctions (1984, 7, 12–16). Evil "lies in the failure to do something universally necessary" (Midgley 1984, 131). It is the absence of goodness and "the failure to live as we are capable of living" (Midgley 1984, 8, 16).[9] She admits that the idea of a strong but negative motivation seems "weird," and despite an interesting discussion of Nietzschean, Freudian, and Darwinian theories of moral motivation illustrated by an array of literary examples, she does not provide a more concrete statement of what evil in fact is, or in this case, what it is not.

Eve Garrard's theory of evil emerges out of a discussion concerning what it means to be virtuous. Borrowing the term "silencing" from John McDowell's (1978) analysis of the virtuous person, Garrard asks us to imagine two individuals, both of whom perform a praiseworthy act. For example, imagine that two people commit to spending their free time volunteering for Habitat for Humanity. One of these individuals actually prefers to spend her leisure time on herself. However, she also disapproves of being self-centered in this way and with some inner reluctance overcomes the desire to be self-absorbed. The other individual feels no inner reluctance. She is

> so gripped by her view of the moral necessity of the required act (perhaps of the lives it will save and the pain it will avert) that considerations of self-interest fall away from her, and she does what she should do effortlessly, even gladly, without struggle or regret.
>
> *(Garrard 1998, 49)*

McDowell and Garrard contend that the difference between these two individuals is that the second is virtuous precisely insofar as she does not need to overcome any inner reluctance to do the right thing. The virtuous person is defined by the fact that for her temptations are not outweighed by more virtuous considerations, but rather are "silenced" altogether in the presence of reasons to do the right thing. (See also, Garrard 2002).

For Garrard, the perpetrator of an evil action is the inverse of the virtuous person. The evildoer does not allow moral reasons to be outweighed by contrary considerations; rather she psychologically silences moral reasons altogether.[10] For example, imagine that in 1968 two US soldiers from Charlie Company arrive at My Lai and have different reactions to what they have just been ordered to do. One soldier deliberates over whether he ought to carry out the orders of his commanding officer to participate in the ensuing gang rape and massacre of the villagers. He considers the suffering of his future victims but allows these considerations to be outweighed by his duty (as he sees it) to obey orders. The other soldier does not consider the suffering of his victims at all. He is "psychologically blind" to reasons to do the right thing and he unreflectively participates in the atrocity. He neither struggles with moral reasons nor decides that non-moral reasons outweigh moral ones. For Garrard, this latter soldier performs an evil act precisely because he is insensitive to the presence of significant (moral) reasons against his acting.[11]

Also focusing on which psychological feature is absent from a perpetrator's moral psychology, Adam Morton argues:

> A person's act is evil when it results from a strategy or learned procedure which allows that person's deliberations over the choice of actions not to be inhibited by barriers against considering harming or humiliating others that ought to have been in place.
>
> *(Morton 2004, 57)*

Basically, a perpetrator of evil lacks the psychological and moral boundaries that when present hinder the performance of harmful acts. Evil occurs due to the deterioration of these psychological barriers.

There are two conceptual problems with these accounts. First, they are too restrictive as are the positive accounts we already assessed. Although Garrard's and Morton's theories may identify actions that are evil, the definitions do not characterize every instance of evil. Perpetrators of evil may act on motivations not accounted for by "psychological blindness" to moral reasons or a lack of moral barriers. Second, by focusing on psychological deficiencies, Garrard's and Morton's theories stray from moral evaluation and cross into discussion of what are arguably psychological illnesses. Individuals with the psychological defects they describe might be exempt from moral evaluation due to their inability to control their actions. If all perpetrators of atrocities were psychologically ill, then their actions could not accurately be considered to be evil, since evil is purportedly a category of moral evaluation.

If current perpetrator accounts fail to explain evil, and if we have alternative harm-based and situationist theories that seemingly deepen our understanding of evil's essential features without any detailed analysis of perpetrators' moral psychology, then what have perpetrators got to do with understanding evil at all? The Kantian account of evil provides an answer to this question.

First, Kant states that the essence of evil is located not in the characteristics of an action, even one of grave violence, but rather in the moral psychology of the perpetrator of the act because evil originates in a perpetrator's moral psychology (Wood 1999; Muchnik 2010). For Kant, individuals naturally have the capacity to act either according to sensuous inclinations (what he calls self-love) or incentives to follow moral principles (what he calls the moral law). The way in which the individual prioritizes moral and non-moral incentives relative to one another defines her moral character as either good or evil (Kant 1998, 6:29). The subordination of moral principles to our sensuous desires is the root of all evil.

> [T]he difference, whether the human being is good or evil, must not lie in the difference between the incentives that he incorporates into his maxim (not in the material of the maxim) but in their *subordination*...It follows that the human being (even the best) is evil only because he reverses the moral order of his incentives in incorporating them into his maxims...[H]e makes the incentives of self-love and their inclinations the condition of compliance with the moral law—whereas it is the latter that, as the supreme condition of the satisfaction of the former, should have been incorporated into the universal maxim of the power of choice as the sole incentive.
>
> *(Kant 1998, 6:36)*

Although Kant's use of technical vocabulary can seem confusing, his analysis is at its core quite intuitive. To put it more simply, Kant defines evil as the ubiquitous tendency of human agents to prefer the satisfaction of their sensuous desires over adherence to morality.

Second, Kant contends that since it cannot be that agents are morally responsible for having natural sensuous desires—having desires is a matter of fact rather than something freely chosen—some other factor must ground our moral responsibility for evil. To this end, Kant explains that prioritizing the satisfaction of our desires over moral law is free and, hence, imputable to us.

> [W]e are only talking of a propensity to genuine evil, i.e. moral evil, which, since it is only possible as the determination of a free power of choice...must reside in the

> subjective ground of the possibility of the deviation of the maxims from the moral law…[T]he will's capacity or incapacity arising from this natural propensity to adopt or not adopt the moral law in its maxims can be called *the good or evil heart.*
>
> *(Kant 1998, 6:29)*

Again, Kant's terminology can be confusing. In this passage, he emphasizes that although we naturally possess both sensuous and moral incentives, how we prioritize our incentives is a free choice. For this reason, we are morally responsible beings.

So far we have seen *that* Kant ascribes evil to individuals' moral psychology but not *why he does so*. Kant argues that what is so morally troublesome about certain psychological states—he mentions envy, ingratitude, and joy in others' misfortune as examples (what he refers to as "vices of culture" (1998, 6:27)—is that they hide behind reason and are compatible with morally good outward, empirical conduct. An individual can perform acts that appear to be moral, both to others and to herself, all the while being motivated by immoral incentives. Kant insists that these sorts of acts that only outwardly adhere to morality cannot be constitutive of it because they do not reflect the moral quality of the individual's character. The acts are in empirical accordance with morality but are not done for moral reasons.

But why should an individual's reasons or moral character be morally relevant as long as her actions are in accordance with morality? Kant tells us that the mere absence of suffering at the current moment is no guarantee of its absence in the future. Indeed, if an individual does not have a good moral character, that is, if she has not prioritized moral incentives over sensuous ones, then it is only contingent whether she will act according to the moral law (See also, Goldberg 2017b, 412). In other words, unless the character of an individual is morally good, then it is always possible, and Kant would say quite likely, that at some future time, the individual will cause harm to others.

Although Kant presumably could not have anticipated the atrocities that marked the twentieth century, his insight has proven to be true. Historical studies have shown that when circumstances provided people with the opportunity to participate in atrocities, many did so. The fact that the perpetrators of these acts had never performed acts of evil previously did not have any bearing on their ability to do so when given the chance. If we focus only on empirical evil—the actual suffering of victims—then we might think that the absence of such suffering is indicative of a morally good state of affairs. But immoral incentives can be cloaked in outwardly good actions. As a result, without good moral character, empirical evil is always lurking around the corner. We never know when circumstances will encourage certain individuals' immoral incentives to cause actual suffering. Therefore, if we only attend to evil's empirical features, we arrive at the site of evil too late, only after it has transpired. We miss the source of evil that is present in an individual's moral psychology prior to its outward manifestation.

This is the first lesson we can adopt from Kant. To understand evil we have to comprehend the moral psychological conditions that make possible its eventual occurrence. Suffering is the outcome of evil, not its genesis. If we want to identify the source of evil, we have to turn to perpetrators' moral psychology. I add to Kant's view the contention that by focusing on evil's origin rather than its grave consequences we open up the possibility of preventing it, or at least decreasing the frequency of its occurrences. If evil originates in an individual's moral psychology, then good moral character is the best guarantee against future acts of evil.

The second lesson concerns ascriptions of moral responsibility for evil. We remarked earlier that many notable historical and psychological studies support situationism—the position that ordinary individuals can be encouraged to participate in acts of extraordinary evil due to situational, societal, and political pressures. If one accepts the truth of situationism, then one might also conclude that almost every person is capable of perpetrating evil under certain circumstances. By accepting the claim that situations have such enormous influence over how we act, one might further conclude that moral responsibility for evil action is mitigated due to evil-making circumstances.[12] However, to conclude that perpetrators of atrocities are not fully responsible for their evil actions is counterintuitive and calls into question the possibility of labeling their acts "evil," which is purportedly a term of *moral* evaluation.

Kant is aware that when we examine the moral choices people make there is a great deal that we can discover regarding these choices. Of course, upbringing, education, culture, and political circumstances can affect how people make moral choices. And yet, even with extensive knowledge of the conditions belonging to one's external situation, we still want to know why one person chooses to perform morally good acts and another chooses to do evil (Bernstein 2002, 44). However, for Kant this information remains "inscrutable" to us (1998, 6:21). The reason one person chooses good and another evil remains "inscrutable" due to each person's freedom to choose good or evil. To offer an explanation of why one person chooses evil rather than good is to determine the causes that led to the choice. But for Kant, our moral choices are not causally determined even if they are influenced by external circumstances. Therefore, there can be no causal explanation of why an individual chooses evil over good (or vice versa). We cannot explain why people make the moral choices they do because it is ultimately a matter of one's freedom.

I think that Kant's language here is too strong, even if his more general insight is correct. We do not have to insist that the ultimate ground of a person's moral choices is "inscrutable" to recognize that understanding why an individual makes the moral choices she does is not only extremely challenging but also exceedingly important, especially to the field of Perpetrator Studies. Why one individual chooses to participate in an atrocity and another individual situated in the same circumstances does not is a critical issue. Although we can learn a great deal about moral decisions that lead to atrocity by examining perpetrators' situations, the analysis of situations does not provide a complete answer to this question. Ultimately, we have to understand the moral psychology of perpetrators to gain insight into the nature of evil. Although there are identifiable conditions and certain situations that tend to motivate many ordinary people to perform acts of evil, this is not sufficient reason to conclude that every person who finds herself in the relevant situation is determined to do evil. It may imply that we are severely morally challenged when it comes to avoiding doing evil, but we may all still be held responsible despite this challenge.

Conclusion

There are several prima facie reasons for thinking that we can determine evil's necessary, sufficient, and significant conditions without focusing on the moral psychology of perpetrators. First, evil actions seem to be evil regardless of the motivations and intentions by which they are performed. In support of this idea, there are several harm-based accounts of evil action that offer plausible theories of evil without attending to the specifics of perpetrators' moral psychology. Furthermore, many empirical studies strongly imply that any person can become a perpetrator of evil due to certain evil-producing circumstances; the situation, not the individual perpetrator, informs us about evil. Moreover, many theories of evil that do focus on perpetrators' moral psychology are beleaguered by conceptual flaws. Taken together, these considerations might provide us with persuasive reasons to conclude that perpetrators are irrelevant to understanding the nature of evil. To counter this conclusion, I adopted two lessons from Kant's theory of evil. The first lesson is that evil is an invisible enemy that hides behind reason and even good conduct, revealing that its empirical manifestation is only symptomatic of its source, which is located in our moral psychology. Consequently, an absence of evil harm in the present is no guarantee of its future non-occurrence. Hence, a theory that focuses only on the occurrence or non-occurrence of evil harm cannot be a complete account of evil. Second, even if the thesis of situationism is true, we cannot adequately explain why different people make different moral choices in similar circumstances. This explanatory gap indicates that individuals, not their situations, are responsible for their moral choices. As a result, we can ascribe moral responsibility to perpetrators even if they face challenging situational pressures. Again, we arrive at this conclusion by focusing on the moral psychology of moral choice. Finally, if Kant is correct that scholars of evil must focus on the moral psychology of perpetrators in order to understand evil, and if the current theories that do so are inadequate, then there is much promise for future research in this direction.

Notes

For critical comments and suggestions on an earlier version of this chapter, I would like to thank Paul Formosa and Susanne Knittel.

1 See Goldberg (2017a) for an analysis of this definition as it relates to the notion of a worthwhile life.
2 Todd Calder rejects the possibility that action without actual harm can qualify as evil. He argues that risking significant harm is not sufficient for evil action, although it might be representative of evil personhood (Calder 2015, 125–126).
3 Calder admits that "significant" is vague but contends that it is "easy enough to get the general idea" (2013, 188).
4 Paul Formosa also offers an intriguing theory of evil that distinguishes evil from mundane wrongdoing by a unique quality of harm. Specifically, he calls the harm of evil action "life-wrecking" harm. However, I do not know if it is accurate to claim that his view is "harm-based" because he explicitly advocates for a "combination theory of evil" that includes the relevance of the perpetrator's intention, motive, situation, and circumstances (Formosa 2008, 230).
5 Stanley Milgram's (1974) experiments are considered the touchstone of the situationist argument. It is later and most prominently endorsed and expanded in the works of Christopher Browning (1992) and Philip Zimbardo (2008). See also, De Swaan (2015, 14, 28–40) for a critical analysis.
6 One might argue that pro-social capacities are only superficial having selfish or aggressive goals as their true motivation. This may be true, but it is plausible that human nature has multiple tendencies, some towards cooperation or even altruism and others towards selfishness and aggression.
7 One might object that the findings just described are a result of psychological research showing that my putative thesis is false. However, these findings are a result of research into human psychology in general and not perpetrator psychology.
8 This categorization is borrowed from Formosa (2008).
9 One of the arguments Midgley gives in support of her position is that the view opposing her own is Manichaeism, which is untenable. However, I reject Midgley's dualistic position that either evil is privation or "a radically distinct force in the world" (1984, 17). In (2016), I argue that good and evil are logical contraries. My position does not entail Manichaeism.
10 See also Goldberg (2017b, 407–409) for a discussion of Garrard's theory as a possible interpretation of Kant's theory that self-love is the single root of evil.
11 Note that Garrard's theory does not require harm at all. See also Garrard (1998, 45–46).
12 I am not stating that the defenders of situationism draw this conclusion. I am only pointing out that one could conclude that the thesis of situationism, especially strong versions of it, leads to possibly exculpating or mitigating moral responsibility.

References

Bernstein, Richard J. 2002. *Radical Evil: A Philosophical Interrogation*. Cambridge, MA: Polity Press.

Browning, Christopher. 1992. *Ordinary Men: Reserve Police Battalion 101 and the Final Solution in Poland*. New York: Harper Collins.

Calder, Todd. 2013. "Is Evil Just Very Wrong?" *Philosophical Studies* 163: 177–196.

Calder, Todd. 2015. "Evil and Its Opposite." *Journal of Value Inquiry* 49: 113–130.

Card, Claudia. 2002. *The Atrocity Paradigm: A Theory of Evil*. Oxford: Oxford University Press.

De Swaan, Abram. 2015. *The Killing Compartments: The Mentality of Mass Murder*. London: Yale University Press.

Formosa, Paul. 2008. "A Conception of Evil." *The Journal of Value Inquiry* 42: 217–239.

French, Peter A. 2011. *War and Moral Dissonance*. Cambridge: Cambridge University Press.

Garrard, Eve. 1998. "The Nature of Evil." *Philosophical Explorations: an International Journal for the Philosophy of Mind and Action* 1: 43–60.

Garrard, Eve. 2002. "Evil as an Explanatory Concept." *The Monist* 85(2): 320–336.

Goldberg, Zachary J. 2016. "Evil, 'Evil', and Taking Responsibility." In *Wozu ist das Böse Gut?* edited by Birgit Recki, 17–36. Münster: Mentis.

Goldberg, Zachary J. 2017a. "Evil and a Worthwhile Life." In *Reflections on Ethics and Responsibility: Essays in Honor of Peter A. French*, edited by Zachary J. Goldberg, 145–164. Cham, Switzerland: Springer.

Goldberg, Zachary J. 2017b. "Can Kant's Theory of Radical Evil Be Saved?" *Kantian Review* 22(3): 395–419.

Kant, Immanuel. 1998. *Religion within the Boundaries of Mere Reason*. Translated and edited by Allen Wood and George di Giovanni. Cambridge: Cambridge University Press.

McDowell, John. 1978. "Are Moral Requirements Hypothetical Imperatives?" *Proceedings of the Aristotelian Society* 52: 13–42.

McGinn, Colin. 1997. *Ethics, Evil, and Fiction*. Oxford: Clarendon Press.

Midgley, Mary. 1984. *Wickedness: A Philosophical Essay*. London: Routledge & Kegan Paul.

Milgram, Stanley. 1974. *Obedience to Authority: An Experimental View*. New York: Harper & Row.

Morton, Adam. 2004. *On Evil*. London: Routledge.

Muchnik, Pablo. 2010. *Kant's Theory of Evil: An Essay on the Dangers of Self-love and the Aprioricity of History*. Lanham, MD: Lexington Books.

Perrett, Roy. 2002. "Evil and Human Nature." *The Monist* 85(2): 304–319.

Russell, Luke. 2007. "Is Evil Action Qualitatively Distinct from Ordinary Wrongdoing?" *Australasian Journal of Philosophy* 85(4): 659–677.

Russell, Luke. 2014. *Evil: A Philosophical Investigation*. Oxford: Oxford University Press.

Steiner, Hillel. 2002. "Calibrating Evil." *The Monist* 85(2): 183–193.

Thomas, Laurence. 1993. *Vessels of Evil: American Slavery and the Holocaust*. Philadelphia: Temple University Press.

Waller, James. 2002. *Becoming Evil: How Ordinary People Commit Genocide and Mass Killing*. Oxford: Oxford University Press.

Waller, James E. 2014. "The Ordinariness of Extraordinary Evil: The Making of Perpetrators of Genocide and Mass Killing." In *Ordinary People as Mass Murderers: Perpetrators in Comparative Perspectives*, edited by Olaf Jensen and Claus-Christian W. Szejnmann, 145–164. New York: Palgrave Macmillan.

Wood, Allen. 1999. *Kant's Ethical Thought*. London: Cambridge University Press.

Zimbardo, Philip. 2008. *The Lucifer Effect: Understanding How Good People Turn Evil*. New York: Random House.

7

The Making of a Torturer

Jessica Wolfendale

Liberal democracies that perpetrate torture represent an apparent paradox: a flagrant violation of human rights by states supposedly dedicated to protecting human rights. In liberal democracies, the political, social, and legal narratives used to justify torture portray torture as an individual act motivated by important moral values. This individualized torture narrative then shapes the moral framework through which the public, policy-makers, and individual torturers view torture, and masks the institutional nature of torture perpetration. This interaction between an individualized torture narrative and the moral framework of torture distinguishes democratic perpetrators (Critchell et al. 2017, 9–10) from non-democratic perpetrators of torture. Yet, the implementation of a torture program in a democratic state is remarkably similar to the implementation of a torture program in a non-democratic state. In both cases, torture is an institutionalized practice given moral and political meaning through broad social and political narratives. This chapter uses the post-9/11 US torture program as a case study of a democratic perpetrator in order to explore the interaction of democratic narratives of torture, state implementation of torture, and the moral psychology of individual torturers. This permits a way of thinking about torture perpetration that goes beyond a myopic focus on torture as an individual act to understand the interaction and mutual reinforcement of different forms of torture perpetration. This analysis also offers a starting point from which to consider how to resist and oppose torture narratives that sustain democratic torture, a question I explore in the conclusion of this chapter.

Democratic Torture and Non-Democratic Torture

In *Torture and Democracy*, Darius Rejali explains how torture in liberal democracies emerges within a "national security model" (2007, 46). In this model, torture may first be used during a conflict by military and/or police forces—sometimes without the knowledge of military or political leaders—outside the borders of the state and almost exclusively against non-citizens. Democratic institutions, such as the judiciary and the press, may fail to stop the use of torture, leading to a situation in which the "police and the military soon operate outside the law ... they form a closed state within the state" (Rejali 2007, 47). According to Rejali, the use of torture by the French in Algeria in the 1950s and 1960s fits this pattern (2007, 47–49). In contrast, torture in authoritarian states tends to be justified as necessary to protect the state's internal security and is used primarily against citizens perceived to be opponents of the regime.[1]

The post-9/11 US torture program fits broadly within the national security model but differs in important ways. Unlike French torture in Algeria, the post-9/11 torture program was explicitly authorized by the government and given political and legal approval. This marks an important shift in US torture. Prior to 9/11, the use of torture by American military and intelligence forces was covert and was not publicly endorsed by the US government. For example, from the 1940s to the 1960s, the CIA sponsored research on psychological torture methods (McCoy 2006) and during the Vietnam War conducted a covert torture and assassination program known as the Phoenix Program (Rejali 2007, Chapter 21). In the 1970s and 1980s, the infamous School of the Americas (now the Western Hemisphere Institute for Security Cooperation) was known to teach torture methods to military and intelligence officials from military dictatorships in Latin and South America (Weschler 1990).

In contrast to this history of covert torture, the post-9/11 torture program was publicly defended by politicians, journalists, ethicists, and lawyers. This represents an unprecedented shift towards the public acceptance of torture and offers a unique opportunity to trace the narrative frameworks that play a crucial role in the implementation of torture within a democratic state and help create democratic perpetrators of torture.

The Ticking Bomb Scenario and Individualization of Torture

The post-9/11 torture debate was often framed around the ticking bomb scenario: a hypothetical situation in which we are asked to consider whether it is permissible to torture a terrorist to find out the location of a bomb that will explode shortly. The use of this scenario is common in philosophical debates about torture—often as a way of casting doubt on absolutist positions on torture (Allhoff 2012; Steinhoff 2013)—but it also plays an important role in the legal and political justification of torture in democratic states and in fostering public acceptance of torture. In 1976, after the European Commission of Human Rights had found that the "five techniques"[2] used against suspected IRA members by British forces amounted to torture, the British press defended the use of torture by "describing a situation in which a captured terrorist knew where a bomb had been planted in a school filled with children" (Conroy 2000, 137). In 1999, the Israeli Supreme Court ruled that torture was illegal but that security officials accused of torture could plead necessity in ticking time-bomb cases (Luban 2014, 81–82). In the US, reference to ticking bomb-type scenarios appears in the August 1, 2002, memo on the "Standards of Conduct for Interrogation" (hereafter the Torture Memo) prepared by the Office of Legal Counsel for the White House. The memo argues that the necessity defense could be available to military personnel charged with torture in circumstances very like those that characterize standard ticking bomb scenarios:

> A detainee may possess information that could enable the United States to prevent attacks that potentially could equal or surpass the September 11 attacks in their magnitude. Clearly, any harm that might occur during an interrogation would pale to insignificance compared to the harm avoided by preventing such an attack.
>
> *(Cole 2009, 92)*

Thus, the ticking bomb scenario plays an important role in shaping torture narratives within democratic states. The persistence of the ticking bomb scenario is explained by the ways in which different elements of the scenario seem to reconcile the use of torture with liberal democratic values.

First, the ticking bomb narrative portrays torture as a tactic that is being considered only because of the extreme threat posed by terrorism, and that has never been used before and will never be used again. The depiction of the resort to torture as unprecedented enables a form of collective "amnesia" about a state's history of torture, even though every state that has used the ticking bomb scenario to justify torture *has* used torture before (Rejali 2007). Thus, President Bush stated in 2005, "We do not torture" (Riechman 2005), despite overwhelming evidence of the use of torture at the time and the extensive history of US torture referred to earlier. Another example of this amnesia occurs in the memoir of James Mitchell, one of the psychologists responsible for designing and implementing the CIA's enhanced interrogation program. According to Mitchell, the CIA told Congress that they recruited him and another psychologist for the enhanced interrogation program because, "we [the CIA] would have been derelict had we not sought them out when it became clear that CIA would be *heading into the uncharted territory of the program*" (Mitchell 2016, 48, emphasis added). Describing the decision to develop an enhanced interrogation program as "heading into uncharted territory" neatly elides the extensive history of CIA research on torture, use of torture, and training of torturers.

The second function of the ticking bomb scenario is to focus our attention onto the individual torturer rather than the system of which he is a part. In the ticking bomb scenario, torture is depicted as a "single, ad hoc, decision about whether to torture, by officials who ordinarily would do no such thing" (Luban 2014, 60). The scenario invites us to think about torture "from the torturer's point of view" (Luban 2014, 55) rather than from the victim's perspective. The ticking bomb scenario frames the use of torture as a necessary evil, undertaken only to save lives. Thus, torture is acknowledged as evil, as "abhorrent both to American law and values and to international norms," as the first sentence of the December 30, 2004, Office of Legal Counsel memo states (Cole 2009, 128),[3] but we are invited to admire the torturer, since he is motivated only by the desire to save lives. This focus on a single individual's motives and actions ignores the reality of state torture as a systematic practice involving policies, procedures, infrastructure, and institutional support.

By framing the choice to use torture in this way, the ticking bomb scenario reconciles the use of torture with the liberal state's commitment to the protection of human rights and the rejection of tyranny (Luban 2014, 56). The ticking bomb scenario thereby generates reasons for torture that seem, on the face of it, endorsable by reasonable citizens in a democratic state, because they are consistent with legitimate state purposes.[4] This depiction of the torturer's motives is reflected in the discussion of the necessity defense in the Torture Memo, which states that the defense requires that it "must actually be the defendant's intention [in using torture] to avoid the greater harm" (Cole 2009, 92). Since, according to the memo, such a defense could be available to a defendant charged with torture, the memo's authors clearly believe that torture can be used with the sole intention of saving lives.

An additional function of the individualizing of torture in the ticking bomb narrative is drawing a distinction between "good" torturers and "bad" torturers. The good torturer is motivated by the need to save lives. He will only torture to gain the information he needs, and he will not torture again. By implied comparison, the bad torturer is unprofessional and sadistic. He has no moral qualms about torturing anyone he is asked to torture.

This difference between "good" and "bad" torturers is evident in the media and political coverage of torture scandals that have occurred in democratic states. During the Bush Administration, the White House maintained a website containing victims' accounts of torture and execution under Saddam Hussein's regime (The White House 2003). Such testimony helped justify the supposed necessity of removing Hussein through military force and highlighted the moral goodness of the US in comparison. In response to the revelations of torture and abuse at Abu Ghraib prison in 2003—revelations that threatened the supposed moral difference between Hussein's torturers and US troops—the Bush Administration described the guards involved as "bad apples" whose actions were not characteristic of the military as an institution (Editorial Board 2014). The "bad apple" analysis of the events at Abu Ghraib dominated discussion of US torture after 2003, resulting in far less discussion of the torture program that was occurring at Guantanamo Bay and elsewhere at the same time. The view that the torture program at Guantanamo Bay (in contrast to the torture at Abu Ghraib) was professional, justified, and legitimate is evident from the decision to transfer the commander of Guantanamo Bay to Iraq to "clean up" the prisons there (Hersh 2005, 32). James Mitchell also describes the events at Abu Ghraib as the actions of a few rogue individuals and worries about the negative impact of the scandal on the CIA's enhanced interrogation program: "I knew the CIA program would take a hit because of the stupid and self-indulgent criminal activities of a few bored and poorly supervised military officers" (2016, 231). In Mitchell's eyes, the torture at Abu Ghraib had nothing to do with the CIA interrogation program, which, in his view, was (at least initially) professional, lawful, and necessary. Indeed, he suggests that the professionalism of the CIA program prevented even worse abuses:

> I think in retrospect the troublesome things done later on by the few officers who did go outside approved guidelines illustrates how bad it could have been throughout the CIA's interrogation program without a carefully crafted list of techniques approved by the Department of Justice and closely monitored during implementation.
>
> *(Mitchell 2016, 42)*

The individualizing narrative of torture thus serves to distinguish professional, legitimate torture from abusive, unprofessional torture in a way that enables those involved to identify their actions and motives as being lawful, honorable, and justified.

This narrative also affected how US courts and the Bush Administration interpreted the intent requirement in the legal definition of torture. The Convention against Torture and Other Cruel, Inhuman, or Degrading Treatment or Punishment (CAT) defines torture as involving "any act, by which severe pain or suffering, whether physical or mental, is *intentionally inflicted* on a person for such purposes as obtaining from him or a third person information or a confession" (Bagchi 2009, 3, emphasis added). Despite evidence that the CAT Drafting Committee intended the intent requirement to mean *general intent*,[5] US courts and the Bush Administration interpreted the intent requirement to mean *specific intent*. This means that, for an individual to be guilty of the crime of torture, he would have to act with "the intent to accomplish the precise criminal act that [he] is later charged with" (Bagchi 2009, 15). The Torture Memo spells this out explicitly:

> … a defendant is guilty of torture only if he acts with the express intention of inflicting severe pain or suffering on a person within his custody or physical control. … Further, a showing that an individual acted with a good faith belief that his conduct would not produce the result that the law prohibits negates specific intent … Where a defendant acts in good faith, he acts with an honest belief that he has not engaged in the proscribed conduct.
>
> *(Cole 2009, 45–46)*

Thus, "even if the defendant knows that severe pain will result from his actions, if causing such harm is not his objective, he lacks the specific requisite intent" (Cole 2009, 45). This means that a torturer who intends only to gain information from a terrorist may not be guilty of torture, if causing severe pain and suffering was not his primary objective but rather a foreseeable but unintended consequence of his goal of getting information. Given the Torture Memo's argument that a defendant charged with torture who intended to prevent a terrorist attack might have access to a necessity defense, the memo offers an argument for the view that torturing with the intention of preventing terrorism may be justified and may not be torture at all.

The individualistic conception of torture is appealing for several reasons. Firstly, as described above, it allows us to draw a distinction between good and bad torturers. Secondly, focusing on individual torturers offers an easy way of allocating moral blame for the use of torture. Our moral evaluation of torture is simply an evaluation of an individual torturer's motives. While there are contexts in which these questions are important, such as in some cases of legal punishment, the individualistic narrative of torture distorts our understanding of the processes that support the use of torture and, as Martha Huggins argues, "overly empowers" individual perpetrators, who may be seen as "uniquely and perhaps inherently evil, motivated largely by internal psychological and biological factors" (Huggins 2000b, 55). Thus, atrocity narratives that focus on individual perpetrators help "to guarantee the relative invisibility of the structural processes that have given perpetrators the power to violate others" (Huggins 2000b, 52).

The ticking bomb narrative of torture distracts us from the fact that the *state* will implement torture, not individuals. We forget *who* will be doing the torturing, and *why* the question of torture is being asked at all. Yet, while the individualized narrative of torture is misleading and dishonest, it is essential to democratic state perpetration of torture because it creates a "torture fantasy" that gives meaning and purpose to the acts of individuals within a democratic torture culture.

The Democratic State as Perpetrator

The torture narrative discussed above distorts our understanding of torture by distracting us from the fact that the meaning, function, and indeed the very possibility of a torturer's actions *require* a pre-existing torture culture. Creating a torture culture requires several steps that give the individual torturer's actions meaning and purpose.

First and foremost, a torture culture requires a class of torturable victims. In the standard ticking bomb scenario, the victim is a terrorist whose guilt is not in doubt. This victim, unlike the clear majority of real-life torture victims, *deserves* to be tortured, and so the torturer is absolved of moral guilt for torturing him. In some accounts, the torture victim is responsible for his own torture because his unjust actions created the circumstances in which the use of torture is necessary (McMahan 2005–2006, 244). This portrayal of the torture victim thereby helps create a torture culture by providing a justification for the use of torture and by creating a class of torture victims who (because of their actions) lack the moral status that would make torturing them a violation of their rights. In the post-9/11 US torture culture, terrorists, suspected terrorists, and people suspected of having information about terrorism constituted the class of torturable victims. Those subject to torture were, in the words of former Secretary of State Donald Rumsfeld "the worst of the worst" (Lithwick 2009).

The classification of torture victims as "terrorists" follows a familiar pattern in the history of democratic torture: the category of "terrorist" was used to justify torture in Northern

Ireland, Israel, and Algeria (Rejali 2007). Yet, the category of "terrorist" is not an objective term but is itself a construction based on pre-existing narratives about the definition of terrorism, the extent of the threat posed by terrorism, and the moral status of terrorists (Jackson 2005). In the US torture narrative, it is no coincidence that the terrorist in the ticking bomb scenario is typically an Islamic terrorist, rather than (say) a white supremacist terrorist. So even though "terrorist" can describe many forms of political violence committed for many different reasons, it is only because of a pre-existing narrative about the threat of Islamic terrorism that the victim in the ticking bomb scenario is placed in the category of "terrorist" *and* into the category of terrorists who may be tortured.

Thus, while the US torture program did not appear to select torturable individuals purely based on their membership in a collective, in practice the distinction between victim-as-guilty-individual and victim-as-member-of-a-collective was porous. Many of those subjected to torture (such as the prisoners in Abu Ghraib) were targeted not because of their individual actions but because of their perceived membership in a group (Muslims) portrayed as threatening the very existence of the United States. That torture victims are, in reality, selected on the basis of their membership in a torturable collective is neatly obscured by the individualizing narrative of torture, which focuses our attention on whether this *specific* person may be tortured. It is no coincidence that many discussions of US torture focus on whether torture was justified in specific cases, such as the torture of Abu Zubaydah (e.g., see Mitchell 2016, Chapters 1 & 2). The criminal actions of individuals are taken to provide further evidence of the menace of the collective to which they are assigned.

The characterization of a person as a member of a "torturable" class is necessary because the decision to torture a person involves a refusal to see the victim's status *as a person* as setting limits on what may be done to them. Likewise, state torture represents a refusal to accept constraints on the state's power over its perceived enemies (Bagchi 2009, 35). Because torture is a violation of a person's fundamental physical and psychological integrity (an attack on personhood itself), to justify torture the torture victim must be viewed as *already* less than a person. We can trace the torture victim's degraded status in the history of torture. In ancient Greece and Rome, initially only slaves could be tortured. Eventually, however, the class of those who could be tortured widened to include "lower-end citizens, the *humiliores*, and in time, the emperors did not care about anyone's civic immunity" (Rejali 2007, 527). A similar pattern occurred in Italy in the late Middle Ages, when Italian republics introduced torture into the criminal justice system. At first, torture was only permitted against non-citizens and slaves—"[c]tizens had dignity and were thus inviolable" (Rejali 2007, 50)—but eventually citizens could be tortured if they were of bad moral reputation (Rejali 2007, 50).

This history reveals that those who were initially classified as "torturable" were *already* viewed as having lesser moral standing. It was permissible to torture them not because of what they had done or any information they possessed, but because of *who they were*. If torture was simply a tool for gaining confessions or information, it would be used against all relevant persons. The fact that torture was restricted, at least initially, only to those who already lacked moral standing reveals that the decision to use torture is not governed by an objective belief in the effectiveness of torture but by a belief that only people of lesser moral standing deserve to be tortured. Because torture is inherently degrading and depersonalizing, it should only be done to those who lack dignity and personhood.

History also shows us that torture, once introduced, expands beyond any initial constraints. While torture was initially restricted to slaves and noncitizens in Rome and Greece, the pool of torture victims eventually spread far beyond those bounds. A similar pattern occurred in the use of torture in military dictatorships in Latin and South America in the 1970s and 1980s. During the "Dirty War" in Argentina, military officers were initially reluctant to use torture. But, towards the end of the military dictatorship: "hardened young officers were placing bets on who could kidnap the prettiest girl to rape and torture … Escalation, is the rule, not the aberration" (Luban 2006, 48). Because torture aims to dehumanize and depersonalize its victims, torture becomes self-justifying: if a person is tortured, it must be deserved. By engaging in torture, the torturer implicitly affirms that they do not recognize any limits on what may be done to a person under their control, and so there is no reason to accept moral limits on who may be tortured.

Similarly, the creation of a torture culture within a state represents a refusal "to acknowledge limits on state power" (Bagchi 2009, 35). The Torture Memo puts this quite explicitly, arguing that "laws that seek to prevent the President from gaining the intelligence he believes necessary to prevent attacks upon the United States" would be unconstitutional (Cole 2009, 90). Once it has been accepted that there are no limits on state power, moral constraints on the use of torture fall away.

As we will see in the final section of this chapter, the creation of the category of torture victim and the denial of any limits on state power are the first steps in structuring and giving meaning to the purpose of state torture in both democratic and non-democratic states. In democratic torture narratives, however, the torture victim is framed as a terrorist, and so the purpose of torture is to save lives and protect the state. This purpose then shapes the motives and intentions of individual torturers. Many of those involved in the creation and implementation of the US torture program describe their motives in these terms. James Mitchell, for example, describes the Senate investigation into the CIA torture program as a "witch-hunt" aimed at "smearing … the CIA and the people who worked hard to protect America" (2016, 233). Thus, framing torture as a necessary evil to protect the state is not simply propaganda: it has a real impact on the ways in which those involved in implementing a torture program justify and make sense of their actions.

The creation of torture culture in democratic states also requires defining torture in such a way as to distinguish legitimate from illegitimate torture (or "torture lite" from "real" torture (Wolfendale 2009)). The US torture memos reveal a concerted effort to define torture so narrowly that the techniques proposed by the CIA, including waterboarding, would not meet the definition of torture. The Torture Memo argues that only acts that cause damage "ordinarily … associated with … injury such as death, organ failure, or serious impairment of body functions" (Cole 2009, 47) meet the threshold of torture, and so the techniques under consideration do not meet this threshold. A 2005 memo evaluating CIA interrogation techniques steps back somewhat from this definition of torture but still argues that *none* of the techniques, including waterboarding "inflicts severe pain or suffering or prolonged mental harm" (Cole 2009, 27) either individually or when used in combination. This denial that the enhanced interrogation methods are torture helps sustain the distinction between "good" and "bad" torturers discussed above. As we saw earlier, James Mitchell described the Abu Ghraib torturers as "poorly supervised," untrained, and "bored" (Mitchell 2016, 231). Yet, by characterizing the Abu Ghraib guards as flawed individuals acting alone, he fails to see the relationship between the abuse they committed and the torture program of which he was an integral part. Understanding why the guards believed that *these* prisoners were torturable, and understanding why they chose the forms of abuse that they did (such as the use of dogs and sexual humiliation), requires seeing their actions in the context of the torture culture of which they were a part.

Comparing Democratic and Non-Democratic Torture

As described above, democratic torture narratives depict torture victims as external enemies of the state, characterize the motive for using torture as the desire to save lives, and describe the techniques used as either not torture at all, or as not "real" torture. These elements play an essential role in resolving the apparent contradiction between the use of torture and the democratic commitment to human rights. In contrast, torture in non-democratic states is framed around a somewhat different narrative in part because there is no need to reconcile the use of torture with democratic values, and so non-democratic torture narratives do not need to deny that *torture* is being used. In addition, while non-democratic and democratic torture narratives share a focus on national security as the primary justificatory framework for the use of torture, non-democratic torture narratives locate the supposed threat to security internally rather than externally. In his study of torture in Brazil, Uruguay, and Argentina during the 1970s and 1980s, Lawrence Weschler describes the "national defense doctrine" that spread throughout military and political leadership in those countries and was strongly influenced by American Cold War thinking. This doctrine emphasized "that strengthening the national system against possible external attack was in fact less important than shoring up institutions against an 'internal enemy' that might be trying to undermine them" (Weschler 1990, 58). This means the class of torturable victims in non-democratic torture cultures tends to be citizens rather than foreigners. However, in both democratic and non-democratic states, this class of victims is characterized as deserving of torture by virtue of their perceived dangerousness.

There are therefore differences between democratic and non-democratic torture that reflect the relative importance attached to reconciling the use of torture with the values ascribed to the state. Yet, in practice, the implementation of democratic and non-democratic torture cultures is remarkably similar.

The Reality of a Torture Culture

Whether it occurs in a democratic or non-democratic state, a torture program requires the involvement and complicity of thousands of people. James Mitchell's description of the interrogation of Abu Zubaydah offers an insight into the sheer number of people (and the institutions they represent) involved in even a single act of torture:

> The team on-site consisted of the chief of base; a handful of operations officers, several analysts and targeters; a reports officer; medical personnel, including a physician; an operational psychologist … an Arab translator … a lot of guards; and a subject matter expert on law enforcement interrogations.
>
> *(Mitchell 2016, 58–59)*

Brasil: Nunca Mas, a book documenting hundreds of cases of torture during the military dictatorship in Brazil, describes many forms of participation and collaboration involved in the torture culture in Brazil. The book lists 444 torturers by name, as well as

> … those who participated in arrests, roundups, and investigations; those who were in charge of investigations; the medical examiners … doctors who participated in torture or signed death certificates … collaborators and informers; members of repressive organizations, federal and state; those who acted as court recorders and stenographers … judges in military courts.
>
> *(Cited from Weschler 1990, 52)*

Torture cultures in both democratic and non-democratic states thus require political and legal support, public acquiescence, and the participation of military personnel, intelligence personnel, medical personnel, psychologists, and psychiatrists. The prominent role played by psychologists, the legal profession, and the medical profession in the creation of a torture culture is particularly striking. The complicity of the legal system cuts across all stages of the creation of a torture culture: from legal opinions authorizing the use of specific techniques (as we saw in the torture memos), to the creation of legal defenses available to military or intelligence personnel charged with torture, to legal proceedings that allow or rely on evidence gained under torture. The medical profession also plays a crucial part in legitimizing torture, by assisting in the illusion of professional, legitimate torture, and by providing services that are essential to the implementation of a torture culture, including falsifying death certificates, directly supervising torture victims, providing medical records to interrogators, and failing to report the use of torture (see e.g., Weschler 1990, 126–127). As we have seen, psychologists played a central role in research on torture techniques in the US in the 1940s and 1950s and designed and implemented the post-9/11 torture program (Mitchell 2016). Psychologists played a similarly important role in the formation of the torture culture that developed in Uruguay during the military dictatorship. The interrogation and imprisonment practices at Libertad prison in Uruguay, for example, were designed by psychologists to "demolish the mental, emotional, and moral integrity of [the] inmate populations" (Weschler 1990, 131), and psychologists and psychiatrists occupied important roles within the prison system.

Non-democratic and democratic torture cultures also have in common the creation of the image of the "good" torturer against whom "bad" torturers are unfavorably compared. I've already mentioned James Mitchell's admiration for the professionalism of the CIA interrogation program, but all torture cultures emphasize self-control, discipline, and professionalism as qualities of good torturers (Huggins 2000a; Wolfendale 2007, 177–182). This encourages the perception of torture as a legitimate tool for fighting threats to the state and enables individual torturers to reconcile their actions with their self-image as good people and dedicated military professionals.

Finally, all torture cultures exceed their initial boundaries. Torture victims are initially selected on the basis of some supposedly objective criteria (that they are terrorists, for example). But whatever initial constraints are placed on who may be tortured soon fall away. As we have seen, this occurred in the military dictatorships in Latin America (for example, in Argentina); it occurred in the torture cultures of ancient Greece and Rome, and in Italy in the middle ages; and it occurred in the post-9/11 US torture culture. This is because the decision to use torture is a decision to reject any moral constraints on individual and state power. Torture is therefore always a form of tyranny, whether it occurs in a democratic or a non-democratic state.

Conclusion

While torture is implemented in democratic and non-democratic states in very similar ways, democratic and non-democratic states utilize different narratives in order to rationalize and give meaning to the practice of torture. This chapter's analysis of the differences between these justificatory narratives sheds light on the nature of democratic perpetrators and the unique ways in which liberal democracies attempt to resolve the tension between the use of torture and the commitment to liberal values. In addition, the analysis of democratic torture narratives offered in this chapter suggests at least two possible approaches to resisting such narratives that would benefit from further development. Firstly, given the central role played by the military, legal, and medical professions in the implementation of torture, it is important to explore ways in which these professions could incorporate education about torture narratives into professional training, in order to mitigate the likelihood of such narratives being adopted and sustained within those institutions. Secondly, the use of the ticking bomb scenario in academic, legal, and popular debates about torture must be resisted. Such resistance could take the form of counter-narratives and of moral pressure on those who contribute to torture narratives. Arguably, opposing torture narratives could even be construed as a moral obligation on the part of those who are in a position to challenge torture narratives, given the extraordinary harm caused by torture.

Notes

1 However, as I will explain, while the justificatory narratives for torture are different in democratic and non-democratic states, the torture programs that emerge are very similar.
2 The five techniques were hooding, sleep deprivation, food deprivation, noise bombardment, and forced standing (Conroy 2000, 6).
3 This memo defines torture less narrowly than the Torture Memo but states in a footnote that "we have reviewed this Office's prior opinions addressing issues involving treatment of detainees and do not believe that any of their conclusions would be different under the standard set forth in this memorandum" (Cole 2009, 17–18).
4 Aditi Bagchi argues that torture is a state crime because the reasons underlying state use of torture are *not* reasons that reasonable constituents could endorse (Bagchi 2009, 26).
5 A person meets the criteria of general intent if she meant to perform the proscribed act in question and knew that she was performing the proscribed action. It does not require that she intended to bring about all the foreseeable consequences of the action.

References

Allhoff, Fritz. 2012. *Terrorism, Ticking Time-Bombs, and Torture: A Philosophical Analysis*. Chicago, IL: University of Chicago Press.

Bagchi, Aditi. 2009. "Intention, Torture, and the Concept of State Crime." *Penn State Law Review* 114: 1–48.

Cole, David. 2009. *The Torture Memos: Rationalizing the Unthinkable*. New York: The New Press.

Conroy, John. 2000. *Unspeakable Acts, Ordinary People: The Dynamics of Torture*. New York: Alfred A. Knopf.

Critchell, Kara, Susanne C. Knittel, Emiliano Perra, & Ugur Ümit Üngor. 2017. "Editors' Introduction." *Journal of Perpetrator Studies* 1: 1–27.

Editorial Board. 2014. "Abu Ghraib – Ten Years On." *The New York Times*, April 22, 2014. www.nytimes.com/2014/04/23/opinion/abu-ghraib-10-years-later.html

Hersh, Seymour. 2005. *Chain of Command: The Road from 9/11 to Abu Ghraib*. New York: Harper Perennial.

Huggins, Martha. 2000a. "Legacies of Authoritarianism: Brazilian Torturers' and Murderers' Reformulation of Memory." *Latin American Perspectives* 27: 57–78.

Huggins, Martha. 2000b. "Reconstructing Atrocity: How Torturers, Murderers, and Researchers Deconstruct Labels and Manage Secrecy." *Human Rights Review* 1(4): 50–70.

Jackson, Richard. 2005. *Writing the War on Terrorism: Language, Politics, and Counter-Terrorism*. Manchester, UK: Manchester University Press.

Lithwick, Dahlia. 2009. "Bad Men: How Many Terrorists Are Left at Guantanamo, Anyway?" *Slate*, January 22, 2009. www.slate.com/articles/news_and_politics/jurisprudence/2009/01/bad_men.html

Luban, David. 2006. "Liberalism, Torture, and the Ticking Bomb." In *The Torture Debate in America*, edited by Karen J. Greenberg, 35–84. New York: Cambridge University Press.

Luban, David. 2014. *Torture, Power, and Law*. New York: Cambridge University Press.

McCoy, Alfred. 2006. *A Question of Torture: CIA Interrogation from the Cold War to the War on Terror*. New York: Henry Holt and Company.

McMahan, Jeff. 2005–2006. "Torture, Morality, and Law." *Case Western Reserve Journal of International Law* 37: 241–248.
Mitchell, James E. 2016. *Enhanced Interrogation: Inside the Minds and Motives of the Islamic Terrorists Trying to Destroy America*. New York: Crown Forum.
Rejali, Darius. 2007. *Torture and Democracy*. Princeton, NJ: Princeton University Press.
Riechman, Deb. 2005. "Bush Declares: 'We Do Not Torture'." *The Washington Post*, November 7, 2005. www.washingtonpost.com/wpdyn/content/article/2005/11/07/AR2005110700521.html
Steinhoff, Uwe. 2013. *On the Ethics of Torture*. Albany, NY: State University of New York Press.
The White House. 2003. "Tales of Saddam's Brutality." The White House, September 29, 2003. https://georgewbush-whitehouse.archives.gov/news/releases/2003/09/20030929-14.html.
Weschler, Lawrence. 1990. *A Miracle, a Universe: Settling Accounts with Torturers*. Chicago, IL: University of Chicago Press.
Wolfendale, Jessica. 2009. "The Myth of Torture Lite." *Ethics and International Affairs* 23(1): 47–61.
Wolfendale, Jessica. 2007. *Torture and the Military Profession*. Abingdon, UK: Palgrave-Macmillan.

8

Linking Perpetrator Characteristics to Jihadist Modus Operandi

An Exploratory Study

Teun van Dongen

Introduction

One of the things that make terrorism a difficult problem to counter is its elusiveness. Put simply, we don't know where, when, and how terrorists are going to strike. As a result, security measures tend to be reactive in the sense that they reflect the nature of one or more recent attacks. A case in point concerns the placement of obstacles to prevent vehicle attacks in cities all over Europe. After the deadly vehicle attacks in Nice (July 2016), Berlin (December 2016), and Barcelona (August 2017), local governments began erecting barriers to keep their populations safe from attacks with what appeared to have become the jihadist weapon of choice ("European cities add barriers to thwart vehicle attacks," 2017).

But while this response is understandable, it also raises the question whether there are ways to act in a less reactive and a more pre-emptive way. The main argument of this chapter is that this is possible. By taking into account the characteristics of the potential perpetrators (i.e., the members of the jihadist movement), one can develop more informed estimates regarding the nature of the attacks that are to be expected. It will be demonstrated that it is possible to draw up perpetrator typologies that correlate with elements of the modus operandi of jihadist terrorist attacks, which means that there are things about a potential terrorist perpetrator that could help us make an educated guess as to what kind of attack this perpetrator will commit should he decide to strike. There is, however, much work to be done to develop such insights, because, remarkably, research regarding terrorist perpetrators often does not address modus operandi.

Motivation

Traditionally, much research on the perpetrators of jihadist terrorist attacks is focused on the motivation of the perpetrators, presumably because insights in what drives terrorists can inform measures to keep people from becoming terrorists in the first place. The 9/11 attacks understandably sparked academic interest in the mind of a suicide bomber. Some authors stressed the importance of religion (Juergensmeyer 2003), whereas others argued that the socio-economic and political stagnation of the Middle East caused a frustration that led some young men to give their lives to the causes espoused by Al Qaida (Atran 2004). Yet others explained suicide terrorism as a rationally deployed instrument to achieve clearly identifiable political goals (Pape 2003; Sedgwick 2004). Questions about jihadist terrorist motivation became even more prominent as a result of the emergence of homegrown jihadist terrorism in the West. The jihadist bombings in Madrid (2004) and London (2005), which involved perpetrators who were born and raised in Western Europe, prompted researchers to ask why seemingly normal young people would want to engage in terrorist activities (Cesari 2008; European Commission's Expert Group on Violent Radicalization, 2008; Dalgaard-Nielsen 2010). The rise of the Islamic State raised similar questions, such as how an organization that commits such grotesque acts of cruelty could possibly appeal to young people from all over the Western world (Coolsaet 2016; Gustafsson & Ranstorp 2017).

Given the complexity of human motivation, it is not surprising that the list of motivating factors that have been suggested is quite long. Some authors have argued that joining a jihadist terrorist cell or network is a way to satisfy certain personal needs, They claim that young men especially see jihadist terrorism as a way to gain status (Bjørgo 2016) or to end an identity crisis or a crisis of faith (Wiktorowicz 2005). Thrill-seeking (Cottee & Hayward 2011) has been suggested as a motive as well, as has loyalty to friends or family members (Nesser 2010; Sageman 2004, 2008). In the latter case, peer pressure and the need to belong to a collective play important roles (Neumann 2016). Most authors agree that such factors are not mutually exclusive and can indeed hang together. Simon Cottee, for instance, drew on classic criminological theories about youth delinquency to demonstrate that jihadists seek the notoriety and the group identity of the jihadist movement to cope with their frustration over their inability to gain social status in more conventional ways (Cottee 2011).

Other authors have explained the motivation of jihadist terrorists on a more political level, claiming that jihadist terrorist attacks are responses to anger about Western military intervention in the Muslim world and the perceived humiliation and marginalization of Muslims in Western countries (Kepel 2017), be it on the labor market, in political discourse, or through the application of heavy-handed security measures. There are also scholars, however, who have downplayed the importance of such fairly specific social or political grievances in the motivations of jihadist terrorists. According to Olivier Roy, for instance, jihadist networks and recruiters managed to seize and deploy for their own purposes an unfocused anti-systemic rage on the part of the perpetrators of jihadist terrorist attacks. In his assessment, the current wave of jihadist terrorism is not the result of the radicalization of Islam, but rather of the Islamization of radicalism (Roy 2017). There are also authors who believe that the political ambitions of jihadist terrorists are derived from deeply held religious beliefs. They explain jihadist terrorism as a way to realize a religiously inspired ideal of the perfect society (Dawson, Amarasingam, & Bain 2016; Wood 2016; Hegghammer 2017).

Modus Operandi

The works discussed in the previous section deepened our understanding of what drives a jihadist terrorist, but they do not offer (nor do they claim to offer) any causal links or correlations between types of motivations and terrorist modus operandi. In the last years, however, research regarding terrorist perpetrators has broadened to include *what* terrorist perpetrators are doing, as opposed to *why* they are doing it. The progress that has thus been made is threefold. First, a series of studies deepens our understanding of the modus operandi of the so-called lone actor terrorist. Gill et al., for instance, mapped a series of characteristics (e.g., employment status and religious conversion) and actions (e.g., training and weapon use) to see how lone-actor terrorist attacks are being planned (Gill, Horgan, & Deckert 2014). In a similar vein, Schuurman et al. examined a large number of lone actor terrorists to see whether they somehow behaved in similar ways in the period preceding the attack (Schuurman, Bakker, Gill, & Bouhana 2017). The authors looked at, among other things, the ways in which the perpetrators maintained operational security, acquired weapons, and collected operational intelligence about their targets. While both groups of authors stress the wide variety they found in their samples, they point out some commonalities as well. Both found that lone actors often have some connections with organizations or movements, inform others about their extremist ideas and plan, and prepare their attacks rather carefully.

Second, there has been progress in developing our understanding of the modus operandi of jihadist terrorism. Several studies have focused on the actual jihadist terrorist attacks and thus talk directly about modus operandi in the way it is understood in this chapter. Nesser and Stenersen looked at the weapons and target selection of jihadist terrorists in Europe and found an increase in indiscriminate attacks (i.e., attacks not aimed at a specific individual or a specific group of people, e.g., policemen or Jews) and a diversification in the use of weapons (Nesser & Stenersen 2014). In a follow-up study about jihadist terrorists in Europe after the emergence of the Islamic State, the same authors concluded that the way in which attacks were organized, planned, and executed had not changed fundamentally since the meteoric rise of the Islamic State (Nesser, Stenersen, & Oftedal 2016). The latest installment in this category is Hemmingby's analysis of the weapon use and target selection of jihadist terrorists in Western Europe from 1994 to 2016 (Hemmingby 2017). In this article, Hemmingby notes a clear risk aversion on the part of jihadist terrorists, as they tend to stay away from hard targets, especially when operating alone. Like Nesser, Stenersen, and Oftedal, Hemmingby sees no significant change in jihadist terrorism in Europe as a result of the emergence of the Islamic State.

The studies in these two categories (i.e., lone actor terrorists and jihadist terrorists in Europe) all provide valuable insights regarding the actions terrorists undertake before and during their attacks, but they offer little in the way of explanations and correlations. Gill, Horgan, and Deckert show that there are differences between lone actor terrorists from different ideological currents. Otherwise, the analyses discussed above do not relate their variables to other variables. This being the case, their conclusions are not of much help in coming up with analyses on the basis of which one could make an informed estimate of what kinds of attack one should expect.

There are authors who do address such relations, but there is certainly no abundance of studies of this kind. In the first years after 9/11 there were some authors who, on the basis of anecdotal evidence at best, argued that a terrorist organization's proclivity towards indiscriminate terrorist attacks and the use of weapons of mass destruction depends on the organization's ideology (Hoffman, B. 1995; Laqueur 2000; Quillen 2002; Hayden 2007). According to such analyses, nationalist terrorist organizations are more careful in their attacks because they don't want to endanger the lives of their potential supporters. As a result, they are less inclined to commit indiscriminate attacks and to pursue weapons of mass destruction.

The last years saw the publication of several studies with a stronger empirical basis. Abrahms, Ward, and Kennedy, for instance, performed a statistical analysis to demonstrate that jihadist terrorist organizations that are affiliates of other groups are more likely to attack civilian targets than parent organizations (Abrahms, Ward, & Kennedy 2018). Hsu & Apel's made a statistical analysis on the effects of the placement of metal detectors at airports (Hsu & Apel 2015). They confirm the substitution effect established by previous studies (Enders & Sandler 1993) but also claim that metal detectors actually keep potential perpetrators from committing terrorist attacks at all. A third noteworthy example, although not about jihadist terrorism, is the study by Asal et al., who sought to explain the differences in the ability of Provisional IRA units to avoid civilian casualties and kill high-value targets (e.g., "military personnel, military infrastructure, police, or politicians") in operations that include the use of IEDs (Asal, Gill, Rethemeyer, & Horgan 2015). Their analysis concludes that units that have received more training are better at keeping the numbers of civilian casualties down and at targeting high-value targets.

In sum, there has been significant progress in research regarding terrorist perpetrators, but few studies examine the ways in which terrorist perpetrator characteristics and modus operandi hang together. Consequently, there is as yet no clear-cut answer to the question of what perpetrator characteristics could help us make an informed estimate of the types of terrorist attacks we should be expecting. Abrahms, Ward, and Kennedy generated a valuable insight in this regard, but they only addressed one element that one could consider a perpetrator characteristic. The next section will, using data regarding jihadist terrorism in the West, outline an example of the other factors we could examine. In doing so, it will take an approach that is more common in criminological studies than in terrorism studies, as several criminologists have examined links between perpetrator characteristics and types of crime. One such study addressed the ways in which perpetrators of spousal homicide are different from all other perpetrators of homicide (Belfrage & Rying 2004), and another set out to find whether characteristics of the perpetrators of fraud related to the organizational characteristics of the organizations they victimized (Holtfreter 2005).

Towards Terrorist Perpetrator Typologies Based on Operational Characteristics

In order to design perpetrator typologies that tell us more about the kind of attacks a terrorist perpetrator is going to carry out, we have to focus on operational characteristics, that is, characteristics that refer to the way the terrorist perpetrator operates. Two fairly simple such characteristics are training and cooperation, both of which can easily be imagined to have a bearing on a perpetrator's modus operandi. Regarding training, we could ask ourselves whether a certain terrorist underwent training in a terrorist training camp run by Al Qaida, the Islamic State, or another major terrorist organization. Regarding cooperation, we could ask ourselves whether a perpetrator attacked alone or in a collective, with other perpetrators. If we consider these variables to be binary (the possible scores are "yes" and "no"), there are four terrorist perpetrator types in this typology (see Table 8.1).

This typology does have some explanatory value regarding terrorist modus operandi in the West, specifically with regard to the use of improvised explosive devices (IEDs), the homemade bombs assembled from freely available ingredients like fertilizer, bleach, and shrapnel. In order to make this point, all jihadist terrorist attacks in Europe, the US, and

Table 8.1 Typology of jihadist terrorists

	TRAINING: Yes	TRAINING: No
COOPERATION: Yes	**Trained collectives**	**Untrained collectives**
COOPERATION: No	**Trained loners**	**Untrained loners**

Canada in the period from the Madrid bombings of March 2004 until September 1, 2017, have been scored on the following three variables (see Table 8.2):

- *Training*: has at least one of the perpetrators received training in a training camp run by Al Qaida, the Islamic State, or another terrorist organization?
- *Cooperation*: was the attack carried out by more than one person?
- *Use of IEDs*: did the perpetrator(s) use one or more IEDs?

The first two questions are meant to assign a perpetrator type to the perpetrator(s) of a given attack; the purpose of the third question is to see whether there is a connection between the perpetrator types and the use of IEDs. In other words, do these perpetrator types tell us anything about the likelihood that they used IEDs in their attacks?

In the compilation of the list of jihadist terrorist attacks in the West, two main criteria have been applied. First, only acts of violence that were actually carried out have been included on the list; foiled attacks have been left out. Foiled attacks may tell us something about terrorist ambitions, but the modus operandi of an attack changes constantly during the planning stage and sometimes even during the attack, so one can only definitively establish a modus operandi after an attack has been carried out.

Second, for an attack to qualify as an act of terrorist violence, it must have been intended "to have far-reaching psychological repercussions beyond the immediate victim or target" (Hoffman 2006, 40). As terrorism is also a form of political violence, those repercussions are intended to bring about a certain political effect. In the case of jihadist terrorists, such effects include the withdrawal of Western troops from predominantly Muslim countries or the cessation of the perceived slandering of Mohammed in cartoons and other forms of satire. Another, but much less common, goal is putting a stop to the Western way of life in general. Attacks for which there is convincing evidence that the perpetrator(s) intended to send a message to coerce or intimidate governments and/or populations into changing their behavior in ways that contribute to one of these items on the jihadist political agenda have been added to the list. Statements of allegiance to jihadist organizations or to individual leaders of such organizations have been considered evidence of a jihadist political motive as well, as has praise of jihad in general.

Another issue that needs addressing concerns simultaneous attacks. Attacks that were planned by members of the same cell to be carried out more or less simultaneously (i.e., in a matter of minutes from each other) count as one attack. For instance, the London bombings of July 7, 2005, have been counted as one attack with four perpetrators, not as four separate attacks. A series of attacks by the same perpetrator(s), on the other hand, has been counted as separate incidents. For instance, Mohammed Merah's shootings of March 11, 15, and 19, 2012, have been counted as three separate attacks, not as one drawn-out attack. Some researchers have counted Merah's three attacks as one incident (Hegghammer & Nesser 2015), but there were three days between the first and the second attack and between the second and the third attack. This being the case, Merah's attacks lacked the element of simultaneity that was present in the 2005 London bombings. Also, it is hard to see how Merah could have been on the attack during these three-day intervals. He was not shooting or following his targets, so his attacks were separated by time periods during which he must have done something else. The same logic has been applied to similar cases.

In order to collate a list of terrorist attacks, I took advantage of existing inventories that have been drawn up for other research projects (Nesser 2015; Barrett 2016; Government Accounting Office 2017; Vidino, Marone, & Entenmann 2017). It should be noted, though, that not all the attacks on these lists have been included in Table 8.2. In some cases, attacks

Table 8.2 Training, cooperation and IED-use by jihadist terrorists in the West

Date	*City*	*Training*	*Cooperation*	*IED*
3-11-2004	Madrid	Yes	Yes	Yes
11-2-2004	Amsterdam	No	No	No
7-7-2005	London	Yes	Yes	Yes
7-21-2005	London	Yes	Yes	Yes
3-3-2006	Chapel Hill (US)	No	No	No
7-28-2006	Seattle	No	No	No
7-31-2006	Hamm/Koblenz	No	Yes	Yes
6-29-2007	London	No	Yes	Yes
6-30-2007	Glasgow	No	Yes	Yes
5-22-2008	Exeter (UK)	No	No	Yes
6-1-2009	Little Rock (US)	No	No	No
10-12-2009	Milan	No	No	Yes
11-5-2009	Fort Hood (US)	No	No	No
12-24-2009	Detroit	Yes	No	Yes
1-1-2010	Aarhus	No	No	No
5-1-2010	New York	Yes	No	Yes
5-14-2010	London	No	No	No
12-11-2010	Stockholm	Yes	No	Yes
4-29-2011	Stuttgart	No	No	No
3-11-2012	Toulouse	Yes	No	No
3-15-2012	Montauban	Yes	No	No
3-19-2012	Toulouse	Yes	No	No
2-5-2013	Copenhagen	No	No	No
4-15-2013	Boston	No	Yes	Yes
5-22-2013	London	No	Yes	No
5-27-2013	Paris	No	No	No
4-27-2014	Seattle	No	No	No
5-24-2014	Brussels	Yes	No	No
6-1-2014	Seattle	No	No	No
6-25-2014	West Orange (US)	No	No	No
10-20-2014	St. Jean-sur-Richelieu (Can.)	No	No	No
10-22-2014	Ottawa	No	No	No
10-23-2014	New York	No	No	No
12-20-2014	Joué-lès-Tours	No	No	No
1-7-2015	Paris	Yes	Yes	No
1-9-2015	Paris	No	No	No
2-9-2015	Nice	No	No	No
2-14-2015	Copenhagen	No	No	No
2-15-2015	Copenhagen	No	No	No
5-3-2015	Garland	No	Yes	No
6-26-2015	St. Quentin-Fallavier	No	No	No
7-16-2015	Chattanooga (US)	No	No	No

(Continued)

Table 8.2 (Cont.)

Date	*City*	*Training*	*Cooperation*	*IED*
8-21-2015	Oignies (Fra.)	Yes	No	No
11-4-2015	Merced (US)	No	No	No
11-13-2015	Paris	Yes	Yes	Yes
12-2-2015	San Bernardino	No	Yes	Yes
12-5-2015	Leytonstone (UK)	No	No	No
12-1-2016	Valence	No	No	No
1-7-2016	Philadelphia	No	No	No
1-11-2016	Marseille	No	No	No
2-11-2016	Columbus (US)	No	No	No
2-18-2016	Rochdale	No	Yes	No
2-22-2016	Hannover	No	No	No
3-22-2016	Brussels	Yes	Yes	Yes
4-16-2016	Essen (Ger.)	No	Yes	Yes
6-12-2016	Orlando	No	No	No
6-13-2016	Magnanville (Fra.)	No	No	No
7-14-2016	Nice	No	No	No
7-18-2016	Würzburg (Ger.)	No	No	No
7-24-2016	Ansbach	No	No	Yes
7-26-2016	St. Etienne du Rouvray (Fra.)	No	Yes	No
8-6-2016	Charleroi (Bel.)	No	No	No
9-17-2016	New York and Seaside Park	No	No	Yes
9-27-2016	St. Cloud (US)	No	No	No
11-28-2016	Columbus (US)	No	No	No
12-19-2016	Berlin	No	No	No
2-3-2017	Paris	No	No	No
3-18-2017	Paris	No	No	No
3-22-2017	London	No	No	No
4-7-2017	Stockholm	No	No	No
4-20-2017	Paris	No	No	No
5-22-2017	Manchester	Yes	No	Yes
6-23-2017	London	No	Yes	No
6-6-2017	Paris	No	No	No
6-19-2017	Paris	No	No	Yes
6-20-2017	Brussels	No	No	Yes
7-28-2017	Hamburg	No	No	No
8-9-2017	Paris	No	No	No
8-17-2017	Barcelona	No	No	No
8-18-2017	Cambrils	No	Yes	No
8-18-2017	Turku	No	No	No
8-26-2017	London	No	No	No

have been left out, mostly because the political motivation of the perpetrator was not entirely clear. The information on the attacks and the intentions of the perpetrators has been drawn mostly from online news reports, in most cases by reputable outlets like CNN, the BBC, *The Guardian*, *Der Spiegel*, *The Washington Post*, and *The New York Times*. Scholarly accounts and government reports have been used for some of the better-known attacks in the set.

From the data that have been thus collected, it is possible to discern a pattern regarding the use of IEDs by jihadist terrorists in the West: "yes" scores on "training" and/or "cooperation" clearly increase the likelihood that a perpetrator or a group of perpetrators will have used IEDs (see Table 8.3). Untrained loners are much less likely to use IEDs than perpetrators who are trained or are working in groups. About half of the perpetrators in the latter two categories used IEDs, compared to 11% of the untrained loners. The difference with the trained collectives is even more striking: five out of the six attacks by trained collectives involved the use of IEDs. The numbers of trained loners, untrained collectives, and trained collectives are small, so some caution is warranted, but it is probably not a coincidence that perpetrators in those categories are more likely to have used IEDs than the untrained loners.

Much has been made of the bomb recipes and explosive manuals that are available online, with some observers warning that terrorists are using the internet as a "virtual training camp" (UNODC 2012, 8; Weimann 2006, 119–123). Bomb experts, however, have pointed out that many of the online manuals are flawed (Cruickshank 2015, 142). Moreover, making a bomb is a risky enterprise. First, some of the ingredients are very unstable and might explode prematurely, or not at all. Second, the perpetrator might give himself away. Bomb making is a process that leaves all kinds of traces, like smells or burn wounds on the perpetrator's body. In 2008, a group of worshipers at a mosque in Bristol alerted the police after they noticed such burn wounds on the hand and feet of young man who frequented the mosque. The man was arrested and convicted for preparing a suicide bombing in a shopping mall (Ellis, Pantucci, & Chaplais 2015, 16). Also, building a powerful IED tends to take a lot of work. The Norwegian right-wing terrorist Anders Breivik spent months working on the explosives he used in his attacks (Pidd 2012), as did the perpetrators of the London bombings of July 7, 2005 (Gilmore, Cole, Briggs, & Soria 2011, 7). Also, the pictures of the apartment of the London bombers showed that building an IED requires space and various kinds of equipment as well as manpower and probably perseverance ("Inside the 7/7 terrorists' flat ... where every room was filled with explosives," 2011).

All of this being the case, it is understandable that terrorist perpetrators who have no training and who operate alone (the untrained loners) will choose a weapon that is easier to acquire and easier to use. They can stay under the radar, minimize their workload,

Table 8.3 Distribution of jihadist terrorists in the West over categories in the typology

		TRAINING: Yes	TRAINING: No
COOPERATION	Yes	Trained collectives: 83% IED use (5 out of 6)	Untrained collectives: 46% IED use (6 out of 13)
COOPERATION	No	Trained loners 44% IED use (4 out of 9)	Untrained loners: 11% IED use (6 out of 54)

and still be reasonably sure that their attacks will cause at least some casualties. For organizations that provide training, on the other hand, it is understandable that they will train their recruits in the fabrication of explosives. IEDs have the potential to kill larger numbers of people than other kinds of attacks, which is clear from the fact that many of the most lethal jihadist attacks in the West were IED attacks (there are seven attacks on the list that killed more than twenty people, and five of those were IED attacks). From this perspective, it makes sense for Al Qaida or the Islamic State to train new recruits to carry out attacks in the West, as that is the kind of investment that is most likely to pay off in terms of the casualty rate.

Conclusion

As the exercise in the previous section has shown, it may well be possible to use perpetrator typologies to make an informed estimate about the modus operandi of the attack. If the research results presented above are anything to go by, there appears to be a connection between perpetrator type and the use of IEDs in jihadist terrorist attacks. Such insights could be of value in the investigation of specific terrorist cells as well as in assessing a jihadist terrorist threat in general. In investigating specific cells, intelligence or police officers could use the links between perpetrator types and modus operandi to decide what to do first. If an investigation concerns a trained collective, it makes sense to start by looking for clues of an impending IED attack. In assessing the general threat, it might be good to monitor trends in the jihadist movement and link them to possible attack types. For instance, if a jihadist movement is becoming more cohesive (i.e., the perpetrators work in groups and are in touch with organizations that can provide training), one should be more aware of the possibility of an IED attack than when the movement is fragmenting.

It may be worth noting that the jihadist terrorist threat to the West is currently undergoing such a process of fragmentation. Before the fall of the Caliphate, the Islamic State recruited, trained, and instructed fighters to commit attacks in Europe. It even had a special unit to organize terrorist attacks in the West, the Emni. The perpetrators of the terrorist attacks in Paris (November 2015) and Brussels (March 2016) were both organized by the Emni (Speckhard & Yayla 2017). Without the control of large swaths of territory, the Islamic State is having a hard time sending trained collectives like the ones that committed the terrorist attacks in Paris and Brussels on a mission to commit terrorist attacks in Europe. There is some speculation that the Islamic State's Libyan branch is taking over the role of the Emni (Saal 2017), but as yet the terrorist threat to Europe appears to emanate from perpetrator types that are less likely to commit IED attacks.

But while the typology developed in the previous section can help us estimate the nature of the terrorist attacks from the jihadist terrorist movement, we need to learn much more than simply that there might be a connection between perpetrator type and the likelihood of IED attacks. The jihadist modus operandi is a much broader phenomenon, which also includes target location, victim selection, and escape mode (unless it's a suicide attack). If we can find links between perpetrator types and any of these other variables, we will be able to get a firmer grip on the terrorist threat. All of this will take a lot of research and requires us, as this chapter was intended to demonstrate, to design typologies on the basis of other factors than motivation and pathways to terrorism. Moreover, the operational considerations that could explain the relation between perpetrator type and IED use might well apply to other types of terrorism. Indeed, Gill et al. demonstrated that terrorists with very different ideological convictions make similar considerations in the planning and execution of a terrorist attack (Gill, Marchment, Corner, & Bouhana 2018). This would mean that the IED use of other terrorist movements may need to be examined in similar ways. This chapter was just one modest attempt regarding one terrorist movement, so new perspectives are still sorely needed.

References

Abrahms, Max, Matthew Ward, & Ryan Kennedy. 2018. "Explaining Civilian Attacks: Terrorist Networks, Principal-Agent Problems and Target Selection." *Perspectives on Terrorism* 12(1): 23-45.

Asal, Victor, Paul Gill, Karl R. Rethemeyer, & John Horgan. 2015. "Killing Range: Explaining Lethality Variance within a Terrorist Organization." *Journal of Conflict Resolution* 59(3): 401-427.

Atran, Scott. 2004. "Mishandling Suicide Terrorism." *Washington Quarterly* 27(3): 67-90.

Barrett, James. 2016. "A Complete List of Radical Islamic Terror Attacks on US Soil under Obama." *The Daily Wire*. December 7, 2016. Retrieved from www.dailywire.com/news/11410/complete-list-radical-islamic-terror-attacks-us-james-barrett#

Belfrage, Henrik, & Mikael Rying. 2004. "Characteristics of Spousal Homicide Perpetrators: A Study of All Cases of Spousal Homicide in Sweden 1990-1999." *Criminal Behaviour and Mental Health* 14(2): 121-133.

Bjørgo, Tore. 2016. *Preventing Crime: A Holistic Approach*. Basingstoke and New York: Palgrave Macmillan.

Cesari, Jocelyne. 2008. "Muslims in Europe and the Risk of Radicalism." In *Facing the Fourth Foreign Fighters Wave: What Drives Europeans to Syria and Islamic State. Insights from the Belgian Case*, edited by Rik Coolsaet, 97-108. Hampshire: Asghate Publishing Limited.

Coolsaet, Rik. 2016. *Facing the Fourth Foreign Fighters Wave: What Drives Europeans to Syria and Islamic State. Insights from the Belgian Case*. Brussels: Egmont Royal Institute for International Relations.

Cottee, Simon. 2011. "Jihadism as a Subcultural Response to Social Strain: Extending Marc Sageman's 'Bunch of Guys' Thesis." *Terrorism and Political Violence* 23(5): 730-751.

Cottee, Simon, & K. Hayward. 2011. "Terrorist (e)Motives: The Existential Attractions of Terrorism." *Studies in Conflict & Terrorism* 34(12): 963-986.

Cruickshank, Paul. 2015. "Learning Terror: The Evolving Threat of Overseas Training to the West." In *Understanding Terrorism Innovation and Learning: Al-Qaeda and Beyond*, edited by Magnus Ranstorp & Magnus Normark, 137-195. New York and Abingdon: Routledge.

Dalgaard-Nielsen, Anja. 2010. "Violent Radicalization in Europe: What We Know and What We Do Not Know." *Studies in Conflict & Terrorism* 33(9): 797-814.

Dawson, Lorne, Amarnath Amarasingam, & Alexandra Bain. 2016. *Talking to Foreign Fighters: Socio-Economic Push Versus Existential Pull Factors*. Canadian Network for Research on Terrorism, Security and Society Retrieved from www.tsas.ca/wp-content/uploads/2018/02/TSASWP16-14_Dawson-Amarasingam-Bain.pdf

Ellis, Clare, Rafaello Pantucci, & Lorien Chaplais. 2015. *Lone-Actor Terrorism: Literature Review*. London: RUSI.

Enders, Walter, & Todd Sandler. 1993. "The Effectiveness of Antiterrorism Policies: A Vector-Autoregression-Intervention Analysis." *American Political Science Review* 87(4): 829-844.

"European Cities Add Barriers to Thwart Vehicle Attacks." 2017. *The New York Times*. August 22, 2017. Retrieved from www.nytimes.com/2017/08/22/world/europe/europe-attacks-safety-barriers.html

European Commission's Expert Group on Violent Radicalisation. 2008. *Radicalisation Processes Leading to Acts of Terrorism*. Retrieved from www.nuansa.nl/uploads/b6/4a/b64ad3af6f9aae9d74f341088d70d8fa/20080500_cscp_report_vries.pdf

Gill, Paul, John Horgan, & Paige Deckert. 2014. "Bombing Alone: Tracing the Motivations and Antecedent Behaviors of Lone-Actor Terrorists." *Journal of Forensic Sciences* 59(2): 425-435.

Gill, Paul, Zoe Marchment, Emily Corner, & Noémie Bouhana. 2018. "Terrorist Decision Making in the Context of Risk, Attack Planning, and Attack Commission." *Studies in Conflict & Terrorism* DOI: 10.1080/1057610X.2018.1445501

Gilmore, Margaret, Jennifer Cole, Rachel Briggs, & Valentina Soria. 2011. *Anatomy of a Terrorist Attack: What the Coroner's Inquest Revealed about the London Bombings*. London: RUSI.

Government Accounting Office. 2017. *Countering Violent Extremism: Actions Needed to Define Strategy and Assess Progress of Federal Efforts (No. GAO-17-300)*. Washington, DC: United States Government Accounting Office.

Gustafsson, Linus, & Magnus Ranstorp. 2017. *Swedish Foreign Fighters in Syria and Iraq: An Analysis of Open-Source Intelligence and Statistical Data*. Stockholm: Centre for Asymmetric Threat Studies.

Hayden, Nancy Kay. 2007. *Terrifying Landscapes: A Study of Scientific Research into Understanding Motivations of Non-State Actors to Acquire and/or Use Weapons of Mass Destruction*. Albuquerque: Sandia National Laboratories.

Hegghammer, Thomas (ed.). 2017. *Jihadi Culture: The Art and Social Practices of Militant Islamists*. Cambridge: Cambridge University Press.

Hegghammer, Thomas, & Petter Nesser. 2015. "Assessing the Islamic State's Commitment to Attacking the West." *Perspectives on Terrorism* 9(4): 14-30.

Hemmingby, Cato. 2017. "Exploring the Continuum of Lethality: Militant Islamists' Targeting Preferences in Europe." *Perspectives on Terrorism* 11(5): 25-41.

Hoffman, Bruce. 1995. *Holy Terror: The Implications of Terrorism Motivated by a Religious Imperative*. Santa Monica: RAND Corporation.

Hoffman, Bruce. 2006. *Inside Terrorism (Revised & Enlarged)*. New York: Columbia University Press.

Holtfreter, Kristy. 2005. "Is Occupational Fraud 'Typical' White-Collar Crime? A Comparison of Individual and Organizational Characteristics." *Journal of Criminal Justice* 33: 353-365.

Hsu, Henda Y. & Robert Apel. 2015. "A Situational Model of Displacement and Diffusion Following the Introduction of Airport Metal Detectors." *Terrorism and Political Violence* 27(1): 29-52.

"Inside the 7/7 terrorists' flat … where every room was filled with explosives." 2011. *Daily Mail*. February 1, 2011. Retrieved from www.dailymail.co.uk/news/article-1352560/7-7-inquest-Inside-terrorists-flat-room-filled-explosives.html

Juergensmeyer, Mark. 2003. *Terror in the Mind of God: The Global Rise of Religious Violence*. (3rd ed.). Berkeley, Los Angeles and London: University of California Press.

Kepel, G. 2017. *Terror in France: The Rise of Jihad in the West*. Princeton and Oxford: Princeton University Press.

Laqueur, Walter. 2000. *The New Terrorism: Fanaticism and the Arms of Mass Destruction*. New York: Oxford University Press.

Nesser, Petter. 2010. "Joining Jihadi Terrorist Cells in Europe: Exploring Motivational Aspects of Recruitment and Radicalization." In *Understanding Violent Radicalisation: Terrorist and Jihadist Movements in Europe*, edited by Magnus Ranstorp, 87-115. London: Routledge.

Nesser, Petter. 2015. *Appendix: Chronology of Jihadism in Europe 1994–2015*. London: Hurst Publishers.

Nesser, Petter, & Anne Stenersen. 2014. "The Modus Operandi of Jihadist Terrorists in Europe." *Perspectives on Terrorism* 8(6): 2-24.

Nesser, Petter, Anne Stenersen, & Emilie Oftedal. 2016. "Jihadi terrorism in Europe: The IS-Effect." *Perspectives on Terrorism* 10(6): 3-24.

Neumann, Peter. 2016. *Radicalized: New Jihadists and the Threat to the West*. London: I.B. Tauris.

Pape, Robert. 2003. "The Strategic Logic of Suicide Terrorism." *American Political Science Review* 97(3): 343-361.

Pidd, Helen. 2012. "Anders Behring Breivik Spent Years Training and Plotting for Massacre." *The Guardian*. August 24, 2012. Retrieved from www.theguardian.com/world/2012/aug/24/anders-behring-breivik-profile-oslo

Quillen, Chris. 2002. "A Historical Analysis of Mass Casualty Bombers." *Studies in Conflict and Terrorism* 25(5): 279-292.

Roy, Olivier. 2017. *Jihad and Death: The Global Appeal of Islamic State*. London: Hurst Publishers.

Saal, Johannes. 2017. "The Islamic State's Libyan External Operations Hub: The Picture So Far." *CTC Sentinel* 10(11): 19-23.

Sageman, Marc. 2004. *Understanding Terror Networks*. Philadelphia: University of Pennsylvania Press.

Sageman, Marc. 2008. *Leaderless Jihad: Terror Networks in the Twenty-First Century*. Philadelphia: University of Pennsylvania Press.

Schuurman, Bart, Edwin Bakker, Paul Gill, & Noémie Bouhana. 2017. "Lone Actor Terrorist Attack Planning and Preparation: A Data-Driven Analysis." *Journal of Forensic Sciences* 63(4): 1-10.

Sedgwick, Mark. 2004. "Al-Qaeda and the Nature of Religious Terrorism." *Terrorism and Political Violence* 16(4): 795-814.

Speckhard, Anne, & S. Ahmet Yayla. 2017. "The ISIS Emni: Origins and Inner Workings of ISIS's Intelligence Apparatus." *Perspectives on Terrorism* 11(1): 2-16.

UNODC. 2012. *The Use of the Internet for Terrorist Purposes*. Vienna:.United Nations Office on Drugs and Crime.

Vidino, Lorenzo, Francesco Marone, & Eva Entenmann. 2017. *Fear Thy Neighbour: Radicalization and Jihadist Attacks in the West.* Milan: ICCT, ISPI and George Washington University.
Weimann, Gabriel. 2006. "Virtual Training Camps: Terrorists' Use of the Internet." In *Teaching Terror: Strategic and Tactical Learning in the Terrorist World*, edited by James J.F. Forest, 110-132. New Delhi: Viva Books.
Wiktorowicz, Quintan. 2005. *Radical Islam Rising: Muslim Extremism in the West.* Oxford: Rowman & Littlefield.
Wood, Graeme. 2016. *The Way of the Strangers.* New York: Random House.

1.3 Perpetrators and the Law

9

Nazi Perpetrators and the Law

Postwar Trials, Courtroom Testimony, and Debates about the Motives of Nazi War Criminals

Hilary Earl

Introduction

The Italian philosopher Giorgio Agamben observed that the vocation of the survivor of the Nazi Holocaust is to remember, to give voice to the millions of victims who have been permanently silenced; in short, to bear witness (Agamben 1998, 26). According to the founder of Oneg Shabbat[1] Emmanuel Ringelblum, the impulse to bear witness began early in the destruction process, during ghettoization when "everyone wrote," of their experiences, not just historians and journalists (Wieviorka 2006, 1–2). This impulse did not end with the war. When he returned from Auschwitz, for example, Primo Levi said he felt "an unrestrainable need to tell [his] story to anyone and everyone" (quoted in Agamben 2002, 16). For survivors such as Levi, giving testimony is rooted in the need to make the truth of the devastating tragedy known (Des Pres 1976). This impulse has given rise to the survivor narrative, what French scholar Annette Wieviorka refers to as the act of "witnessing," both during the violence and especially in the years after it (Wieviorka 2006, 1–144). Since 1945, thousands of survivor memoirs and even more oral histories have been written, published, and recorded—an archive of personal experiences and testimony unparalleled in modern history. For the perpetrators of these crimes, however, there rarely was such an inducement to tell the truth, nor any desire to record their personal experiences. Certainly, there was no Spielberg or Yale project devoted to amassing the narrative of the perpetrator.[2] This should not be surprising. After all, few admitted to participating in the crimes of the Third Reich when guilt and complicity were implicated by such a confession, and criminal prosecution and possibly death were the likely outcomes. Even after prosecution, few perpetrators were willing to speak. Exceptions include Franz Stangl, the Kommandant of Treblinka death camp, and Albert Speer, the Armaments Minister of the Third Reich. Both men willingly spoke to investigative journalist Gitta Sereny who gave voice to their criminal pasts in the form of biographies (Speer 1976). However, in doing so she has been criticized by some for being overly sympathetic to her subjects, one of the pitfalls of knowing your subjects too well (Sereny 1974, 1995).

The judicial reckoning that Nazi officials faced for the crimes they perpetrated before and during the Second World War—beginning with the International Military Tribunal at Nuremberg in 1945 (IMT), and continuing until recently in Australia, the United States, Canada, Germany, Poland, Russia, and other European countries—has ensured that very few, if any former Nazis would *voluntarily* explain their aberrant behavior, which, without exception, ended with the Third Reich itself.[3] Nazi perpetrators, as it turned out, lived lives that were free from violence after the war (Earl 2015). Thus, understanding what motivated otherwise non-violent, mentally stable individuals to participate in persecution, mass murder, and genocide, acts that social-psychologist James Waller has referred to as "extraordinary human evil," is left for scholars to interpret (Waller 2002, 12). However, if we lack explanations from participants about their actions, how are we to fully understand the human mechanisms of genocide? This confessional absence forces us, for better or worse, to use the documentation we do have at our disposal, including interrogation records and testimonies given at postwar trials. As problematic as these can be, they are available in abundance.

In the decades following the war, thousands of individual perpetrators, from the highest-ranking Nazi to the lowliest reserve policeman and camp guard, were called as witnesses to testify against their colleagues or to directly answer for the crimes they themselves had committed. It is in the courtroom then, that perpetrators have spoken—albeit involuntarily—of their experiences. In doing so, they have left a vast repository of testimony, interrogations, affidavits, and other documentation for scholars to utilize. Perhaps the best known case is that of Adolf Eichmann's 1961 trial in Jerusalem that has been written about extensively and which set in motion an entire historiography of perpetrator narratives, the most famous of which is undoubtedly Hannah Arendt's 1963, *Eichmann in Jerusalem: A Report on the Banality of Evil.*

Since the publication of Arendt's now famous observations about Eichmann's motives, many scholars have used trial documents and testimony to access and develop a better understanding of the behavior of participants of genocide—mostly men—and the functioning of the state apparatus in the commission of the "Final Solution." This chapter examines the relationship between the law—especially the postwar trials of German perpetrators—perpetrator motives and behavior, and genocide. It critically evaluates some of the major themes and debates in Nazi Perpetrator Studies as they relate to law, especially the benefits and shortcomings that arise in utilizing Nazi perpetrator testimony.

Listening to Perpetrators: Trial Testimony, the "Banality of Evil," and the Genesis of Interpretations of "Perpetrator Motive"

The use and historical credibility of pre-trial interrogations, affidavits, trial testimony, and documentation is a charged one, particularly when it comes to reconstructing historical events and explaining human behavior. Why? Not only because human memory is fallible and selective but also, and equally as important, because in the context of the courtroom where individuals are fighting for their lives, the propensity for perjury (the deliberate act of stating something you know to be false as truth) is great. That testimonies are fabricated, details forgotten, defenses mounted, or lies told should be neither surprising nor unexpected to scholars. Yet, some have reconstructed historical narratives of the Nazi destruction of Europe's Jews using evidence derived expressly from a legal setting. On the one hand, doing so can elicit incredible results. One such example is Raul Hilberg's masterful *Destruction of the European Jews* in which he uses the documents amassed to prosecute the Third Reich's leading personnel in 13 trials held between 1945 and 1949 known collectively as the Nuremberg

Trials, to construct an interpretation of the "Final Solution" as a giant and well-oiled bureaucratic "machinery" (Hilberg 1961). On the other hand, though, even the brilliant Hilberg fell prey to the seductive arguments of the Nuremberg defendants, some of whom were completely believable but who were also fighting for their lives.

To illustrate the way in which Nuremberg testimony skewed and possibly complicated the historical record, we can turn to our historical understanding of the timing and nature of the *Führerbefehl*, Hitler's alleged order to murder all of Europe's Jews. Because no documented order by Hitler to murder all European Jews has ever been located, some historians (Hilberg included) relied on perpetrator testimony to determine the precise nature and timing of this decision. In this instance, Otto Ohlendorf, the head of *Einsatzgruppe* D (one of 4 mobile killing units deployed in the Soviet Union in the summer of 1941 to kill Russian, Ukrainian, and other Jews in the occupied eastern territories) gave direct testimony at Nuremberg about the nature and timing of the order. On the witness stand, Ohlendorf clearly and convincingly recalled that he had been given the order to murder all Soviet Jews *prior* to the deployment of the *Einsatzgruppen* on June 22, 1941, and that it had come from his superiors. Because of the dearth of documentary evidence and for a variety of other reasons I will not expound on here, many historians took Ohlendorf's testimony at face value (Hilberg 1961, 177). As a result, the court and later those scholars who used court transcripts to interpret the genesis of the "Final Solution" believed that the decision to murder all Soviet Jews was taken in the late spring or early summer of 1941, prior to the invasion of the Soviet Union and that it had come from Hitler. This conclusion supports an "intentionalist" interpretation of the origins of the genocide in the East and firmly locates Hitler at the center of the decision-making process. Years later some evidence surfaced that suggested that Ohlendorf might have deliberately lied at his trial about the timing and delivery of the *Führerbefehl* in order to cast blame on Hitler directly, and most importantly in the legal context, to avoid a death sentence himself. At Nuremberg, a defense of "superior orders," while not enough to exonerate an individual, was enough to mitigate a death sentence (Earl 2003). Whether or not Ohlendorf was telling the truth about the timing and delivery of the order will not be addressed here; what is important is that in a criminal trial—particularly at Nuremberg where the stakes were so high because of the existence of the death penalty—it was tempting for defendants to perjure themselves.[4] Even if a defendant does not intentionally lie, memories are fallible (Earl 2006, 2009).

Inaccurate and skewed testimony is not limited to the Nuremberg Trials. As Christian Gerlach has noted in the case of Adolf Eichmann's 1961 trial, his "statements [too] are fundamentally unreliable, and none of them can, by themselves, provide firm ground for any factual interpretation" of events (Gerlach 2001, 442). The reason of course is that criminal trials are adversarial and defendant testimony is most frequently given in an attempt to establish legal innocence, not necessarily to document historical events. In fact, by their very nature, criminal trials may be impediments to the establishment of the historical record, when by excluding or altering historical facts a defendant can demonstrate innocence. This is precisely what Adolf Eichmann did at his trial in 1961. His performance convinced many that he was a desk murderer—killing because it was his job, not because he hated his victims. While the Jerusalem court did not believe Eichmann was innocent—ruled on irrefutable documentary evidence against him—the trial also functioned as an oral history project for survivors who were called to testify in large numbers even when their testimony had little or nothing to do with the legal charges against Eichmann. Survivor testimony was welcomed in the courthouse in Jerusalem largely because survivors were denied a voice at Nuremberg, where prosecutors relied almost exclusively on documents as opposed to direct witnesses because it was feared that survivor testimony would not be believed because its content was so outrageous. Certainly legal truth and historical accuracy are not one and the same. They diverge especially when, in an attempt to determine guilt or innocence, the court privileges witness testimony over historical documentation, thus establishing a testimonial record and not a documentary one. In a criminal court, testimony *is* evidence and is generally privileged because documents cannot be cross-examined, whereas witnesses can be. For judges, comportment and testimony are tests of credibility; for historians, memory is always selective and while testimony *is* documentation, it should not be accepted uncritically by scholars. This is not to suggest that *de facto* all perpetrator testimony is perjured or even unreliable, but rather in the context of a legal proceeding, the historian would be well advised to understand the context of a testimony and secure corroborating evidence before drawing a conclusion. The tension between witness testimony and documentary evidence played out particularly badly in the trial of John Demjanjuk—a Ukrainian national believed to be the notorious Ivan the Terrible of Treblinka death camp. At his trial in Israel (he was also tried in the United States and in 2009 in Germany), he was prosecuted and found guilty based almost exclusively on witness testimony. The witnesses, as it turned out, were wrong. Demjanjuk was not at Treblinka and was not "the" Ivan the Terrible. Rather, as documents later showed, he was terrible, but at Sobibor death camp and not Treblinka (Douglas 2016).

Testimony can be informative if it is not used exclusively for historical reconstruction. For instance, in my research on the leadership corps of the SS-*Einsatzgruppen*, I use testimony to help explain and understand aberrant human behavior, especially how and why twenty-four high-ranking and well-educated SS men willingly participated in state violence (Earl 2009). Establishing a willingness or intention to commit genocide is crucial since, by virtue of the legal definition of genocide, it only occurs when it is intended. However, since genocide is a corporate act, and legally it requires intention, it is difficult to discern whether or which individual members of the perpetrator group held the pertinent intention. Disaggregating a collective intention among the group's individual members is both complex and controversial, but it also helps us understand individual human action in the context of violent conflict and hierarchical structures (May 2010). Exactly how and why individuals are implicated in genocide was of interest to the scholarly community immediately.

In the decades after the war, interpreting perpetrator behavior types was exclusively the purview of psychologists and social-psychologists. The prototype of Nazi SS personnel as easily recognizable monsters who killed because they were brainwashed to believe in a murderous ideology remained the conventional explanatory paradigm until it was challenged in the 1960s by Arendt's controversial observations of Eichmann. Her observations about one SS officer gave birth to the study of perpetrator motive as a sub-genre of Holocaust and genocide studies that to this day has not abated and to which this volume, at least in part, owes its genesis.

Arendt attended Eichmann's trial and related her observations of him in a series of articles in *The New Yorker* magazine, which she later turned into *Eichmann in Jerusalem*. Arendt took Eichmann, a Lieutenant Colonel in the SS and head of IV B4, the office in charge of Jewish affairs, at his word, depicting him as a relatively ambitious man who claimed he was neither a hater of Jews nor a first-hand killer, yet whose conscientious bureaucratic activities helped facilitate the murder of as many as 1.5 million innocent people. Eichmann was middle-aged, rather ordinary looking, with dark glasses and balding head. Certainly, his appearance did not at all conform to the image of the stereotypical SS man conveyed in our imaginations or a man who was responsible for the murder of so many. One of the great breakthroughs that

Arendt made in understanding perpetrator motive was that Eichmann's murderous behavior did not necessarily correspond with stereotypes of SS men. He was neither mad nor a monster nor brainwashed, far from it, she argued. Instead, he was a conscientious bureaucrat, a rather ordinary albeit ambitious man whose routine work in office IV B4 helped facilitate the murder of millions of innocent people (Arendt 1963, 22–23). He was the epitome, she noted, of the "banality of evil" a phrase that has become a hackneyed yet familiar (and contested) part of our lexicon in Perpetrator Studies (Arendt 1963, 252). As one of Eichmann's biographers has ruefully noted, it is a difficult concept to shake in understanding Eichmann as well as other SS perpetrators of his stature (Cesarani 2007). Some scholars directly question Arendt's ostensibly uncritical acceptance of Eichmann's testimony, suggesting that he was not the obedient follower he portrayed himself to be nor was he the law-abiding citizen and "banal desk murderer" Arendt persuaded us he was. Rather, Eichmann was an initiator, with agency, who enjoyed exercising his power over those who were powerless. As it turns out, he was overly zealous, a committed and virulent antisemitism even before the Nazis "seized" power and certainly after they did (Safrian 1996; Stangneth 2014, xvii, 6–7, 49–50, 96–97).

While courtrooms have generated a vast array of perpetrator-related documents, it is incumbent on scholars to consider the environment in which the testimony is given. In assessing a defendant's testimony in a legal context, the entire narrative must be considered. It is not enough to analyze fragments of testimony; the trial, like a book, must be read in its entirety. Only in this way will a scholar have a complete view of the defense strategy and counter narrative (Stangneth 2014, xv–xxi, 178–179). Not attending the entire trial was one of Arendt's great mistakes, and it undoubtedly led to an incomplete view of Eichmann and his defense.

Perpetrator Motive: Ordinary Men or Ordinary Germans?

While the Eichmann debate still rages in some circles, Christopher Browning managed to change the conversation about perpetrator motive when, in 1992 he published his now famous and important book *Ordinary Men: Reserve Police Battalion 101 and the Final Solution in Poland*. He argued that Arendt's thesis is inapplicable in the context of shootings on the Eastern front where the perpetrators killed their victims face-to-face (Browning 1992). They were anything but "banal" desk murderers because they killed their victims including women and children at close range. A pathbreaking interpretation, not just because he moved away from Arendt's thesis, but also because he took it a step further. Using trial testimony, Browning argued that there are different types of perpetrators; the men of PB 101 were firsthand killers and unlike Eichmann, "ordinary," by which he meant non-ideological men who were motivated to kill largely because of situational factors such as peer pressure. As pathbreaking, insightful, and measured as Browning's analysis certainly is, it rankled some scholars who still saw antisemitism (ideology) as the only motive for murder.

Browning's nemesis was Daniel Goldhagen, whose 1996 book *Hitler's Willing Executioners* used the same trial testimony and interrogation records as Browning, yet he came to a radically different conclusion than Browning (Goldhagen 1996). At the heart of the disagreement—referred to as the "ordinary men or ordinary Germans" debate—was the role ideology played in the murderous actions of the perpetrators. Goldhagen's thesis revolves around the monocausal idea that Germans willingly and happily killed because they were born hating Jews (he refers to this as "eliminationist antisemitism"). Goldhagen accused Browning of not fully considering the role of antisemitism as a motivating factor, which all defendants, he observed, universally and deliberately avoided as an explanation for their behavior because to do so in a postwar German courtroom was to ensure a verdict of guilty (Goldhagen 1996, 467).[5] In this case, Goldhagen notes, a testimonial absence in the courtroom speaks volumes about motive.

Another core disagreement between Goldhagen and Browning is the latter's willingness to use self-exculpatory testimony—a highly contested area—by members of the Order Police (*Ordnungspolizei*) to explain individual motivation for participating in the mass slaughter of Jews in the East. Interpreting perpetrator testimony and assessing its reliability, Browning admits, is often an exercise in historical intuition and judgment. The subjective nature of the interpretation process inevitably ensures that "different historians reading the same set of interrogations would," in all likelihood, produce different narratives just as he and Goldhagen did (Browning 1998, 30). In other words, no matter how rigorous a historian is in analyzing testimony, there is always an element of personal bias at play.

Even though historical fact is produced in large measure by the historians' interpretative craft, using the postwar testimony of perpetrators has the potential to blur the lines between "fact" and "interpretation" more than other types of historical analysis (Scott 2001, 86–87). This blurring can have grave consequences, especially when dealing with perpetrators and the historian's narration of their horrific acts. For instance, in narrating the perpetrator experience, Goldhagen embellishes witness testimony to such an extent, a process Nancy Wood refers to as "literary digression," that the outcome borders on the sensational; some have even described it as obscene (Wood 1999, 93). Aside from the obvious, the problem with this approach is that, while appealing to a voyeuristic public (Goldhagen's book was a best seller), it also offers the reader a "fantasy of witnessing" the horrors of the victim experience, to which some would argue neither Goldhagen "nor his readers are morally entitled" (Wood 1999, 93).

Relying on documentation from perpetrator-centric trials as Arendt, Hilberg, Goldhagen, and Browning have done has undoubtedly skewed scholarly interpretations of victim experiences and contributed to the specious view that victims went to their deaths like sheep to the slaughter (Hilberg 1961). The Eichmann trial in 1961 was the first perpetrator trial where Jewish witnesses were invited to give direct testimony about their experiences during the war that often had nothing to do with the criminal charges against the defendant. While these narratives gave voice to the victim experience, they did not mitigate the skewed interpretation of victim behavior. Even Arendt, who was present for some of the testimony, adopted Hilberg's view that victims were passive. Whether or not victims testify at trials, any scholar working with trial documents to explain perpetrator behavior must be aware of the courtroom context, including testimonial absences, witness absences, and most especially victim perspectives, which certainly will be radically different from those of the perpetrators.

Perpetrator Trials, Testimony, and the "Making of a Murderer"

Testimony, uncritically appropriated by historians, has proved to be limiting and problematic, and sometimes efforts to understand perpetrators are misunderstood as apology; the perpetrators are seen mistakenly as victims of German society, puppets of Hitler, or otherwise their explanations—insanity, sadism, superior orders, to name a few—somehow justify their appalling and inhuman behavior.[6] Yet this does not mean *a priori* that perpetrator testimony holds no value. I want to suggest here that trial documents, this vast archive of perpetrator testimony, is one of the most voluminous, detailed, and rich sources of perpetrator "voice" that scholars have at their disposal. Its utility is not only in relationship to the history of trials themselves; testimony can also be used to help us better understand how and why genocide happens. To truly understand the unfolding of the "Final Solution," a human-generated criminal action, we must try to understand—as objectively as possible and with little sensationalism and sympathy for the individual murderers—those who perpetrated it. Using credible documentation such as trial testimony can help us advance this aim. For instance, using the testimony can help us establish a person's "route to crime" (de Mildt 1996) or how exactly a person becomes a murderer. In many cases, criminal prosecutors amassed vast biographical information about individual defendants, frequently supplemented by the defendants themselves when they were questioned on the witness stand. This process enables historians to reconstruct an individual's path to murder. Using the methods of historical biography helps scholars better understand how otherwise non-violent people become genocidal murderers (Earl 2009, 46–95).

For instance, trial documents, particularly material culled from the twelve group proceedings at Nuremberg conducted by the Americans between 1946 and 1949, offer ample material with which to profile the social characteristics of an identifiable group of perpetrators. Especially relevant to the ongoing discussion about perpetrator behavior types and motivation, these trials dealt exclusively with the crimes committed by the Third Reich between 1939 and 1945, including those that led to the Final Solution and other crimes against humanity. The testimonies of these defendants and other trial documents help elucidate the common attributes of the various core groups of perpetrators, not an insignificant undertaking and certainly an important aspect of understanding how cohorts came to their jobs as killers (Wildt 2003). Perhaps most importantly to our understanding of perpetrator mentality and motive, scholars can use trial testimony to assess how perpetrators represented themselves in a public and legal forum, that is, their comportment at trial and conversely how they wanted to be perceived by their audience.

A good example of how trial testimony helps us understand how perpetrators are made comes from the *Einsatzgruppen* trial (1947–1948). The men tried here were not desk murderers like Eichmann, nor do they fit into Browning's situational firsthand killers model. Rather, these men must be categorized differently, as a type of *hybrid killer*: high-ranking SS men like Eichmann who were deployed in the field like the men of Reserve Police Battalion 101, yet who never pulled the trigger themselves. My research demonstrates that without exception, these men were of strong character. Many possessed charismatic traits; they were, for the most part, well-educated professionals with minds and wills of their own, anything but "banal," "insane," or automatons. Some were ideologically motivated, and others came to the killing process through their work in the Reich Security Main Office. They were all ambitious and career-driven, and some were even likeable. Others were the epitome of the nasty, jackbooted SS man we see represented in popular film. Literally thousands of pages of testimony and documentation from the trial of the *Einsatzgruppen* and other Nuremberg Trials attest to the fact that these men were anything but puppets of the regime (Earl 2009).

Scholarly interpretation aside, there seems to be a more fundamental reason for our uneasiness in understanding perpetrator behavior. It would seem that to admit that the perpetrators of genocide are human, not monsters, forces us to admit that we too, under the right circumstances may be capable of committing similar acts (Browning 1992).[7] This is difficult for many to accept. It is, after all, much more comforting to imagine that perpetrators are removed from us, so inhuman that we share none of the same characteristics or tendencies. By casting the perpetrator as the "incomprehensible other," we are able to distance ourselves from them. If this were true, if perpetrators were evil incarnate, the vast number of perpetrators of the Nazi Holocaust would have been unable to integrate into German society after the war, rather they would have continued to kill regardless of the new context in which they found themselves living. The truth seems to be otherwise. That said, to recognize their humanness is not to suggest that we are able to relate to their actions or empathize with their crimes, but rather it does imply that we need to find a new paradigm by which to understand how otherwise non-violent men can perpetrate such violent acts (Hinton 2004, 2016). Listening to the perpetrators is one such way. As Donald Bloxham, a comparative genocide scholar and the author of numerous books on genocide and war crimes trials has said, this shift in the historiography is a way of "cutting through the courtroom apologia" to get at the real motive for perpetration (Bloxham 2004, 414).

Sparked originally by Browning's *Ordinary Men*, this "legal turn" in perpetrator history now offers a more complicated depiction of the SS and policemen in the field. Unfortunately, though, this picture does not allow for easy characterizations such as Arendt relied on so many years ago. Instead, it yields a myriad of personality types and variable factors that more accurately reflect the complex human reality of events on the ground, how and why individuals become implicated in state violence such as genocide, and how they live their lives after they are released from prison.

Conclusion

As Allied justice was coming to an end in 1949 and Germans were regaining their sovereignty, West Germans took justice into their hands and opened their own investigations into Nazi crimes. Norbert Frei, one of Germany's leading experts on the postwar period, has noted that since 1949, 106,496 investigations were opened against perpetrators living in West Germany. Of these 6,498 had sentences brought against them (Frei 2002). No one has tallied the number of perpetrators prosecuted across Europe and the rest of the world although it is probably safe to assert that only a fraction of those who committed crimes were ever held to account in any meaningful way. The truth is that war crimes trials are an imperfect way to contend with the corporate crime of genocide. While individual and group trials account for some measure of justice, this is but a small fraction of those who contributed to the crime. What about the hundreds of thousands of perpetrators who escaped justice? What became of them and what did they have to say about their wartime actions? Unfortunately, as Gerald Steinacher, Ernst Klee, and others have noted, many fled prosecution using various networks of escape across Europe (Klee 1991; Steinacher 2011).[8] And for those who did not escape, most managed to live lives unfettered by their Nazi past, leaving no trace whatsoever of what motivated them to participate in the crimes of the Third Reich (Ullrich 2011; Messenger & Paehler 2015).

In explaining perpetrator attitudes and motivation, scholars have attempted to compartmentalize behavior into identifiable paradigms such as "desk murderers," "ordinary men", or "ideological killers". While unquestionably there is merit and utility in employing models of perpetrator types, particularly when looking at the issue of motivation, the truth is that perpetrator behavior and experiences are unique and often divided along gender lines. Women were also drawn into the killing process, although for much different reasons than men. Early research on this subject suggests that while some women have directly engaged in the murder process, such as those involved in medical experiments and tried at Nuremberg and elsewhere,[9] their roles tended to be indirect, as enablers, accomplices, and helpers, rather than as firsthand killers (Lower 2013).

With few exceptions, the vast majority of postwar trials were of defined groups of Nazis such as the *Einsatzgruppen* leaders and personnel, the men of Reserve Police Battalion 101,

Auschwitz personnel, *Wehrmacht* officers, judicial figures, German doctors, and German government officials. Even so, group trials are fundamentally about individual behavior. The laws that governed and the ideas that conditioned these trials were rooted in democratic-liberal ideas that ultimately hold an individual responsible for his own actions, not an arbitrarily and often expeditiously defined group. Even though Browning and others have used trial documentation to explain perpetrator motivation collectively, this really flies in the face of the legal conceptions that underpinned all of the Allied and German war crimes trials. Thus, if we are looking for answers to why "groups" behaved as they did, the courtroom may not be the best location to secure an answer. The courtroom is a venue though, as this essay has demonstrated, to begin assessing the individual perpetrator's comportment and personality, as in no other environment is the individual so vulnerable, exposed, and confronted with his or her actions.

As I have intimated here, it is possible to reconstruct the self-understanding of the perpetrators, not only by reading, observing, and analyzing their comportment at trial, but also by taking seriously and evaluating the reasons they have given for their own behavior. In undertaking such an effort, we can return human agency to perpetrators, both men and women, who in courts of law have understandably attempted to strip themselves of all accountability. From reading Otto Ohlendorf's or Adolf Eichmann's trial testimony and interrogation records a picture of a more complex individual than has been traditionally offered emerges. By moving away from traditional readings of these legal documents, we can expand the existing paradigm to include additional nuances and a more wide-ranging and inclusive view of individual perpetrators.

Notes

1 Oneg Shabbat was a group of Jewish scholars devoted to amassing an archive of experiences of those imprisoned in the Warsaw ghetto during World War II.

2 Some perpetrators have written about their experiences; for instance, Rudolf Höss, the former commandant of Auschwitz wrote his memoirs in 1947 while awaiting his trial in Poland. Joseph Goebbels, Hitler's propaganda minister, left a vast archive of his experiences in the form of a diary, and Albert Speer is probably the most well known memoirist of the Third Reich.

3 Oskar Gröning, the so-called bookkeeper of Auschwitz who was tried and prosecuted by a German court for crimes he committed while a guard in Auschwitz, may be the first perpetrator to speak publicly about his role. See, for example, "Profile: Oskar Groening 'book-keeper' of Auschwitz," BBC News, July 15, 2015. Accessed November 10, 2017 www.bbc.com/news/world-europe-32336353.

4 Death penalties were doled out at Nuremberg until 1949 and in Israel in 1961 at the Eichmann trial. West Germany outlawed the death penalty in 1949.

5 Because of the propensity to lie, fabricate, or otherwise deny their criminal behavior, Goldhagen believes, "the only methodological position that makes sense is to discount *all* [his emphasis] self-exculpating testimony that finds no corroboration from other sources."

6 Social scientists once believed that the Nazi perpetrators displayed abnormal personalities. Proponents of this view analyzed psychological data collected while the major Nazi war criminals were awaiting trial at Nuremberg and concluded they were pathological, unhealthy individuals. See for example, Miale and Selzer (1975). More recently, social scientists have challenged this orthodoxy, arguing that there was no such thing as a homogenous Nazi personality type. See for example, Dimsdale (2016).

7 Browning writes, "if the men of Reserve Police Battalion 101 could become killers under such circumstances, what group of men cannot?" (Browning 1992, 189).

8 Klee may have been the first to highlight the flight of Nazi war criminals with the help of the Protestant and Catholic churches. More recently Gerald Steinacher has written about the extensive networks of escape throughout Europe.

9 Irma Grese was a female SS guard at Ravensbrück and later the warden of Bergen-Belsen; she was tried and sentenced for crimes against humanity at the Bergen-Belsen trial. Herta Oberhauser was

a female physician who was the only woman tried at Nuremberg in the so-called doctors' trial in 1946. She was found guilty for the crimes she committed against inmates at Ravensbrück and sentenced to twenty years. Her sentence was later reduced, and she along with many war criminals were released from prison in 1952. Oberhauser practiced medicine for a time but had her medical license revoked in 1958, and she died in 1978. See *Trials of War Criminals before the Nuernberg Military Tribunals under Control Council Law No. 10* (Green Series), "The Medical Case" (Washington: Government Printing Office, 1949).

References

Agamben, Giorgio. 1998. *Remnants of Auschwitz: The Witness and the Archive.* New York: Zone Books.

Arendt, Hannah. 1963. *Eichmann in Jerusalem: A Report on the Banality of Evil.* New York: The Viking Press.

Bloxham, Donald. 2004. "From Streicher to Sawoniuk: The Holocaust in the Courtroom." In *The Historiography of the Holocaust*, edited by Dan Stone, 397–419. London: Palgrave.

Browning, Christopher. 1992. *Ordinary Men: Reserve Police Battalion 101 or the Final Solution in Poland.* New York: Harper Collins.

Browning, Christopher. 1998. "German Memory, Judicial Interrogation, Historical Reconstruction: Writing Perpetrator History from Postwar Testimony." In *Probing the Limits of Representation: Nazism and the "Final Solution,"*, edited by Saul Friedlander, 22–36. Cambridge, MA: Harvard University Press.

Cesarani, David. 2007. *Becoming Eichmann: Rethinking the Life, Crimes, and Trial of a "Desk Murderer."* Boston: Da Capo Press.

de Mildt, Dick. 1996. *In the Name of the People: Perpetrators of Genocide in the Reflection of their Post-War Prosecution in West Germany.* Leiden: Martinus Nijhoff.

Des Pres, Terrence. 1976. *The Survivor: An Anatomy of Life in the Death Camps.* New York: Oxford University Press.

Dimsdale, Joel E. 2016. *Anatomy of Malice: The Enigma of the Nazi War Criminals.* New Haven: Yale University Press.

Douglas, Lawrence. 2016. *The Right Wrong Man. John Demjanjuk and the Last Great Nazi War Crimes Trial.* Princeton: Princeton University Press.

Earl, Hilary. 2003. "Scales of Justice: History, Testimony, and the Einsatzgruppen Trial at Nuremberg." In *Lessons and Legacies VI: New Currents in Historical Research*, edited by Jeffry Diefendorf, 325–351. Evanston: Northwestern University Press.

Earl, Hilary. 2006. "Confessions of Wrong-doing or How to save yourself from the Hangman? An Analysis of British and American Intelligence Reports of the Activities of Otto Ohlendorf, May-December 1945." In *Secret Intelligence and the Holocaust*, edited by David Bankier, 301–326. New York and Jerusalem: Enigma Books and Yad Vashem.

Earl, Hilary Earl. 2009. *The Nuremberg SS-Einsatzgruppen Trial, 1945–1958: Atrocity, Law, and History.* New York: Cambridge University Press.

Earl, Hilary. 2015. "'Bad Nazis and other Germans': The fate of SS-*Einsatzgruppen* Commander Martin Sandberger in postwar Germany." In *From Nazis to West Germans: Self Invention, Recast Identities and the Politics of the Past after 1945*, edited by David Messenger and Katrin Paehler, 61–90. Lexington: University of Kentucky Press.

Frei, Norbert. 2002. *Adenauer's Germany and the Nazi Past. The Politics of Amnesty and Integration*, trans. Joel Golb. New York: Columbia University Press.

Gerlach, Christian. 2001. "The Eichmann Interrogations in Holocaust Historiography." *Holocaust and Genocide Studies* 15(3): Winter, 428–452.

Goldhagen, Daniel. 1996. *Hitler's Willing Executions: Ordinary Germans and the Holocaust.* New York: Alfred A. Knopf.

Hilberg, Raul. 1961. *The Destruction of the European Jews.* Chicago: Quadrangle.

Hinton, Alexander Laban. 2004. *Why Did They Kill? Cambodia in the Shadow of Genocide.* Berkeley: University of California Press.

Hinton, Alex Laban. 2016. *Man or Monster? The Trial of a Khmer Rouge Torturer.* Durham, NC: Duke University Press.

Klee, Ernst. 1991. *Persilscheine und falsche Pässe. Wie die Kirchen den Nazis halfen.* Frankfurt am Main: Fischer Taschenbuch Verlag.

Lower, Wendy. 2013. *Hitler's Furies: German Women in the Nazi Killing Fields.* Boston and New York: Houghton Mifflin Harcourt.

May, Larry. 2010. *Genocide: A Normative Account.* Cambridge: Cambridge University Press.

Messenger, David & Katrin Paehler (eds.). 2015. *From Nazis to West Germans: Self Invention, Recast Identities and the Politics of the Past after 1945.* Lexington: University of Kentucky Press.

Miale, Florence R. & Michael Selzer. 1975. *The Nuremberg Mind: The Psychology of the Nazi Leaders.* New York: Quadrangle.

Safrian, Hans. 1996. *Eichmann und seine Gehilfen.* Frankfurt: Fischer Taschenbuch Verlag. English translation, *Eichmann's Men,* translated by Ute Stargardt. 2010. New York: Cambridge University Press.

Scott, Joan. 2001. "After History?" In *Schools of Thought: Twenty-five Years of Interpretive Social Science,* edited by Joan W. Scott and Debra Keates, 85–103. Princeton: Princeton University Press.

Sereny, Gitta. 1974. *Into that Darkness: An Examination of Conscience.* New York: Vintage.

Sereny, Gitta. 1995. *Albert Speer: His Battle with Truth.* New York: Vintage.

Speer, Albert. 1976. *Inside the Third Reich,* trans. Richard and Clara Winston. New York: The MacMillan Co.

Stangneth, Bettina. 2014. *Eichmann before Jerusalem. The Unexamined Life of a Mass Murderer.* New York: Alfred A. Knopf.

Steinacher, Gerald. 2011. *Nazis on the Run. How Hitler's Henchmen Fled Justice.* Oxford: Oxford University Press.

Ullrich, Christina. 2011. *"Ich fühl' mich nicht als Mörder". Die Integration von NS-Tätern in die Nachkriegsgesellschaft.* Darmstadt: Wissenschaftliche Buchgesellschaft.

Waller, James. 2002. *Becoming Evil: How Ordinary People Commit Genocide and Mass Killing.* New York: Oxford University Press.

Wieviorka, Annette. 2006. *The Era of the Witness.* Ithaca and London: Cornell University Press.

Wildt, Michael. 2003. *Generation des Unbedingten. Das Führungskorps des Reichssicherheitshauptamtes.* Hamburg: Hamburger Edition.

Wood, Nancy. 1999. *Vectors of Memory: Legacies of Trauma in Postwar Europe.* London: Bloomsbury.

10

When Perpetrators Become Defendants and then Convicts

Mark A. Drumbl

In recent decades, the courtroom has emerged ideationally as the iconic place in and through which to deliver justice in the aftermath of atrocity. This move synchronizes with the emergence of international criminal law as a reflexive accountability mechanism—a normative preference catalyzed at Nuremberg. As for punishment, courtrooms become twinned with jailhouses: perpetrators of massive human rights abuses are to be sentenced to terms of imprisonment. The emergence of the courtroom and the jailhouse as the "best practice" when it comes to accountability for massive human rights abuses means that certain perpetrators become defendants and, if found guilty, then become convicts. This chapter unpacks two themes. First, how do the representational practices of the criminal trial constrict the agency, conduct, and actions of the perpetrator? This chapter posits that the hydraulics of criminal law distort the agency of the perpetrator. The prosecutorial impulse exaggerates the individual responsibility exercised by many perpetrators, including higher-level authorities, in particular the massive numbers of perpetrators who operate below the levels of the top leadership whose handiwork is essential to the collectivization of atrocity. On the other hand, the defense tends to artificially minimize perpetrator agency to increase the likelihood of an acquittal. This chapter takes up the trial of Issa Sesay (a senior leader of the rebel Revolutionary United Front in Sierra Leone) as a case study of these hydraulics.

Second, this chapter examines how and why international institutions punish defendants who are found guilty. This is the stage where perpetrators transform from defendants to convicts. Questions emerge as to whether the sentencing rationales of international criminal law (primarily retribution and deterrence) are attainable in the context of mass atrocity.

From Nuremberg to Everywhere

At the time, and for several decades thereafter, it was not evident that the proceedings conducted by the International Military Tribunal at Nuremberg (IMT) in 1945–1946 would serve as any sort of precedent or fixture. Beginning with the end of the Cold War in the 1990s, however, Nuremberg became evoked as a benchmark as the push to create international courts and tribunals acquired political traction. Unlike its companion trials at the International Military Tribunal for the Far East (Tokyo Tribunal), the IMT proceedings are referentially taken as the start of a very big project, cast by many—including in the Introduction to this book (the *Handbook of Perpetrator Studies*)—as "epochal." What is more, proceedings subsequent to the IMT also conducted in Nuremberg under the auspices of the American Military Tribunal also serve in folkloric fashion as a point of genesis. The trajectory—well-worn in the literature—"from Nuremberg to The Hague" evokes the progressive development of international law as a bulwark against human rights abuses (Sands 2003).

The IMT famously held: "Crimes against international law are committed by men, not by abstract entities, and only by punishing individuals who commit such crimes can the provisions of international law be enforced" (Nuremberg Trial, Vol I, 1947–1949, 223). The IMT battled to ensure that personal responsibility would not be obscured by the muck and murk of the anonymity of collective violence. Over time, these words have come to encapsulate a normative preference, namely, that the pursuit of post-conflict justice is best served through the selective prosecution and punishment of individual defendants. Courts of law have become mainstreamed as the reflexive first option to hold accountable those persons responsible for the commission of extraordinary international crimes such as genocide, crimes against humanity, aggression, or war crimes. Nuremberg saw some due process defects (as did the Tokyo trials), to be sure. Contemporary institutions strive to reduce these defects. The impartiality of contemporary institutions is far from unassailable, but efforts to promote fairness and equality of arms are more robust than those evident at Nuremberg.

In sum, then, the atrocity trial is the *primus inter pares* of transitional justice mechanisms. The architecture of justice, hence, involves courtrooms and jailhouses. The narrative of justice maps onto individual culpability, rules of evidence, legal technique, and microscopic proofs. Judges are the arbiters of guilt or innocence and assessors of right or wrong. The frame of punishment, moreover, has become defined as sequestered incarceration along the penitentiary model. The IMT had sentenced convicts to death, to be sure, but this form of punishment is no longer operationally available under contemporary international criminal processes.

International criminal law dazzles by dint of its ambition. The claim that courtrooms can distil terribly complex episodes of collective atrocity is a bold one. So too, is the claim that the jailhouse can punish the enemies of all humankind. These ambitions, nevertheless, have prompted concrete action, notably, considerable institution building over the past two decades. Forerunner institutions such as the *ad hoc* International Criminal Tribunals for the former Yugoslavia (ICTY 1993) and Rwanda (ICTR 1994) have concluded their work. Enforcement of their ongoing sentences and residual appeals is overseen by a Mechanism for International Criminal Tribunals (MICT). The topography of post-conflict justice also includes the permanent International Criminal Court (ICC 2002, currently with 123 state parties) (Rome Statute 1998); hybrid tribunals such as the Special Court for Sierra Leone (SCSL 2002, which closed down after completing its work but like the *ad hoc* tribunals is also overseen by its own Residual Mechanism); the Extraordinary Chambers in the Courts of Cambodia (ECCC); and the Special Tribunal for Lebanon (STL). The institutions of international criminal law are neither spectral nor illusory. They are very real. No doubt, they often move languidly, while incurring great costs and consuming large tranches of UN budgets. Still, the political economy of judicialized accountability is a going concern.

These institutions have also generated reams of substantive law, thereby serving an important expressive, social constructivist, and jurisprudential function. Over the past decade, international criminal law has advanced rapidly in terms of codification and interpretation. Crimes, and elements of crimes, are set out in great detail. The case law interpreting textual documents is robust. Processes of codification and interpretation have, for the most part, been progressive: these processes expand the ground covered by law. Crimes committed against women, which have been long ignored, have now become a focus of attention. Groundbreaking judgments condemn conduct that ranges far beyond massacre, including child soldiering, intentional attacks upon cultural property, and pillage. Liability theories such as joint criminal enterprise, indirect co-perpetration, and superior responsibility widen the scope of potential perpetrators. International criminal law regulates more and more: at times elegantly, at times tenaciously. Its place has solidified within post-conflict peace negotiations, thereby tainting the amnesty and jaundicing the pardon. The peace *versus* justice debate is becoming a relic of the past: Regardless of whether criminal justice thwarts peace or stimulates it, the fact remains that criminal justice has intractably wended its way into, and now entwines with, peace negotiations.

International criminal law transcends the international plane. It seeps into national jurisdictions. Over the past decade, national courts have increasingly prosecuted and punished perpetrators of genocide, crimes against humanity, and wide-scale war crimes. The iconic status of the atrocity trial remodels national legal orders and guides the micro-politics of post-conflict transitions. In sum, the emergence of the courtroom as the "best practice" when it comes to accountability for massive human rights abuses means that certain select perpetrators become defendants and, if found guilty, then become convicts.

The Hydraulics of the Criminal Trial

The adversarialism of criminal procedure triggers a prosecutorial impulse to essentialize the accused perpetrator as perfectly evil. Critical legal scholar Sofia Stolk remarks that, in their opening statements, international prosecutors caricaturize perpetrators with a view to presenting them as despicable, animalistic, and monstrous (Stolk 2017, 112–118). This strategic move is understandable. After all, it helps instrumentalize convictions and weightier sentences. It builds moral outrage. Obversely, I also have found that the defense, exercising the responsibility they have to zealously represent the accused, also participates in a competing game of essentialization that inflates the innocence, cluelessness, and powerlessness of the perpetrator. I have discussed elsewhere specific examples of these dual hydraulics in the ICC's ongoing trial of former Lord's Resistance Army (LRA) child soldier Dominic Ongwen (Drumbl 2016a, 2016b) and Nazi collaborator trials held in Israeli courts in the 1950s and 1960s (Drumbl 2016c, 2017). The reductive parsimony of criminal trials may also distort the historical record and neglect the reality that many individuals who harm others in times of atrocity may themselves be compromised, victims, or individuals who exercised their agency in contradictory ways.

The trial of Issa Hassan Sesay constitutes an example. Sesay was born on June 27, 1970, in Freetown, Sierra Leone. He ultimately served as the Interim Leader of the rebel Revolutionary United Front (RUF) from 2000 to 2003 while its actual leader (and founder) Foday Sankoh was detained. The RUF inflicted grievous violence throughout Sierra Leone during the country's armed conflict in the 1990s and early 2000s. It led a brutal insurrection against the government, then led by President Ahmad Kabbah, rife with mass rape, amputation, and deployment of children to commit heinous atrocities in its military campaigns (ominously called "Operation Spare No Soul" and "Operation No Living Thing"). From 1993 to 1997, Sesay served as an RUF Regional Area Commander. From April 1997 to December 1999, he was an RUF Battle Group Commander. Sesay also had senior connections with another rebel group, the AFRC.

The Special Court for Sierra Leone (SCSL) indicted Sesay on March 7, 2003. Together with two other RUF leaders (Kallon and Gbao)—all three accused of forming a joint criminal enterprise—Sesay went to trial starting in 2004. Sankoh had died before the start of the trial and hence was not prosecuted despite having initially being indicted. The SCSL separately (and subsequently) convicted Charles Taylor, the President of Liberia, for conduct that *inter alia* involved his support of the RUF. Sesay was found guilty on February 25, 2009, of sixteen counts of war crimes and crimes against humanity, including acts of terrorism, collective punishments, extermination, murder, rape, sexual slavery, other inhumane acts (forced marriage), outrages upon personal dignity, cruel treatment, use of child soldiers, enslavement, pillage, and attacks against UN peacekeepers. He was sentenced on April 8, 2009, to a hefty prison term of fifty-two years (Sesay et al. Sentencing Judgment 2009). The SCSL Appeals Chamber upheld the trial convictions against Sesay, along with his sentence, on October 26, 2009.

Sesay is now in the Mpanga Prison in Rwanda. This is because Rwanda signed an agreement with the SCSL to incarcerate SCSL convicts. Sesay is serving out his fifty-two-year sentence. He does so with considerable complaints from the monotonous menus to the fact he cannot call his family on Sundays to the quality of the reading materials made available to him (Mwenda 2012). Reaction to his complaints is not particularly sympathetic. At trial, Sesay was portrayed as a monster. In his opening statement, Chief Prosecutor David Crane evoked the harshest language of outrage. "May it please the Court," Crane began, "this is a tale of horror, beyond the gothic into the realm of Dante's inferno. They came across the border, dark shadows, on a warm spring day […] These dogs of war, these hounds from hell […]" (Stolk 2017, 112–118).

Yet Sesay was a more complex character. Like Ongwen in the LRA, Sesay was forcibly abducted into the RUF, albeit unlike Ongwen, this was at the age of nineteen (the age of Ongwen's abduction remains unclear, but is estimated as young as nine and no older than fourteen). The defense argued that Sesay's forced conscription and "subsequent loss of youth" put him in the category of being "another of Sankoh's many victims" (Sesay et al. Sentencing Judgment, 2009, para. 69).[1] During his testimony, Sesay stated that he was afraid to leave, as someone who had previously tried to flee had died in the attempt. He did not want to train for war, but he also wanted to survive. Like Ongwen, Sesay had a complicated relationship with other rebel leadership and faced threats from them.

Sesay played a pivotal role in decommissioning and demilitarizing the RUF. Between 1999 and 2002, he significantly disarmed the RUF, thereby weakening the group to the extent that the war was brought to an end. The defense seized on this to present Sesay as a moderate who pushed for disarmament even though the incarcerated RUF leadership and Charles Taylor requested him not to do so. Without Sesay's leadership in the RUF, it is unclear whether the civil war would have ended (BBC News 2008). The defense introduced considerable evidence in this regard, including formal statements by the former Special Representative of the UN Secretary-General to Sierra Leone and the former President of the Economic Community of West African States (ECOWAS), a regional group of sixteen countries that had sent peacekeepers. The defense also insisted that Sesay had less authority and control and direct involvement than the prosecutor alleged.

The defense raised all these points at trial as well as at sentencing (to plead for mitigation of punishment). The prosecution, however, convinced judges to look the other way. These realities of Sesay as perpetrator were stripped from the construction of Sesay as defendant. In fact, the SCSL flatly ruled that the fact that he was forcibly recruited into the RUF was irrelevant, even when it came to mitigation of sentence, in part because of Sesay's own agency. The sentencing judges concluded that his "forced recruitment cannot mitigate the crimes which Sesay later committed, as we consider that he could well have chosen another path" (Sesay et al. Sentencing Judgment 2009, para. 220). The judges found that Sesay's leadership role was at a very senior level (Sesay et al. Sentencing Judgment 2009, para. 228). Judges also dismissed in mitigation his efforts to bring about peace and reconciliation (Sesay et al. Sentencing Judgment 2009, para. 228).[2] On the other hand, the SCSL found that its convictions of Sesay for attacking peacekeepers stood "in contrast to these clear statements describing Sesay as a reliable partner in the peace process" (Sesay et al. Sentencing Judgment 2009, para. 227). On this latter point, however, Judge Boutet dissented. He would have mitigated Sesay's sentence because of his peace efforts. Judge Boutet held that he

> entirely believe[d] the evidence of Sesay when [Sesay] testified that some of the top ranking officers of the RUF were against disarmament just as they were against Sesay for disarming without making the release of Sankoh from prison as a condition precedent.
>
> *(Sesay et al. Sentencing Judgment 2009, Boutet opinion, para. 62)*

He added that "[t]here may well have been no peace if Sesay did not embrace the peace process and take the bold and risky initiative to encourage disarmament" (Sesay et al. Sentencing Judgment 2009, Boutet opinion, para. 67).[3] But majority rules in legal process—in zero-sum fashion—so this judge's findings had no effect on the outcome.

Sesay's punishment is heavy by international standards.[4] His sentence exceeds Charles Taylor's (fifty years) and Radovan Karadžić's (forty years). His sentence also was the longest among the three RUF defendants: Kallon received forty years and Gbao twenty-five years. As the next section of this chapter discusses, it is utterly implausible that Ongwen would receive anything similar in length in light of the ICC's sentences to date in other finalized cases of fourteen, twelve, and nine years.

The SCSL judgments, however, are not the only venues in which Sesay's perpetration has been presented. He is also the subject of a well-received feature-length documentary, *War Don Don*, made by US filmmaker Rebecca Richman Cohen in 2010. In the Krio language, "war don don" means "the war is over": Cohen's film explores the dénouement of armed conflict in Sierra Leone and the arrival of the SCSL through the prism of the proceedings against Sesay. *War Don Don* unwraps these questions through a variety of devices: Cohen's recorded conversations with many key players; footage of the trial; graphic victim testimony; images of casualties and child soldiers; presentation of background information about Sierra Leone and the SCSL; and the filmmaker and crew following the SCSL Outreach Team as it meets with often skeptical Sierra Leoneans throughout the country to explain what exactly the SCSL is doing and why it was worthwhile to spend a couple of hundred million dollars on it. Cohen refrains from the use of authoritative or narrative voice-over. Instead, the film unfurls through the voices of respondents. Its "stars" are Sesay, his prosecutors, his defense lawyers, and many people of Sierra Leone.

This documentary presents Sesay in a more nuanced fashion than the criminal trial did. The film allows viewers room to form their own assessments regarding Sesay's culpability and the form that "truth" takes. The RUF judgments permit some small space for public discernment, by virtue of the existence of a thin dissenting judgment. That said, because dissents are separate (and materially irrelevant to the outcome), the film, by its very design, offers a more interactive, integrated, and subtle portrayal. Unlike the actual trial, of course, the film itself does not produce a verdict. It is not consequential in this regard.

Chief Prosecutor Crane flatly states in *War Don Don* that he believes Sesay "has no soul." Stephen Rapp, another prosecutor, contends that Sesay is responsible for the acts of all the forces, no matter if they were under his direct control or not. He states that, even if Sesay was not directing troops to perpetrate amputations and rapes, "cowardice has criminal consequences." The prosecutors aim to stress that Sesay was a senior commander of the RUF. Yet, considering the organization of the RUF, the film also gestures towards the possibility that the crimes of which Sesay was convicted were virtually out of his control. Sareta Ashraph, a member of the defense team, explains to Cohen that the prosecution looked at the RUF as a traditional army, with traditional command structure, when rather it was a guerrilla army with its own idiosyncratic loyalties and command structures. Eldred Collins (a founding member of the RUF) adds in the film that Sesay was only a battlefield commander; he was appointed to Interim Leader not by the RUF, but instead by heads of other West African states. To be sure, all of these comments are made in hindsight, well after the events, but so too is testimony at a criminal trial.

War Don Don shows defense lawyer Wayne Jordash critiquing the SCSL on a radio show, saying that it was more focused on punishing someone for atrocities rather than truly completing a fact-finding mission. Jordash adds that the SCSL was unable to acknowledge the existence of some middle ground between good and evil. *War Don Don* also features a Sierra Leonean villager who similarly inquires how the SCSL, a court, ever could navigate this terrain. The defense also references the "favors" trial witnesses received for testifying for the prosecution. These witnesses included other war criminals the SCSL chose not to prosecute, or had even pardoned, some of whom received financial inducements for their testimony. The prosecutors do acknowledge in the film that their witnesses were not good people, but Crane justifies his approach as a necessary, though unappealing, part of the process: he refers to working with these witnesses as "dancing with the devil."

A trial process determines a defendant to be one of two things—guilty or innocent—and this process will, as this section has suggested, trigger a process of reductive parsimony. A guilty defendant then becomes a convict to be sentenced. This means that a quantification process must begin. How much time to serve? And why? The next section of this chapter explores the interface of law with punishment in the context of the perpetrator of mass atrocity and collective violence.

From Defendant to Convict

The ICC can sentence an offender to up to 30 years' jail-time, with a possibility of "life imprisonment when justified by the extreme gravity of the crime and the individual circumstances of the convicted person" (Rome Statute 1998, art. 77(1)). There is no minimum sentence. When determining an appropriate sentence, ICC judges shall "take into account such factors as the gravity of the crime and the individual circumstances of the convicted person" (Rome Statute 1998, art. 78(1)). The ICTY and ICTR proceed similarly. The ICTR and ICTY may incarcerate a convict for a term up to life. Since there is no mandatory minimum sentence, ICTR and ICTY judges therefore have the power to impose any sentence ranging from one-day imprisonment to life imprisonment for any crime within their jurisdiction. The Statute of the SCSL formally precludes life sentences and stipulates that juvenile offenders (persons between fifteen and eighteen years of age) are to be treated with clemency so as to encourage their rehabilitation.[5] All of these institutions only exercise jurisdiction over natural persons, thereby obscuring the role that corporate entities (legal persons) may play in atrocity and thereby further narrowing the construction of the kind of perpetrator that can even become a defendant or convict.

Convicts are eligible for consideration for early release after they have served two-thirds of their sentence. This is the practice at the *ad hoc* tribunals and included in the formal language of the Rome Statute, the ICC's constitutive treaty. The Rome Statute also permits reparations to be made to victims (Rome Statute 1998, art. 75). Nearly all convicts are indigent, however. This means that reparative orders are made through the Trust Fund for Victims. The Fund is capitalized by voluntary grants from organizations and governments (thirty-four donor countries so far) (Smeulers et al., 2013, 22).[6] The Trust Fund nonetheless disclaims any punitive orientation and operates within a restorative paradigm. Hence, it is not formally part of the ICC's penalty schematic.

The SCSL has sentenced its nine convicts to an average term of nearly thirty-nine years. As of the beginning of 2017, the ICTY has finalized eighty-two sentences.[7] Five of these are life sentences (6% of the total). Among the seventy-seven determinate sentences, the median term is fifteen years and the mean term is fifteen and 54/100 years. The minimum determinate sentence is two years in length, and the maximum life sentence is forty years. Even if the five life sentences are included in the median calculations (coded at a value of 100), the ICTY median sentence still remains fifteen. The ICTR has finalized fifty-nine sentences. Seventeen of these are life sentences. Among the forty-two determinate sentences, the median sentence is twenty-five years, and the mean sentence is twenty-four and 67/100 years. The shortest determinate sentence issued by the ICTR is 6 years, while the maximum is 47 years. Owing to the comparatively larger number of life sentences awarded by the ICTR (28.9 % of the total), including the life sentences (coded at a value of 100) in the median calculations would increase the median sentence to thirty years.

As of the time of writing, the ICC has sentenced three convicts: Thomas Lubanga, Germain Katanga, and Ahmad al-Faqi al-Mahdi. They received sentences of fourteen, twelve, and nine years respectively. A fourth convict, Jean-Pierre Bemba Gombo, had been sentenced at trial to eighteen years but was subsequently acquitted on appeal in June 2018 on the basis that, *inter alia*, as a matter of law he lacked command responsibility over the conduct in question. Bemba was the former Vice-President of the DRC. After his release from the ICC, he returned to the DRC to run for President.

Ahmad al-Faqi al-Mahdi, a radical Islamist, was sentenced in 2016 to nine years in a case emerging out of the Mali situation. Al-Mahdi had pleaded guilty. He was charged in relation to his role in demolishing nine historic shrines, and the door of a renowned mosque (Sidi Yahia), in Timbuktu, Mali. Al-Mahdi's prosecution and sentencing was the first for the ICC with regard to the war crime of destruction of cultural heritage. In terms of the gravity of the crime, Judge Pangalangan noted that crimes against property are generally of lesser gravity than crimes against persons, but also underscored the symbolic value, religious salience, and affective attachment generated by the Timbuktu shrines. He explicitly linked the crime to human suffering.

Thomas Lubanga, a rebel leader in the DRC, was convicted as a co-perpetrator of the war crime of conscripting and enlisting children under the age of fifteen years and using them to participate actively in hostilities in a non-international conflict. His was the ICC's first conviction and sentence. The special vulnerability of children was recognized in his fourteen-year sentence. Germain Katanga, also a DRC rebel leader, was convicted as an accessory to one count of murder as a crime against humanity and to four counts of war crimes (murder, attacking a civilian population, destruction of property and pillaging) for a 2003 attack. Katanga was sentenced to twelve years.

International criminal judges gesture towards important rationales when they impose sentences for mass atrocity crimes. Retribution and general deterrence are the two most prominently cited punishment goals (Bemba Sentencing Judgment 2016, para. 10).[8] These are largely drawn from the penological practices of ordinary criminal law, that is, the law applicable at the national level in times of peace. In the RUF sentencing judgment, the Trial Chamber ruled that "the goals and objectives of sentencing in the sphere of international criminal law derive essentially from the doctrines underlying penal sanctions in the domestic or national law setting" (Sesay et al. Sentencing Judgment 2009, para. 12). This superimposition seems somewhat facile, however. While the perpetrator of collective violence such as genocide and persecution may share many elements in common with the perpetrator of an isolated act of murder or sexual violence in times of peace, a broad array of evidence suggests the existence of conceptual, psychological, etiological, and motivational differences between perpetrators of extraordinary international crimes and ordinary common crimes (Drumbl 2007).

Although there are many divergent schools of retributivism, what retributivists generally share is an understanding that the infliction of punishment rectifies the moral balance, in particular, through condemnation of the criminal conduct. Simply put, punishment is what the perpetrator deserves. Punishment, therefore, is to be proportionate to the extent of the harm caused by the crime and to the perpetrator's degree of intentionality. When it comes to extraordinary international criminality, however, tension may arise, in particular at the lower ranks of offenders, insofar as crimes of terrible gravity may in fact be committed by persons with low intent—the phenomenon of administrative or occupational massacre within a totalitarian apparatus. In any event, the ICTY Appeals Chamber has emphasized that "retribution should not be misunderstood as a way of expressing revenge or vengeance" (Prosecutor v. Kordić and Čerkez 2004, para. 1075). Rather, it has conceived of retribution as the "expression of condemnation and outrage of the international community" (Prosecutor v. Nikolić 2003, para. 86). The ICC proceeds similarly. In this regard, retributive motivations wander in the direction of expressivism. The expressivist punishes to strengthen faith in rule of law among the general public, as opposed to punishing simply because the perpetrator deserves it or will be deterred by it. From an expressivist perspective, punishment proactively embeds the normative value of law within the community. This in theory leads to positive general prevention.

General deterrence considers that the purpose of prosecuting and punishing individuals who commit mass atrocity is utilitarian in nature, that is, to dissuade others from offending in the future. Specific deterrence implies that punishing the offender will deter that one offender from re-offending. When the activity of international criminal justice institutions is taken as a whole, the focus of deterrence remains oriented towards general deterrence. From a deterrence perspective, punishment is inflicted because of the consequentialist effect of reducing the incidence of crime.

On occasion, international judges also refer to other penological rationales including rehabilitation, incapacitation, and reconciliation. These rationales, however, are not particularly salient. It is unfortunate that rehabilitation figures so marginally, insofar as many convicts (for example from the ICTY) are now being released for having served their sentences. They return home to face very different fates; there are no common policies to promote what would be understood as meaningful re-integration.

Whether the sentencing practices of international institutions attain their avowed penological goals remains an unsettled question. The evidence is mixed regarding whether and to what extent punishing a perpetrator dissuades other perpetrators, either in the same region or elsewhere, from offending, notably in the case of collective discrimination-oriented crimes such as genocide, extermination, and persecution. A recent study conducted under the auspices of the International Nuremberg Academy grappled with the inherent difficulties in measuring deterrence, in the first place, and then correlating it with the interventions of international courts and tribunals. Entitled *Two Steps Forward, One Step Back*, this excellent study found some unsystematized and impressionistic evidence of deterrent effect within ten post-conflict case studies (Schense and Carter 2016). It also identified a number of challenges to deterrence, specifically, selectivity in prosecutions (when only one "side" is prosecuted), witness security, and the perceived severity of sentencing.

The likelihood of getting caught is more influential than any other factor in discouraging criminal conduct. Yet the likelihood of getting caught and prosecuted by an international institution in cases of atrocity crimes sadly remains low. In terms of retribution, the severity of a prison sentence may never be able to reciprocate the gravity of egregious international crimes. Meting out just deserts in such cases ominously suggests the abandonment of core principles of international human rights law (whether in terms of the length of sentence or conditions of confinement). Many ICTY and ICC convicts received sentences that were no longer than those routinely meted out to ordinary common criminals in many national justice systems.

Conclusion

International criminal law iconographically ripples through the imaginative space of post-conflict justice. It has ascended as the reflexive "way" to fight impunity. One effect of this ascension—as this chapter discusses—is to massage the construction of the perpetrator, who passes into the figure of the defendant and then the convict. Another broader effect, of course, is to deprioritize other justice methods, which become seen as "alternate." These other methods are varied; they include truth commissions, public inquiries, and traditional ceremonial rituals. How are perpetrators presented in these other processes? A fertile ground of inquiry for the discipline of Perpetrator Studies would be to unpack how these justice modalities representationally construct the perpetrator and how the public absorbs these representations. Until these other methods are given more room to operate, however, and until they lose their subaltern status within the international legal imagination, only limited opportunity will arise to engage in any such studies.

Notes

1 The defense also added that Sesay's "limited life choices" and "lack of training in the dictates of international humanitarian law" should mitigate the severity of sentence as well.

2 "The Chamber finds that the Defense has proved mitigating circumstances on the basis of a balance of probabilities in relation to Sesay's real and meaningful contribution to the peace process in Sierra Leone following his appointment as interim leader of the RUF, however, the Chamber does not accept Sesay's explanation of his reasons for failing to prevent or punish the perpetrators of the attacks against the UNAMSIL personnel, a direct affront to the international community's own attempts to facilitate peace in Sierra Leone."

3 Judge Boutet added in this paragraph that "If Sesay were not on board the peace process, peace would in any event have certainly been achieved in Sierra Leone but, I dare say, at a renewed, continued, and bloody cost, which, we must admit, Sesay pre-empted and prevented."

4 During sentencing arguments, the prosecution requested sixty years; the defense argued for a sentence in the ten to fifteen year range (Sesay et al. Sentencing Judgment, 2009, paras. 54, 76).

5 No juvenile ever was charged, however.

6 *See* www.trustfundforvictims.org/sites/default/files/imce/summary_EN_LR_ONLINE.pdf.
7 All of the ICTR and ICTY data are compiled and analyzed by Barbora Holá and shared with the author on January 7, 2017 (tables on file with the author). A handful of sentences have since been issued, for example the life sentence issued by an ICTY Trial Chamber to Ratko Mladić on November 22, 2017.
8 Citing also the ICC *Katanga* sentencing decision, ICTY *Popović* et al appeal judgment, and ECCC *Kaing* appeal judgment); *Prosecutor v. Stakić* ICTY (IT-97-24-A), Judgment, March 22, 2006, para. 402 (stating that "the Appeals Chamber notes that the jurisprudence of the Tribunal and the ICTR consistently points out that the two main purposes of sentencing are deterrence and retribution"); Sesay et al. Sentencing Judgment, 2009, para. 13.

References

BBC News. 2008. "Kabbah Ends Honeymoon for Trial." BBC News. May 16, 2008. Available at http://news.bbc.co.uk/2/hi/africa/7405481.stm.

Drumbl, Mark A. 2007. *Atrocity, Punishment, and International Law*. New York: Cambridge University Press.

Drumbl, Mark A. 2016a. "A Former Child Soldier in the Hague, as an Accused." *African Yearbook on International Humanitarian Law* 1(1): 144–150.

Drumbl, Mark A. 2016b. "Shifting Narratives: Ongwen and Lubanga on the Effects of Child Soldiering," available at https://justiceinconflict.org/2016/04/20/shifting-narratives-ongwen-and-lubanga-on-the-effects-of-child-soldiering/.

Drumbl, Mark A. 2016c. "Victims Who Victimise." *London Review of International Law* 4(2): 217–246.

Drumbl, Mark A. 2017. "Histories of the Jewish 'Collaborator': Exile, Not Guilt", available on SSRN at https://papers.ssrn.com/sol3/papers.cfm?abstract_id=3009231.

Mwenda, Andrew M. 2012. "Lavish Life of a War Criminal inside a Rwandan Jail." *The East African* (May 5).

Prosecutor v. Kordić and Čerkez (IT-95-14/2-A), ICTY Appeals Judgment, 17 December 2004.

Prosecutor v. Momir Nikolić (IT-02-60/1-S), ICTY Judgment, 2 December 2003.

Prosecutor v. Sesay, Kallon, and Gbao, Case No. SCSL-04-15-T, Sentencing Judgment (Special Court for Sierra Leone, Trial Chamber I, April 8, 2009).

Rome Statute of the International Criminal Court, 2187 UNTS 90, 17 July 1998, entered into force 1 July 2002.

Sands, Philippe. (ed.). 2003. *From Nuremberg to The Hague: The Future of International Criminal Justice*. Cambridge, UK: Cambridge University Press.

Schense, Jennifer and Linda Carter. (eds.). 2016. *Two Steps Forward, One Step Back: The Deterrent Effect of International Criminal Tribunals*. Nuremberg: International Nuremberg Principles Academy.

Situation in the Central African Republic in the Case of the *Prosecutor v. Jean-Pierre Bemba Gombo*, ICC-01/05-01/08 (Trial Chamber III), Decision on Sentence pursuant to Article 76 of the Statute, 1 September 2016.

Smeulers, Alette et al. 2013. "Sixty-Five Years of International Criminal Justice: The Facts and Figures." *International Criminal Law Review* 13(1): 7–41.

Stolk, Sofia. 2017. *A Solemn Tale of Horror: The Opening Statement of the Prosecution in International Criminal Trials*. Free University of Amsterdam (doctoral thesis).

Trials of the Major War Criminals before the International Military Tribunal, Nuremberg, 14 November 1945 – 1 October 1946 Vol 1, Judgment (International Military Tribunal, Nuremberg, 1947–1949).

War Don. 2014. DVD. Dir. Rebecca Richman Cohen. USA: DMGI Studios.

11

Unsettling Accounts

Perpetrators' Confessions in the Aftermath of State Violence and Armed Conflict

Leigh A. Payne

The South African Truth and Reconciliation Commission (TRC) involved a novel process by which perpetrators of apartheid-era violence could confess to past violence in exchange for amnesty from prosecution. Many aspects of the TRC process have been criticized, not least the failure to prosecute those who did not confess or who were denied amnesty after confession. Less questioned is the premise underlying the TRC amnesty process, that perpetrators' confessions could lead to reconciliation.

This chapter takes up that challenge. Using a performative analysis, it shows that the confessional script, acting, timing, staging, and audience tend to lead towards dialogic conflict, rather than reconciliation. "Contentious co-existence," however, can enhance democratic practice. To make this point, the chapter draws on confessions in the South African TRC but also those in Argentina, Brazil, Chile, Colombia, and Spain.

Perpetrators' Confessions and the Truth and Reconciliation Assumption

The South African Truth and Reconciliation Commission (TRC) provided perpetrators with an option of making a full and truthful confession to past political violence and receiving an amnesty from prosecution. Criminal prosecution of apartheid-era perpetrators would occur only if they failed to provide a full and truthful confession or if they did not come forward to confess.

The desire for the end to violence and for reconciliation in a new South Africa motivated this unique transitional justice arrangement. Unlike the standard practice around the world at the time of granting a blanket amnesty to perpetrators of past violations, South Africa's novel process conditioned amnesty on perpetrators' public confessions. The process was designed to advance truth and acknowledgment of wrongdoing; it would make clear that someone committed acts that harmed individuals to restore the dignity of those victims.[1] A form of accountability would result from the confession and the public act of accepting responsibility for violent acts. In addition to the restorative form of accountability through confession, victims would receive official recognition and financial and collective reparations for past violence.

The logic behind the mechanism assumed that perpetrators would want to avoid a prison sentence and thus could be induced to participate. The assumption was based on perpetrators' calculation that they *would* be held accountable in a court of law *unless* they confessed. Those who did not expect their names to emerge from victims' testimony or from commission investigations had a strong reason to remain silent to avoid the stigma of having tortured, killed, or disappeared people. Leaders of some branches of the security forces (such as the army) boldly defied the process, arguing that they and their troops had dutifully served the country and would not confess to wrongdoing. The attitude taken by the high command sent a message to lower ranking perpetrators regarding the degree of support they would receive from the security apparatus if they remained silent and possible repercussions if they did not.

In the end, those who bet on staying quiet seem to have come out ahead. Very few perpetrators have been held accountable in court for apartheid-era crimes. Those who failed to confess, and those who did and were denied amnesty by the TRC, have not faced the expected consequences of court hearings, criminal sentences, and imprisonment. This has thus been a controversial aspect of the TRC. Victims were denied the minimal symbolic form of accountability promised by perpetrators' confessions to past violence. They were further denied justice for violence carried out by those perpetrators who did not participate fully in the process. Lastly, the reparations program provided far less financial support to fewer victims than had been anticipated. Victims widely felt betrayed by the outcomes of the TRC.

Despite a plethora of studies on the TRC and its outcomes, few question the logic behind the confession-reconciliation assumption. This chapter accepts the first part of the logic: when perpetrators speak out, they contribute to truth and acknowledgment of past violence. It challenges the notion, however, that such truths will lead to reconciliation. Dialogic conflict, instead, emerges when perpetrators confess, unsettling rather than settling accounts with the past.

Contentious co-existence that tends to result from perpetrators' confessions may not contribute to reconciliation but has the potential to put democracy into practice through the basic democratic values of political expression, participation, and contestation (Dahl 1971). Moreover, as perpetrators begin to refine their narratives about the past, through interaction with the public, they employ a language that tends to reinforce, rather than undermine, human rights values. A performative approach reveals the dynamics of this process.

Elements of Confessional Performances

A dramaturgical methodology (Goffman 1959, 1976) identifies five essential characteristics of a confessional performance: script (what is said in the confessional text), actor and acting (how the perpetrators present themselves), timing (when perpetrators confess and in what political context), staging (where confessions take place in formal political institutions or in informal settings such as the media), and audience (who observes and interprets the presentation).

Perpetrator Script

The TRC may have expected that perpetrators invited to confess in exchange for amnesty would express remorse and ask for forgiveness. Indeed, there were times when the head of the TRC, Archbishop Desmond Tutu, shocked and disappointed at perpetrators' insensitivity to victims, explicitly provided the words of contrition perpetrators should use to heal the nation.[2] If remorse is rare in an exchange relationship—where truth is bartered for amnesty—it is even less common when no inducement exists for perpetrators to speak about their past, for example, when they enjoy a blanket amnesty for their acts, as was the case in the early years after the transitions from authoritarian rule and war in Latin America, or when they face a credible threat of prosecution for their past acts.

Instead of remorse, perpetrators employ a range of narrative devices to avoid guilt, blame, or stigma. Denial is an obvious and common one. While this may seem to contradict the notion of confession, perpetrators sometimes admit that wrongdoing occurred, while denying their own involvement in it. Or perpetrators might confess that a particular event occurred in which victims faced harm, but deny that it was a criminal act. The denial reflects the notion that all wars, including "just wars," involve the killing of combatants and "collateral damage" that harms innocent bystanders. This narrative device allows perpetrators to deny or disguise acts of criminal violence as warfare. Denial is a kind of script that makes it nearly impossible for victims to reconcile. In these confessions, truth and acknowledgment, and therefore personal responsibility for wrongdoing, are avoided. Denial continues to perpetuate the justifications of past violence and thus the harm to victims.

An illustration of this kind of denial can be found in the confession by Adolfo Scilingo, an Argentine naval officer who admitted to throwing living people from a plane to their death in the ocean. He confessed to a journalist, Horacio Verbitsky, who urged him to recognize the harm he had done as part of the repressive apparatus. Scilingo responded with a kind of denial: "No navy officer participated in kidnapping, torture, and clandestine eliminations. The entire navy participated in detentions, interrogations, and the elimination of the subversives" (Verbitsky 1996, 35–36; Payne 2008, 46).

Heroic confessions are similar. Those perpetrators who come forward to promote their past acts as brave and patriotic sacrifices to save the nation cannot provide the sort of narrative that is likely to lead to reconciliation with victims. These are not uncommon. They seem to emerge from a particular type of socialization that convinced perpetrators to carry out abuses in the first place. To distinguish themselves from the kind of deviants who push from a plane drugged, stripped, living children, women, and men to their death in the ocean below, those who later confessed to these acts had to reconstruct a palatable version of their stories. Scilingo, as in his statement above, used the language of heroic sacrifice to the nation.

It is difficult to extract heroism from the tawdry clandestine forms of violence carried out in authoritarian regimes. And, yet, perpetrators do so. A very well-known perpetrator in Argentina, another navy captain, Alfredo Astiz, did not confess to infiltrating the Mothers of Plaza de Mayo, who organized to try to find their disappeared children. He did not mention in his confession that by posing as a brother of a disappeared, he identified which of the mothers in the group would themselves disappear. Instead, he boasted about his military prowess:

> Do you know why a military man kills? For a lot of reasons: for love of his country, for machismo, for pride, for duty.... I am the best man in this country, technically speaking, to kill a politician or a journalist .
>
> *(Cerruti 1998; Payne 2008, 75)*

Denial and heroic narratives constitute a set of "vital lies" (Goleman 1985; Payne 2008, 19–20), the deliberate or unconscious way perpetrators create stories that make sense of their past, how they remember, or want to remember, those events. Victims and their supporters assume these lies and fictions are deliberate obfuscations. And yet, sometimes perpetrators lack the language to directly confront what they have done; they have been socialized to think of their past in a particular way and they have lived with that past by understanding it in that way.

At other times, perpetrators simply cannot retrieve the details of past acts. Rather than denial or lies, amnesia best describes these types of confessions. One of the apartheid era policemen, Captain Jacques Hechter, knew that the TRC had testimony against him and the other members of the Vlakplaas death squad. He needed to confess to avoid prosecution. And yet, due to amnesia, he could not corroborate the stories told by his colleagues. As he said,

> I can remember the electrocution, but only after it was told to me. I can more or less remember the specific place where it happened. It was on a farm. There was a gate. I remember the narrow dirt road. It's a white, white chalk road. I can remember lots of trivialities. There were also guinea fowl. Those are the kinds of things I remember. But the actual serious deeds, I can't remember them.
>
> *(South Africa's Human Spirit 2000, 3.1.4; Payne 2008, 242–244)*

Amnesia and silence over the past make it nearly impossible for victims to feel that they can reconcile; how can one get at truth, acknowledgment, and victims' dignity when the perpetrator of those acts has no memory of them, or cannot speak of them?

While remorse may be the confessional script most likely to contribute to truth, acknowledgment, and victims' dignity, such contrition is rare. When it is expressed, victims often doubt the sincerity behind the words. They see remorse, instead, as instrumental, a way to verbally manipulate memory of the past to the perpetrator's benefit, such as confession in exchange for amnesty.

Betrayal confessions are much more likely to be believed. Betrayal confessions emerge when people feel that they are taking the fall for an entire institutional apparatus of violence. Rather than going down alone, they name the names of others, document acts of violence, and share the blame and responsibility. Facing a life sentence, the head of the South African Vlakplaas death squad, Eugene de Kock, famously betrayed his colleagues saying, "I have nothing to lose." He added, "I do not deny that I am guilty of the crimes, many of them horrible, of which I was accused. But I am not the only guilty one" (Payne 2008, 251–278). He then exposed the acts ordered and carried out by the commanders who had betrayed him.

What perpetrators say about their past acts—the confessional script—matters in terms of contributing to truth, acknowledgment, and victims' dignity. This script can shape victims' sense of whether the individuals have taken responsibility for their past acts or if they are avoiding that responsibility.

Perpetrator as Actor, Acting

What perpetrators say is often reinforced by how they present themselves. These include the "expressive equipment, the items that we most intimately identify with the performer himself and that we naturally expect will follow the performer wherever he goes" (Goffman 1976, 91). These are not just the clothing or props that might signal rank, office, or authority; they can also include non-verbal gestures or body language. Some of these traits are less easily altered than uniforms—such as age, race, gender, size, speech patterns, posture—and yet, they send a message that may reinforce or undermine that which the performer hopes to convey.

Thapelo Mbelo, a black South African policeman, confessed to the TRC about his participation in the Guguleto Seven massacre of young anti-apartheid activists. His confession did not end with his application for amnesty; he also met with the family members of those he had killed. In front of television cameras and facing a hostile audience of victims, Mbelo apologized for what he had done. His body and his movements matched his contrition. He turned his back to the camera and himself towards his victims, creating an intimate connection with those he had harmed. He cried. He bent his tall frame to make himself smaller than he was, to fit inside the embrace of each mother, sister, and brother that he approached begging forgiveness. Even those who could not forgive the act seemed to find a way to accept the sincerity of his remorse (Payne 2008, 56–57).

Argentine Navy admiral and junta leader Emilio Massera appeared in court accepting "responsibility but not guilt," claiming that "[n]o one should have to defend himself for winning a just war" (Ciancaglini and Granovsky 1995, 203). The way he carried himself and how he dressed stressed his power and authority: "erect posture and clenched jaw, navy-commander uniform with brass buttons and medals of honor, starched collar, polished shoes, and manicured fingernails" (Payne 2008, 99). Massera, in the dock, but cloaked in legitimacy, received a guilty verdict and a life sentence for his past atrocities. His attempts at exerting his power through script, appearance, and performance failed to convince the judges of the appropriateness of his past acts.

It is not uncommon to hear surprise that someone who committed atrocity appeared to be so normal, so kind. Perpetrators themselves engage in a kind of "doubling" (Lifton 1986), in which they present themselves as the good spouse, parent, neighbor, friend, making it unimaginable that they could commit atrocity. Whether consciously or not, this becomes a way of hiding past acts of violence. We seem to think that we know what perpetrators look like, even when we are constantly surprised when they do not appear in that gruesome image.

In confessional performances, perpetrators have an opportunity—within some constraints—to present themselves in a particular way to reinforce a particular image of innocence of wrongdoing. Perpetrators can employ "the whole theatrical array of gestures, demeanors, costumes, props, and stage devices" to "[i]mpress or bamboozle an audience" (Lincoln 1994, 5). They do not always achieve their ends, however. As Erving Goffman notes,

> To be awkward or unkempt, to talk or move wrongly, is to be a dangerous giant, a destroyer of worlds. As every psychotic and comic ought to know, any accurately improper move can poke through the thin sleeve of immediate reality.
>
> *(Goffman 1961, 80)*

Timing of Perpetrators' Confessions

The timing of perpetrators' confessions sometimes depends on the creation of a particular institutional incentive, as in the case of the South African TRC or the Colombian Justice and Peace Law (975) explored further below. When perpetrators wait until an institutional process makes it instrumental to confess, victims tend to perceive these confessions as insincere, motivated by self-protection rather than contrition. Yet sometimes the timing—even late confessions—can reflect contrition.

Perpetrators have come forward after recovering from addiction. They have also confessed to past acts of violence after a religious conversion in which they are born again. These types of clean breaks with past violence have allowed perpetrators to sometimes make very persuasive forms of confession. At other times, however, these confessions seem to suggest that the violent acts victimized the perpetrators, tormented them, and turned them into drug addicts or alcoholics. Or they can suggest that they do not bear responsibility for acts under the influence or in an earlier life.

When apartheid policeman Jeffrey Benzien applied for amnesty for his perfection of a particular (wet bag[3]) torture technique, he attempted to explain the impact of his torture on his life. He stated,

> [t]he method employed by me is something that I have to live with and no matter how I try to interpret what I did, I still find [it] deplorable I find it exceptionally difficult, sitting here in front of the news to everybody, I concede that no matter how bad I feel about it, what was done to you and your colleagues, must have been worse. Believe me, I am not gloating or trying to prove that I am somebody who I am not.
>
> *(Payne 1997, 120)*

He referred to a failed marriage and family life, depression, anxiety, addiction, and insomnia. His psychologist presented a report claiming that he suffered from post-traumatic stress disorder (PTSD). His victims and their lawyers questioned this diagnosis since PTSD results from a situation of intense fear and helplessness, not the context of total power over victims that Benzien enjoyed. "They viewed the PTSD defense as a cynical attempt on Benzien's part to reverse roles and portray himself as the victim of trauma after he had brutally traumatized his victims" (Payne 2008, 236).

Timing may also allow perpetrators to expiate themselves through participation in the truth process. Marcia Merino and Luz Arce participated in the Chilean post-authoritarian truth processes by recounting what they knew about specific events. They had both been militants on the left who were picked up shortly after the coup, severely tortured, and convinced to cooperate with Pinochet's secret police, DINA, eventually as agents. After the dictatorship, they wrote confessional memoirs about their activities. They also offered valuable testimony used to construct the facts surrounding certain acts of violence in which they were involved. For Luz Arce, these were acts of contrition for her role in the repressive apparatus. As she stated,

> I believe that I have to pay a price—due to my own actions and those of others. For a long time I have understood that I have to pay a price to live in my country… . I ask for pardon, but I don't expect it.
>
> *(Arce 1993, 19)*

She did not get it. Both she and Merino moved away from Chile, unable to rebuild their lives there, at least in the early years after the dictatorship and despite their effort to contribute to truth-gathering efforts.

Timing can, however, work against perpetrators hoping to contribute to truth processes. The Brazilian Air Force officer Pedro Corrêa Cabral (1993) wrote a novel recounting his role in hiding the bodies of the 1970s Araguaia massacre.[4] As he stated,

> [m]y objective was not and is not to take anyone to trial, but rather, as the saying goes, to sweep the dirt out from under the rug and to reveal this dark page of Brazilian history that must be understood so that new generations understand what happened.
>
> *(Payne 2008, 202)*

He also found his writing to be a form of spiritual healing and a way to attempt to recover the armed forces' image by condemning those acts of the past. As an evangelical Christian, he felt that he had a Christian duty to the victims.

The timing of his confession did not work in his favor, however. Under his armed forces' contract, he could not disclose information about his activities until he resigned from active duty. He thus waited to tell his story. Without notes from the time and due to trauma-induced amnesia, his memory was faulty. Moreover, the region had been napalmed to destroy evidence of the massacre. The late timing, therefore, prevented Cabral from providing the details he had hoped to reveal to the Human Rights Commission and to fulfill his moral responsibility to the families of the victims whose bodies he had helped hide.

Cabral's novel and subsequent testimonies set off a number of other confessional acts by those who had participated in the Araguaia massacre. This is not unusual. Marguerite Feitlowitz (1998) speaks of the "Scilingo effect" in which perpetrators of Argentina's state terror came forward to confess after Scilingo's interviews with Verbitsky became public. Some did so because they believed that Scilingo had signed a deal with Hollywood for his story and they too wanted payment. Others, such as Julio Simón, discussed below, saw confession as a pathway to fame, and thus appeared on talk shows sometimes facing victims' families in violent confrontations.

Timing, in other words, played an important role in victims' interpretations of the sincerity of the confession. It can contribute to doubts about the sincerity of the confession. But even very late confessions, after much of the truth about past acts is already revealed, still unsettle audiences and catalyze debate.

Staging Perpetrators' Confessions

Where perpetrators confess shapes how the act is interpreted. As mentioned above, institutional arrangements like the South African TRC and the Colombian Justice and Peace processes offer a stage for perpetrators' confessions. These stages are often seen cynically as ways in which perpetrators can protect themselves rather than ways to get at victims' needs for truth, acknowledgment, dignity, and accountability.

Media stages, such as that discussed above with regard to Scilingo, seem to offer perpetrators a chance to make some money, even if they appear unrepentant. Such was the case with the Argentine torturer Julio Simón. He appeared on several television programs and confessed to torture, defending his acts in one by saying "[w]hat I did, I did for my Fatherland, my faith, and my religion. Of course I would do it again" (Feitlowitz 1998, 212). At times Simón seemed almost bored and yet his body often shook. "He tried to recover his pluck at the end of each sentence by delivering a punctuating thrust of his chin into the air or a cold glare at the interviewer" (Payne 2008, 131). Although his televised confessions did not reveal any sadistic tendencies, only justifications, the program spliced in testimonies from victims recounting the horrors of Simón's acts. Similarly, in Simón's more lucrative appearance on the *Mediodía con Mauro* television show, torture of one of his victims was simulated. The re-enactment involved a young, beautiful actress playing the blind and pregnant Mónica

Brull. She is stripped, shocked with electric prods, and raped while the perpetrator resembling Simón smokes and laughs in perverse pleasure at her pain (Payne 2008, 130–132).

The infamous Chilean torturer Osvaldo Romo, whose nickname was "Big Fat Romo" (Guatón Romo), could look larger and more threatening, or less menacing, depending on the stage. Denounced in more than eighty incidents of rape in Pinochet-era clandestine detention centers, he later faced trial. Seeing him in the courtroom was a revelation to some of those victims who had imagined him larger: "he no longer towered over them physically or metaphorically" (Payne 2008, 123). Romo's expanse and degree of vileness also varied by the stage or media outlet. In the documentary film *La Flaca Alejandra* (Castillo and Girard 1994), he sits in a dark corner, far from the camera, and exudes no sense of threat. In the Univision television show *Primer Impacto* (1998), he fills the frame, as a dirty, sweaty, monster who uses his body to show how torture was carried out. Camerawork thus contributes to the portrayal of the individual, often removing perpetrators' control over their confessional performances.

The stage for confession is not a neutral space. The stage itself influences how audiences perceive the individual: as a criminal in the dock, as a torturer peddling his story to the media for profit, as a repentant perpetrator in an intimate encounter with his victims, or as someone who is ready and willing to harm again. How the perpetrator appears only partially depends on deliberate choices made by that individual. The public rarely sees an original, live, and uncut version of that performance. Instead, we observe an edited, redacted, enhanced, or invented performance that produces, or tries to produce, a particular meaning or slant.

The Audience to the Confession

The success of the staging of the confessional act in producing meaning depends on an audience. Indeed, audiences are key to the interpretation of all aspects of the confessional performance—script, actor and acting, timing, and staging. The audience is not a single entity that views performances similarly. It is comprised of diverse individuals and groups that come to the performance with their own personal experiences and worldviews. Victims of violence are part of that audience, but so too are fellow perpetrators. The public nature of the confessional acts analyzed in this study means that the performances reach an audience whose past was not directly affected by these perpetrators, including new generations and bystanders. Their direct experience with that past occurs with the confessional act, brought into their lives through radio, television, or other media.

Because of the unsettling nature of perpetrators' confessions, efforts are sometimes made to censor them. The confession of the sadistic Chilean torturer, Osvaldo Romo, was broadcast in the U.S. and discussed in the Chilean print media before it was shown on Chilean television. In Chile, the program was criticized for "advising, stimulating, and calmly provoking the feared person [Romo]" without consideration of its impact on audiences of victims. It was argued that "[t]hese people have already suffered a lot and should not continue being assaulted by the harmful words of this former agent" and "[w]e are still too affected, too diseased" to experience this confessional performance (Confesiones 2001). Other audiences presented a different argument for censoring the program, seeing it as an effort to frighten or intimidate those investigating past violence, using Romo to show that perpetrators are still around and capable of acting against their enemies (Payne 2008, 120–123).

Audiences' desire to silence perpetrators' confessions is not atypical or unique to Chile. Scilingo received death threats and threats against members of his family in an effort to silence him, threats he assumed came from his fellow military officers. The country's president, Carlos Menem, referred to Scilingo as a scoundrel and myth-maker, aiming to discredit and silence his confession. The Mothers and Grandmothers of the Plaza de Mayo vehemently rejected the idea of letting the Scilingos of the past dictate how it would be remembered (Payne 2008, 51–52).

And yet, some of the lawyers working with Argentine victims considered Scilingo's declarations "useful," a way to morally condemn past violence when justice was not possible. Long-term human rights activist (and the father of a disappeared daughter) Emilio Mignone forcefully called for other perpetrators to "tell their stories, that ten, twenty officials like Scilingo overwhelm the navy with their declarations and that the institution has to reconsider its position" (Rodríguez 1995). Martin Abregú, another well-known human rights advocate, echoed this view, "Do we love Scilingo? Of course not! But we don't want him or other Scilingos to stop talking" (Sims 1995).

Emerging from situations of repression or armed violence, audiences' desire to control speech, the desire to silence perpetrators' confessions is understandable. Silence about the past is preferable to perpetrators' control over memory through narratives of heroism or denial. Silence has the potential to prevent a renewed cycle of hatred, revenge, and violence from polarizing confessions.

Such is the case in Spain. When perpetrators of violence have spoken out, audience response is silence. The "pact of oblivion" is believed to inoculate against another cycle of violence that will tear apart the country, communities, and families again. The fear of violence seems to be dying off along with the older generation. The grandchildren of Franco's victims have begun to reclaim their families' past. With the exhumations of the bones hidden away in mass graves, silenced truths about the past are also dug up. New audiences to perpetrators' confessions have responded differently, daring to contest the settled version on the past without fear of reprisal (Aguilar and Payne 2016).

Similarly, the confessions by paramilitaries under the 2005 Colombian Justice and Peace Law (Law 975) initially met with little response from victims. This could be partially explained by the institutional arrangements in which victims were kept at a distance from perpetrators for fear of intimidation or violent reprisal. But it also resulted from the continued paramilitary power to use violence against their enemies, particularly in conflict zones (Payne 2009). With the peace negotiations in Havana in 2016, victims found a secure environment in which to challenge perpetrators' acts and demand acknowledgment of wrongdoing. Despite efforts by some observers to denigrate these perpetrator-victim encounters, for much of Colombian society they reflected an important shift in power relations that gave victims the moral and political authority to speak.

Unsettling Accounts

Although perpetrators' confessional performances are not common, they occur. When they do, they unsettle accounts. They are not necessarily "the truth" about the past, but versions or accounts. They are a form of public accounting for past action. They have the opportunity to change the balance of those accounts, shifting the responsibility of past violence away from victims and towards perpetrators. Yet they are unsettling. They are unsettling in content: the revelation of past atrocity. They break, or unsettle, the silence about the past, catalyzing debate. When perpetrators speak about the violent past, they do not usually contribute to "settling accounts with the past," but rather to unsettling and unleashing different versions of that past.

The unsettling is not necessarily desirable. Fellow perpetrators and their supporters would prefer silence to the public accounting of past violence. Victims may also wish to silence confessions, particularly when they promote anew heroic versions of the past and denial of wrongdoing. There is thus a desire to impose "gag rules" on perpetrators to strengthen the post-authoritarian, post-conflict democracy. Such an argument builds on Stephen Holmes's notion that "repression can be perfectly healthy for democracy" or "tongue-tying may be one of constitutionalism's main gifts to democracy" (Holmes 1995, 203, 204).

In contrast to that view, this chapter has shown that gag orders are not possible: perpetrators' accounts about the past are unavoidable. Moreover, audience responses to confessional acts can prove positive for democracy and human rights. Confessions open up contentious debate about the past in which victims have an opportunity to challenge the perpetrator-version of the past. Talk becomes a political resource, a way in which victims begin to reassert their narrative power to express their political views and to participate in contested political processes. Contentious debate leads to the refining of political arguments, especially arguments about human rights (Benhabib 1996; Mansbridge 1996; Young 1996; Mouffe 2013). Rejecting gag rules, and instead contesting perpetrators' views, puts democratic values in practice through the acts of political expression, participation, and contestation. Reconciliation, tending towards the goal of harmony, does not accurately reflect the agonistic nature of these confrontations over the past, or even the messy nature of democracy. Contentious co-existence does.

Contentious co-existence—the achievement of non-violent democratic dialogic contestation over the past—depends on public performance, but more importantly on audience engagement with that performance. When perpetrators do not speak out, as happened in Brazil, the catalyst for debate over the past fails to emerge. Yet even in Brazil, the Youth Uprising (Levante Popular da Juventude) movement has responded to military performances of power and other positive versions of the repressive past, to publicly "out" perpetrators and their human rights violations (Cristina and Marques 2017). As the range of experiences show, formal processes such as the South African TRC or the Justice and Peace Law in Colombia are thus not necessary, and certainly not sufficient, in opening up debate about the past.

Sheldon Wolin contends that "democracy was born in transgressive acts" (Wolin 1996, 37). Perpetrators' confessional performances embody this notion. They first reveal in public the undemocratic acts of past violence, unsettling a silence and subjecting abuses to debate. Audiences engage those performances, critically interpreting perpetrators' confessional scripts, acting, timing, and staging. Those once subject to the power of perpetrators regain their democratic right and responsibility—through speech—to challenge those versions of the past. In doing so, they confront other audiences cautioning and threatening against the reopening of the past to debate. By performing their rights, they confirm them. By condemning past violence, they reinforce the political change and the recognition of democratic rights. In this way, perpetrators' confessional performances unintentionally and paradoxically advance truth and acknowledgment, the dignity of victims, and a form of accountability for past violence.

Notes

1 An abundance of literature covers the unique TRC amnesty process and the controversies surrounding its assumptions; see, for example: Chapman and van der Merwe (2008), du Bois-Pedain (2012), James and Van de Vijver (2001), Posel and Simpson (2002), Sarkin (2004).

2 For an example, see the famous exchange between Tutu and Winnie Madikizela-Mandela over the soccer club killing (Payne 2008, 70–71; South Africa's Human Spirit IV:10).

3 He would soak in water a standard prison bag used to hold detainees' personal goods until the fibers swelled. He would then place the bag over the prisoner's head, suffocating him, to extract

a confession. Those who experienced the wet bag method felt that Benzien had taken them to their death repeatedly (Payne 2008, 230–239).

4 Cabral wrote a fictional account to allow him to tell a more emotional story and to fill in details he had forgotten. In his words, "[i]f I wrote a journalistic account I would run the risk of it being cold, sterile. And if I decided to write an autobiography, it would turn out to be a silly book" (Payne 2008, 206).

References

Aguilar, Paloma and Leigh A. Payne. 2016. *Revealing New Truths about Spain's Violent Past: Perpetrators' Confessions and Victim Exhumations*. London: Palgrave Macmillan.

Arce, Luz. 1993. *El infierno*. Santiago: Planeta.

Benhabib, Seyla. 1996. "Toward a Deliberative Model of Democratic Legitimacy." In *Democracy and Difference: Contesting the Boundaries of the Political*, edited by Seyla Benhabib, 67–94. Princeton, NJ: Princeton University Press.

Cabral, Pedro Corrêa. 1993. *Xambioá: Guerrilha do Araguaia*. Rio de Janeiro: Editora Record.

Castillo, Carmen and Guy Girard. 1994. *La Flaca Alejandra: Vidas y muertes de una mujer chilena*. Bry-Sur-Marne Cedex, France: Institut Nacional de L'audiovisuel, Channel 4.

Cerruti, Gabriela. 1998. "El asesino está entre nosotros." *Trespuntos*, 14 January, 6–11.

Chapman, Audrey R. and Hugo van der Merwe (eds.). 2008. *Truth and Reconciliation in South Africa: Did the TRC Deliver?* Philadelphia: University of Pennsylvania Press.

Ciancaglini, Sergio and Martín Granovsky. 1995. *Nada más que la verdad: El juicio a las juntas*. Buenos Aires: Editorial Planeta Argentina.

Confessiones. 2001. "Confesiones de Romo: Locura del verdugo o locura de la sociedad?" *Rocinante*, 2 March.

Cristina, Odete and Francisco Marques. 2017. "A debandada do Levante Popular da Juventude para o colo da UJS na UNE." *Esquera Diario*, 21 June. Accessed on 13 February 2018 www.esquerdadiario.com.br/.

Dahl, Robert A. 1971. *Polyarchy: Participation and Opposition*. New Haven: Yale University Press.

du Bois-Pedain, Antjie. 2012. "Accountability through Conditional Amnesty: The Case of South Africa." In *Amnesty in the Age of Human Rights Accountability: Comparative and International Perspectives*, edited by Francesca Lessa and Leigh A. Payne, 238–262. Cambridge: Cambridge University Press.

Feitlowitz, Marguerite. 1998. *A Lexicon of Terror: Argentina and the Legacies of Torture*. New York: Oxford University Press.

Goffman, Erving. 1959. *The Presentation of Self in Everyday Life*. New York: Anchor Books.

Goffman, Erving. 1961. *Encounters: Two Studies in the Sociology of Interaction*. Indianapolis: Bobbs-Merrill.

Goffman, Erving. 1976. "Performances." In *Ritual, Play, and Performance: Readings in the Social Sciences/Theatre*, edited by Richard Schechner and Mady Schurman, 89–96. New York: Seabury Press.

Goleman, Daniel. 1985. *Vital Lies, Simple Truths: The Psychology of Self-Deception*. New York: Simon and Schuster.

Holmes, Stephen. 1995. "Gag Rules or the Politics of Omission." In *Passions and Constraint: On the Theory of Liberal Democracy*, edited by Stephen Holmes, 202–235. Chicago: University of Chicago Press.

James, Wilmot and Linda Van de Vijver (Editors). 2001. *After the TRC: Reflections on Truth and Reconciliation in South Africa*. Athens, OH: Ohio University Press.

Lifton, Robert Jay. 1986. *The Nazi Doctors: Medical Killing and the Psychology of Genocide*. New York: Basic Books.

Lincoln, Bruce. 1994. *Authority: Construction and Corrosion*. Chicago: University of Chicago Press.

Mansbridge, Jane. 1996. "Using Power/Fighting Power: The Policy." In *Democracy and Difference: Contesting the Boundaries of the Political*, edited by Seyla Benhabib, 46–66. Princeton, NJ: Princeton University Press.

Mouffe, Chantal. 2013. *Agonistics: Thinking the World Politically*. London: Verso.

Payne, Leigh A. 2008. *Unsettling Accounts: Neither Truth nor Reconciliation in Confessions of State Violence*. Durham and London: Duke University Press.

Payne, Leigh A. 2009. *Testimonios Perturbadores: Ni verdad ni reconciliación en las confesiones de violencia de estado*. Translated by Julio Paredes. Includes an additional chapter on Colombia, "Epílogo: Representaciones de Poder." Bogotá: Universidad de los Andes.

Posel, Deborah and Graeme Simpson (eds.). 2002. *Commissioning the Past: Understanding South Africa's Truth and Reconciliation Commission.* Johannesburg: Witwatersrand University Press.

Primer Impacto. 1998. "En Confianza." Televised Interview by Mercedes Soler with Osvaldo Romo Mena. Broadcast on Univision, 17 May.

Rodríguez, Andrea. 1995. "Que haya otros que cuenten," *Página/12*, 5 March.

Sarkin, Jeremy. 2004. *Carrots and Sticks: The TRC and the South African Amnesty Process.* Antwerp and Oxford: Intersentia.

Sergio Ciancaglini and Martín Granovsky. *Nada más que la verdad: El juicio a las juntas.* Buenos Aires: Editorial Planeta Argentina, 1995.

Sims, Calvin. 1995. "In Exposing Abuses, Argentine Earns Hate," *New York Times*, 29 October.

South Africa's Human Spirit: An Oral Memoir of the Truth and Reconciliation Commission. 2000. 5 vols. CD-ROM. Johannesburg: SABC News Production. www.sabctruth.co.za/.

Truth and Reconciliation Commission, Amnesty Hearing for Jeffrey T. Benzien, Cape Town, South Africa, 14 July 1997, 120

Verbitsky, Horacio. 1996. *The Flight: Confessions of an Argentine Dirty Warrior.* Translated by Ester Allen. New York: New Press.

Wolin, Sheldon S. 1996. "Fugitive Democracy." In *Democracy and Difference: Contesting the Boundaries of the Political*, edited by Seyla Benhabib, 31–45. Princeton, NJ: Princeton University Press.

Young, Iris Marion. 1996. "Communication and the Other: Beyond Deliberative Democracy." In *Democracy and Difference: Contesting the Boundaries of the Political*, edited by Seyla Benhabib, 120–135. Princeton, NJ: Princeton University Press.

12

The Coercive Effects of International Justice

How Perpetrators Respond to Threats of Prosecution

David Mendeloff

Scholars have long debated whether the International Criminal Court (ICC) can deter future genocidal acts, crimes against humanity, and war crimes.[1] But what impact, if any, do ICC actions have after deterrence has failed and war crimes are already being perpetrated? International criminal tribunals have historically conducted prosecutions in the aftermath of wars, once killing has stopped. Increasingly, though, they have focused investigations on conflicts where civilian abuses are actively underway. These cases are pursued partly with the intention of using the threat of prosecution to stop ongoing violence (Mendeloff 2018). Assumptions about the coercive effects of wartime prosecutions inform the way the ICC operates, how states respond to wartime atrocities, and how human rights organizations advocate for appropriate responses to civilian violence. Are these assumptions valid? Does the threat of criminal prosecution effectively coerce perpetrators of wartime atrocities to restrain their abusive behavior?

This chapter assesses what we know—and don't know—about the coercive effects of international justice in active conflicts. Recent scholarship on the impact of criminal tribunals offers important insights, revealing the complex interaction between violent perpetrators and international prosecutions and showing that legal sanction may impact violence in varied ways. This work has mostly confirmed that wartime coercion of violent actors is extremely difficult, operating under very limited conditions and in combination with other more forceful measures to limit violence. Debate continues, however, over the precise mechanisms and conditions under which wartime prosecution restrains perpetrators, encourages more violence, or has no effect at all.

This chapter is divided into two parts. Part I provides an overview of the nature of international prosecutions in active conflicts and distills key insights from literature on coercive diplomacy, criminal deterrence, and civilian violence that frames our expectations around prosecutorial threats and the conditions for their success. Part II surveys recent empirical research on the impact of international prosecutions on war termination and civilian violence. It concludes with a discussion of unanswered questions and avenues for future research.

The Nature of Wartime Criminal Prosecutions

The pursuit of criminal accountability in wartime, rather than after wars have ended, is a relatively recent phenomenon. The International Criminal Tribunal for the Former-Yugoslavia (ICTY) was the first to pursue war criminals actively perpetrating abuses (McAllister 2014, 24). Since its creation in 2002, the ICC has increasingly investigated ongoing crimes. More than half its investigations have been launched in the midst of active conflicts with the intention, in part, of using the threat of prosecution to stop ongoing violence (Mendeloff 2018). Some have hailed more aggressive wartime prosecutions as crucial to eradicating impunity. Others have argued that it has no effect on perpetrators' behavior (Ku and Nzelibe 2006) or even prolongs violent conflict by incentivizing perpetrators to "spoil" efforts to negotiate peace for fear of imprisonment (Snyder and Vinjamuri 2003/04; Licklider 2008).

For many years, legal scholars and political scientists have subjected this so-called "peace vs. justice" debate to considerable scrutiny. The debate has continued partly because of ongoing conceptual and empirical challenges. First, there are relatively few cases of coercive prosecution in active conflicts, so there is a tendency to over-generalize from particular experiences. Second, because these investigations take place in war zones, good quality data is not easily accessible to researchers; our knowledge of individual cases is incomplete and subject to differing interpretations. Third, while political scientists have increasingly utilized broad cross-national statistical analyses to assess the impact of international justice on a wide range of phenomena, very few studies have focused exclusively on *civilian violence in active conflicts*. In addition, much of this work has focused on the effects of ICC membership—rather than the Court's investigations and prosecutions. Those that have done so have largely examined the broader deterrence question—do ICC actions prevent future violence where we might otherwise expect it?—rather than cases of *deterrence failure*—that is, the impact on perpetrators who have already committed to using unlawful violence, for whatever reason, and are actively perpetrating atrocities. International security scholars refer to this as "compellence"—the use of threats and limited punishment to change unlawful or undesirable behavior (Schelling 1966). In short, the question addressed here is not does the ICC prevent atrocity crimes but, does it help to stop those crimes, and if so, how?[2] Before discussing recent scholarship that touches most directly on this question, I begin with an overview of the general logic of wartime prosecutions and our expectations for effective coercion.

Expectations for Effective Prosecutorial Coercion

Should we expect wartime prosecution, and the possibility of criminal punishment of atrocity crimes, to curtail unlawful violence, exacerbate it, or have no effect at all? What conditions might increase the likelihood of effective coercive prosecution? At least three bodies of literature offer important insight into these questions: coercive diplomacy and strategic bargaining; domestic criminal deterrence; and causes of wartime civilian violence. All three suggest that effective coercion is likely to be limited to a fairly narrow range of conditions.

Coercive Diplomacy

Coercive diplomacy is a bargaining strategy that entails using threats, limited punishment, and inducements to encourage compliance by shaping the cost-benefit calculations of states or individuals engaged in a proscribed behavior. This can be future-oriented and preventative (deterrence) or present-oriented and reactive (compellence). Much of the debate about ICC impact, for example, is about whether legal sanction imposes sufficient costs on perpetrators. Many expect the ICC to have limited coercive impact because it has very weak enforcement: the ICC has no standing police force to execute warrants and must rely on the (inconsistent) cooperation of ICC member states (Hillebrecht and Straus 2017). This makes threats of punishment extremely mild. Yet, others have argued that the Court's actions are not entirely painless. While actual punishment may be slight, targets of investigation face social stigma that in some cases may be considerable (Sikkink 2011).

In addition to imposing sufficient costs, effective compellence requires credible assurances, inducements, or rewards for compliant behavior (Byman and Waxman 2002, 9; Davis 2000; Kydd 2000; George 1991, 68; Schelling 1966, 74). Without credible assurances—for example, that prosecution will be dropped when perpetrators comply, or offering amnesties—threats of prosecution are unlikely to persuade (Snyder and Vinjamuri 2003/04). If there are no obvious benefits to compliance, only the promise of punishment, targets of prosecution will have a strong incentive to avoid compliance and "gamble for resurrection"—escalate their violent behavior in the hopes of winning the war on the battlefield or forcing a more favorable bargain (Krcmaric 2015). This makes the structure of prosecutorial threats particularly important. The logic of coercive diplomacy dictates that threats of prosecution work best when they can be credibly enforced, when they avoid actors whose cooperation is needed to end violence (Rodman 2008), and *before* indictments and arrest warrants are issued (Mendeloff 2018).

Criminal Deterrence

The logic of criminal deterrence rests on similar rationalist assumptions of coercive diplomacy. Individuals engage in cost-benefit calculations when making a decision to commit a crime. When the cost of punishment outweighs the benefits, individuals will moderate their behavior and stop or avoid criminal conduct. Economists and criminologists who study how potential and actual offenders respond to legal sanctions generally agree that certainty of punishment, rather than its severity or celerity (immediacy), is the most important determinant of deterrent effectiveness (Nagin 2013, 85). Many suggest that the ICC has an extremely low certainty of punishment that stems from weak enforcement. Among the large number of potential crimes committed, the ICC investigates only a very small fraction, and fewer still are successfully prosecuted. Many who have been indicted by the ICC remain at large. However, while this may be true in the context of general deterrence, it is not necessarily so once the Court intervenes in a conflict. Given that nearly all of the Court's investigations have led to some indictments, the certainty of punishment in this context is considerably greater (Prorok 2017, 218).

However, recent research in criminology, social psychology, and behavioral economics has begun to explode many of the simplistic rationalist assumptions of deterrence theory. The most important for understanding prosecutorial coercion is that individual assessments of the costs of punishment are almost entirely subjective. While the objective certainty of punishment may be high, this does not mean that offenders will update their cost-benefit calculations predictably (Kennedy 2009; Kleiman 2009). What matters is how they *perceive* the certainty of punishment. Perceptions in turn are shaped by a range of cognitive, emotional, and environmental factors that vary across individuals. Thus, different individuals will respond to the same legal sanction in very different ways. To assess how perpetrators respond to particular threats of punishment requires knowledge of their motivations for offending and their social environment. Indeed, many criminologists have found informal, extra-legal social sanctions, rather than formal legal punishment, to be a much more powerful disincentive for criminal behavior (Paternoster 2010).

This suggests that prosecutorial coercion at the international level should be most effective when the Court can credibly communicate painful costs for continued transgressions, even if arrest is unlikely. For example, the Court's real power may lie in its ability to signal to perpetrators sufficiently painful informal or extra-legal costs that follow from investigations, rather than formal punishment itself. Because those costs are subjective, prosecutorial threats will work best when they are carefully matched to the specific conflict environment and the perpetrator's underlying motivations for violence.

Wartime Violence

The literature on wartime civilian violence also suggests a narrow set of conditions under which prosecutorial coercion is likely to work. Civilian violence is driven largely by motivations that are not readily amenable to legal coercion, even those that might entail extra-legal costs. A robust research program in political science on the sources of civilian violence has pointed to three broad motivations for violence.[3] The first are *military-strategic incentives*. A great deal of violence is driven by strategic and instrumental logic shaped by particular wartime situational conditions (Valentino 2004, Chapter 3). Government forces and rebels intentionally target and terrorize civilians as a way to achieve military objectives or to enhance their bargaining positions by inflicting punishment in the hopes of extracting concessions. Deliberate civilian violence has been used to ensure control of territory and to intimidate the adversary's supporters (Kalyvas 2006); to demonstrate power, especially in asymmetrical conflicts (Arreguin-Toft 2005; Valentino, Huth, and Balch-Lindsay 2004); and to seize resources needed to sustain the war effort (Metelits 2010; Wood 2010, 2014a).

That much civilian violence is rational and instrumental suggests that it should be amenable to coercion when the perceived costs of legal sanction, or associated extra-legal social costs, surpass the military-strategic value of civilian violence. In many cases, however, short-term military expediency is a powerful motivation that is hard to override (Cronin-Furman 2013). Since perceptions of costs are strongly influenced by an individual's particular situation, even an objectively credible and certain promise of punishment may be discounted.

In other cases, civilian violence is not a result of clear-eyed, instrumental military-strategic calculation but of particular *organizational structures and dynamics*. The chaotic environment of wartime presents opportunities for abuses that need to be reined in by military discipline that prohibits unlawful behavior. When military organizations lack effective discipline and control over rank-and-file soldiers, opportunistic violence is much more likely. Even leaders who might wish to curtail this violence might be unable to do so. In other cases, violence has been used deliberately for organizational reasons: to incentivize recruitment of soldiers (Humphreys and Weinstein 2006) or in the case of wartime rape, to strengthen discipline and group cohesion (Cohen 2016; Wood 2009). It follows that prosecutorial threats should be most effective against individuals with clear command and control over the rank-and-file perpetrators and where organizational incentives for violence are relatively weak.

Finally, armed groups may engage in deliberate targeting of civilians because of particular exclusionary group identities, ideological programs, political interests, and emotions that actively foment, or are indifferent to, civilian violence, mass killing, and genocide (Petersen 2002; Valentino 2004, Chapter 3; Kaufman 2006, 2015; Gutiérrez-Sanín and Wood 2014; Straus 2015; Balcells 2017). Armed groups that lack strong social connections or shared norms and values with the population will exercise little restraint in the use of violence (Weinstein 2007). Similarly, governments and rebel groups that rely on the political support of the domestic population or international audiences that value human rights are more likely to eschew unlawful violence and impose discipline on the rank and file (Fazal 2017; Jo 2015; Stanton 2016; Wood 2014b).

It follows, then, that prosecutorial coercion should be most effective when there is little ideological or political incentive for targeting civilians and where there is obvious political value to treating civilians well. The promise of punishment, particularly its informal, extra-legal costs, might serve to focus the attention of elites on the political benefits of restraint. Yet, because such groups are the least likely to commit atrocity crimes, or to do so intentionally, these conditions are likely to be rare and unusual. Further, this logic would seem to apply more readily to deterrent threats, rather than compellent demands after deterrence has failed and violence is underway. Revenge and retaliation can be a powerful incentive for violence (Balcells 2017). Once it is unleashed, it can become very difficult to restrain.

What Do We Know about Coercive Effects of International Prosecution?

The logic of coercion, criminal deterrence, and wartime violence point to a narrow range of conditions under which we would expect effective prosecutorial coercion. Is this reflected in actual experience? Scholars have generated a large body of research on the impact of international justice and national-level accountability efforts on wide range of phenomena—democratic consolidation, rule of law, human rights behavior, victim satisfaction, social repair and political reconciliation, and deterrence of human rights violations and atrocity crimes. Few studies, however, have focused exclusively on the effects of wartime prosecutorial activity on ongoing violence. Often the question of prosecutorial compellence is folded into broader examinations of general deterrence or human rights impact. Existing studies offer important insights but tend to obscure the salient questions: does prosecution generally restrain active perpetrators, exacerbate violence, or have no effect at all? More important, what explains the variation in the effects of wartime prosecution? Is it primarily exogenous factors—the character and timing of prosecutorial threats—or endogenous factors—the underlying motivations for violence and the strategic wartime environment? Below I assess recent research that speaks most directly to these questions.

International Tribunals and War Termination

A number of recent studies have examined the relationship between international prosecution and conflict termination, asking if threats of legal punishment help to either hasten an end to civil wars or prolong them. This is an important line of inquiry because civilian violence, particularly mass violence and genocide are highly correlated with civil wars (Valentino 2014, 94–96). Ending those wars is one way to limit that violence. There is mixed evidence here. Beth Simmons and Allison Danner (2010) argue that states join the ICC to entice rebel groups to negotiate an end to civil wars. Because rebels rarely trust governments to stick to the terms of a negotiated settlement, states signal their commitment to act in good faith by subjecting themselves to the ICC's jurisdiction. Indeed, Geoff Dancy (2017, 638–639) has found that countries that ratify the Rome Statute in the midst of civil wars end those wars through negotiated settlements at a higher rate than non-ratifying states. But the source of variation among ICC states remains unclear. The vast majority of civil wars, even in those states that join the ICC in the midst of fighting, remain completely unaffected by the presence of the ICC.[4]

More important, these data tell us little about the effects of international *prosecution* on the prospects of war termination. Studies that have examined this impact directly reach less sanguine conclusions. Dancy (2017, 643) and Dancy and Eric Wiebelhaus-Brahm (2018, 57), for example, find no evidence that international prosecutions shorten the duration of wars. Others find that it actually prolongs them (Krcmaric 2015). Allyson Prorok (2017), for example, finds no impact when domestic punishment alternatives are worse than the potential costs of international prosecution.[5] But when there is little or no domestic punishment alternative, ICC prosecutions on average *increase* the duration of wars.

To the extent that prosecutions prolong fighting, what explains that behavior? Do perpetrators gamble for resurrection because prosecution is perceived to be highly credible and costly, or because it is a hollow threat that suggests a weakness to be exploited? Do belligerents continue fighting because prosecution prevents negotiated bargains by foreclosing the possibility of amnesties? Dancy (2017), for example, has questioned this claim by showing that amnesty deals are actually *more likely* to be offered by ICC states than by non-ICC states. Yet, it is unclear whether *actual prosecution and indictment* had been pursued in any of these cases. The more germane question is whether perpetrators believe that states can credibly commit to amnesty deals when they are under investigation (Ginsburg 2009). Anecdotal evidence is mixed. In the Uganda situation, for example, Mark Kersten (2016, 101–108) finds that indictments of Lord's Resistance Army (LRA) leaders had no impact on the Juba peace talks, while Patrick Wegner (2015, 232–261) finds that the Court's refusal to waiver on those indictments, despite the pleas of the Ugandan government, scuttled the talks. Alternatively, Jacqueline McAllister (2014) shows how ICTY indictments of key Bosnian leaders may have facilitated the Dayton accord that ended the Bosnian war.[6]

To answer these questions may require disaggregating the various phases of international prosecution.[7] Do initial investigations have the same war-prolonging effects as indictments or arrests or trials? Michael Broache (2015) and Richard Steinberg (2017) have found that physical arrest of suspects, as distinct from indictments, may catalyze war termination. Both offer persuasive evidence that the arrest of suspects in the Democratic Republic of Congo (DRC) had a "decapitation" effect, breaking down the organizational cohesion of rebel militias, facilitating their collapse. However, Broache (2015, 175) finds that prosecutorial interventions that preceded these arrests exacerbated warfighting by spurring the creation of the M23 rebel group. In their study of the impact of ICC intervention on conflict mediation efforts in Africa, J. Michael Greig and James Meernik (2014) find a similar pattern.

International Tribunals and Civilian Violence

Studies of international tribunal impact on conflict termination speak only indirectly to civilian violence. Ultimately, we want to understand how and whether the coercive use of wartime prosecution can limit or restrain perpetrators from engaging in specific unlawful behavior. Does the arrest of leaders encourage restraint among the rank and file? If civilian violence is inflicted for instrumental reasons, does the capture of leaders change the value of that strategy? More important, how does international prosecution short of arrest and trial, shape the perpetrators' behavior?

A number of recent studies, both cross-national and detailed case analyses, have found that coercive effects of wartime prosecution are highly contingent on the motivations for violence, the underlying structure of the conflict, and the particular form of prosecution. In short, this work has shown that coercive effects appear to occur under limited conditions, namely when targeted rebel groups or states need to appease domestic or international audiences who support rule of law and international humanitarian norms.

In a systematic cross-national study of the potential general deterrence effect of the ICC, Hyren Jo and Beth Simmons (2016) find that states that have ratified the Rome Statute experience less civilian killing than non-ratifiers, and that ICC intervention is associated with lower levels of unlawful violence by rebel groups who are motivated by a need to enhance their legitimacy with domestic and international audiences. Though these effects are quite modest, particularly with regard to rebel groups (468), they are suggestive of some coercive effect. Similarly, Allyson McAllister and James Meernik (2016) find that across African conflicts states that have ratified the Rome Statute and demonstrate a commitment to rule of law tend to engage in lower levels of unlawful civilian violence.

However, this does not tell us precisely how perpetrators respond to ICC interventions in their civil wars. The Jo and Simmons study, for example, focuses on general deterrence effects rather than compellence specifically. Indeed, when McAllister and Meernik (2016) and Dancy (2017) look at cases where the ICC has undertaken investigations, they find no net impact on civilian violence: in some cases, ICC interventions are associated with increased violence; in others—the Central African Republic and Nigeria—they are associated with an overall increase. However, we need to explain precisely that variation. Because these studies focus on average effects and aggregate all forms of prosecutorial action—preliminary investigations, full investigations, indictments, arrests, and trials—into a single variable, they may be masking potential coercive effects of different prosecutorial phases. It is impossible to know from these data if some forms of prosecution are more impactful than others.

Broache (2015) addresses that problem in a superb study of the impact of ICC intervention on civilian violence in the DRC. He finds that civilian violence varies with phases of prosecution: ICC action has little effect on civilian violence, either positive or negative, in its early stages. But as the investigation becomes more aggressive and suspects are named and warrants issued, civilian violence increases, encouraging targeted leaders to "gamble for resurrection." Yet, once warrants are executed, violence attenuates as arrest facilitates the collapse of armed groups.

Broache's study also offers insight into how the underlying sources of violence shape responses to Court action. Reasons initial ICC investigations had little effect on behavior were the low perceived certainty of punishment and a lack of organizational and social restraint on violence. Broache reports, for example, how rank-and-file soldiers in the CNDP believed that crimes would not be illegal if ordered by a superior and how they saw atrocities as integral to their identity as rebels (Broache 2015, 168–170).

McAllister's 2014 study of ICTY impact on civilian violence in the Bosnian, Croatian, Kosovo, and Macedonian wars offers another granular level of understanding of the coercive effects of international justice. Overall, the ICTY had very little impact on civilian violence. But in some cases, it did appear to moderate behavior. Her study suggests that international prosecution can restrain war criminals when states actively cooperate in enforcement (increasing the certainty of punishment) and when violent groups rely on the support of civilian populations.

While the study does not directly control for different phases of prosecution, the ICTY seemed to have the most power in cases where it intervened with less aggressive, more informal threats. Aggressive prosecution in Bosnia, Croatia, and Kosovo had little effect on perpetrator behavior. But the mere threat of prosecution seemed to have some persuasive power in Macedonia in 2001, where violence was relatively limited in scope and intensity (McAllister 2014, 179–257).

The ICTY experience also reveals how rare these conditions for restraint actually are. Meernik (2015), McAllister and Meernik (2016), and Jo and Simmons (2016) find that groups that seek to appease domestic or international audiences, or that demonstrate a basic commitment to rule of law and international humanitarian norms (through, for example, ratification of the Rome Statute), are more susceptible to prosecutorial coercion. But since these actors are least likely to engage in unlawful violence—and when they do are unlikely to commit acts of violence that trigger ICC jurisdiction—the range of cases where prosecutorial pressure can operate is particularly small. Further, since restraint is already overdetermined in these cases, the distinct importance of international prosecution remains unclear. The threat of punishment is supposed to focus attention on the political benefits of restraint, but why are actors not already aware of those benefits? And if they have already transgressed by engaging in unlawful violence, why did their political interests prove insufficient to restrain them in the first place?

Conclusion

The logic of coercive bargaining, criminal deterrence, and civilian violence mostly militate against successful prosecutorial coercion and suggest a fairly narrow set of conditions under which it is likely to work. Recent scholarship on the impact of international tribunals on civilian violence is generally consistent with these expectations: Effective compellence of wartime violence is indeed rare; the Court's impact varies across and within cases, and it seems to correspond to both the underlying sources of violence and the particular type of prosecutorial action.

More fine-grained analyses of ICC interventions can sharpen our understanding of the dynamics of prosecutorial interventions and can help us better understand and distinguish among the complex sources of that behavior. Future research should focus on a number of issues. First, it should disaggregate civilian violence: much of the research discussed here focuses on intentional killing. We know much less about the Court's impact on other atrocity crimes, such as sexual violence, and non-lethal violence that may fall below the standards of "gravity" that trigger ICC jurisdiction. This is important because perpetrators might respond to prosecution by simply changing tactics, using lethal violence more selectively, or substituting it for other forms of violence, similar to what criminologists identify as "crime switching." One perverse consequence of more robust prosecutions is that perpetrators continue to offend but carefully hide their crimes (Wippman 1999/2000).

Second, future research should seek to explain how prosecutorial action interacts with other domestic and international measures to end violence. Few scholars believe that the ICC alone can force belligerents to cease unlawful violence. Indeed, when it seems to have worked, it has done so in the presence of other coercive measures (Rodman 2013). But what role does prosecution play? Do the other forceful actions enhance the Court's potency by increasing the certainty of punishment? Does prosecution serve as a catalyst or "focal point" for national and international attention and action (Jo and Simmons 2016; Dancy 2017)? Or is legal action merely ancillary? And how likely is it that ICC attention might be used by states as a substitute for more forceful action (Ku and Nzelibe 2006)?

Finally, future research should examine how wartime prosecutions impact other international justice goals. The ICC is intended to do much more than restrain ongoing violence—a narrow slice of the Court's broader agenda that includes providing accountability for mass atrocity, deterring future atrocity crimes, imposing an obligation on states to prosecute those crimes, and strengthening a global anti-impunity norm. While its wartime coercive power may be limited, the Court may be more effective at advancing these other goals. For example, recent research suggests possible positive effects of ratification and complementarity on states' human rights behavior (Meernik 2015; Dancy and Montal 2017; Appel 2018). Does wartime prosecution complicate these efforts? The most serious potential impact is on the Court's reputation. Because legal restraint of wartime violence is rare, the ICC interventions in active conflicts are more likely to fail than succeed. To the extent that success of the Court's other goals rests on its credibility to prosecute, this is a serious concern.

This survey of the coercive effects of international justice also demonstrates the critical importance of the emerging interdisciplinary field of Perpetrator Studies: to understand how international prosecutions impact wartime violence requires more than knowledge of international law or the ICC. We must understand the motivations and perceptions of those who commission and perpetrate civilian abuses. Ultimately, the answers to many of our outstanding questions are found in fine-grained, ethnographic studies of perpetrators that utilize important insights from criminology, behavioral economics, social psychology, and political science.

Notes

This chapter was submitted for publication on November 12, 2017 and subsequently revised on February 16, 2018.

1 A growing body of empirical research has examined this question. See for example Kim and Sikkink (2010, 2012–2013), Meernik (2015), Krcmaric (2015), Jo and Simmons (2016), Dancy (2017), Appel (2018).
2 The term "atrocity crimes" encompasses genocide, crimes against humanity, and war crimes (Schabas 2016).
3 An excellent overview of the literature is Valentino (2014).
4 While roughly 30% of wars in states that have joined the ICC during active conflicts end with a negotiated settlement, nearly 70% continue unaffected or end on the battlefield (Dancy 2017, 638–639).
5 This finding is consistent with those who argue that the ICC has little general deterrence impact because domestic punishment alternatives are often a much more powerful incentive to behavior than a relatively weak ICC. See Cronin-Furman (2013) and Ku and Nzelibe (2006).
6 The Ugandan and Bosnian cases, however, are not entirely analogous. At Juba, the LRA leaders facing international indictment were also the ones required to negotiate peace. At Dayton, Serbian President Milošević was needed to negotiate peace, not the indicted Bosnian leaders. This logic is persuasively described by Rodman (2008).
7 While Dancy and Wiebelhaus-Brahm (2018) disaggregate types and targets of prosecution, they treat "international trials" as a single variable.

References

Appel, Benjamin J. 2018. "In the Shadow of the International Criminal Court: Does the ICC Deter Human Rights Violations?" *Journal of Conflict Resolution* 62(1): 3–28.

Arreguin-Toft, Ivan. 2005. *How the Weak Win Wars: A Theory of Asymmetric Conflict.* Cambridge: Cambridge University Press.

Balcells, Laia. 2017. *Rivalry and Revenge: The Politics of Violence during Civil War.* Cambridge: Cambridge University Press.

Broache, Michael Patrick. 2015. *Evaluating the Effects of International Criminal Court Prosecutions on Atrocities during Ongoing Armed Conflict.* Dissertation, Columbia University.

Byman, Daniel & Matthew Waxman. 2002. *The Dynamics of Coercion: American Foreign Policy and the Limits of Military Might*. Cambridge: Cambridge University Press.

Cohen, Dara Kay. 2016. *Rape during Wartime*. Ithaca, NY: Cornell University Press.

Cronin-Furman, Kate. 2013. "Managing Expectations: International Criminal Trials and the Prospects for Deterrence of Mass Atrocity." *International Journal of Transitional Justice* 7(3): 434–454.

Dancy, Geoff. 2017. "Searching for Deterrence at the International Criminal Court." *International Criminal Law Review* 17: 625–655.

Dancy, Geoff & Florencia Montal. 2017. "Unintended Positive Complementarity: Why International Criminal Court Investigations May Increase Domestic Human Rights Prosecutions." *American Journal of International Law* 111(3): 689–723.

Dancy, Geoff & Eric Wiebelhaus-Brahm. 2018. "The Impact of Criminal Prosecutions During Intrastate Conflict." *Journal of Peace Research* 55(1): 47–61.

Davis, James W., Jr. 2000. *Threats and Promises: The Pursuit of International Influence*. Baltimore, MD: Johns Hopkins University Press.

Fazal, Tanisha M. 2017. "Rebellion, War Aims & the Laws of War." *Daedalus* 146(1): 71–82.

George, Alexander L. 1991. *Forceful Persuasion: Coercive Diplomacy as an Alternative to War*. Washington, DC: USIP Press.

Ginsburg, Tom. 2009. "The Clash of Commitments at the International Criminal Court." *Chicago Journal of International Law* 9(2): 499–514.

Greig, J. Michael & James D. Meernik. 2014. "To Prosecute or Not to Prosecute: Civil War Mediation and International Criminal Justice." *International Negotiation* 19(2): 257–284.

Gutiérrez-Sanín, Francisco & Elisabeth Jean Wood. 2014. "Ideology in Civil War: Instrumental Adoption and Beyond." *Journal of Peace Research* 51(2): 213–226.

Hillebrecht, Courtney & Scott Straus. 2017. "Who Pursues the Perpetrators? State Cooperation with the ICC." *Human Right Quarterly* 39(4): 162–188.

Humphreys, Macartan & Jeremy Weinstein. 2006. "Handling and Manhandling Civilians in Civil War." *American Political Science Research* 100(3): 429–447.

Jo, Hyeran. 2015. *Compliant Rebels: Rebel Groups and International Law in World Politics*. Cambridge: Cambridge University Press.

Jo, Hyeran & Beth A. Simmons. 2016. "Can the International Criminal Court Deter Atrocity?" *International Organization* 70(2): 443–475.

Kalyvas, Stathis N. 2006. *The Logic of Violence in Civil War*. Cambridge: Cambridge University Press.

Kaufman, Stuart J. 2006. "Symbolic Politics or Rational Choice? Testing Theories of Extreme Ethnic Violence." *International Security* 30(4): 45–86.

Kaufman, Stuart J. 2015. *Nationalist Passions*. Ithaca, NY: Cornell University Press.

Kennedy, David M. 2009. *Deterrence and Crime Prevention*. London: Routledge.

Kersten, Mark. 2016. *Justice in Conflict: The Effects of the International Criminal Court's Interventions on the Ending Wars and Building Peace*. Oxford: Oxford University Press.

Kim, Hun Joon & Kathryn Sikkink. 2010. "Explaining the Deterrence Effect of Human Rights Prosecutions for Transitional Countries." *International Studies Quarterly* 54: 939–963.

Kim, Hun Joon & Kathryn Sikkink. 2012-2013. "How Do Human Rights Prosecutions Improve Human Rights after Transition?" *Interdisciplinary Journal of Human Rights Law* 7(1): 69–90.

Kleiman, Mark A. R. 2009. *When Brute Force Fails: How to Have Less Crime and Less Punishment*. Princeton, NJ: Princeton University Press.

Krcmaric, Daniel. 2015. *The Justice Dilemma: International Criminal Accountability, Mass Atrocities, and Civil Conflict*. Dissertation, Duke University.

Ku, Julian & Jide Nzelibe. 2006. "Do International Criminal Tribunals Deter or Exacerbate Humanitarian Atrocities?" *Washington University Law Review* 84(4): 777–833.

Kydd, Andrew. 2000. "Trust, Reassurance, and Cooperation." *International Organization* 54(2): 325–357.

Licklider, Roy. 2008. "Ethical Advice: Conflict Management vs. Human Rights in Ending Civil Wars." *Journal of Human Rights* 7(4): 376–387.

McAllister, Jacqueline. 2014. *On Knife's Edge: The International Criminal Tribunal for the Former Yugoslavia's Impact on Violence against Civilians*. Dissertation, Northwestern University.

McAllister, Jacqueline & James Meernik. 2016. "Casting a Shadow over War Zones: The International Criminal Court's Impact on Rebel and Government Forces' Use of Violence against Civilians," Paper presented at the CEEISA-ISA Joint International Conference, Ljubljana, Slovenia. http://web.isanet.org/Web/Conferences/CEEISA-ISA-LBJ2016/Archive/a7a5720e-fe27-48a6-8144-b816c183957d.pdf

Meernik, James. 2015. "The International Criminal Court and the Deterrence of Human Rights Atrocities." *Civil Wars* 17(3): 318–339.

Mendeloff, David. 2018. "Punish or Persuade? The Compellence Logic of International Criminal Court Intervention in Cases of Ongoing Civilian Violence." *International Studies Review.* 18(3): 395-421.

Metelits, Claire. 2010. *Inside Insurgency: Violence, Civilians, and Revolutionary Group Behavior.* New York: New York University Press.

Nagin, Daniel S. 2013. "Deterrence: A Review of the Evidence by a Criminologist for Economists." *Annual Review of Economics* 5: 83–105.

Paternoster, Raymond. 2010. "How Much Do We Really Know About Criminal Deterrence?" *The Journal of Criminal Law and Criminology* 100(3): 765–823.

Petersen, Roger D. 2002. *Understanding Ethnic Violence: Fear, Hatred, and Resentment in Twentieth Century Eastern Europe.* Cambridge: Cambridge University Press.

Prorok, Allyson. 2017. "The (In)compatibility of Peace and Justice? The International Criminal Court and Civil Conflict Termination." *International Organization* 71(2): 213–243.

Rodman, Kenneth A. 2008. "Darfur and the Limits of Legal Deterrence." *Human Rights Quarterly* 30(3): 529–560.

Rodman, Kenneth A. 2013. "Justice Is Interventionist: The Political Sources of the Judicial Reach of the Special Court for Sierra Leone." *International Criminal Law Review* 13: 63–91.

Schabas, William A. 2016. "Atrocity Crimes (Genocide, Crimes against Humanity and War Crimes)." In *The Cambridge Companion to International Criminal Law*, edited by William A. Schabas, 199–213. Cambridge: Cambridge University Press.

Schelling, Thomas C. 1966. *Arms and Influence.* New Haven, CT: Yale University Press.

Sikkink, Kathryn. 2011. *The Justice Cascade: How Human Rights Prosecutions are Changing World Politics.* New York: Norton.

Simmons, Beth A. & Allison Danner. 2010. "Credible Commitments and the International Criminal Court." *International Organization* 64(2): 225–256.

Snyder, Jack & Leslie Vinjamuri. 2003/04. "Trials and Errors: Principle and Pragmatism in Strategies for International Justice." *International Security* 28(3): 5–44.

Stanton, Jessica. 2016. *Violence and Restraint in Civil War: Civilian Targeting in the Shadow of International Law.* Cambridge: Cambridge University Press.

Steinberg, Richard H. 2017. "Decapitation by Arrest: International Justice and Demobilization in Congo." Unpublished manuscript, www.polisci.ucla.edu/sites/default/files/u245/richard_steinberg_paper_04-10-17.pdf

Straus, Scott. 2015. *The Making and Unmaking of Nations: War, Leadership, and Genocide in Modern Africa.* Ithaca, NY: Cornell University Press.

Valentino, Benjamin A. 2004. *Final Solutions: Mass Killing and Genocide in the 20th Century.* Ithaca, NY: Cornell University Press.

Valentino, Benjamin A. 2014. "Why We Kill: The Political Science of Political Violence Against Civilians." *Annual Review of Political Science* 17: 89–103.

Valentino, Benjamin, Paul Huth, & Dylan Balch-Lindsay. 2004. "'Draining the Sea': Mass Killing and Guerrilla Warfare." *International Organization* 58(2): 375–407.

Wegner, Patrick S. 2015. *The International Criminal Court in Ongoing Intrastate Conflicts: Navigating the Peace-Justice Divide.* Cambridge: Cambridge University Press.

Weinstein, Jeremy M. 2007. *Inside Rebellion: The Politics of Insurgent Violence.* Cambridge: Cambridge University Press.

Wippman, David. 1999/2000. "Atrocities, Deterrence, and the Limits of International Justice." *Fordham International Law Journal* 23(473): 473–482.

Wood, Elisabeth Jean. 2009. "Armed Groups and Sexual Violence: When Is Wartime Rape Rare?" *Politics and Society* 37: 131–161.

Wood, Reed M. 2010. "Rebel Capability and Strategic Violence against Civilians." *Journal of Peace Research* 47(5): 601–614.

Wood, Reed M. 2014a. "From Loss to Looting? Battlefield Costs and Rebel Incentives for Violence." *International Organization* 68(4): 979–999.

Wood, Reed M. 2014b. "Opportunities to Kill or Incentives for Restraint? Rebel Capabilities, the Origins of Support, and Civilian Victimization in Civil War." *Conflict Management and Peace Science* 31(5): 461–480.

Part 2
Intersections

2.1 Perpetrators—New Theoretical Approaches

13

Gendering the Perpetrator

Gendering Perpetrator Studies

Clare Bielby

Gender is constitutive of how we think about the perpetrator, perpetration, and violence. Even on an etymological level, gender is written into the category: "to perpetrate" derives from the Latin *per* (completely) and *patrare* (to carry out/bring into existence) from *pater* (father). Still today, and not least on account of crucial work conducted by feminist activists and scholars since the 1970s in drawing attention to violence against women, the categories of "perpetrator" and "victim" tend to be gendered male and female respectively. As a result, there has been little discursive space to imagine women's perpetration, whilst the gender of the male perpetrator has tended to be taken for granted. Against that backdrop, this chapter seeks to gender both the category of the perpetrator and the field now coming to understand itself as interdisciplinary Perpetrator Studies, where gender analysis, as V. Spike Peterson reminds us, is "neither just about women, nor about the addition of women to male-stream constructions"; rather it "is about transforming ways of being and knowing" (1992, 205).

Texts that are coming to count as part of the "canon" of Perpetrator Studies and to provide its conceptual tools seldom address gender, taking the male subject as universal. Hannah Arendt's *Eichmann in Jerusalem* (2006/[1963]) showed little interest in Adolf Eichmann as a gendered subject, whilst Stanley Milgram's obedience experiments of the early 1960s (Milgram 1974/2010) and Philip Zimbardo's Stanford prison experiment of 1971 (Zimbardo et al. 1973) only involved male subjects whose gender was not thematized. Meanwhile Christopher Browning's groundbreaking *Ordinary Men: Reserve Police Battalion 101 and the Final Solution in Poland* barely makes reference to masculinity (1992).[1]

Perpetrator Studies is a vast area of enquiry, drawing on genocide, Holocaust, terrorism, and violence studies, amongst other fields. That makes the task of writing a chapter on perpetration and scholarship in the field (in my case with regard to gender) extremely challenging. In this chapter, I focus on gendered approaches within historiography of the Holocaust and National Socialism and on what has come to be known as terrorism studies.[2] The Holocaust is arguably foundational to the field of Perpetrator Studies, and there are striking parallels in how both fields have addressed gender.

Another challenge is the question of which (violent) subjects should count as "perpetrators" when, as Nancy Scheper-Hughes and Philippe Bourgois assert, "violence is in the eye of the beholder" (2004, 2), and what counts as violence and perpetration is—to some degree at least—historically and culturally contingent. Up until 1991 in the UK for example, "rape" did not exist within marriage—at least in a legal sense: the man who forcefully had sex with his wife did not count as a "rapist" or a "perpetrator." Similarly, and although it is relatively straightforward to apply the term "perpetrators" to National Socialist actors, in the context of Nazi Germany, many of what we now understand as acts of perpetration did not count as perpetration, neither in a legal sense nor with regard to wider cultural understandings. What, then, is the yardstick we should use to measure whether someone counts as a "perpetrator"? If we cannot go by what counted as "perpetration" at the time, is "perpetrator" a designation that we, as scholars, impose on historical actors as a form of moral condemnation? If so, how do we account for our own subjectivities and the contingency of our own cultural and historical moment? Are we simply going by today's legal constructions of "perpetration" or some "gut instinct" of what is "moral" and "right"? At what point, for example, does a soldier in a legal or "just" war become a "perpetrator," when what counts as legal and "just" is culturally dependent and reflects the moral standards and/or political interests of those in power? As feminist theorists have demonstrated, what tends to be constructed as political perpetration ("unjust wars," "terrorism"), and hence invites moral condemnation, is a gendered and racialized issue. With reference to terror in particular, Laura Sjoberg observes, "Terror is often represented as the product of the fears and problems of a small (often masculine). elite part of the population" (2011, 236).

Male Perpetrators of Violence against Women

So-called "second-wave" feminism's "discovery" and interrogation of the topic of male, largely "personal" violence against women is not the most intuitive place to start this chapter. Interdisciplinary Perpetrator Studies seems to understand itself as focusing on what has been constructed as the "high" politics of "political" violence.[3] Meanwhile, feminist scholarly and activist work around violence against women has been—certainly in its early days—squarely focused on women as victims and on the importance of women voicing *their* experiences of violence, rather than on the (male) perpetrator. But crucially, feminists not only drew attention to the gendered nature of "personal" violence; they also insisted that male violence against women was a political, rather than merely a private, issue. The feminist maxim "the personal is political" could be equally applied to the topic of violence against women.

Feminist scholars working on the subject have had productive exchanges on what to understand under the term "violence": should it be limited, for example, to instances of physical force and coercion, or should the threat of these and more "everyday" examples of abuse and harassment also constitute violence? Significantly, they have also emphasized the gendered nature of forms of knowledge with regard to "political" violence. References to "sex wars," so commonplace within feminism, particularly in the 1970s, functioned in part to highlight the implicit gendering of conventional constructions of "war." As Liz Kelly asks in 2000: "When is a war a war, and what constitutes peace from the perspective of women?" (47). Since the very earliest "second-wave" feminist work on sexual violence (Griffin 1971; Brownmiller 1975), "personal" violence against women has been framed as "terrorism" and male perpetrators as "terrorists."[4] Feminist scholars have also sought to frame violence against women as "genocide," mobilizing terms such as "gendercide" (Warren 1985) and "femicide" (Radford 1992; Russell & Harmes 2001).

In this context, it is probably not surprising that feminists were for a long time reluctant to investigate the subject of women who perpetrate violence, which "must be seen in the light of well-founded fears that such investigations could be used to mask male violence" (Jacobs et al. 2000, 12). An additional factor was the desire, evident in women's studies scholarship, particularly of the 1970s and 1980s, to posit women as the "'better' part of the human race" (Herkommer 2014, 101). How feminist scholarship and activism dealt with the phenomenon of woman engaging in urban terrorism in mostly western contexts from the late 1960s, as well as debates within German feminist historiography with regard to women's roles in National Socialism, are revealing here.

Early Feminist Approaches to Terrorism and the *Historikerinnenstreit*: Women as Perpetrators in the 1970s and 1980s

Feminist first steps to address the challenging subject of women as perpetrators in the context of terrorism and National Socialism bear striking parallels. Broadly speaking, these steps were the result of two developments: firstly, women's studies establishing itself as an academic field and seeking to excavate—in the Foucauldian sense—a history of women as historical and political actors and secondly, the high incidence of women perpetrators in the urban terrorism that occurred from the late 1960s in countries such as West Germany, Italy, the USA, and Japan, and the misogynistic responses that these "exceptional" women elicited. In all these contexts, women terrorists were demonized, for example as hysterics, mothers gone awry, *femmes fatales*, lesbians, and/or monsters, in ways that echo how National Socialist women had been represented in public discourse since the end of the Second World War. The disciplines of sociology, criminology, and law, among others, also weighed in, with legal specialist H.H.A. Cooper's essay "Woman as Terrorist" a notable example. Cooper attributed terrorism in women to pathology, thereby disavowing women's ability to make (political) decisions for themselves. He also sexualized women's participation, asserting "that a primary cause of female terrorism is erotomania" (Cooper 1979, 154) and positing the woman terrorist's dependency on men.

Another strategy that plays out in public discourses in the 1970s is blaming feminism for women terrorists and thereby delegitimizing both. For example, in West Germany, women's terrorism, embodied most famously through RAF cofounders Ulrike Meinhof and Gudrun Ensslin, was blamed on an "excess of women's emancipation."[5] As has been documented, feminists within West Germany's New Women's Movement did respond to this, showing solidarity with militant women and heavily criticizing misogynistic public discourses at the time (Melzer 2015, 109–151). In fact, these responses should be seen as some of the first feminist interventions in Perpetrator Studies, certainly with regard to "high" politics.[6] However, on account of developments within western forms of feminism from the second half of the 1970s, the often ambivalent nature of feminists' relationship to (women's) violent perpetration has been forgotten or even written out of the New Women's Movement (Melzer 2015; Bielby 2017; Karcher 2017). Cultural/difference feminism and so-called "maternalist" positions, for example, were positing women as inherently peaceful and "naturally" opposed to violent conflict due to their capacity for maternity, which arguably held back gendered, feminist approaches to Perpetrator Studies. Furthermore, not only did those positions fundamentally misrepresent women's complex relationship to violence, they are also indicative of more general problematic tendencies within western forms of feminism, particularly in the 1980s. "An assumed peaceful disposition," Patricia Melzer argues,

> releases Western women from examining calls for solidarity and their own privilege, which allows a pacifist strategy. Instead of constituting an ahistoric, universal truth, women's presumed nonviolence is actually a discursively produced assumption based on the privileging of specific voices and actions.
>
> (Melzer 2015, 234)

Somewhat surprisingly, the most significant early feminist contribution to terrorism studies comes from precisely that cultural feminist position: Robin Morgan's *The Demon Lover: The Roots of Terrorism* of 1989 (2001). The text gets around the dilemma of what to do with a terrorist woman through positioning her as a victim rather than a perpetrator: a role occupied by the male terrorist. Morgan suggests that it is because of their emotional and sexual attachments to men that women become involved in armed activism. "Female terrorists are rare, almost always 'tokens,'" she asserts, "and invariably involved because of their love for a particular man, a personal demon lover who draws them in" (2001, xviii).

As with early feminist work on terrorism, women were the focus of the first gendered approaches within German historiography of the Second World War. Broadly speaking, feminist historians understood patriarchy as foundational to National Socialism, which meant that, similar to Morgan's analysis, women could easily be conceptualized as its victims (Lehker 1984, 68). As Christina Herkommer explains, the so-called "victimhood thesis" was represented by two main positions (2014, 101–103): firstly, one that focused on the "real" or everyday life of women during the National Socialist period, for example as determined by National Socialist sterilization policy[7]; secondly, a position that explored women's active participation in National Socialism, not least in crimes, linking that participation to women's oppressed status more generally.[8] As the 1980s progressed and as broader debates within women's studies in West Germany developed, feminist historians started to explore women's roles as perpetrators. As Herkommer has conceptualized (2014, 104–107), there were three main approaches: firstly the idea of women as *Mittäterinnen* (joint perpetrators) alongside men and patriarchal structures (Thürmer-Rohr 1987); secondly the notion that women are perpetrators because of carrying out their gendered roles, for example as housewife and/or mother, and thus supporting a violent system. An example of this position is Claudia Koonz's *Mothers in the Fatherland* of 1987. The third approach homed in specifically on women's direct involvement in National Socialist extermination policies, for example Angelika Ebbinghaus's *Opfer und Täterinnen* of 1987, a text comprised of the biographies of women perpetrators that clearly positions them as responsible agents. This text provoked nothing like the controversy of Koonz's text, the publication of which (in German translation) led to what has been termed by one of the historians centrally involved in the debate, Gisela Bock, a *Historikerinnenstreit* (1992): a fierce debate over whether women under National Socialism should be seen as victims or perpetrators in their socially allocated role.

The Long 1990s: Gender Trouble; Perpetrator Trouble

Tensions within feminist historiography of National Socialism eased as the 1990s progressed. More nuanced perspectives that emphasized the multiplicity of women's positions as "perpetrators, victims, fellow travellers and bystanders" and, reflecting the influence of Browning's work, as "ordinary women" emerged (Bock 1997). This was indicative of developments within German historiography and German culture more generally.[9] It also reflects developments within (West) German feminism from the "difference" model of gender to an understanding of binary gender as constructed and of all gender as performative. Indeed, Judith Butler's groundbreaking *Gender Trouble: Feminism and the Subversion of Identity* (1999), published in German translation in 1991, was paradigm shifting in Germany where it had an "especially strong impact on discussions of gender and politics" (Butler 1999, x).

In the 1990s feminist historians began to focus on women's involvement in National Socialist extermination policy, for example women associated with the SS (Schwarz 1997a, 1997b), working as doctors, nurses, administrators (Schwarz 1992), and as concentration camp guards (Schwarz 1994; Heike 1995). That development brought into sharp relief the idea of women's *Handlungsraum* (scope for action), this, according to Herkommer, started to become a focus in the 1990s (2014, 111). Despite Butler's encouragement to deconstruct all genders, historians of the Holocaust and National Socialism were slow to apply these insights to male perpetrators. One notable exception is German historian Thomas Kühne who made first steps in approaching masculinities from a historical perspective in his edited collection *Männergeschichte—Geschlechtergeschichte* (1996). Although the volume is not specifically interested in violent perpetrating masculinities, it includes important early contributions to the field, including Kühne's own essay on male "comradeship," particularly during the Second World War. Continuing with this line of enquiry, Kühne has gone on to analyze male soldiers as gendered subjects in his groundbreaking *Kameradschaft: Die Soldaten des Nationalsozialistischen Krieges und das 20 Jahrhundert* (2006).

Kühne was clearly influenced by critical masculinity studies; a field dominated by sociologists that had taken off in the late 1980s, gaining momentum in the 1990s through the publication of groundbreaking texts such as R.W. Connell's *Masculinities* of 1995. In that text, Connell elaborated on the idea of "hegemonic masculinity" and discussed men's violence. In fact, from the mid-1980s, men's violence was becoming a important topic for the field (Kaufman 1987), with violence theorized as constitutive of masculinity (Connell 1985; Messerschmidt 1993; Hearn 1998) and "personal" and "political" violence analyzed alongside each other (Connell 1985). As Jeff Hearn asserts in 1998, the topics of violence and sexual violence should be "central within the framework, not just another 'topic' within studies of men" (13). As with feminist approaches to violence against women discussed above, this field should be seen as making an important contribution to the gendering of, and (pro)feminist approaches to, Perpetrator Studies. The fact that it was largely sociologists writing about "low" politics and "personal" violence has meant that these important insights could be ignored by those disciplines dealing with the "high" politics of war and terrorism.

Interestingly, there was comparatively little work conducted on terrorist women (or men) from a gendered perspective in this period. Notable contributions, such as oral historian Luisa Passerini's article on women who had been involved in Italian underground organizations (1992) and Gilda Zwerman's study on women who had participated in armed US organizations (1994), were based on interviews with those militant women. Otherwise, the decade was significant for bringing the idea of sexual violence in times of war and specifically rape as genocide to the fore. That was a response to the horrific incidence of rape during the Bosnian conflict (Stiglmayer 1994; Allen 1996) and the Rwandan genocide, the latter of which saw women participating in acts of perpetration "in unprecedented fashion" (Jones 2008, 234). Writing in 2000 in the wake of Bosnia and Rwanda, Liz Kelly reflects on connections between sexual violence against women in times of "war" and "peace," which serve to problematize "conventional distinctions in political theory between 'public' and 'private', 'war' and 'peace'" (Kelly 2000, 45). As she concludes, "sexual violence connects 'war' and 'peace' as conventionally defined, and […] these conventional definitions rely on a construction of 'war' which women's experiences belie" (61).

Perpetrator Studies in the Twenty-first Century

Gendered and feminist scholarship on the Holocaust and National Socialism in the twenty-first century has continued to be influenced by constructivist approaches to the sex/gender binary and the idea that gender is performatively constituted. Feminist work on representation and discourse has also shaped the field. Following Gudrun Schwarz's and Irmtraud Heike's leads in the 1990s, historians have continued to focus on women concentration camp guards and those involved in the SS more generally (Schwartz 2005; Erpel 2007; Mailänder Koslov 2009; Mühlenberg 2011), with emphasis on women's investment in perpetration with regard to aspects such as career progression (Tzani 2011). There have also been more holistic approaches highlighting the diversity of ways in which women functioned as perpetrators (and bystanders). As well as considering women in the SS, for example, Kathrin Kompisch explores the involvement of women in the criminal police, the *Gestapo*, women as so-called *Schreibtischtäterinnen*, and women associated with the *Wehrmacht* (2008). Women doctors, nurses, and midwives who participated in Nazi extermination policy have also become a subject of interest (Lehnert 2003; Lower 2013).

A new focus has been the gendered and sexualized representations, particularly of women concentration camp guards, as the epitome of deviance and perversity, both during their trial and in public discourse more widely in the postwar context (Duesterberg 2002; Przyrembel 2002; Kretzer 2005). Meanwhile, publication of the edited volume *Gedächtnis und Geschlecht: Deutungsmuster in Darstellungen des nationalsozialistischen Genozids* (Eschebach et al. 2002) marked a move towards the investigation of gender as an analytical, rather than empirical, category. German feminist art historians have been especially attentive to that approach, with a particular focus on the postwar context. In fact, Irit Rogoff and Kathrin Hoffmann-Curtius had identified a "feminization" of postwar discourses on National Socialism as early as 1993 and 1996, respectively, whilst Silke Wenk has more recently explored the strategy of "pornographization" within postwar discourse (2002).

There has been reluctance to apply this gendered-analytical approach to the National Socialist period itself. As Claus-Christian Szejnmann observes in 2008: "There are still hardly any attempts at a systematic gender perspective in Perpetrator Studies [of the Holocaust]" (Szejnmann 2014, 46). Recently published volumes of essays do start to move in that direction, with the title of Christina Herkommer and Elke Frietsch's collection suggestive of a broader gendered interest: *Nationalsozialismus und Geschlecht: Zur Politisierung und Ästhetisierung von Körper, "Rasse" und Sexualität im "Dritten Reich" und nach 1945* (2009).[10] The volume includes essays that address masculinity and gender more generally as an analytical category. However, the focus remains on women and femininity.

Meanwhile and somewhat predictably, since 9/11 terrorism studies has fortified itself as an academic field that, dominated by the disciplines of international relations and political science, tends to ignore gender. It focuses furthermore on contemporary forms of terrorism and mirrors the language on and ideology of the "war on terror," never really questioning the contingent nature of conceptions of "the terrorist" and "terrorism" (Hamilton 2010, 96).[11] As Carrie Hamilton has argued, those specializing in terrorism show little to no interest in questions such as:

> Why the majority of activists who commit terrorist acts have been male, how constructions of masculinity and femininity in given historical contexts help to determine who becomes an armed activist, how and why, or what experiences male and female activists have once inside an organisation that uses terrorism.
>
> *(2010, 98)*

More widely, and as with scholarship on the Holocaust and National Socialism, studies that offer a gendered and/or feminist perspective to terrorism have largely focused on women. Whilst the limited work on terrorism and women from the 1970s tended to focus on left-wing and nationalist armed organizations in western contexts, since 9/11 there has been a marked shift to women and terrorism in Islamic and nationalist contexts around the Middle East (Hamilton 2010, 99). Much of this work fails to critically interrogate categories such as "female terrorist" and "woman" and is not informed by feminist theory (Hamilton 2010, 99).[12] A striking example is the work of Mia Bloom, who has published widely on women suicide bombers and personalizes their motivation, positioning them as victims (see for example Bloom 2005) and hence echoing the work of Cooper (1979) and Morgan (2001).

The most fruitful feminist/gendered approaches to women and terrorism have been shaped by developments in feminist theory since the 1990s: intersectionality, gender theory, post-structuralism, the politics of representation (Hamilton 2010, 99–100). Many studies take a comparative, global approach (Sjoberg & Gentry 2007; Eager 2008), which, whilst insightful can be limiting as the authors do not always have a finely grained understanding of the different historical contexts under scrutiny, which can lead to overgeneralizations. By and large, approaches that focus on one or two specific case studies are more successful because they are able to clearly locate the examples of terrorism in their historical and cultural contexts (Hamilton 2007; Alison 2009; Glynn 2013). Interestingly, many of these studies go back to examples of terrorism of the twentieth century (Hamilton 2007; Glynn 2013) and/or focus on ethno-nationalist contexts (Hamilton 2007; Alison 2009), rather than on so-called Islamic terrorism. Feminist scholarship on representation and discourse, especially with regard to the mass media and new social media (Sjoberg and Gentry 2007; Bielby 2012; Glynn 2013), has also made a valuable contribution. This is not least because discourse and communication are constitutive of the meaning of terrorism.

In the last decade, there have been a number of highly productive collections of essays and journal special issues on the subject of terrorism and women but also gender more broadly. Karen Alexander and Mary Hawskesworth's edited volume *War & Terror: Feminist Perspectives* (2008), based on two special issues of *Signs: Journal of Women in Culture and Society*, is notable for exploring terrorism and gender alongside war, interrogating similarities and differences in how the categories of gender and race intersect with "political" violence in diverse contexts. The volume addresses women as perpetrators and/or victims, problematizing the artificial binary opposition of victim/perpetrator. Influenced also by feminist scholarship on violence against women, the volume is attentive to "hitherto unnoted continuities between what is considered the 'extraordinary violence' of war and the 'ordinary violence' to which women are subjected in peacetime" (Hawkesworth 2008, 6). As Hawkesworth asks: "If women experience neither peace nor liberation in the aftermath of revolutionary violence, what exactly does demilitarization mean for women?" (13). The volume also interrogates violence as a productive force, "shifting the analytical frame from a focus on war as an instrument of statecraft and a means of destruction to war as a mode of production and reproduction" (5). That idea of violence as generative can be applied to the production of gendered perpetrator subjectivities but also to the gendering and racialization of discourse in a more abstract sense, taking us close to recent bio-political and queering approaches to gender and terrorism. Whilst these studies can be highly insightful, they tend to lose sight of the subject (Wilcox 2015), with Jasbir K. Puar, for example, positing the model of assemblages (2007). They are therefore of limited value for interdisciplinary Perpetrator Studies, although it may be productive to start thinking about "perpetrator assemblages."

Another significant volume is Laura Sjoberg and Caron Gentry's *Women, Gender, and Terrorism* of 2011. Like Hawkesworth and Alexander's volume, this text considers diverse examples of women's terrorism through feminist, gendered, and racializing lenses, although the focus is on the contemporary world and Islamic terrorism in particular. As stated in the introduction, it is fruitful to see terrorism as "a process" rather than an essence (Sjoberg et al 2011, 11), which helps to get around the contingency and subjective nature of the term. In her thoughtful conclusion to the volume, Sjoberg raises the issue of gendered forms of knowledge around terrorism (2011, 236–237), critically engaging with questions of "who and what counts as terrorist" and the "theoretical frames we use to deal with terrorism," such as subaltern and post-colonial approaches (237). Crucial to this endeavor, she argues, is breaking down traditional divisions, constructed in international relations and elsewhere, between "the personal" and "the political" realms. Amongst other things, this division and its gendering has led to a personalization of women's motivations for participating in terrorist organizations and a construction of the male terrorist as a rational, autonomous, ungendered political subject who is unaffected by personal considerations. Both of these constructions, she argues, are a misrepresentation of terrorist and political agency more generally. Drawing on feminist philosophers of the late 1990s, she argues that male and female terrorists, as all subjects, are "relationally autonomous"; that is, they have "agency and independent identity" but their choices "are constrained by their relationships with others" (232).

Towards a Critical Feminist Perpetrator Studies: Some Ways Forward

Interdisciplinary, Gendered Approaches to Perpetrator Studies

Perpetrator Studies needs to be attentive to the multiple ways in which constructions and embodied experiences of violence, perpetration, and gender intersect, where gender is understood as it intersects also with categories such as race, ethnicity, class, age, sexuality, and dis/ability. Gender does not offer *the* key to understanding perpetration. But it does shed crucial light, providing one of the critical lenses that Perpetrator Studies should utilize. Scholarship on women as perpetrators in relation to the Holocaust and Nazi Germany, but also in the context of terrorism, is clearly well developed, but there are obvious deficits when it comes to interrogating men and masculinities, as well as employing more systematic, gendered-analytical approaches. With regard to masculinity, Perpetrator Studies would do well to draw on the scholarship conducted on "personal" violence and masculinity, but also on militarism and the military within critical masculinity studies,[13] particularly within the discipline of sociology. The fact that it has so rarely done so is proof of the need for genuinely interdisciplinary methodologies that combine sociological approaches such as these with fine-grained, area-studies approaches that are attuned to cultural and historical specificity. Women's and gender studies can provide an important model here since, according to Kath Woodward and Sophie Woodward, these fields are "distinctive in their engagement with interdisciplinarity," having developed "through a synergy between thought and activism" (Woodward & Woodward 2015).

Perpetrating Subjects

Feminist scholarship has been highly attentive to the dangers of essentializing and reifying identity categories, not least those associated with the perpetration of violence. As Miranda Alison argues: "Narrating women who have suffered violent or abusive events in war as victims […]

is disempowering, inaccurate, and constitutes further victimization" (2009, 119). There are dangers too in reifying acts of violence with the result that violence becomes decontextualized, even fetishized. One way around this is to regard perpetration as a dynamic process, a form of *doing* (perpetrating) rather than *being* (the perpetrator) and a form of *doing* intimately bound up with many others, not least the *doing* of one's gender (Bielby & Murer 2018). Critical feminist work on terrorism has employed this perspective. Hamilton, for example, explains that she uses "the words terrorism and terrorist to apply to certain *tactics* or *forms* of violence, typically associated with insurgent and illegal armed movements, but not to refer to those movements themselves, or to their members" (2010, 95). A great deal is at stake here. Not only does the reification of violence and of identity categories run the risk of misrepresenting the process of perpetration within scholarship, it can also perpetuate wider tendencies to focus on—even fetishize—the ever more "extraordinary" acts of violence that seem to characterize the post-9/11 world. As a result, we become less able and willing to apprehend those more "ordinary" (Hawkesworth 2008, 6) or—to cite Rob Nixon—"slow" forms of violence, which seem to disproportionately affect women and/or people of color.[14] According to Nixon, there is a "representational bias against slow violence" (2011, 13)—that is, the violence "that occurs gradually and out of sight, a violence of delayed destruction that is dispersed across time and space, an attritional violence that is typically not viewed as violence" (2). As he argues, this bias was fortified through the 9/11 terrorist attacks "which reinforced a spectacular, immediately sensational, and instantly hyper-visible image of what constitutes a violent threat. The fiery spectacle of the collapsing towers was burned into the national psyche as *the* definitive image of violence" (13). Critical feminist Perpetrator Studies must therefore situate acts of perpetration in the context of those "slow" or "objective" (Žižek 2008) forms of violence that are so often misrecognized.

Perpetrating Agency

The notion of the "relational autonomy" of subjects who commit acts of terrorism (Sjoberg & Gentry 2011), regardless of their gender, can be usefully applied within Perpetrator Studies. As Sjoberg argues, the acts and behavior of "terrorists"—as of all subjects—emanate from both conscious decision-making and how subjects are moved and affected by others. It is not just women's but in fact all agency in the context of perpetration (and more widely) that is "complex, contingent, contextual, and relational" (2011, 235). This understanding works against fantasies of (male) autonomy, typical of liberalism, which are echoed in much of the work within international relations, political science, and terrorism studies more generally. As Paul Reynolds argues, feminist approaches to knowledge in particular have done crucial work in drawing attention to "[t]he idea that an agent and their actions cannot be removed from their situatedness in social and cultural contexts"; "an important corrective to the universal, one-dimensional rational 'man' of liberal philosophy" (2015, 204). Reynolds advocates an understanding of agency (over autonomy) that balances "self-constitution with being constituted, subject to forms of fluidity, plurality, plasticity and interdependence, dialectically, with the agents, cultures, situatedness, customs and practices within which they interrelate" (205).

Perpetration as "in the Eye of the Beholder"

The central feminist tenet that "the personal is political" alerts us to the contingent and gendered nature of what constitutes the political of "political" violence, and of what counts as violence and perpetration more generally. As feminist applications of "high" political terms such as "terrorism," "femicide," "gendercide," and "war" to the "low" politics of violence against women and gendered relations more generally make clear, knowledge around "political" violence is always gendered (raced and classed), representing the fears and interests of certain privileged groups: usually heterosexual white men. Critical feminist Perpetrator Studies must therefore continuously interrogate the gendered politics of representation at stake when we use terms such as "political violence" and "perpetration." We need to ask whose interests and experiences we are representing and privileging when we apply these terms and knowledges. There is no universal or neutral notion of "perpetration" and we should be alert to the contingent, gendered nature of our own value judgments, if indeed application of the term "perpetration" is a way to delegitimize something. Again, feminist scholarship, so alert to the (gendered) values implicit in supposedly "objective"/"malestream" knowledge production, can offer tools to better take account of our own positionality, investments, and subjective bias. Feminist reflexivity, so fundamental to feminist constructions of knowledge, particularly in the social sciences, is an important model. As Gayle Letherby points out, since the 1970s feminists have been criticizing "male-dominated knowledge production and the methodological claims made by researchers who argued that their work was objective and value free" (2015, 78). Acknowledging that all research is subjective and biased, feminists have instead advocated a reflexive approach to scholarship that takes account of the fact that research "is contextual, situational, and specific, and […] will differ systematically according to the social location (as gendered, raced, classed, sexualised person) or the particular knowledge-producer" (Stanley 1993, 49). Feminist reflexivity furthermore accounts for the fact that "we need to consider how the researcher as author is positioned in relation to the research process" (Letherby 2015, 87). Letherby advocates "theorised subjectivity": "what is practicable, desirable and necessary," she asserts, "is the theorisation of the subjective (which includes the researcher's motivation and practice […] and its significance to knowledge production" (88). This comes close to what Donna Haraway has termed "situated and embodied knowledge" (1988, 583); that is "politics and epistemologies of location, positioning, and situating, where partiality and not universality is the condition of being heard to make rational knowledge claims" (589). In adopting a reflexive and situated approach to research on and knowledge around perpetration, then, critical feminist Perpetrator Studies can start to account for the contingency and subjective nature of all work on perpetration.

Notes

1 As Adam Jones points out, Browning "placed the emphasis squarely on the 'ordinary' rather than the 'men'" though he does note for example the "'macho' vision" that underpinned aspects of the killing (2008, 236).
2 For a critical overview of terrorism studies, see Hamilton (2010, 96–98).
3 According to Laura Sjoberg and Sandra Via, "[h]igh politics refers to the traditional sites of power in global politics, such as state governments and international organizations, as opposed to the 'low' politics of everyday life with which most feminist work is concerned" (2010, 13).
4 See also Barry 1979/1984; Sheffield 1987; Card 1991.
5 On that, see Bielby (2012), particularly chapter 1.
6 As Cynthia Enloe observes, feminist and gendered analyses are not necessarily the same thing though there is "substantial overlap" (2010, xi).
7 See Bock 1986.
8 See for example Mitscherlich 1985.
9 See Niven 2002.
10 See also Gehmacher and Hauch 2007.

11 A welcome intervention has been the emergence of "critical terrorism studies," the name of a journal launched in 2008.
12 See for example Gonzalez Perez 2008; Ness 2008.
13 See for example Higate 2003.
14 Nixon is not specifically concerned with gender, but his theory requires this gendered analysis.

References

Alexander, Karen & Mary E. Hawkesworth, eds. 2008. *War & Terror: Feminist Perspectives*. Chicago: University of Chicago Press.

Alison, Miranda. 2009. *Women and Political Violence: Female Combatants in Ethno-National Conflict*. London: Routledge.

Allen, Beverly. 1996. *Rape Warfare: The Hidden Genocide in Bosnia-Herzegovina and Croatia*. Minneapolis, MN: University of Minnesota Press.

Arendt, Hannah. [1963] 2006. *Eichmann in Jerusalem: A Report on the Banality of Evil*. London: Penguin.

Barry, Kathleen. [1979] 1984. *Female Sexual Slavery*. New York: New York University Press.

Bielby, Clare. 2012. *Violent Women in Print: Representations in the West German Print Media of the 1960s and 1970s*. Rochester, NY: Camden House.

Bielby, Clare. 2017. "West Germany's *neue Frauenbewegung* and the Productive Potential of Feminist *Gegengewalt*." *Forum for Modern Language Studies* no. 534: 379–404.

Bielby, Clare & Jeffrey Murer, eds. 2018. *Perpetrating Selves: Doing Violence, Performing Identity*. London: Palgrave Macmillan.

Bloom, Mia. 2005. *Dying to Kill: The Allure of Suicide Terror*. New York: Columbia University Press.

Bock, Gisela. 1986. *Zwangssterilisation im Nationalsozialismus. Studien zur Rassenpolitik und Frauenpolitik*. Opladen: Westdeutscher Verlag.

Bock, Gisela. 1992. "Ein Historikerinnenstreit?" *Geschichte und Gesellschaft* no. 18: 400–404.

Bock, Gisela. 1997. "Ganz normale Frauen. Täter, Opfer, Mitläufer und Zuschauer im Nationalsozialismus." In *Zwischen Karriere und Verfolgung: Handlungsräume von Frauen im nationalisozialistischen Deutschland*, edited by Kirsten Heinsohn et al., 245–277. Frankfurt am Main: Campus.

Browning, Christopher. 1992. *Ordinary Men: Reserve Police Battalion 101 and the Final Solution in Poland*. New York: HarperPerennial.

Brownmiller, Susan. 1975. *Against Our Will: Men, Women and Rape*. London: Secker and Warburg.

Butler, Judith. 1999. *Gender Trouble: Feminism and the Subversion of Identity*. London: Routledge.

Card, Claudia. 1991. "Rape as a Terrorist Institution." In *Violence, Terrorism and Justice*, edited by Raymond G. Frey and Christopher W. Morris, 296–319. Cambridge: Cambridge University Press.

Connell, Raewyn W. 1985. "Masculinity, Violence and War." In *War/Masculinity*, edited by Paul Patton and Ross Poole, 4–10. Sydney: Intervention.

Connell, Raewyn W. 1995. *Masculinities*. Cambridge: Polity.

Cooper, H.H.A. 1979. "Woman as Terrorist." In *The Criminology of Deviant Women*, edited by Freda Adler and Rita J. Simon, 150–157. Boston: Houghton Mifflin.

Duesterberg, Julia. 2002. "Von der 'Umkehr aller Weiblichkeit'. Charakterbilder einer KZ-Aufseherin." In *Deutungsmuster in Darstellungen des nationalsozialistischen Genozids, Gedächtnis und Geschlecht*, edited by Insa Eschebach et al., 237–243. Frankfurt am Main: Campus.

Eager, Paige W. 2008. *From Freedom Fighters to Terrorists: Women and Political Violence*. Aldershot: Ashgate.

Ebbinghaus, Angelika, ed. 1987. *Opfer und Täterinnen. Frauenbiographien des Nationalsozialismus*. Nördlingen: Franz Greno Verlag.

Enloe, Cynthia. 2010. Foreword to *Gender, War, and Militarism: Feminist Perspectives*, edited by Laura Sjoberg and Sandra Via, xi–xiii. Santa Barbara: Praeger.

Erpel, Simone, ed.. 2007. *Im Gefolge der SS: Aufseherinnen des Frauen-KZ Ravensbrück*. Berlin: Metropol.

Eschebach, Insa et al., eds. 2002. *Gedächtnis und Geschlecht. Deutungsmuster in Darstellungen des nationalsozialistischen Genozids*. Frankfurt am Main: Campus.

Frietsch, Elke & Christina Herkommer, eds. 2009. *Nationalsozialismus und Geschlecht. Zur Politisierung und Ästhetisierung von Körper, "Rasse" und Sexualität im "Dritten Reich" und nach 1945*. Bielefeld: transcript.

Gehmacher, Johanna & Gabriella Hauch, eds. 2007. *Frauen- und Geschlechtergeschichte des Nationalsozialismus: Fragestellungen, Perspektiven, neue Forschungen*. Innsbruck: Studien Verlag.

Gonzalez Perez, Maria. 2008. *Women and Terrorism: Female Activity in Domestic and International Terror Groups*. London: Routledge.

Glynn, Ruth. 2013. *Women, Terrorism and Trauma in Italian Culture*. Basingstoke: Palgrave Macmillan.

Griffin, Susan. 1971. "Rape: The All-American Crime." *Ramparts* no. 10: 26–35.

Hamilton, Carrie. 2007. *Women and ETA: The Gender Politics of Radical Basque Nationalism*. Manchester: Manchester University Press.

Hamilton, Carrie. 2010. "Towards a Historiography of Gender and 'Terrorism'." *Zeitgeschichte* no. 372: 95–110.

Haraway, Donna. 1988. "The Science Question in Feminism and the Privilege of Partial Perspective." *Feminist Studies* no. 143: 575–599.

Hawkesworth, Mary. 2008. "War as a Mode of Production and Reproduction: Feminist Analytics." In *War & Terror: Feminist Perspectives*, edited by Karen Alexander and Mary E. Hawkesworth, 1–31. Chicago: University of Chicago Press.

Hearn, Jeff. 1998. *The Violences of Men: How Men Talk about and How Agencies Respond to Men's Violence to Women*. London: Sage.

Heike, Irmtraut. 1995. "Johanna Langefeld. Die Biographie einer KZ-Oberaufseherin." *Werkstattgeschichte* no. 12: 7–19.

Herkommer, Christina. 2014. "Women under National Socialism: Women's Scope for Action and the Issue of Gender." In *Ordinary People as Mass Murderers: Perpetrators in Comparative Perspective*, edited by Olaf Jensen and Claus-Christian W. Szejnmann, 99–119. Basingstoke: Palgrave Macmillan.

Higate, Paul. 2003. *Military Masculinities: Identity and the State*. London: Praeger.

Hoffmann-Curtius, Katrin. 1996. "Feminisierung des Faschismus." In *Die Nacht hat zwölf Stunden dann kommt schon der Tag: Antifaschismus, Geschichte und Neubewertung*, edited by Claudia Keller & LiteraturWERKstatt Berlin, 45–69. Berlin: Aufbau Verlag.

Jacobs, Susie et al. 2000. "Introduction: States of Conflict." In *States of Conflict: Gender, Violence and Resistance*, edited by Susie Jacobs et al., 1–23. London: Zed Books.

Jones, Adam. 2008. "Gender and Genocide." In *The Historiography of Genocide*, edited by Dan Stone, 228–252. Basingstoke: Palgrave Macmillan.

Karcher, Katharina. 2017. *Sisters in Arms: Militant Feminisms in the Federal Republic of Germany since 1968*. New York: Berghahn.

Kaufman, Michael. 1987. "The Construction of Masculinity and the Triad of Men's Violence." In *Beyond Patriarchy: Essays by men on Pleasure, Power, and Change*, edited by Michael Kaufman, 1–29. Oxford: Oxford University Press.

Kelly, Liz. 2000. "Wars against Women: Sexual Violence, Sexual Politics and the Militarized State." In *States of Conflict: Gender, Violence and Resistance*, edited by Susie Jacobs et al., 45–65. London: Zed Books.

Kompisch, Kathrin. 2008. *Täterinnen: Frauen im Nationalsozialismus*. Vienna: Böhlau.

Koonz, Claudia. 1987. *Mothers in the Fatherland: Women, the Family and Nazi Politics*. New York: St Martin's Press.

Kretzer, Anette. 2005. "'His or Her Special Job'. Die Repräsentation von NS-Verbrecherinnen im ersten Hamburger Ravensbrück-Prozess und im westdeutschen Täterschaftsdiskurs." *Beiträge Zur Geschichte der nationalsozialistischen Verfolgung in Norddeutschland* no. 7: 134–150.

Kühne, Thomas. 1996. *Männergeschichte – Geschlechtergeschichte. Männlichkeit im Wandel der Moderne*. Frankfurt am Main: Campus.

Kühne, Thomas. 2006. *Kameradschaft: Die Soldaten des Nationalsozialistischen Krieges und das 20 Jahrhundert*. Göttingen: Vandenhoeck & Ruprecht.

Lehker, Marianne. 1984. *Frauen im Nationalsozialismus. Wie aus Opfern Handlanger der Täter wurden, eine nötige Trauerarbeit*. Frankfurt am Main: Materialis Verlag.

Lehnert, Esther. 2003. *Die Beteiligung von Fürsorgerinnen an der Bildung und Umsetzung der Kategorie "minderwertig" im Nationalsozialismus*. Frankfurt am Main: Mabuse Verlag.

Letherby, Gayle. 2015. "Gender-Sensitive Method/ologies." In *Gender & Women's Studies*, fourth edition, edited by Victoria Robinson and Diane Richards, 76–94. Basingstoke: Palgrave Macmillan.

Lower, Wendy. 2013. *Hitler's Furies: German Women in the Nazi Killing Fields*. London: Chatto & Windus.

Mailänder Koslov, Elissa. 2009. *Gewalt im Dienstalltag: Die SS-Aufseherinnen des Konzentrations- und Vernichtungslager Majdanek*. Hamburg: Hamburger Edition.

Melzer, Patricia. 2015. *Death in the Shape of a Young Girl: Women's Political Violence in the Red Army Faction*. New York: New York University Press.

Messerschmidt, James. 1993. *Masculinities and Crime: Critique and Reconceptualization of Theory*. Lanham, MD: Rowman & Littlefield.

Milgram, Stanley. [1974]2010. *Obedience to Authority: An Experimental View*. New York: Pinter & Martin.

Mitscherlich, Margarete. 1985. *Die friedfertige Frau. Eine psychoanalytische Untersuchung zur Aggression der Geschlechter*. Frankfurt am Main: Fischer.

Morgan, Robin. 2001. *The Demon Lover: The Roots of Terrorism*. New York: Washington Square Press.

Mühlenberg, Jutta. 2011. *Das SS-Helferinnenkorps: Ausbildung, Einsatz und Entnazifizierung der weiblichen Angehörigen der Waffen-SS 1942–1949*. Hamburg: Hamburger Edition.

Ness, Cindy. 2008. *Female Terrorism and Militancy: Agency, Utility, and Organization*. London: Routledge.

Niven, Bill. 2002. *Facing the Nazi Past: United Germany and the Legacy of the Third Reich*. London: Routledge.

Nixon, Rob. 2011. *Slow Violence and the Environmentalism of the Poor*. Cambridge, MA: Harvard University Press.

Passerini, Luisa. 1992. "Lacerations in the Memory: Women in the Italian Underground Organizations." *International Social Movement Research* no. 4: 161–212.

Przyrembel, Alexandra. 2002. "Der Bann eines Bildes. Ilse Koch, die 'Kommandeuse von Buchenwald'." In *Gedächtnis und Geschlecht. Deutungsmuster in Darstellungen des nationalsozialistischen Genozids*, edited by Insa Eschebach et al., 45–267. Frankfurt am Main: Campus.

Puar, Jasbir K. 2007. *Terrorist Assemblages: Homonationalism in Queer Times*. Durham, NC: Duke University Press.

Radford, Jill. 1992. *Femicide: The Politics of Woman Killing*. Farmington Hills, MI: Twayne Publishers.

Reynolds, Paul. 2015. "Women's Agency and the Fallacy of Autonomy: The Example of Rape and Sexual Consent." In *Women and Violence: The Agency of Victims and Perpetrators*, edited by Herjeet Marway and Heather Widdows, 197–215. London: Palgrave Macmillan.

Rogoff, Irit. 1993. "Von Ruinen zu Trümmern. Die Feminisierung von Faschismus in deutschen historischen Museen." In *Denkräume zwischen Kunst und Wissenschaft*, edited by Silvia Baumgart et al., 258–285. Berlin: Reimer.

Russell, Diana E.H. & Roberta A. Harmes, eds. 2001. *Femicide in Global Perspective*. New York: Teachers College Press.

Scheper-Hughes, Nancy & Philippe Bourgois. 2004. "Introduction: Making Sense of Violence." In *Violence in War and Peace: An Anthology*, edited by Scheper-Hughes and Bourgois, 1–31. Malden, MA: Blackwell.

Schwartz, Johannes. 2005. "Geschlechtsspezifischer Eigensinn von NS-Täterinnen am Beispiel der KZ-Oberaufseherin Johanna Langefeld." In *Frauen als Täterinnen im Nationalsozialismus*, edited by Viola Schubert-Lehnhardt, 56–82. Gerbstedt: Mansfeld Druck.

Schwarz, Gudrun. 1992. "Verdrängte Täterinnen. Frauen im Apparat der SS 1939–1945." In *Nach Osten. Verdeckte Spuren nationalsozialistischer Verbrechen*, edited by Theresa Wobbe, 197–227. Frankfurt am Main: Neue Kritik.

Schwarz, Gudrun. 1994. "SS-Aufseherinnen in nationalsozialistischen Konzentrationslagern 1993–1945." *Dachauer Hefte* 10: 32–49.

Schwarz, Gudrun. 1997a. "Frauen in der SS: Sipperverband und Frauenkorps." In *Zwischen Karriere und Verfolgung: Handlungsräume von Frauen im nationalsozialistischen Deutschland*, edited by Kirsten Heinsohn et al., 233–244. Frankfurt am Main: Campus.

Schwarz, Gudrun. 1997b. *Eine Frau an seiner Seite. Ehefrauen in der "SS-Sippegemeinschaft."* Hamburg: Hamburger Edition.

Sheffield, Carole J. 1987. "Sexual Terrorism: The Social Control of Women." In *Analyzing Gender: A Handbook of Social Science Research*, edited by Beth B. Hess and Myra M. Ferree, 171–189. Newbury Park: Sage Publications.

Sjoberg, Laura & Caron E. Gentry. 2007. *Mothers, Monsters, Whores: Women's Violence in Global Politics*. London: Zed Books.

Sjoberg, Laura & Caron E. Gentry, eds. 2011. *Women, Gender, and Terrorism*. London: University of Georgia Press.

Sjoberg, Laura & Sandra Via. 2010. "Introduction." In *Gender, War, and Militarism: Feminist Perspectives*, edited by Laura Sjoberg and Sandra Via, 1–13. Santa Barbara: Praeger.

Spike Peterson, V. 1992. "Transgressing Boundaries: Theories of Knowledge, Gender and International Relations." *Millennium* no. 212: 183–206.

Stanley, Liz. 1993. "On Auto/Biography in Sociology." *Sociology* no. 271: 41–52.

Stiglmayer, Alexandra, ed. 1994. *Mass Rape: The War against Women in Bosnia-Herzegovina*. Lincoln: University of Nebraska Press.

Szejnmann, Claus-Christian W. 2014. "Perpetrators of the Holocaust: A Historiography." In *Ordinary People as Mass Murderers: Perpetrators in Comparative Perspective*, edited by Olaf Jensen and Claus-Christian Szejnmann, 25–54. Basingstoke: Palgrave Macmillan.

Thürmer-Rohr, Christina. 1987. *Vagabundinnen. Feministische Essays*. Berlin: Orlanda Frauenverlag.

Tzani, Fotini. 2011. *Zwischen Karrierismus und Widerspenstigkeit: SS-Aufseherinnen im KZ-Alltag*. Bielefeld: Lorbeer Verlag.

Warren, Mary A. 1985. *Gendercide: The Implications of Sex Selection*. Totowa, NJ: Rowman and Allanheld.

Wenk, Silke. 2002. "Rhetoriken der Pornografisierung: Rahmungen des Blicks auf die NS-Verbrecher." In *Gedächtnis und Geschlecht: Deutungsmuster in Darstellungen des nationalsozialistischen Genozids*, edited by Insa Eschebach et al., 269–294. Frankfurt am Main: Campus.

Wilcox, Lauren B. 2015. *Bodies of Violence: Theorizing Embodied Subjects in International Relations*. Oxford: Oxford University Press.

Woodward, Kath & Woodward, Sophie. 2015. "Gender Studies and Interdisciplinarity." *Palgrave Communications*, 1. Available at: www.nature.com/articles/palcomms201518.

Zimbardo, Philip et al. 1973. "A Study of Prisoners and Guards in a Simulated Prison." *Naval Research Review* 30: 4–17.

Žižek, Slavoj. 2008. *Violence: Six Sideways Reflections*. London: Profile.

Zwerman, Gilda. 1994. "Mothering on the Lam: Politics, Gender Fantasies and Maternal Thinking in Women Associated with Armed, Clandestine Organizations in the United States." *Feminist Review* no. 47: 33–56.

14

Posthumanism and Perpetrators

Jonathan Luke Austin

Who is responsible? Why did *they* do "it"? Were *they* born like this? What pushed *them* over a threshold into violence? Questions like these have been at the heart of Perpetrator Studies. They are questions that focus on human beings as figures whose social, political, cultural, and psychological composition makes terrible things possible: questions that thus prefigure our understanding of perpetrators as puzzling distortions of what makes more or less "normal" human life possible. But what if the emergence of perpetrators was related to something fundamentally *non*human? What if violence committed between individuals, collectivities, or states was about more than what goes on in our minds, shared societal commitments, and other such fundamentally human preoccupations? Recent "posthumanist" developments in social theory, sociology, and philosophy all suggest these questions need to be asked.[1] They hint that understanding the figure of the perpetrator—however much of a "flesh and blood" human this figure may be—requires looking outside the confines of human bodies, minds, and societies. What happens, then, if we displace—*without erasing*[2]—human beings from the center of our accounting for the possibility of genocide, ethnic cleansing, torture, and other atrocities?

This contribution provides a starting point for engaging with the question of posthumanism and perpetrators. As an approach, posthumanism represents a broad school of thought—made up of diverse sets of theoretical and empirical commitments—beginning with the basic insight that "nonhuman" things (tools, technologies, natural phenomena, etc.) matter for, and have influence over, human behavior. Put in its most simple terms, what ties posthumanist approaches together is a rejection of the belief that material things are merely neutral carriers of human intentionality: material objects are not simply the props through which human life plays out but actively shape, direct, and transform human behavior. Exploring the work of perpetrators through posthumanism can thus expand our understanding of the conditions of possibility for perpetration by adding an appreciation of how the "nonhuman" also works to make significant difference in why, how, and when human beings become perpetrators of violence. The perspective allows us to see how violence is often more than human in its coordinates.

The chapter proceeds in three main sections. The first section begins by expanding on the theoretical underpinnings of the posthumanist claim that studying "nonhuman" objects or systems is important for understanding social phenomena. These insights are then connected to the study of the perpetration of violence and a brief review of the nascent literature within Perpetrator Studies drawing on this approach is offered. The next section focuses on the perpetration of torture to demonstrate at length three key insights that posthumanist theory offers to perpetrator studies. Specifically, it is shown that material objects can sometimes A) pre*script* human behavior, B) *circulate* knowledge of violence, and C) *compel* human beings to act violently. The first of these claims focuses on how material objects contain scripts for violent behavior that subconsciously provide cues and repertoires of possible (violent) action. The second claim highlights how the spatial circulation of material objects leads to the unintentional spreading of particular patterns of (perpetrating) violence over the world. The final claim demonstrates how nonhuman objects and their scripts also contain "affective" capacities that, more than suggesting or directing violence, can be seen as "compelling" human beings to perpetrate violent acts. Each of these claims is supported by concrete empirical examples. The third and final section of the chapter outlines the challenges that posthumanism poses to Perpetrator Studies concerning, in particular, the issue of adjudicating responsibility, before closing in on the promises the approach nonetheless offers the field.

The Importance of the Nonhuman

Perpetrator Studies has always had a humanistic focus. To some degree, this focus has its origins in Hannah Arendt's (1958, 1963) deconstruction of Adolf Eichmann's *personal* role in the Holocaust and the legacy of that work in shaping inquiries into perpetrators (c.f.: Browning 1993; Huggins et al. 2002). But human beings—it will be clear—do not live (intersubjectively) alone in the world. Perpetrators are surrounded by tools, technologies, infrastructures, natural environmental features, and many other things that collectively make the world a complicated place. These "nonhuman" objects alter, instruct, affect, and make demands upon human beings, perpetrators or not. Indeed, the easiest way to see the importance of the post-human attribution of "agency" to material objects is to step away from the most egregious instances of perpetration in human history (the Holocaust, the Killing Fields of Cambodia, etc.) and to a more "everyday" form of violence where social and political discourses already partially incorporate an understanding of posthumanist claims. For example, debates over gun control in the United States have long focused on the fact that the number of human perpetrators who carry out massacres, acts of domestic violence, or terrorist incidents is dramatically increased by the widespread availability of firearms. As Bruno Latour writes:

> "Guns kill people" is a slogan of those who try to control the unrestricted sale of guns. To which the National Rifle Association replies with another slogan, "Guns don't kill people, people kill people". The first slogan is materialist: the gun acts by virtue of *material* components irreducible to the social qualities of the gunman. On account of the gun the law-abiding citizen, a good guy, becomes dangerous. The NRA, meanwhile, offers (amusingly enough, given its political views) a *sociological* version more often associated with the Left: that the gun does nothing in and of itself or by virtue of its material components. The gun is a tool … a neutral carrier of human will.
>
> *(1999, 176–177)*

If you, the reader, believe that gun control of one sort or another is a good thing then you are *already* a posthumanist (or "materialist") thinker. The example of gun control suggests that the mere possession or availability of weapons *transforms* human beings into a potentially more dangerous form than they would be in its absence. But even if readers do not support gun control, then the material safety measures found in automobiles, aircraft, and modern construction projects similarly demonstrate how the materiality of the world alters human behavior.[3] Indeed, it is possible to be even more basic here. The reader of this chapter is—hopefully—sitting comfortably, in an ergonomically designed chair. In the absence of such materially provided comfort, we all behave differently: we become fatigued, bad tempered, and work less effectively. Another case in point: psychologists have shown how individuals behave "better" and are more generous when childhood toys like teddy bears are present (Gino and Desai 2012). All these examples demonstrate the basic claim of posthumanism: material objects like guns, teddy bears, and chairs all possess "agency" in the sense that they change human behavior.[4]

This basic principle of posthuman thought—that human beings or their collectivities do not act in isolation from material, environmental, and other nonhuman aspects of the world—has many different, more specific, theoretical expressions. These include approaches integrating feminist thought (Haraway 1988, 2016), the use of quantum or complexity theory to understand the relation between humans and nonhumans (Barad 2003, 2007), the use of pragmatist sociology or philosophy (Harman 2007; Stengers 2010), a greater focus on technology (Hayles 1999; Hansen 2000; Harman 2002, 2005, 2016), and beyond (Wolfe 2010). Within Perpetrator Studies, specifically, the approach is still nascent, despite basic elements of the claims of posthumanism being found in much earlier psychological studies of violence (Berkowitz and Lepage 1967), core theoretical texts that explore the emergence of violence (Scarry 1985), as well as some attention to these issues being displayed in the classical studies of Zimbardo and Milgram (Milgram 1963; Zimbardo 2007, c.f.: Stengers 1997). Nonetheless, a growing trend integrating posthumanist thought into Perpetrator Studies has begun.

Recent work within perpetrator studies employing elements of posthumanism includes studies by Clegg et al. (2012, 2013) and Cunha et al. (2014, 2015) of the Cambodian genocide. There, Clegg, Cunha, and their colleagues explore how everyday objects like books, chairs, uniforms, walls, and weapons work to A) "authorize" violence by legitimizing its ideological basis, B) "make sense" of and give meaning to violence for individual perpetrators, and C) "enable" violence by perpetrators by providing both the means for its use and specific "scripts" for perpetrators to follow. In a similar vein, I have explored the perpetration of torture through posthumanist approaches, developing a "non-purposeful" account of the emergence of this form of political violence in which material objects and natural environments play a central role in suggesting the possibility of torture to acting human subjects (Austin 2016b, 2017a, 2017b, 2019b). In particular, I trace how the circulation of material objects is especially important in contributing to the "standardization" of specific techniques of perpetration (e.g., waterboarding) across borders and state type. Others have drawn on similar approaches to explore the role of material agency in developing drone warfare (Leander 2013; Kindervater 2017), germ warfare (du Plessis 2017), concentration camps (Netz 2004; Meiches 2015), and beyond (c.f.: Bousquet et al. 2017).

Perpetrators and Posthumanism in Action

To see the value of posthumanism for Perpetrator Studies, we can now turn to a second "real world" example that is more typical in its contours for the field than gun control in the United

States necessarily is. Consider the following US soldier's description of a prisoner he detained "in the field" during the occupation of Iraq who was:

> Bound to a chair and interrogated. During the course of the interrogation the team beat him, shocked him at various places on his body with the electrical cord torn from a lamp. That technique was suggested by a squad member who claimed to have seen it used in a movie.
>
> *(Tsukayama 2014, 186)*

This single short example contains evidence of at least *three* ways in which material objects both make perpetration (of torture, in this case) possible and—indeed—produce the figure of the perpetrator. In the remainder of this text, I focus on these three elements, which are most commonly employed within "pragmatist" approaches to posthumanism (including Actor-Network Theory and variants of assemblage theory[5]). Nonetheless, most posthumanist approaches would agree with their relevance even where they also identify a multitude of other "agentic" effects of the nonhuman.[6] The three "effects" of nonhuman agents found in the above example are: 1) the (pre)scripting of human behavior through the presence of non human objects, 2) the global "circulation" of and "convergence" in violent practices across borders through the ways material objects move, and 3) the affective "compelling" of violence by nonhuman objects. Abstractly, these will seem unclear. Taking the example of the US soldier cited above and other examples, I will therefore now unpack each of these effects in turn.

Prescripting Perpetration

Seemingly innocuous little objects like lamps can lay out "scripts" for human behavior in particular settings. Within Actor-Network Theory, this process is described as occurring through the socio-technical "black-boxing" of different "capacities" (c.f. DeLanda 2016) in material objects (Brown and Capdevila 1999; Barron 2003). Put simply, the idea here is that any material object, especially those that are more technologically advanced, represents a degree of "congealed labor" compressed into material form: these objects "do things" that would otherwise require the work of (usually) many human beings to achieve (Latour 1999, 189). Speed bumps on roads, for example, reduce excessive speeding by motorists and prevent accidents, without the need for the police to be present. In doing so, they *de facto* "replace" the labor of the police in this respect.

In our opening example, a group of US soldiers used electrical torture on a prisoner based on the ways that one soldier had previously become aware of or been "subjectified" towards the possibility of modifying an everyday lamp for that purpose through a cinematic frame of reference. Much as a chair prescripts our behavior in certain ways—a chair is for sitting down on—so everyday objects can equally prompt violent repertories of actions within human minds: scripting particular ways of perpetrating violations of human rights or humanitarian law. In the case of the lamp, this object contains the capacity to harm individuals (electricity), the tools needed to apply that harm (wires, cables), and—most importantly—is already available in everyday rooms, including the one you are sitting in. Whereas, in the past (i.e., the Inquisition), torture was most frequently employed through the use of objects *designed* for that purpose (i.e., any of the objects found in a macabre "Torture Museum"), today the labor needed to torture is congealed in everyday objects, which "suggest" their use in these ways when human beings have knowledge of that capacity (i.e., through movies) (Austin 2016b).

Take another example. In my own interviews with Syrian perpetrators of torture, a man named *Ali* was describing to me the use of an AK-47-variant assault rifle to carry out the torture technique known in the Middle East as the *falaqa*, which involves the immobilization of the victim's feet and their whipping (Edston 2009). In this case, the immobilization of the feet was achieved with the AK-47 rifle, which provides a "brace" on which the victim's feet can be laid and raised up, held on either side by two perpetrators, whilst a third whips the feet. *Ali* described the use of the AK-47 for this purpose thus:

> You see how good this tool is? *It tells you what to do?* Once you've played a game or seen it on TV or something ... that's how it works. Even for you! I've seen the *falaqa* used like this before. When we were training [after conscription to the Syrian army], they [higher rank soldiers] used it against us, and—well—this is just a children's punishment here. We've seen it on TV, everywhere ... That's how we know, I guess.[7]

Material objects like rifles, *Ali* suggest here, *tell people what to do*. They provide a repertoire of scripts for perpetrators that can be drawn upon at moments of violence and so order the particular direction in which violent abuse moves, without a great deal of human deliberation. In order to see how this precisely occurs, however, we now also need to look more precisely at how men like *Ali* or that aforementioned soldier become slowly "subjectified" towards these possibilities in different ways.

Circulating Perpetration

The preceding example of the use of a lamp to torture a body reflects a second aspect of importance in considering the role of material objects in perpetration: *circulation*. That US soldier came to be aware of the possibility of using a lamp for torture through motion pictures. In other cases, individuals become aware of how to torture through novels, comic books, children's games, sporting rituals, etc.: a host of different representational artifacts whose purpose was not originally to disseminate information on torture (Rejali 2007; Austin 2016b, 2017a). What is critical to understand about these representational artifacts, and the way they integrate material objects (e.g., lamps), is that they circulate freely across time and space. In the terms of Bruno Latour (2005, 207–216), these objects are "circulating subjectifiers" that allow knowledge of "how to" perpetrate violence to circulate through our normal lives. And these circulating subjectifiers have led—in posthumanist thought—to a certain "convergence" in the types of violence seen across the world (Keeley 1996; Rejali 2007; Austin 2016b; Austin and Bocco 2017). Torture, for example, occurs in strikingly similar ways across the world: US soldiers can be found using *precisely* the same techniques of harm in Guantanamo Bay as North Korean soldiers employ, without any direct cooperation in their work (Austin 2016b, 3–4).

The ways in which material objects (whether lamps, movies, or novels) circulate prescriptions for perpetration across borders has become increasingly important given that most forms of violent abuse are *not* trained for (Rejali 2007). It is through these material conditions of possibility, instead, that most people learn "how to" perpetrate abusive violence.

Take another example to affirm this point. In the Northern Iraqi town of Sulaymaniyah lies an abandoned prison. That prison—now converted into a museum—contains a bare set of rooms filled with a few objects, here and there: chairs, tables, hooks, etc. One object (depicted in Figure 14.1) is of particular interest. This object is a military field telephone, which has a rather interesting history. The development of small and portable field radios

Figure 14.1 An M-63 Field Telephone used for torture found at the Amna Suraka Prison in Sulaymaniyah, Iraq, author's photograph.

was central to opening up the possibility of rapid military mobilities. Like many such objects—the jerrycan, the rifle, the armored vehicle—its advantages as a warfaring ally were quickly realized across the world. The result was imitation. In the former Yugoslavia, a small manufacturing company named *Iskra Mehanizmi* was tasked with developing a variant of the US military TA-314 series field telephones. They created the M-63 Field Telephone.[8] Circuitously, the telephone reached Iraq at an unknown date, alongside thousands of Kalashnikov rifles and other equipment imported from Eastern Europe. Having arrived in Iraq, the object led several lives. It was involved in the everyday military operations of the Baathist state. But it also coordinated the movement of Iraqi forces during the Anfal Genocide and—eventually—enabled the use of electrical torture against the bodies of thousands of Kurds in Sulaymaniyah over many years. It became—without any purpose or design—a prominent and in fact globalized tool of torture.

The possibility of using field telephones like these for electrical torture seems to have first been discovered by the French in colonial-era Algeria (Rejali 2001). Shortly, the procedure would reach Vietnam where US forces orchestrated what they euphemistically termed "Bell Telephone Hours" that precisely echoed the methods of the French (Burke 2004, 110). From there, the procedure traveled to Iraq and far beyond. Indeed, the procedure even returned to the domestic sphere of the United States. One veteran of Vietnam named Jon Burge, for example, later became a Chicago police detective who was accused of, in 1985, torturing an African American named Leonard Hinton (Conroy 2005). Hinton described going underground to a basement where "his hands were handcuffed above his head, his pants and shorts were pulled down, his ankles were handcuffed ... " and then:

> The officer with the moustache and with the glasses with the black hair, he came in with a rod, and one was carrying a box, a black box … There was a cord to the long rod … The handle on it was black and they plugged the wire into the box … Then they put something in my mouth … it was cloth … and they tied it so I couldn't holler … Then they took the rod, long part, and they placed it under my genitals … [It was] a pain out of this world. I couldn't describe it … They said, "Are you ready to talk yet?" The other said, "I don't think he's ready to talk yet." He hit me with it again. […] Then … he touched it in the crack of my rectum … Then he took that [cloth] out of my mouth. I said, "I am ready to talk. Tell me what you want me to say, sir. Please stop."
>
> *(Conroy 2005)*

The circulation of electrical torture has depended precisely on the way that its conditions for possibility (its "congealed labor") are compressed into little boxes like field radios or *Tasers* and the knowledge of how to use these devices for harm is spread through films, novels, and other representational artifacts. These objects circulate freely across borders and generally do so quite legitimately but in doing so also carry the capacity and knowledge to perpetrate torture.

Compelling Perpetration

The prescripting and circulating of perpetration through material objects, as described above, relates at its most basic level to the way that nonhuman things can "suggest," "hint," or "whisper" the possibility of violence to individuals. But nonhuman objects can also do more than that: sometimes they can directly *compel* violence. Consider the following example:

> The environment here is completely different. It's like living in the Wild West or something—the normal rules don't seem to apply. For example, here we kill people for driving too close to us, so I guess soldiers figure what's the big deal about a restraint chair or double litters, after all "it's still a lot better than what Saddam was doing to them."
>
> *(Keller 2007, 55)*

These words come from a US Soldier—Michael Keller—who was stationed in Abu Ghraib *after* the revelations of torture there became public. Keller is justifying the use of a "restraint chair" and/or "double litters" (two stretchers placed underneath and on top of a detainee with weight placed on the top to compress the body) based on the "completely different" world he had come to live in. In this case, certain material objects (chairs or stretchers) contain scripts for violence that individuals like Keller became aware of through various circulating subjectifiers. However, when then placed in a particular "situation" or "taskscape" (the "Wild West") (Ingold 2000; Collins 2007) that incorporates various human and nonhuman elements, these factors then worked to *compel* violence by creating a different world without any "normal rules." They not only made violence possible but worked to *make it happen.*

Nonhuman objects, environments, and phenomena can thus "compel" violence based on the ways they are collectively assembled in certain environments. In the terms of posthumanist theory, this relates to the "assemblage" or "actor-network" that is relationally constructed around acting human beings (DeLanda 2016). These assemblages construct situations that place certain stresses or pressures on human beings—the fear of death, emotions of anger and fear, etc.—that force them to do "something." In a situation in which "something must be done" (e.g., "state of emergency"), nonhuman objects and their scripts for action can directly compel violence by providing a straightforward and immediately available path to take. Indeed, most firsthand accounts from torturers stress the lack of "choice" they had in their actions along these lines.[9]

In circumstances like these, direct human choice or purposefulness becomes less salient, as the precise direction in which humans act is at least partially affectively delegated to non-human circumstances. Here, then: "responsibility for action must be shared among the various [inter]actants" found in a particular situation (Latour 1999, 170). A helpful analogy can be drawn here with police shootings in the United States, which will help "de-dramatize" our claims by distancing us from the socio-political complexities of torture. In one recent police shooting, an African-American man named Charles Kinsey was non-fatally shot by police while assisting an autistic man whom police incorrectly feared was holding a gun and had thus surrounded. Kinsey recounts:

> I thought it was a mosquito bite, and when it hit me I had my hands in the air, and I'm thinking, "I just got shot!" I'm saying, "Sir, why did you shoot me?", and his words to me were, "I don't know."
>
> *(Chappell 2016)*

The policeman who shot Kinsey is reported as also having been asked by another officer, "Why did you shoot this guy?," to which the shooter replied again, "I don't know" (Bagg 2016). This immediate assertion by perpetrators of a lack of knowledge of "why" they carried out their acts (whatever they might say later in the court room) reflects the ways in which particular "situations" in which violence occurs are filled with nonhuman elements that affectively compel violence without cognitive deliberation (Austin and Bocco 2017). Indeed, within both this story and that of the US soldier with which we opened, we find 1) a situation that affectively "cues" violence, 2) material objects with the capacity to be used for violence (the gun, the lamp) and which suggests a particular script for how to perpetrate violence; and 3) scripts for violence derived from a popular-cultural representative artifacts (movies, notions of the "hard" police officer, etc.). Indeed, to return to our earlier example of the use of a lamp to carry out electrical torture, that particular story comes from an individual who was initiated into these events entirely by "surprise" (Tsukayama 2014, 162). He was—before going to Iraq—an ordinary individual who became a torturer to a great degree through the posthuman dynamics described herein. The consequences for his self-worth and psyche were substantial: he describes how, whilst in Iraq and after his return to the United States, he "kept telling [him]self it was somebody else [who tortured], it wasn't me ... I just kept believing that it was somebody else that did it," because "I ... thought that they [second person] were a monster. (Pause) That that person had no place back in the States. I had no place back in the States" (Ibid: 212).

The Importance of Considering Posthumanism

As mentioned earlier, the three preceding posthuman insights into the perpetration of violence only scratch the surface of the more extended ontological and epistemological claims made by posthumanist thought.[10] But they provide a good grounding for beginning to think about how posthumanism can connect to Perpetrator Studies in very concrete terms. Nonetheless, challenges specific to Perpetrator Studies do exist in employing posthumanist thought, which we must now touch upon. Indeed, one quite strong objection to thinking in posthuman terms about perpetrators will likely be immediately obvious from this discussion: the question of accountability and responsibility. Integrating posthumanist thought into the study of political violence seems to risk diluting our capacity to attribute responsibility to individual perpetrators, those who enabled them, and the broader society in which they emerged. The suggestion that nonhuman objects prescribe, circulate, and compel the perpetration of political violence can appear to denude human beings of agency and, so, our ability to "judge" right and wrong in particular circumstances.

This concern is real and important. However, a strong distinction must be made between more theoretical and sociological accountings of perpetration and the distinct concerns of legal or political thinking about perpetrators (Austin and Bocco 2017; Austin 2019a). Posthuman forms of sociological accounting are fundamentally about complexifying our understanding of how events happen in the world (Law 2004). The approach provides a set of "terms and sensitivities" that allow us to deepen our understanding of how perpetration happens by incorporating the nonhuman (Mol 2011). And the importance of this task lies in the simple fact that despite the vast array of more humanist accountings for the perpetration of violence in the literature, the figure of the perpetrator continues to escape our full understanding and—moreover—the perpetration of innumerable crimes only continues in human history. Seeking a deeper posthuman understanding of perpetration is—thus—just one further effort to better understand this most pressing of human concerns, perhaps for the benefit of all society.

Indeed, and to conclude, there are therefore at least three good reasons for incorporating the philosophy, theory, and sociology of posthumanism into Perpetrator Studies more widely. The first relates to the general significance that both victims and perpetrators of violence attribute to nonhuman objects. In the aftermath of the Argentine "Dirty War," for example, the names for innumerable everyday objects—barbecues, tickets, trucks, egg cartons, etc.—have all now become inescapably linked to particular practices of violence (respectively, the burning of dead bodies, the sign of imminent execution, the means used to transport prisoners for execution, the sound-proofing used on the walls of torture chambers) (Feitlowitz 1998). Indeed, accounts of the perpetration of violence are suffused with references to nonhuman objects and their distortion towards causing pain (Scarry 1985). Incorporating posthumanist thought allows us to better understand the role of these objects and thus their significance both during and *after* periods of violence have occurred.

Secondly, posthumanist approaches deepen our understanding of the emergence of violence by—perhaps paradoxically—dramatically *humanizing* the figure of the perpetrator. If the approach reveals, quite often, that perpetrators are "compelled" into their acts by the different human and nonhuman elements that make up particular situations, then we gain a deeper understanding of the powerlessness that many perpetrators have attested to across the course of history. This may make some uneasy, of course (Austin, 2019b). The third, and perhaps most important reason, relates to what many feel must remain an overarching goal of Perpetrator Studies: moving explanation and understanding towards *preventing* the emergence of perpetrators. If posthuman approaches can show that the non-human environments in which violence occurs are contributory factors in encouraging perpetration, then we open up a quite new avenue through which to consider possibilities for preventing the emergence of perpetrators by altering those material environments (Austin 2016a, Austin 2019b).

Notes

1 For a review of these approaches see Wolfe (2010).
2 It is very important to note that posthumanist thought is explicitly *not* about effacing the human subject as of central importance to understanding the workings of the world, as certain *anti-*

humanist approaches suggest. Instead, and as this discussion stresses throughout, posthumanism only "displaces" human subjects from the *center* of sociological accounting (avoiding placing any particular subject at such a center). For a full discussion here, see Pickering (1993, 1995).

3 For descriptions of these examples see *inter alia* Soekkha (1997), Sivak and Tsimhoni (2008).

4 The notion of nonhuman objects possessing agency is controversial. At its most minimal level, posthumanism uses this term merely to focus on the fact that material objects "make-difference" on human beings, although others are far more radical in their interpretations. See, for discussions, Sayes (2014), Pickering (2001).

5 On Actor Network Theory, see Latour (2005), Mol (2011), Law (2009), and on assemblage theory, see DeLanda (2016), Coyne (2008).

6 For a good introductory review of these alternative effects, see Wolfe (2010).

7 Interview conducted by the author in Beirut, Lebanon. Names of respondents are anonymized. For full details on these interviews see Austin (2016b, 2017a).

8 See https://tinyurl.com/ycu29554.

9 For examples see (Keller 2007; Lagouranis 2007; National Defense Intelligence College 2006; Tsukayama 2014).

10 For further reading here, see the references throughout the paper, and/or for a good introduction, see Wolfe (2010).

References

Arendt, Hannah. 1958. *The Human Condition*. Chicago: The University of Chicago Press.

Arendt, Hannah. 1963. *Eichmann in Jerusalem*. New York: The Viking Press.

Austin, Jonathan Luke. 2016a. *The Germination of Abusive Violence and Its Restraint*. Geneva: The Violence Prevention Initiative.

Austin, Jonathan Luke. 2016b. "Torture and the Material-Semiotic Networks of Violence across Borders." *International Political Sociology* 10(1): 3–21.

Austin, Jonathan Luke. 2017a. *Small Worlds of Violence: A Global Grammar for Torture*. Geneva: Graduate Institute Geneva.

Austin, Jonathan Luke. 2017b. "We Have Never Been Civilized: Torture and the Materiality of World Political Binaries." *European Journal of International Relations* 23(1): 49–73. 10.1177/1354066115616466.

Austin, Jonathan Luke. 2019a. "A Parasitic Critique for International Relations." *International Political Sociology* 13(2): 215–231. 10.1093/ips/oly032.

Austin, Jonathan Luke. 2019b. "Towards an International Political Ergonomics." *European Journal of International Relations* 25(4): 979–1006.

Austin, Jonathan Luke & Riccardo Bocco. 2017. "Becoming a Torturer: Towards a Global Ergonomics of Care." *International Review of the Red Cross* 901.

Bagg, Marissa. 2016. "New Video Shows Moments Before and After Man Was Shot by North Miami Police Officer." *NBC Miami*, July 21.

Barad, Karen. 2003. "Posthumanist Performativity: Toward an Understanding of How Matter Comes to Matter." *Signs: Journal of Women in Culture and Society* 28(3): 801–831.

Barad, Karen. 2007. *Meeting the Universe Halfway: Quantum Physics and the Entanglement of Matter and Meaning*. Durham: Duke University Press.

Barron, Colin. 2003. "A Strong Distinction between Humans and Non-Humans is No Longer Required for Research Purposes: A Debate between Bruno Latour and Steve Fuller." *History of the Human Sciences* 16(2): 77–99.

Berkowitz, Leonard & Anthony Lepage. 1967. "Weapons as Aggression-eliciting Stimuli." *Journal of Personality and Social Psychology* 7(2): 202–207.

Bousquet, Antoine, Jarius Grove, & Nina Shah. 2017. "Becoming Weapon: An Open Call to Arms." *Critical Studies on Security* 5(1): 1–8.

Brown, Steven D. & Rose Capdevila. 1999. "Perpetuum Mobile: Substance, Force and the Sociology of Translation." In *Actor Network Theory and After*, edited by John Law and John Hassard, 26–50. Oxford: Blackwell Publishers.

Browning, Christopher R. 1993. *Ordinary Men: Reserve Police Battalion 101 and the Final Solution in Poland*. London: HarperCollins.

Burke, Carol. 2004. *Camp All-American, Hanoi Jane, and the High-and-tight: Gender, Folklore, and Changing Military Culture*. New York: Beacon Press.
Chappell, Bill. 2016. "North Miami Officer Was Aiming At Man With Autism, Union Chief Says." *National Public Radio*.
Clegg, Stewart R., Miguel Pina Cunha, & Armenio Rego. 2012. "The Theory and Practice of Utopia in a Total Institution: The Pineapple Panopticon." *Organization Studies* 33(12): 1735–1757.
Clegg, Stewart R., Miguel Pina Cunha, Armenio Rego, & Joana Dias. 2013. "Mundane Objects and the Banality of Evil: The Sociomateriality of a Death Camp." *Journal of Management Inquiry* 22(3): 325–340.
Collins, Randall. 2007. *Violence: A Micro-Sociological Theory*. Princeton: Princeton University Press.
Conroy, John. 2005. "Tools of Torture." *Chicago Reader*, February 3.
Coyne, Richard. 2008. "The Net Effect: Design, the Rhizome, and Complex Philosophy." *Futures* 40: 552–561.
Cunha, Miguel Pina, Stewart Clegg, & Armenio Rego. 2014. "The Ethical Speaking of Objects: The 'Object-Ive' World of Young Khmer Rouge Combatants." *Journal of Political Power* 7(1): 35–61.
Cunha, Miguel Pina, Stewart Clegg, Armenio Rego, & Jorge F.S. Gomes. 2015. "Embodying Sensemaking: Learning from the Extreme Case of Vann Nath, Prisoner at S-21." *European Management Review* 12: 41–58.
DeLanda, Manuel. 2016. *Assemblage Theory*. Edinburgh: Edinburgh University Press.
du Plessis, Gitte. 2017. "War Machines Par Excellence: The Discrepancy Between Threat and Control in the Weaponisation of Infectious Agents." *Critical Studies on Security* 5(1): 45–61.
Edston, Erik. 2009. "The Epidemiology of Falanga." *Torture* 19(1): 27–32.
Feitlowitz, Marguerite. 1998. *A Lexicon of Terror: Argentina and the Legacies of Torture*. Oxford: Oxford University Press.
Gino, Francesca & Sreedhari D. Desai. 2012. "Memory Lane and Morality: How Childhood Memories Promote Prosocial Behavior." *Journal of Personality and Social Psychology* 102(4): 743–758.
Hansen, Mark. 2000. *Embodying Technesis: Technology beyond Writing*. Ann Arbor: The University of Michigan Press.
Haraway, Donna. 1988. "Situated Knowledges: The Science Question in Feminism and the Privilege of Partial Perspective." *Feminist Studies* 14(3): 575–599.
Haraway, Donna J. 2016. *Staying with the Trouble*. New York: Duke University Press.
Harman, Graham. 2002. *Tool-Being: Heidegger and the Metaphysics of Objects*. Peru, IL: Open Court.
Harman, Graham. 2005. *Guerrilla Metaphysics: Phenomenology and the Carpentry of Things*. Peru, IL: Open Court.
Harman, Graham. 2007. "The Importance of Bruno Latour." *Cultural Studies Review* 13(1): 31–49.
Harman, Graham. 2016. *Immaterialism*. London: Polity.
Hayles, Katherine N. 1999. *How We Became Posthuman: Virtual Bodies in Cybernetics, Literature, and Informatics*. Chicago: The University of Chicago Press.
Huggins, Martha, Mika Haritos-Fatouros, & Phillip G. Zimbardo. 2002. *Violence Workers: Police Torturers and Murderers Reconstruct Brazilian Atrocities*. Berkeley, CA: University of California Press.
Ingold, Tim. 2000. *The Perception of the Environment: Essays on Livelihood, Dwelling and Skill*. London: Routledge.
Keeley, Lawrence H. 1996. *War before Civilization: The Myth of the Peaceful Savage*. Oxford: Oxford University Press.
Keller, Michael. 2007. *Torture Central: Emails from Abu Ghraib*. New York: iUniverse, Inc.
Kindervater, Katherine Hall. 2017. "The Technological Rationality of the Drone Strike." *Critical Studies on Security* 5(1): 28–44.
Lagouranis, Tony. 2007. *Fear Up Harsh: An Army Interrogator's Dark Journey through Iraq*. London: Penguin.
Latour, Bruno. 1999. *Pandora's Hope: Essays on the Reality of Science Studies*. Cambridge, MA: Harvard University Press.
Latour, Bruno. 2005. *Reassembling the Social: An Introduction to Actor-Network Theory*. Oxford: Oxford University Press.
Law, John. 2004. *After Method: Mess in Social Science Research*. London: Routledge.
Law, John. 2009. "Actor Network Theory and Material Semiotics." In *The New Blackwell Companion to Social Theory*, edited by Bryan S. Turner, 141–158. London: Blackwell.
Leander, Anna. 2013. "Technological Agency in the Co-Constitution of Legal Expertise and the US Drone Program." *Leiden Journal of International Law* 26(4): 811–831.

Meiches, Benjamin. 2015. "A Political Ecology of the Camp." *Security Dialogue* 46(5): 476–492.
Milgram, Stanley. 1963. "Behavioral Study of Obedience." *The Journal of Abnormal and Social Psychology* 67(4): 371–378.
Mol, Annemarie. 2011. "Actor-Network Theory: Sensitive Terms and Enduring Tensions." *Kölner Zeitschrift fur Soziologie und Sozialpsychologie* 50(1): 253–269.
National Defense Intelligence College. 2006. *Educing Information, Interrogation: Science and Art.* Washington: National Defense Intelligence College.
Netz, Reviel. 2004. *Barbed Wire: An Ecology of Modernity.* Middletown: Wesleyan University Press.
Pickering, Andrew. 1993. "The Mangle of Practice: Agency and Emergence in the Sociology of Science." *American Journal of Sociology* 99(3): 559–589.
Pickering, Andrew. 1995. *The Mangle of Practice: Time, Agency, and Science.* Chicago: The University of Chicago Press.
Pickering, Andrew. 2001. "Practice and Posthumanism: Social Theory and a History of Agency." In *The Practice Turn in Contemporary Theory*, edited by Theodore R Schatzki, Karin Knorr-Cetina and Elike Von Savigny, 172–183. London: Routledge.
Rejali, Darius. 2001. "Electric Torture: A Global History of a Torture Technology." *Connect: art.politics.theory.practice* (June 2001): 101–109.
Rejali, Darius. 2007. *Torture and Democracy.* Princeton: Princeton University Press.
Sayes, Edwin. 2014. "Actor-Network Theory and methodology: Just what does it mean to say that non-humans have agency?" *Social Studies of Science* 44(1): 134–149.
Scarry, Elaine. 1985. *The Body in Pain: The Making and Unmaking of the World.* Oxford: Oxford University Press.
Sivak, Michael & Omer Tsimhoni. 2008. "Improving Traffic Safety: Conceptual Considerations for Successful Action." *Journal of Safety Research* 39: 453–457.
Soekkha, Hans M. 1997. *Aviation Safety: Human Factors.* AH Zeist: VSP.
Stengers, Isabelle. 1997. *Power and Invention: Situating Science.* Minneapolis: University of Minnesota Press.
Stengers, Isabelle. 2010. *Cosmopolitics.* Minneapolis: University of Minnesota Press.
Tsukayama, John K. 2014. *By Any Means Necessary: An Interpretive Phenomenological Analysis Study of Post 9/11 American Abusive Violence in Iraq.* St Andrews, UK: Unpublished PhD Dissertation.
Wolfe, Cary. 2010. *What is Posthumanism?* Minneapolis: University of Minnesota Press.
Zimbardo, Phillip G. 2007. *The Lucifer Effect: Understanding How Good People Turn Evil.* New York: Random House.

15

Notes on the Subaltern

Or, How Postcolonial Critique Meets the Perpetrator

rashné limki

Let me begin with an image: the body of a child, drained of life and color. Its mouth slightly parted; white, unblinking spots where there were once, perhaps, seeing eyes. Its torso—broken flesh, broken bone—encased in broken stone.[1]

Then the story: December 3rd, 1984. The populace of the city Bhopal in central India is gassed with twenty-seven tons of methyl isocyanate that leaked from a pesticide factory: "It felt like somebody had filled our bodies up with red chillies, our eyes tears coming out, noses were watering, we had froth in our mouths" (Champa Devi Shukla, quoted by International Campaign for Justice in Bhopal 2014). Within 24 hours, this city-turned-gas-chamber claims over 2,000 lives, devastated over 150,000 bodies, thousands of which were—which *are*—yet to be born. The next morning, a father buries his child. "Unable to bear the thought of never seeing her again," we are told, "he brushed away the dirt for one last look."

The catastrophe in Bhopal has been described as an act of corporate killing (Jones 1988), the effect of a moral disregard for socioeconomically subjugated populations (Fortun 2000; Mukherjee 2010). Thus, the image represents not only the violation of a particular child but also the many bodies similarly devastated and those yet awaiting this fate. The destruction of the body, the irruption of organic matter, visible in the image, then, speaks the singular and historical act of killing. To think the event as such (i.e., as killing) evokes the question of perpetration. That is, it compels us to ask after the performers and performance of acts of injury. Following this line of inquiry, some studies of Bhopal have produced a detailed account of particular actors, corporate and political, involved in the variety of decisions that precipitated the leak, thereby tracing a line between doer(s) and deed (cf. Ali 1987; Chouhan et al. 1994). Others have taken a broader view, seeking to historicize the event through a consideration of the sociopolitical and economic particularities that engendered the event (cf. Guillette 2008; Shrivastava 1987). To be sure, each of these approaches is concerned with the question of accountability, not merely for the purpose of redress but also for thinking through the possibilities of preventing similar disasters in the future. Yet, evaluations of accountability are contingent upon the location of agency—whether within individual or structural contexts—so that investigations of perpetration are concerned, in fact, with agency as the condition of possibility for the act.

In this chapter, I interrogate the significance of agency in contexts such as Bhopal. In particular, I focus on Bhopal as activity against the subaltern and outline the implications of asking the question of perpetratorship therein. Insofar as Perpetrator Studies is concerned with the figure of the perpetrator, it assumes the agency of a self-knowing subject whose performative capacity is embedded in particular ethico-political rationalities (cf. Feldman 1991). Moreover, given that scenes of violation are constituted through the triangulation of subject, object, and act, the rationale that describes agency simultaneously describes its object. For instance, in the case of Bhopal, the rationalization of agency lies between the poles of economic fundamentalism[2] and economic and political expediency.[3] Accordingly, the victims of the leak are either ill-fated objects of rescue or expendable objects of contempt.

Within the contemporary global regime of human rights, the latter description seems inadmissible, so the figure of the perpetrator is approached as a transgressor against an established moral order. Yet, the image of the child, I suggest, is a representation not merely of transgression but, more crucially, of repetition. That is, as I will argue in this chapter, where perpetration as transgression signifies a wrongful *rupture* in the moral order; the perpetration of violence against subaltern bodies is part of an ongoing history of killing, one whose rationality flows from the description of the subaltern as expendable. Thus, acts of violence against subaltern bodies are a repetition of killing as *constitutive* of the moral order.

Understanding violence against the subaltern as such requires us to re-think approaches to perpetration. In order to do so, I will introduce the figure of the subaltern and outline how postcolonial studies can contribute to the encounter between Perpetrator Studies and the subaltern. Thereafter, I will use the concept of agential separability to critique our (possible) investments—as witness/researcher/writer—in the figure of the perpetrator and acts of perpetration, especially in relation to the violation of subaltern bodies.

I begin, however, with a brief outline of the imperative to re-think approaches to perpetration.

Re-encountering Perpetrator Studies

As already noted, Perpetrator Studies generally seeks to address the figure of the perpetrator and to comprehend the conditions that facilitated associated acts of perpetration. This approach tends towards the evental wherein historical consideration focuses largely upon the context for the acts rather than their own historicity. To consider the historicity of an act is to recognize not only its material but also its onto-epistemic lineage. Such an approach would necessitate a shift away from the figure of the perpetrator towards the signifying effects of perpetration. In particular, it requires a rethinking of the relation between doer and deed. Most accounts of agency posit a causal relation between doer and deed, wherein the doer is imagined separate from, and prior to, the deed. This description of agency follows from the notion of action as an effect of will.

Contrary to this view, Nietzsche's oft-cited critique of agency asserts that "there is no 'being' behind the doing, acting, becoming" he writes, "'the doer' has simply been added to the deed by the imagination—*the doing is everything*" (1956, 178–79; added emphasis). This follows from his postulation of will not as an effect of reason (as per Kant) but as "simply a matter of commanding and obeying, on the groundwork … of a society constructed out of many 'souls'" (2002, 20; see also, 1956, 190–91). Here, soul is a "subject-multiplicity" or "a society *constructed out of drives and affects*" (2002, 14; added emphasis). Thus, Nietzsche views the idea of will as that which "merely captures the idea that mental entities have an urge to be realized" (Risse 2007, 65). All activity, then, is simply actualization.

For Nietzsche, the agent is not the source of an act but is rather a rationalizing myth that *serves the purpose* of identifying a contemporaneous origin or source of injury. As such, the appending of doer to deed is an effect of the law of contract that requires a responsible subject in order to dispense punishment for the infliction of suffering (1956, 194–98). This approach to agency as invention signals a rejection of the Kantian notion of morality as a system of *a priori* principles, the understanding and abiding of which are imperative for the ethical (or human) subject. Instead, Nietzsche argues, "morality [must be] understood as *a doctrine of the power relations* under which the phenomenon of 'life' arises" (2002, 20; added emphasis). That is, morality is a system of ends, one that seeks to formalize the subjugation of certain affects and drives that, through a dominating power, come to be described as evil to others that come to be described as good. It is through this dynamic of valorization that the appearances of an ideal life and moral world are created. It is also, therefore, within this context alone that any interpretation of activity and ascription of accountability becomes possible.

If we accept this proposition, then focusing on the figure of the perpetrator and the singularity of perpetration inhibits our ability (1) to interrogate the historicity of the moral framework that evaluates action as perpetration and (2) to comprehend perpetration as a historical force, or drive, that produces the world as we perceive it. A concern, instead, with the signifying effects of perpetration would provide insight into the creation of the contemporary global moral order and the significance of the drives that have been suppressed therein, drives that are ultimately unleashed in perpetrative activity.

As already indicated, in this chapter I seek to approach violence against subaltern bodies, such as that evidenced in Bhopal, as iterative activity that rehearses their institution as expendable objects. If, as Nietzsche proposes, it is only a moralizing force that demands that the suppression of "bad" drives in relation to the "good," then it is this same force—the judgment of a moralistic order—that mistakenly anticipates the life of the subaltern and laments its death. I substantiate this proposition in the next section through an engagement with this figure. Thereafter, I propose postcolonial critique as a methodology that can help us approach perpetration as the actualization of the subaltern as expendable.

Encountering the Subaltern

In 1968, Union Carbide India Limited (UCIL) (a subsidiary of the US Union Carbide Corporation), set up its Pesticides and Formulations plant in Bhopal, at the behest of the Indian government. The development of this plant was in keeping with India's post-independence industrialization project intended towards economic growth and national prosperity. The choice of Bhopal as the site for this production facility was deliberate due to its status as a fledgling city and the capital of the relatively "undeveloped" state of Madhya Pradesh. Given this circumstance, the government required opportunities to expand employment as well as to create a confidence-building precedent that could attract greater foreign investment.

The state's push towards industrial growth was concomitant with the devalorization of traditional methods of agriculture, resulting in an economically untenable rural to urban migration. Indeed, a substantial portion of the communities outside the factory walls were made up of first- and second-generation migrants displaced from their rural communities by the imposition of mechanized agriculture (Mukherjee 2010). These people, who were lured to urban areas for the economic betterment promised by the state's development visions, settled in colonies outside the factory "without papers." This precarious situation coerced a silence that they hoped would protect them from evacuation by the city (Chouhan et al. 1994).

Eventually, in order to improve its own image, UCIL distributed land deeds in these communities despite the fact that they had failed to establish the necessary safety zones. But the residents themselves had little idea that "the plant was producing one of the most dangerous compounds ever conceived by the chemical industry" (Guillette 2008, 174). In fact, a project manager for the plant described the development of this project as "analogous to planting a bomb near where people live and children play" (Fortun 2001, 117).

The pain and suffering that unfolded in the aftermath of the Bhopal gas leak epitomize the experience of suffering as "actively created and distributed by the social order itself" (Das 1995, 138). Whether it be the physical pain described by survivors like Champa Devi Shukla (quoted above) or the spectacular representation of pain on the child's body in Rai's image—each iteration is ultimately an embodied "stamp of the authority of society upon the docile bodies of its members" (1995, 138). That is, pain is the actualization of an originary onto-epistemic injury that instituted the subaltern within the economy of death. I substantiate this further by describing how the subaltern is constituted as a collection of traces.

An engagement with the figure of the subaltern may begin with a consideration of the Gramscian definition of subalternity as the condition of being subjugated by hegemonic power. Specifically, subalternity demarcates a political location that is sharply distinct from and in strong opposition to elite domination. Furthermore, this distinction may be understood as the basis for the formation of a unified subaltern identity and hence of collective action (cf. Guha 1981; Green 2010). Within the postcolonial, and specifically Indian, context, this description of the subaltern was appropriated by The Subaltern Studies Collective[4] in an endeavor to recuperate the historical agency of the underclasses—and the Indian peasant, in particular—from their suppression within colonial and national/ist historiography. Through this historicization, the work of the Collective came to record the mis-/displaced representations of the subaltern wrought by hegemonic (colonial and bourgeois nationalist) ideals. In so doing, these writings were able to present the subaltern as "that impossible thought, figure, or action without which the dominant discourse cannot exist and which is acknowledged in its subterfuges and stereotypes" (Prakash 1994, 1483). In other words, even though the writings of the Collective were committed to historical rectification and recovery, their account of the subaltern implicated the violent, and violating, itinerary of colonial, and ultimately "Western," power in absenting the subaltern. Their work thus anticipated the condition of the subaltern as trace.

The trace may be understood as the mark of an erasure enacted in the constitution of a given object (Derrida 1973, 1997). An object emerges *qua* object (i.e., functions as signifier) by entering into a "system of differences" (1973, 145). In particular, the object is structured through the erasure of all that is different or other. This is the condition of possibility for the appearance of objects as such. The trace, then, is the "silent mark" (1973, 132)—the mark of that which has been rendered absent, invisible—in the production of appearances. To be sure, this mark is contained, albeit elided, in the appearance, so that trace is, in fact, constitutive of the it. Indeed, the trace belongs to the structure of the object, it is that which "opens appearance and signification" (1997, 65).

The "postcolonial turn" in subaltern studies, and specifically the work of literary theorist Gayatri Chakravorty Spivak, takes up this notion of the trace to offer a critical description of the subaltern. While the Subaltern Studies Collective undertook to describe the historico-materialist erasure of the subaltern under colonialism, Spivak's work furthers this description through a consideration of the subaltern as an effect of onto-epistemic erasures. Specifically, she draws attention to the erasure of particular modes of existence that are the condition of possibility for the emergence of the human as phenomenon. As such, the subaltern is the mark of these erasures, indeed is "a site of unlisted traces" (1999, 6) that constitutes the human. Practically speaking, then, the subaltern appears as "a position without identity" constituted through an exclusion from "institutional [onto-epistemic and, hence, sociopolitical] infrastructure" (Spivak 2005, 476). This exclusion then renders the speech of the subaltern unhearable and its activity unrecognizable as such. Spivak's description of the subaltern thus recognizes this figure as an effect of onto-epistemic disappearance.

Now, in Derrida's view, the fidelity of an object is contingent upon the continued erasure (i.e., the guarantee of the non-exposure) of the trace. For the irruption of the trace would bring into crisis not only the coherence of the object as signifier but also its primacy in relation to its others.[5] Moreover, in the instance where a trace does become revealed, its constitution as object—as a nameable and knowable entity—always already effects new erasures. That is, insofar as the trace is the condition of possibility for the emergence of objects, the apparent liberation of a trace (i.e., making present that which is absented) always already entails further absenting.[6]

Following a Derridean phenomenology, then, I suggest that insofar as the subaltern is the trace that constitutes the human, the suppression of subalternity—its continued invisibility—is the condition of possibility for the appearance of humanity. Furthermore, the irruption of subalternity as disappeared difference always already threatens the signification and primacy of humanity. The perpetual material and epistemic effacement of the subaltern guarantees the ontological security of the human. As such, expendability is the essential characteristic—the ontological condition—of the subaltern.

Thus, in the case of contemporary activity against the subaltern, focus on the figure of the perpetrator as agent of injury elides both the originary and iterative violence. In order to remain faithful to the subaltern as trace, it is necessary to comprehend activity against the subaltern as an ongoing doing, the realization of an urge, albeit conditioned, to expunge subalternity to assure the unfolding of humanity. Killing, then, is merely the manifestation of a drive that realizes the subaltern as expendable. In the following section, I propose postcolonial critique as a methodology that facilitates this recognition.

The Methodology of Postcolonial Critique

Over three decades on, the chemical plant in Bhopal still stands as a toxic rem(a)inder of the events of 1984. Even as its after-effects continue to wreak havoc on the lives of survivors, Union Carbide Corporation (UCC, now Dow Chemicals) has been excused from formal liability for the leak. However, as an expression of moral responsibility,[7] UCC contributed approximately $130 million to various emergency, health, and vocational funds. During this period, it simultaneously argued against the litigation of any claims against it, especially within the US judicial system. This move was substantiated by assertions of an unresolvable "cultural difference" between India and the US, one that imputed deficient, indeed perverse, moral-cultural "values" (Fortun 2001).[8]

This circumstance had serious implications for any possibility of justice for the workers and residents of Bhopal. The presumed cultural deficiencies of survivors rendered them unreliable sources who produced exaggerated accounts of injury. Moreover, the inability of survivors to translate injury into scientific/medical language removed their own experiences and understanding from carrying juridical import, thereby subjugating self-knowledge to institutional claims to scientific and legal expertise (cf. Das 1995; Jasanoff 2007). Consequently, in a performance of moral duty, the Indian government and UCC undertook to negotiate a settlement under the principle of *parens patriae*. In so doing, they deprived victims of the leak the right to represent themselves and to opt out of proxy representation. Instead, the government viewed this curtailment of the rights as "[t]he appropriate response ... such that the largest good of the largest number is served. Justice, then, was a utilitarian quantification" (Fortun 2001, 40).

This circumstance epitomizes how, for the subaltern, every appearance is a disappearance. In the first instance, the subalternity of the survivors of Bhopal always already denied them the sociopolitical infrastructure required to be seen and heard (Spivak 2005). Moreover, absent access to this infrastructure, they lacked recognizable agency, where agency names "institutionally validated action, assuming collectivity" (2005, 475). This apparent lack of agency validated the state's paternalistic intervention. Moreover, in order to reclaim agency, it became necessary for survivors to "metonymize/synecdochize [themselves], understand the part by which [they were] connected to that abstract whole so that [they could] claim it" (2005, 483). This is evident in the requirement to narrate injury through the rational discourses of science and law. This refiguring of speech is the re-enactment of an originary erasure (i.e., the negation of any existential difference). In other words, in order to make themselves seeable and hearable, survivors had to disappear their onto-epistemic selves. Every appearance is a disappearance.

The repetition of epistemic pain evident herein is authorized by the juridical imperative to designate a "doer" and a "deed." That is, in order to arrogate accountability and provide redress, the state must identify a wrong doer—here, UCC—as the source of material injury—and indicate a wrongful act—here, negligence. Yet, material and epistemic pain are not related as cause and effect. Rather, given the ontological condition of the subaltern, material injury is merely the repetition of the originary onto-epistemic injury that produced the subaltern as the other of the human. Moreover, the ongoing onto-epistemic suppression of survivors rehearses the rendering of the subaltern as trace. The material and epistemic pain evidenced in Bhopal are thus entangled (i.e., they "lack an independent, self-contained existence") (Barad 2007, ix). As such, material and epistemic pain are not separate but can be made to appear as if separate (non-mutual) through the in(ter)vention of the figure of the perpetrator. More importantly, this apparent separation absents the epistemic violence inherent in material injury. In the next section, I will propose an underlying purpose for the investment in material injury and the associated imperative for accountability as it emerges in Perpetrator Studies. In this section, however, I focus on how postcolonial critique remains faithful to the subaltern by asserting the material and epistemic pain as entangled.

If colonialism names "the historical process whereby the 'West' attempts systematically to cancel or negate the cultural difference and value of the 'non-West'" (Gandhi 1998, 16), then postcolonial critique marks an opening towards these negations that approaches what is lost therein. Specifically, it signals an attentiveness to subjugations, or foreclosures, of particular modes of knowing and existence as effected by the universalizing of "Europe" i.e., the institution of a spatio-temporally specific ontoepistemology as world historical).

Consequently, postcolonial critique is the practice of traveling the "fault lines [of dominant discourse] in order to provide different accounts, to describe histories revealed in the cracks of the colonial archaeology of knowledge" (Prakash 1994, 1486). This archaeology entails an accounting of humanism, the fundamental proposition of Enlightenment that enabled the imposition of universality as the condition of onto-epistemic subjugation.

Colonial subjugation is the institution of native modes of existence and knowing as differentially human. In this context, postcolonial critique advances itself through anti-humanist contention.[9]

In particular, the method of postcolonial critique consists of historicizing the subaltern. To be sure, such historicization does not merely entail the rectification of and recovery from the edifice of history but rather necessitates a confrontation with "sites of legitimation and authorization" (Feldman 1991, 2) that suppress subalternity. Insofar as the figure of the human is designated as the agent of History, to historicize the subaltern is to ask after the historical practices that have foreclosed her from this phenomenon of the human. Below I engage Hortense Spillers' account of violence perpetrated against the African body under coloniality as an instance of such historicization.[10]

In her text "Mama's Baby, Papa's Maybe," Spillers notes that the African slave trade with/in the Americas is generally regarded as a case of "high crimes against the flesh" (1987, 67). Here, injury is seen to proceed through flesh in its "seared, divided, ripped-apartness, riveted to the ship's hole, fallen, or 'escaped' overboard" (1987, 67). Flesh, according to Spillers, is the primary medium through which the body is written as text—*before body there is flesh*—so that the violation of body is the disintegration of a text and thus the dissolution of person to mere matter. She explicates this circumstance as the "theft of the body" (1987, 67) that inaugurated the New World order. During the Middle Passage the body *qua* body is in suspension—dissolved of all its indigenous signification and produced as undifferentiated mass it awaits a new inscription—through name, identity, signification—that will be gained only upon reaching land at the other end (1987, 72). As such, the relation between body and person is severed through material violation from which follows the external imposition of meanings and uses. This represents a theft, a "severing of the captive body from motive will and desire" (1987, 67). Spillers' account of injury thus affirms how the instrument of torture, wielded by/for the slave master upon flesh, also effects onto-epistemic effacement.

Moreover, the distinction between body and flesh, according to Spillers, is the primary distinction between liberated and captive subject-positions. To wit, the black female body, as the objectified other, is produced through instruments of torture, through acts of material wounding. The markings of torture thus effected—what Spillers refers to as a "hieroglyphics of flesh"—become invisible once the body materializes within a cultural code organized through skin color. Yet, despite this invisibility, the hieroglyphs are transferred across generations so that the body, marked by color and other culturally identifiable determinants, remains vulnerable to "protocols of 'search and destroy'" enacted by and for the state (1987, 67). The liberation of the black female from captivity and her restoration as subject is thus always already an impossibility. Indeed, the unfolding of violation follows from the imperative to keep the black female body, and all that it has been made to signify, the absented presence—the trace—that constitutes humanity. All ongoing activity against this figure is a *historically authorized* doing of an originary material and onto-epistemic deed. All activity against the subaltern is thus a signifying performance.

Insofar as postcolonial critique recognizes these enactments as such, it demands an attentiveness to the historicity of perpetration, the replication of a practice exemplified in Spillers' account above. Such historicization reveals how the emergence of the subaltern and the subject as, respectively, external to and the objectification of the human are an effect of "a doctrine of the power relations" (Nietzsche 2002, 20). Indeed, these power relations effect, and are effected by, material practices that affirm a specific articulation of morality—one that posits the figure of the subaltern as ethically degraded and hence expendable. Consequently, postcolonial critique insists on recognizing acts of injury against the subaltern not as transgressions against, but instead as fundamental to, the contemporary moral order.

To comprehend activity against the subaltern through the figure of a perpetrator, then, is to fundamentally misapprehend her. Such readings of perpetration betray a faith in the moral order of liberal humanism, in the liberalized fiction of the human. Liberal humanism seeks to liberate the subaltern as trace—that is, to make forms of existence previously ejected from humanity appear as such. In other words, liberal humanism assumes the possibility of rendering the figure of the subaltern as subject. Only then can activity against the subaltern be held as immoral and/or unlawful, so that the designation of a perpetrator becomes viable. Yet, as evidenced above, the condition of possibility for the (institutional) appearance of the figure of the subaltern as a legible entity is its (onto-epistemic) disappearance. The subaltern, thus, is not an easily recuperable subject-position. Accordingly, one becomes compelled to ask what purpose a concern with the figure of the perpetrator and an ensuing demand for accountability serves in relation to activity against the subaltern.

In order to attempt a response, the final section of this chapter advances an ethical concern with the notion of agential separability.

Agential Separability: How Postcolonial Studies Meets the Perpetrator

The case of Bhopal, as outlined in this chapter, reveals how for the subaltern recuperation is the re-enactment of annihilation. The subaltern *qua* subaltern has no place within humanity; to make it occupy such a space is to deny its essence. Concerns with "responsibility" and "accountability" within the contemporary human rights regime compel the legibility of the subaltern. Such legibility, however, is merely a legitimation of the human, one that rehearses the subaltern as the mark of death.

Recalling the Nietzschean description of morality as a system of ends, it may be argued that the pursuit of accountability for the subaltern as an object of perpetration becomes imperative primarily in order to institutionalize appearances of "good" and "evil." The pursuit of accountability, however, is not identical to the pursuit of justice. From the perspective of postcolonial critique, this necessitates, in the first instance, staying with the subaltern as trace. In the previous section, I suggested that such faithfulness to subaltern makes imperative a practice of historicization that comprehends perpetration as a signifying gesture.

Furthermore, the possibility of justice for those abandoned by humanity—those that remain unseen and unheard within it—lies not in some form of restoration that "deal[s] with a past [but rather with] retribution [that] seeks to create a certain kind of present moment and future," a moment that can begin to "build [community] anew *where it never before existed*" (Stauffer 2015; added emphasis). That is, justice entails repair intended towards a renewed form of relations rather than mere redress (i.e., "fixing" that which has been destroyed to some imagined original form). This form of reparative justice requires, in the first instance, creating anew the conditions for seeing and listening. This makes imperative the turning of the gaze from the subaltern back onto ourselves as observers in an attempt to comprehend our own relationality with the subaltern. To do so, we must recognize ourselves as separable from subalternity.

Agential separability is a condition of "*exteriority within (material-discursive) phenomena*" (Barad 2003, 825). Barad offers this concept as a critique of the ontological determinism that establishes differences as fixed. Agential separability affirms difference as neither *a priori* nor absolute distinction, but rather the consequence of an *agential cut* made by instruments of observation and comprehension that produces separation within phenomena (2007, 140). Thus, for instance, agential separability allows us to comprehend how the notion of rational agency produces a cut within the phenomenon of the human in order to produce the subaltern as *different* from the subject and *external* to the human.

Crucially, agential separability reconfigures the notion of agency as "not an attribute but the ongoing reconfigurings of the world" (2003, 818). That is, agency is not a causal force acting between entities (i.e., between a subject who has agency and an object that lacks it) but rather designates a relational force that facilitates the *mutual becoming* of separable entities. It is "*a matter of intra-acting; it is an enactment, not something that someone or something has .... It is the enactment of iterative changes to particular practices ...*" (2007, 178 original emphasis). Agency, then, does not presume action according to a motive exercised by already constituted entities. Rather, *it lies in the iterative performance of material-discursive practices that affirm entities as different.* Thus, reading activity against the subaltern through the figure of the perpetrator—specifically, through a causal description of agency—is itself a part of the violent "doing."

Alternately, a refiguration of agency—one that moves away from a juridical concern with causality to an ethical concern with separability—allows us to recognize how the liberal humanist order produces a cut between the figure of the perpetrator as *wrong doer* and the observer as *judge* to establish them as morally distinct entities. This separation allows the observers to distance themselves not only from the perpetrators but also from the act of perpetration. Insofar as perpetration is iterative activity, the observers are also able to disregard their existence as an effect of the originary cut that ejected the subaltern from the field of humanity. This, I propose, is the tacit investment in grasping the figure of the perpetrator in relation to activity against the subaltern.

Given its ethical investment in historicizing the subaltern, postcolonial critique forces a recognition of the observer as separable from, and hence a co-produced effect of, the observed. It thereby compels a self-implicating reckoning with onto-epistemic complicity in ongoing activity against the subaltern. It is as such that postcolonial critique meets the perpetrator.

Notes

1 "Burial of an unknown child," captured by the Indian photographer, Raghu Rai.
2 Specifically, the faith in developmentalism as key to social, and indeed human, progress.
3 In his study of the crisis, Paul Shrivastava describes Bhopal as "a textbook example of a rapidly developing city that sought—and obtained—sophisticated Western-style industrialization without making a commensurate investment in industrial infrastructure or rural development" (1987, 57). Indeed, the state's push towards industrial growth through the concomitant devalorization of traditional methods of agriculture resulted in an economically untenable rural to urban migration. Moreover, the location of the Union Carbide factory violated the city's own zoning codes. But Union Carbide sought to appease these concerns by funding a public park. In return, Municipal Commissioners who sought to move the factory were replaced by those who were more amenable to state and corporate aspirations (Ali 1987, 175). The promise of economic growth thus seemed to warrant the expedient execution of business deeds.
4 The Subaltern Studies Collective was initially comprised of the historians Ranajit Guha, Shahid Amin, David Arnold, Partha Chatterjee, David Hardiman, and Gyanendra Pandey. The first volume of their collected works was published in 1982. Guha's 1983 text "Elementary aspects of peasant insurgency in colonial India" is generally viewed as the foundational text of this project.
5 "All the coupled oppositions on which philosophy is constructed," notes Derrida, emerge of "a necessity such that one of the terms appears as ... the other as 'differed' within a systematic ordering of the same" (1973, 149).

6 To quote Derrida:

> The trace has, properly speaking, no place, for effacement belongs to the very structure of the trace. Effacement must always be able to overtake the trace; otherwise it would not be a trace but an indestructible and monumental substance. In addition, and from the start, effacement constitutes it as a trace—effacement establishes the trace in a change of place and makes it disappear in its appearing. …
>
> *(1973, 156)*

7 In a statement commemorating the anniversary of leak, the then-CEO of UCC, Warren Andersen noted:

> We saw Bhopal for what it was—a terrible tragedy involving real people who had either lost family members or had suffered injuries, in some cases serious injuries. They needed medical relief, prompt aid in any form possible, and an early settlement which would help restore their lives and bring long-term relief. They didn't need what they ultimately got—armies of lawyers and politicians who spent years claiming to represent them and deciding what was in their best interests. *We saw Bhopal in moral—not in legal—terms. Although we had good legal defences—the plant wasn't ours and it later was established that the tragedy had been caused by employee sabotage—we didn't want to spend years arguing those issues in court while the victims waited.* We therefore said immediately that Union Carbide Corporation would take any moral responsibility for the disaster.
>
> *(printed in Fortun 2001, 99; emphasis added)*

8 Arguing for the dismissal of claims filed by survivors of the leak in U.S. courts, the defense for UCC sought to highlight

> the practical impossibility for American courts and juries, imbued with US cultural values, living standards and expectations, to determine living standards for people living in the slums or "hutments" surrounding UCIL, Bhopal, India, [thus] confirm[ing] that the Indian forum is overwhelmingly the most appropriate. *Such abject poverty and the vastly different values, standards and expectations which accompany it are commonplace in India and the third world. They are incomprehensible to Americans living in the United States.*
>
> *(Amnesty International 2004, 51; emphasis added)*

Indeed, the invocation of such difference enabled UCC to advance a sabotage theory that relied on the image of "a typical worker—stupid, vindictive, prone to lying" (Chouhan et al. 1994).

9 This description of "postcolonial" differs from the more common temporal understanding of the term. For a critique of this temporal association, see Shohat (1992).

10 Although Spillers' work focuses on blackness and sits firmly with the tradition of black thought, her account of the violence of slavery as subalternizing violence has much to offer the project of postcolonial critique. It is as such that I engage her work without any allusion of uniformity or agreement between black and postcolonial history and critique.

References

Ali, Syed Ashfaq. 1987. *A Guide to Bhopal.* Bhopal: Jai Bharat Publishing House.

Amnesty International. 2004. "Clouds of Injustice: Bhopal Disaster 20 Years on." Amnesty.org. https://www.amnesty.org/en/documents/ASA20/015/2004/en/

Barad, Karen. 2003. "Posthumanist Performativity: Toward an Understanding of How Matter Comes to Matter." *Signs: Journal of Women in Culture and Society* 28(3): 801–831.

Barad, Karen. 2007. *Meeting the Universe Halfway: Quantum Physics and the Entanglement of Matter and Meaning.* Durham: Duke University Press Books.

Chouhan, T. R., and Others with International Coalition for Justice in Bhopal. 1994. *Bhopal, the Inside Story: Carbide Workers Speak out on the World's Worst Industrial Disaster.* Mapusa, Goa: Other India Press.

Das, Veena. 1995. *Critical Events: An Anthropological Perspective on Contemporary India*. Delhi: Oxford University Press.

Derrida, Jacques. 1973. "Differance." In *Speech and Phenomena, and Other Essays on Husserl's Theory of Signs*, edited by David B. Allison and Newton Garver, 129–160. Evanston: Northwestern University Press.

Derrida, Jacques. 1997. *Of Grammatology*. Baltimore: Johns Hopkins University Press.

Feldman, Allen. 1991. *Formations of Violence: The Narrative of the Body and Political Terror in Northern Ireland*. Chicago: University of Chicago Press.

Fortun, Kim. 2000. "Remembering Bhopal, Re-Figuring Liability." *Interventions* 2(2): 187–198.

Fortun, Kim. 2001. *Advocacy after Bhopal: Environmentalism, Disaster, New Global Orders*. Chicago: University of Chicago Press.

Gandhi, Leela. 1998. *Postcolonial Theory: A Critical Introduction*. New York: Columbia University Press.

Green, Marcus. 2010. "Gramsci Cannot Speak: Presentations and Interpretations of Gramsci's Concept of the Subaltern." *Rethinking Marxism* 14(3): 1–24.

Guha, Ranajit. 1981. "On Some Aspects of the Historiography of Colonial India." *Subaltern Studies* 1: 1–8.

Guillette, Elizabeth. 2008. "The Foul Odor of Capital: The Union Carbide Disaster in Bhopal." In *Capitalizing on Catastrophe: Neoliberal Strategies in Disaster Reconstruction*, edited by Nandini Gunewardena and Mark Schuller, 173–188. Plymouth: Alta Mira Press.

International Campaign for Justice in Bhopal. 2014. "Reliving 'That Night'" *International Campaign for Justice in Bhopal*. www.bhopal.net/what-happened/that-night-december-3-1984/reliving-that-night/.

Jasanoff, Sheila. 2007. "Bhopal's Trials of Knowledge and Ignorance." *Isis: A Journal of the History of Science* 98(2): 344–350.

Jones, Tara. 1988. *Corporate Killing: Bhopals Will Happen*. London: Free Association Books.

Mukherjee, Suroopa. 2010. *Surviving Bhopal: Dancing Bodies, Written Texts, and Oral Testimonials of Women in the Wake of an Industrial Disaster*. New York: Palgrave Macmillan.

Nietzsche, Friedrich W. 1956. *The Genealogy of Morals*. Translated by Francis Golffing. New York: Doubleday and Company.

Nietzsche, Friedrich W. 2002. *Beyond Good and Evil*. Edited by Rolf-Peter Horstmann and Judith Norman. Cambridge: Cambridge University Press.

Prakash, Gyan. 1994. "Subaltern Studies as Postcolonial Criticism." *The American Historical Review* 99(5): 1475–1490.

Risse, Mathias. 2007. "Nietzschean 'Animal Psychology' versus Kantian Ethics." In *Nietzsche and Morality*, edited by Brian Leiter and Neil Sinhababu, 57–82. Oxford: Oxford University Press.

Shohat, Ella. 1992. "Notes on the 'Post-Colonial'." *Social Text* 31/32: 99–113.

Shrivastava, Paul. 1987. *Bhopal: Anatomy of a Crisis*. Cambridge, MA: Ballinger.

Spillers, Hortense J. 1987. "Mama's Baby, Papa's Maybe: An American Grammar Book." *Diacritics* 17(2): 64–81.

Spivak, Gayatri Chakravorty. 1999. *A Critique of Postcolonial Reason: Toward a History of the Vanishing Present*. Cambridge: Harvard University Press.

Spivak, Gayatri Chakravorty. 2005. "Scattered Speculations on the Subaltern and the Popular." *Postcolonial Studies: Culture, Politics, Economy* 8(4): 475–486.

Stauffer, Jill. 2015. *Ethical Loneliness: The Injustice of Not Being Heard*. New York: Columbia University Press.

16

Perpetrators, Animals, and Animality

Kári Driscoll

Introduction: Border Control

In late 2015, the journal *Totalitarismus und Demokratie* published an article entitled "Der deutsch-deutsche Schäferhund—Ein Beitrag zur Gewaltgeschichte des Jahrhunderts der Extreme" [*The East and West German Shepherd: A Contribution to the History of Violence in the Century of Extremes*], which presented a series of revelations about the employment of dogs by border police in East and West Germany between 1961 and 1989.[1] Drawing on previously unexamined archival sources, the author, Christiane Schulte, claimed that the first victim of the Berlin Wall had not been a human but rather a police dog named Rex, and furthermore that the German shepherds used by the border police on both sides of the Wall had been direct descendants of those deployed by the Nazis at Buchenwald and Sachsenhausen. The same, moreover, was true of dogs used by the border police in present-day Germany. The article thus traced a continuity of biopolitical violence, of which these dogs were both perpetrators and victims, from the Third Reich to the Cold War and right through to the migrant crisis which had reached its height in the summer of 2015.

If this sounds a little too good to be true, that's because it was. On February 15, 2016, "Schulte" (not her real name) and various unnamed co-authors revealed that the article had been an elaborate hoax: the archival sources detailing the pedigree of the dogs as well as the identities of the canine victims of the Berlin Wall had been fictitious, and the exaggerated claims of the piece had been intended as a parody of the emerging field of animal studies (or human–animal studies), which they characterize as the latest academic fad, full of empty rhetoric and absurd theories about nonhuman "agency." The incident was a source of great embarrassment to the journal, which promptly withdrew the article, and the ensuing scandal has had reverberations in the academic world beyond Germany, sparking a debate about the state of political and academic discourse and the relevance and legitimacy of fields such as animal studies for the study of history, biopolitics, totalitarianism, and genocide.

As usual, the hoax reveals more about its perpetrators than it does about the object of their scorn. The argument they present against animal studies is both spurious and disingenuous and is based on a number of unexamined assumptions as well as a willful misrepresentation of the aims of the field. This becomes abundantly clear in the conclusion to their 2016 exposé where they express their horror at the thought that animal studies "may soon make inroads into comparative genocide studies." It is one thing, they opine, to study human–animal relations and to "denounce cruelty to animals," but this must not come at the cost of a concept of "society" that is separate from "nature," since, they argue, "as soon as the distinction between natural and cultural history is abolished, it becomes impossible to distinguish the racism of the transatlantic slave trade from the 'speciesism' of an industrial pig farm" (Schulte et al. 2016a, n.p.; my translation). There are several basic problems with this argument, starting with the rather surprising implication that industrialized slaughter belongs to "natural history"! Much like the dogs they write about in their article, Schulte and co. are preoccupied with the policing of boundaries, both epistemological and ontological. This extends to disciplinary boundaries as well: earlier in the same piece, the authors criticize the field of animal studies for approaching the question of the animal in the language of philosophy and sociology (i.e., with reference to "agency," rather than remaining within the "proper" confines of biology and zoology). By the same token, the comparative study of totalitarianism and genocide is likewise suspect because of its interdisciplinary approach to structures of violence and injustice, which in the authors' view serves as a license for moral and political relativism (Schulte et al. 2016b, 143).

The main problem, however, is the authors' appeal to a rigid distinction between nature ("natural history") and (human) culture. Their ultimate worry seems to be that blurring this boundary will make it impossible to draw distinctions between different forms of violence and that everything will blend together in a sea of false equivalence. Their position thus buys into a zero-sum logic whereby recognizing speciesism (which they tellingly put in scare quotes) as a form of violence with political and ethical implications would be to relativize and hence diminish the violence of slavery or genocide. To be sure, it is of course vital that we be able to distinguish between different forms of violence perpetrated against different groups, but the solution cannot be to fall back on a reified nature/culture binary that is irreducibly problematic and has been untenable at least since Lévi-Strauss (1969; cf. Derrida 1978). Far from being a universal and transhistorical given, the dichotomy between nature and culture is a comparatively recent and specifically Western notion (Soper 1995; Descola 2013), which, moreover, is complicit in the very violence the authors claim to denounce, since it was in large part this dichotomy, coupled with the rhetoric of human exceptionalism and mastery over "nature," that served as the justification of colonialism, slavery, and "scientific" racism in the first place (Spiegel 1988; Wynter 1994; Huggan and Tiffin 2010; Smith 2015; Boisseron 2018).

Rather than simply dismissing this hoax as a misguided and ultimately reactionary gesture—though it is that[2]—I propose that we take it seriously as an object lesson on the importance of the question of the animal and the discourse of species for the understanding of genocide and political mass violence. Schulte's intervention, I argue, is in fact precisely what it claims to be, namely a "contribution to the history of violence"—not only in the way the authors themselves perpetuate a tradition of epistemic violence by insisting upon a nature/culture boundary which has historically been used to disenfranchise and oppress others, but also because, contrary to the authors' stated intentions, the article itself actually *does* make a fairly convincing case for why attention to the entanglements of humans and nonhumans in systems of oppression can yield new insights into processes of perpetration, injustice, and political violence. The hoaxers' own characterization of their deception makes it seem as though all of the sources were made up and transparently absurd, and this is a narrative that was largely perpetuated by the media response to the scandal. In actual fact, however, the majority of the texts cited are genuine, just as the historical continuities between the Nazi concentration camps and their subsequent reuse by the Soviet occupying forces and later by the GDR are well documented, as is the deployment of dogs at these sites. Thus, even if the genealogical evidence for a direct family *relation* was fictitious, there is no denying that there is a "family resemblance" between these dogs and the sites of (bio)political violence where they were in active service.[3]

The bulk of the article draws extensively on Marie-Luise Scherer's classic 1994 reportage *Die Hundegrenze* [*The Dog Border*], which is based on interviews and journalistic investigations into the use and function of dogs along the inner-German border. One of the security installations along the death strip was a series of dog runs (*Hundelaufanlagen*), consisting of steel cables fitted with a metal ring to which the dogs' leashes were secured. In this way, each dog could patrol a section of the wall unsupervised. As Scherer explains, in order to prevent the dogs from attacking each other, a stop was placed at either end of each cable. As a result, between each dog run there was a gap of at least half a meter, which afforded a window of opportunity for potential human escapees. In the 2015 article, "Schulte" writes:

> The border fortifications can thus be described as a biopolitical paradox, characterized by the mutually incompatible uncertainty principles of two systems of control: the control of animals and that of humans.
>
> *(2015, 330; my translation)*

Notwithstanding the authors' stated opinion that the concept of animal "agency" is so much fashionable nonsense, the gap in the totalitarian control mechanism they describe here simply *is* the product, or rather the effect, of the guard dogs' agency and the regime's efforts to curb it. Hence, in this instance, they are absolutely right to say that paying attention to the entanglement of humans and nonhumans in systems of oppression reveals the "limits of the total" (ibid.). Unfortunately, however, because they take it for granted that what they are writing is nonsense, the authors fail to draw the logical conclusion from this insight, namely that their own efforts to police the human–animal border are likewise doomed to fail. A key insight of animal studies is that this border is not singular, universal, indivisible, and insurmountable, but rather porous and internally incoherent, defined by ruptures, gaps, and inconsistencies. It is, as Jacques Derrida writes, a "plural and repeatedly folded frontier," which, moreover, "has a history" (2008, 30–31), something Schulte and co. also choose to ignore. The normative categories of "Man" and "Animal" are not stable ontological givens, but rather discursive formations that have been historically produced and continue to be strategically enforced. Contrary to the hoaxers' assertions, the aim of animal studies is precisely *not* to abolish or wish away the human–animal distinction, but rather to complicate and "thicken" it, to multiply its differences and discontinuities, in order to show how the limit is not "single and indivisible" but rather multiple, fractured, and folded in on itself in complex and often contradictory ways, not the least of which is the fact that this border serves not only to separate "what calls *itself* man" from "what *he* calls the animal" (Derrida 2008, 40), but also to separate "the animal" within the human. The human–animal border is thus in an important sense an "inner" border as well, the enforcement and transgression of which is fraught with biopolitical and ethical consequences.

The "question of the animal," Derrida insists, is "not one question among others," but rather

> represents the limit upon which all the great questions are formed and determined, as well as all the concepts that attempt to delimit what is "proper to man," the essence

> and future of humanity, ethics, politics, law, "human rights," "crimes against humanity," "genocide," etc.
>
> *(Derrida and Roudinesco 2004, 63)*

Hence, it is a question that a field such as Perpetrator Studies must take seriously. In what follows I will consider the entanglements of the question of the animal with the question of the perpetrator with the aim of moving beyond the unexamined anthropocentrism that has characterized much of the research in Perpetrator Studies. My basic contention is that the forms of political and collective violence with which the field is concerned have always been a multispecies affair, both figuratively *and* literally. Therefore, in order to be able to arrive at a richer and more nuanced understanding of its own fundamental questions—such as "who or what is a perpetrator?" and "what do genocides kill?"—Perpetrator Studies must adopt a more-than-human frame of reference. I will proceed in three stages: First, I will revisit the question of "dehumanization" in order to consider how the language of animality haunts the discourse of genocide in the metaphorical or symbolic representation of both victims and perpetrators and how this figurative use of animals and animality both invites and forecloses comparisons to the treatment of actual nonhuman animals. I will then explore the concept of genocide itself and the extent to which it can and should be applied to the extermination of nonhumans (e.g., in the case of the near-eradication of the North American buffalo in the nineteenth century and in the context of the currently unfolding sixth mass extinction). Finally, I will consider the extent to which animals can be considered perpetrators and not just victims of political and genocidal violence. Here I will revisit the question of nonhuman agency, with particular reference to the role of dogs as agents of (bio)political violence.

Animals as Victims, Victims as Animals

In *Minima Moralia*, Theodor W. Adorno notes that public "indignation over cruelty diminishes in proportion as the victims are less like normal readers." This, he says, tells us at least as much about these observers as it does about the victims:

> The constantly encountered assertion that savages, blacks, Japanese are like animals, monkeys for example, is the key to the pogrom. The possibility of pogroms is decided in the moment when the gaze of a fatally-wounded animal falls on a human being. The defiance with which he repels this gaze—"after all, it's only an animal"—reappears irresistibly in cruelties done to human beings, the perpetrators having again and again to reassure themselves that it is "only an animal," because they could never fully believe this, even of animals.
>
> *(Adorno 2005, 105)*

These observations serve as a powerful reminder not only that the mechanisms of "othering" and racialization are closely interwoven with the discourse of species, but also that this process of "animalization" affects not only other humans but *also* animals, who, in other words, must themselves be "animalized" in order for their deaths to be of no concern. Such animalization, then, is not simply "natural" or universal but rather culturally and historically specific. Adorno frames this logic of animalization (dehumanization) in terms of an ethics and a politics of recognition. The failure to recognize the other as similar to oneself is predicated on a refusal to return the other's gaze. This refusal in turn stems from an unconscious fear of being recognized as familiar by the other and is ultimately grounded in a disavowal of one's *own* animality. Yet because of this disavowal, as Adorno goes on to emphasize, the image of

Man that emerges and serves as the normative standard against which others (human and nonhuman) are judged is in fact fundamentally skewed and can only be upheld by repeated recourse to biopolitical violence, whereby those traits and behaviors that do not fit Man's flattering self-image as rational, civilized, and elevated above "mere" animal desires and needs are continually repressed, externalized, and projected onto others who must then be either "corrected" or eliminated in order to preserve this image of Man.[4]

Such violence sometimes manifests itself in physical acts, but for the most part it is systemic and epistemic, bound up with particular dynamics of power/knowledge that determine who or what "counts" as human and therefore deserves (legal, moral, conceptual) recognition. A familiar, and indeed understandable, response to dehumanizing violence is to reassert the humanity of the target group by insisting that they are *not* animals. The problem with such reaffirmations of "humanity" and human dignity, however, is that they leave uninterrogated the logic underlying dehumanization, which is the *a priori* distinction of the moral, political, and ethical significance of human life as opposed to nonhuman life. A cornerstone of the tradition of Western humanism, as animal studies doyen Cary Wolfe emphasizes, is

> the tacit agreement that the full transcendence of the "human" requires the sacrifice of the "animal" and the animalistic, which in turn makes possible a symbolic economy in which we can engage in what Derrida will call a "noncriminal putting to death" of other *humans* as well by marking *them* as animal.
>
> *(Wolfe 2003, 6; cf. Derrida 1995, 278)*

In other words, the logic of dehumanization which countenances the exploitation and killing of individuals and groups by representing them as animals hinges entirely on the prior assumption that the lives of animals don't matter purely and simply because they are not human. This also explains why the language of animality perennially haunts the discourse surrounding genocide and biopolitical violence, both in the rhetoric of the perpetrators (who like to cast their victims as insects or vermin) and in the descriptions after the fact of the perpetrators as "beasts" or, alternatively, "butchers" and the victims as "lambs to the slaughter," an so on.[5] At the same time, this logic of human exceptionalism also informs the injunctions *against* drawing comparisons between violence done to humans and violence done to animals. The discomfort elicited by such comparisons is of course understandable, given the associations they inevitably evoke with the history of racist discrimination and marginalization and given the pervasiveness of violence against animals in all cultures, but the refusal to entertain the parallel is ultimately beholden to the same anthropocentrism and the willful turning away from the gaze of the animal that Adorno describes.[6]

There are clear and well-documented continuities between modern technologies of animal control and slaughter and the development of the *univers concentrationnaire*.[7] Indeed, this is what makes the commonplace that "the Jews died like cattle" plausible in the first place. Nevertheless, the converse assertion, that "cattle die like Jews," remains controversial (cf. Coetzee 1999; Pick 2011). This comparison is of course one that animal rights activists have frequently made, perhaps most notoriously PETA (People for the Ethical Treatment of Animals) in their 2003 campaign "Holocaust on Your Plate," which juxtaposed iconic images of emaciated concentration camp prisoners with pictures of battery hens and piles of human corpses with piles of animal carcasses along with statistics of the number of animals killed annually in the US. As Angi Buettner (2011) observes in her nuanced discussion of this campaign, the "Holocaust on Your Plate" relies on the status of the Holocaust as a master trope for industrial mass murder, which, for better or worse, has made it the point of comparison for other genocides and mass atrocities. In this way, such comparisons participate in a broader cultural dynamic that Michael Rothberg refers to as "multidirectional memory." In his 2009 book of that name, Rothberg examines the intersections of the memory of the Holocaust and the memory of slavery and colonialism in public and cultural discourse. He is particularly concerned to show how the conception of memory and commemoration as a competition for the scarce resources of space, money, attention, and recognition is counterproductive and even harmful in that it tends to work against solidarity and "the creation of new communal and political identities" (2009, 11). Building on Rothberg's work in her book *Unthinking Mastery*, decolonial scholar Julietta Singh compellingly argues that "extending the concept of multidirectional memory to include the mass torture of animals can enable new conversations between Holocaust, postcolonial, literary, and animal studies rather than confirming a competitive hierarchy among them" (2018, 145). Such an approach can help us to move beyond the sort of zero-sum logic that informs the "Schulte" hoax and towards a multidirectional or intersectional model that is open to comparisons and parallels that may at first appear "unseemly" (Rothberg 2009, 17), but that thinks about such intersections as productive, especially if they challenge our own preconceptions about who or what merits ethical consideration and critical attention.

What Do Genocides Kill?

At base, the "animal turn" presents a corrective to the disregard for the question of the animal that has characterized scholarship especially in the humanities and social sciences. In so doing, it poses a challenge to fundamental assumptions regarding the "proper" object of disciplinary concern and knowledge production. When it comes to the intersection of Perpetrator Studies and Animal Studies, a case in point would be the concept of genocide. Within Genocide Studies, the nature and constitution of the *genos* is a matter of ongoing debate. In an article entitled "What Do Genocides Kill?" Christopher Powell describes it as an "essentially contested concept," adding that different definitions of *genos* "presume different theories about the nature of social life" (2007, 529–530). He distinguishes between a "liberal" and a "post-liberal" conception, where the former imagines society to be the sum total of the individuals that make it up, whereas the latter conceives of it as more than the sum of its parts. On this view, "genocide is the killing or destruction of that 'something more,' and we need to specify just what that 'something more' is to define 'genocide' rigorously" (528; cf. Card 2003). This characterization of the *genos* helpfully leaves space for a notion of social life that is not limited to the human. Nevertheless, the field of Genocide Studies remains largely anthropocentric in its articulation. In his recent book *Redefining Genocide*, for instance, Damien Short powerfully links the concept of genocide to colonialism and environmental devastation. He insists that genocide has an "inherently colonial character" and as such cannot be regarded merely as synonymous with "mass murder." Moreover, he writes, the crime of genocide is specifically cultural in nature: "it destroys a human cultural grouping, a '*genos*'" (2016, 3). Important as Short's intervention is, this delimitation of *genos* to the human is questionable, particularly in light of the strong link that he makes between genocide and settler colonialism. As Indigenous scholar and filmmaker Tasha Hubbard argues, for instance, the near-eradication of the North American buffalo (bison) in the nineteenth century—numbers went from tens of millions to just a few hundred by century's end—constitutes a genocide, not only, as others have argued, because it was seen as a means to the ultimate displacement and eradication of the native populations, but also because within

Plains Indigenous cultures, the buffalo are regarded as "First People"—ancestors, relatives, and teachers—and hence form part of the *genos*. "According to Indigenous ways of knowing," Hubbard writes, "humans do not hold exclusive title to personhood, and therefore neither to genocide" (2014, 295). From this perspective, to insist that genocide applies only to humans is to impose Euro-American categories in a way that perpetuates the legacy of colonial violence at an epistemic level: "Genocide and denial of genocide work in conjunction, and the buffalo genocide is no exception" (299).[8]

Moreover, the buffalo themselves had a social structure and a cultural life, including practices of mourning for the dead, that were catastrophically disrupted by settler colonial violence.[9] Hence, while various scholars have proposed concepts such as "ecocide" (Zierler 2011) and "speciocide" (Mazis 2008) to describe the large-scale destruction of animal populations and ecosystems by humans, such concepts are in fact superfluous within a framework that does not restrict the concepts of personhood, culture, or society to human beings. In other words, as Audra Mitchell argues in reference to Hubbard, "the systematic destruction of the buffalo is not *like* genocide, nor is it *exclusively* a tool for carrying out genocide against human peoples. It *is* genocide in its own right" (2017, n.p.). By the same token, Mitchell continues, what Western scientists refer to as the "sixth mass extinction event" is more properly understood not as "an unfortunate, unintended consequence of desirable 'human' activities" such as urban and scientific development, global economic growth, and international trade, but rather as a series of genocides perpetrated, often quite deliberately, by Western governments and corporations in the context of (neo-)colonial expansionism and resource extraction. The massive scale of the currently unfolding loss of biodiversity requires careful attention to the macroscopic causes and effects, including especially its implication in global capital flows. Furthermore, it should serve as a stark reminder that one cannot separate human "society" from nonhuman "nature"; the two are fundamentally and irreducibly entangled. These entanglements, however, are not homogeneous or universal but rather culturally, geographically, and historically specific. Hence, as multispecies ethnographer Thom van Dooren writes, in reality "there is no single 'extinction' phenomenon. Rather, in each case there is a distinct unraveling of ways of life, a distinctive loss and set of changes and challenges that require situated and case-specific attention" (2016, 7). Drawing on perspectives from Holocaust Studies, van Dooren emphasizes the importance of bearing witness to these unravelings and of telling the story of these vanishing species "in a way that significantly *implicates* us—causally, perhaps emotionally, and certainly ethically" (4). Implication, here, has a dual significance, referring, on the one hand, to the responsibility we as humans bear for species extinction, and, on the other, to the various complex ways in which the human–animal relationship is articulated in multispecies communities or *genea*.

Van Dooren's emphasis on the need for "situated and case-specific attention" resonates with Christopher Powell's definition of *genos* as a relational formation. Such a definition of *genos*, Powell writes, requires "an empirical understanding of how [social] identities have functioned historically to connect people through practical relations that foster a shared sense of self." "Ironically," he continues, "the study of genocide can contribute to this investigation: because genocide attacks the processes by which [social] figurations exist, [it] in a sense expose[s] those processes and reveal[s] their importance" (2007, 544). As we have seen, genocidal processes radically unmoor the category of the human. Hence, a multispecies Perpetrator Studies can help understand how "human" and "animal" are constructed and deconstructed as subject positions within the dualistic logic of biopolitics, and in turn grant us a richer and more nuanced understanding of the processes involved in the perpetration and aftermath of (bio)political mass violence.

Animals as Perpetrators

As the buffalo genocide illustrates, "the historical horror of settler colonization has always been a multispecies endeavor" (Taschereau Mamers 2019, 12). This applies not only to the *victims* of colonial violence but also to its *agents*. As Alfred Crosby notes in his pathbreaking history of the biological expansion of Europe, settlers did not arrive as individual immigrants but "as part of a grunting, lowing, neighing, crowing, chirping, snarling, buzzing, self-replicating and world-altering avalanche" (2004, 194; quoted in Swart 2007). European settlers brought with them an array of animals, from domestic animals and livestock to vermin and microbes, which played a crucial role in the colonial project. Sheep, for instance, "were deployed as agents for the expansion of white settlement" in the Americas and in Australia, contributing to the displacement of indigenous populations "and the transformation of the endemic ecosystem" (Armstrong 2016, 97; cf. Melville 1997). The ubiquitous use of the European honey bee (*apis mellifera*) for the pollination of crops around the world is another example of how nonhumans are enlisted in the destruction of ecosystems and the Indigenous cultures that depend on them (McHugh 2019). In other cases, native species such as elephants were conscripted in the colonial exploitation of resources and extraction of capital (Saha 2017). In all of these examples, the respective species are implicated in (bio)political processes because of their particular characteristics and abilities. No doubt whatever guilt or responsibility these animals bear for these processes is only "by association," yet those processes could not have taken place in this way without their involvement. Clearly, it is inadequate, therefore, to conceive of them as purely passive objects or "tools" in the hands of human actors. Instead, scholars in animal and environmental studies have increasingly sought to elaborate a theory of agency that is not limited to human actions and hence not synonymous with traditional humanist concepts such as intentionality or "free will."

Historical geographer Philip Howell (2018) distinguishes between three different ways in which animal agency has been theorized: "ascribed," "agonistic," and "assembled." The first brackets the question of whether animals *actually have* agency in some ontological or metaphysical sense and asks how agency (or quasi-personhood) has been *ascribed* to nonhuman animals by individuals and groups in different cultures and at different times. In the case of the status of buffalo as "First People" within Indigenous cultures, for instance, the relevant question is not "Yes, but are they *really* people?"; nor is it particularly helpful (or feasible) to ask whether the buffalo think of *themselves* as people. Another salient example of "ascribed" agency is the history of animal trials. As Howell writes,

> even if we do not accept at face value the notion that priests, lawmakers and laypeople endowed pigs, dogs, horses, oxen, cats, fish, even swarms of insects, with moral agency and responsibility, the historical fact that culpability for crimes and sins could in some circumstances be extended to nonhumans is striking, and deserves our attention as historians of attitudes if not necessarily of the animals themselves.
>
> *(2018, 203)*[10]

Howell's second category, "agonistic" agency, describes a conception of agency as a form of resistance or recalcitrance and pays less attention to the way animals are perceived by humans than to the actions of the animals themselves and their (historical) effects. A proponent of this view is Fahim Amir, who proposes that we "conceive of animals as agents of political resistance" rather than focusing only on their vulnerability and our responsibilities toward them as "moral patients."[11] "The entire apparatus of fences, cages, enclosures, surveillance and monitoring systems," he writes, "is a response to the monstrous agency of animals, and a confirmation of the world-forming power of that agency" (Amir 2018, 15; my translation).

The third category Howell identifies is "assembled agency," which is also sometimes referred to as "relational" (Roscher 2018) or "distributive" (Bennett 2010) agency. Rather than being the property of this or that individual, agency by this definition is instead an emergent effect of the interaction between various agents. Perhaps the clearest example Howell discusses is guide dogs for the blind, where "the agency of the (disabled) human is dependent in large part upon the agency of the animal" (2018, 208) and vice versa. In this instance, it is difficult to argue that the dog's agency "is no more significant than that of a cane or a stick" (ibid.). The dog and the human form an agential assemblage based on reciprocal training and communication, and their agency is both greater and qualitatively different than it would be for either party independently. The same, of course, is true of police and military dogs as well as other service animals employed by states in conflict situations.

Conclusion: The Dog Border Revisited

In conclusion, let us revisit the question of the "dog border," which may serve as an illustration of both "agonistic" and "assembled" agency. The aforementioned "gap" between the dog runs is a perfect example of the former. In an effort to limit the agency of the human population, the East German regime enlists the help of dogs, whose own agency must similarly be curtailed, first by means of the leash and second by means of the gaps, which in turn produces the unintended side effect of allowing room for human agency. In her 2015 article, Schulte describes this as a "biopolitical paradox" resulting from the incommensurability of two systems of control. In fact, however, the paradox is an intrinsic feature of *one* system, namely of biopolitics, which, as theorized by Giorgio Agamben, functions via the "inclusive exclusion" of animal life (*zoē*) within political life (*bíos*) (1998, 5–8). The "dog border" is thus a sort of literal manifestation of the logic of biopolitics, whereby the gap in the totality of its control represents the "zone of indeterminacy" between *zoē* and *bíos*, "the place of a ceaselessly updated decision in which the caesurae and their rearticulation are always dislocated and displaced anew" (Agamben 2004, 38). This no man's land represents the site where biopolitical subjectivity is produced (i.e., it is here that the recognition of the "human" is decided). A byproduct of this process is a form of life that is excluded from the privileges of political sovereignty but is nevertheless subject to biopolitical violence—"noncriminal putting to death"—or what Agamben calls *bare life*. At a theoretical level, the unilateral ascription of agency to humans and its converse denial to animals is itself an iteration of this "inclusive exclusion," and as such a further example of the way conceptual border policing is complicit in the system of biopolitics it supposedly critiques.

With respect to "assembled" agency, we might read the dog runs themselves in terms of what in Perpetrator Studies is referred to as the "scope for action" (in German, "*Handlungsraum*") available to individuals implicated in systems and processes of political violence (see Herkommer 2008; Bajohr 2016). It is by now commonly accepted that responsibility for and complicity in acts of perpetration cannot be assessed purely on the basis of intention but must take into account an individual's *Handlungsraum*, which is nothing other than the capacity for agency within a given sociopolitical system and historical situation. Which is to say: even in humans, agency is always contingent and only ever expressed in relation to a given set of circumstances, many of which will be beyond the individual's control. Moreover, the theory of *Handlungsräume* reveals agency to be distributed unequally among participants or actors in a system of relations. There is no inherent reason to treat these participants self-evidently as human, least of all with respect to situations in which their "humanity" is precisely what is at stake—be it a concentration camp, a slave plantation, a civil rights demonstration, or in Abu Ghraib.[12] Moreover, the routine involvement of *actual* animals, such as police dogs, in the perpetration of "dehumanizing" violence should at the very least serve as a reminder that the opposition between human and animal is never simply binary and that its enforcement can never be politically neutral. It is for this reason above all that Perpetrator Studies cannot afford to ignore the question of the animal.

Notes

The research and writing of this chapter was made possible in part by a VENI grant from the Dutch Research Council (NWO). I would like to thank Susan McHugh, Mieke Roscher, and the editors for their comments and support.

1 The title, arguably the cleverest aspect of the entire enterprise, is a pun on the "deutsch-deutsche Grenze," or inner-German border between the GDR (East Germany) and the Federal Republic (West Germany), and "deutscher Schäferhund" or German Shepherd (Alsatian).

2 Essentially, the hoax is a latter-day rehashing of the Sokal hoax, which had likewise sought to lampoon the idea of nonhuman agency some twenty years previously. Moreover, as historical geographer Philip Howell notes, the hoax also recalls a "fake" article published in the *Journal of Social History* in 1974, which had asserted, satirically as it turned out, the "full historical power" of domestic animals. "Given the passage of time," Howell writes, it is "almost exponentially dispiriting to see the same gesture trotted out" by Schulte and co. (Howell 2018, 197). Evidently, the very concept of nonhuman agency is sufficiently traumatic to trigger a sort of "repetition compulsion" among those for whom "agency" must remain synonymous with "intentionality" and "free will" and hence the prerogative of the rational human(ist) subject.

3 On the role of guard dogs at Nazi concentration camps, see Perz (1996), Möhring (2011), and Tindol (2013). One might also note here the nontrivial parallels between the history of dog breeding and the history of racist and eugenicist thinking. Thus, Dominick LaCapra notes that "kennel clubs, along with similar breed registries for other species, may be among the last bastions of unexamined racism, reproducing, vis-à-vis other animals, barriers and attitudes that have been challenged with respect to humans" (2009, 155; cf. Sax 2000; Skabelund 2008; Roscher 2016).

4 The mechanism Adorno is describing here corresponds to that which Giorgio Agamben will later refer to as the "anthropological machine," a discursive apparatus whereby a concept of "the human" is continually produced by means of an "inclusive exclusion" of "the animal" (2004, 33–38). For a discussion of the anthropological machine, see Calarco (2008, 79–102) and Pettman (2011, 1–36).

5 On the rhetoric of animalization in antisemitism, see Geller (2018) and Urban (2018).

6 That being said, going back to Adorno's observation about the lack of concern among "normal" (white, middle-class) audiences elicited by the suffering and death of people of color, it is important to acknowledge that concern for animal suffering can indeed at times serve as a screen that permits people to "look away" from crimes in which they may themselves be implicated but which they would rather not think about (cf. Arseneault 2013; Salih 2014). This also applies to the hypocrisy of labeling culturally specific practices relating to animals as "barbaric" (e.g., halal slaughter, the consumption of dog meat, etc.) while simultaneously tacitly condoning the unfathomable suffering of animals on factory farms and in biomedical laboratories in the West (cf. Huggan and Tiffin 2010, 135–38).

7 See, for example, Bauman (1989), Sax (2000), Patterson (2002), Netz (2004), and Shukin (2009).

8 One very illuminating example of how colonial biopolitical violence disrupts more-than-human communities is the so-called Mountie Sled Dog Massacre of the 1950s and '60s, in which the Canadian government led a campaign to eradicate the *qimmiit*, Inuit sled dogs, who had traditionally been an integral part of Inuit culture and identity (see McHugh 2019, 122–154).

9 See Hubbard (2014) and King (2013, 134–144). The same is true of other species whose lifeways have been disrupted by poaching, culling, and habitat loss through human expansion. A particularly striking example of the effects of such social disruption is the epidemic of inter-species violence

perpetrated by juvenile elephants in South Africa against rhinoceroses. In her 2009 book *Elephants on the Edge*, psychologist G.A. Bradshaw argues that the elephants' behavior was a symptom of post-traumatic stress resulting from the collapse of familial and societal relations upon which elephant culture depends. Bradshaw deliberately refers to the acts as *violence*, a term usually reserved for human beings, in order to underscore its social and psychological dimensions and to trouble the human–animal binary. In that context, she also refers to the war documented by Jane Goodall between two rival communities of chimpanzees in Gombe National Park, Tanzania, in the 1970s (see Goodall 1990, 98–111). "Despite a desire by many other scientists to discredit her on the grounds of anthropomorphic projection," Bradshaw writes, "species parallels were marked. Chimpanzees were observed engaging in multiple, systematic gang- or group-led killings, infanticide, and finally the eradication of one clan by the other (what one might call, in the case of humans, ethnic cleansing)" (2009, 40). Evidently, Bradshaw is wary of transposing the vocabulary of genocide onto violence between nonhumans. Nevertheless, the occurrence of coordinated intercommunity killings among chimpanzees should at the very least serve to complicate negative assertions of human exceptionalism regarding the "distinctively human" nature of "victimization, torture, or genocide" (LaCapra 2009, 156).

10 The criminal prosecution and capital punishment of animals is generally associated with the European middle ages (Evans 1906; Dinzelbacher 2002; Srivastava 2007; Sykes 2011), but in fact continued well into the twentieth century, for instance in the case of the elephant Topsy executed by electrocution at Coney Island 1903 and whose death was captured on film by Thomas Edison (Doane 2002, 140–171; Stallwood 2018), and of "Murderous Mary," another Asian elephant hanged in Tennessee in 1916 (Oliver 2013, 166–187).

11 On the distinction between "moral agents" and "moral patients," see Cavalieri (2001, 28–31) and Wolfe (2010, 2013).

12 For a particularly insightful analysis of Abu Ghraib in relation to the production of biopolitical subjectivity, see Boggs (2013, 41–76).

References

Adorno, Theodor W. 2005. *Minima Moralia: Reflections from Damaged Life*. Translated by E.F.N. Jephcott. London: Verso.

Agamben, Giorgio. 1998. *Homo Sacer: Sovereign Power and Bare Life*. Translated by Daniel Heller-Roazen. Stanford, CA: Stanford University Press.

Agamben, Giorgio. 2004. *The Open: Man and Animal*. Translated by Kevin Attell. Stanford, CA: Stanford University Press.

Amir, Fahim. 2018. *Schwein und Zeit. Tiere, Politik, Revolte*. Hamburg: Nautilus.

Armstrong, Philip. 2016. *Sheep*. London: Reaktion Books.

Arseneault, Jesse. 2013. "On Canicide and Concern: Species Sovereignty in Western Accounts of Rwanda's Genocide." *ESC: English Studies in Canada* 39(1): 125–147.

Bajohr, Frank. 2016. "Neuere Täterforschung." In *Nationalsozialistische Täterschaften. Nachwirkungen in Gesellschaft und Familie*, edited by Oliver von Wrochem and Christine Eckel, 19–31. Berlin: Metropol.

Bauman, Zygmunt. 1989. *Modernity and the Holocaust*. Cambridge: Polity.

Bennett, Jane. 2010. *Vibrant Matter: A Political Ecology of Things*. Durham, NC: Duke University Press.

Boggs, Colleen Glenney. 2013. *Animalia Americana: Animal Representations and Biopolitical Subjectivity*. New York: Columbia University Press.

Boisseron, Bénédicte. 2018. *Afro-Dog: Blackness and the Animal Question*. New York: Columbia University Press.

Bradshaw, Gay A. 2009. *Elephants on the Edge: What Animals Teach Us about Humanity*. New Haven, CT: Yale University Press.

Buettner, Angi. 2011. *Holocaust Images and Picturing Catastrophe: The Cultural Politics of Seeing*. Farnham, NH: Ashgate.

Calarco, Matthew. 2008. *Zoographies: The Question of the Animal from Heidegger to Derrida*. New York: Columbia University Press.

Card, Claudia. 2003. "Genocide and Social Death." *Hypatia* 18(1): 63–79.

Cavalieri, Paola. 2001. *The Animal Question: Why Nonhuman Animals Deserve Human Rights*. Translated by Catherine Woollard. Oxford: Oxford University Press.

Coetzee, J. M. 1999. *The Lives of Animals*. Edited and with an introduction by Amy Gutmann. Princeton, NJ: Princeton University Press.
Crosby, Alfred W. 2004. *Ecological Imperialism: The Biological Expansion of Europe 900–1900*. 2nd ed. Cambridge: Cambridge University Press.
Derrida, Jacques. 1978. "Structure, Sign, and Play in the Discourse of the Human Sciences." In *Writing and Difference*, translated by Alan Bass, 278–293. Chicago: University of Chicago Press.
Derrida, Jacques. 1995. "'Eating Well', or the Calculation of the Subject." Translated by Peter Connor and Avital Ronell. In *Points … Interviews, 1974–1994*, edited by Elisabeth Weber, 255–287. Stanford, CA: Stanford University Press.
Derrida, Jacques. 2008. *The Animal That Therefore I Am*. Edited by Marie-Louise Mallet. Translated by David Wills. New York: Fordham University Press.
Derrida, Jacques & Elisabeth Roudinesco. 2004. "Violence against Animals." In *For What Tomorrow: A Dialogue*, translated by Jeff Fort, 62–76. Stanford, CA: Stanford University Press.
Descola, Philippe. 2013. *Beyond Nature and Culture*. Translated by Janet Lloyd. Chicago: University of Chicago Press.
Dinzelbacher, Peter. 2002. "Animal Trials: A Multidisciplinary Approach." *Journal of Interdisciplinary History* 32(3): 405–421.
Doane, Mary Anne. 2002. *The Emergence of Cinematic Time: Modernity, Contingency, the Archive*. Cambridge, MA: Harvard University Press.
Donaldson, Sue and Will Kymlicka 2011. *Zoopolis: A Political Theory of Animal Rights*. Oxford: Oxford University Press.
Evans, Edward Payson. 1906. *The Criminal Prosecution and Capital Punishment of Animals*. London: Heinemann.
Geller, Jay 2018. *Bestiarium Jadaicum: Unnatural Histories of the Jews*. New York: Fordham University Press.
Goodall, Jane. 1990. *Through a Window: My Thirty Years with the Chimpanzees of Gombe*. Boston, MA: Mariner Books.
Herkommer, Christina. 2008. "Women under National Socialism: Women's Scope for Action and the Issue of Gender." In *Ordinary People as Mass Murderers: Perpetrators in Comparative Perspectives*, edited by Olaf Jensen and Claus-Christian W. Szejnmann, 99–119. Basingstoke: Palgrave Macmillan.
Howell, Philip. 2018. "Animals, Agency, and History." In *The Routledge Companion to Animal–Human History*, edited by Hilda Kean and Philip Howell, 197–221. London: Routledge.
Hubbard, Tasha. 2014. "Buffalo Genocide in Nineteenth-Century North America: 'Kill, Skin, and Sell'." In *Colonial Genocide in Indigenous North America*, edited by Andrew Woolford, Jeff Benvenuto, and Alexander Laban Hinton, 292–305. Durham, NC: Duke University Press.
Huggan, Graham & Helen Tiffin. 2010. *Postcolonial Ecocriticism: Literature, Animals, Environment*. London: Routledge.
King, Barbara J. 2013. *How Animals Grieve*. Chicago: University of Chicago Press.
LaCapra, Dominick. 2009. *History and Its Limits: Human, Animal, Violence*. Ithaca, NY: Cornell University Press.
Lévi-Strauss, Claude. 1969. *The Elementary Structures of Kinship*. Rev. ed. Edited by Rodney Needham. Translated by James Harle Bell, John Richard von Sturmer, and Rodney Needham. Boston, MA: Beacon Press.
Mazis, Glen. 2008. "The World of Wolves: Lessons about the Sacredness of the Surround, Belonging, the Silent Dialogue of Interdependence and Death, and Speciocide." *Environmental Philosophy* 5(2): 69–92.
McHugh, Susan. 2019. *Love in a Time of Slaughters: Human-Animal Stories against Genocide and Extinction*. University Park, PA: Pennsylvania State University Press.
Melville, Elinor G. K. 1997. *A Plague of Sheep: Environmental Consequences of the Conquest of Mexico*. Cambridge: Cambridge University Press.
Mitchell, Audra. 2017. "Decolonising against Extinction Part II: Extinction Is Not a Metaphor – It Is Literally Genocide." *Worldly IR* (blog), 27 September.
Möhring, Maren. 2011. "'Herrentiere' und 'Untermenschen'. Zu den Transformationen des Mensch-Tier-Verhältnisses im nationalsozialistischen Deutschland." *Historische Anthropologie* 19(2): 229–244.
Netz, Reviel. 2004. *Barbed Wire: An Ecology of Modernity*. Middletown, CT: Wesleyan University Press.
Oliver, Kelly. 2013. *Technologies of Life and Death: From Cloning to Capital Punishment*. New York: Fordham University Press.

Patterson, Charles. 2002. *Eternal Treblinka: Our Treatment of Animals and Holocaust.* New York: Lantern Books.

Perz, Bertrand. 1996. "'...müssen zu reißenden Bestien erzogen werden.' Der Einsatz von Hunden zur Bewachung in den Konzentrationslagern." *Dachauer Hefte* no. 12: 139–158

Pettman, Dominic. 2011. *Human Error: Species-Being and Media Machines.* Minneapolis: University of Minnesota Press.

Pick, Anat. 2011. *Creaturely Poetics: Animality and Vulnerability in Literature and Film.* New York: Columbia University Press.

Powell, Christopher. 2007. "What Do Genocides Kill? A Relational Conception of Genocide." *Journal of Genocide Research* 9(4): 527–547.

Roscher, Mieke. 2016. "Das nationalsozialistische Tier: Projektionen von Rasse und Reinheit im 'Dritten Reich'." *TIERethik* 8(2): 30–47.

Roscher, Mieke. 2018. "New Political History and the Writing of Animal Lives." In *The Routledge Companion to Animal–Human History*, edited by Hilda Kean and Philip Howell, 53–75. London: Routledge.

Rothberg, Michael. 2009. *Multidirectional Memory: Remembering the Holocaust in the Age of Decolonization.* Stanford, CA: Stanford University Press.

Saha, Jonathan. 2017. "Colonizing Elephants: Animal Agency, Undead Capital and Imperial Science in British Burma." *BJHS Themes* 2: 169–189.

Salih, Sara. 2014. "The Animal You See: Why Look at Animals in Gaza?" *Interventions* 16(3): 299–324.

Sax, Boria. 2000. *Animals in the Third Reich: Pets, Scapegoats, and the Holocaust.* New York: Continuum.

Scherer, Marie-Luise. 1994. "Die Hundegrenze." *Der Spiegel*, no. 6 (7 February): 94–115. https://www.spiegel.de/spiegel/print/d-13684223.html

Schulte, Christiane [pseud.]. 2015. "Der deutsch-deutsche Schäferhund – Ein Beitrag zur Gewaltgeschichte des Jahrhunderts der Extreme." *Totalitarismus und Demokratie* 13(2): 319–334.

Schulte, Christiane, et al. 2016a. "Kommissar Rex an der Mauer erschossen?" *Telepolis*, 15 February. https://heise.de/-3378291.

Schulte, Christiane, et al. 2016b. "Kritische Wissenschaft braucht einen Begriff von Gesellschaft." *sub\urban: Zeitschrift für kritische Stadtforschung* 4(2/3): 137–144.

Short, Damien. 2016. *Redefining Genocide: Settler Colonialism, Social Death and Ecocide.* London: Zed Books.

Shukin, Nicole. 2009. *Animal Capital: Rendering Life in Biopolitical Times.* Minneapolis: University of Minnesota Press.

Singh, Julietta. 2018. *Unthinking Mastery: Dehumanism and Decolonial Entanglements.* Durham, NC: Duke University Press.

Skabelund, Aaron. 2008. "Breeding Racism: The Imperial Battlefields of the 'German' Shepherd Dog." *Society & Animals* no. 16: 354–371.

Smith, Justin E. H. 2015. *Nature, Human Nature, & Human Difference: Race in Early Modern Philosophy.* Princeton, NJ: Princeton University Press.

Soper, Kate. 1995. *What Is Nature? – Culture, Politics, and the Non-Human.* Oxford: Blackwell.

Spiegel, Marjorie. 1988. *The Dreaded Comparison: Human and Animal Slavery.* Preface by Alice Walker. London: Heretic Books.

Srivastava, Anila. 2007. "'Mean, dangerous, and uncontrollable beasts': Mediaeval Animal Trials." *Mosaic* 40(1): 127–143.

Stallwood, Kim. 2018. "Topsy: The Elephant We Must Never Forget." In *Animal Biography: Re-Framing Animal Lives*, edited by André Krebber and Mieke Roscher, 227–242. London: Palgrave Macmillan.

Swart, Sandra. 2007. "'But Where's the Bloody Horse?': Textuality and Corporeality in the 'Animal Turn'." *Journal of Literary Studies* 23(3): 271–292.

Sykes, Katie. 2011. "Human Drama, Animal Trials: What the Medieval Animal Trials Can Teach Us about Justice for Animals." *Animal Law Review* 17(2): 273–311.

Taschereau Mamers, Danielle. 2019. "Human–Bison Relations as Sites of Settler Colonial Violence and Decolonial Resurgence." *Humanimalia* 10(2): 10–41.

Tindol, Robert. 2013. "The Best Friend of the Murderers: Guard Dogs and the Nazi Holocaust." In *Animals and War: Studies of Europe and North America*, edited by Ryan Hediger, 105–121. Leiden: Brill.

Urban, Monika 2018. *Von Ratten, Schmeißfliegen und Heuschrecken. Judenfeindliche Tiersymbolisierungen und die postfaschistischen Grenzen des Sagbaren.* Köln: Herbert von Halem Verlag.

van Dooren, Thom. 2016. *Flight Ways: Life and Loss at the Edge of Extinction*. New York: Columbia University Press.
Wolfe, Cary. 2003. *Animal Rites: American Culture, the Discourse of Species, and Posthumanist Theory*. Chicago: University of Chicago Press.
Wolfe, Cary. 2010. *What Is Posthumanism?* Minneapolis: University of Minnesota Press.
Wolfe, Cary. 2013. *Before the Law: Humans and Other Animals in a Biopolitical Frame*. Chicago: University of Chicago Press.
Wynter, Sylvia. 1994. "'No Humans Involved': An Open Letter to My Colleagues." *Forum N. H. I.: Knowledge for the 21st Century* 1(1): 42–73.
Zierler, David. 2011. *The Invention of Ecocid e: Agent Orange, Vietnam, and the Scientists Who Changed the Way We Think about the Environment*. Athens: University of Georgia Press.

17
Understanding Perpetrators' Use of Music

M.J. Grant

An emerging body of research documents the many ways in which music has been used in genocide, war crimes, and torture.[1] Nevertheless, there is continuing resistance to the idea that music has any real significance in such contexts. The playing of music during acts of torture and killing, for example, is often dismissed as an attempt to drown out other noises, such as shots or screams. Such an interpretation robs music of its potential to frame and give meaning to social action; in the process, we lose a potentially rich source of evidence for understanding how perpetrators organize and make sense of their actions. This chapter will highlight the benefits as well as some of the challenges of paying more focused attention to perpetrators' uses of music. The main focus will be mass shootings in the Holocaust; this is preceded by a brief overview of some ways in which music has been used to promote, prepare, and carry out atrocities.

Music and Atrocities: A Brief Introduction

There are multiple ways in which music can be implicated in atrocities, including the violent act itself. As the examples below demonstrate, music may reinforce distinctions between in-group and out-group; it may help ritualize and thus provide a sense of personal distance from the acts concerned for perpetrators; and by imposing a soundtrack that reinforces the exclusion of the victims, music can be an attempt to silence victims' voices acoustically in the very act of silencing them permanently. In the specific case of genocide, music has been shown to play significant roles at all stages in the genocidal process (Grant et al. 2015).

In order to analyze and understand the connections between musical practices and atrocities, it can be helpful to distinguish between three broad contexts within which music can be employed.

First is the use of music in propaganda and other systems of (mis-)information. Directed at the general public as a whole, or specific subsets thereof, music can attract attention to, or emphasize and influence the emotional reception of, a political message. Equally, however, it can help deflect attention away from the true nature or consequences of a particular course of action, by presenting these actions as something they are not or by using music to "normalize" the discursive framework. An example of the former can be seen in the ways that musical life in Nazi ghettoes and camps was (quite literally) orchestrated to give the impression to nearby residents and humanitarian delegations that detainees were treated well (Fackler 2007). The latter case is well documented in the case of the Rwandan radio station RTLM before and after the genocide there (McCoy 2009). RTLM attracted a broad audience precisely because of the range and popularity of the music broadcast. Though the playlists included pro-Hutu and anti-Tutsi songs such as those written and performed by star musician Simon Bikindi (some of which were presented in evidence when Bikindi was tried at the International Criminal Tribunal for Rwanda; see Parker 2015), this was only one element of a diverse and international playlist. This strategy ensured wide audiences and helped normalize the genocidal undertones of certain tracks by placing them in this wider program.

The second broad context concerns how music is employed before and particularly in the aftermath of mass killing to help perpetrators cope with their actions. Take for example this command issued by Colonel Montua of the *Polizeiregiment Mitte* in 1941:

> 1. By order of the Higher SS and Police Leader [...] all male Jews between the ages of 17 and 45 convicted as plunderers are to be shot according to martial law. The shootings are to take place away from cities, villages, and thoroughfares. [...]
> 2. The battalion and company commanders are especially to provide for the spiritual care of the men who participate in this action. The impressions of the day are to be blotted out through the holding of social events in the evenings.
>
> *(Qtd. in Browning 1992, 13–14)*

Such "spiritual care" and "social events" have long been used to help soldiers relax and recuperate during war; music—be it in the form of informal singsongs or performances by military musicians—is often an essential component.[2] In Nazi concentration and extermination camps, imprisoned musicians were often forced to play on command for high-ranking members of the SS, especially just after they had been involved in mass killing (Brauer 2016). Following Shirli Gilbert, who argues that listening to classical music "provided a framework within which the SS could maintain a self-image of refined German culture and personal 'decency,' not apart from but precisely in the context of the activities in which they were involved" (Gilbert 2005, 187), Brauer suggests that

> this cultivated "enjoyment" of music was intended to demonstrate moral superiority and, on some level, a sense of normality. This bourgeois notion of music was based on the German Romantic understanding of music as something good, moral, and beautiful, a means of producing and solidifying a sense of ethics. [...] By fostering this habitus, the SS styled itself as an organization composed of cultured, civilized, and educated people, which was contrasted directly with the image of the humiliated prisoners.
>
> *(Brauer 2016, 25)*

This brings us to the third context: the use of music concurrently with, and often as a component of, extreme violence. Forcing prisoners to play or sing is not merely a form of exploitation: often, through the physical effort as well as the humiliation and mental strain involved, it constitutes a severe act of violence against them. Brauer argues for example that "[m]usic had a dual purpose for the SS: to shore up their own sense of self while destroying that of the prisoners" (Brauer 2016). Thus, music's use during violence may be directed at the victims or serve as a psychological aid to the perpetrators; the two possibilities are never mutually exclusive.

There is a long history of the use of music in connection with torture and ill-treatment (Grant 2014). As well as forced singing and playing, this can entail subjecting prisoners to music played live or from recordings. The most widely debated example to date is that of US practices in the "War on Terror" (see especially Cusick 2008, 2013); related techniques, which use music as part of a complex and psychologically devastating system of sensory deprivation/sensory overload, have however been used since at least the 1970s in many countries. As well as such sophisticated methods of psychological torture, perpetrators often use music in ways that seem more spontaneous. Testimony from a former prisoner of the Greek military in the early 1970s, discussed by Papaeti, demonstrates for example how perpetrators themselves sang to create a punishment scenario for the further humiliation of prisoners; the song concerned, *Tarzan* by Yannis Markopoulos, was popular at the time:

> "In the evening," he told me, "the soldiers would return to the prisons drunk and they would sing the Tarzan song in order to terrorize us. They would enter the cells for the so-called 'tea party' or 'tea party with toast.'" "Tea party" here refers to guards surrounding a detainee, shouting and cursing. While beating him, they would throw him against the bed or the chair. "Tea party with toast" was a similar torture, but with even more brutal beatings. During this time, B remembers them singing the "Tarzan" song. He told me: "This was not music. This was terror. It was part of the system."
>
> *(Papaeti 2013, 75)*

The remainder of this chapter will look in more detail at one particular set of historical examples: the use of music and related sonic practices during the mass shootings of the Holocaust. By exploring the available evidence in this case, this discussion will demonstrate the kinds of information that can be teased out when we treat the recourse to music during atrocities as a significant rather than trivial element of these situations.

Cognitive Dissonances

In 1941, the commandants of the Nazi concentration camps were ordered to Sachsenhausen for instruction in how best to kill Soviet prisoners of war:

> In a barrack which was divided into different sections, the [Soviet] commissars and *politruks* were gathered together at one end, and then led one by one through a dark corridor to the execution cell, to the sound of a radio at full blast [*laut aufheulend*]. At the opposite end of this large room there was a slat with a slit in it, behind which there was an adjustable stand. The execution was carried out by a shot in the neck from a barrel to which an auxiliary barrel had been added.
>
> *(Franz Ziereis, commandant of Mauthausen concentration camp, cited from Orth 2000, 174)*

The method described above was subsequently used for the execution of Soviet POWs in other camps (Orth 2000, 175), though whether a radio or other form of amplified sound was used in those cases is not clear. But why use a radio at all? Two possibilities immediately present themselves. First, it may have been intended to ensure those waiting at the other side of the building did not hear the shots. Second, precisely because it was radio—an informal, everyday source of sound—it may have served to reassure prisoners. Both of these tactics might decrease the chance that prisoners would rise up against their fate.

The Sachsenhausen "model execution" provides one explanation as to why music was also used during mass killings of Jews from 1941 onwards. It is difficult to ascertain just how often these massacres were accompanied by music: unless the playing of music struck witnesses as unusual or significant, they would be unlikely to mention it, and until recently, few if any interviewers would be likely to ask. The examples discussed in this and the next section, however, demonstrate that even fragmentary references to music can provide new forms of evidence for understanding the situational dynamics of these killings.

Harald Welzer's exploration of the various frames of reference guiding the decision-making of perpetrators is particularly useful here (Welzer 2005). These frames of reference can take many forms: more stable frames such as those provided by law or organizational culture (here particularly, military and police codes of behavior and practice, both formal and informal); the immediate situational frames of how other people are currently behaving; and knowledge (firsthand or reported) about how others have behaved in similar situations in the past. In other words, music may have been used at some of these mass killings simply because it had been used thus previously. Whether those doing so grasped the original meaning or function of the music, or whether this was even relevant for the situation at hand, is not important here; what *is* important is that by replicating elements of previous executions those concerned could quell some of their uncertainties and guilt, safe in the knowledge that they were only doing what others had done before.

I have presumed that music was probably the main feature of the radio broadcasts played during the "model" executions in Sachsenhausen. Ziereis does not refer to music specifically, but this could be because the precise music playing seemed irrelevant. In the examples discussed below, on the other hand, it is notable that those eyewitnesses who mention music speak specifically about the kind of music chosen. The main reason for this is probably the cognitive dissonance they experienced between the type of music played and what they knew to be happening.

The first examples concern the mass shooting of Jewish prisoners at Majdanek concentration camp in November 1943, during what the Nazis termed *Aktion Erntefest* (Harvest Festival Action). Here, too, we have a statement from one of those implicated, made in the context of criminal proceedings in Germany in the 1960s:

> We had to cordon off a path [*Laufweg*] around 15 meters wide between the hall already mentioned and the pit where the shootings took place. [...] In the hall, the Jews had to undress, because they were naked when they came out on the other side. Then they had to walk/run [*laufen*] along the track we had cordoned off to the shooting site, which was about 1000 meters away. SD [*Sicherheitsdienst*] men, who also stood along this area, drove the Jews on using riding crops. Dogs were set at them as well. If a Jew collapsed with exhaustion, the others had to carry/drag him to the shooting site. [...] During the shootings music was transmitted via loudspeakers, clearly with the purpose of drowning out the sound of the shots.
>
> *(Former member of Mounted Police Battalion III, cited in Mallmann, Rieß & Pyta (eds.). 2003; my translation)*

The pit into which the bodies were to fall and the practice of making victims undress before execution—de-individualizing as well as degrading them—are typical aspects of other Nazi mass shootings, as is the fact that victims were shot only at the designated site, even if they had to be carried there.[3] Loud music was also used at subsequent massacres in *Aktion Erntefest* at the Budzyn and Krasnik camps, with Browning concluding that this was "a vain attempt to cover up the noise of the shooting" (Browning 1992, 140). The use of music is the only apparent similarity to the Sachsenhausen example, and the situation as a whole was completely different, not least because of the sheer numbers involved and the identity of the victims.

In their discussion of the soundscape of Majdanek, from which the quotations below are drawn, Joanna Posłuszna and Łukasz Posłusny point out that the sounds of beatings and shootings were part of everyday life in the camp and frequently discussed in survivor testimony (2015). Prisoners were generally under no illusions as to what their captors were capable of; they lived in constant fear of acts of great brutality. From this perspective, it is not surprising that the music that emanated from the loudspeakers that day did anything but reassure them, especially since this was only one of several highly unusual things to happen. "Morning of 3 November," recalled Jerzy Kwiatkowski,

> [b]efore the roll call started, we notice that behind the barbed wire, at regular intervals machine guns were set, with their barrels aimed at the camp; next to them groups of SS men were wearing military coats and combat gear. They had apparently stood there all night. And we say to ourselves, dicke Luft, something sinister is in the air.
>
> *(Cited from Posłuszna and Posłusny 2015, 117)*

Kwiatkowski goes on to recount how Jews were ordered to present themselves and eventually led out through the gates towards the crematorium:

> We look at the road running to Lublin, and at the road leading to the camp, both are teeming with people over whom hover clouds of dust. Numerous cars and military troops move towards the crematorium. In an unprecedented move, a mass of human tide flows in one direction. Suddenly we hear some music, some pitiful Tango Milonga and then a waltz by Strauss. It is music from records broadcast through a loudspeaker. The sound comes from the direction of the crematory. Where has the loud-speaker come from? This has never been used before. The music keeps going incessantly. Disc after disc. A plane is making circles low over the camp; it is such a horrible drone that I cannot hear my own voice. There were short breaks between the discs and then you could hear a muffled "ta ta ta—ta ta ta", like the shots from a handheld machine gun. [...] The loudspeaker plays for the whole day and from time to time there is a series of shots from the machine gun. New columns of Jewish men and women keep moving along the road next to our field. The twilight falls, the sound of music still fill[s] the air. The night comes, the music stops, the slaughter is over [...].
>
> *(Cited from Posłuszna and Posłusny 2015, 117–118)*[4]

The respite was only temporary: the shootings, and their musical accompaniment, resumed the next day.

As Kwiatkowski recalls, it was clear to observers that something very different and very wrong was happening—an impression underlined, rather than assuaged, by the sound of music. Neither does the music completely cover the sound of the shots. We should also note Kwiatkowski's specific reference to the music played: dance music, specifically a tango and a waltz (other survivors remembered foxtrots; Fackler 2007). This must have presented a particularly crass contrast to the sound of shooting. Another survivor of Majdanek, Stefania Perzanowska, also remembers waltz music:

> Shots! By the Beautiful Blue Danube.[5] Music and the distant rattle of machine guns. Tired and stressed, yet full of expectations, we sat on benches, tables, and bunks. We waited, listening intently to the melodies and the sounds of gunfire we hadn't heard for a while. [...] Shots again. Salvos of machine guns and the music from megaphones. Basia bursts into mournful crying. Regina echoes her. One begins the prayer for the dying. We all kneel down. Poles, Jews, Russians. We pray for those who died in agony, for those standing in the face of death, for battered men, sick women, and children who do not know hatred. Megaphones blare. Machine guns rattle [...].
>
> *(Cited from Posłuszna and Posłusny 2015, 118)*[6]

The passages above, and others cited by the authors, are unusual in the emphasis laid on aural impressions—perhaps because the other prisoners could not see what was actually happening and were thus forced to make sense of the days' events, then and since, through auditory evidence. These remain fleeting impressions, which is not uncommon. Researchers are not the only ones likely to put little stress on musical accompaniments to atrocities: eyewitnesses, too, are for obvious reasons more likely to prioritize other memories and experiences. In addition, many if not most people have difficulty describing music, whether this is music they know and love or music that is linked to traumatic events (Cusick 2013). Thanks to a number of recent studies specifically on the role of music in Nazi atrocities, we know that the use of music during or as punishment, including executions, was by no means limited to Majdanek. In some cases, the music for these punishments was provided by camp orchestras or bands.[7] A photograph taken in Mauthausen concentration camp in 1944, for example, shows prisoners being led to their execution by members of the camp band;[8] the Sachsenhausen camp orchestra similarly played dance music and marches during public floggings and executions (Gilbert 2005, 132). Many of these uses of music demonstrate striking parallels to historical uses of music in punishment in both military and civilian contexts, as I will discuss later.

Countless examples exist from other camps as well. Testimony from Treblinka tells of musicians being required to entertain soldiers during mass killings (Naliwajek-Mazurek 2013). There is at least one report that dance music was played through loudspeakers during the massacre at Babi Yar, near Kiev, where 33,771 Jewish children, women, and men were shot in late September 1941. Michael Berenbaum, who presents this example, suggests that the music "drowned out the screams of the victims" (cited here from Moreno 2006, 269). Given that the victims had all reported to the site voluntarily, believing they were to be relocated, it may be that the light entertainment music was intended to keep up the pretense as long as possible.[9] Using music to deceive people as to their fate was not limited to mass murder by shooting: in Auschwitz-Birkenau from 1944 on, music from camp orchestras "welcomed" new truckloads of people during the selection process. Again, the popular repertoire played gave no inkling to the new arrivals that many would be taken directly to the gas chambers (Gilbert 2005, 177–178).

In the case of Majdanek, too, it is possible that the music was meant to reassure the victims:[10] *Aktion Erntefest* took place in response to uprisings in several other camps and ghettoes; given the sheer number of prisoners, the perpetrators may have been afraid of losing control of the situation if prisoners realized what was about to happen. After the victims left the hall, however, the charade was discontinued: they were forced forward between rows of soldiers brandishing whips. The historical military punishment of running the gauntlet could well have been an active frame of reference here.

Novozlatopol

Novozlatopol is a small commune in Ukraine, founded on the arrival of Jewish agricultural workers in the mid-nineteenth century. At the outbreak of the Second World War, around half of the population (about 1,100 people) was Jewish.[11] It was one of many rural communities in occupied Eastern Europe to witness mass shootings of the Jewish population. Nazi forces arrived in early October 1941; in November and December, around 800 Jews from Novozlatopol and surrounding communities were shot.

The testimony gathered in Novozlatopol is significant because it touches on aspects of musical practice during mass shootings that, to my knowledge, are quite unusual.[12] Several different eyewitnesses record broadly similar accounts, and the musical elements of the mass shootings seemed important enough to have passed into local memory. Polina Savchenko, a local high school teacher, recounts one such story:

> It is said that in a village near Novozlatopol there was a musician. He played the *buben*[13] and he was requisitioned several times to play it during executions. He couldn't bear it. One day, when he was being taken home, he saw a young girl hiding behind the hospital. He said nothing. He went back in secret and saved her and her son.
>
> *(Cited from Desbois 2008, 140–141)*

A similar story, but with a very different ending, was given by eyewitness Ivan Litchnitski.[14] He had witnessed the shootings from a hiding place in a hayloft and also saw many of the preparations carried out the night before. His uncle had been requisitioned to guard the Jews who had been rounded up. As Desbois recounts from Litchnitski's testimony,

> One of the villagers had been requisitioned to play the Ukrainian drum every morning. One day, the drummer had not been able to take it any longer. Seeing a Feldgendarme beating Jewish children, he had thrown himself at him. The German had shot him and thrown his body in the pit along with the Jews from the 15 villages.
>
> *(Desbois 2008, 136)*

It is unclear whether the drummer had been told to play during the shootings. From the context, it is also possible that he played for a type of morning "roll call," a military tradition also copied in the concentration camps. Historically, however, drums often accompanied military punishment and execution rituals across Europe—not frame drums, but drums nonetheless. Military tradition may therefore have been a primary frame of reference for this massacre and the drum a primary element in creating that frame. Alternatively, and given the widespread use of frame drums in folk music traditions—including in dance music—it is possible that the perpetrators were again following the example of other mass shootings and executions where popular music had been employed.

Litchnitski also recounted that, in Desbois' words, "other peasants had been recruited in the morning to bang saucepans to muffle the cries of the Jews" (Desbois 2008, 136). Litchnitski is not the only person to have recalled the sound of banging metal. Maria Savovska, who would have been thirteen at the time, testified that "the shouting was heard all over the village. Local residents were forced to hit buckets with sticks in order to cover the cries" (Savovska 2002). Testimony from Tatyana Zogot, a woman active in the Jewish community of Novozlatopol, stated that

> in order to cover the sounds of the shouting and lamenting and the children's crying the policemen suspended a rail and beat it to cover up the terrible noises of the people who were innocent victims of the fascists and their henchmen, the [local] policemen.
>
> *(Zogot n.d.)*

This account is similar to testimony given by Ivan Plyasovitsa and included in the 1944 report of the Soviet Extraordinary State Commission, established to investigate Nazi atrocities on Soviet territory. Plyasovitsa would have been around twenty-two years old at the time of the massacre:

> The Jews were taken to the pits: those who did not resist were shot while those who resisted were thrown into the pit alive. In order to cover the sounds of the screaming and groaning of those who were being thrown into the pits the German henchmen struck broken buckets and boxes and even turned on a tractor. In spite of that it was impossible to cover the sounds of the screaming and groaning because they were so loud.
>
> *(Plyasovitsa 1944)*

This statement sheds a new light on events: many of the victims were buried alive, and it was seemingly in a failed attempt to silence *their* voices that the perpetrators resorted to loud noise, variously described as coming from pots, buckets, or a metal rail, as well as a tractor. This explanation seems plausible: such noises are more likely to attract attention than deflect it. Given that surely no one in the small community could still be under the impression that the Jews were being gathered together for transportation to Palestine, as they had been told, there would be little point in trying to mask the sound of the shots.

There is a further possible explanation as well. Some of the objects mentioned—especially saucepans and buckets—are typical of those used in historical traditions of public shaming and folk justice. A range of such traditions, in which creating such a cacophony was central, were found across Europe from the Middle Ages to the recent past. Generally discussed by scholars under the umbrella term "charivari," the names given to individual traditions—such as "rough music" (England) and "*Katzenmusik*" ("cat music," Germany)—often point to the essential sonic feature that links them. Such practices were collective, carried out either by the community at large or certain sub-groups within that community; the targets were generally people deemed to have contravened local moral laws. As well as drawing attention to the ritual, scholars have suggested that the cacophony of a charivari functioned as a sort of anti-music or paramusic, clearly marking a disharmony in the community (Thompson 1992). Most of the related German practices had died out by the later nineteenth or early twentieth century, but instances have been reported of Nazi-era punishments in Germany that consciously referenced these traditions (Hinrichs 1982, 306).

Could the sonic practices at Novozlatopol have constituted such a "paramusic"? The historical context suggests that this is entirely plausible. Thomas Kühne has argued that "in Germany around 1930, shame culture [...] attained a level that was unusual for an industrialized society" (Kühne 2010, 29). He describes shame culture as a morality driven not by individual responsibility for one's actions, but by "obedience, duty, and suffering" (28). Kühne attributes this development to Germany's defeat in the First World War, and the burden of collective guilt placed on Germany in its aftermath. The Nazi ethos both spoke to this feeling of national humiliation and fed on the central tenets of a shame culture—many of which are foundational aspects of military culture as well—with the promise of a *Volksgemeinschaft*, a national community. Essential to this kind of community, however, is that it defines itself by exclusion as much as inclusion. The primary "others" against which the Nazi community defined itself were the Jews. Practices of public shaming of Jewish people took place in Germany long before the events discussed above. Michael Wildt, for example, discusses a case from the eastern German town of Osterode in 1935, in which a Jewish shopkeeper who had been accused of hitting a boy (after pursuing some boys who had stuck defamatory posters to his windows) was forced to parade through the streets wearing a sign proclaiming that "This dirty Jew hit a German boy!" while being subjected to shouts, taunts, and kicks (Wildt 2003, 23–24).

The connection between music and violence under the Nazis is strongest in their treatment of Jewish people. Although music had been a consistent feature of discipline and punishment in Sachsenhausen from its inception, the use of music to mark off, humiliate, and inflict violence on Jewish prisoners was unlike anything meted out against other prisoners (Brauer 2009). Brauer suggests that this specifically musical ill-treatment was related to the belief that Jews were dominating German musical life, a belief that predated Nazism but became much stronger as a result of Nazi propaganda. This prejudice rested on the idea that the Jews were innately "musical people" (*innate* musicality, as opposed to *cultured* musicality, has in white European thought long been associated with racial "inferiors").[15] At the same time, and crucially for our consideration of what happened at Novozlatopol, anti-Semitism in Europe has long cultivated the trope of Jewish people as creators of disruptive noise. As Ruth HaCohen has explored, descriptions of the sounds of Jewish worship are particular targets for such treatment (2011). She quotes for example from Johann Christian Edelmann's 1749 description of the sound of Jews praying at a synagogue in Frankfurt as "*Katzengeschrey* (cat-calls)" and "*Katzen-Töne* (catlike tones)." Both terms are uncannily close to the word *Katzenmusik*, the most common German name for charivari or "rough music" traditions.

Conclusion

The question of what motivated Nazi perpetrators remains as controversial as it is challenging (Orth 2000, 53–54, Orth 2010). There are relatively few subjective accounts from perpetrators themselves, and many of these—stemming from testimony provided sometimes many years after the atrocities and in the context of criminal proceedings—must be approached with even more care than normal. Perhaps the word "motivation" is itself misleading, given the complex situational dynamics involved. Welzer's outline of three questions that any social-psychological study of mass murder must pose is perhaps a better way to frame the research question:

> [H]ow the perpetrators understood and interpreted the situation in which they killed, which internal rationale accounted for how they made sense of their actions (bearing in mind that this rationale may appear completely irrational to outsiders), and what the social and mental processes and situational dynamics were that formed the basis of their decision to kill.
>
> *(Welzer 2005, 43, my translation)*

Musical practices may constitute frames of reference in Welzer's sense: by situating the killing within the cultural framework of military action or criminally sanctioned execution; by drawing attention away from the reality of what is happening; or, more subtly, by uniting individuals through a single soundtrack, like the beat of a common drum. Where music is an element in such situations, it may still transpire to be tangential; it may, however, reveal aspects of the mindset and motivation of killers not apparent by other means.

How perpetrators use music is only one side of the story: how the music is perceived by their victims—what it does to *their* situation—is another issue entirely. We can never know how those murdered by the Nazis experienced this music and these sounds in their final moments; studies such as those discussed earlier indicate, however, that for some people at least, the music likely added to their suffering. Bearing witness to their experience is a further reason for understanding how music was used against them.

Notes

1 A significant proportion of this research focuses on atrocities committed by the Nazis and will be discussed in more detail later. Other conflicts investigated include the civil war in Sierra Leone (Richards 2007; Nuxoll 2015) and the wars in former Yugoslavia (e.g., Baker 2013). Research into the use of music in the genocide in Rwanda, also referenced separately in this chapter, has often focused on the legal implications of the trials pertaining to incitement to genocide. Several recent studies focus on the of music in torture, also touched on below.
2 Browning recounts how Police Reserve Battalion 101 was joined, on the eve of one massacre, by a police entertainment troupe from Berlin, members of which were enthusiastic to join in the killing (Browning 1992, 113).
3 Welzer argues that such incidents point to how the perpetrators focused on fulfilling their task exactly as expected or ordered, again a way to deflect responsibility (2005, 152).
4 Original source: Jerzy Kwiatkowski, *485 dni na Majdanku*, Lublin 1988.
5 The name of one of Johann Strauss Jr.'s most famous waltzes.
6 Original source: Stefania Perzanowska, *Gdyi myśli wrancają do Majdanka*, Lublin 1970.
7 Such bands were a standard feature of Nazi concentration camps. See, for example, Brauer (2009, 2016); Fackler (2007); and Gilbert (2005) for more information.
8 Viewable at www.bpk-images.de/, image no. 30013239.
9 Moreno cites from Michael Berenbaum's *Witness to the Holocaust* (New York: Harper Collins, 1997), 145.
10 A more conclusive discussion would seek to establish the exact location of the loudspeakers, for example, in order to establish who (and where) the intended auditors were.
11 Information taken from www.yadvashem.org/untoldstories/database/index.asp?cid=595, accessed November 16, 2017.
12 Much of the information below is drawn from Desbois (2008). Additional references come from testimony held at the World Holocaust Memorial Centre Yad Vashem.
13 A Ukrainian frame drum.
14 Documentation on the Novozlatopol massacre held in Yad Vashem includes testimony gathered in 2002 from a man named Ivan Vishnitsky. This is apparently the same person.
15 Hence the prejudices surrounding the "natural rhythm" of people of African heritage. Roma, too, are often typified as musical, perhaps because in many regions they have had to rely on a marginalized existence as traveling musicians.

References

Baker, Catherine. 2013. "Music as a Weapon of Ethnopolitical Violence and Conflict: Processes of Ethnic Separation during and after the Break-up of Yugoslavia." *Patterns of Prejudice* 47/4–5: 409–429.

Berenbaum, Michael. 1997. *Witness to the Holocaust*. New York: Harper Collins.

Brauer, Juliane. 2009. *Musik im Konzentrationslager Sachsenhausen*. Berlin: Metropol.

Brauer, Juliane. 2016. "How Can Music Be Torturous? Music in Nazi Concentration and Extermination Camps." *Music and Politics* X/1, online, http://dx.doi.org/10.3998/mp.9460447.0010.103.

Browning, Christopher. 1992. *Ordinary Men: Reserve Police Battalion 101 and the "Final Solution" in Poland*. New York: Harper Collins.

Cusick, Suzanne G. 2008. "'You Are in a Place That Is Out of the World … ': Music in the Detention Camps of the 'Global War on Terror'." *Journal of the Society for American Music* 2/1: 1–26.

Cusick, Suzanne G. 2013. "Toward an Acoustemology of Detention in the 'Global War on Terror'." In *Music, Sound and Space: Transformation of Public and Private Experience*, edited by Georgina Born, 275–291. Cambridge: Cambridge University Press.

Desbois, Patrick. 2008. *The Holocaust by Bullets: A Priest's Journey to Uncover the Truth behind the Murder of 1.5 Million Jews*. Translated from the French by Catherine Spencer. New York: Palgrave Macmillan.

Fackler, Guido. 2007. "Music in Concentration Camps 1933–1945." *Music and Politics* 1/1, online, http://dx.doi.org/10.3998/mp.9460447.0001.102.

Gilbert, Shirli. 2005. *Music in the Holocaust: Confronting Life in the Nazi Ghettoes and Camps*. Oxford: Oxford University Press.

Grant, M. J. 2014. "Pathways to Music Torture." *Transpositions: Musique et sciences sociales*, 4/2014, special issue *Music and armed conflict since* 1945, online, http://transposition.revues.org/494.

Grant, M. J., Cornelia Nuxoll, Mareike Jacobs, Rebecca Möllemann & Simone Münz. 2015. "Music, the 'Third Reich', and the '8 Stages of Genocide'." In *Music and Genocide*, edited by Wojciech Klimczyk and Agatha Świerzowska, 23–68. Frankfurt am Main etc.: Peter Lang.

HaCohen, Ruth. 2011. *The Music Libel against the Jews*. New Haven: Yale.

Hinrichs, Ernst. 1982. "Le charivari et les usages de réprimande en Allemagne. État et perspectives de la recherche." In *Le Charivari*, edited by Jacques Le Goff and Jean-Claude Schmitt, 297–306. Paris etc.: EHESS/Mouton.

Kühne, Thomas. 2010. *Belonging and Genocide: Hitler's Community, 1918–1945*. New Haven: Yale University Press.

Mallmann, Klaus-Michael, Volker Rieß & Wolfram Pyta (eds.). 2003. *Deutscher Osten 1939-1945: Der Weltanschauungskrieg in Photos und Texten*. Darmstadt: Wissenschaftliche Buchgesellschaft.

McCoy, Jason. 2009. "Making Violence Ordinary: Radio, Music and the Rwandan Genocide." *African Music* 8/3: 85–96.

Moreno, Joseph J. 2006. "Orpheus in Hell: Music in the Holocaust." In *Music and Manipulation: On the Social Uses and Social Control of Music*, edited by Steve Brown and Ulrik Vogelsten, 264–286. New York: Berghahn Books.

Naliwajek-Mazurek, Katarzyna. 2013. "Music and Torture in Nazi Sites of Persecution and Genocide in Occupied Poland, 1939–1945." *The world of music (new series)* 2/1 (June 2013), thematic issue *Music and Torture | Music and Punishment*, guest editors M.J. Grant and Anna Papaeti: 31–50.

Nuxoll, Cornelia. 2015. "'We Listened to It Because of the Message': Juvenile RUF Com- batants and the Role of Music in the Sierra Leone Civil War." *Music and Politics* 9/1, online, http://dx.doi.org/10.3998/mp.9460447.0009.104.

Orth, Karin. 2000. *Die Konzentrationslager SS. Soziostrukturelle Analysen und biographische Studien*. Göttingen: Wallstein.

Orth, Karin. 2010. "The Concentration Camp Personnel." In *Concentration Camps in Nazi Germany: The New Histories*, edited by Jane Caplan and Nikolaus Wachsmann, 44–57. London: Routledge.

Papaeti, Anna. 2013. "Music, Torture, Testimony: Reopening the Case of the Greek Military Junta (1967-1974)." *the world of music (new series)* 2013/1, thematic issue *Music and Torture | Music and Punishment*, guest editors M.J. Grant and Anna Papaeti: 67–89.

Parker, James. 2015. *Acoustic Jurisprudence: Listening to the Trial of Simon Bikindi*. Oxford: Oxford University Press.

Plyasovitsa, Ivan. 1944. "Testimony on the Massacres in Novozlatopol Included in The report of the Soviet Extraordinary State Commission," from www.yadvashem.org/untoldstories/database/chgkSovietReports.asp?cid=595&site_id=752.

Posłuszna, Joanna & Łukasz Posłusny. 2015. "The Aural Landscape of Majdanek." In *Music and Genocide*, edited by Wojciech Klimczyk and Agatha Świerzowska, 105–120. Frankfurt am Main etc.: Peter Lang.

Richards, Paul. 2007. "The Emotions at War: A Musicological Approach to Understanding Atrocity in Sierra Leone." In *Public Emotions*, edited by S. Perri Six C. Squire Radstone and A. Treacher, 62–84. London: Palgrave Macmillan.

Savovska, Maria. 2002. "Testimony on the Massacres in Novozlatopol," from www.yadvashem.org/untoldstories/database/writtenTestimonies.asp?cid=595&site_id=752.

Thompson, E. P. 1992. "Rough Music Reconsidered." *Folklore* 103/1: 3–26.

Welzer, Harald. 2005. *Täter: Wie ganz normale Menschen Massenmörder werden*. Frankfurt am Main: Fischer.

Wildt, Michael. 2003. "Gewaltpolitik. Volksgemeinschaft und Judenverfolgung in der deutschen Provinz 1932 bis 1935." *WerkstattGeschichte* 35: 23–43.

Zogot, Tatyana. n.d. "Testimony on the Massacres in Novozlatopol," from www.yadvashem.org/untoldstories/database/writtenTestimonies.asp?cid=595&site_id=752.

18

Information Technologies and Constructions of Perpetrator Identities

Adam Henschke

Information, Security, and Values

The capacity of information technologies to identify and respond to perpetrators of mass violence creates an expectation that states should use these technologies to provide security to their citizens. One of the recommendations of the 9/11 Commission Report was that US intelligence agencies needed to make better use of the information they had on potential terrorists (National Commission on Terrorist Attacks upon the United States 2004, 417). In the intervening years, the power of information technologies has increased, and so too have the claims about what these information technologies can do to identify the perpetrators of mass violence before such events occur. Some propose that security agencies could analyze their existing intelligence to predict terrorist attacks (Woollacot 2015). Others are doing "research on support tools and methods that help law enforcement officers in ongoing investigations of web extremism … [to develop] techniques that can be used to detect indicators supporting that someone has intent to commit a terror attack" (Brynielsson et al. 2013, 2). Following the shooting at Stoneman Douglas High School in Florida in February 2018, US President Trump criticized the Federal Bureau of Investigation for not monitoring and responding to social media posts by the shooter to prevent the tragedy (Graham 2018). In short, there are continued pushes to use these and other informational tools to protect civil society against perpetrators of mass violence.

However, in liberal democratic societies there are constraints around intelligence and surveillance technologies, particularly for domestic use. The 9/11 Commission Report, for instance, recognized that "the sharing and uses of information must be guided by a set of practical policy guidelines that simultaneously empower and constrain officials, telling them clearly what is and is not permitted" (National Commission on Terrorist Attacks upon the United States 2004, 419). One way to explore the constraints is to view how elements of the construction of a "virtual identity" for potential perpetrators of mass violence inform and guide decision-making.

In this chapter, I draw from US, UK, and Australian cases to show how value judgments can be woven into these automated systems. The chapter covers the argument that automated informational technologies play a role in the active construction of virtual identities and that these virtual identities are of core interest to Perpetrator Studies. First, I introduce the notion of virtual identities and their relation to surveillance and perpetrator identification. Then I examine value sensitive design, and I conclude with examples that demonstrate particular concerns when information technologies go wrong in the context of mass violence and state actions.

Virtual Identities: Making Information Useful

Vast amounts of personal information are currently produced and collected through people's online behavior and with surveillance technologies. To make this information more useful for preventing acts of violence, it needs to be structured and analyzed. One set of methods uses the information to construct what we can call a "virtual identity." A virtual identity is "some information set in the world that calls to mind a person. Virtual identity refers to a particular type of information which encourages the observer to experience the information as Personal Information" (Henschke 2017, 122). A virtual identity, then, is a photo, a diagram of a person's social network, or a map of a person's movements through a city that encourages the observer of the information to experience the information as relating to a person or people in some way. In the context of this discussion, the purpose of constructing these virtual identities is to make the identification of perpetrators of mass violence easier and more accurate.

We can look to three methods of constructing these virtual identities: the comparison of surveillance data with existing biometric databases, characterization of individuals through metadata analysis, and flagging of suspicious behavior through artificial intelligence pattern recognition. When considered in the context of national security and law enforcement, each of these methods can construct a virtual identity that suggests that the target of the information is a potential perpetrator of violence.

Biometrics are used in surveillance to make an identity claim between a suspect and a known perpetrator of violence. In late 2017, the Council of Australian Governments "signed off on a facial biometric agreement to give state and federal police real-time access to passport, visa, citizenship, and driver's license images for criminal investigations including those involving suspected terrorists" (Cooper 2017). The mechanism that the virtual identity construction relies on here is the similarity and likelihood that the given target of suspicion is a known threat. The background condition is that there is a potentially violent actor, and biometrics are used to quickly and perhaps automatically test if anyone in a large group of people in a public space could be the perpetrator. The combination of biometrics with informational analytics can increase the power of the identification in at least three ways. First, the range of source data for biometrics expands beyond photo matching—facial recognition, ears, iris recognition, voice, and even a person's walking patterns can be used as part of a recognition effort (Azom et al. 2015; Reid et al. 2014; Dubois and Bresciani 2015; Dovydaitis et al. 2017). Second, the new source of information can be compared against an existing biometric database. Third, these comparisons can be done automatically and rapidly.

The second method involves the use of metadata to identify the character of the target of attention. Social network analysis, for example, is frequently touted as a way to identify membership in terrorist groups (Ressler 2006; Mullins and Dolnik 2010; Mullins 2013). In social network analysis, rather than focusing on the content of what a person might be saying, personal connections and social relations are potential indicators of their status as terrorists.[1] Here, the metadata is used to characterize an individual or group as terrorists in reference to whom they know and are interacting with. By virtue of these interactions, the target's virtual identity includes a characterization as a risk due to the potential connection to perpetrators of mass violence.

The third method involves various forms of artificial intelligence or machine learning to flag suspicious activity. A recent review article of video surveillance systems suggests that suspicious activity detection is a key technique of intelligent video surveillance techniques. The suspicious events included loitering individuals, unattended/missing objects, intruder detection, abnormal activity, and abnormal behavior (Mathur and Bundele 2016). For instance, video surveillance can be analyzed to detect if "a pedestrian moves with a different speed and in a different direction" in a crowd (Kapoor and Pateriya 2016, 415). Given that the use of artificial intelligence to identify abnormal or suspicious behaviors removes human operators from the process, on the face of it, this may seem to be the method most removed from human values. In these methods, however, humans are involved in the training stage of the machine learning to provide an initial determination of what is normal behavior and what is abnormal or strange. The virtual identity here is constructed from what the human trainers have judged to be abnormal or suspicious behavior.

Values in Informational Analytics

This is all relevant because humans design values into technologies; the idea that all technologies are value neutral is a coarse simplification. This idea derives from "value sensitive design":

> If our moral and political discourse on user autonomy, patient centered-ness and citizen centered-ness, our privacy, security is to be more than an empty promise, these values will have to be expressed in the design, architecture and specifications of systems. If we want our information technology—and the use that is made of it—to be just, fair and safe, we must see to it that it inherits our good intentions.
>
> *(van Den Hoven 2007, 69)*

For example: if surveillance cameras are placed in public toilets but are kept out of the offices of politicians, we can conclude that the privacy of the average citizen is not of high value, but that the privacy of politicians is valued higher than transparency.[2] Something as simple as the location of a surveillance camera carries with it a set of values; it expresses a set of design choices that favor one set of values over another.

In terms of the processing of information to create virtual identities, we will see that three value judgments are involved in particular steps in the creation of virtual identities: choosing security over privacy, that metadata is of limited moral value, and of suspicion and abnormality. Note that this is not a comprehensive list; instead, the point is to show how certain values are part of the automated processes of creating virtual identities.

At a national security summit in Australia in late 2017, a range of political leaders stated that security is of greater value than a value like privacy, saying

> [w]e are going to have to curtail the rights and freedoms of a small number of people in order to keep the vast majority of Australians safe" and that "[a]ll of us are having to reconsider our civil rights and compromise on those things but I think the vast majority of the public wants us to put security first.
>
> *(Daniel Andrews and Gladys Berejiklian quoted in Bickers 2017)*

Valuing security over privacy is expressed in the use of driver's license data as part of biometric analysis to identify terror suspects at airports. The information has already been collected for other government agencies; it is already part of the bureaucratic system. Individual privacy is valued less than the need to provide general security to the citizens.

When considering the use of metadata about people, metadata's value is derived from recognizing that it has practical value, not that it might be considered private. In terms of value tradeoffs, because the metadata is publicly available and therefore not secret, this personal information is treated as having significant practical value while having minimal moral value. This approach draws from the concept of privacy being synonymous with secrecy. As Daniel Solove writes, "One of the most common understandings of privacy is that it constitutes the secrecy of certain matters. In this view, privacy is violated by the public disclosure of previously concealed information" (Solove 2008, 21). In contrast, a concept of privacy-as-intimacy, like that described by Julie Inness (1992) considers that even publicly available personal information can be deemed private in virtue of an intimate relation between a person and personal information. In moving beyond a singular conception of privacy-as-secrecy, I have argued in depth in *Ethics in an Age of Surveillance* (2017) that seemingly "morally innocuous" personal information like metadata can and ought to be considered private.

The proponents of metadata's utility see it as valuable in terms of its use. As a former Australian Prime Minister stated:

> We're talking here about metadata ... It's just the data that the system generates ... To use an old fashioned metaphor if you like, if you look at a letter, you've got the address, you've got the sender, you've got the date stamp, where it was posted and what time it was posted. [Metadata is] the electronic version of what is on the front of the letter that we want to keep. The contents of the letter, well people can only get access to that with a warrant.
>
> *(Abbott 2015)*

The reasoning is that because metadata is not secret it is not private and so we do not need to apply significant moral value to it. Or at least, its moral value is close to insignificant whereas its utility is paramount. This then builds into the previous reasoning of security trumping privacy—people's metadata is of such limited moral value that any security-orientated use is easily justified.

The final value is in the determination of strangeness and abnormality required to identify suspicious behaviors: what behaviors count as normal and what behaviors deviate from that normal? Machine learning and certain forms of artificial intelligence that form the basis for the automated surveillance analysis described above require humans to provide the initial training data that forms the basis for the artificial judgments on strange and abnormal behaviors. For this sort of technology to work at all, humans program in values like normal/abnormal, values that are core to the technology's function. Again, humans and the values that they hold are central to the automated processes.

Virtual Identities Shaping Responses to People

In this section, I defend the claim that there are morally relevant aspects in the automation of information technologies when they are involved in the creation of virtual identities for the purposes of identifying potential perpetrators of mass violence. Much like the recognition that there are values in the way these technologies are designed, there are values in how the constructs and outputs of these technologies are applied. That is, the construction of identities for perpetrators matters. The argument at its most basic is that the form given to the perpetrator identities affects how users respond to and apply the virtual identities.

The simplest example of this is the designation of someone as a perpetrator in the first place. Consider that a surveillance operator receives an alert that given people on a CCTV screen are flagged as a possible terrorist risk: perhaps at an ID check, metadata reveals that they are on a terrorist no-fly list. Alternatively, maybe their biometrics match that of terrorist suspects from another state. Or maybe they are walking abnormally, and that abnormal gait suggests that they may be carrying something suspicious on their body. In all scenarios, the identities constructed for the target people is that of perpetrators and so warrants some form of response by a human operator.

Following this designation as potential perpetrators, it is now up to the operator to respond to that designation. Are the targets actually threats? Should they be cleared of the character assessments? Should they be followed, should the surveillance be continued? Or should the police be called in to detain or arrest the targets? Confronted with the character assessments, the surveillance operators are now in a position of responsibility, and they are required to act in some way.

This may seem problematic, but perhaps it is not *especially* problematic. Police on patrol, security officers at airports, CCTV operators all do this as part of their daily jobs. The special relevance here relates to the technological design. First, as Richard Thaler and Cass Sunstein have argued, the defaults in a socio-technological system matter (2009). If X is a given default in a system, we are inclined to retain that default. Even in an area like national security, we see repeatedly that the default settings on passwords remain unchanged, creating major cybersecurity vulnerabilities (Palmer 2018). Defaults matter, and as we have seen, the design of technologies involves values. The designation of a person as "perpetrator" warranting follow-up is not simply a request for response. It carries with it the default setting that the focus of attention is problematic in some way.

A counter-argument to this point is that though flagging peoples makes them persons of interest, our operators are not automatons. It is their *job* to assess the situation. The technology is simply indicating that a situation needs to be assessed. While this may be true, it does not always represent the reality of how people make decisions. Daniel Kahneman's descriptions of cognitive biases and mental effort (2011, 31–49) suggest that when we are tired, when our cognitive processes are "drawn down," we are more likely to accept an argument *as it is presented* (2011, 46). That is, our capacity to respond to and *challenge defaults* is in part dependent on our state of mind. Stress, tiredness, and boredom can play a big role in how effective an operator is at challenging or simply accepting the default settings. Following the construction of a virtual identity where the target of surveillance is designated as a perpetrator and so presented to the operator as a potential risk or threat, it is now up to the operator to *reject* the suggestion that the target of the surveillance is worthy of suspicion. However, the capacity to reject this is dependent on factors like tiredness, stress, or the number of other tasks running at the time.

Getting It Wrong

The claims that there are values designed into surveillance technologies and that these values might significantly guide operators' decisions and behavior might both be accurate, but the next question to ask is: why should we care? Human values guide and are subtly fed into technologies, and those design decisions can then guide and impact user decisions. The final section of this chapter will show two ways in which the design features in information technologies shape virtual identities in ways that are morally relevant.

Risk of False Positives: From Deaths to Discrimination

The first set of worries arises when the technologies get it wrong and incorrectly identify a person as a perpetrator, as guilty, or as simply suspicious. Liberal democracies pride themselves on their criminal justice institutions, seeing the rule of law and the right to a fair trial as parts of an essential legal, social, and moral fabric that separates them from autocratic or despotic regimes. A presumption of guilt or suspicion runs contrary to that, undermining the notion of innocent until proven guilty.

The worst-case scenario is if the automated processes misidentify a person as a terrorist or dangerous criminal and then that person is physically harmed or killed because of misidentification. The shooting of Jean Charles da Silva de Menezes in London in 2005 is proof that this can happen. In the de Menezes case, the victim was misidentified as a terror suspect; his behaviors were seen to be suspicious, indicating that he might be about to commit a terrorist attack, and he was subsequently shot by police officers (Miller and Gordon 2014, 188–194). This case clearly displays the risks of getting identification wrong: he was mistaken for someone else, and officers misinterpreted his character identity when his behaviors were seen as suspicious. In the subsequent inquiry, one of the chief problems stemmed from the communication of relevant information: the virtual identity was constructed for de Menezes as guilty and suspicious, and there were communication failures in correcting that virtual identity (Miller and Gordon 2014, 188). While the de Menezes case is an extreme example, it shows how faulty information can lead to problematic identity constructions that can have lethal consequences in situations of stress and imminent danger.

A second set of concerns can be seen when we look at people being put on "no-fly lists." Here, a piece of metadata is added to a person's travel data because of some suspicion about a risk to national security. Following the 9/11 terrorist attacks, airport security around the world was substantially tightened. One measure was to be more vigilant in assessing and preventing threats from getting onto planes. Functionally, being on a no-fly list means that a person may be prevented from traveling, or face significant delays or problems while traveling. While these processes were and are controversial (Florence 2006), the particular concern here is when a person is mistakenly placed on the no-fly lists. This is an issue because the processes around inclusion, finding out, and appealing the inclusion or being removed from a no-fly list are complex, opaque, and may require considerable effort and resources. In a US Judiciary Committee hearing, US Senator Edward Kennedy drew attention to how hard it was for him to get off a no-fly list (Florence 2006, 2151). It seems that being on a no-fly list is quite "sticky"—once you are on, it is hard to get off.

The issue of false positives for no-fly lists draws out the problems in "black boxing" virtual identity construction. One of the key processes that both causes the harms and increases the magnitude of the harms is when the operators are unaware of how or why people have been flagged. If they are on a no-fly list, thought to be acting suspiciously, or fit some pattern that artificial intelligence has determined warrants following up, the operators are unlikely to know just *why* they are flagged. While some situations might be easily resolved—the operators check if the person is the known terrorist, or upon questioning the target see that the reason for the strange gait is blisters on the heels—other situations might not be so easily resolved. Like the no-fly list, if the operators cannot find out why the person has been flagged, and/or have no capacity to update or fix the details of the virtual identity, then the restrictions and interference may remain. Furthermore, if the targets don't know that their lives are being impacted because of an inaccurate virtual identity, and if the ways or processes of amending that virtual identity are limited, we have a "negligent information harm" that arises when "information is constructed that targets an individual or group, but the data is not accurate, resulting in harm to a person" (Henschke 2017, 257).

Given the threats posed by international terrorism, perhaps we must all accept some interference in our lives in order to feel safe. The reasoning is that the odd false positive is the price we have to pay for our collective security. The issue here is not so much about giving up certain rights and civil liberties. Rather, the issue of concern is about the distribution of harms and benefits. That is, who bears the majority of the cost, and who reaps the majority of the reward? Policing and security agencies have long been criticized for targeting particular minority groups—young black males for instance—which causes a disproportionate number of that minority group to be pulled into the criminal justice realm resulting in statistically higher numbers of those minorities in prisons (Dunham and Lawford-Smith 2017).[3] In the decades following the 9/11 attacks, passengers and civil rights advocates have raised the concern about racial profiling on commercial flights (Khaleeli 2016).

For instance, let us consider that we turn identification of potential anti-social behaviors over to machine learning processes. A series of computer technicians train the analytics to recognize potential anti-social behaviors and then the machine learning algorithms develop a series of processes that are rolled out to automatically alert CCTV operators to the anti-social behaviors. However, it turns out that rather than identifying anti-social behaviors, the algorithms are identifying teenaged dark-skinned males.[4] The undesired outcome is that the automated processes perpetuate existing discrimination by drawing from existing social inequalities and the unconscious biases of the designers (Winner 1980, Dunham and Lawford-Smith 2017). It is easy to say that this is the price I have to pay for such automated processes, when I am not likely to bear the costs of misidentification. And, as before, given the technological nature of the decision-making that forms the virtual identities, just how or why a particular set of people is targeted is opaque, challenging for operators to counter, and hard to amend.

The overall point is not so much that false positives are bad. That should be obvious. Instead, I want to draw out the range of impacts that false positives can have when thinking of automated surveillance and identity constructions for potential perpetrators of mass violence—from the extreme end of accidentally killing an innocent person, to the direct interference in a person's free movement, to the subtle end that perpetuates existing discrimination. Importantly, I want to show how information technologies and virtual identity construction can play subtle and at times near invisible roles in bringing about these unwanted outcomes.

Risk of False Negatives: From Security Failures to Resource Distribution

With these significant problems of false positives, and recalling that the defaults and settings are the province of designers, maybe the solution is to recalibrate the systems so that there is more likelihood of false negatives than false positives. However, recall that there is a background expectation by citizens that the state will keep them safe against perpetrators of mass violence. When considering shocking crimes like terrorist attacks or school shootings, the notion of a zero-tolerance policy is endorsed and perpetuated by political leaders. "Notional considerations of civil liberties do not trump the very real threat, the very real threat of terror in our country today" (Daniel Andrews, quoted in Bickers 2017).[5]

The issue here is that technology can impact our assessment of security policy. Consider these scenarios. In the first, a counter-terrorism operation is aborted, due to the fear that the suspect is in fact an innocent person, a case of mistaken identity. Much like the de Menezes shooting, in this scenario, the decision to abort the operation is made under high stress and with limited, potentially faulty information. Unfortunately, it turns out that the call was wrong, and the suspect conducts an attack, killing four innocent people and harming nine others. Such an incident would of course provoke reflection and criticism and would likely require an inquiry and internal investigation. Contrast this with a second scenario where a counter-terrorism operation is canceled resulting in four people killed and nine injured. However, rather than the decision to cancel being made by people in the high-pressure scenario, the operation was canceled automatically, due to the default settings in the information analysis process.

The outcomes may be functionally equivalent—four killed and nine injured in both cases—but because the decision-making occurred prior to the specific outcome, I would expect that public outcry and criticism of such decision-making could be much higher.[6] We see examples of this when it becomes public that terrorists were "known to police" prior to their conducting an attack. The man who bombed Ariana Grande's concert at the Manchester Arena in May 2017, Salman Ramadan Abedi, "was known to the security services but was not part of any active investigation or regarded as a high risk. He was viewed as a peripheral figure in much the same way as the Westminster attacker, Khalid Masood" (Cobain et al. 2017). Technologies might exasperate this criticism of security agencies in that though we can more easily excuse mistakes made by people while under stress, the decisions of engineers and designers made months or years prior to an attack cannot be excused by the immediate stress. Further is the worry that the false negatives created by the default settings can create a false sense of confidence in the operators. Following Thaler and Sunstein's work on defaults and Kahneman's work on cognitive biases, it is hard to argue with a computer. And while it might be easier for the operator to flag than to "deflag" an individual, that only works if the operators have time and the cognitive capacity to pay attention to the scenes under surveillance. If they are busy, understaffed, tired, working with poorly designed interfaces, etc., it can be very difficult to recognize and correct a false negative.

This leads to a further worry about the widespread introduction of, and subsequent reliance on, these automated processes to identify risks and threats. The concern here is if these technologies are seen as the solution to the problem of perpetrators of mass violence, they can draw substantial resources away from traditional policing methods. In the UK election campaign of 2017 that followed the terrorist attack on Manchester Arena, the sitting Prime Minister Theresa May was criticized in her role as Home Secretary that her preference for technological solutions permitted substantial cuts to traditional policing (Walker and Walker 2017). This demonstrates the public criticism of decision-making that favors technological solutions to social problems. Hence, while surveillance technologies can be extremely useful, they are not a substitute for traditional methods like community policing and human intelligence.

Conclusion

This chapter makes two points. First, following the recognition that values play a major role in the design, operation, and application of information technologies, we must recognize that we may need to make a hard decision between preferring false positives over false negatives, or vice versa, and that that decision may come at a significant cost. Second, sitting underneath this, we need to see that these new technologies are not going to be silver bullets that easily and simply solve security problems. What they are more likely to do is either highlight existing problems, challenges, and value trade-offs or create a new layer of complexity in decision-making.

While perpetrators of mass violence present a challenge to which liberal democracies must respond, we need to be thoughtful and careful in how we apply information technologies in these situations. By looking at information technologies and their application to perpetrators of mass violence with reference to how virtual identities are constructed, we see how values play a role in technological design and policy and are hopefully better able to recognize the real challenges that come from getting the identities wrong.

Notes

1 I recognize here that metadata is a contextually variable notion. For the purposes of this chapter, and in the general context of surveillance and information technologies, the relevant distinction between information and metadata is that metadata is not about the content of a communication. For the social networks, metadata refers to who is communicating with whom, when and by what means, rather than the content of the communications. This largely follows Luciano Floridi's accounts of metadata (2011). See also my discussion of metadata in (Henschke 2017, 186–188, 197–198).

2 This is to suggest neither that cameras should be placed in politician's offices nor that transparency is a value that should trump privacy in the political space at all times. As Christopher Moran points out, there is a set of reasons public servants might expect confidentiality and secrecy in their professional dealings (Moran 2012). The point is to demonstrate how values shape the decisions around surveillance.

3 I note here that the connections between racial profiling and police behavior are highly contentious (Bowling and Phillips 2007; Miller 2010; Waddington et al. 2004).

4 This scenario is based on an apocryphal story about machine learning, tanks, and camouflage: "Once upon a time, the US army decided to develop a computer system for detecting camouflaged tanks. They built a neural network—a kind of artificial brain—and trained it on hundreds of photos of tanks hidden among trees, and hundreds of photos of trees without any tanks, until it could tell the difference between the two types of pictures … Upon further investigation, it turned out that the soldiers taking the photos had only had a tank to camouflage for a couple of days, when the weather had been great. After the tank was returned, the weather changed, and all the photos without a tank in them were taken under cloudy skies. As a result, the network had not learned to discriminate between tanks, but between weather conditions: it was very good at deciding if the weather in the photograph was sunny or overcast, but not much else. The moral of the story is that machines are great at learning; it's just very hard to know what it is that they've learned" (Bridle 2018).

5 Such posturing generates a cynicism about the motivations of politicians. "[W]e have a political class that feels it must inoculate itself against allegations of weakness. Our politicians are more fearful of the politics of terrorism—of the charge that they do not take terrorism seriously—than they are of the crime itself" (Snowden 2016). This is not to endorse either view, but to draw out the fact that decisions around terrorism policy are politically and socially fraught and that automating the surveillance systems will not resolve these issues.

6 The criticism of designers and politicians after a pedestrian, Elaine Herzberg, was run down and killed by a self-driving vehicle in Arizona shows that the public criticizes technologies differently than a human driving the car or making decisions (Levin 2018).

References

Abbott, Tony. 2015. Prime Minister: Joint Doorstop Interview. Office of the Prime Minister.

Azom, Valentine, Aderemi, Adewumi, & Jules-Raymond, Adewumi. 2015. "Face and Iris Biometrics Person Identification Using Hybrid Fusion at Feature and Score-Level." *2015 Pattern Recognition Association of South Africa and Robotics and Mechatronics International Conference* (PRASA-RobMech), 26-27 Nov. 2015: 207–212.

Bickers, Claire. 2017. "National Security COAG Meeting: Australian Airports to Get Facial Recognition Software." *News.com*, October 5, 2017.

Bowling, Ben & Coretta, Adewumi. 2007. "Disproportionate and Discriminatory: Reviewing the Evidence on Police Stop and Search." *The Modern Law Review* 70: 936–961.

Brindle, James. 2018. "Known Unknowns." *Harpers Magazine*, July 2018. https://harpers.org/archive/2018/07/known-unknowns/

Brynielsson, Joel, Andreas, Adewumi., Fredrik, Adewumi., Lisa, Adewumi., Christian, Adewumi, & Pontus, Svenson. 2013. "Harvesting and Analysis of Weak Signals for Detecting Lone Wolf Terrorists." *Security Informatics* 2(11).

Cobain, Ian, Frances Perraudin, Steven Morris, & Nazia Parveen. 2017 Salman Ramadan Abedi Named by Police as Manchester Arena Attacker." *The Guardian*, May 24, 2017.

Cooper, Benjamin. 2017. "Australia to Tighten Airport Security Further after Foiled Attack." *Reuters*, October 22, 2017.

Dovydaitis, Laurynas, Tomas Rasymas, & Vytautas Rudžionis. 2017. "Speaker Authentication System Based on Voice Biometrics and Speech Recognition." *International Conference on Business Information Systems*. Cham. Springer International Publishing: 79–84.

Dubois, Amandine & Jean-Pierre Bresciani. 2015 "Person Identification from Gait Analysis with a Depth Camera at Home." *2015 37th Annual International Conference of the IEEE Engineering in Medicine and Biology Society* (EMBC), 25-29 Aug. 2015: 4999–5002.

Dunham, Jeremy & Holly Lawford-Smith. 2017. "Offsetting Race Privilege." *Journal of Ethics and Social Philosophy* 11(2): 1-23.

Florence, Justin. 2006. "Making the No Fly List Fly: A Due Process Model for Terrorist Watchlists." *Yale Law Journal* 115: 2148–2182.

Floridi, Luciano. 2011. "Semantic Conceptions of Information."*The Stanford Encyclopedia of Philosophy (Spring 2011 Edition)*, Edward N. Zalta (ed.), https://plato.stanford.edu/archives/spr2011/entries/information-semantic/.

Graham, Chris. 2018. "Florida Shooting: Donald Trump Blames FBI's Russia Probe for Failure to Spot Suspect's Warning Signs." *Telegraph*, February 18, 2018.

Henschke, Adam. 2017. *Ethics in an Age of Surveillance: Virtual Identities and Personal Information.* New York: Cambridge University Press.

Inness, Julie. 1992. *Privacy, Intimacy and Isolation*. New York: Oxford University Press.

Kahneman, Daniel. 2011. *Thinking, Fast and Slow*. New York: FSG.

Kapoor, Surbhi, & Pushpendra Kumar Pateriya. 2016. "A Study on Various Methods Used in Automatic Video Surveillance." *6th International Conference - Cloud System and Big Data Engineering (Confluence)*: 413–416.

Khaleeli, Homa. 2016. "The Perils of 'Flying While Muslim'." *The Guardian UK*, August 8, 2016.

Levin, Sam. 2018. "'Uber Should Be Shut Down': Friends of Self Driving Car Crash Victim Seek Justice." *The Guardian*, March 20, 2018.

Mathur, Garima & Mahesh Bundele. 2016. "Research on Intelligent Video Surveillance Techniques for Suspicious Activity Detection: Critical Review." *2016 International Conference on Recent Advances and Innovations in Engineering (ICRAIE)*: 1–8.

Miller, Joel. 2010. "Stop and Search in England: A Reformed Tactic or Business as Usual?" *British Journal of Criminology* 50: 954–974.

Miller, Seumas & Ian A Gordon. 2014. *Investigative Ethics: Ethics for Police Detectives and Criminal Investigators.* Malden: Blackwell Publishing.

Moran, Christopher. 2012. *Classified: Secrecy and the State in Modern Britain*. Cambridge: Cambridge University Press.

Mullins, Sam. 2013. "Social Network Analysis and Counter-Terrorism: Measures of Centrality as an Investigative Tool." *Behavioral Sciences of Terrorism and Political Aggression* 5: 115–136.

Mullins, Sam & Adam Dolnik. 2010. "An Exploratory, Dynamic Application of Social Network Analysis for Modelling the Development of Islamist Terror-Cells in the West." *Behavioral Sciences of Terrorism and Political Aggression* 2: 3–29.

National Commission on Terrorist Attacks upon The United States 2004. "The 9/11 Commission Report: Final Report of the National Commission on Terrorist Attacks upon The United States." Washington, DC: US Government.

Palmer, Danny. 2018. "New IoT Security Rules: Stop Using Default Passwords and Allow Software Updates." *ZDNet*, available at www.zdnet.com/article/new-iot-security-rules-stop-using-default-passwords-and-allow-software-updates/, accessed 06/10/2018.

Reid, Daniel A., Mark S. Nixon, & Sarah V. Stevenage. 2014. "Soft Biometrics; Human Identification Using Comparative Descriptions." *IEEE Transactions on Pattern Analysis and Machine Intelligence* 36: 1216–1228.

Ressler, Steve. 2006. "Social Network Analysis as an Approach to Combat Terrorism: Past, Present, and Future Research." *Homeland Security Affairs* 2: 1–10.

Snowden, Edward. 2016. "Whistleblowing is Not Just Leaking: It' an Act of Political Resistance." Occupy.com. May 4, 2017. https://www.occupy.com/article/snowden-whistleblowing-not-just-leaking-—-it's-act-political-resistance?qt-article_tabs=3#sthash.MVFyGzjS.dpbs

Solove, Daniel. 2008. *Understanding Privacy*. Harvard: Harvard University Press.
Thaler, Richard H. & Cass R. Sunstein. 2009. *Nudge: Improving Decisions about Health, Wealth and Happiness*. New York: Penguin.
Van Den Hoven, Jeroen. 2007. "ICT and Value Sensitive Design." In *The Information Society: Innovation, Legitimacy, Ethics and Democracy in Honor of Professor Jacques Berleur s.j.*, edited by Goujon, Philippe, Lavelle, Sylvian, Duquenoy, Penny, Kimppa, Kai & Laurent, Véronique, 67-72. Boston: Springer.
Waddington, Philip A. J., Kevin Stenson, & David Don 2004. "In Proportion: Race, and Police Stop and Search." *British Journal of Criminology* 44: 889–914.
Walker, Rowena & Peter Walker. 2017. "Under-Fire Theresa May Hits Back over Police Cuts." *The Guardian*, June 5, 2017.
Winner, Langdon. 1980. "Do Artefacts Have Politics?" *Daedalus* 109: 121–136.
Woollacot, Emma. 2015. "The Algorithm that Can Predict Isis's Next Move – Before They Even Know What It Is." *New Statesman*. September 24, 2015.

19

Climate Change Perpetrators

Ecocriticism, Implicated Subjects, and Anthropocene Fiction

Rick Crownshaw

Of late, studies in the humanities of the perpetration of mass violence have started to demonstrate eco-critical tendencies and potentialities. Such research has explored the ecological dimensions of mass violence, as in the ways in which the so-called natural world has been instrumentalized and entangled with the processes of genocide, enslavement, and colonial settlement (see, e.g., Levene 2012; Rapson 2015; Snyder 2015; Short 2016). This chapter capitalizes on the synergy between such environmentally oriented research and Perpetrator Studies to rethink the very definition of violence and its perpetration and the figure of the perpetrator. In particular, in the following I will define anthropogenic climate change as a form of mass violence and will use its literary representation—in this case Richard Ford's post-Hurricane Sandy novel, *Let Me Be Frank With You* (set in the aftermath of the storm in 2012 and published in 2014)—to apprehend its perpetrators. This chapter finds that literary realism depicts seemingly unlikely acts of violence through routinized participation in a fossil-fueled economy of the US. The chapter seeks thereby not to universalize perpetration but to navigate the difficulties of attributing agency and ethical responsibility and to remember violence that will always be latent, hidden in plain sight, and instituted by ideological and psychical attachments to the social, political, and cultural regimes of fossil-fueled capitalism.

Key to rethinking violence is a recalibration of the scales by which we measure its acts and impacts. Hurricane Sandy may have made landfall on the northeastern seaboard with lethal force, but as a consequence of climate change, that violence was slow and "long in the making" (Nixon 2011, 3). As Rob Nixon defines it, "slow" violence "occurs gradually and out of sight, […] [it is] delayed destruction that is dispersed across time and space, attritional [and] typically not viewed as violence at all […]. Neither spectacular nor instantaneous, but rather incremental and accretive" (2011, 2). Inherent, then, in the consumption of fossil fuels is a form of violence that manifests itself belatedly in extreme hydrological and meteorological events—floods and hurricanes—of climates changed by the after-effects of cumulative CO_2 emissions. Less noticeable but no less extreme, this violence manifests itself in the planet's sixth mass extinction event of flora and fauna no longer sustained by climate-changed ecosystems, or what is left of them (Kolbert 2015). As report after report of the Intergovernmental Panel on Climate Change has stated, even a rise of 1.5–2.0 degrees centigrade in planetary temperature above preindustrial levels will have profound, longstanding, and often lethal effects on "health, livelihoods, food security, water supply, and human security" during the twenty-first century (IPCC 2018), the human death toll to date from extreme weather events and conditions, eco-systemic failure, resource depletion, and conflict notwithstanding. So, although dispersed and belated, this violence is not necessarily less impactful, or less collectively massive, than the typical (e.g., genocidal) cases Perpetrator Studies usually draws upon, not least because of its planetary scale. After all, climate change has probably been the most culturally pronounced characteristic of the Anthropocene, our new geological epoch defined by the primacy of humanity's geophysical agency (Crutzen and Stoermer 2000; Crutzen 2002). Although the epoch's inception dates vary (see, e.g., Chakrabarty 2009; Lewis and Maslin 2015), the current orthodoxy points to the Great Acceleration of oil extraction and consumption, along with radioactive fallout from atomic warfare and nuclear testing, in the post-1945 period (but particularly from 1950) (Zalasiewicz et al. 2017), given the consistent imprint of these processes in the geological record.

Despite its impact (albeit cumulative), slow violence poses representational challenges to cultures habitually geared to the punctual. Although he mainly has in mind the work of postcolonialist writer-activists rather than mainstream American realists, for Nixon literature has the potential to "apprehend threats imaginatively that remain imperceptible to the senses, [… and] played out across a time span that exceeds the instance of observation" (2011, 15). However, Ford's novel does not enunciate the relationship between global warming and extreme weather events (see Sobel 2014) and the American oil-fueled society narrated by its seemingly innocuous protagonist, but the author stages that dissociative narrative with dramatic irony. The weather and its effects become increasingly uncanny, and by implication, so do the otherwise normative and banal routines, structures, and settings of fossil-fuel consumption. In other words, the narrator's failure to articulate the relation between hydrocarbons and climate—his cognitive dissonance—becomes increasingly conspicuous and questionable, and the realities his narrative constructs become less stable. For the critical reader, then, the normative realities of the narrator's oil-based American life give way to glimpses of the ecological implications of such living. This destabilization of the real corresponds with recent analyses of contemporary American "pragmatic" realism, particularly Ford's, and its writers' investment in an external reality, but one that is not timeless and metaphysical but historically contingent and only accessible through the inadequacies of language and culture (see, e.g., McGuire 2015, xvii–xix). As we shall see, then, literary eco-criticism can inform Perpetrator Studies by, in this case, scrutinizing petro-normativity, and the (petro)realism in which it is emplotted, to elicit the perpetration of violence otherwise overlooked. If, for Nixon, "*imaginative writing can help make the unapparent appear, making it accessible and tangible by humanizing drawn-out threats inaccessible to the immediate senses*" (2011, 15; emphasis in original), Ford's novel demonstrates that making the unapparent apparent is not just a matter of overcoming the issue of scale but also of mediation.

Here it is useful to deploy the notion of "implicatedness" as the basis on which perpetration can be redefined in environmental but nonetheless very ordinary terms. Michael Rothberg's conception of implicatedness modifies classical trauma studies' focus on the psychological dynamics and dimensions of the traumatic event. A modifying sociological approach can analyze the structures through which trauma is exercised in addition to the traditional focus on the affective singularity of the traumatic event. To recognize the structures that institute trauma, such as global capitalism's, is to recognize the maleficient and beneficient participants in those structures and the ways that beneficiaries can become maleficiaries.

This is particularly the case when the effects of global capitalism are felt in terms of anthropogenic climate change, which belatedly threatens the developed, industrialized world—the Global North and its "implicated" subjects—from which it originated, as well as those usually first to feel its effects in the Global South (Rothberg 2013a, xiv–xv). So, "the deliberately open-ended term 'implication'" gathers

> together various modes of historical relation that do not necessarily fall under the more direct forms of participation associated with traumatic events, such as victimization and perpetration. [...] These subject positions move us away from overt questions of guilt and innocence and leave us in a more complex and uncertain ethical and moral terrain—a terrain in which most of us live most of the time.
>
> *(Rothberg 2013b, 41; see also Rothberg 2019)*

On that terrain, we will find Ford's protagonist, Frank Bascombe, given his implication in the perpetration of climate change through an active participation in the fossil-fueled economy, his oil-based social mobility.

The novel opens with Bascombe on his way to meet the man who purchased his old house from him, to view what little is left of that property after the hurricane has hit, and to provide financial advice from an ex-realtor's perspective on what to do with what is left. On this journey, Bascombe navigates the geography of American modernity: highways, gas stations, strip malls, suburban housing tracts, and finally, exclusive residential coastal developments alongside older, more established beachside properties. His narration of this landscape does not articulate the relation between the extreme weather that has battered this fossil-fueled topography and the extraction and consumption of oil that has shaped the terrain and which resources the lives lived thereon—and indeed everywhere. There are various, related ways of explaining this cognitive dissonance.

Patricia Yaeger's seminal conception of the "energy unconscious" is particularly useful in this respect. The concept is inspired by Fredric Jameson's "political unconscious" and the ways in which texts, if historicized, reveal the symbolization of class conflicts embedded in modes of production, or, more precisely, strive to contain and resolve the realities of social conflict at the imaginary, textual level of the novel. Yaeger et al. refines this theory, asking what happens if we periodize literature not in terms of centuries or the history of ideas but according to the energy sources that made literary composition, production, and reception possible (2011, 305–10). If literary criticism drills down into the textual unconscious, it can elicit the overlooked embeddedness of oil in cultural production: the American petroscape (a built environment organized around the consumption of oil) that engenders Ford's realism and enables the peripatetic (automobilized, driven) narration that opens the novel. Affording context and content, the consumption of oil is not just a reality effect. The enunciation of the expenditure of energy—the consumption of oil—becomes a way of asserting a particular character's socioeconomic position, and the myth of resource abundance to which he or she subscribes, and masks the unseen labor, socioeconomic class system, and social iniquities upon which the social mobility of the narrator and his fueled life are predicated (as well those exploited farther afield in the global system of oil extraction and supply) (Yaeger 2011, 309). In this novel, though, the most glaring contradiction that this ideology of form struggles to contain is the difficulty of reconciling or even associating the seemingly inconsequential daily acts of fossil fuel consumption with their environmental repercussions, of which the physical imprint (on lives and landscapes) is writ large across the narrative.

Stephanie LeMenager might describe this cognitive dissonance as an example of petro-melancholia: an aesthetics that fails to imagine an alternative to a fossil-fueled capitalist modernity and the dismantling of "our self-subjection to oil capital" (Imre Szeman 2011, 324, quoted in LeMenager 2014, 11, 16–7), an aesthetics geared not to mourning infinite, easily accessible oil, but the disavowal of the reality of less easily extractable if not precarious future reserves. This aesthetic screens past, present, and future environmental consequences of extraction and consumption. Such melancholic texts underscore a forgetful attachment to oil through the representation of embodied routines of consumption—the living of oil—which are in effect habitual, embodied routines of forgetting (LeMenager 2014, 6, 104). Indeed, Bascombe's meditation on the American socio-economic landscape as he drives to his former, storm-ruined property is punctuated (fueled, even) by stopping for gas (Ford 2015, 3–4).

We could place Bascombe's journey in a larger trajectory of neoliberalism, which for Matthew Huber is inextricable from the Great Acceleration of oil extraction, refinement, distribution, and consumption that characterizes the American postwar period (and which informs the Anthropocene's inception). The massive increase in fossil-fuel extraction and consumption and therefore the intensification of production throughout the twentieth and early twenty-first century led to a perception that energized, mechanized production was freed from the laboring body. So thought the relatively new, more socially mobile, and suburbanized, professional middle classes of the postwar period who were themselves energized by intensified regimes of fossil-fuel consumption.

The distance they traveled, geographically speaking, from sites of less mobile labor, industrial production, and the racially and ethnically mixed demographics of the city also facilitated a cognitive distance from those spaces. That distance, geographical and cognitive, was and is maintained by an ideology concomitant with petrocapitalism—neoliberalism—that sees living as a private enterprise in which the neoliberal subject is producer of his or her own life, so long as the right social, financial, political, and professional choices have been made along the way. Under the regime of this structure of feeling, "the material and technological objects that fill the spaces" of neoliberal life are seen as the expression of this entrepreneurialism.

This is a privatized life quarantined from (and forgetful of) the industrial labor upon which it rests and the local, national, and international geographies, systems, and state-sponsored infrastructures of fossil-fueled capitalism, the "taken-for-granted hydrocarbons" that energize American life (Huber 2013, 19–20, 23), and finally, the ecological implications of fossil-fueled living—felt most keenly in the extreme weather that motivates the novel's narrative. This privatized and supposedly entrepreneurial life has been most at home in the suburban plot, ownership of which, along with the very idea of home ownership had become aligned with neoliberalism (Knapp 2011, 506). Although retired from the real estate business and therefore from superintending the exchange of suburban property that domiciles neoliberal ideologies, Bascombe is still fully implicated in the fossil-fueled energy regimes upon which his socio-economic status depends, that have literally fueled his social mobility, but which also, of course, have environmental repercussions.

As Bascombe is implicated in (slow) violence, it is significant that, when he visits his former home and neighborhood, he describes the spectacle of the hurricane's aftermath and the cleanup operation in terms of war. As David Palumbo-Liu argues, in a post-9/11 America, the failure of the War on Terror to shore up the national fantasy of American democratic and moral exceptionalism led to the appropriation of other threats against which the homeland could be seen as vulnerable and then pre-emptively strengthened, thereby securing national identity (2006, 152). Climate change served the purposes of hegemonic affirmation. As Robert Marzec puts it, after 9/11 the "nation-state collective fantasy of Homeland Security" evolved into a "new planetary ecological-state fantasy of 'natural security'" or an "eco-security imaginary" (Marzec 2015a, 73–8, 79; see also, Marzec 2015b). Securing the environment became the means of securing the state at home and abroad, given the relation of climate change, resource scarcity, conflict, and terrorism. This does not mean stabilizing the environment, or in this case the climate, but rather adapting to its continued mutation. Commandeering rather than stemming environmental threat ensures hegemonic perpetuity. The post-9/11 securitization of the environment sheds light on the constellation of imagery and figures deployed by Bascombe that entangles war, terrorism, and environmental catastrophe. In these scenes in the novel, SWAT teams provide security for the clean-up operations, along with the National Guard in "desert issue," which suggests an alertness against terrorist attacks and alludes to the theater in which the War on Terror was fought. "State Health" workers clearing debris wearing "hazmat suits," necessary to protect against contaminants released by storm damage, but which also suggest the threat of biological terrorism or chemical warfare; in essence, though, the storm is a bio-chemical threat caused by changing atmospheric conditions. The detritus from this site of destruction is likened to that removed from Ground Zero; the vehicles used in detritus-removal are likened to the vehicles used by insurgents in Afghanistan. The sand washed and blown from the beach makes Sea-Clift look like "Riyadh" (Ford 2015, 23–4) (and the oil reserves of Saudi Arabia have been integral to the US global oil industry, since its early twentieth-century origins, and are related to America's military interventions in the Middle East to defend its resource interests there [see Mitchell 2013]). As Yaeger suggests, the phenomenology of energy (driving, filling up at a gas station, or just about any human action in the novel) relates the text to "its originating modes of production as quasi objects" (2011, 310), and here the figurative language returns us to the resource-production over which wars are fought and against the environmental repercussions of which the nation is marshaled. The impact of the hurricane reminds Arnie, owner of Bascombe's former and now destroyed home, of the attack on the Twin Towers, which, local residents claim, could once be glimpsed from the beach their houses used to line (Ford 2015, 42). The hurricane and what it stands for have superseded 9/11 in the national imaginary, suggesting that Bascombe's energetic implicatedness has been pressed into the service of national fantasy. Not just a perpetrator of climate change, he has been drawn into (an imaginary and ineffective) war against the threat it poses.

However, if this *is* a "post-combat zone," as Bascombe suggests, it is unclear who has won. In the same scene, Bascombe reminisces about his time in the Marines: when scouting the US-Mexico borderlands, he could not discern from the abandoned dwellings he saw there whether they were in state of dereliction or repair, regression, or progression. The same applies to the ruined houses and battered towns Bascombe witnesses on the New Jersey shoreline, stranded between a state of "being and not being," the "possibility" of redevelopment unreadable, illegible from their ruins. Bascombe describes homes (and homeland) not necessarily secured against the threat (terror) of climate change, his implicatedness notwithstanding (Ford 2015, 24). Indeed, later in the novel Bascombe is still haunted by his inability to read the future:

> Once it was possible to cast my eye over almost any piece of settled landscape here-around and know how it would look in the future; what uses it'd be set to by succeeding waves of human purpose—as if a logic lay buried within, the genome of its later what's-it.
>
> *(Ford 2015, 117)*

Given the ambiguous figuration of environmental catastrophe and how it bodes for the future of the homeland and climate, Bascombe's narration (and its orchestration by Ford) implies that the novel, while not avowedly environmentalist, is not strictly in accord with neoliberalist and nationalist narratives. As such, the novel affords the possibility of refocusing what Bascombe witnesses: the "slow violence" of his own (and others') making. His narration is less implicated in his implicatedness than expected. In fact, Bascombe's narratorial musings develop increasing signs of what Dipesh Chakrabarty might describe as "species thinking" (2009), a species self-consciousness that implies a sense of how humanity's collective agency is shaping the planet. His species self-consciousness gestures beyond the usual humanist scope of the novel genre and defies literary (eco)criticisms of the genre's delimited temporal and spatial scales in the face of the planetary nature of the Anthropocene (see Clark 2015, 59, 80, 103, 181–2). For example, in pronouncing "complex life will resume here," on the devastated shoreline of Sea-Clift (Ford 2015, 49), he is describing the social in terms of an ecosystem. In describing the rebuilding, redevelopment, and general social mobility noted on the New Jersey shore, particularly in terms of the trade in real estate, Bascombe, sounding more like an anthropologist than ex-realtor, meditates on the ceaselessness of collective human behavior: "No one wants to stay any place. There are species-level changes afoot" (Ford 2015, 73). That is certainly the case—we are, after all, in a new epoch—and Bascombe gestures towards the trajectory of species measured across geological time or across an extended temporality:

> plenty happens in the suburbs—in the way that putting a drop of water under an electron microscope reveals civilizations with histories, destinies, and an overpowering experience of the present.
>
> *(Ford 2015, 78–9)*

The *longue durée* of history—"civilization, with histories, destinies"—culminates in the cumulative effects of the species' impact on the planet, in this case, the climatic manifestation of a history of fossil-fuel use, the "overpowering experience of the present" that has perturbed the world of the novel.

From the putatively parochial nature of the suburbs, a sense of planetary change can be gleaned, and this is correspondent with recent literary criticism of American suburban realism (Ford's included). This criticism has found that, after 9/11, the suburbs are no longer imagined as a refuge from American and global history, for example, the vicissitudes of global capitalism and the repercussions of the terrorist attacks (Knapp 2011, 501–2, 503–4), and now they are no longer imagined as isolated from the Anthropocene but rendered permeable to ecological, geological, and planetary contexts. Rather than written or narrated according to the former master narratives of the suburban imaginary ("the neoliberal values that have come to be synonymous with suburbia—individuality, security, and mastery," [Knapp 2011, 501–2]), the suburbs are focalized through the figure of the "everyman": "the hapless, ineffectual everyman. It is he who demonstrates how to live with lack by being so obviously lacking, and who effectively counters the narrative of American exceptionalism by being so emphatically unexceptional" (Knapp 2011, 503–4). Indeed, Bascombe admits to not having a "trajectory" in life (Ford 2015, 193–4). We have seen how the idea of exceptionalism resonates in ideological terms, but ambiguously so, in Bascombe's narratorial deployment of a post-9/11 "natural security" imaginary (to recall Marzec's phrasing). Now that unexceptionalism resonates in the novel's gestures beyond human exceptionalism—the prevailing idea that the human species is somehow transcendent of and extricable from the natural environment (with which it is actually and inextricably entangled), which it others and instrumentalizes. Unexceptionalism also resonates in the ordinariness of petro-cultural participation, which has extraordinary climatic consequences.

If an eco-critical Perpetrator Studies is able to use literature to identify violence and its ecological implications to de-reify an interpellated, energized neoliberal subject and his narrative, in other words, to see beyond the perspective of the perpetrator, then this raises questions of agency and responsibility. What is seen beyond that perspective is the way in which human agency activates the nonhuman world, an activation that literature can make imaginable. Human activity—the burning of fossil fuels—sets in motion a chain of action; the environment and its materials are lent an emergent catastrophic agency that exceeds human control. In Jane Bennett's theory of "vibrant materialism," this "material agency" would be explained as "the capacity of things […] not only to impede or block the will and designs of humans but also to act as quasi agents or forces with trajectories, propensities, or tendencies of their own" (2010, viii–ix). For Bennett, then, the "locus of agency is always a human-nonhuman working group" (xvii), an always contingent and emergent confederation of actants (23–4).

However, it is one thing to engage in an inversive hermeneutics, in which the novel's "foreground becomes background and background becomes foreground," as the weather and its environmental contexts takes center stage, becomes a protagonist rather than just a metaphor for human drama, and where its literal and literary presence is a materialization of "the climates of history," no matter how mediated (Taylor 2016, 10–5; see also Trexler 2015, 13). It is another thing if ecocriticism dethrones the human protagonist altogether and protagonizes the environment to the extent that its putative agency subsumes the anthropogenesis of climate change. Here, then, Perpetrator Studies in dialogue with ecocriticism frames the humanness of perpetration.

Bascombe entertains the idea of the environment as protagonist, particularly his ex-wife's belief that the storm is a "'super-real change agent,' which it surely was." She and her online community of "hurricane conspirators" think "the storm is responsible and will go on being responsible for any damn thing they need it to be [Parkinson's Disease in Ann's case]. […] Agency is, of course, what Ann and all these zanies are seeking" (Ford 2015, 142–3). The agency of the storm, in its embryonic stages, generated atmospheric force fields to which Ann's neural physiology was peculiarly susceptible, supposedly.

Bascombe dismisses the idea of an agentic storm—insightfully commenting that the weather has been appropriated to symbolize national disquiet at a time of presidential elections and to enable anyone to claim to be a hurricane victim (Ford 2015, 179)—but his continuing dismissal of nonhuman agency speaks volumes about the actual nature of climate change. In fact, the mythology aired on local talk radio is rather uncanny:

> Callers have pointed out a "strange ether" the storm is suspected of having unearthed from the sea's fundament, and that's now become a permanent part of our New Jersey atmosphere, causing an assortment of "effects" we'll all only know about many years from now, but that won't be good.
>
> *(Ford 2015, 178–9)*

Although couched in the supernatural, this is actually a fairly reasonable description of the ways that, as water temperatures rise, the oceans release their stores of carbon dioxide, exacerbating green-house-gas-induced global warming and its meteorological and other effects, in turn warming the oceans further and releasing more carbon, and so on. The future "effects" of this "strange ether," also known as carbon dioxide, will certainly have many climatic repercussions in the future that are difficult to predict with accuracy. This description of climate change, no matter its guise, is too conspicuous to take Bascombe's dismissal at face value. So, although Bascombe rejects the agency of things that Ford has made uncanny, through the provocative uncanniness of those things the author stages a consideration of the agential—if not for the narrator then for the provoked critical reader. However, the problem with the idea of things having agency is that they, not humans, become implicated in the perpetration of climate change.

Bennett might think otherwise:

> The notion of confederate agency does attenuate the blame game, but it does not thereby abandon the project of identifying [...] the sources of harmful effects. To the contrary, such a notion broadens the range of places to look for sources.
>
> *(2010, 37)*

However, for environmental historian Andreas Malm, this kind of new materialist thinking, in its reversal of human exceptionalism, collapses the distinctions between the natural and the social (Malm 2018, 58–9). In his critique of that indistinction, Malm finds that new materialism's conceptualization of the agency of things is ambiguous enough to accommodate some notion of intentionality, or quasi-intentionality. For example, the accumulated atmospheric CO_2, emitted by human intentional actions (the burning of fossil fuels), effects (climate) change and so borrows something like intention. For Malm, human intentionality cannot be so transferred, and thus he discounts the idea of nonhuman agency altogether (2018, 26, 46). (Here, I think Bennett would actually agree with Malm; for her it is the assemblage of human and nonhuman rather than a transference of the properties of one to another that effects change. The agency of things catalyzes change; it does not intend change. In fact, in Malm's critique, the distinctions between agency and intention become blurred.) For Malm, only by maintaining the distinction between the natural and the social, and by recognizing that a natural material entity can have both natural *and* social properties (the chemical potential of crude oil *and* how humans realize it, for instance), which are not the same, can critical theory identify what society does to nature (2018, 61, 73, 82, 93). For Malm, the logical endpoint of new materialism is the potential for agency to extend as far as, well, any thing, because any thing has the potential to effect material change (to be in a confederation of actants). For Malm, the logical outcome of this universalization of agency is that ultimately environmental catastrophe is not anthropogenic (2018, 89), and, if put into the terms of this chapter's argument, things, not humans, can become perpetrators (or implicated subjects) of climate change. This chapter is cognizant of Malm's concerns over nonhuman agency for just those reasons but recognizes the differentiation of human and nonhuman properties in some (Bennett's, for example) if not all new materialisms. Nonetheless, Malm's critique and Bascombe's skepticism remind us of the humanness of perpetration.

While Ford's novel stages a consideration of agency and lends itself to the eco-critical theorization of agency, the dialogue between eco-criticism and Perpetrator Studies adds further nuance to the conception of agency in this context—in terms of the differentiation of responsibility and intentionality. An eco-critical Perpetrator Studies can identify the perpetration of slow violence inherent in normative behavior—for example, stopping for gas—but does Bascombe *intend* future hurricanes to form, the likes of which have just hit the Jersey shoreline? No. But is he responsible? Yes, because his actions, multiplied across North American society in particular, and his species more unevenly, contribute to the accumulation of greenhouse gas emissions and their effects. That said, given the ways that the novel lends itself to an identification of violence and implies an ecological context to fossil-fueled living, if read ecocritically, and, therefore, given the ways the novel encourages the questioning of a neoliberalist, cognitively dissonant, and exceptionalist perspective, the distance between intentionality and responsibility seems to close. Nevertheless, as an ecocritical Perpetrator Studies has shown, no matter how apparent violence is, the material structures, systems, and processes through which oil is lived together with the concomitant cultures and ideology through which oil is experienced allows the idea of responsibility to be deferred and ensures intention is out of the question.

As we see, the application of Rothberg's implicatedness enables the analysis of the structures of responsibility in its reconceptualization of (the very humanness of) perpetration. The concept of implicatedness also develops Rothberg's conceptualization of multidirectional memory in which cultural memories are not seen as discrete, impermeable, and the exclusive preserve of different social groups and so essential to their identities but rather as always traveling across cultural borders, always in dialogue with and co-constituting other memories (and identities) (2009, 5, 11). In the context of this analysis, multidirectional memory studies can map the structural relations between different histories of (fast and slow) violence and so relate different histories of implicatedness—implicatedness in implicatedness. Where notions of responsibility and intention have been ideologically bracketed, such a network of implicatedness provides alternative routes to liability—for acts of historical and contemporary violence and their legacies (Rothberg 2013b, 57). So, it is to multidirectional memory that this chapter turns in its conclusions on the possibilities of ecocritical Perpetrator Studies and the ways in which literature can chart, implicitly and explicitly, networks of historical responsibility.

Most of the history articulated by Bascombe takes the form of personal, subjective reminiscence of the life stories of people he has met (including the properties in which they have lived), of the use and development of local real estate, be it residential, commercial, or municipal, and of the nature of suburbs over time. Given the horizons of this localized, personalized, and propertied historical memory, the articulation of other kinds of history is often awkward. Sally, Bascombe's wife, feels compelled to share with him the story of thirty-eight Sioux warriors, hanged "on one big scaffold [...] all at once" by the US Cavalry in Minnesota in 1862 following the Dakota uprising (Ford 2015, 19–8). Sally is embarrassed to retell the story that she just has read, including its final detail, that of the warriors' final words from the scaffold: "I'm here." Although unmoved when he first heard the story, Bascombe uses the same final words to describe his own act of witnessing the scene of devastation at Sea-Clift: "And today I'm willing to say 'I'm here' to whoever can hear me, and for whatever good it might to do to man or beast" (Ford 2015, 22). This is surely meant ironically and as a provocation to the reader. Arguably, what he wants to provoke, or what Ford wants to provoke by orchestrating the irony, is the differentiation between victims and perpetrators. Bascombe is an implicated subject, implicated not only in a fossil-fueled energy regime—the living of oil—and its climatic repercussions, but also in the (internal) colonialism of the white settler society whose appropriation of land, ethnic cleansing, and genocidal violence has ultimately made that living possible—a "manifest domesticity" that rests on Manifest Destiny (Kaplan 1998). So, as Rothberg would put it, these related scenes could be read not as the colonization of the historical victims' experience but the mobilization of alternative paths to the past through the recognition of an affiliation with the perpetrators (of settlement) and/or of implication in the perpetration of ongoing, analogous traumas (of climate change) and so a sense of historical responsibility through multidirectional memory work (Rothberg 2013b, 57).

For Bascombe, remembrance continues at home. Although property may be the materialization of privatized life, in this novel houses always disclose more than they enclose. Bascombe's house is no exception and continues to house the irrepressible theme of race. Around the center of the novel, Bascombe is visited by an African American women, Charlotte Pines, displaced by the hurricane, who lived in his house when she was a girl (from 1959–69). After awkward small talk and her (granted) request to look at the basement, she recounts the terrible story of what happened down there (unknown to Bascombe until this moment, despite its local infamy). Her story is of the psychosis of her father whose professional success, middle class status, and Italian opera-singing wife neither assuaged his internalization of the racist culture in which he lived nor eased his assimilation into his place of work or the neighborhood. Consequently driven psychotic, Charlotte's father murdered his wife and son in the basement, and, lying in wait for his daughter to return home from school, decided to kill himself rather than her (Ford 2015, 107).

The emergence of racial history from the foundations of white settlement continues to the novel's end. The novel ends with Bascombe's visit to an old acquaintance, Eddie Medley, whose body and fortune are spent. Medley lies dying of pancreatic cancer, tended to by an African American nurse whose ministrations inside the house are paralleled outside by African American Ezekiel Lewis, who is delivering the fuel oil on which the property runs. Both African American figures are somewhat romanticized by Bascombe for their moral integrity and good citizenry, stalwart qualities embodied through an enunciated physical presence (Ford 2015, 232–8). In the first instance, these characterizations cast a critical light on the decrepitude of privileged white masculinity (housed within), the sovereignty of which promises to be waning in the era of Obama (his second election has just taken place). Indeed, the aging Bascombe's narrative is replete with meditations on mortality and the failures and betrayals of the body—that of his own and of other white men (and sometimes women). More than that, though, we must focus on what Lewis is doing: fueling white life, or rather fueling the end of white life. More allegorical than literal, this scene bodies forth the labor usually obscured by perceptions of energy released from oil and reveals, as oil is pumped into the mausoleum of a neoliberal subject, that the life blood of Americans may not be that sustaining. The transition of America's fossil-fuel economy to oil promised freedom from the dependence on energy stored in laboring bodies (see Nikiforuk 2012). The compressed energy stored in this highly mobile liquid form notwithstanding, the promises made about oil have continued to mask the history of instrumentalized bodies. Here, though, the association of labor, race, and energy is legible (although allegorized), indeed irrepressible.

Despite his seeming obliviousness to the retelling of the settler-colonial past, and his proclaimed self-immunization from any unsettling historical knowledge, the storm has provoked Bascombe's historical sensibility (Ford 2015, 108). He has become more receptive to American history, writ small in stories like Charlotte's, writ bigger in the closing scenes set outside Medley's house, and writ expansively, ecologically even, if we now look back retrospectively at the associations in Bascombe's narrative among oil, energy, race, class, climate, the human and nonhuman. An ecocritical approach has made these associations scrutable and apprehensible, has demonstrated the ways literature can trace violence across time and space, and therefore contributes to current debates about the Anthropocene and responsibility. There has been concern that some conceptions of the Anthropocene have universalized both the agency of humans in bringing about the epoch and the precariousness of their lives in the face of planetary change (e.g., see Wenzel 2017). Although ecocriticism's differentiation of the Anthropos usually looks to the relations between the Global North and South, and is informed by a postcolonialist methodology, this chapter, with Perpetrator Studies in mind, has added historical and ideological complexity, specificity, and nuance to the (otherwise unremarkable) figure of the American perpetrator of an ordinary, yet ecological, form of violence. And Perpetrator Studies has primed ecocriticism to define literary critically apprehended and particularized perpetration in very human terms, no matter the environmental mediation of that violence.

References

Bennett, Jane. 2010. *Vibrant Matter: A Political Ecology of Things*. Durham, NC: Duke University Press.

Chakrabarty, Dipesh. 2009. "The Climate of History: Four Theses." *Critical Inquiry* 35(2): 197–222.

Clark, Timothy. 2015. *Ecocriticism on the Edge: The Anthropocene as a Threshold Concept*. London: Bloomsbury.

Crutzen, Paul. 2002. "The Geology of Mankind." *Nature* 415: 23.

Crutzen, Paul & Eugene Stoermer. 2000. "The Anthropocene." *Global Change Newsletter* 41(1): 17–18.

Ford, Richard. 2015. *Let Me Be Frank with You*. London: Bloomsbury.

Huber, Matthew T. 2013. *Lifeblood: Oil, Freedom, and the Forces of Capital*. Minneapolis: University of Minnesota Press.

IPCC 2018. "Special Report: Global Warming of 1.5 °C." Geneva: World Meteorological Association. www.ipcc.ch/report/sr15/.

Kaplan, Amy. 1998. "Manifest Domesticity." *American Literature* 70(3): 581–606.

Knapp, Kathy. 2011. "Richard Fords Frank Bascombe Trilogy and the Post-9/11 Suburban Novel." *American Literary History* 23(3): 500–528.

Kolbert, Elizabeth. 2015. *The Sixth Extinction: An Unnatural History*. London: Bloomsbury.

LeMenager, Stephanie. 2014. *Living Oil: Petroleum Culture in the American Century*. Oxford: Oxford University Press.

Levene, Mark. 2012. "From Past to Future: Prospects for Genocide and Its Avoidance in the Twenty-First Century." In *The Oxford Handbook of Genocide Studies*, edited by Donald Bloxham and Dirk Moses, 1–12. Oxford: Oxford University Press.

Lewis, Simon L. & Mark A. Maslin. 2015. "Defining the Anthropocene." *Nature* 519: 171–180.

Malm, Andreas. 2018. *The Progress of the Storm: Nature and Society in a Warming World*. London: Verso.

Marzec, Robert P. 2015a. "Climate Change and the Evolution of the 9/11 Security State." In *Narrating 9/11: Fantasies of State, Security, and Terrorism*, edited by John Duvall and Robert P. Marzec, 70–97. Baltimore: Johns Hopkins University Press.

Marzec, Robert P. 2015b. *Militarizing the Environment: Climate Change and the Security State*. Minneapolis: University of Minnesota Press.

McGuire, Ian. 2015. *Richard Ford and the Ends of Realism*. Iowa City: University of Iowa Press.

Mitchell, Timothy. 2013. *Carbon Democracy: Political Power in the Age of Oil*. London: Verso.

Nikiforuk, Andrew. 2012. *The Energy of Slaves: Oil and the New Servitude*. Vancouver, BC: Greystone Books.

Nixon, Rob. 2011. *Slow Violence and the Environmentalism of the Poor*. Cambridge, MA: Harvard University Press.

Palumbo-Liu, David. 2006. "Preemption, Perpetual War, and the Future of the Imagination." *Boundary 2* 33(1): 159–169.

Rapson, Jessica. 2015. *Topographies of Suffering: Buchenwald, Babi Yar, Lidice*. New York: Berghahn.

Rothberg, Michael. 2009. *Multidirectional Memory: Remembering the Holocaust in the Age of Decolonization*. Stanford: Stanford University Press.

Rothberg, Michael. 2013a. "Beyond Tancred and Clorinda: Trauma Studies for Implicated Subjects." In *The Future of Trauma Theory: Contemporary Literary Criticism*, edited by Gert Buelens, Sam Durrant, and Robert Eaglestone, xi–xvii. London: Routledge.

Rothberg, Michael. 2013b. "Multidirectional Memory and the Implicated Subject: On Sebald and Kentridge." In *Performing Memory in Art and Popular Culture*, edited by Liedeke Plate and Anneke Smelik, 39–58. London: Routledge.

Rothberg, Michael. 2019. *The Implicated Subject: Beyond Victims and Perpetrators*. Stanford: Stanford University Press.

Short, Damien. 2016. *Redefining Genocide: Settler Colonialism, Social Death and Ecocide*. London: Zed Books.

Snyder, Timothy. 2015. *Black Earth: The Holocaust as History and Warning*. London: Vintage.

Sobel, Adam H. 2014. *Storm Surge: Hurricane Sandy, Our Changing Climate, and Extreme Weather of the Past and Future*. New York: Harper Wave.

Taylor, Jesse Oak. 2016. *The Sky of Our Manufacture: The London Fog in British Fiction from Dickens to Woolf*. Charlottesville: University of Virginia Press.

Trexler, Adam. 2015. *Anthropocene Fictions: The Novel in a Time of Climate Change*. Charlottesville: University of Virginia Press.

Wenzel, Jennifer. 2017. "Turning over a New Leaf: Fanonian Humanism and Environmental Justice." In *The Routledge Companion to the Environmental Humanities*, edited by Ursula K. Heise, Jon Christensen, and Michelle Niemann, 165–173. London: Routledge.

Yaeger, Patricia, Ken Hiltner, Saree Makdisi, Vin Nardizzi, Laurie Shannon, Imre Szeman, & Michael Ziser. 2011. "Editor's Column: Literature in the Ages of Wood, Tallow, Coal, Whale Oil, Gasoline, Atomic Power, and Other Energy Sources." *PMLA* 126(2): 305–326. doi:10.1632/pmla.2011.126.2.305.

Zalasiewicz, Jan, Colin N. Waters, Alexander P. Wolfe, Anthony D. Barnosky, Alejandro Cearreta, Matt Edgeworth, & Erle C. Ellis et al. 2017. "Making the Case for a Formal Anthropocene Epoch: An Analysis of Ongoing Critiques." *Newsletters on Stratigraphy* 50(2). doi:10.1127/nos/2017/0385.

2.2 Aftermaths, Responsibility, Trauma, and Memory

20

Moral Responsibility and Evil

Paul Formosa

Introduction

We often describe the perpetrators of mass violence and genocide as evil. For example, to call what the Nazis did merely wrong is to undersell the moral gravity of the genocide they perpetrated. What the Nazis did was evil, not merely wrong. However, if we are to describe the perpetrators of genocide and other horrendous crimes as evil, then we need to be able to hold them morally responsible for their actions (Formosa 2008). But this is no easy task, since perpetrators of evil seem to give rise to a paradox of responsibility (Watson 2004, 9). On the one hand, the more extreme the evil, the more we want to blame the perpetrator. On the other hand, the more extreme the evil, the greater our doubts about the sanity and moral responsibility of the perpetrator. After all, how could any sane and morally responsible person perpetrate such horrific deeds? But this creates a problem: how can perpetrators of extreme evils be both especially blameworthy and yet not responsible for what they do? The key to resolving this paradox is to understand that moral responsibility has what Gary Watson (1996) calls "two faces," answerability (being responsible *to* someone) and attributability (being responsible *for* something), and that not all types of perpetrators of evil are equally responsible for what they do. I will make this argument as follows. First, we shall look at the concept of evil and categorize the different types of perpetrators of evil. With this background in place, we can see that some types of perpetrators of evil are more morally responsible for their evildoing than others. This requires seeing moral responsibility as a matter of degree. While this might seem a straightforward move to make when thinking about moral responsibility, in the field of philosophy this is simply not the case. In the vast philosophical literature on moral responsibility, there is surprisingly little direct and sustained discussion of *degrees* of moral responsibility. Instead, the focus is almost exclusively on whether people are *ever* morally responsible *at all* for what they do (Faraci & Shoemaker 2010), and there is very little focus on how to give a philosophical account, as I shall do here, of why some perpetrators are *more or less* morally responsible than others.

However, before proceeding with this argument, it is worth making a quick point about methodology in the context of an interdisciplinary handbook. This chapter is a work in analytic moral philosophy. Philosophers tend to invent bizarre and contrived examples to make a *conceptual* point, often while drawing cavalierly on real historical examples. Contrived examples are used to illustrate fine-grained distinctions and to demonstrate the limitations of alternative views and, as such, the accuracy of the historical allusions made in examples rarely matters when it comes to making those conceptual points. This approach has its limitations. Bizarre and unrealistic examples can be misleading, and the details of real historical examples can matter. Despite these weaknesses, the conceptual clarity and analytic rigor it introduces can help to enrich, in combination with other disciplinary approaches, our understanding of perpetrators.

Evil Actions and Evil Persons

A perpetrator of evil is an agent who perpetrates an evil action. But while you cannot be the perpetrator of a good action, you can be the perpetrator of a bad or wrongful action without also being the perpetrator of evil. An evil action, in the sense that concerns us here, is a sub-category of moral wrongs. We need this special sub-category because some wrongs seem, due to their extreme moral gravity, to be of a different moral kind to lesser wrongs. For example, telling an unjustified minor lie, while wrong, seems to be of a different moral kind to horribly torturing children for fun. What is the nature of this moral difference (Russell 2007)? Four main types of theories of evil try to make sense of this difference. These theories differ over whether the extremely heinous motives of the perpetrator (*Perpetrator Views*), the reactions of others in response to such acts (*Response Views*), the horrific harm inflicted on victims (*Victim Views*), or some combination of these three factors (*Mixed Views*) transforms a mere wrong into an evil action (Formosa 2008). We need not decide here which theory of evil is the best (but for relevant discussion, see Garrard 1998; de Wijze 2002; Morton 2004; Barry 2013; Formosa 2013; Kramer 2014; Russell 2014). Whichever theory is best, these three factors (alone or in combination) can explain why, for example, unjustifiably telling a minor lie to a friend is wrong but not evil, whereas the sadistic torture of children for fun is evil and not merely wrong. Roughly, the moral difference is that torturing children for fun incomprehensibly inflicts a very great harm for an extremely heinous motive, whereas telling unjustified minor lies does not. This explains why the former is evil and the latter is merely wrong.

Due to their extreme moral gravity, evil actions raise important questions about the moral responsibility of perpetrators of evil that do not typically arise in the case of mere wrongs. For example, we can typically understand why someone might unjustifiably tell a small lie to avoid a minor difficulty. After all, lying is something that we have all done, and for this reason we are not, in general, particularly puzzled about the moral responsibility of liars. But evil acts are unlike lying in this regard. Most of us will never perform acts that are anywhere near the same moral ballpark as, for example, the sadistic torture of children. We cannot even *imagine* ourselves ever perpetrating such evil acts. Indeed, we struggle to understand how *anyone* could perpetrate such acts (Russell 2014). This puzzlement leads us to wonder how anyone could be both a morally responsible agent like ourselves and yet still perpetrate such morally extreme acts.

Before we can address this puzzlement, we first need to see that not every perpetrator of evil is also an evil person. What makes someone an evil person? Luke Russell (2014) argues that there are two key views here: *Aggregate Views*, which hold that an evil person is someone who perpetrates a sufficient number of evil acts; and *Dispositional Views*, which hold that an evil person is someone who is disposed to perpetrate evil acts. The difference between an evil person and a perpetrator of evil who is not also an evil person is, on aggregate views, that the former has perpetrated more evil actions than the latter, and on dispositional views, that the former is more disposed to perpetrate evil actions than the latter.

On Russell's preferred dispositional view, an evil person is "strongly and highly fixedly disposed to perform evil actions when in autonomy-favoring conditions" (2014, 173). While many of us might be disposed to perpetrate evils under relatively harsh conditions, such as during wartime or under the influence of powerful authority figures (as in the infamous Milgram experiments (Doris 2002)), only evil persons are disposed to perpetrate evil in conditions where they can do what they *really* want to do. To see this difference, consider the example of a fictional German (call him Heinz) who gets swept up in the Nazi war machine and ends up perpetrating multiple evil actions. However, in more autonomy-favoring conditions (such as in a modern, peaceful, and liberal democracy), Heinz would neither perpetrate nor be disposed to perpetrate evil. But while Heinz might count as an evil person on aggregate accounts, since he perpetrated multiple evil actions, he doesn't count as an evil person on Russell's dispositional account. This is because, once outside the Nazi state in more autonomy-favoring conditions, Heinz is not disposed to perpetrate evil. The flipside of this point is that many of us, who are not disposed to perpetrate evil in autonomy-favoring conditions, might become perpetrators of evil if we were placed in a situation like Nazi Germany. But this alone doesn't make us evil persons.

Three Types of Perpetrators of Evil

Not all perpetrators of evil are the same. To see why, we need to think of a spectrum of conditions, from strongly *evil-encouraging* conditions (such as wartime or the charismatic influence of corrupting authority figures), to strongly *evil-discouraging* conditions (such as peacetime in a just state with strongly enforced sanctions against evildoing), and everything in between (Formosa 2007). By applying our understanding of evil actions and evil persons to this spectrum of conditions, we can map out at least three different types of perpetrators of evil. These are: 1) *Banal*; 2) *Non-banal*; and 3) *Evil person* perpetrators of evil. People who are not evil persons are not disposed to perpetrate evil in autonomy-favoring or evil-discouraging conditions that allow them to do what they really want.[1]

Banal perpetrators of evil are motivated to inflict evil by banal everyday concerns, such as avoiding trouble, doing one's job well, fitting in, seeking promotion, doing what one is told, and so on. Arendt famously claims that Adolf Eichmann was motivated to be involved in the Nazi genocide, not by anti-Semitic hatred, but by banal everyday concerns such as these (Arendt 1965). While Arendt's claims about Eichmann's motives and supposed thoughtlessness have been heavily criticized (Felman 2001; Stangneth 2014), these criticisms do not undermine the conceptual point that *some* perpetrators of evil (even if this doesn't include Eichmann) are banal perpetrators of evil (Formosa 2006, 513). As Christopher Browning puts it, "she [Arendt] had the right type [banal perpetrators of evil], but the wrong guy [Eichmann]" (Schuessler 2014). Banal perpetrators of evil are not disposed to perpetrate evil in a wide variety of situations because acting on banal concerns does not normally lead to evildoing. Nonetheless, under strongly evil-encouraging conditions, acting on banal motives can lead to evildoing. For these reasons, many of us who never perpetrate evil under evil-discouraging conditions (such as being well-off in a peaceful democratic state), might become banal perpetrators of evil were we unlucky enough to find ourselves in strongly evil-encouraging conditions (such as in Nazi Germany).

Non-banal perpetrators of evil are motivated to inflict evils by non-banal concerns, such as racial hatred or extreme greed, without being evil persons who are disposed to perpetrate evil in autonomy-favoring situations. While banal motives typically *only* lead to evil in evil-encouraging situations, since banal motives alone don't typically lead to evildoing otherwise, non-banal motives, given their nature, can lead to evil in *many* situations. To see the difference, imagine that a fictional Henry is not disposed under autonomy-favoring conditions either to perpetrate evil or to have racist motives. Henry is not the sort of person who really wants to have or to act on motives of racial hatred. However, after suffering one very bad day in which he is the victim of multiple unjustified harms inflicted by several members of a single race, Henry is overcome by non-banal motives of racial hatred that, though he is not usually disposed to act on, he nonetheless does act on in this case. When he subsequently perpetrates an evil action, he does so for non-banal motives of racial hatred, even though he is not an evil person who is disposed to perpetrate evil in autonomy-favoring situations. In contrast, *evil persons* are disposed to perpetrate evil even under conditions that favor doing what they really want to do. Since evil persons are disposed to perpetrate evil even when they are not in evil-encouraging situations, they must have motives that direct them towards evildoing in all sorts of situations. These motives must be morally pernicious motives, such as hatred or a thirst for power, which can lead to evil in the absence of evil-encouraging situational forces. For our fictional Henry to count as an evil person, he would have to not only act on motives of racial hatred after a very bad day, but also be disposed to act on such heinous motives even under autonomy-favoring conditions that allow him to do what he really wants to do.

Moral Responsibility

Having set out three different types of perpetrators of evil, we can now examine their moral responsibility. Moral responsibility for an action is typically understood to depend on the presence of certain agential capacities being causally connected in the right way to the agent's action in the absence of excusing and exempting conditions. According to contemporary views, these agential capacities include (one or more of) self-control; doing what you (or your deep self) really wants to do; understanding what you do; normative competence; sanity; autonomy; consciousness; reasons-responsiveness; free will; being able to do otherwise; being the subject of reactive attitudes; being part of the moral community; being able to engage in moral discourse; and so on (Watson 1987; Frankfurt 1988; Wolf 1990; Fischer & Ravizza 1998; Fischer et al. 2007; Mele 2009; McKenna 2012; Pickard & Ward 2013; Vargas 2013; 1996; Levy 2014). We need not decide here which of these are the relevant capacities needed for having moral responsibility. Instead, for ease of presentation, we shall simply assume here that a basic threshold level of the capacities for self-control and normative competence are required for moral responsibility. When these capacities are absent, a person is in an exempting condition. For example, someone who has been drugged against his will and no longer has any self-control is in an exempting condition. Even in the absence of an exempting condition, an agent can be in an excusing condition. For example, someone forced to do something at gunpoint is typically excused from moral responsibility, while retaining self-control and normative competence.

Watson (1996) argues that there are two different "faces" of moral responsibility: attributability and answerability (for a critical discussion see Levy (2005)). These two faces exist because responsibility is a "triadic relationship: an individual (or group) is responsible *to* others *for* something" (Watson 2004, 7). Attribution-responsibility is being responsible *for* something. This takes the form of aretaic (or character) assessments of what an action reveals about you in terms of your virtues, vices, commitments, and practical identities. Answerability-responsibility is being responsible *to* others. This involves our practices of responding to an action and forming reactive attitudes such as resentment. While attribution and answerability typically go together, Watson argues that someone can be responsible *for* something (attribution) without being responsible *to* anyone (answerability). For example, imagine someone who chooses a dull but secure occupation over a riskier but more rewarding one. We might regard her choice as unwise and something that she is responsible for (attribution) in the sense that her choice reveals something significant about her character and commitments, but we don't hold her responsible to us for it (answerability) since it is none of our business what she does (Watson 1996, 231). This means that we don't develop reactive attitudes towards her because of this choice, even though we regard it as *her* choice that reveals something about the sort of person that she is.

Watson's distinction between two faces of responsibility is central to his attempts to make sense of the moral responsibility of evildoers. Watson wonders, in examining the real-world case of the murderer Robert Harris, why it is that learning about Harris's shocking personal background leads to an "ambivalence toward the vicious criminal who is himself a victim of an abusive childhood" (Watson 1996, 240; see also, Watson 1987, 275). Nothing we learn about Harris's background leads us to believe that he is in an exempting or excusing condition. But his abusive background seems to *temper* our answerability assessments of his actions. While his murderous actions really are *his* actions, we shouldn't *hold* him *fully* responsible for them because of his bad background (Watson 1996, 240).[2] After all, if we had endured a similarly bad background, we might have turned out as bad as Harris, and Harris isn't responsible for his poor upbringing.

Watson's example of Harris emphasizes the fact that moral responsibility comes in degrees. This important point is rarely given the attention it deserves in theoretical discussions of moral responsibility (Ciurria 2015; Nelkin 2016). In Watson's example, an abusive childhood *mitigates some degree* of Harris's blameworthiness, even though Harris must still answer for his crimes. However, an abusive childhood can be more or less abusive. An upbringing might be so abusive that it impairs the agent's capacities to such an extent that she is exempt from all blame. But usually an abusive background mitigates blame rather than exempts an agent from all blame (Strawson 2008). In contrast, Harris's abusive background doesn't seem to impact our attribution-responsibility assessments (Watson 1996, 240). When Harris perpetrates evil, *his* character, identity, and practical commitments are being expressed in his actions. Harris *really is* cruel and indifferent, and we can rightly attribute these qualities to him, even though his background helped to make him like that.

This point about degrees of responsibility is backed up by empirical work by David Faraci and David Shoemaker (2010) on our intuitions about Susan Wolf's well-known example of JoJo. In Wolf's example, JoJo is the son of an evil dictator who is raised in an undeveloped society to become a ruthless dictator himself. When JoJo acts in evil and sadistic ways, he is acting in accordance with his deep self. He is doing what he really wants, on reflection, to do. Nonetheless, Wolf argues that JoJo is not responsible for his actions because he is "insane," as he lacks the "*ability* cognitively and normatively to understand and appreciate the world for what it is" (Wolf 1987, 387). While JoJo has self-control, he lacks (on Wolf's account) the normative competence needed to be morally responsible for his actions. But whereas Wolf claims that JoJo is not *at all* morally responsible for his actions, Faraci and Shoemaker convincingly draw on empirical evidence to show that most people judge that JoJo is *somewhat* morally responsible for his actions, even though his *degree* of moral responsibility is limited by his poor upbringing. Whereas Wolf claims that JoJo's background completely *exempts* him from responsibility, Faraci and Shoemaker instead claim his background only *mitigates* his degree of responsibility. While JoJo is isolated, he is not *so* isolated that he is unable to develop at least some level of normative competence, and thus he retains some degree of responsibility for his actions. This is a significant and important move, since JoJo's case generalizes for Wolf to cover a wide variety of perpetrators of evil, including Nazis of the 1930s and American slave owners of the 1850s (Wolf 1987). Rather than having to say with Wolf that Nazis or slave owners in those periods were not responsible for their actions, we can instead assess their relative degree of responsibility in proportion to their circumstances. This is a significant outcome.

But how do we measure *degrees* of responsibility? While this question is relatively neglected in the literature on moral responsibility, what literature there is seems to agree that responsibility (in the answerability sense) varies conversely with difficulty. As Faraci and Shoemaker (2010, 319) put it in their discussion of JoJo, "the more difficult [the incorporation of the relevant moral awareness], the less blameworthy." Dana Nelkin (2016, 374) similarly argues that "how blameworthy" an agent is, is "a function of (in part) how difficult it would be for her to take" an "opportunity to act well" that is open to her. Angela Smith (2005, 268) argues that because it is harder for people from bad backgrounds to modify their normative attitudes, they are less blameworthy for having them. Claims of this sort are hardly new. Immanuel Kant (1996, 6:228) makes a similar point: "the degree to which an action can be imputed (*imputabilitas*) has to be assessed by the magnitude of the obstacles that had to be overcome."

Generalizing from this literature, we can say that in terms of blameworthiness, roughly, the harder the obstacle to acting well agents must overcome, the lesser degree of responsibility (in terms of answerability) they bear for acting badly, all else being equal. For example, imagine two similar moral agents, Eric and Gary. Eric is in a strongly evil-discouraging situation in which it is very easy to act well. In contrast, Gary is in a strongly evil-encouraging situation in which it is very hard to act well. Both perpetrate the same evil action: they murder several children. But Gary had to overcome a large barrier in order not to perpetrate evil. For example, Gary was greatly in need of money and he was ordered by a menacing authority figure to murder several children for a large fee or be subject to a severe but non-life-threatening beating. In contrast, Eric had to overcome no such barrier to acting well. His situation provided no encouragement or inducement to murdering children. Indeed, his situation discouraged it, with appropriate prevention and law enforcement arrangements in place and no external benefits to be gained by murdering the children. Nonetheless, after careful planning, Eric murders several children. While both Gary and Eric murder several children, given that Gary had to overcome a large obstacle to acting well and Eric didn't, Gary is less blameworthy for his action than Eric.

The obstacles that agents face might be *formative*—their bad upbringings helped either to make them bad persons with strong desires to do evil or stunted their moral capacities—or *situational*—they are placed in contexts where there are strong situational forces to do evil—or *both*. Further, formative and situational factors are interconnected (Nelkin 2016, 370). For example, bad situations can be highly stressful and temporarily limit moral capacities. In Watson's example of Robert Harris, who killed multiple people in cold blood, the obstacles to acting well were primarily formative rather than situational. Indeed, it is just this relative absence of situational forces that makes his crime so shocking and incomprehensible. His violence on that day was completely uncalled for by his situation. While nothing in his situation strongly encouraged Harris to murder in cold blood that day, his bad upbringing did add formative obstacles to his acting well. Given who he was, Harris seemingly *wanted* to murder, and this desire was something that he had to overcome to act well. Further, his bad background seemed to *stunt* his moral capacities of self-control and normative competence. In contrast, Arendt's example of Eichmann is a case where the obstacles to acting well are primarily situational rather than formative. If Arendt is right (which is, of course, strongly contested), Eichmann was perfectly normal in a formative sense. He was no different to "a common mailman" (Arendt 1965, 145). But there were strong situational forces that pushed Eichmann into becoming morally implicated in the evils perpetrated by Nazi Germany. In contrast to Harris, the violence in which Eichmann was morally implicated wasn't completely unprovoked by his situation. If Eichmann hadn't done what he did, then someone else might have acted similarly, a claim that we cannot make about the murders that Harris perpetrated precisely because of the lack of evil-encouraging situational forces in this case. Of course, both factors could be present at once. For example, if Harris was offered large monetary inducements to kill, then formative and situational forces would combine to provide even larger obstacles to his acting well. Generalizing from this example allows us to make sense of the common intuition that it is less blameworthy when someone from a very bad background or in a very bad situation commits a crime, whereas it is more blameworthy when someone from a very good background or in a very good situation commits that same crime, all else being equal (Smith 2005, 268).

This approach allows us to move beyond the binary bluntness of exempting and excusing conditions towards a more nuanced spectrum of degrees of responsibility, determined by relevant mitigating and aggravating factors. In terms of evildoing, enduring a bad background, acting in an evil-encouraging situation, and having stunted moral capacities are mitigating factors. In contrast, enjoying a good background, acting in an evil-discouraging situation, and having highly developed moral capacities are aggravating factors. There are, of course, other mitigating and aggravating factors,[3] such as "the degree or level of an offender's intent, voluntariness, [and] knowledge" (Corlett 2001, 108), as well as the reprehensibility of the perpetrator's motives. With this account of degrees of moral responsibility in place, we can now consider the relative moral responsibility of the three different types of perpetrators of evil outlined above.

Perpetrators of Evil and Moral Responsibility

First, *banal perpetrators of evil* tend to perpetrate evil only in strongly evil-encouraging situations. Banal perpetrators of evil therefore must typically overcome evil-encouraging situational forces to avoid perpetrating evil. The greater these obstacles to avoiding evildoing are, the less blameworthy the banal perpetrator of evil is for their evildoing. Since it can be comparatively hard to avoid evildoing in strongly evil-encouraging situations, such as when one is part of a vast bureaucracy implementing genocide, those who perpetrate evil in such situations will tend, all else being equal, to have lower degrees of answerability. The fact that banal perpetrators of evil have banal everyday motives for their evildoing is a further mitigating factor that lowers their degree of blameworthiness.

However, while the degree of moral responsibility of banal perpetrators of evil is mitigated because of their circumstances, they can still bear significant degrees of responsibility for their evildoing. To see this point, we can compare the degree of responsibility of Eichmann (assuming, for the moment, that he was a banal perpetrator) to that of the Jewish *Sonderkommandos*. Primo Levi emphasizes the way that the Nazis attempted to "shift onto others—specifically the victims—the burden of guilt" by morally implicating them in the work of the death camps (Lee 2016, 277). The Jewish *Sonderkommandos* were required, among other things, to herd Jews to the gas chambers "by lying to them," help collect items of value from the dead, and cremate bodies. In exchange for their work, which they had to accept on pain of death, they received slightly better conditions. But after doing this work for a while, they were gassed themselves, which resulted in an average life expectancy of three months on the job (Lee 2016, 277). The psychological traumas of such a job, combined with poor treatment, may have been enough to undermine the threshold level of moral capacities needed for responsibility, thereby amounting to an exempting condition.

But even if the *Sonderkommandos* weren't in an exempting condition, the extreme gun-to-the-head style coercion they faced would surely amount to an excusing condition. Either way, they would seem to be not *at all* responsible for their actions. This is clearly in contrast with Eichmann who was in neither an exempting nor an excusing condition and thereby remained *somewhat* morally responsible for his actions (Formosa 2006). Finally, even if some Jews who cooperated with the Nazis were in neither excusing nor exempting conditions, the pressures they faced to become complicit in Nazi evildoing would likely have been far greater than the pressures that Eichmann ever faced. This would make them, assuming they retained at least some degree of responsibility for their actions, much less blameworthy than the likes of Eichmann. Indeed, part of what is so shocking about Eichmann is just how little pressure it took for him to commit such horrendous acts.

Unlike banal perpetrators of evil, *non-banal perpetrators of evil* and *evil persons* can perpetrate evil in evil-discouraging situations. Agents who perpetrate evil in evil-discouraging situations are more responsible (in the answerability sense) than agents who do not, all else being equal. Such agents act badly even when acting badly is harder to do. This makes them more blameworthy. This explains why we are so shocked by evil actions that are not the result of evil-encouraging situational forces. The fact that non-banal perpetrators of evil and evil persons act on highly reprehensible motives is a further aggravating factor that makes them even more blameworthy. These factors, in combination, help to explain why non-banal perpetrators of evil and evil persons tend to be much more blameworthy for their evil actions than banal perpetrators of evil, all else being equal.

However, in the absence of external evil-encouraging pressures, we may worry about the responsibility of non-banal perpetrators of evil and evil persons. If their situation does not pressure them into perpetrating evil, then their own flawed moral characters must cause them to act so badly. But given their flawed moral characters, which are often the result of harsh formative backgrounds, could they really have done otherwise? If the backgrounds of perpetrators of evil really are so bad that they cause them to fall below threshold levels of the capacities for normative competence and self-control, then they completely lack moral responsibility as they are in an exempting case. While adopting this approach to evildoers might seem compassionate, it can also be patronizing and disrespectful if it is inappropriate, as it involves seeing perpetrators as passive victims of their circumstances rather than as active agents who owe us an explanation for their actions (Smith 2005). However, if the backgrounds of perpetrators of evil are not *that* bad, then they can be *somewhat* morally responsible for what they do relative to the difficulty of their circumstances, as we saw above in the case of JoJo. While such perpetrators of evil may suffer normative competence and self-control deficits, those deficits are mitigating rather than exempting conditions.

Evil and the Limits of Moral Responsibility

So far, we have focused on cases where the perpetrators of evil are morally responsible. But some of the worst perpetrators of evil, such as psychopaths, do not seem to be responsible for what they do. While psychopaths make up about 1 percent of the general population, they make on some estimates up to about 25 to 30 percent of the US prison population (Watson 2011, 307). While high-level psychopaths might be intelligent, they also suffer "severe deficits in their emotional, interpersonal, and self-control capacities" (Shoemaker 2011a, 627). Are these deficits so severe as to completely undermine the moral responsibility of psychopaths? While there is much debate on this topic (Clancy 2016), both Watson and Shoemaker argue that high-level psychopaths are not blameworthy because they are "*unreachable* by the language of moral address" (Watson 2011, 308), since they lack the capacity to *understand* moral demands *as* moral demands (Shoemaker 2011b). Nonetheless, when psychopaths perpetrate evil, we can attribute to them aretaic qualities, such as charm, dishonesty, meanness, and cruelty. Psychopaths really do have these qualities, and we can therefore justifiably attribute these qualities to them. But even though psychopaths retain attribution-responsibility, they lack answerability-responsibility because of the severe deficits in their capabilities for normative competence (at least if we accept Watson's and Shoemaker's claims in this regard).

Psychopaths, so understood, are a case of attribution without answerability. Even if psychopaths cannot be blamed for their evil actions, their evil actions are not like natural disasters which we cannot attribute to anyone. However, other cases that involve the infliction of extreme harms may involve neither answerability nor attribution. For example, imagine that Michelle accidently swallows a highly poisonous mushroom. Under the irresistible influence of this drug, Michelle perpetrates horrible deeds, such as the torture of small children. But in this case, unlike in the case of a psychopath, we cannot attribute this act to Michelle since she isn't *really* cruel, *and* Michelle is not answerable for what she does since she lacks any degree of normative competence and self-control while she is under the influence of the drug. In this case, however, it no longer looks as if we have an evil *action* at all, since evil actions deserve our strongest form of *moral* condemnation. But the extreme harm that Michelle inflicts is better thought of as an unfortunate and horrific event, rather than an evil action, since it doesn't warrant our strongest form of moral condemnation.

Conclusion

We want to hold perpetrators of evil morally responsible for what they do, and yet perpetrators of evil seem to raise a paradox of responsibility. On the one hand, perpetrators of evil seem to be highly blameworthy due to the horrific nature of their acts. On the other hand, they don't seem to be blameworthy at all due to their morally flawed natures and (often) difficult circumstances. I have attempted to resolve this paradox here by developing a philosophical account of degrees of moral responsibility. I did that, first, by developing an account of different types of perpetrators of evil, from the banal person who only perpetrates evil under evil-encouraging conditions, to the evil person who perpetrates evil even under evil-discouraging conditions. Next, I examined Watson's account of the two faces of responsibility and moved beyond a focus on exempting and excusing conditions by developing a philosophical account of degrees of mitigation and aggravation. This allows the unique formative and situational forces in each case to play a key role in assessing individual degrees of responsibility. The approach developed here thus provides us with an important set of conceptual tools for assessing the moral responsibility of perpetrators by providing a bridge between philosophical work on moral responsibility, which often takes an all-or-nothing approach to responsibility, and detailed work in other disciplines, which focuses on matters of degree and historical specificity. This is an important outcome, since being able to make sense of the moral responsibility of perpetrators of evil is essential to seeing perpetrators, not as passive entities pushed around by their backgrounds or circumstances, but as active agents who remain answerable to others for their actions.

Notes

1 Although autonomy-favoring and evil-discouraging conditions are not necessarily co-extensive, they generally overlap and for our purposes we shall consider them to be roughly equivalent.

2 However, Watson is not totally explicit on this point. He (Watson 1996, 240) merely says that there "is an *inclination to doubt* (my emphasis) that such a person can rightly be held accountable, at least fully," not that it would be *wrong* to hold him fully accountable.
3 This point is an important feature of many criminal codes. For example, the *New South Wales Crimes (Sentencing Procedure) Act 1999* lists over thirty distinct mitigating and aggravating factors in sentencing.

References

Arendt, Hannah. 1965. *Eichmann in Jerusalem: A Report on the Banality of Evil.* New York: Penguin Books.

Barry, Peter Brian. 2013. *Evil and Moral Psychology.* New York: Routledge.

Ciurria, Michelle. 2015. "Moral Responsibility Ain't Just in the Head." *Journal of the American Philosophical Association* 1(4): 601–616.

Clancy, Sean. 2016. "Psychopaths, Ill-Will, and the Wrong-Making Features of Actions." *Ergo* 3(29): 755–777.

Corlett, J. Angelo. 2001. "Making Sense of Retributivism." *Philosophy* 76(295): 77–110.

de Wijze, Stephen. 2002. "Defining Evil: Insights from the Problem of 'Dirty Hands'." *The Monist* 85(2): 210–238.

Doris, John M. 2002. *Lack of Character.* Cambridge: Cambridge University Press.

Faraci, David & David Shoemaker. 2010. "Insanity, Deep Selves, and Moral Responsibility: The Case of JoJo." *Review of Philosophy and Psychology* 1(3): 319–332.

Felman, Shoshana. 2001. "Theaters of Justice: Arendt in Jerusalem, the Eichmann Trial, and the Redefinition of Legal Meaning in the Wake of the Holocaust." *Critical Inquiry* 27(2): 201–238.

Fischer, John Martin, Robert Kane, Derk Pereboom & Manuel Vargas 2007. *Four Views on Free Will.* Oxford: Blackwell.

Fischer, John Martin & Mark Ravizza. 1998. *Responsibility and Control.* New York: Cambridge University Press.

Formosa, Paul. 2006. "Moral Responsibility for Banal Evil." *Journal of Social Philosophy* 37(4): 501–520.

Formosa, Paul. 2007. "Understanding Evil Acts." *Human Studies* 30(2): 57–77.

Formosa, Paul. 2008. "A Conception of Evil." *Journal of Value Inquiry* 42(2): 217–239.

Formosa, Paul. 2013. "Evils, Wrongs and Dignity: How to Test a Theory of Evil." *Journal of Value Inquiry* 47: 235–253.

Frankfurt, Harry. 1988. *The Importance of What We Care about.* Cambridge: Cambridge University Press.

Garrard, Eve. 1998. "The Nature of Evil." *Philosophical Explorations* 1(1): 46–60.

Kant, Immanuel. 1996. "The Metaphysics of Morals." In *Practical Philosophy*, edited by Mary J. Gregor, 353–604. Cambridge: Cambridge University Press.

Kramer, Matthew H. 2014. "The Nature of Evil." *The American Journal of Jurisprudence* 59(1): 49–84.

Lee, Sander H. 2016. "Primo Levi's Gray Zone." *Holocaust and Genocide Studies* 30(2): 276–297.

Levy, Neil. 2005. "The Good, the Bad and the Blameworthy." *Journal of Ethics & Social Philosophy* 1(2): 1–16.

Levy, Neil. 2014. *Consciousness and Moral Responsibility.* Oxford: Oxford University Press.

McKenna, Michael. 2012. *Conversation and Responsibility.* Oxford: Oxford University Press.

Mele, Alfred. 2009. "Moral Responsibility and Agents' Histories." *Philosophical Studies* 142(2): 161–181.

Morton, Adam. 2004. *On Evil.* New York: Routledge.

Nelkin, Dana Kay. 2016. "Difficulty and Degrees of Moral Praiseworthiness and Blameworthiness." *Nous* 50(2): 356–378.

Pickard, Hanna & Lisa Ward. 2013. "Responsibility without Blame." In *The Oxford Handbook of Philosophy and Psychiatry*, Vol. 1., edited by K.W.M. Fulford et al, 1134–1154. Oxford: Oxford University Press.

Russell, Luke. 2007. "Is Evil Action Qualitatively Distinct from Ordinary Wrongdoing?" *Australasian Journal of Philosophy* 85(4): 659–677.

Russell, Luke. 2014. *Evil: A Philosophical Investigation.* Oxford: Oxford University Press.

Schuessler, Jennifer. September 3, 2014. "Book Portrays Eichmann as Evil, but Not Banal." *The New York Times*: C1.

Shoemaker, David. 2011a. "Attributability, Answerability, and Accountability." *Ethics* 121(3): 602–632.

Shoemaker, David. 2011b. "Psychopathy, Responsibility, and the Moral/conventional Distinction." *Southern Journal of Philosophy* 49: 99–124.

Smith, Angela M. 2005. "Responsibility for Attitudes: Activity and Passivity in Mental Life." *Ethics* 115 (2): 236–271.

Stangneth, Bettina. 2014. *Eichmann before Jerusalem*. New York: Random House.

Strawson, P F. 2008. *Freedom and Resentment and Other Essays*. Abingdon: Routledge.

Vargas, Manuel. 2013. *Building Better Beings: A Theory of Moral Responsibility*. Oxford: Oxford University Press.

Watson, Gary. 1987. "Responsibility and the Limits of Evil." In *Responsibility, Character, and the Emotions*, edited by Ferdinard Schoeman, 256–286. Cambridge: Cambridge University Press.

Watson, Gary. 1996. "Two Faces of Responsibility." *Philosophical Topics* 24(2): 227–248.

Watson, Gary. 2004. *Agency and Answerability*. Oxford: Oxford University Press.

Watson, Gary. 2011. "The Trouble with Psychopaths." In *Reasons and Recognition*, edited by R. Jay Wallace et al., 307–331. Oxford: Oxford University Press.

Wolf, Susan. 1987. "Sanity and the Metaphysics of Responsibility." In *Responsibility, Character, and the Emotions*, edited by Ferdinand Schoeman, 46–62. Cambridge: Cambridge University Press.

Wolf, Susan. 1990. *Freedom within Reason*. Oxford: Oxford University Press.

21

Restorative justice and the challenge of perpetrator accountability

Margaret Urban Walker

Mass violence—atrocity, systemic torture or terror, genocide—invites the characterization "monstrous." Such episodes combine the two features at the core of that notion: immense scale and extreme abnormality, deformity, or deviation. Yet episodes of mass violence are in fact horrifyingly ordinary. In the world as we have it, they are things that happen, somewhere, practically every day.[1] When these things happen, they fail our hopes and violate our sense of moral decency, but we cannot realistically say that they violate our well-informed expectations.

When monstrous violence occurs, it can give rise to the corresponding thought about those who perform or participate in it: that they, or some of them, are "monsters." We know from social psychology studies (most famously those of Stanley Milgram), however, that many otherwise ordinary people can be induced to behave badly.[2] Study of actual atrocity crimes confirms what the lab experiments suggest: there are situational dynamics and circumstantial features that create conditions for many people to go drastically out of bounds in perpetrating violence.[3] James Waller calls this the "ordinariness of extraordinary evil" (Waller 2007, xvii). This is not to say, nor has it been shown, that "anyone" can be induced to engage in extreme, indiscriminate, or mass violence given the "right" circumstances.[4] It is sobering enough to accept the more modest but well-established conclusion: many otherwise ordinary people will (under certain conditions) behave violently. They will do so by their own initiative, in conformity with a group, or under orders from authorities. They may do so in discrete episodes such as massacre or mass rape, or routinely, as in the case of torturers and executioners where torture or extra-judicial execution is a systemic practice. Mass crimes and systemic violence require mass or systemic participation; if even some participants are "monsters," there turn out to be a lot of those.

The charged idea of the "monster" who commits or contributes knowingly to atrocity is arguably unhelpful. Alexander Hinton, in his close study of the trial of "Duch" (originally Kaing Guek Eav), commandant of the Khmer Rouge torture center S-21, suggests that the image of the monster "naturalizes" genocidal violence as either the natural behavior of a lower, animal-like creature or the sadistic cruelty of a psychological deviant. No doubt there is, as Hinton says, an impulse to affirm that "we are not like that" (Hinton 2016, 30). But "monstrous" is also a term of extreme moral opprobrium, an ascriptive category for people and acts that are beyond the human moral pale, even if they are the acts of human beings. This use is not entirely misleading or misplaced. These crimes strain our ordinary ways of scaling wrongs and challenge notions like "proportionality" in punishment or compensation.[5] Atrocity crimes yield many perpetrators of monstrous violence with greatly varied kinds of responsibility, awareness, and motivation. They tax our understanding, ingenuity, and humanity in trying to fathom appropriate and just responses. Widespread participation in these crimes can threaten us with accepting the fact that, in many cases, "they are very much like us."

The theory and practice of transitional justice has developed rapidly in recent decades to address the question of dealing with mass atrocity and repression in ways that are just and meaningful for victims of violence, perpetrators of violence, and communities riven by, but also often complicit in, violence. In practice, transitional justice has fallen woefully short of addressing the needs and rights of victims.[6] I argue here that it has fallen short in theory and practice on the issue of dealing with perpetrators in just and meaningful ways as well. Aside from criminal prosecution (inevitably the fate of few participants in atrocity), opportunities for alternative forms of accountability and for just and meaningful reintegration of perpetrators, sensitive to individual differences, have been little explored, despite hopeful appeals to "restorative justice."[7] Restorative justice-based practices, I argue, do have potential to expand the scope, complexity, and depth of perpetrator accountability, with distinctive benefits to victims, communities, and perpetrators themselves. The practices needed, however, have so far been barely imagined. The emerging multidisciplinary field of Perpetrator Studies promises to deepen our understandings of the psychology, sociology, politics, and ethics of perpetrator accountability and restoration (Critchell et al. 2017). I make a start on the question of *just and morally meaningful reintegration of perpetrators* at the intersection of transitional justice and Perpetrator Studies.

Transitional justice and the challenge of perpetrator accountability

Given the alarming but predictable frequency of mass violence, we ought to be prepared to deal purposefully with its aftermath. Only in recent decades has a dedicated body of theory and practice attempted to define a general and concerted approach to the occurrence and consequences of mass violence and systemic repression, the field called "transitional justice."[8] Paul Seils of the International Center for Transitional Justice identifies transitional justice with "justice-focused processes that societies undertake in the aftermath of large-scale human rights violations, normally in the relatively recent past," under "fragile conditions, where the justice system and protection of rights have significantly or totally failed" (Seils 2017, 2).[9] I foreground this definition because it keeps in focus that transitional justice is about *justice*.[10] For my present purposes, it helps to narrow the question of how adequately transitional justice is prepared to address perpetrators, what it means to require of perpetrators what they owe to others and to acknowledge what may be owed to them.

I believe that the "justice" in transitional justice is most usefully understood to refer to varied practices of accountability in response to a violent past. "Accountability" means being liable to answer to others in the matter of one's conduct and thereby being exposed to the consequences of their judgment, which may include assignment of responsibility and retributive or reparative demands.[11] Demands may include penalty or punishment; restitution, compensation, and social, psychological, and moral support; respectful acknowledgment and remembrance; and reform of institutions that allow or harbor abuse. Practices of accountability attempt to assess and to render what is "due" those affected. In the case of putative wrongdoing, failure to render what is due is itself an injustice added to the original wrong. What is due in these cases includes acknowledgment of the reality of the wrong and responsibility for its redress and repair (Walker 2006b). While liability to punishment following criminal prosecution and conviction may be the most obvious institutional example, accountability practices can take varied forms. The standard "menu" of transitional justice practices privileges trials, truth commissions, multiform reparations (including gestures of apology and memorialization), and guarantees of non-repetition (including institutional reforms and perpetrator vetting).

There is an evident shortfall of perpetrator accountability in contexts of mass violence and repression. Criminal prosecution, a perpetrator-centered practice whose point is to impose individual legal responsibility, has enjoyed premier status as an accountability measure, at least among international experts.[12] The fact remains that only a small (and often a miniscule) number of responsible individuals will ever be subject to a criminal process after mass violence. Vetting programs that screen actors involved or complicit in human rights abuses to be excluded from eligibility for public positions often suffer from weak and inconsistent implementation or political manipulation that undermines their status as a justice measure, by failing to penalize perpetrators in a meaningfully discriminate way.[13] At the same time, amnesty from criminal prosecution is the most widely used response to mass violence and political repression in comparison to transitional justice mechanisms (Olsen et al. 2010, 181–188). In practice, amnesties and programs that demobilize and reintegrate combatants (DDR) are pragmatic, non-justice-focused measures that (whether or not justifiably) either bypass or conflict with justice demands by allowing perpetrators to evade accountability. They can effectively reward perpetrators with impunity and, in the case of DDR, material benefits.[14] There is a missing piece in the accountability matrix of transitional justice as conventionally understood. It elevates practices of accountability to victims by states (access to justice, truth-telling, and reparations) and accountability of perpetrators to states (criminal prosecution for a few and vetting). What is missing in both theory and practice is the requirement and the opportunity after mass violence for direct accountability of perpetrators to their victims (and to society more generally) in ways that can reach more widely and that offer morally meaningful reintegration of perpetrators in ways recognizable as justice. What might such practices be like?

Restorative justice has been widely advanced as an alternative framework for approaching transitional justice (Llewellyn and Philpott 2014). Restorative justice thinking originated in response to ordinary criminal justice systems as "a progressive alternative to the increasing use of imprisonment and other exclusionary measures to control crime and dispense justice" (Johnstone 2013, xi.) Despite its emergence in response to too much, not too little, criminal prosecution, restorative justice has potential as a response to the perpetrator accountability gap. The proposal at the core of restorative justice is to connect the victim and the offender directly (when both are prepared and willing) with the support of relevant communities so that the *victim and the victim's harm are addressed directly by the perpetrator.*[15] Restorative justice practices, such as victim-offender dialogue or community conferencing or circles, create dynamics that can break down emotional distance and denial in offenders confronted with the reality of their victims (Braithwaite 2002, 73–136). They have potential to "leverage responsibility," as I have put it, by moving offending parties from denial or defensive self-justification towards a more demanding perception of the effects of what they have done (Walker 2006a, 385). By doing so, they can produce a deeper or more satisfying experience of justice for victims (Strang 2002). The perpetrator's active accountability contributes to redress, affording the victim validation, vindication, and possibly agreed-upon forms of amends or atonement. In the best case, the perpetrator earns an opportunity for self-respecting reintegration into the community as one who has accepted responsibility and become an agent, rather than a target, of justice. At the center of restorative justice is repair of relationships: victim and offender; victim and community; offender and community. Rather than victim-centered or perpetrator-centered, restorative justice is relationship-centered (Llewellyn 2006, 94).

South Africa's Truth and Reconciliation Commission (TRC) appealed to restorative justice as the self-described ethos of its proceedings, injecting the idea into transitional justice thinking. But South Africa's claim to restorative justice at the TRC is tenuous. Perpetrators of gross violations of human rights were accountable to the TRC, to whom they submitted their applications for amnesty in exchange for their confession of politically motivated crimes, not directly to the victims of those crimes. The benefit of perpetrator accountability went to the perpetrator, who might receive amnesty, not to the victim.[16] Victims participated in parallel by giving reports of human rights abuses they suffered to a separate committee of the TRC. While perpetrators got relatively speedy amnesty verdicts, victims waited years for a meager reparations payment from the South African state. Victims were at one point publicly criticized by then-President Thabo Mbeki for seeking reparations at all (Hamber 2009, 103–108). Direct interaction between victims and perpetrators was not part of the formal structure of the TRC (Llewellyn 2006, 99–100). Yet restorative justice depends on what victims and perpetrators do *together* to produce accountability and a satisfactory experience of justice.[17] The TRC in fact roughly reproduced the incomplete accountability matrix mentioned earlier: perpetrators were invited to be accountable to a state-authorized mechanism and victims were given a platform and ultimately slight reparations by the state. This is not restorative justice in either process or outcome.[18]

Restorative Justice for Perpetrators

Despite the gap between the restorative justice principle and its actual practice, the TRC prompts a valuable question. Can and should restorative justice in some credible form be implemented more widely in the aftermath of mass atrocity and repression? There are many reasons truly restorative practices could be a desirable development for victims and communities. Many individual restorative meetings might produce more, and more detailed, information about particular crimes, patterns, and policies, extending and enhancing the work of truth commissions, while responding more fully to individual victims.[19] Victims of political violence might reap some of the benefits that controlled empirical studies have shown crime victims get from restorative practices, including greater satisfaction than with conventional criminal process, reduced negative feelings, and (surprisingly) empathy for offenders.[20] Here, I explore three possible contributions that restorative transitional justice practices, suitably scaled and implemented, could make *for perpetrators of violence.*

First, "reintegration" of perpetrators after violence is a practical necessity that is most often handled by amnesties (formal or de facto), DDR programs, or some combination of these. These procedures, as remarked earlier, are not justice measures, but rather expedient attempts to redirect and neutralize actors previously involved in violence. An attempt at "just reintegration" would look to modes and terms of re-entry that offer perpetrators the possibility of asserting agency in positive ways that justify self-respect, as well as deal with intense feelings or troubling memories with which some previously violent actors may struggle. Although the topic of what perpetrators need (much less deserve) will provoke resistance from some, it is a core principle of restorative justice that the experience of justice is to be shared among all parties to its practices. Even if offenders deserve punishment for serious crimes, they also deserve recognition of their humanity, citizenship, and needs for self-respect and belonging. Yet some practitioners question how adequately restorative justice practice in criminal contexts attends to the needs of offenders. Among needs identified by many offenders are the need to explain their behavior and the world from which they come, to better understand the reality of harms they have caused, to express remorse and sadness, to apologize, and to have their experiences heard and acknowledged along with the victim's (Toews and Katounas 2004, 107–118).

Restorative formats that allow direct engagement between victims and offenders can enhance fulfillment of these needs. Perpetrators of violence can gain, in many cases for the first time, a true and full grasp of the nature and extent of the harms they have caused to others. Given the organized, systematic, and even routinized nature of much political violence, confrontation with the consequences of one's actions may be even more demanding (and the pull to resist or rationalize more tempting) for the perpetrator than in purely individual cases. John Conroy, writing on the practice of torture, records this comment of one torturer: "Everybody did these things all the time. It wasn't something so bad. It wasn't something that dropped from the sky. It was something that you saw every day" (1990, 204). Conroy himself observes,

> The man who feels 'nothing personal' against his victim, who takes comfort in the belief that he is not as bad as some other torturer, who believes that he was not so bad because his victim did not die, never sees the extent of the damage, never considers that he has assaulted generations yet unborn.
>
> *(Conroy 1990, 183)*

One price that offenders typically pay in restorative justice participation is what some researchers call the "shock" of being confronted with what they have actually done (Sherman & Strang 2011, 156). These encounters open a path to earned self-respect by motivating offenders to take responsibility but also to contribute actively to a mutually agreed outcome that might include concrete reparation or constructive action. At the same time, victims get to reach offenders directly with their anger, pain, and loss and to witness genuine moments of remorse, as well as apologies.[21]

Second, restorative processes offer an opportunity to deal with the challenging reality of "complex victims" or perpetrators of crimes who are themselves victims (Borer 2003; Bouris 2007). Some "child soldiers," adolescents or children accepted, induced, coerced, or born into participation in armed conflict, commit atrocities. These cases trouble the clear victim-perpetrator binary that tends to be assumed in accountability practices, for they are at once coerced or exploited victims but also perpetrators of serious crimes. Mark Drumbl advocates restorative practices such as community work projects and local reinsertion rituals for the reintegration of child soldiers; he cautions against the tendency to insulate these actors from accountability, treating their age as a uniformly exculpating factor. To do so is to treat these individuals as "fungible," creating reintegration hurdles for communities who "care about conduct during conflict, that is, why and how did the child join fighting forces and, once there, what did he or she do" (Drumbl 2012, 22). Virginie Ladisch concurs that the role of passive victim "does not allow [the young soldiers] to deal with their own possible feelings of remorse or their community's potential resentment" (Ladisch 2013). Adult perpetrators, too, may have acted under various degrees and kinds of duress, as when locals are coercively pressed into paramilitary activity but also commit crimes against other community members (Martinez et al. 2016, 17–19). In Timor-Leste, before it achieved independence from

Indonesia, occupying Indonesian security forces extensively and coercively recruited Timorese, while the resistance organized secretly, leaving a legacy of profound mistrust, since it was "impossible to know with certainty who was doing what for or against the cause" (Drexler 2013, 88).

Societies emerging from insurgency, civil conflict, or violently authoritarian regimes face politically controversial decisions about whether those who have themselves committed crimes, or were members or supporters of armed groups responsible for atrocities, can in turn be seen as victims when their own rights are grossly violated. In the striking case of Cambodia's infamous torture center, "many S-21 guards were recruited as children and about one-third of the staff was eventually executed there," as were many intellectuals and cadres of the Khmer Rouge regime itself (Bernath 2016, 54). In Northern Ireland, a proposed "recognition payment" to relatives of all those killed in the protracted civil conflict, regardless of their political association, was rejected by all sides in a hail of public criticism (Moffett 2016, 158).[22]

Cases of victimized perpetrators, complex mixes of participation and resistance, and loyalties that forbid recognition of those on opposing political or ideological sides create large gray zones in many conflicts. In cases of complex perpetrator-victim statuses, there are strong temptations either to see the victimhood aspect as wholly exculpating (child soldiers) or the perpetration of (or complicity in) wrongs as wholly disqualifying for "real" victimization (tortured insurgents). Participatory restorative practices could offer flexible and plural modes of accountability to victims and communities, allowing for nuanced responses to this complexity. Drumbl suggests, in the case of child soldiers, "endogenous ceremonies, reinsertion rites, reparative mechanisms, and community service," as restorative paths (2012, 207). It might be possible for individuals to participate in distinct (and distinct kinds of) encounters that address both their responsibilities for harming others and their suffering at others' hands. Restorative justice conferences often do lead to examining serious victimization in the background or circumstances of the wrongdoer as well as his or her culpable wrongdoing.[23]

Third, and finally, restorative practice opens up the possibility of meaningfully differentiating among those responsible for violence and giving violent actors agency in differentiating themselves from others by their willingness to respond to their victims. Restorative justice practices provide an opportunity to discover whether monstrous conduct in fact reveals hopelessly depraved, callous, or malignant character or instead something more mixed, ambiguous, or uncertain. It does this by inviting those responsible for terrible harms to become accountable and take responsibility by directly engaging with the victims of their wrongdoing (or their survivors), addressing the consequences of what they did and the suffering it caused. Broad availability of restorative practices for willing victims and perpetrators is a uniquely effective path to fairer judgment by victims and communities of perpetrators' candor, awareness, and sense of responsibility. However various or confused were the intentions and motives of violent actors in the event, restorative practice allows the same offenders to make clarifying moral judgments about their responsibilities after the fact and to act as those judgments require. John Braithwaite says, "Restorative justice is not about picking good apples for reconciliation and bad apples for deterrence; it is about treating everyone as a good apple as the preferred first approach" (2002, 120).

At the same time, anyone who has studied mass violence and repression knows how routine it is for those responsible to continue to defend themselves and their conduct or to deny or misrepresent it.[24] I have argued that moral repair is always a communal responsibility regardless of where individual responsibilities lie, precisely because relief and justice for victims cannot be hostage to the unavailability or intransigence of those individually (or collectively) responsible (Walker 2006b, 29–34). A community's support for the availability of restorative practices, however, seems not only an effective but also a just way to prompt offenders to discover and demonstrate, for themselves and others, which kind of apples they actually are.

Conclusion

I have suggested some possible virtues of implementing restorative practices in contexts of mass political violence. But as with transitional justice generally, there is the theory and then there is the—often disappointing—reality. A number of (more or less) restorative experiments in transitional contexts merit close study as models: Rwandan *gacaca*, Timor-Leste's Community Reconciliation Process, Sierra Leone's Fambul Tok, Indonesian *gotong royong*, and locally adapted traditional practices in Mozambique, Uganda, and Burundi. These approaches, often adopting and adapting traditional practices with cultural legitimacy, embody a varying mix of restorative features such as direct engagement of victim and perpetrators, moments of truth-telling, offers of material or symbolic amends, and rituals of cleansing or reacceptance into community. At the same time, all can function as cautionary tales: compulsory and routinized participation and inadequate protection for victims (Rwanda); limited duration and restriction to low-level offenses, such as property crimes (Timor-Leste); gains for communities at the expense of the well-being of victims (Sierra Leone); reliance on traditional or religious authority structures weakened by conflict or on hierarchical and exclusionary social relations of age or gender (Uganda, Mozambique); or emotional and practical conciliation without individual accountability or truth (Indonesia).[25] A core conundrum is the problem of scale; sheer numbers of victims and perpetrators invite innovation in designing practices (where possible) that are widely but effectively repeatable, invite flexible local adaptation, allow for participation in groups, or can be kept available within communities for longer-term or serial use.

Restorative practices, of course, cannot replace other accountability practices. They are additions and enhancements, not replacements, for the established repertory of transitional accountability measures. Criminal prosecutions, at the very least for those who command and control mass death and suffering or those who show particular dedication, pleasure, or zeal in carrying out atrocities, is an indispensable testament to the resolve to combat impunity. But it is universally understood that this resource-intensive device will reach only a small fragment of those responsible. Restorative practices create a wider net and can be open even to those subject to criminal sanction. Truth commissions are absolutely necessary for comprehensive public accounting and societal reckoning, as well as to identify the nature and extent of violence and target reparations and reform. Truth commissions, however, can neither offer participation to, nor guarantee investigation on behalf of, the entire universe of individual victims. Financial and political commitment to reparations, the transitional measure that alone speaks directly and unilaterally to the rights and needs of victims, needs to be extended and fortified. Preventive institutional reform is owed to society as a whole and victims alike; its absence mocks the pretension of redress. Restorative practices, however, could add to these other measures dimensions of individual accountability for more perpetrators, greater satisfaction for more victims, and opportunities for empowerment and agency for both. The field of Perpetrator Studies provides the multidisciplinary resources to explore the psychological effects, social meanings, cultural fit, political dynamics, legal propriety, and moral adequacy of such practices in specific contexts.

Notes

1 Glover (2012) presents a set of case studies of war, atrocity, and repression that span the twentieth century.
2 Central studies are Milgram (1974); Kelman and Hamilton (1989); Zimbardo (2007).
3 Studies include Conroy (1990); Browning (1992); Staub (2003); Waller (2007); Klusemann (2012).
4 Waller (2007, 269), succumbs to this generalization: "The unsettling truth is that any deed that perpetrators of genocide and mass killing have ever done, however atrocious, is possible for any of us to do—under particular situational pressures."
5 Seils (2015, 10), says, "If a maximum sentence, for example, is 40 years in jail, regardless of whether the convicted committed 1 murder or 100 murders, the proportionality from a retributive point of view is doubtful."
6 See, for example, de Greiff (2017, para. 81) on a reparations implementation gap of "scandalous proportions."
7 Llewellyn and Philpott (2014) represent this thematic turn.
8 The literature now is vast and overlaps with work on "reconciliation." General works on transitional justice include (Minow 1998; Teitel 2000; Daly and Sarkin 2007; Eisikovits 2010; Olsen et al. 2010; Winter 2014; Maddison 2016; Murphy 2017; McAuliffe 2017). Human societies, of course, have always navigated the aftermath of conflict; what is new is the idea of principled approach with claimed cross-societal application. See Elster (2004); Arthur (2009).
9 A definition of transitional justice by the UN Secretary General includes justice, accountability, and reconciliation as aims (UN Secretary General 2004, para. 8). Seils (2017, 2–4 and 10–12) argues, persuasively in my view, that reconciliation has distinct aims and entails processes, like trauma healing and community development, that are not inherently justice-focused. Olsen et al. (2010, 35–36), an influential empirical study of the impact of transitional justice measures, includes amnesty as a relevant measure while conceding that amnesty is not standardly defined as a transitional justice measure, but is rather a "practical mechanism" to secure peace.
10 de Greiff (2012) is a deeply thought argument for how transitional justice measures in concert can embody justice. See also Murphy (2017).
11 On accountability, see Walker (2014); Van Ness (2014).
12 Arthur (2009, 355), reports that a 1988 field-defining conference at the Aspen Institute had already focused on "a particular set of measures," including prosecutions, truth-telling, reform of an abusive security apparatus, and victim compensation; the strong impression, however, is that criminal liability was the driving issue.
13 On vetting, see Waldorf (2017, 54–59). For a broad ranging examination, see Mayer-Rieckh & de Greiff (2007).
14 Freeman (2010, 1) notes that amnesties are "uncontroversial" in security focused DDR thinking, while viewed as "sources of impunity" from a transitional justice perspective. See UN High Commissioner for Human Rights 2009 on acceptable amnesties under human rights constraints.
15 Zehr (1990) is a classic statement. Braithwaite (2002) provides sophisticated theoretical treatment. Johnstone (2013) is a useful compendium. See also Winter (2014, 190ff) on the role of redress for authorized state wrongdoing.
16 See Hamber (2009, 147–150) and Chapman & van der Merwe (2008, 289–291) on the shortfall of truth for individual victims.
17 On the role of emotional and interpersonal dynamics in restorative justice practice, see Rossner (2011); Sherman & Strang (2011).
18 On restorative justice at the TRC, see Hamber (2009, 132–133) and the studies in Chapman & van der Merwe (2008). Llewellyn (2006, 98–100) defends the TRC's exercise of restorative justice.
19 Waldorf (2010) gives an overview of the importance of information from perpetrators.
20 Sherman and Strang (2011). Whether restorative justice reduces re-offending longer term, and hence is a beneficial form of reintegration for communities, is an unsettled matter. See Rosser (2011, 169).
21 Sherman and Strang (2011, 156) describe this breakthrough moment as typical in victim-offender conferences.
22 On the problem of "innocence" as a criterion of victimhood, see McEvoy and McConnachie (2012). For a model of the politics of victimhood, see Druliolle (2015).

23 Sherman and Strang (2011, 156), emphasize that this occurs; see also Toews and Katounas (2004, 109–110), on neglect of the offender's own deprivation or victimization.
24 See Cohen (2001) on many modes of denial, individual and social. Payne (2008), explores different modalities of disclosure, evasion, and self-exoneration in perpetrators' confessions.
25 On Rwanda, see Brounéus (2008); Clark (2010). On Timor-Leste, see McAuliffe (2008). On Sierra Leone, see Cilliers et al. (2016). On Uganda and Mozambique, see Huyse and Salter (2008). On Indonesia, see (Braithwaite 2011).

References

Arthur, Paige. 2009. "How Transitions Reshaped Human Rights: A Conceptual History of Transitional Justice." *Human Rights Quarterly* 31: 321–367.

Bernath, Julie. 2016. "'Complex Political Victims' in the Aftermath of Mass Atrocity: Reflections on the Khmer Rouge Tribunal in Cambodia." *International Journal of Transitional Justice* 10: 46–66.

Borer, Tristan Anne. 2003. "A Taxonomy of Victims and Perpetrators: Human Rights and Reconciliation in South Africa." *Human Rights Quarterly* 25: 1088–1116.

Bouris, Erica. 2007. *Complex Political Victims*. Bloomfield, CT: Kumarian Press.

Braithwaite, John. 2002. *Restorative Justice and Responsive Regulation*. New York: Oxford University Press.

Braithwaite, John. 2011. "Partial Truth and Reconciliation in the *Longue Durée*." *Contemporary Social Science: Journal of the Academy of Social Sciences* 6: 129–146.

Brounéus, Valerie. 2008. "Truth-Telling as Talking Cure? Insecurity and Retraumatization in the Rwandan Gacaca Courts." *Security Dialogue* 39: 59–76.

Browning, Christopher. 1992. *Ordinary Men: Reserve Police Battalion 101 and the Final Solution in Poland*. New York: Harper Collins.

Chapman, Audrey & Hugo van der Merwe (eds.). 2008. *Truth and Reconciliation in South Africa: Did the TRC Deliver?* Philadelphia: University of Pennsylvania Press.

Cilliers, Jacobus, Oeindrila Dube, & Bilal Siddiqi. 2016. "Reconciling after Civil Conflict Increases Social Capital but Decreases Individual Well-being." *Science* 12 May 352(6287): 787–794.

Clark, Phil. 2010. *The Gacaca Courts, Post-Genocide Justice and Reconciliation in Rwanda: Justice without Lawyers*. New York: Cambridge University Press.

Cohen, Stanley. 2001. *States of Denial: Knowing about Atrocities and Suffering*. Cambridge, UK: Polity Press.

Conroy, John. 1990. *Unspeakable Acts, Ordinary People: The Dynamics of Torture*. Berkeley and Los Angeles: University of California Press.

Critchell, Kara, Susanne C. Knittel, Emiliano Perra & Uğur Ümit Ungör. 2017. "Editor's Introduction." *Journal of Perpetrator Research* 1: 1–27.

Daly, Erin & Jeremy Sarkin. 2007. *Reconciliation in Divided Societies: Finding Common Ground*. Philadelphia: University of Pennsylvania Press.

de Greiff, Pablo. 2012. "Theorizing Transitional Justice." In *Transitional Justice, Nomos 51*, edited by Melissa Williams, Rosemary Nagy, and Jon Elster, 31–77. New York: New York University Press.

de Greiff, Pablo. 2017. "Report of the Special Rapporteur on the Promotion of Truth, Justice, Reparation and Guarantees of Non-Recurrence." UN Doc. A/69/518, 14 October.

Drexler, Elizabeth F. 2013. "Fatal Knowledges: The Social and Political Legacies of Collaboration and Betrayal in Timor-Leste." *International Journal of Transitional Justice* 7: 74–94.

Druliolle, Vincent. 2015. "Recovering Historical Memory: A Struggle against Silence and Forgetting? The Politics of Victimhood in Spain." *International Journal of Transitional Justice* 9: 316–335.

Drumbl, Mark A. 2012. *Reimagining Child Soldiers in International Law and Policy*. New York: Oxford University Press.

Eisikovits, Nir. 2010. *Sympathizing with the Enemy: Reconciliaton, Transitional Justice, Negotiation*. Dordrecht: Martinus Nijhoff.

Elster, Jon. 2004. *Transitional Justice in Historical Perspective*. New York: Cambridge University Press.

Freeman, Mark. 2010. "Amnesties and DDR Programs." Research Brief, International Center for Transitional Justice, February.

Glover, Jonathan. 2012. *Humanity*, 2nd Edition. New Haven: Yale University Press.

Hamber, Brandon. 2009. *Transforming Societies after Political Violence: Truth, Reconciliation, and Mental Health*. Dordrecht: Springer.

Hinton, Alexander Laban. 2016. *Man or Monster? The Trial of a Khmer Rouge Torturer*. Durham: Duke University Press.

Huyse, Luc & Mark Salter (eds.). 2008. *Traditional Justice and Reconciliation after Violent Conflict*. Stockholm: International Institute for Democracy and Electoral Assistance.

Johnstone, Gerry. 2013. *A Restorative Justice Reader*, 2nd Edition. New York: Routledge.

Kelman, Herbert C. & V. Lee Hamilton. 1989. *Crimes of Obedience*. New Haven: Yale University Press.

Klusemann, Stefan. 2012. "Massacres as Process: A Micro-Sociological Theory of Internal Patterns of Mass Atrocities." *European Journal of Criminology* 9: 468–480.

Ladisch, Virginie. 2013. "In Reintegration Programs, Seeing Former Child Soldiers as More than Just Victims." *Al Jazeera*, 20 November 2013. www.ictj.org/news/more-than-just-victims, accessed 7 September 2019.

Llewellyn, Jennifer J. 2006. "Restorative Justice in Transitions and Beyond: The Justice Potential of Truth-Telling Mechanisms for Post-Peace Accord Societies." In *Telling the Truths: Truth Telling and Peace Building in Post-Conflict Societies*, edited by Tristan Anne Borer, 83–113. Notre Dame: University of Notre Dame Press.

Llewellyn, Jennifer J. & Daniel Philpott (eds.). 2014. *Restorative Justice, Reconciliation, and Peacebuilding*. New York: Oxford University Press.

Maddison, Sarah. 2016. *Conflict Transformation and Reconciliation: Multi-level Challenges in Deeply Divided Societies*. New York: Routledge.

Martinez, Denis, Gabriela Flores & Oliver Rogers. 2016. "We Struggle with Dignity: Victims' Participation in Transitional Justice in Guatemala." Research Report, Impunity Watch, May.

Mayer-Rieckh, Alexander & Pablo de Greiff (eds.). 2007. *Justice as Prevention: Vetting Public Employees in Transitional Societies*. New York: Social Science Research Council.

McAuliffe, Padraig. 2008. "East Timor's Community Reconciliation Process as a Model for Legal Pluralism in Criminal Justice."*Law, Social Justice & Global Development Journal (LGD)*.http://www.go.warwick.ac.uk/elj/lgd/2008_2/mcauliffe.

McAuliffe, Padraig. 2017. *Transformative Transitional Justice and the Malleability of Post-Conflict States*. Cheltenham, UK: Edward Elgar.

McEvoy, Kieran & Kirsten McConnachie. 2012. "Victimology in Transitional Justice: Victimhood, Innocence, and Hierarchy." *European Journal of Criminology* 9: 527–538.

Milgram, Stanley. 1974. *Obedience to Authority*. New York: Harper & Row.

Minow, Martha. 1998. *Between Vengeance and Forgiveness: Facing History after Genocide and Mass Violence*. Boston: Beacon Press.

Moffett, Luke. 2016. "Reparations for 'Guilty Victims: Navigating Complex Identities of Victim-Perpetrators in Reparations Mechanisms." *International Journal of Transitional Justice* 10: 146–167.

Murphy, Colleen. 2017. *The Conceptual Foundations of Transitional Justice*. New York: Cambridge.

Olsen, Tricia D., Leigh A. Payne, & Andrew G. Reiter. 2010. *Transitional Justice in Balance: Comparing Processes, Weighing Efficacy*. Washington, DC: US Institute of Peace.

Payne, Leigh. 2008. *Unsettling Accounts: Neither Truth nor Reconciliation in Confessions of State Violence*. Durham, NC: Duke University Press.

Rossner, Meredith. 2011. "Reintegrative Ritual: Restorative Justice and Micro-sociology." In *Emotions, Crime and Justice*, edited by Susanne Karstedt, Ian Loader and Heather Strang, 169–191. Portland, OR: Hart Publishing.

Seils, Paul. 2015. "Squaring Colombia's Circle: The Objectives of Punishment and the Pursuit of Peace." Briefing Paper, International Center for Transitional Justice, June.

Seils, Paul. 2017. "The Place of Reconciliation in Transitional Justice." Briefing Paper, International Center for Transitional Justice, June.

Sherman, Lawrence & Heather Strang. 2011. "Empathy for the Devil: The Nature and Nurture of Revenge." In *Emotions, Crime and Justice*, edited by Susanne Karstedt, Ian Loader and Heather Strang, 145–167. Portland, OR: Hart Publishing.

Staub, Ervin. 2003. *The Psychology of Good and Evil: Why Children, Adults, and Groups Help and Harm Others*. New York: Cambridge University Press.

Strang, Heather. 2002. *Repair or Revenge: Victims and Restorative Justice*. New York: Oxford University Press.

Teitel, Ruti G. 2000. *Transitional Justice*. New York: Oxford University Press.

Toews, Barb & Jackie Katounas. 2004. "Have Offender Needs and Perspectives Been Adequately Incorporated into Restorative Justice?" In *Critical Issues in Restorative Justice*, edited by Howard Zehr and Barb Toews, 107–118. Monsey, NY: Criminal Justice Press.

United Nations High Commissioner for Human Rights. 2009. *Rule-of-Law Tools for Post-Conflict States: Amnesties*. New York and Geneva: United Nations.

United Nations Security Council. 2004. "The Rule of Law and Transitional Justice in Conflict and Post-Conflict Societies: Report of Secretary General." UN Doc. S/2004/616, 23 August.

Van Ness, Daniel W. 2014. "Accountability." In *Restorative Justice, Reconciliation, and Peacebuilding*, edited by Jennifer J. Llewellyn and Daniel Philpott, 118–137. New York: Oxford University Press.

Waldorf, Lars. 2010. "Ex-Combatants and Truth Commissions." Research Brief, International Center for Transitional Justice, February.

Waldorf, Lars. 2017. "Institutional Gardening in Unsettled Times: Transitional Justice and Institutional Contexts." In *Justice Mosaics: How Context Shapes Transitional Justice in Fractured Societies*, edited by Roger Duthie and Paul Seils, 40–83. New York: International Center for Transitional Justice.

Walker, Margaret Urban. 2006a. "Restorative Justice and Reparations." *Journal of Social Philosophy, Special Issue: Reparations* 37: 377–395.

Walker, Margaret Urban. 2006b. *Moral Repair: Reconstruction Moral Relations after Wrongdoing*. New York: Cambridge University Press.

Walker, Margaret Urban. 2014. "Moral Vulnerability and the Task of Reparations." In *Vulnerability: New Essays in Ethics and Feminist Philosophy*, edited by Catriona MacKenzie, Wendy Rogers, and Susan Dodds, 110–133. New York: Oxford University Press.

Waller, James. 2007. *Becoming Evil: How Ordinary People Commit Genocide and Mass Killing*, 2nd Edition. New York: Oxford University Press.

Winter, Stephen. 2014. *Transitional Justice in Established Democracies: A Political Theory*. Basingstoke, UK: Palgrave Macmillan.

Zehr, Howard. 1990. *Changing Lenses: A New Focus for Crime and Justice*. Scottsdale, PA: Herald Press.

Zimbardo, Philip. 2007. *The Lucifer Effect: Understanding How Good People Turn Evil*. New York: Random House.

22
The Contours and Controversies of Perpetrator Trauma

Saira Mohamed

Introduction

Over more than a century, the study of trauma has proceeded in fits and starts, initially as a medical and psychological phenomenon and later, after the Second World War, flourishing in a range of fields in the social sciences and humanities in explorations of the nature of trauma, its significance, and its representation. The field of Perpetrator Studies, meanwhile, arises from more recent developments and continues to grow in both reach and depth. The idea of perpetrator trauma—in its simplest encapsulation, the trauma that is experienced by the person who commits some wrong because of committing that wrong—exists at the intersection of those two fields, but it carries its own distinct set of features and difficulties as well.

This chapter examines the idea of perpetrator trauma. By identifying and probing the contours of the concept as well as its controversies, this chapter seeks to present a sketch of the concept and to raise a number of questions for further inquiry and research. Ultimately, the chapter defends the study of perpetrator trauma, calling attention to the potential for recognition of perpetrator trauma to contribute to greater comprehension of trauma, as well as to a more nuanced understanding of perpetrators, the choices they make, and the appropriate avenues for reckoning with those choices.

What Is Perpetrator Trauma?

Perpetrator trauma refers to the idea that perpetrators can experience their own crimes or wrongs as trauma. To understand perpetrator trauma, it is helpful first to pull apart the two pieces of the concept: trauma and perpetrators.

At its most general, trauma refers to a psychological injury that exists apart from the event that causes the psychological injury. As trauma is both a "clinical concept" and a "cultural trope" (Farrell 1998, 14), definitions of trauma fall across a wide spectrum, from the colloquial to the clinical to the theoretical. Merriam-Webster defines trauma as "a disordered psychic or behavioral state resulting from severe mental or emotional stress or physical injury" (Merriam-Webster, n.d.). Studies from medicine, psychology, and related fields, meanwhile, use the term to refer to an "emotional response to a terrible event," in the words of the American Psychological Association (2018a).[1] Humanities-based research has focused primarily on trauma as "a wound inflicted not upon the body but upon the mind" (Caruth 1996, 3).

Crucial to the understanding of trauma is the notion that the psychic trauma exists separately from the event that causes the trauma. Psychological and psychiatric explanations focus on how the intensity of the experience prevents the person undergoing that experience from properly processing it at the time it is happening. Rape or assault, for example, thus gives rise to the trauma, the psychological injury, because that violent event "overwhelm[s] both psychological and biological coping mechanisms" (van der Kolk 1987, xii), or "overwhelm[s] the ordinary human adaptations to life" (Herman 1992, 33). Humanities-based renderings of trauma also have seized on the idea of a failure to process and have depicted that failure as an absence—of awareness, of understanding, of language. Felman and Laub describe trauma as "an event without a witness" (1992, 69). Along similar lines, Caruth, whose study *Unclaimed Experience* was foundational in trauma theory, writes that

> [t]rauma is not locatable in the simple violent or original event in an individual's past, but rather in the way that its very unassimilated nature—the way it was precisely *not known* in the first instance—returns to haunt the survivor later on.
>
> *(1996, 4)*

The notion of an "unspeakable" act reflects this association between a horrific experience and the inability to comprehend and articulate it. Because of the "absolute inability to know" the traumatic event at the time it takes place, trauma is also characterized by "belatedness," (which in turns derives from Freud's *Nachträglichkeit*), where the traumatic event that is not understood or known at the time gives rise after a period of latency to recurrence of those events (Caruth 1996, 4, 148).

Those who experience trauma may undergo a range of symptoms of posttraumatic stress, including flashbacks, nightmares, dissociation, or feelings of alienation (APA 2013, 271–274). While psychological and psychiatric approaches to trauma promote a range of treatments, such as cognitive behavior therapy and prolonged exposure therapy (APA 2018b), narrative and expression are the key in the humanities to working through trauma. As trauma consists of an unknowing, trauma thus must be known, enunciated, in order for it to be addressed. But trauma must not only be spoken; it also must be *listened to* (Caruth 1996, 11; Felman and Laub 1992, 69). In this regard, trauma theory is closely connected to theories of witnessing and testimony; both fields are situated largely in questions of the Holocaust and other mass atrocity crimes (see, for example, Felman and Laub 1992).

This is, to be sure, merely a sketch of prominent threads in the study of trauma, and there are other approaches as well. More recent studies, for example, have sought to release trauma from its attachment to Western conceptualizations in order to consider more deeply such topics as collective trauma, intergenerational trauma, historical trauma, structural trauma, and perpetrator trauma (Rothberg 2008, 230; Andermahr 2015, 501; Dalley 2015, 382–385). While these have opened up new avenues of inquiry, the subject remains closely tied to its roots.

Defining a "perpetrator" for purposes of understanding perpetrator trauma, meanwhile, proves an even more complicated task. Like the term "trauma," the term "perpetrator" has a range of meanings. In the most basic colloquial sense, a perpetrator is a person who *does* something—the subject rather than the object, the agent rather than the party who is acted upon. Moving from the colloquial to the criminal produces a more cabined definition: a perpetrator is a person who does something that the law defines as a crime. This person is distinguished from the victim, who is acted upon, and differs also from the accomplice, typically described as the person who merely assists in the criminal conduct (see, for example, American Law Institute 1962, 29–30). The accomplice is also a criminal actor, even though a secondary one, raising a question about whether perpetrator trauma should encompass trauma on the part of only the principal to the crime and not the accomplice, or whether, if the category should encompass both, research should distinguish in some way between the two. The same question may be asked regarding the person who legally is defined as a perpetrator but does not personally carry out the conduct, as with the concept of indirect perpetratorship in international criminal law or innocent agency in Anglo-American criminal law (Jain 2014, 108–112, 121–122; see also, for example, Rome Statute of the International Criminal Court 1998, 105).

Outside criminal law, the term "perpetrator" occupies a much broader expanse with no clear borders. A perpetrator might be a person who has committed not a crime, but rather a moral wrong that may not be defined as a crime. In some cases, a perpetrator might even be a person who has carried out some act of violence, regardless of whether that act of violence is a moral or legal wrong (see, for example, Whitney Humanities Center 2014, 2). Many studies of trauma have adopted these kinds of more capacious understandings of perpetrator. For example, much of the work that has been done on perpetrator trauma has focused on combat veterans. But these discussions do not strictly limit themselves to veterans who have committed crimes. Rather, they include veterans who have killed, despite the fact that killing in war is not necessarily illegal or wrong (for example, MacNair 2002, 13–27; see also Gibbs 2014, 168–169), and they include veterans who have witnessed such violence, despite the fact that witnessing even a war crime might not necessarily constitute a crime or even a moral wrong (for example, Laufer, Brett and Gallops 1985, 1304–1311; see also Gibbs 2014, 118).[2] Some use the concept of perpetrator trauma to describe the trauma a person experiences when committing some act that does not accord with the usual moral worldview (Whitney Humanities Center 2014, 2), a version of trauma that resembles the experience of "moral injury," a term coined by Jonathan Shay (1994, 18–20). The designation of a person as a perpetrator, then, is not limited to the status under the criminal law of a direct or indirect perpetrator or an accomplice; under this approach, a perpetrator may be understood more expansively as a person who has committed a wrong, whether in the view of the law, of some observer, or even in the mind of the perpetrator.

Putting the two pieces together, then, in its most skeletal form perpetrator trauma would be the trauma, so defined, experienced by an individual in the category of perpetrator, so defined. But scholarly inquiry into perpetrator trauma has been more limited than this broad definition would suggest. For one, although perpetrator trauma could exist in any context, most studies of perpetrator trauma have dealt with mass atrocity or war, following on the trend begun in Perpetrator Studies (see, for example, Critchell et al. 2017, 1). As a result, the subject of perpetrator trauma has primarily addressed perpetrators of genocide, systematic war crimes, or crimes against humanity, wrongdoing characterized by extremes in scale or cruelty.[3]

Moreover, studies of perpetrator trauma have been characterized by an apparent discomfort with the subject due to significant conceptual and ethical difficulties. The following section thus discusses some of the primary controversies around the idea of perpetrator trauma.

Controversies of Perpetrator Trauma

The study of perpetrator trauma has been plagued by questions about whether it is appropriate or, indeed, conceivable to refer to trauma in a person who has perpetrated the wrong giving rise to the trauma. These debates have been more prevalent in the humanities than they have been in psychology and brain sciences.[4] As Gibbs notes about literary studies of trauma, "there is still a strong discomfort with even broaching the notion of the perpetrator" (Craps et al. 2015, 198). This section addresses three sources of reluctance to recognize perpetrator trauma.

First, unease about recognizing perpetrator trauma stems in large part from the prevalent conception of trauma as an experience of victims (Giesen 2004, 114; Mohamed 2015, 1172–1177; see also van der Kolk 1987; van der Kolk and van der Hart 1995; Leys 2000).[5] Trauma studies began as a field of inquiry primarily about the Holocaust, and even as it has grown, it has continued to overlap significantly with research on victims of the Holocaust and other mass atrocities (Kaplan 2005, 1). Moreover, the understanding of trauma as rooted in silence, and as healing through voice, has overlapped significantly with studies of testimony and witnessing of victims (Gibbs 2014: 18–19). For much of its history, accordingly, the concept of trauma has been associated with victims. In the most prevalent conception of trauma, victims suffer and are silenced; they are to be acknowledged, heard, and healed. Perpetrators, by contrast, are responsible for that suffering, the ones who did the silencing. Because the recognition of trauma also entails the restoration of voice, it would be unthinkable to amplify the voice of the perpetrator.

Those studies of trauma that do consider perpetrators, meanwhile, often seek to cast those perpetrators as victims, thus rendering the contemplation of their trauma more consonant with traditional concepts of trauma and more palatable. One version of the perpetrator-as-victim narrative concerns the lack of choice of perpetrators in occupying the social or political spaces in which they commit the crimes that give rise to their trauma. The rise of attention to and research on trauma and PTSD in Vietnam War veterans, for example, took place in the context of the anti-war movement and the association of those veterans with that movement. Alongside candor about the crimes those veterans had perpetrated was a sense that they also had been victims of a system in which the powerful prosecuted an immoral war using vulnerable, young men with no choice in front of them as pawns (Mohamed 2015, 1175 and n.82; Summerfield 2001, 95). Discussing memoirs of more recent wars, Gibbs notes a similar dynamic in the representation of American veterans of the wars in Afghanistan and Iraq as victims of a destructive form of masculinity forced on them by society and military culture (Gibbs 2014, 19, 161–209). Dalley (2015, 383) notes that the "most iconic examples" of perpetrator trauma in literature "come from child soldier novels," a focus that of course is consistent with the figure of perpetrator as victim, as child soldiers can be understood as victims of undeniably horrific circumstances of duress or coercion, even when they are also perpetrators of equally horrific wrongs (Drumbl 2012).

Another way in which a traumatized perpetrator is represented as a victim is through the notion that the perpetrator has been victimized in history. Dandicat's *The Dew Breaker*, for example, depicts a perpetrator of atrocities as a victim of the forces of history and power (Dandicat 2004; Armendariz 2010, 54). In perhaps the most comprehensive study of perpetrator trauma in film, Morag presents the concept of the "persecuted perpetrator" to capture in Israeli perpetrators the notion of the "inter-generational trauma of the Holocaust." In this figure, Morag presents the perpetrator as belonging to a persecuted people and thus having to face the "identity crisis" of being a person who is both a member of the second and third

Holocaust generations and indeed a perpetrator (Morag 2013, 27–32). In both Dandicat's novel and the films Morag examines, the perpetration of wrongdoing is real; the perpetrators' actions are explained, even mitigated, by their histories of victimization.

Because of this association of trauma with victims, some theorists have responded to the notion of perpetrator trauma with resistance. Perhaps the most prominent example is the reaction to Caruth's discussion of Freud's interpretation of Tasso's *Jerusalem Delivered*, in which Tancred "'unwittingly kills his beloved Clorinda.'" Later, when Tancred strikes his sword at a tree, blood pours out, and he hears Clorinda's voice crying out that Tancred has hurt her again. To Caruth, it is a story of Tancred's trauma: when he kills Clorinda, there is a void, an absence of knowing, and the unknown act comes back to him later in the form of the "witness of the crying voice" (Caruth 1996, 2–3). But Caruth's interpretation strikes some as simply incongruous, for trauma cannot exist in the person who caused the injury. In challenging Caruth, Amy Novak writes, as if the point is beyond argument: "But Tancred does not experience the trauma; Clorinda does" (Novak 2008, 32). Others have responded more strongly. Describing the "chilling implications" (Leys 2000, 297) of Caruth's account,[6] Leys writes:

> [I]f … the murderer Tancred can become the victim of the trauma …, then Caruth's logic would turn other perpetrators into victims too—for example, it would turn the executioners of the Jews into victims …. On Caruth's interpretation, … not only can Tancred be considered the victim of a trauma but that even the Nazis are not exempt from the same dispensation.
>
> *(2000, 297)*

Even those who do not show such resistance recognize the significance of the inquiry. Morag, writing about perpetrator trauma in Israeli film, asks whether, if trauma research dealt with the Israeli ex-soldier, "would it 'victimize' him, that is, make him an inevitable—albeit reluctant—victim?" (2012, 11)

Second, recognition of perpetrator trauma is further complicated by the related association of trauma with moral status. As trauma has expanded from a medical phenomenon to a cultural and social one, trauma has shifted "from a neutral category that identifies an experience that is universal (at least in its possibility) to a label that validates, even extols, the suffering of those whose experiences warrant recognition" (Mohamed 2015, 1173; citing Fassin and Rechtman 2009, 5). This association of trauma with moral status stems in part from the association of trauma with victims and the corresponding moral status of victims (Card 2002, 166–187; Thomas 1999, 202–210). This moral status may derive from the fact that, because suffering would most readily be forgotten, its recognition demands, in Judith Herman's words, "a political movement powerful enough … to counteract the ordinary social processes of silence and denial" (Herman 1992, 9). Only victims of wrongs, and not perpetrators of them, can demand such recognition and respect.

Third, acknowledgment of perpetrator trauma raises difficult ethical questions also because of an understanding of the consequences of bearing witness to trauma. Whitehead explains, "Trauma theory readjusts the relationship between reader and text, so that reading is restored as an ethical practice" (2004, 8). Laub also sees bearing witness to trauma as altering the relationship between reader and text:

> [T]he listener to trauma comes to be a participant and a co-owner of the traumatic event: through his very listening, he comes to partially experience trauma in himself.

> The relation of the victim to the event of the trauma, therefore, impacts on the relation of the listener to it, and the latter comes to feel the bewilderment, injury, confusion, dread and conflicts that the trauma victim feels.
>
> *(2015, 57)*

Both accounts raise questions, then, about the propriety of perpetrator trauma, given the role of the witness to the trauma; what witness would want to be the "co-owner" or "participant" in the perpetrator's trauma?

Towards Greater Understanding of Perpetrator Trauma

These controversies are broad-ranging and significant, deriving from the origins and original orientations of fields of study, the ethical and political difficulties of granting witness and recognition to individuals who have committed terrible acts, and the limited data available on how those individuals experience those acts. But these controversies are also rooted in cramped visions of trauma, of victims and perpetrators, and of representation and acknowledgment. It is important to dismantle these myths about perpetrator trauma both for the future of trauma studies and for the future of Perpetrator Studies.

As a threshold matter, trauma is not confined to victims, and, as LaCapra writes, "victim is not a psychological category" (LaCapra 2001, 79; see also Rothberg 2009, 90). As was clear in the early days of trauma research, the psychological injury of trauma is a human experience that has no relation to the category of victim or perpetrator. One's status as a victim does not ensure that one will experience trauma. It is here that skeptics about perpetrator trauma falter in their analysis; when Leys criticizes Caruth (1996) for identifying Tancred as a "victim of trauma" (Leys 2000, 295), she conflates the victim of trauma with the victim of the event giving rise to the trauma. The two are of course different; one may be both a perpetrator of a crime and a victim of trauma arising out of that crime, and one may be a victim of a crime and not a victim of trauma arising out of that crime. As Rothberg writes, "[t]he categories of victim and perpetrator derive from either a legal or a moral discourse, but the concept of trauma emerges from a diagnostic realm that lies beyond guilt and innocence or good and evil" (Rothberg 2009, 90). Moreover, if trauma can be separated from the status of victimhood, it may be possible to dismantle the notion that trauma is associated with some moral status. As Craps notes, "calling someone a trauma survivor or trauma victim does not in and of itself confer any moral capital on that person" (2013, 15).[7]

The recognition of trauma as a condition that has no connection to status as a perpetrator or victim should not be understood as a call to loosen or dissolve the categories of victim and perpetrator. While there may be value to thinking through the ways in which a person can occupy the position of both perpetrator and victim and the ways in which those categories are blurred at their edges, as depicted so elegantly by Primo Levi's concept of the "gray zone" (1986/2017, 25), the argument here is not intended to sound in that register.

Moreover, the tendency of some trauma narratives to cast perpetrators as victims is destructive in its own right. Such reimagining of a perpetrator as a victim may assist in what Katz describes as perpetrators' efforts to "pacify [their] subjectivity" in order to "transition from subject to object" and thus render themselves blameless in the decision to commit crime (1998, 8).[8] It also carries the risk of impeding efforts to better understand the experience of perpetrators.

Indeed, this potential for greater understanding of perpetrators, their choices, and their motivations is one of the primary reasons to acknowledge perpetrator trauma, to free it from its distorting and constraining myths, and to confer upon it status as a topic worthy of scholarly inquiry. Specifically, investigating perpetrator trauma not only can contribute to better understandings of trauma, but also can contribute to better understandings of perpetrators. By "understanding," I mean to use the term in its primary sense: to be aware of the nature of the choices and characteristics of perpetrators. Despite the tendency for some to condemn as "obscene" any attempt to understand perpetrators of mass violence (Rosenbaum (1998) 2014, xv–xvi), understanding need not entail identification or forgiveness. Indeed, understanding can be a process that enables condemnation, too; to grasp what a perpetrator has done is, of course, a goal of a criminal trial. Understanding the choices and characteristics of perpetrators may contribute also to efforts at preventing crimes in the future.

Recognizing perpetrator trauma has been impeded by the association of articulating that trauma with healing it. While some might find recovery from trauma on the part of perpetrators unimportant or even undesirable, the field of transitional justice, among others, would find value in the rehabilitation and recovery of perpetrators, if nothing else because the peaceful survival of communities may depend on it (Mohamed 2015, 1201–1206). If we accept the understanding of trauma as an experience of unknowing, or a crisis of narrativization (Caruth 1996, 4; Morag 2012, 93), then the creation of a narrative may facilitate recovery from trauma on the part of perpetrators. To the extent rehabilitation of perpetrators is desirable, that alignment signals greater value in such narratives. Moreover, it may shape views on what are appropriate mechanisms for post-atrocity justice or reconciliation. Given that trials are not necessarily effective in generating narratives from perpetrators, a focus on perpetrator trauma requires reckoning with the possibility that other forms of redress, such as truth commissions, may serve to create narratives where they have gone missing because of trauma.

This call for further study of perpetrator trauma is not intended to suggest that the field of inquiry is free from difficulty. There are still, to be sure, questions to answer about the implications of recognizing trauma in perpetrators of crimes or wrongdoing. One concerns the relative status of victims and perpetrators, and the ethical implications of recognizing perpetrator trauma. Specifically, to the extent that trauma, rather than victimhood, bestows some moral status on a person, there is a risk that examining trauma on the part of perpetrators might inappropriately minimize the significance of the trauma of victims (see Blackie, Hitchcott and Joseph 2017, 79; Williamson 2014).

Moreover, the question is open whether perpetrator trauma demands not only recognition, but also remedy. On the one hand, perpetrators who experience their crimes as trauma may be more unwilling to express remorse, more prone to dissociation from reality, more likely to continue to hate and victimize. If reconciliation is to be realized, then treating perpetrators who suffer the aftereffects of trauma may be worth the resources it will entail (Mohamed 2015, 1204–1205; Staub 2006, 872). On the other, to the extent that resources are finite, any investigation of trauma in perpetrators takes away from other needs, such as treatment of victims.

Still, there are vast opportunities for future work in the study of perpetrator trauma. For example, the foundational question of whether or how trauma exists differently for perpetrators of wrongs is ripe for exploration, as is further research in how perpetrator trauma is represented and understood differently from victim trauma. Studies of perpetrator trauma can open up productive inquiries into how the perpetrator's experience of trauma varies depending on the role the person plays in the ultimate wrong that is undertaken. A few studies have focused on PTSD in perpetrators (for example, Schaal et al. 2012, 450–452), but more work needs to be done. There is room for greater differentiation between those who perpetrate violence and those who witness it (see, for example, Laufer, Brett, and Gallops 1985, 1307–1309), as well as for studying trauma across different categories of perpetrators, bystanders, and accomplices. Alette Smeulers, for example, offers a typology of perpetrators in mass atrocity crimes that considers both the extent of a person's participation and the motivation for participating (Hilberg 1992, 3–103; Smeulers 2008, 243–260); Michael Mann has categorized perpetrators as "elites, militants, and core constituencies" (Mann 2005, 20). Does the experience of trauma differ between, say, the criminal mastermind, who plans the crime for his own gain, and the conformist, who has no role in planning but goes along with the crime motivated by pressure to conform with peers? Does the elite thought leader, who does not plan particular attacks but instead creates a psychological climate so that others will engage in violence, experience trauma arising out of atrocity crime differently from the foot soldier, and should different experiences of trauma across categories of perpetrators influence legal or moral assessments of their blameworthiness (see Mohamed 2017, 782)? How does the burgeoning study of collective and transgenerational trauma illuminate the understanding of perpetrator trauma (see Giesen 2004, 131; Schwab 2010, 83)? How is the perpetrator's experience of trauma—whether of post-traumatic stress or of post-traumatic growth—affected by the particular traumatic experience in the first place?

As studies of perpetrator trauma move forward, there should be greater precision in the use of the term "perpetrator trauma." Specifically, in order to best serve the field of Perpetrator Studies, it is important that the term refer to the trauma experienced by a person who is indeed a perpetrator of wrongdoing. Accordingly, scholars should distinguish trauma experienced by individuals in the military from perpetrator trauma. A person who engages in lawful combat may indeed experience trauma arising out of that combat, but that is not perpetrator trauma if that combatant is not a perpetrator of any wrong. Even if that person experiences trauma because of feelings of moral ambivalence or disagreement with the underlying war, the classification of perpetrator still should not be applied. This is not to suggest that the trauma is not real. But it is disruptive to studies of perpetrator trauma and to studies of perpetrators more generally, to include those who are not perpetrators, and it is potentially destructive to those individuals to categorize them as perpetrators. It is, therefore, also inadvisable to conflate the category of perpetrator trauma with moral injury. But ultimately, further study of the subject, properly defined, can open up greater understanding about perpetrators, their choices, and their crimes, and perhaps also about how they may be reintegrated into society and how similar crimes may be prevented in the future.

Notes

1 For further formulations of trauma, see also Cardeña, Butler and Spiegel (2003, 229–231); Briere, Scott, and Jones (2015, 25, 31). The types of events that are understood to give rise to trauma have changed over time. The original formulation in the *Diagnostic and Statistical Manual of Mental Disorders* (DSM) described traumatic events as those "generally outside the range of usual human experience" that caused symptoms such as "reexperiencing the traumatic event; numbing of responsiveness to, or reduced involvement with, the external world; and a variety of autonomic, dysphoric, or cognitive symptoms" (APA 1980, 236). Greater understanding of the prevalence of trauma, including rape, domestic violence, or other forms of abuse (Russell 1984) has engendered greater understanding that traumatic events are extraordinary not in their uncommonness, but rather in the sense that they are beyond a person's capacity to experience them as routine life events. Accordingly, the next version of the DSM dropped the reference to usual human experience and referred to trauma as an experience involving "actual or threatened death or serious injury, or a threat to the physical integrity of self or others" that evoked "intense fear, helplessness, or horror" (APA 1994, 427–428),

while the most recent similarly refers to traumatic events as those involving "actual or threatened death, serious injury, or sexual violence" (APA (American Psychiatric Association) 2013, 271).

2 DSM-IV and DSM-V specify that the traumatic event giving rise to PTSD can be either experienced directly or witnessed (APA 1994, 424; APA (American Psychiatric Association) 2013, 271).

3 One notable exception is MacNair, who addresses what she calls "perpetration-induced traumatic stress" on the part of many groups engaged in non-criminal violence, including executioners, abortion practitioners, and animal shelter workers responsible for euthanasia (MacNair 2002, 31–42, 71–81, 87–88).

4 For a few examples of discussions of perpetrator trauma, see Caruth (1996, 2–3); LaCapra (2001, 79); MacNair (2002); Morag (2013); Staub (2006, 872).

5 Jan Assmann points out, moreover, that even Freud in *Moses and Monotheism* was examining "traumatization of the perpetrator" (2006, 50).

6 Interestingly, in describing Caruth's account, LaCapra refers to Tancred as a "perpetrator-victim" (2001, 182).

7 A groundbreaking representation of perpetrator trauma without suggestion that the perpetrator is a victim is Joshua Oppenheimer's film *The Act of Killing* (2013), which presents through the leitmotif of reenactment, as well as through depiction of apparent symptoms of PTSD, trauma on the part of a former death-squad leader in Indonesia who is not a victim and indeed who feels no remorse. The result is a startling study of trauma, one that properly separates the experience of trauma from remorse and victimhood and thereby strips the concept of trauma of any moral valence.

8 LaCapra (2001, 79) helpfully notes: "[T]he gray zone serves to raise the question of the existence and extent of problematic—at times more or less dubiously hybridized—cases, but does not imply the rashly generalized blurring or simple collapse of all distinction, including that between perpetrator and victim."

References

American Law Institute. 1962. *Model Penal Code: Official Draft and Explanatory Notes.* Philadelphia: American Law Institute.

Andermahr, Sonya. 2015. "'Decolonizing Trauma Studies: Trauma and Postcolonialism'—Introduction." *Humanities* 4(4): 500–505.

APA (American Psychiatric Association) 1980. *Diagnostic and Statistical Manual of Mental Disorders, Third Edition: DSM-III.* Washington: American Psychiatric Association Publishing.

APA 1994. *Diagnostic and Statistical Manual of Mental Disorders, Fourth Edition: DSM-IV.* Washington: American Psychiatric Association Publishing.

APA 2018a. Trauma. www.apa.org/topics/trauma/.

APA 2018b. Clinical Practice Guidelines for the Treatment of Posttraumatic Stress Disorder. www.apa.org/ptsd-guideline/treatments/index.aspx.

APA 2013. *Diagnostic and Statistical Manual of Mental Disorders, Fifth Edition: DSM-V.* Arlington: American Psychiatric Association Publishing.

Armendariz, Aitor Ibarrola. 2010. "The Language of Wounds and Scars in Edwidge Danticat's *The Dew Breaker*, a Case Study in Trauma Symptoms and the Recovery Process." *Journal of English Studies* 8: 23–56.

Assmann, Jan. 2006. *Religion and Cultural Memory.* Translated by Rodney Livingstone. Stanford: Stanford University Press.

Blackie, Laura E. R., Nicki Hitchcott, & Stephen Joseph. 2017. "Looking for Post-Traumatic Growth in Perpetrators of the 1994 Genocide in Rwanda: A Discussion of Theoretical and Ethical Issues." *Journal of Perpetrator Research* 1(1): 64–84.

Briere, John N., Catherine Scott, & Janelle Jones. 2015. "The Effects of Trauma." In *Principles of Trauma Therapy: A Guide to Symptoms, Evaluation, and Treatment*, 2nd ed., edited by John N. Briere & Catherine Scott, 25–61. Los Angeles, CA: Sage Publications.

Card, Claudia. 2002. *The Atrocity Paradigm: A Theory of Evil.* Oxford: Oxford University Press.

Cardeña Etzel, Lisa D. Butler, & David Spiegel. 2003. "Stress Disorders." In *Clinical Psychology*, edited by George Stricker, Thomas A. Widiger, 229–249. Vol. 8 of *Handbook of Psychology*, general editor Irving B. Weiner. Hoboken, NJ: John Wiley & Sons.

Caruth, Cathy. 1996. *Unclaimed Experience: Trauma Narrative, and History*. Baltimore: John Hopkins University Press.

Craps, Stef. 2013. *Postcolonial Witnessing: Trauma out of Bounds*. New York: Palgrave Macmillan.

Craps, Stef, Bryan Cheyette, Alan Gibbs, Sonya Andermahr & Larissa Allwork. 2015. "Decolonizing Trauma Studies Round-Table Discussion." *Humanities* 4(4): 905–923.

Critchell, Kara, Susanne C. Knittel, Emiliano Perra, and Uğur Ümit Üngör. 2017. "Editors' Introduction." *Journal of Perpetrator Research* 1(1): 1–27.

Dalley, Hamish. 2015. "The Question of 'Solidarity' in Postcolonial Trauma Fiction: Beyond the Recognition Principle." *Humanities* 4(3): 369–392.

Dandicat, Edwidge. 2004. *The Dew Breaker*. New York: Knopf.

Drumbl, Mark A. 2012. *Reimagining Child Soldiers in International Law and Policy*. Oxford: Oxford University Press.

Farrell, Kirby. 1998. *Post-Traumatic Culture: Injury and Interpretation in the Nineties*. Baltimore: The Johns Hopkins University Press.

Fassin, Didier & Richard Rechtman. 2009. *The Empire of Trauma: An Inquiry into the Condition of Victimhood*. Translated by Rachel Gomme. Princeton: Princeton University Press.

Felman, Shoshana & Dori Laub. 1992. *Testimony: Crises of Witnessing in Literature, Psychoanalysis, and History*. New York: Routledge.

Gibbs, Alan. 2014. *Contemporary American Trauma Narratives*. Edinburgh: Edinburgh University Press.

Giesen, Bernhard. 2004. "The Trauma of Perpetrators: The Holocaust as the Traumatic Reference of German National Identity." In *Cultural Trauma and Collective Identity*, edited by Jeffrey C. Alexander, Ron Eyerman, Bernard Giesen, Neil J. Smelser, and Piotr Sztompka, 112–154. Berkeley: University of California Press.

Herman, Judith Lewis. 1992. *Trauma and Recovery*. New York: Basic Books.

Hilberg, Raul. 1992. *Perpetrators Victims Bystanders: The Jewish Catastrophe, 1933–1945*. New York: Harper Perennial.

Jain, Neha. 2014. *Perpetrators and Accessories in International Criminal Law: Individual Modes of Responsibility for Collective Crimes*. Oxford and Portland: Hart Publishing.

Kaplan, E. Ann. 2005. *Trauma Culture: The Politics of Terror and Loss in Media and Literature*. New Brunswick, NJ: Rutgers University Press.

Katz, Jack. 1998. *Seductions of Crime: Moral and Sensual Attractions in Doing Evil*. New York: Basic Books.

LaCapra, Dominick. 2001. *Writing History, Writing Trauma*. Baltimore: John Hopkins University Press.

Laub, Dori. 2015. "Bearing Witness or the Vicissitudes of Listening." In *Testimony: Crises of Witnessing in Literature, Psychoanalysis, and History*, edited by Shoshana Felman and Dori Laub, 57–74. New York: Routledge.

Laufer, Robert S., Elizabeth Brett, & M. S. Gallops. 1985. "Symptom Patterns Associated with Posttraumatic Stress Disorder Among Vietnam Veterans Exposed to War Trauma." *American Journal of Psychiatry* 142(11): 1304–1311.

Levi, Primo. 1986/2017. *The Drowned and the Saved*. New York: Simon and Schuster.

Leys, Ruth. 2000. *Trauma: A Genealogy*. Chicago: University of Chicago Press.

MacNair, Rachel M. 2002. *Perpetration-Induced Traumatic Stress: The Psychological Consequences of Killing*. London; Westport: Prager.

Mann, Michael. 2005. *The Dark Side of Democracy: Explaining Ethnic Cleansing*. Cambridge; New York: Cambridge University Press.

Merriam-Webster. n.d. "Trauma." Accessed May 22, 2018. www.merriam-webster.com/dictionary/trauma.

Mohamed, Saira. 2015. "Of Monsters and Men: Perpetrator Trauma and Mass Atrocity." *Columbia Law Review* 115(5): 1157–1216.

Mohamed, Saira. 2017. "Leadership Crimes." *California Law Review* 105(3): 777–836.

Morag, Raya. 2012. "Perpetrator Trauma and Current Israeli Documentary Cinema." *Camera Obscura* 27(2): 93–133.

Morag, Raya. 2013. *Waltzing with Bashir: Perpetrator Trauma and Cinema*. London: I.B. Tauris & Co.

Novak, Amy. 2008. "Who Speaks? Who Listens? The Problem of Address in Two Nigerian Trauma Novels." *Studies in the Novel* 40(1–2): 31–51.

Oppenheimer, Joshua, 2013. *The Act of Killing*. London: Dogwoof Pictures.

Rome Statute of the International Criminal Court 1998. U.N.T.S. 2187, 90–158.

Rosenbaum, Ron. (1998) 2014. *Explaining Hitler: The Search for the Origins of His Evil*. Boston: DaCapo Press.

Rothberg, Michael. 2008. "Decolonizing Trauma Studies: A Response." *Studies in the Novel* 40(1–2): 224–234.
Rothberg, Michael. 2009. *Multidirectional Memory: Remembering the Holocaust in the Age of Decolonization.* Stanford: Stanford University Press.
Russell, Diana. 1984. *Sexual Exploitation: Rape, Child Sexual Abuse, and Sexual Harassment.* Beverly Hills: Sage.
Schaal, Susanne, Roland Weierstall, Jean-Pierre Dusingizemungu, & Thomas Elbert, 2012. "Mental Health 15 Years after the Killings in Rwanda: Imprisoned Perpetrators of the Genocide against the Tutsi versus a Community Sample of Survivors." *Journal of Traumatic Stress* 25: 446–453.
Schwab, Gabriele. 2010. *Haunting Legacies: Violent Histories and Transgenerational Trauma.* New York: Columbia University Press.
Shay, Jonathan. 1994. *Achilles in Vietnam: Combat Trauma and the Undoing of Character.* New York: Scribner.
Smeulers, Alette. 2008. "Perpetrators of International Crimes: Towards a Typology." In *Supranational Criminology: Towards a Criminology of International Crimes*, edited by Alette Smeulers and Roelof Haveman, 233–365. Antwerp: Intersentia.
Staub, Ervin. 2006. "Reconciliation after Genocide, Mass Killing, or Intractable Conflict: Understanding the Roots of Violence, Psychological Recovery, and Steps toward a General Theory." *Political Psychology* 27(6): 867–894.
Summerfield, Derek. 2001. "The Invention of Post-Traumatic Stress Disorder and the Social Usefulness of a Psychiatric Category." *BMJ* 322: 95–98.
Thomas, Laurence Mordekhai. 1999. "Suffering as a Moral Beacon: Blacks and Jews." In *The Americanization of the Holocaust*, edited by Helene Flantzbaum, 198–210. Baltimore: Johns Hopkins University Press.
van der Kolk, Bessel A. 1987. *Psychological Trauma.* Washington: American Psychiatric Publishing.
van der Kolk, Bessel A., & Otto Van der Hart, 1995. "The Intrusive Past: The Flexibility of Memory and the Engraving of Trauma." In *Trauma: Explorations of Memory*, edited by Cathy Caruth. Baltimore: Johns Hopkins Press.
Whitehead, Anne. 2004. *Trauma Fiction.* Edinburgh: Edinburgh University Press.
Whitney Humanities Center. 2014. Workshop Report: The Trauma of the Perpetrators? Politics, Ethics and Representation. https://whc.yale.edu/sites/default/files/files/Traumaoftheperpetratorworkshop2015.pdf.
Williamson, Caroline. 2014. "Towards a Theory of Collective Posttraumatic Growth in Rwanda: The Pursuit of Agency and Communion." *Traumatology: An International Journal* 20(2): 91–102.

23

The Intergenerational Effects of Mass Trauma in Sculpting New Perpetrators

Lane Benjamin and Melike M. Fourie

Introduction

The intergenerational transmission of traumatic memory should be of special interest in post-conflict countries where youth have grown up with the legacies and memories of state violence. The problem of reversion to violence has not yet been considered adequately in the copious literature on trauma and memory studies. Scholars in psychology and in the peace-building field have argued that past traumas tend to be passed on intergenerationally and that the "memory" of the humiliation associated with past trauma often provokes violence in communities that have suffered collective experiences of trauma (Brave Heart and DeBruyn 1998). This violence may be directed at the self, against close others, or collectively against those perceived to be enemies. These arguments about the link between past trauma and current violence are compelling; however, the micro-dynamics of the legacies of human rights crimes and how these are re-enacted in the individual and the collective is an area that demands investigation.

South Africa may be best known for its apartheid government, which from 1948 to 1994 was responsible for the systematic oppression of black South Africans, while white South African supremacy was maintained. Although younger generations were not exposed to the levels of violence and discrimination that existed during the apartheid era, structural legacies of this collective trauma continue to perpetuate (economic and social) inequality and prejudice, which, in turn, fuel destructive intergenerational cycles of violence. It is against this backdrop of historical mass atrocity and its transgenerational effects that victims often turn into perpetrators themselves. Post-apartheid South Africa has witnessed the emergence of different forms of violence, including crowd violence, xenophobic violence, unspeakable forms of rape, and gang and domestic violence. As can be deduced from the above, much of this insidious violence is disproportionately skewed, with poorer, previously disadvantaged communities bearing the brunt of it. Sadly, narratives related to those who commit these crimes tend to distinguish between "good citizens" and "evil perpetrators," with the latter committing senseless acts of violence against the former.

This chapter seeks to illuminate the connection between violence at the level of the state and an increase in violence at the level of the individual. Specifically, it explores the intersectionality that exists between victims of state violence and perpetrators in the aftermath of that violence, as these are often situated within the same body. In South Africa, many individuals who have perpetrated violence have experienced as much, if not more, violence in their own lives as a result of colonialism and the historical apartheid context, thereby creating a very indistinct boundary between victims and perpetrators of violence. In what follows, we offer a more complex perspective of the commonly perceived duality between victims and perpetrators in the context of a low-income so-called "colored" community that has suffered extensive intergenerational trauma and community violence. "Colored" in this context refers to people of mixed (i.e., black and white) descent, according to the South African Population Registration Act of 1950. To bolster our argument, we draw on neuroscientific evidence in the areas of traumatic stress and early brain development to show how threatening and unstable environments provide the perfect fertilization ground for perpetrators of violence.

The intergenerational transmission of traumatic memory in post-conflict countries, where youth have grown up with the legacy of violence, highlights the need to understand the problem of reversion to violence and the potential backlash from groups who were direct victims under oppressive regimes. It should be noted that this chapter was not devised to provide justification for the violent acts of individuals growing up in violent environments. Nor does it preclude the fact that many people growing up in violent neighborhoods are able to succeed despite their adversity, and do not use violence as a means to cope. Rather, it serves to shed light on the experience of perpetrators whose unresolved past traumas often set in motion a cycle of violence that is then enacted upon others. Drawing on insights regarding the young brain's neurobiological adaptation to threat, this chapter aims to make transparent the indelible relationship between growing up in an environment of chronic violence and the transformation into youth and adult perpetrators of this same violence.

Intergenerational Trauma in South Africa

Violence in South Africa is comparatively high. The aftermath of colonization and structurally engineered racial inequality, known as apartheid, has contributed significantly to the high rates of contemporary violence in South Africa (Amtaika 2010). Despite more than two decades of democracy, the majority of South Africans remain socio-economically and psychologically disenfranchised. The result is that violence has become a tool of the marginalized to communicate their frustration and to force their agenda into view.

Evidence of the systemic effects of structural violence are deeply embedded in the fiber of many low-income communities. In a 2006 Western Cape situational analysis, for example, it was found that violence is the leading cause of death among adolescents (Dawes et al. 2006). Even more harrowing was that children appeared to be exposed to high levels of violence within their own homes, where perpetrators are typically male and known to the child. This landscape of violence in South Africa is comparable to other first nations in the global south who have experienced the intergenerational effects of historical trauma (Levine and Kline 2007).

In 2001, Memmott and colleagues coined the term "dysfunctional community syndrome" in a report on the indigenous communities in Australia, which describes their findings of Aboriginal communities as having multiple experiences of violence that were increasing in both number and intensity. These accounts span five to six generations and emanate from the trauma of colonization of the Aboriginal people: the victimization and enslavement of the first generation of men spilled over into subsequent generations, who suffered from low self-esteem and unhealthy identity formation and who then began to abuse alcohol and drugs. These behaviors exacerbated the effects of the initial trauma and perpetuated further violence. In later generations, domestic violence began to increase with cumulative effects in terms of family dysfunction. Limited access to government support and other resources only reinforced Aboriginal people's feelings of exclusion and inferiority, which led to a breakdown in community relationships and functioning. Ultimately, a cycle of violence is perpetuated and becomes entrenched as victims turn into perpetrators and unresolved trauma continues to be transmitted to the next generation.

Similarly, in South Africa, our history of colonialism and generations of apartheid discrimination no doubt contributed markedly to our current reality where feelings of exclusion and fragmentation of communities continue and where crime and violence are ubiquitous in many oppressed communities. This chapter is based on our research exploring conceptualizations of trauma and resilience in one such community in the Western Cape and years of clinical experience gleaned from working in the non-profit sector.

Context of violence in community A

Due to the apartheid government's notorious Group Areas Act in 1966, non-white (black and colored) residents were displaced and relocated from the city center of Cape Town to the area now known as the Cape Flats. Community A was one of the neighborhoods established in this manner around 1969. So-called colored people who were relocated to Community A suffered the trauma of losing their homes, family members (in some cases), and sense of community. These violations have had devastating repercussions for generations to come, and have meant that families have carried the bitterness, anger, and loss of identity and culture for many years (Jeppie and Soudien 1990).

Community A's unemployment rates are substantial (45%); police statistics bear evidence to extraordinarily high rates of violence (Crime Stats SA 2016). The high exposure to violence in children provides further evidence of the climate of enduring violence in which young people are brought up and socialized. For example, a localized study on polyvictimization in Community A found that in a sample of 617 Grade 7 learners (aged 12–15 years), almost all (98.9%) reported witnessing violence in their community; 40% had experienced direct threat or assault; 76.9% reported witnessing domestic violence; 68.9% had seen someone get shot in the neighborhood; and 93.1% had experienced more than one type of violence (Kaminer et al. 2013). Furthermore, research shows that young people in South Africa who have been victims of violence are six times more likely to commit a crime compared to those who have not been victimized (Burton et al. 2009).

Within this complex socio-economic background, Community A has become notorious for high rates of gang violence that have plagued the area for decades. While several interventions have attempted to address gang violence and the shattering effects it has on the community, the multi-systemic nature of the gang culture has made it difficult to create an integrated and effective plan of action. Considering the extent of violence that occurs on the streets, schools, and within the family, Community A could be described as an "urban war zone" (Garbarino 2015).

Childhood Neurobiology and the Victim-Perpetrator Cycle

While children may not have suffered direct exposure to historical trauma, they often live in environments that remain haunted by the ongoing transmission of the negative effects of that trauma (Frosh 2013). This may be communicated both implicitly, through the things that remain unsaid by parents, aunts, and uncles and a deeply subjective inner voice that "*something has happened,*" and explicitly, through the lasting physical effects of oppression. The latter often results in children becoming victims of and witnesses to intense experiences of violence in the form of child abuse, rape, intimate partner violence, suicide, assaults, and murder (Memmott et al. 2001). Children who grow up amid such violence frequently display violent behavior themselves, in that they accept and internalize violence as a normal way to resolve conflict and interact with others. Consider, for example, the cases of Chadley and Mikhail below (not clients' real names), shared by counsellors elicited in research interviews (Benjamin 2014):

> Chadley, a six year old boy, whose single mother had rejected him, directed much of his anger at his three-year-old sister and his peers. The school counsellor recollected how Chadley would always carry a weapon in the form of a pen or a sharp stick. She explained how he would often walk around at school, acting out his aggression and pretending to stab whomever he passed.
>
> At fifteen, Mikhail was referred for counseling due to experiences of trauma at home. During these sessions, it became known that his parents were both drug addicts, and that he and his brother had been exposed to violent crimes from an early age due to their parents' gang involvement. Becoming involved in gangs was therefore the natural succession plan for them as well. During counseling, Mikhail expressed suffering from vegetative symptoms and was unable to sleep as a result of inflicting violence on others.

Traditionally, the experience of trauma has been situated firmly within the experience of the victim. However, cumulative traumatic memories in cases such as those described above are illustrative of deep soul wounds stemming from historical trauma that blur the distinctions between victim and perpetrator. Through our work in these contexts, we have often experienced this overlap in victim and perpetrator identities: as the stories of individuals who have committed heinous crimes unfold, so too do histories of racial oppression, rejection, betrayal, abuse, and violence. The effects of unresolved trauma are transmitted across attachment relationships between parents and children, extended families, and ultimately society. These traumatic effects are exacerbated by ongoing stress, loss, and oppression perpetuated by the inequality of society, which manifests in further anger, abuse, and violence, fueling cycles of violence. We believe it is only through a deeper understanding of the neurobiological and developmental maladaptations that occur in maltreated children like these that we may reflect more critically on how society frames our understanding of the victim-perpetrator dyad.

Neurobiological Adaptations to Threat

Over the last three decades, Bruce Perry and colleagues have pioneered work on the neurobiology of children growing up in adverse conditions, specifically also detailing the impact of chronic violence on the developing brain (Perry 1997, 2001; Anda et al. 2006; Brandt et al. 2014). This work has greatly informed our understanding of the factors that predispose children to violent crime and has resulted in nuanced approaches to therapeutic work with severely traumatized children. To understand the significance of this work, one needs to grasp some basic concepts about normal brain functioning.

The most important starting point to any understanding of brain function and human behavior is the idea that the brain has developed with survival as its primary goal. Humans have not always thrived on earth, in fact, for the largest part of our evolutionary history, life was characterized by persisting threat and violence between and within species. Therefore, our bodies have incorporated any genetic adaptation that helped us survive. With this idea in mind, it is helpful to consider the triune theory of the brain, which proposes that the human brain is comprised of three distinct, hierarchically organized "subbrains"—each being the product of a separate age in evolutionary history (MacLean 1990). Although there are many critiques against this compartmentalization of the brain, it nevertheless provides a useful rough distinction of brain function.

1. The evolutionarily oldest part is the brainstem, also known as the survival or instinctual brain. It is the first part of our brain to develop and is the most resistant to change. It houses vital control centers that are critical for basic survival, including rudimentary approach/avoidance behaviors.
2. On top of the brainstem is the "limbic brain," which regulates emotional responses. Here we find three important structures involved in the stress response, namely the amygdala, hypothalamus, and hippocampus. When the external environment changes in a threatening way, the amygdala alerts the hypothalamus, which activates the appropriate system to move the body into a heightened physiological arousal state. The hippocampus facilitates memory and learning.
3. The neocortex or "thinking brain" forms the newest, outermost layer of the brain. Whereas the brainstem and limbic system are often regarded as the lower "primitive" brains, the neocortex is regarded as the higher, more evolved brain. The neocortex houses the prefrontal cortex, which enables complex, higher-order cognitive functioning, such as problem solving, language, and abstract thinking.

A second important insight into basic brain function is the brain's incredible capacity to develop in a "use-dependent" fashion, in the sense that *that* which gets used, gets developed. From animal and human research, we know that sensory deprivation can have devastating and sometimes permanent consequences in terms of sensory dysfunction (Perry and Pollard 1997). The flipside is that that which *is* present (in this case, violence) significantly shapes the neurobiological development of the child. A common misconception in examining the neurobiology of violent populations is to assume underlying genetic differences (e.g., whole blood serotonin levels); however, nothing could be further from the truth (Perry 1997). Their *experiences* differ qualitatively, which, in turn, give rise to the critical neurobiological hallmarks associated with violence.

A final insight is that the brain is most sensitive to disruptive environmental inputs during early childhood, when the greatest structural organization takes place. David Hubel and Torsten Wiesel's ground-breaking work on vision-deprived kittens, for example, has led researchers to infer that certain "critical periods" exist during infancy and early childhood (from 0–3 years), during which atypical experiences result in permanent alterations in brain development (Perry et al. 1995; Wiesel & Hubel 1963). The notion of "critical periods" has subsequently been replaced with "sensitive periods," because more recent research suggests that adverse early experiences are enduring but not necessarily permanent (Weder and Kaufman 2011). Nevertheless, the nature and timing of early maltreatment remain critical in determining the extent of subsequent deficits in important human qualities, such as empathy, attachment, and affect regulation. This is because the brain develops sequentially (from the inside out), such that disruption of developmental processes early on will have ripple effects on the development of higher-order structures.

Key to understanding the neurobiological adaptations to threat is that the brain's capacity for impulse control is related to its higher-order cortical and subcortical areas' ability to regulate excitatory activity originating from more primitive brain areas. Constant exposure to threat or traumatic stress in early childhood has the effect of increasing brainstem excitatory activity, while neglect decreases the modulatory capacity of the cortex. Taken together, the way in which the adult brain regulates its automatic reaction to threat (whether perceived or real) is directly related to the intensity and timing of sensory exposure to threat during early childhood. It is ironic that the very neurobiological adaptations that enable children to survive their violent surroundings potentially predispose them to enact aggressive, impulsive, and violent behavior towards others later in life.

For the child growing up in a relatively nurturing and secure environment, the brain responds to threat with an instinctive, contained stress response geared to allow the body to avoid or remove the threat (i.e., fight or flight). This involves the hypothalamus activating the body through the secretion of stress hormones (cortisol and adrenaline), as well as through activation of the autonomic nervous system. A hyper-aroused state is thus temporarily induced, but under normal conditions the individual is able to return to a baseline relaxed physiological state once the threat is removed.

However, when a child grows up in a persistent state of fear, the stress-response neurobiology becomes permanently activated and maladaptive (Perry 2001). Alongside several adverse effects in the body, chronic stress results in over-stimulation of neurons in various brain areas, which negatively impacts neurobiological development over time. Notably, chronic stress enhances the amygdala's reactive processing of incoming stimuli—a state that can be described as hypervigilant. This means that the child becomes hypersensitive to negative emotional signals so that even mild or moderate stressors may elicit a full-blown stress response (Heim and Nemeroff 2001). In addition, the cortex becomes turned down and less able to facilitate higher-order functions like problem solving, language, and logical thinking, resulting in several cognitive distortions.

Without access to the thinking brain, which acts like a brake to instinctive, impulsive, and aggressive reactions, it is no wonder that a child whose brain developed under constant low-level fear is primed for violent behavior. This use-dependent organization of the brain is evident in many young children growing up in environments like Community A, where the need to survive daily threats result in violent, reactive behavior. Males, in particular, show this pattern of response because they are more likely to move into classic fight or flight, whereas females are more likely to dissociate in response to threat, thus disengaging from the external world (Perry 2001). The child can also begin to perceive threats that may not exist and react aggressively to triggers that are non-threatening. This is because the process that allows them to distinguish between safe and threatening situations—neuroception—is no longer functional (Porges 2011). Cases abound where, for example, a ten-year old boy will instinctively react to a classmate taking a pencil without asking by stabbing him with a pair of scissors, because he perceived the classmate's behavior as threatening.

Attachment Quality

A crucial insight into brain function is that our neurobiology develops in relation to others. As Perry states, "There is no more specific 'biological' determinant than a relationship" (1997, p. 3). Sadly, perpetrators of violence against young children are very often those who are supposed to nurture and protect them (Gould 2015).

At some point in our evolutionary history, our social connectedness became so integral to our survival that our brains developed unique strategies to keep us connected (De Waal 2006). Whenever we feel lonely or separated from others, our brains instigate an acute distress response in the body aimed at re-establishing contact. Anyone who has suffered a broken heart can attest to the physical distress associated with this separation. When separation from a loved one is prolonged, despair may set in and is associated with widespread disruption of several bodily rhythms, including cardiovascular function, circadian rhythms, and immune system regulation (Lewis et al. 2001). In fact, separation despair and depression have been described as close cousins (Panksepp 2010).

Losing our connectedness to others thus profoundly affects our overall sense of well-being and disrupts normal brain function. This is particularly true when the brain is at its most vulnerable in infancy and early childhood. A healthy, secure attachment between infant and caregiver is necessary for trust to be established and for the infant to feel safe and secure when distressed (Bowlby 1998). Furthermore, the capacity for empathy is determined by these early attachment relationships, which, in turn, set the tone for future relationships and emotional behavior throughout life (Watt 2007; Chaitin and Steinberg 2008; Locher et al. 2014). Parents that are emotionally available and responsive to the child foster secure attachments and encourage the child to explore the mind of the parent, thereby facilitating the child's capacity to mentalize and understand the minds of others (Fonagy 2000).

By contrast, an environment that hinders the ability of the child to establish a sense of safety and trust with caregivers will influence the child's social and emotional outcome. Families who endured historical and ongoing violence are often unable to create a calm and safe environment for child rearing amidst the general chaos, unpredictability, and financial insecurity of the environment. In fact, the systemic effects of intergenerational trauma are perhaps most evident in the negative effects it has on the attachment relationship (Van der Kolk 2007). In such communities, caregivers are burdened by their own histories of unresolved trauma and distress and may not have the emotional resources to provide a safe space for their children (Benjamin and Carolissen 2015).

Strikingly, up to 82% of infants in high psychosocial risk environments have insecure, disorganized attachments with their caregivers (Benoit 2004). It is disorganized in the sense that such children do not know how to respond to their caregivers, who are simultaneously their haven of safety and source of fear and distress. This kind of attachment is recognized as a powerful predictor for serious psychopathology and maladjustment (including aggressive behavior) in later life and is extremely resistant to therapy or replacement experiences (Benoit 2004). Deep-seated, toxic shame stemming from these early experiences imprint on the child's psyche that he is worthless, undeserving, and unlovable (Gould 2015). Children with insecure attachments also typically internalize negative working models of the world. For example, they see others as hostile and uncaring and regard interpersonal interactions as potentially dangerous and painful (Herman 1992). Such negative internal working models are likely to foster disdain, fear, and mistrust of others and undermine the development of empathy (Briere and Spinazzola 2005).

In post-apartheid South Africa, the media often shines a spotlight on gang or community violence in ways that overlook the fact that historical legacies of colonialism and apartheid remain at the origin of this violence, thus exacerbating the profound sense of disconnection among individuals, communities, and history. Specifically, many, but not all, who perpetrate community violence likely developed the characteristics underlying their violent behavior in their own homes—from intrafamilial violence and neglect during childhood—as a result of unresolved historical trauma. In Community A, for example, most children are raised by single parents or grandparents, with parents absent due to imprisonment, death, drug addiction, divorce, or separation. Where parents *are* physically present, some children may experience emotional neglect, rejection, abandonment, and abuse.

Without the protective experiences of healthy early attachment relationships, the capacity for connection and empathy is diminished or lost for many children growing up in chronically violent settings. The parts of their brains that facilitate empathy and remorse literally did not develop, as these are experience-based capabilities (Perry 2012). Not being able to value another human's life, or having an appreciation for the painful consequences of violence, becomes a useful coping strategy and enables someone with a lower capacity for attachment to enact violent impulses (Huesmann and Kirwil 2007). This lack of empathy is evident in individuals who regularly assert power over others with little perceived remorse and who rationalize vengeance as self-defense.

A Culture of Violence

All human beings have similar neurobiological responses to threat. However, the psychosocial environment within which these threats persist will affect how responses are enacted and whether they become maladaptive (Gilbert 2014). Notably, those who turn out to be violent are more likely to have had direct or indirect encouragement to be violent (Rhodes 1999). Where the environment inculcates a belief that violence is the normative response to conflict, it is transferred through family and community members and becomes embedded in the belief systems of children. In the current community context, it evokes social constructions of masculinity, such that young people learn that violence is a means of earning respect. Belief systems such as these continue to fuel cycles of violence.

In many developing countries, historical legacies of violence have meant that men have been engaged in political wars that reinforce aggressive, protective aspects of masculinity and that undermine expression of emotion and empathy (Cabrera 2002). Toughness, machismo, defending one's honor, pride, and risk-taking are some of the attributes ascribed to masculinity ideals (Seedat et al. 2009). Competition for power and authority between men, which often involves the use of force, is another reason both perpetrators and victims of violence are predominantly male. It is important to note, however, that men are not the only ones perpetuating negative stereotypes of masculinity. Women, often without conscious awareness, also play a role in promoting and reinforcing stereotypes of patriarchal power.

In South Africa, boys growing up in homes with absent father figures are more likely to display aggressive behavior (Holborn and Eddy 2011). Moreover, because these youths are exposed to fewer positive male role models, they become drawn to models of men in gangs who emulate power and relative wealth within their community. Gangs have long been known to provide the security and space for belonging that young people seek in impoverished, violent environments (Covey 2010). Gang membership is also associated with a perceived higher social standing within the socio-economic ranks of the community. Young men are privy to these perspectives and it is not difficult to see why crime, as a form of income, becomes appealing—not only does it serve to provide a form of subsistence and relative independence, but the violence and aggression bring a sense of restored power that inflates their self-esteem. In fact, appetitive violence in this context appears to serve a psychologically adaptive function, in that offenders showing this pattern of aggression typically show better functioning and fewer concerns about future threat than those who are reactively aggressive (Weierstall et al. 2013). While so much of this violence thus appears senseless, belief systems that foster violence and ignore the laws of biology continue to prevail, resulting in violence that *does* make sense given the context.

Conclusion

Not all children growing up in violent communities will grow up to be violent offenders. However, the toxic combination of impoverished and unsafe neighborhoods, hypervigilant brains wired for threat, childhood neglect and abuse, and powerful and aggressive male role models encourage those who have experienced historical trauma to become predisposed to falling into a mode of psychological re-enactment of the violent oppression they have suffered. Having insight into the ways in which these young perpetrators' stories unfold provides us with a more complex perspective into acts of perpetration that might otherwise be construed as "pure evil"—it compels us to acknowledge and contextualize these stories as part of our historical legacy. In addition, a deeper understanding of what the young brain requires to develop normally challenges assumptions that violent perpetrators from historically oppressed communities have distinct neurobiological genotypes. Rather, what has and continues to be different are the environments in which they grow up and thus the way in which their neurobiological development is shaped. Violent offenses in these communities will continue to escalate until the historical trauma is acknowledged and opportunities are created to mourn this collective loss. In addition, significant economic disparities and inequity that fuel familial and societal fragmentation, social injustice, and systemic violence need to be addressed. In the meantime, innocent children will survive victimhood only to become potential perpetrators themselves.

References

Amtaika, Alexius. 2010. "Crime Prevention Programmes at the Lower Level of Government in South Africa." *The International Journal of Human Rights* 14(4): 603–623.

Anda, Robert F., Vincent J. Felitti, J. Douglas Bremner, John D. Walker, Charles Whitfield, Bruce D. Perry, Shanta R. Dube & Wayne H. Giles. 2006. "The Enduring Effects of Abuse and Related Adverse Experiences in Childhood. A Convergence of Evidence from Neurobiology and Epidemiology." *European Archives of Psychiatry and Clinical Neuroscience* 256(3): 174–186.

Benjamin, Arlene. 2014. *Community counsellors' experiences of trauma and resilience in a low-income community.* (Unpublished doctoral dissertation) Stellenbosch, South Africa: Stellenbosch University.

Benjamin, Arlene & Ronelle Carolissen. 2015. "'They Just Block it Out': Community Counselors' Narratives of Trauma in a Low-Income Community." *Peace and Conflict: Journal of Peace Psychology* 21(3): 414–431.

Benoit, Diane. 2004. "Infant-Parent Attachment: Definition, Types, Antecedents, Measurement and Outcome." *Paediatrics & Child Health* 9(8): 541–545.

Bowlby, E. & M. John. 1998. *Separation: Anger and Anxiety, Attachment and Loss, Vol. 2: Separation, Anxiety and Anger.* Pimlico: Hogarth Press (Original work published 1973).

Brandt, Kristie, Bruce D. Perry, Stephen Seligman & Ed Tronisk. 2014. *Infant & Early Childhood Mental Health: Core Concepts & Clinical Practice.* Washington, DC: American Psychiatric Publishing.

Brave Heart, Maria Y. & Lemyra M. DeBruyn. 1998. "The American Indian Holocaust: Healing Historical Unresolved Grief." *American Indian and Alaska Native Mental Health Research* 8(2): 56–78.

Briere, John & Joseph Spinazzola. 2005. "Phenomenology and Psychological Assessment of Complex Posttraumatic States." *Journal of Traumatic Stress* 18(5): 401–412.

Burton, Patrick, Lezanne Leoschut & Angela Bonora. 2009. *Walking the Tightrope: Youth Resilience to Crime in South Africa, Monograph Series, No. 5.* Cape Town: Centre for Justice and Crime Prevention.

Cabrera, Martha. 2002. "Living and Surviving in a Multiply Wounded Country, Nicaragua." *Envio* 12: 11–18.

Chaitin, Julia & Shoshana Steinberg. 2008. "'You Should Know Better': Expressions of Empathy and Disregard Among Victims of Massive Social Trauma." *Journal of Aggression, Maltreatment & Trauma* 17 (2): 197–226.

Covey, Robert C. 2010. *Street Gangs throughout the World*. Springfield: Charles C. Thomas Publisher Ltd.

Crime Stats SA. 2016. www.crimestatssa.com/toptenbyprovince.php?ShowProvince=Western%20Cape.

Dawes, Andrew, Wahbie Long, Lameez Alexander & Catherine Ward. 2006. *A Situation Analysis of Children Affected by Maltreatment and Violence in the Western Cape*. Cape Town: Human Sciences Research Council.

De Waal, Frans B.M. 2006. *Primates and Philosophers: How Morality Evolved*. Princeton: Princeton University Press.

Fonagy, Peter. 2000. "Attachment and Borderline Personality Disorder." *Journal of the American Psychoanalytic Association* 48(4): 1129–1146.

Frosh, Stephen. 2013. *Hauntings: Psychoanalysis and Ghostly Transmissions*. Hampshire, UK: Macmillan Publishers Ltd.

Garbarino, James. 2015. *Listening to Killers: Lessons Learned from My Twenty Years as a Psychological Expert Witness in Murder Cases*. Oakland, CA: University of California Press.

Gilbert, Paul. 2014. "The Origins and Nature of Compassion Focused Therapy." *British Journal of Clinical Psychology* 53(1): 6–41.

Gould, Chandre. 2015. "Beaten Bad: The Life Stories of Violent Offenders." *Institute for Security Studies Monographs* 192: 1–144.

Heim, Christine & Charles B. Nemeroff. 2001. "The Role of Childhood Trauma in the Neurobiology of Mood and Anxiety Disorders: Preclinical and Clinical Studies." *Biological Psychiatry* 49(12): 1023–1039.

Herman, Judith L. 1992. "Complex PTSD: A Syndrome in Survivors of Prolonged and Repeated Trauma." *Journal of Traumatic Stress* 5(3): 377–391.

Holborn, Lucy & Gail Eddy. 2011. "First Steps to Healing the South African Family." *South African Institute of Race Relations*.

Jeppie, Shamil & Crain Soudien. 1990. *The Struggle for District Six: Past and Present*. Cape Town, South Africa: Buchu Books.

Kaminer, Debra, Bernice Du Plessis, Anneli Hardy & Arlene Benjamin. 2013. "Exposure to Violence across Multiple Sites among Young South African Adolescents." *Peace and Conflict: Journal of Peace Psychology* 19(2): 112–124.

Levine, Peter & Maggie Kline. 2007. *Trauma through a Child's Eyes*. Berkeley, CA: North Atlantic Books.

Lewis, Thomas, Fari Amini & Richard Lannon. 2001. *A General Theory of Love*. New York: Vintage Books.

Locher, Simon C., Lisa Barenblatt Melike M., Fourie Dan J. Stein & Pumla Gobodo-Madikizela. 2014. "Empathy and Childhood Maltreatment: A Mixed-Methods Investigation." *Annals of Clinical Psychiatry* 26(2): 97–110.

MacLean, Paul D. 1990. *The Triune Brain in Evolution: Role in Paleocerebral Functions*. New York: Plenum Press.

Memmott, Paul, Racheal Stacy, Catherine Chambers & Catherine Keys. 2001. *Violence in Indigenous Communities*. Australia: Attorney General's Department: Canberra.

Panksepp, Jaak. 2010. "Affective Neuroscience of the Emotional Brainmind: Evolutionary Perspectives and Implications for Understanding Depression." *Dialogues in Clinical Neuroscience* 12(4): 533–545.

Perry, Bruce D. 1997. "Incubated in Terror: Neurodevelopmental Factors in the 'Cycle of Violence'." In *Children, Youth and Violence: The Search for Solutions*, edited by Joy Osofsky, 124–148. New York: Guilford Press.

Perry, Bruce D. 2001. "The Neurodevelopmental Impact of Violence in Childhood." In *Child and Adolescent Forensic Psychiatry*, edited by Diane Schetky and Elissa P. Benedek, 221–238. Washington, D.C.: American Psychiatric Press, Inc.

Perry, Bruce D. 2012. "The Death of Empathy?" In *Evolution, Early Experience and Human Development*, edited by Darcea Narvaez, Jaak Panksepp, Allan Schore and Tracy Gleason, 199–201. New York: Oxford University Press.

Perry, Bruce D. & Ronnie Pollard. 1997. "Altered Brain Development Following Global Neglect in Early Childhood." Society for Neuroscience: Proceedings from Annual Meeting, New Orleans.

Perry, Bruce D., Ronnie A. Pollard, Toi L. Blakley, William L. Baker & Domenico Vigilante. 1995. "Childhood Trauma, The Neurobiology of Adaptation, and 'Use-Dependent' Development of the Brain: How 'States' Become 'Traits'." *Infant Mental Health Journal* 16(4): 271–291.

Porges, Stephen W. 2011. *Neurophysiological Foundations of Emotions, Attachment, Communication, and Self-Regulation*. New York: W.W. Norton.

Rhodes, Richard. 1999. *Why They Kill: The Discoveries of a Maverick Criminologist*. New York: Random House, Inc.

Huesmann, L. Rowell & Lucyna Kirwil. 2007. "Why Observing Violence Increases the Risk of Violent Behavior in the Observer." In *The Cambridge Handbook of Violent Behavior and Aggression*, edited by Daniel J. Flannery, Alexander T. Vazsonyi and Irwin D. Waldman, 545–570. Cambridge: Cambridge University Press.

Seedat, Mohamed, Ashley Van Niekerk, Rachel Jewkes, Shahnaaz Suffla & Kopano Ratele. 2009. "Violence and Injuries in South Africa: Prioritising an Agenda for Prevention." *The Lancet* 374(9694): 1011–1022.

Van der Kolk, Bessel A. 2007. "The History of Trauma in Psychiatry." In *Handbook of PTSD: Science and practice*, edited by Matthew J. Friedman, Terence M. Keane and Patricia A. Resick, 19–36. New York: The Guilford Press.

Watt, Douglas. 2007. "Toward a Neuroscience of Empathy: Integrating Affective and Cognitive Perspectives." *Neuro-Psychoanalysis* 9(2): 119–140.

Weder, Natalie & Joan Kaufman. 2011. "Critical Periods Revisited: Implications for Intervention with Traumatized Children." *Journal of the American Academy of Child & Adolescent Psychiatry* 50(11): 1087–1089.

Weierstall, Roland, Martina Hinsberger, Debra Kaminer, Leon Holtzhausen, Solomon Madikane & Thomas Elbert. 2013. "Appetitive Aggression and Adaptation to a Violent Environment among Youth Offenders." *Peace and Conflict: Journal of Peace Psychology* 19(2): 138–149.

Wiesel, Torsten N. & David H. Hubel. 1963. "Effects of Visual Deprivation on Morphology and Physiology of Cells in the Cats Lateral Geniculate Body." *Journal of Neurophysiology* 26: 978–993.

24

One Perpetrator at a Time

The Contribution of Public Health Science to Genocide Prevention[1]

Reva N. Adler

Of genocide, Leo Kuper wrote, "the word is new, the crime ancient" (Kuper 1981). The sacking of Carthage by Rome in 149 B.C., the massacre of Huguenots in sixteenth-century France, the murder of 800,000 Armenians in the Ottoman Empire in 1915, the elimination of six million Jews and one million Sinti and Roma by the Nazis between 1939 and 1945, the execution of 1.7 million Cambodians between 1975 and 1979, and the killing of 800,000 Tutsis and Hutu moderates in Rwanda in 1994 are but a few examples of early and modern episodes of genocide.

Though not customarily thought of as a population health issue, genocide poses a substantial threat to global health in the twenty-first century. Deaths due to genocide have exceeded war-related deaths in every historical period and were eightfold higher in the twentieth century than in all preceding centuries. Genocide-related mortality rates are far greater than rates for other global pandemics, including HIV/AIDS, malaria, and tuberculosis combined. The health consequences of genocide are acute, chronic, and intergenerational, increasing disease burden both immediately and long term.

Traditional theory holds that the risk of catastrophic violence in any jurisdiction increases when a destructive amalgam of armed conflict, autocratic governance, inter-ethnic strife, social exclusion, economic crisis, and idle threats of international intervention is present. More recent scholarship has focused on the conflation of war and genocide, as well as the use of genocide by social and political elites to advance a vision of utopian society, a radical strategic agenda, or domestic military objectives.

As such, genocide may be viewed in aggregated metrics through a macro-dynamic, socio-political lens. For example, it is customary to describe the dynamics of the Nazi Genocide of 1938–1945 as 1) *a ruling German elite, 2) embracing destructive, exclusionary ideology, 3) prosecuting a world war, and 4) leveraging the subsequent crisis to murder as many as seventeen million unarmed disabled, homosexual, Jewish, Romani, and other European civilians*. Viewed in this way, genocide prevention strategies are framed as military, diplomatic, and economic interventions targeting the power, resources, and global enablers of elite, genocidal leaders.

In recent years, the international community has accelerated calls for *primary* prevention of extreme, collective violence, through study of its root causes and development of anticipatory interventions. Within the health sciences, the 2002 WHO World Report on Violence and

Health established violence prevention as an international public health priority. Newer study has focused on empirical research with individual participants in mass atrocity in order to understand the dynamics impelling ordinary citizens to engage in crimes against humanity. The ultimate goal of this research is to interrupt the cycle of violence amongst individuals and groups *before* a crisis ensues.

Within this *micro-dynamic approach*, genocide is viewed as the hands-on interface between killer and victim. From this vantage point, the Nazi Genocide may be described as 1) *the discrete homicide of a single disabled, homosexual, Jewish, Romani, or other European civilian,* 2) *repeated seventeen million times, 3) by individuals and groups comprising the rank and file of European society*. This is no small distinction, as it suggests complementary interventions focused on inuring average citizens to genocidal provocation by ruling elites, long before violence is underway.

Though genocidal governments may incite their citizens to commit violence, it is fundamental that in any genocide, *rank-and-file individuals carry out the actual killing*. As such, any organized, scientific agenda for the prevention of genocide is incomplete without a strategy for transforming the behavior of potential perpetrators. The chapter that follows will advance this discussion by situating genocide within an epidemiological framework, and describing an approach to genocide prevention grounded in public health science and practice.

The Health Outcomes of Genocide

It is estimated that deaths due to a combination of genocide, politicide, and mass murder ("democide") have exceeded war-related deaths in all historical eras (see Table 24.1) (Rummel 1998). Data demonstrate that targeted civilians are at higher risk of death during armed conflict than are military combatants.

Statistics from the 1994 Rwandan Genocide illustrate the impact of genocide on population mortality. Eight hundred thousand individuals, representing 10.2 percent of the total Rwandan population, were killed within 100 days between April and June of that year (Caplan 2000). The genocide-specific mortality rates for Tutsis and a smaller number of politically moderate Hutus was 12,100/100,000/100 days (Adler et al. 2004).

These rates may be compared to those for leading causes of mortality in Sub-Saharan Africa. In 1999, 40,000 individuals, representing 0.6 percent of the Rwandan population, died of AIDS-related illness (WHO 2000), translating to a mortality rate of 1200/100,000/year. Accordingly, for the time period in question, mortality rates for the Rwandan genocide exceeded rates for HIV/AIDS by a factor of ten (Adler et al. 2004).

Tragically, more recent episodes of genocide have been no different. Between August 25 and September 24, 2017, crude mortality rates for Rohingya refugees in Cox's Bazaar, Bangladesh, was 61/1000/day, representing a fifteen-fold increase in the mortality rate of the

Table 24.1 Estimated Numbers of Individuals Who Died in War and Genocide: 5000 BC to 2000 AD

ERA	*War Deaths*	*War Death % **	*Democide*	*Democide % ***
5000 BC—1900 AD	40,269,000	.29	133,147,000	.97
Twentieth Century	110,929,000	4.44	192,284,000	7.70

* *War deaths as a percent of total population.*
** *Deaths due to genocide as a percent of total population* (Rummel 1998, 29).

same population for the six preceding months. During the same time period, twenty-one percent of refugees experienced at least one violent event, including shooting, physical violence, burning of homes, and detentions or kidnappings (Guzek et al. 2017).

The impact of genocide on population health is compounded by increased rates of acute and chronic disease amongst genocide survivors. The health consequences of genocidal violence may be immediate or may manifest after decades. For example, eighty-six percent of a sample of Cambodian refugees surveyed in the United States met the criteria for PTSD (Carlson and Rosser-Hogan 1991). In addition to psychiatric illness, genocide survivors may be more likely to live with a variety of physical illnesses when compared to control groups. A 1981 Norwegian study demonstrated an increased prevalence of cardiovascular disorders, peptic ulcer disease, and respiratory disorders amongst former Nazi prisoners compared to the general public. Notably, these findings were evident more than thirty years after the end of WWII (Eitinger, 1980.).

The population health effects of genocide may not subside within one generation. In 1998, Yehuda compared 100 offspring of Holocaust survivors to 44 matched controls. Though both groups reported the same rates of personal traumatic experience, children of Holocaust survivors reported a higher prevalence of current and lifetime PTSD than the comparison group. Authors theorized both psychological and/or physiological mechanisms for this phenomenon (Yehuda 1998).

Public Health Science and Violence Prevention

In view of the enormous consequences of violent trauma on international health, the science of violence prevention has gradually entered the public health mainstream. Specialists focusing on violence prevention assert that violence, when viewed as a public health problem as any other, may be prevented. They advocate for emphasis to be placed on primary violence prevention, as this lessens the consequences of violence for victims and perpetrators alike. Identification of host (victim), agent-related (perpetrator and/or weapon), and environmental (physical and sociocultural) antecedents is central to this approach. Experts underscore the importance of applying organized, scientific methods, along with targeted interventions, in addressing the problem (Mercy 1988; Hammond 1993; Scott et al. 1999).

The public health approach to violence prevention is anchored in a four-stage process that has proven durable over a thirty-year period. Stages include:

1. **Problem definition and surveillance**, including demographic description and rate calculations, and assessment of those at highest risk for injury
2. **Analysis of all risk and protective factors** contributing to the mode of violence being studied
3. **Development and testing of prevention strategies** based on the information obtained in the first two stages
4. **Widespread adoption** of efficacious findings

Examples of the successful application of this approach are available from the United States, a country with a high level of gun violence when compared to other developed nations in the global north.

In Chicago, a program known as CeaseFire set out in 1999 to reduce gun violence in high-risk neighborhoods. CeaseFire relied on law enforcement databases to target districts with high rates of shootings. Drawing from previous study and the peer-reviewed literature on behavioral change, CeaseFire developed and implemented a direct intervention with key individuals at risk for either harming, or being harmed, through gun violence. "Violence Interrupters" worked on the street to mediate conflicts directly between opponents. Program clients also received counseling and connection to an array of community and educational services. Communities were mobilized to hold monthly events designed to promote non-violent norms amongst potential opponents. In a prospective, controlled evaluation, the CeaseFire program was found to have reduced significantly the number of gun homicides in three of seven targeted neighborhoods (Skogan et al. 2009).

In keeping with the principle of widespread adoption, a follow-on project known as Safe Streets was implemented in Baltimore in 2007. Safe Streets yielded similar results, reducing non-fatal shootings and/or homicides in three out of four experimental neighborhoods, as well as reducing both homicides and non-fatal shootings in bordering communities (Webster et al. 2013). CeaseFire and Safe Streets are but two of a larger number of public health-based programs that have reduced violence in a number of settings, including but not limited to schools (Coker et al. 2018) and prisons (Guerra and Slaby 1990) and between intimate partners (Foshee et al. 2004).

As violence prevention emerged as established practice in the 1990s, a small number of researchers began to apply this approach to the prevention of genocide, one of the most destructive forms of human violence. Starting with problem-definition, researchers reviewed all available surveillance data from real-time journalistic reports, United National Peacekeeping dispatches, and aid organization communiqués. Retrospective information was later added from post hoc reports commissioned by international organizations (e.g., in Rwanda, where press presence was scarce, and local infrastructure was quickly destroyed) (African Rights 1995; Human Rights Watch 1999; Caplan 2000).

As the second step, risk and protective factors for genocide in Rwanda were explored. This phase was accomplished by intensive multidisciplinary research targeting the national, mid-level, and micro-dynamics of genocide (Valentino 2004; Straus 2006; Adler et al. 2008; Fujii 2009; McDoom 2012; Brehm 2017).

Results suggest that at the level of the nation-state, civil armed conflict, manipulated by ruling elites seeking to reinforce their interests, is the most dangerous risk factor for genocide (Valentino 2004; Straus 2006). Failed civil wars, coups d'état, and political assassinations increase the likelihood of genocide nearly fivefold (Brehm 2017). In countries where elites of differing ethnicities or religious affiliations compete for power, the odds of genocide are higher (Brehm 2017).

At the regional level, social ties predict involvement in genocide. McDoom has demonstrated that living within 100 meters of a genocide perpetrator and membership in larger social networks containing perpetrators increase the likelihood of an individual's participation in genocide. People are twice as likely to engage in mayhem if a first-degree relative engages first (McDoom 2014).

At the grassroots, results suggest that typical perpetrators of genocidal violence are average people standing at the epicenter of coextensive household, community-based, and national stressors. The interdependence of these stressors acts to transform otherwise peaceful citizens into agents of mass atrocity.

Specifically at the community level, the interplay of fear and greed between local groups appears to be the most powerful driver of genocidal behavior (Straus 2006; Adler et al. 2008; Fujii 2009). Social psychologists have long observed that groups are more competitive and less cooperative than individual group members (Tajfel 1970). In extreme situations, groups who feel threatened by outside forces are more likely to perceive ethnic differences more intensely, develop antipathy for members of other groups, perceive all outside group members as a homogeneous block, and insist on compliance with intra-group dogma as a test of loyalty.

Through this cascade, it is possible to identify the specific cognitive and emotional pathways exploited by elites in manipulating average citizens to commit atrocity crimes (McDoom 2012).

Addressing the Root Causes of Genocide (ARC-G)

In 2002, the ARC-G research group of the University of British Columbia set out to understand the micro-dynamics of genocide within a public health framework. ARC-G began this inquiry with the following key question: *Can public health-based violence prevention methodology be applied successfully to the prevention of genocide?*

Situated within the second phase of the public health violence prevention method, ARC-G Phase 1 was designed to ascertain the micro-dynamics and pressures experienced by average members of society who participate in genocidal violence. ARC-G Phase one has been described in detail elsewhere (Adler et al. 2007, 2008). In brief, fifty-one civilians convicted of genocide crimes under Rwandan law were interviewed for two hours each. Men and women, youth and adults, and urban and rural dwellers were included in the sample. Data was analyzed in five stages, and risk factors derived after the development and testing of over 700 data codes (Adler et al. 2008).

Background: The Rwandan Genocide

In order to place ARC-G results in context, it is first helpful to have a short summary of the events leading up to and during the Rwandan Genocide.

Rwanda is a small country the size of Sicily, located in what is now the East African Community. Ruled by a Mwami (King) in the nineteenth century, Rwanda was governed by Germany, the League of Nations, and Belgium from 1894 to 1962, when independence was declared and governance passed to politicians from the Hutu majority. By 1980, sporadic pogroms had forced nearly a half million members of the minority Tutsi cultural group to flee to neighboring countries.

In 1990, the Rwandan Patriotic Front (RPF), an army comprising largely displaced Tutsis and a smaller number of affiliated Hutus, invaded Rwanda from the north. The goals of the RPF were to depose President Juvénal Habyarimana and democratize Rwandan governance. Habyarimana responded militarily, in addition to mounting a propaganda campaign branding all Tutsis living in Rwanda as RPF collaborators and traitors.

The Rwandan genocide started on April 6, 1994, with the downing, by surface to air missile, of the airplane carrying President Habyarimana and Burundian President Cyprien Ntaryamira. Though it is still not known who mounted the attack, the Hutu elite immediately blamed the RPF and began rounding up and executing Tutsi civilians across the country.

Between April and July of 1994, approximately 800,000 ethnic Tutsis and politically moderate Hutu civilians were murdered within Rwandan borders. The Rwandan Patriotic Front eventually took over and stabilized the country and has been in power in Rwanda since the end of the genocide in July 1994.

ARC-G Results

On the community level, Rwandans described congenial and close-knit neighborhoods free of ethnic tension prior to the RPF invasion. When the genocide started abruptly on April 6, 1994, the country was plunged into immediate crisis. Study respondents described escalating militarization of civilian communities throughout the country. Militarization was embraced by not only professional soldiers, but also a majority of Rwandan civil society (Human Rights Watch 1999; Dallaire and Beardsley 2005).

Respondents also reported a cluster of experiential pressures that drove their violent behavior during the genocide. The summary that follows outlines the key, interconnected pressures informing their choices to engage in genocidal action (Adler et al. 2008).

Defense of family, self, and nation

Most respondents believed that by participating in the genocide, they were acting as deputized soldiers protecting nation, home, and family during a time of enemy attack. All Tutsis were characterized as traitors and enemy collaborators who deserved death. Adoption of military rules of engagement led to the deterioration of traditional social norms and resulted in new standards condoning murder and mayhem. Reinforcing this, civilian killers were encouraged, lauded, and rewarded by leaders for violent behavior that would have been anathema prior to the war.

Fear

Respondents reported overwhelming fear as the pervasive emotion during the genocide. Respondents were more frightened of Hutu Power extremists, subjectively believing that the penalty for non-participation in the genocide would be death. Some respondents reported fear of the RPF, whom they believed would enslave and kill them.

Greed

Self-enrichment was a widely reported motive for participating in genocide and co-existed alongside all other pressures. Acquisition of material possessions, land, and jobs were cited as important incentives. Leaders manipulated men to kill while they were looting, as a method of being able to retain possession of stolen goods. Many respondents actively avoided joining attack groups but eventually relented after leaders hectored, threatened, or bribed them.

Feeling Overpowered, Confused, or Ambivalent ("Tsunami Effect")

As the Rwandan social landscape deteriorated into massacres and chaos, Rwandan men experienced a "new reality," heightened by the iterating reinforcement of terror, greed, chaos, and relentless pressure from authorities. Respondents describe feeling emotionally overpowered and unable to process events rationally. Some knew the genocide was wrong and catastrophic but felt powerless to change the course of events. Evocatively, three younger participants reported thinking they were living through the biblical Apocalypse. As one younger respondent put it, "you know, I was still young then, and I believed it was really the final day."

Factors Unique to Young Adults

Younger ARC-G respondents described thought processes consistent with their age and stage of neurocognitive development. For example, some younger respondents participated in the genocide as a way of gaining social acceptance and peer approval. Others reported impulsive decision-making and a paucity of fact-finding before taking action. Each of these descriptions aligns with what is known about the maturing brain in adolescents and young adults, and is consistent with adolescent behavior in a broad range of circumstances (Casey et al. 2008; Somerville 2013; Bushman et al. 2016)

ARC-G Conclusions

Surveillance at the macro-dynamic level demonstrates that civil war is critical to the prosecution of genocide by threatened, governing elites. On the ground, civil warfare is also the key scenario fostering the fear, opportunism, and social disruption necessary to the formation of genocidal intent amongst average citizens. Fear of both in-group authority and outgroup aggression, coupled with the opportunity for self or in-group advancement appears to drive deadly behavior when social norms are under attack. Unique risk factors for adolescent and young adult participants suggest future directions for genocide prevention research based on successful violence prevention programming for this age group in other settings.

The Future of Public Health-Based Genocide Prevention Research and Practice

A comprehensive approach to a problem as complex as genocide requires a broad range of coordinated interventions, sustained over a time period that may span decades. Public health tools such as the Haddon Matrix may be particularly helpful in organizing our thinking about multi-level genocide prevention activities at multiple points in time. Developed to inform injury prevention efforts, the Haddon model is scalable and may be applied at the local level as well as internationally (National Academy of Sciences 2003).

A typical Haddon Matrix addressing injury prevention due to car crash is seen in Table 24.2.

In recent years, the Haddon Matrix has also been employed to better understand the micro-dynamics of genocide at regional and community levels. Table 24.3 illustrates one example of an abridged matrix addressing integrated preventive strategies for genocide at the local level.

Table 24.2 Haddon Matrix for Prevention of Injury Due to Car Crash (Haddon 1972)

	HOST (PERSON AFFECTED)	*AGENT OR VEHICLE*	*PHYSICAL ENVIRONMENT*	*SOCIAL ENVIRONMENT*
PRE-EVENT (→ PRIMARY PREVENTION)	Driving skill; Time pressures (in a rush to get home?); Inebriated?	Car design & handling; Anti-lock brakes; Maintenance of car	Road design; Speed limits	Reliance on private, rather than public transportation raises traffic load; Compliance with seatbelt laws
EVENT (→ SECONDARY PREVENTION)	Wearing seatbelt?	Air bags working? Size of car & crash resistance	Weather conditions; Ice on road?	Quality of emergency assistance; Assistance from bystanders
POST-EVENT (→ TERTIARY PREVENTION)	Ability to call for help (phone available?); Knows first aid?	Tendency of car to catch on fire	Emergency vehicle access to collision site	Continued funding for emergency services

Table 24.3 Haddon Matrix for Prevention of Injury due to Genocide

	HOST (TARGETED INDIVIDUALS)	*AGENT (PERPETRATOR/WEAPON)*	*PHYSICAL ENVIRONMENT*	*SOCIO/POLITICAL ENVIRONMENT*
PRE-GENOCIDE (→ PRIMARY PREVENTION)	• Means available to flee dangerous jurisdictions? • Communication lines open to alert external authorities? • Defensive equipment available?	• Are livelihoods available to young adults in developing countries with a demographic youth bulge? • Are programs in place to mediate violence and interrupt local involvement before genocide begins? **ARC-G IS FOCUSED HERE**	• Are victims being separated from broader communities? Can this be stopped? • Are training camps for perpetrators seen and challenged?	• Are borders open? • Are travel documents available to potential victims? • Are weapons being purchased? Can this be stopped? • Do international partners challenge political elites?
GENOCIDE (→ SECONDARY PREVENTION)	• Means available to protect self and family? • Access to Media to alert international community? • Violence Interrupters on the ground?	• Are programs in place to mediate and interrupt violence at the local involvement? • Are community-based organizations activated to intervene in the violence?	• Are safe havens created and defended by the international community? • Is communications equipment available?	• Are bystanders activated to oppose coercive elites and governments? • Are bystanders activated to assist victims?
POST-GENOCIDE (→ TERTIARY PREVENTION)	• International response to aid victims? • Housing, food and medical support available?	• Restorative justice • Education • Community reintegration	• Rebuilding communities • Rehousing returnees	• International support for nation building • Monetary support for victim assistance

As noted earlier, public health initiatives seek to prevent a problem before it starts, an approach known as *primary prevention*. As such, ARC-G study and practice has focused on one critical piece of a much larger puzzle, as highlighted by the grey box in Table 24.3. Specifically, ARC-G seeks to prevent potential genocide perpetrators from succumbing to malevolent provocation, picking up a weapon, and attacking unarmed civilians.

Specific interventions in this domain might include, but not be limited to, direct intervention with key opinion leaders promoting violence; training bystanders and "interrupters" to intercede directly in incipient violence; widespread public advertisement campaigns promoting attitude change towards intergroup bloodshed; development of enhanced, shared social capital between opposing groups; livelihood promotion for vulnerable youth; and community-based mobilization to reinforce non-violent norms. While these activities in isolation are unlikely to prevent genocide at a national level, it is also unlikely that genocide may be prevented at any level without such a strategy in place.

Perpetrator Research and Implications for Genocide Prevention

Informed by successful public health violence prevention trials and earlier ARC-G findings, ARC-G Phase 2 was launched in 2007 with the goal of developing, implementing, and testing a violence reduction program in West Darfur, Sudan. In partnership with the non-governmental organization Fellowship for African Relief-Sudan, the ARC-G team ascertained local risk and protective factors by interviewing combatants from rival factions in and around the town of El Geneina, West Darfur.

During interviews, respondents identified mental health challenges amongst combatants and civilians as a high priority for all groups. Based on these findings, the study team, in partnership with local health officials, launched a program designed to improve mental health care in the region and in doing so, promote positive, shared social capital between combatant communities.

Programming focused on three key domains: 1) Mental Health training for local health care practitioners, 2) Creation of an inter-group Steering Committee to lead the program, and 3) Conflict Resolution training for Steering Committee members and local community leaders. These interventions were chosen for their potential to a) Increase positive intergroup contact around self-identified social goals, b) Promote the non-violent community norms inherent in mental health practice, and c) Advance conflict resolution opportunities and skills amongst and between opposing groups (Centre for the Study of Civil War, The International Peace Research Institute 2006; Skogan et al. 2009; Bock 2012; Al Ramiah and Hewstone 2013; Webster et al. 2013).

The Government of Sudan approved this initiative at the outset, and early results were promising. Regrettably, the project had to be abandoned prior to completion due to withdrawal of government support. Despite its early demise, the FAR-Sudan program is one example of a novel attempt to apply recent scholarship to on-the-ground genocide prevention trials. This and other programming may serve as departure points for future prevention efforts.

Conclusion

Research with genocide perpetrators is the road less traveled and can still evoke skeptical responses from the most knowledgeable audiences. This is curious, as in order to fathom the crime, one must understand the criminal.

Research with genocide perpetrators obliges us to suspend our disbelief and engage with individuals who were once ordinary citizens but who chose to commit unspeakable crimes. This undertaking is not easy, but it is essential if we are to better understand the dynamics of mass atrocities and someday prevent them.

The research described within this chapter represents the leading edge of what is currently known about genocide perpetrators and the pressure that impels them to act. As is the goal of all genocide research, it is hoped that this body of work will form the foundation for future efforts focused on preventing this form of deadly violence for future generations.

Note

1 For Rob.

References

Adler, Reva, Cyanne Loyle, & Judith Globerman. 2007. "A Calamity in the Neighborhood: Women's Participation in the Rwandan Genocide." *Genocide Studies and Prevention: An International Journal* 2(3): 209–233.

Adler, Reva, Cyanne Loyle, Judith Globerman, & Eric Larson. 2008. "Transforming Men into Killers: Attitudes Leading to Hands on Violence during the 1994 Rwandan Genocide." *Global Public Health* 3 (3): 291–307.

Adler, Reva, James Smith, Paul Fishman, & Eric Larson. 2004. "To Prevent, Reach and Rebuild: Health Research and the Prevention of Genocide." *Health Services Research* 39(6 Part 2): 2027–2051.

African Rights. 1995. *Rwanda: Not So Innocent - When Women Become Killers.* London: African Rights.

Al Ramiah, Ananthi, & Miles Hewstone. 2013. "Intergroup Contact as a Tool for Reducing, Resolving and Prevention Intergroup Conflict." *American Psychologist* 68, no. 7(October): 527–542.

Bock, Joseph. 2012. *The Technology of Nonviolence: Social Media and Violence Prevention.* Cambridge, MA: MIT Press.

Brehm, Hollie. 2017. "Re-examining Risk factors for Genocide." *Journal of Genocide Research* 19(1): 61–87.

Bushman, BJ, K Newman, & SL Calvert et al. 2016. "Youth Violence: What We Know and What We Need to Know." *American Psychologist* 71(1): 17–39.

Caplan, Gerald. 2000. *Rwanda: The Preventable Genocide: The International Panel of Eminent Personalities to Investigate the 1994 Genocide in Rwanda.* Addis Ababa: Organization of American States.

Carlson, Eve Bernstein & Rhonda Rosser-Hogan. 1991. "Trauma Experiences, Posttraumatic Stress, Dissociation and Depression in Cambodian Refugees." *American Journal of Psychiatry* 148(11): 1546–1551.

Casey, B J, Rebecca Jones, & Todd Hare. 2008. "The Adolescent Brain." *Annals of the New York Academy of Science* 1124(1): 111–126.

Centre for the Study of Civil War, The International Peace Research Institute. 2006. "A Clash of Generations? Youth Bulges and Political Violence." *International Studies Quarterly* 50(3): 607–629.

Coker, Ann, Heather Bush, Candace Brancato, Emily Clear, & Eileen Recktenwald. 2018. "Bystander Program to Reduce Violence Acceptance: RCT in High Schools." *Journal of Family Violence* 34(3): 153–164.

Dallaire, Romeo & Brent Beardsley. 2005. *Shake Hands with the Devil: The Failure of Humanity in Rwanda.* New York: Carrol and Graf.

Eitinger, Leo. 1980. "The Concentration Camp Syndrome and Its Late Sequelae." In *Survivors, Victims and Perpetrators: Essays on the Nazi Holocaust,* edited by Joel E. Dimsdale, 127–162. New York: Taylor and Francis.

Foshee, VA, KE Bauman, ST Enneit, DG Linder, T Benefield, & C Suchindran. 2004. "Assessing the Long-Term Effects of the Safe Dates Program and a Booster in Preventing and Reducing Adolescent Dating Violence Victimization and Perpetration." *American Journal of Public Health* 94(4): 619–624.

Fujii, Lee Ann. 2009. *Killing Neighbours.* Ithaca, NY: Cornell University Press.

Guerra, Nancy & Ronald Slaby. 1990. "Cognitive Mediators of Aggression in Adolescent Offenders 2: Intervention." *Developmental Psychology* 26(2): 269–277.

Guzek, John, Ruby Siddiqui, Kate White, Crystal Van Leeuwen, & Robert Onus. 2017. *Health Survey in Kutupalong and Balukhali Refugee Settlements, Cox's Bazar, Bangladesh (December 2017).* New York: Doctors without Borders.

Haddon, William A. 1972. "A Logical Framework for Categorizing Highway Safety Phemonema and Activity." *Journal of Trauma* 12(3): 193–207.

Hammond, W.R. 1993. "Psychology's Role in the Public Health Response to Assaultive Violence Among Young African-American Men." *The American Psychologist* 48(2): 142–154.

Hogg, Nicole. 2010. "Women's Participation in the Rwandan Genocide: Mothers or Monsters?" *International Review of the Red Cross* 92(877): 69–102.

Human Rights Watch. 1999. *Leave None to Tell the Story*. New York: Human Rights Watch.

Kuper, Leo. 1981. *Genocide: Its Political Use in the Twentieth Century*. New Haven, CT: Yale University Press.

Loyle, Cyanne. 2009. "Why Men Participate: A Review of Perpetrator Research in the Rwandan Genocide." *Journal of African Conflicts and Peace Studies* 1(9): 26–42.

McDoom, Omar. 2012. "The Psychology of Threat in Intergroup Conflict: Emotions, Rationality, and Opportunity in the Rwandan Genocide." *International Security* 37(2): 119–155.

McDoom, Omar. 2014. "Antisocial Capital: A Profile of Rwandan Genocide Perpetrators' Social Networks." *Journal of Conflict Resolution* 58(5): 865–893.

Mercy, James A. 1988. "New Directions in Violence Prediction: The Public Health Area." *Violence and Victims* 3(4): 285–301.

National Academy of Sciences. 2003. *Preparing for the Psychological Consequences of Terrorism: A Public Health Strategy*. Washington, DC: National Academy of Sciences: 1–17.

Rummel, Rudolph. 1998. *Statistics of Democide Volume One*. Munster: LIT Verlag.

Scott, K.D., J. Schafer, & T.K. Greenfield. 1999. "The Role of Alcohol in Physical Assault Perpetration And Victimization." *Journal of Studies on Alcohol* 60(4): 528–536.

Skogan, Wesley, Susan Hartnett, Natalie Bump, & Jill Dubois. 2009. *Evaluation of Cease Fire-Chicago*. Evanston, IL: Northwestern University: 1–238.

Somerville, Leah. 2013. "The Teen Brain: Sensitivity to Social Evaluation." *Current Directions of Psychological Science* 22(2): 121–127.

Straus, Scott. 2006. *The Order of Genocide: Race, Power and War in Rwanda*. Ithaca, NY: Cornell University Press.

Tajfel, Henri. 1970. "Experiments in Intergroup Discrimination." *Scientific American* 223: 96–102.

Valentino, Benjamin. 2004. *Final Solutions: Mass Killing and Genocide in the Twentieth Century*. Ithaca, NY: Cornell University Press.

Webster, Daniel, Jennifer Whitehill, Jon Vernick, & Frank Curreiro. 2013. "Baltimore's Safe Streets Program on Gun Violence: A Replication of Chicago's Cease Fire Program." *Journal of Urban Medicine: Bulletin of the New York Academy of Medicine* 90(1): 27–40.

World Health Organization. 2000. *Epidemiological Fact Sheet: 2000 Update*. Geneva: UN AIDS/WHO Working Group in Global HIV/AIDS and STI Surveillance.

World Health Organization. 2002. *World Report on Violence and Health*. Geneva: United Nations.

Yehuda, Rachel. 1998. "Vulnerability to Posttraumatic Stress Disorder in Adult Offspring of Holocaust Survivors." *American Journal of Psychiatry* 155(9): 1163–1171.

2.3 Perpetrators and Representation

25

Perpetrators and Perpetration in Literature

Stephanie Bird

In 1946 Jorge Luis Borges "created the ideal Nazi" (1998, 21). In the fictional monologue *Deutsches Requiem*, the Nazi Otto Dietrich zur Linde explains that he does not feel guilt and does not wish to be pardoned for his involvement in torture and murder; he does, though, wish to be understood. He adheres to his belief that Nazism "is intrinsically a *moral* act" and that Hitler was "fighting for *all* nations" to build an order in which violence and not servility rules (Borges 1949/2000, 65). Zur Linde's monologue is unapologetically that of a man who is dying for his beliefs, and it has consequently been charged with being an exculpatory narrative. In 1979, George Steiner, too, provoked considerable criticism for his portrayal of Hitler in *The Portage to San Cristóbal of A. H.* In it, Hitler is put on trial by his captors in the Amazon jungle, and in the final chapter of the novel he offers his self-defense, pointing to the complicity of other nations in the Holocaust and to the fact that his crimes were exceeded by the crimes of others. Similarly, Max Aue, the Nazi protagonist in Jonathan Littell's *The Kindly Ones*, argues that he is no worse than his reader: "I am a man like other men, I am a man like you" (Littell 2006/2010, 24). All three stories, written at very different times, caused controversy for giving the Nazi perpetrator a voice with which to present his motives rather than to display remorse or guilt.

Literary representations of perpetrators that give them a voice, present their point of view, or give access to their subjectivity and motivations frequently cause anxiety, even scandal. Disquiet is variously justified through references to the dangers of mythologizing evil, the "boundaries of appropriate enquiry," the seduction of identification with the perpetrator resulting in uncritical exculpation, and concerns about validating the perpetrator's perspective.[1] Unease is also fueled by ethical worry around the fascination exerted by perpetrators and the sense that enjoyment of their literary representation might be morally inappropriate. Yet Borges and Steiner offer an important counterweight to such concerns. Borges is unapologetic about imagining "the Platonic idea of a Nazi" and giving him a voice (1998, 21), insisting on the separation of his political beliefs from his fiction: "I think a writer's duty is to be a writer [...]. Everybody knows my opinions, but as for my dreams and my stories, they should be allowed their full freedom" (Di Giovanni et al. 1973, 59). Steiner too defended his freedom as a writer when responding to the criticism that he "put in Hitler's mouth [...] provocations and dialectical arguments either unanswered or, indeed, in some degree unanswerable" (1979/1999, 171). He argues that his fictional Hitler's questions are valid and unavoidable but that he has no answers. Indeed, Steiner "has grown to distrust those who confidently and eloquently do," for the many examples of mass murder present us with "unthinkable paradoxes" (174).

Exploring unthinkable paradoxes without the need to resolve them, as well as articulating the realms of dreams, are vital qualities of literature. Fiction can challenge certainty, expectations, and norms and does so by eluding the demands of serious discourse, not having to heed its demand for congruity. Fiction belongs to the realm of play and speculation, where it need not operate in the service of argument or coherence but can articulate multiple perspectives, imagine contradictions, and convey unresolved emotions and motivations. Furthermore, fiction challenges readers to consider their own pleasure in reading about suffering and violence and so may evoke complex, ambivalent, and contradictory responses that cannot easily be reconciled with unambiguous moral expectations or judgments.

There has been a surge in critical interest in perpetrator literature since the 1990s, often with an attendant focus on literature of the same period and a tendency to see it as more nuanced in its exploration of perpetrators than what preceded. Yet fiction has long explored the paradoxes and ambivalence of perpetration, as texts such as José Marmol's *Amalia* (1851/2001), Miguel Ángel Asturias's *Mr President* (1946/1997), and John Hawkes's *The Cannibal* (1949/1962) testify. The forms and genres that perpetrator literature takes are many: historical novels, fictional autobiography, family memoir, crime novels, comedy, counter-factual histories, and those that are unique. Stereotypes of sadistic individuals undoubtedly recur, often alongside more moral figures who have been sucked into complicity and who attempt to mitigate cruelty or to resist somehow. In the Holocaust context, this is most evident in the juxtaposition between the Nazi (SS/Gestapo) and the "good German" (army/police). Nevertheless, even when stereotypes or stereotypical moral configurations are evident, texts may be nuanced or thought provoking, not least because they pose questions about moral compromise and justice. Thus, in Robert Shaw's *The Man in the Glass Booth* (1967), the racy figure of the Nazi disguised as a Jew is used to reflect on the Eichmann trial and Hannah Arendt's response to it (Bird 2018). Edgar Hilsenrath uses the same figure in *The Nazi and the Barber* (1971/2017), taken to grotesque stereotypical extremes, precisely to debunk stereotypes (Bird 2016, 167–198). Crucially, some extremely interesting representations of perpetrators emerge from texts that are not immediately identifiable as perpetrator literature, as the following discussion of Imre Kertész's work demonstrates and Ágota Kristóf's *The Notebook* (1986) illustrates.

In what follows, I draw on texts from different national and historical contexts that exemplify how the various levels of play in narrative fiction complicate and enhance our understanding of perpetration and complicity. They ask crucial questions about perpetrators' moral responsibility and the complicated relationship between their violence on the one hand and their good intentions and positive self-image on the other. They also challenge us to reflect on the role of language and their own modes of representation in constructing and dismantling the figure of the perpetrator.

Accurate Portrayal

Imre Kertész is not commonly thought of as a writer interested in representing perpetrators. Kertész survived deportation to Auschwitz-Birkenau and Seitz as a fourteen-year old boy, and his writing is more immediately associated with the victim's experience. Yet in his fiction, Kertész offers some of the most complex and provocative explorations of perpetrators, their motivation, and their moral responsibility for their crimes. In *Detective Story*, Antonio Martens, secret police agent in a South American dictatorship, recounts his involvement in torture and murder while awaiting execution. Martens's defense lawyer emphasizes the importance of letting a perpetrator relate his own story, asserting that everyone has the right "to speak out and make sense of his fate [...] and to do it in his own way" (1997/2008a, 5). In *Fiasco*, two further perpetrators have a voice. Their accounts complicate the question of where moral culpability for mass murder lies, for both, in different but complementary ways, point to the question of wider complicity. The first perpetrator is the nameless executioner of the section "I, The Executioner" who is awaiting trial for the murder of 30,000 people. He does not speak of what he has done but theorizes that individual perpetrators like him are locked together in "miserable camaraderie" with his audience; they all belong to a world, "which allowed, tolerated, and thus wished for" (1988/2011, 308) his fate. The executioner refuses any simplistic reduction of guilt to an individual, monstrous figure. He points to the "vitality of the relationship" (305) between him and those who condemn him; the "tacit agreement" (307) whereby he is found guilty for deeds the world did nothing to prevent but where his guilt serves to redeem others (305). His audience then uses moral censure to silence him, thereby denying the relevance of his actions to their lives. He, however, insists on the significance of his account for understanding the human condition generally and for exposing the self-righteous innocence of the "not-guilty."

The second account is by Köves, a character who shares aspects of Kertész's biography: Köves too survived the experience of being deported as a boy to be murdered in the Holocaust. He wants to understand how an ordinary man makes choices "under the pressure of external compulsion" and how his first act on the path to perpetrating violence can be "governed by a purely helpful intention" (331). He tells of the gradual process that led him to strike a defenseless prisoner in the face, an act that "may [...] open up the route to the 30,000 corpses" (348): he is called up to the army, pressured to become a prison guard, tries to be decent, and is finally overcome with anger by a prisoner's aloof resistance to his attempts to persuade him to eat. Köves questions the nature of individual choice: he was in a situation not of his choosing, with a choice between two options (sign up or be punished) that casts doubt on whether it can be described as his decision at all. Even though Köves did not himself graduate from striking the prisoner to becoming a mass murderer, his actions have made him aware that any individual may take the steps into perpetration. Crucially, this has implications for representation: as Köves remarks, the color of life is usually grey, a fact that should be reflected in complex stories that can "imagine the simple, grey, absurd act, and the simple, grey, absurd path leading to that act" (332).

Köves's concerns mirror Kertész's. In *Dossier K.,* Kertész suggests that "you can't know" beforehand who will strike a defenseless prisoner in the face, the "first and decisive step, from which there is no turning back" (129). Nor is he an exception. Kertész's worry about the nature of individual choice and culpability is further articulated through the figure of the old boy in *Fiasco*, also a Holocaust survivor. He muses on the motives of Ilse Koch and describes the way that Buchenwald was created by one "state of affairs," which in turn created many others, including the specific context that created Koch herself. The ever-determining state of affairs makes her individuality increasingly insignificant and possible that her role as camp commandant's wife "could have been filled by essentially *anybody* else with similar feelings and actions" (51). Like the cumulative "state of affairs," each step contributes to a given and, at one level, impersonal fate. Yet at the same time as being impersonal, everyone takes the steps that enable that fate to occur. For this reason, everyone is implicated.

This notion of the step-by-step movement into violence has complex moral and aesthetic implications. Kertész is aware that his representation of perpetrators might provide an exculpatory narrative, indeed his alter-ego refers to the executioner's account as "an apology for mass murder" (2006/2013, 130). Similarly, and echoing precisely the anxiety of many critics and readers, the frustrated alter-ego points out that Kertész's understanding of the steps into violence determined within the "state of affairs" means that "*it would be impossible to call any mass murderer to account.*" But, like Borges and Steiner, Kertész is unambiguous in his response: "You are forgetting that as a writer I am not concerned with calling people to account but with accurate portrayal" (129). For him, accurate portrayal is not reducible to facts, but belongs too to the realm of the imagination, which "is also a kind of reality" (130), it is "a sovereign world that [...] follows the rules of art" (10).

Following the rules of art means that the representation of perpetrators eludes prescription, even if the exploration of perpetrators' frailty, motivations, desires, or positive characteristics weakens our willingness to call them to account. The tension between the desire to judge and the empathy evoked through the accurate portrayal of the grey color of life is at the heart of much perpetrator fiction, and it is to this tension I now turn.

A Purely Helpful Intention

Quite apart from the compelling argument that literature is not about imposing judgment, the fear that empathy with a perpetrator is morally compromising is frequently superfluous, since many novels explicitly relativize the point of view of the perpetrator by including graphic descriptions of the violent effects of their actions and policies. Hitler's arguments in *The Portage to San Cristóbal of A.H.* follow a "monologue of horror" (Steiner 1979/1999, 172), in which one of the Nazi hunters lists innumerable and horrific individual atrocities. While Kertész's executioner concerns himself with theories of moral complicity, the reader has not forgotten the earlier descriptions of Mauthausen. Littell's *The Kindly Ones* is written entirely from Max Aue's point of view, but we are not spared relentless and historically accurate details of genocidal violence in all its forms. In Mario Vargas Llosa's *The Feast of the Goat*, Rafael Trujillo's perspective is interlaced with horrific and explicit torture scenes. In Gabriel García Márquez's *The Autumn of the Patriarch*, the loneliness and isolation of the eternal dictator co-exist with his persistent brutality and oppression, including serving up a dissenting general to his comrades at a banquet. There is little opportunity for drifting into empathy with Steiner's old Hitler with palsy or Márquez's eternal dictator who loves and cares for his mother until her death, for their violence is ever present. Nor is it the case that the imaginative portrayal of a perpetrator's point of view necessarily solicits empathy. Aue, for example, repeatedly betrays his compulsive narcissism, ambition, and self-aggrandizement in his stylized narrative, and Trujillo's thoughts show him to be utterly ruthless in all aspects of his life.

An ambivalent path between depicting a perpetrator's involvement in violence and yet evoking empathy for him is trodden by novels in which the perpetrator acts out of an ideological commitment to the social good, or "a purely helpful intention," to cite Kertész. Augusto Roa Bastos's *I the Supreme* is a largely first-person narration by José Gaspar Rodríguez de Francia, the Supreme Dictator of Paraguay from 1814–1840, of his assumption of power, career, aims, and ideas. The novel was written by Bastos in Argentina during his exile from the Paraguayan dictator Alfredo Stroessner from 1947 until 1976; it therefore resonated with contemporary civil rights abuses and political violence. The Supreme Dictator's highly subjective account offers a counter-narrative to the predominantly negative contemporary and subsequent historical assessments presented in the footnotes, that portray him as a violent despot who ruthlessly suppressed opposition. He is scathing about his critics and actively repudiates these accounts, presenting himself in the tradition of the French Revolution as a leader who embodies the absolute will of the people. Francia points to his abhorrence of the enslavement of the masses by the upper classes, his introduction of laws that were the same for all, collectivization of property, and the ending of the domination of the indigenous population by Creoles (Bastos 1974/2000, 39). In addition to his advocacy of enlightened values, a characteristic that further encourages empathy for Francia is his growing capacity for self-examination as he approaches death. This takes the form of self-castigation through the ghost of his dead dog, Sultan, who criticizes Francia's rigid adherence to ideals and his failure to recognize or understand the joys and passions of the body. Francia's defense is that he "always obeyed the great principle of Justice," which demanded "implacable rigor in order to do away with rigor," whatever the human cost. But Sultan is not persuaded, condemning his rhetoric as no more than self-justification (387).

The tension between the absolute adherence to the social good and the ruthless violence that it is held to justify on the one hand and subjective emotion and the value of the individual on the other is at the core of Arthur Koestler's novel, *Darkness at Noon*. Rubashov, one of the old heroes of the revolution, falls victim to the Stalinist purges, is interrogated and finally executed. His commitment to revolutionary ideals involved him in the murder or deaths of individuals who were arbitrarily deemed to have transgressed party discipline. During his imprisonment, Rubashov struggles to reconcile the problematic equation, in which the amorality of the ineluctable progress of history, in the service of which the party operates, is set against the "mystical intoxication" of emotion, or "sentimentality" as he has always thought of it (Koestler 1940/1994, 125). He cannot resolve the equation because what had previously seemed to him to represent a clear moral decision, that it was either right or wrong to sacrifice individuals for the good of the party, is now put into question by the immediacy of human suffering and emotion. Rubashov's doubts and self-examination follow from his incarceration and the inversion of the power structure in which hitherto he has been, in effect, the desk executioner. His far-reaching reconsideration of his position and responsibility for injustice exposes both the seductive role of ideological commitment in the perpetration of violence and the manipulation and exploitation of ideological positions for maintaining positions of power.

Darkness at Noon and, to a lesser extent, *I the Supreme* display a redemptive impulse. The men's suffering invites empathy, and their gradual self-castigating introspection and awareness of their own culpability emphasizes their humanity and potential for moral salvation. However, the redemptive dimensions of the novels are textually privileged through the selective deployment of violence. The protagonists are shown either as victims of violence or distanced from the actual perpetration of violence or both. Francia's "Truth Chamber" is referred to (383), but depictions of violence remain sparse and, in keeping with Francia's perspective, they are reported from a distance. Rubashov enforces party policy that involves sending individuals for execution but does not participate in direct violence. In *Darkness at Noon*, the importance of an individual's proximity to violence is explicitly thematized when Rubashov, for whom death has always been an abstract "logical consequence" (111), is confronted with the sight of his old acquaintance Bogrov, being dragged to execution, whimpering from torture. This sight forces Rubashov finally to imagine the physical reality of Arlova's fate, the lover in whose execution he was implicated.

Rubashov's reflections on his distance from and then direct encounter with violence also function as a figure of reading; a crucial invitation to the reader to reflect upon the purpose of violence, or its absence, in representation. The degree to which violence is dissociated from the perpetrator figure or not directly molds our willingness to empathize with or exonerate those involved in perpetration or to take comfort from the redemptive spark offered by a perpetrator's self-doubt. If, as Kertész's executioner claims, the vilification of the perpetrator serves as a palliative for the consciences of the "not-guilty," the perpetrator's redemption might serve as part of a vital relationship in which the reader's desire for catharsis is too easily satisfied.

"Good People"

I the Supreme and *Darkness at Noon* portray perpetrators for whom murder is a necessary by-product of commitment to the social good, however understood. In two more recent novels, the notion that perpetration can be combined with good intentions is further radicalized by showing how "good people" become entangled in and contribute to systems of violent perpetration. Ironically, these texts do not offer a redemptive narrative. In Martín Kohan's *School for Patriots*, María Teresa is a class assistant in the National School of Buenos Aires, a school whose history is inseparable from Argentina's and which is closely identified with the military junta that took power in the coup of 1976. This identification is made explicit through the figure of Señor Biasutto, the team supervisor, who uses his position at the school to help oppose "ideological infiltration" (Kohan 2007/2012, 42) and who in 1976 drew up lists of students for the Night of the Pencils, when students were kidnapped, disappeared, and murdered by the junta. María's pride in her job, which involves ensuring the students' rigid adherence to school rules, motivates her to escalate her efforts and start spying in the boys' toilet, an activity that after initial qualms, she soon feels comfortable doing. She sees spying as no more than a greater devotion to duty, pre-emptively working to please Señor Biasutto. She is driven by the desire for approval but also from the disavowed pleasure she derives from her surveillance, refusing to conceive of her libidinous devotion to duty as an extension of the violent regime. Indeed, she admires the values of rules and respect that she identifies with it.

School for Patriots is narrated by a third person narrator whose perspective is largely limited to María's own. This coupling of external gaze with interior perception enables us to recognize the significance of María's actions to the wider political situation. It is also key to the novel's systematic exposure of the role of self-deception in facilitating an individual's complicity. María is willfully naïve, failing to see the link between her acute self-consciousness as a plain woman and her pleasure in her secret intimacy with the boys. Avoiding opportunities for reflection, María reassures herself that she is "fulfilling her role" (125). She chooses not to tell her mother about Señor Biasutto's involvement with the lists, because she "might not be able to appreciate that" (143). It is in fact the mother who articulates the anguish of living under the regime, in constant despair that her son has been conscripted and sent to fight in the Falklands. The extensive use of free indirect speech exposes María's self-deception while giving us access to a consciousness that retains a belief in its innocence. This belief persists to the end, even when Señor Biasutto starts to rape María repeatedly. Her horrified realization that the world goes on as normal despite the violence being done to her does not trigger self-reflection or any even rudimentary awareness that the violence is symptomatic of the regime's abuses. Nor does the end of the novel suggest that any such reflection will occur, for she is saved from her plight by the sudden change in regime at the school following the fall of Port Stanley. María's avoidance of reflection exemplifies Hannah Arendt's notion of thoughtlessness, which protects against reality and "against the claim on our thinking attention that all events and facts make by virtue of their existence" (1978, 4). María's refusal to engage in thinking attention allows her to maintain a positive self-image, which persists, is even reinforced, as she herself becomes a victim of the power structures that she has supported.

The importance of self-deception and rationalization as a strategy for upholding a positive self-image is also evident in Nir Baram's *Good People*. Sasha Weissberg, one of the main protagonists, betrays the poet Nadyezhda Petrovna, who is also her father's lover, to the NKVD, the Soviet secret police. She thereby implicates the whole group of intellectuals to which her parents belong. The deal that Sacha believes she is making, that "they could have Nadyezhda, and she wouldn't lose her parents" (Baram 2010/2016, 63) proves naïve, for all in the group are arrested, her parents are sent to a labor camp, and her younger twin brothers are sent to the army. To save herself, she joins the NKVD and gets a job writing up interrogation protocols into coherent and precise confessions in which the prisoners articulate their remorse appropriately. When she is challenged about the betrayal of her family, she defends herself in various ways: she blames the literary circle for being provocative; sees herself as helping them "write decent confessions and express sincere remorse to minimize their suffering and their sentences" (143); points to the agony of her own even greater loss; and argues that she had no choice but to join the NKVD if she wanted to survive and help her twin brothers (343). All these points are true or partially true, but as her husband points out, they are nevertheless part of the "veil of [...] denial" shielding her from understanding "with blood-curdling clarity, the meaning of [her] actions" (359). What Sacha also omits from her justification is the pleasure she derives from the success of her interrogations and her power, laughing at how "easy it was to toy with a person's weaknesses" (146). Even more telling emotionally is her loathing of the poet Nadyezhda, whose affair with her father demeans both her parents in her eyes. Sacha is disappointed to hear that Nadyezhda has survived imprisonment and wishes "that whore dead!" (362), a vitriolic insult that suggests revenge for humiliation formed part of her original motivation in denouncing the poet.

Sacha's despair is formed of the entanglement of perpetration and victimhood, and she struggles to maintain a positive image of herself. Her repeated refrain that she acted "for the twins' sake" is compromised when her entanglement is mirrored back to her by the twins themselves. Her meeting with Kolya, now a malnourished soldier, is devoid of warmth as he communicates his ambivalence towards her following her act of betrayal. The death of her other brother, Vlada, also puts a different perspective on her repeated claim that she had no choice: far from being killed in action in Finland, he was executed for objecting to the Red Army's cruel treatment of civilians. The question of how far Sacha is a good person, as Baram's title asserts, or whether the title casts an ironic shadow, is left open. Indeed, both are possible. The novel presents Sacha's complex mixture of motives and depicts how conflicting emotions and intentions co-exist under pressure of a "state of affairs" in which everyone is mutually suspicious and resistance is dangerous. Any irony cast by the title thus serves to complicate the meaning of "good" and not determine it. Neither of these novels about "good people" offers a redemptive resolution. Instead they present an unsettling recognition of the fluidity and reach of the term "perpetrator."

Full Freedom

The strength of fictional representations of perpetrators and perpetration is their freedom to challenge coherence and dissociate accurate portrayal from any lingering notions of consistency or logic, be that of motive, action or moral positioning. Fiction insists that ambiguity may itself be an accurate state of affairs, even if this fundamentally challenges our moral expectations or desire for redemptive narratives. Such ambiguity is inseparable from fiction's emphasis on the dialogic and often incoherent interplay of voices, perspectives, emotions, and memories. At the level of character, the shock of ambiguity is something that Rubashov learns in *Darkness at Noon*. He explicitly links his growing moral insecurity to the "phenomenon called the 'first person singular'" (Koestler 1940/1994, 90). In his long periods of reflection in prison, he is surprised to discover that his internal monologues are in fact dialogues with a silent partner who refuses his normal processes of deliberation, such as putting himself in the minds of others, logical thought, or eliciting intentions. On the contrary, Rubashov realizes that after many years' silence this silent partner is tangibly asserting itself, but that it "remains out of the reach of logical thought" (92), ambushing him with daydreams and disconnected fragments of memory. Rubashov is not describing the "first person singular" of the rational mind, but the physical reality of emotions and associations that evade "the objective rightness or wrongness of the measure itself" (126). His very distinct experience of the "first person singular" is at odds with the objective rationalism of the Party. It disrupts his understanding of the differences among interior monologue, dialogue, external perspective, and of the limits of reason in understanding subjectivity, forcing him to reappraise his moral value system.

Rubashov's difficulty with reconciling objective grammar with subjective experiences is, in various forms, explored and played with in many novels on perpetrators. In *I the Supreme*, Francia explicitly articulates the conflict between the supreme dictator who pursues and personifies the social good and the supreme dictator who is merely mortal, in his use of **I** and **HE**. He refutes the notion that there are single individuals: "Difficult to be the same man constantly. [...] **I** am not always **I**. The only one who doesn't change is **HE**" (Bastos 1974/2000, 45). In Francia's case this distinction is straightforward, with **HE** offering an externalized, abstract gaze upon the **I**, as well as the rationalization for absolute identification with the nation. The novel overall, however, vividly articulates Francia's assertion that the I is not always I through its many narrative levels: statements dictated by Francia to his scribe, including interjections, comments, and conversations which take place during the dictation; the "Perpetual Circular," Francia's version of Paraguayan history; his entries in his private notebook, which frequently read like stream of consciousness; and opinions vented from beyond the grave. Temporal continuity and coherence of the I is constantly undermined, and with it the notion of a consistent identity. By thematizing interaction of the socially embedded third person with the subjective first person, as well as destabilizing the coherence of the self, these novels further unsettle the idea of a stable perpetrator identity and suggest instead a more fluid interaction between social and individual processes that underlie involvement in perpetration. This is particularly evident in *The Autumn of the Patriarch*, where the narrative voice flows from third to first person, singular and plural, frequently leaving only to context the knowledge of who is speaking: "he would bring the flame of a match close to the thermometers so you can see the oppressive mercury of what I think inside go up and down" (Márquez 1975/2014, 65). The flow is intensified by sentences that run on over pages, blurring clear boundaries between individuals; the first person does not belong to the dictator alone, nor is the "we" of his subjects defined. Márquez thus lyrically expresses the "vitality of the relationship" (to quote Kertész's executioner) between dictator and subjects, perpetrator and accusers, as complex and fluid.

Crucially, the novels' formal qualities are also a means by which literature reflects upon modes of representation, including its own contribution to discourses around perpetration. This is evident in *I the Supreme*, which consists of notes and interjections by the anonymous compiler and footnotes that often include contemporary reports, letters, and histories of the period. The novel plays with narrative forms as part of a strategy to question the veracity of written accounts, the structures of power that determine which accounts are ascribed authority, and the way in which the oral tradition has been suppressed. In *Fiasco*, fictional accounts inhabit each other, so that "I, The Executioner" is written by Berg, a character created by the book's framework protagonist, the old boy, who is himself the author of a Holocaust novel that was initially rejected for publication with the very words that Kertész's own novel *Fateless* was rejected. Köves, the protagonist of the old boy's novel, is himself a younger version of the old boy whose story culminates in the decision to write a novel that will become *Fateless*. In *The Kindly Ones*, Aue is at once a realistic protagonist and first-person narrator, with motives and desires that adhere to fictional realist conventions, and also an anti-realist narrative device. He becomes a means to observe and analyze events even as he participates in them, offering unrealistically accurate insight into a historical period and integrating contemporary historiography into his account. Furthermore, by structuring the novel around Aeschylus's *Oresteia* and the Oedipus myth, the novel exposes the inadequacy of tragedy as a mode of representation for responding to genocide: there is no place for the extraordinary individual and for the redemption of catharsis in the process of mass murder (Bird 2016, 167–198). Thus, all three novels invite us to question the relationship of historical and fictional narratives, how the negative figure of the dictator or perpetrator is mediated and whose interests, and cultural expectations, such mediation serves or challenges.

In Kertész's *The Pathseeker*, perpetrators sit in the theater after a hard day's killing, "sniggering up their sleeves" (1977/2008b, 87) as their brutality is aesthetically transformed into a morally uplifting happy ending. Kertész's criticism of art's aesthetic cover-up is precisely what triggers moral anxiety in relation to perpetrator literature. The question of whether there are (ontological) or should be (ethical) limits to representation in relation to extreme atrocities has been extensively discussed. Yet Kertész is here concerned not with setting limits to representation but with art's potential to distract from the reality of violence. This might be through satisfying the reader's desire for redemption, or through the reader's pleasure in aesthetic transformation, perhaps itself a refined form of sniggering. Such pleasure may be found in an engrossing story, crafted for enhanced suspense. Thus, a thriller-like quality is achieved in *The Feast of the Goat* by intertwining the plot to assassinate the dictator Rafael Trujillo with the gradual revelation that the protagonist, Urania Cabral, was, at age fourteen, given to Trujillo for sex by her father to regain his favor. Pleasure might be felt in response to representations of violence and it is certainly found in the comedy of some texts. In *I the Supreme*, Francia's hyperbolic attacks are very funny even as they are designed to humiliate—calling his scribe "Sancho Pauncho" (Bastos 1974/2000, 57)—and the arbitrariness of his power is rendered grotesquely comic in the image of the falsely imprisoned man who roasts mosquitoes to survive and finally becomes so thin that he escapes through a crack in the wall (269). Crucially, pleasure is undoubtedly offered in language itself, as in the lyrical, effortlessly sensuous and often beautiful depiction of the dictator in Márquez's *The Autumn of the Patriarch*. Perhaps this association of beauty and perpetration, and more broadly of pleasure and perpetration, offends our preferred coupling of beauty and pleasure with the moral good. J. M. Coetzee gestures to such offense when he asks: "If the novelist finds in squalor the occasion for his most soaring poetic eloquence, might he not be guilty of seeking out his squalid subject matter for perversely literary reasons?" (1986) Yet taking pleasure in a fictional representation of perpetration is not equivalent to taking pleasure in the perpetration of violence; different ontological levels are at stake. Nevertheless, these novels challenge us to be cognizant of the pleasure we take in reading about extreme subjects and with it to reflect on the complex, ambivalent emotions that co-exist with moral censure in our response to perpetrators and those complicit with state condoned violence. The novels discussed here do not expunge the violence of perpetration or its effects, but they enrich and complicate our response to it.

Note

1 Anxiety relating to the representation of perpetrators of genocide and collective violence arises in particular from extensive debate around the ethics and possibility of representation, largely in relation to the Holocaust. For an overview of this debate and its influence, see Bird (2016). For discussions relating to perpetrator representation, see Adams and Vice (2015), Crownshaw (2011), Jinks (2016, "Introduction"), McGlothlin (2016).

References

Adams, Jenni & Sue Vice (eds.). 2015. *Representing Perpetrators in Holocaust Literature and Film*. Edgware: Vallentine Mitchell.

Ángel Asturias, Miguel. 1946/1997. *Mr President*. Translated by Frances Partridge. Prospect Heights: Waveland.

Arendt, Hannah. 1978. *The Life of the Mind*. Orlando: Harcourt.

Baram, Nir. 2010/2016. *Good People*. Translated by Jeffrey Green. Melbourne: Text Publishing.

Bastos, Augusto Roa. 1974/2000. *I The Supreme*. Translated by Helen Lane. New York: Dalkey Archive.

Bird, Stephanie. 2016. *Comedy and Trauma in Austria and Germany after 1945: The InnerSide of Mourning*. Cambridge: Legenda.

Bird, Stephanie. 2018. "Nazis Disguised as Jews and Israel's Pursuit of Justice: The Eichmann Trial and the *kapo* Trials in Robert Shaw's *The Man in the Glass Booth* and Emanuel Litvinoff's *Falls the Shadow*." *Holocaust Studies* 24(4): 466–487.

Borges, Jorge Luis. 1949/2000. "*Deutsches Requiem*." In *The Aleph*. Translated by Andrew Hurley. London: Penguin.

Borges, Jorge Luis. 1998. *Jorge Luis Borges: Conversations*. Edited by Richard Burgin. Jackson: University Press of Mississippi.

Coetzee, J. M. 1986. "Into the Dark Chamber: The Novelist and South Africa." In *The NewYork Times*, 12 January. www.nytimes.com/books/97/11/02/home/coetzee-chamber.html. Accessed 13 February 2018.

Crownshaw, Richard. 2011. "Perpetrator Fictions and Transcultural Memory." *Parallax* 17(4): 75–89.

Di Giovanni, Thomas, Daniel Halpern and Frank MacShane (eds.). 1973. *Borges on Writing*. New York: E. P. Dutton & Co.

Hawkes, John. 1949/1962. *The Cannibal*. New York: New Directions.

Hilsenrath, Edgar. 1971/2017. *The Nazi and the Barber*. Berlin: Owl of Minerva Press.

Jinks, Rebecca. 2016. *Representing Genocide: The Holocaust as Paradigm?* London: Bloomsbury.

Kertész, Imre. 1977/2008b. *The Pathseeker*. Translated by Tim Wilkinson. New York: Melville.

Kertész, Imre. 1988/2011. *Fiasco*. Translated by Tim Wilkinson. New York: Melville.

Kertész, Imre. 1997/2008a. *Detective Story*. Translated by Tim Wilkinson. London: Vintage.

Kertész, Imre. 2006/2013. *Dossier K*. Translated by Tim Wilkinson. New York: Melville.

Koestler, Arthur. 1940/1994. *Darkness at Noon*. Translated by Daphne Hardy. London: Vintage.

Kohan, Martín. 2007/2012. *School for Patriots*. Translated by Nick Caistor. London: Serpent's Tail.

Kristóf, Ágota. 1986. *The Notebook*. Translated by Alan Sheridan. London: CB editions.

Littell, Jonathan. 2006/2010. *The Kindly Ones*. Translated by Charlotte Mandell. London: Vintage.

Mármol, José. 1851/2001. *Amalia*. Translated by Helen Lane. Oxford: Oxford University Press.

Márquez, Gabriel García. 1975/2014. *The Autumn of the Patriarch*. Translated by Gregory Rabassa. London: Penguin.

McGlothlin, Erin. 2016. "Empathetic Identification and the Mind of the Holocaust Perpetrator in Fiction: A Proposed Taxonomy of Response." *Narrative* 24(3): 251–276.

Shaw, Robert. 1967. *The Man in the Glass Booth*. London: Chatto & Windus.

Steiner, George. 1979/1999. *The Portage to San Cristóbal of A.H.* Chicago: University of Chicago Press.

Vargas Llosa, Mario. 2001/2012. *The Feast of the Goat*. Translated by Edith Grossman. London: Faber and Faber.

26

Whose Evil Is This? Perpetrators in the Theater

Robert Skloot

As with all serious artistic endeavor, a "theater of perpetrators" engages issues of universal concern, foremost among them the "problems" of justice and truth, guilt and responsibility. Defining these subjects, and then dramatizing their implications in urgent situations, is the distinguishing feature of the work of playwrights of perpetration. Although most theater dealing with historical atrocity has tended to focus on the plight and terror of the victim, an important (and more recent) contribution to our knowledge of historical events and their human "actors" is to be found by investigating the representation of those who commit, condone, and are complicit in the perpetration of evil.

It is no secret why this should be so. All of us, as ethical beings, are driven to understand and assess our behavior towards others and then to relate our finding to the conception of ourselves. Are we good or bad? honest or self-deceiving? generous or selfish? humane or destructive? Are we capable of escaping from a cycle of terror and guilt? Will dealing with a violent past prevent a violent future? Because few if any of us can be added to the company of saints, answers to these questions can be difficult, unsettling, and painful. Nevertheless, concerned playwrights will compel these inquiries, often by presenting ethical conflicts within a historical context full of violence and irreparable harm.

From the theatrical evidence at hand, it would seem that the catastrophic events of the twentieth century, particularly the occurrences of global genocide, have provoked much serious drama of the last several generations. To be sure, earlier playwrights didn't avoid engagement with the subject, as anyone familiar with the tragedies of classical Greece or Shakespeare can attest. But the "century of genocide," beginning with the annihilation of the Herero (1904–07) and the Armenians (1916–23) and extending through and beyond the murderous episodes in Rwanda, Cambodia, and Bosnia, appears to have provided the essential material for ethical explorations. When attention turned to "the concentration camp," wrote Tzvetan Todorov, "evil is the main character" (Todorov 1996, 121).

To earlier concerns with victims and their suffering were now added the inhumane actions of perpetrators. Plays of perpetration sought to explore guilt and responsibility and to disclose the murderous effects of inhumanity on the self and society; playwrights seized and held a prominent (though not always comfortable) place where the ultimate and existential question, "whose evil is this?" could be asked and answered. Where previous portrayals had been simplistic, even propagandistic in their response to grievance, absence, and pain, this change made an important alteration in theater practice: the diminution of the genre of melodrama, the popular dramatic form that highlights the uncomplicated conflict of good vs. evil.[1]

This chapter seeks to examine selected theatrical representations of perpetrators in western drama over several generations from the 1960s until the end of the 1990s. Prior to the examination of a number of plays of perpetration, this chapter will explain a) how a number of components contribute to producing meaning in plays, b) how audience expectation often affects the responses to artistic production, and c) how the post-Holocaust concern with understanding perpetrators frustrates the search for "simple" justice that audiences often expect, even demand. Erik Ehn substitutes for that expectation the goals of investigation and reparation in the introductory comments to his play about the Rwandan genocide: "*Maria Kizito* doesn't seek to explain the source of the genocide or to fix blame. It attempts to enter into the inner life of a perpetrator" (Skloot 2008, 178).

A Note about How the Theater Works

Understanding plays that contain perpetrators involves dealing with a number of complicated factors including the public nature of the theater itself. These factors affect how any play in performance is received. The reception of the theatrical event relies on more than simple speech and movement for meaning and impact. To those two components must be added the constructed setting; the use of light, sound and media, costume and makeup; as well as the dynamic interaction among the actors/characters, all of which are decided and coordinated by the work of the director and her team and continually influenced by the effect of the audience members on the work as a whole in performance. Taken together, all these elements define a unique interpretation of the playwright's text (its meaning), which will be at variance with other interpretations of the same text at some other time and place. Other variables include the skill of the translator's work if the script is heard in a language different from the original and the historical moment at which the text is performed.[2]

The plays that will be discussed later in this chapter all exist in a relationship to the particular time and place of their performance, and all productions of the plays, after their premieres, will be different, sometimes radically so, from earlier ones. Critics who understand the paradoxical nature of theatrical performance (that the text is "always the same and never the same") recognize that as the components of the performance change, the meanings of the event also change. They accept that theater is a dynamic art form that requires an expansive knowledge of stagecraft, an openness to re-visioning what is known and believed, and a resistance to doctrinaire ideologies of art and history.[3]

Audiences, however, in the time span covered by this essay, often rejected the form in which stories of atrocity were dramatized if they varied from a style of realism and an adherence to specific portrayals about how perpetrators and victims were displayed. Dealing with atrocity and genocide demanded that ethical binaries, emotional seriousness (e.g., no comedy), and historical accuracy (e.g., no variance from "facts") would be respected. But this "traditional" approach constrained creativity and prevented new interpretive possibilities that would become increasingly evident in the post-1960s engagement with genocidal issues.

> The best Holocaust theatre [...] recreates the past into an unpredictable present, which means there is freedom in the performance event that may liberate us in ways that we cannot, at the moment of our encounter, anticipate or define. [...] Further disruption

> occurs when we acknowledge that history is changing too, not only in how it is interpreted but because new facts are being discovered all the time that require assessments to be modified.
>
> *(Skloot 2013, 28–29)*

Nonetheless, playwrights in the 1960s became vulnerable to the criticism of "traditional" audiences and critics who objected to "modified" images of victims and of perpetrators, especially when aspects of both identities merged. They rejected any overlap between victims (mostly helpless, sorrowful, innocent, and virtuous) and perpetrators (all-powerful, malevolent, and merciless). They preferred "old interpretations" of texts and history that preserve the stark, rigid assessments of both, a preference that dismissed the theater's performative nature, the complexity of human personality, and the discovery of "new" historical evidence. In short, they knew *before* the theatrical encounter *whose evil it is*, and knowing that meant that systems of law and ethics should determine performances whose task was to deter and punish genocide. The theater, it was argued, should join them on the "right" side of history.[4]

Just How Did We Get Here?

To understand theatrical images of perpetrators, it is necessary to answer a basic question: who are perpetrators? The answer may be found in the work of one of the great Holocaust historians, Raul Hilberg. More than fifty years ago, Hilberg established what he later called his "triptych," a system that defined the typology of persons caught up in the Holocaust. These "actors" belonged to one of three categories: perpetrator, victim, and bystander; this system of categorization has been universally adopted by critics, historians, and others since it was initially advanced in the 1960s (Hilberg 1961, 639–669).[5] Hilberg's importance to our investigation is twofold. First, he recognized early that perpetrators were as deserving of attention and discussion as were the victims. In his summation of his work as a historian, he writes harshly of Holocaust historians whose work focused only on the (Jewish) victims and for what he called in his final book "the fadeout of the perpetrator" (Hilberg 1996, 131).

Hilberg's second influence was to judge negatively the behavior of Jewish elites (community leaders, police, administrators appointed by the Nazis) for being partly responsible for the destruction of the Jewish victims. It was this charge, one that was accepted and later disseminated by Hannah Arendt in her *Eichmann in Jerusalem: A Report on the Banality of Evil* (1964), that caused an explosion of anger among critics who excoriated Hilberg and Arendt for their accusation that victims collaborated in their own destruction. Adam Brown's recent superb discussion *Judging "Privileged" Jews* notes: "Hilberg's brief evaluation of Jewish behavior has stirred up more controversy than any other aspect of his research" (Brown 2013, 79).

In fact, this assertion prefigured, and later certified, the instability of the "triptych" that Hilberg himself designed. Together with Arendt, but from different directions, they advanced a conclusion concerning the difficulty of judging ethically the historical actions of the "actors." Thus, from Hilberg's viewpoint, the victims of the Holocaust (the Jews) shared some features of the perpetrators (the Nazis), and from Arendt's perspective, the purposeful and murderous evil of the perpetrators (represented by Eichmann) was lessened by their drift or indifference in responding to a malignant, bureaucratic environment. In both cases, rigid categories were destabilized, and, in theatrical terms, the sharpness and clarity of historical conflict resulted in a more hybrid and perhaps less fixed expression of the Jewish genocide's "cast of characters" in one of Hilberg's often-used theatrical references (Hilberg 1996, 191).[6]

Dealing with Nazis

Importantly, the 1960s can be seen as the decade when playwrights began to complicate the treatment of Nazi characters, moving away from expressions of a purely "negative" picture of perpetration vis-a-vis a "positive" picture of victimization. The case for the latter may have been made best by the German Erwin Sylvanus whose *Dr. Korczak and the Children* (1957), a one-act play in the manner of Pirandello, presented the historical figure of Janusz Korczak, as an almost saintly figure of courage and resistance. Korczak, director of a Jewish orphanage in the Warsaw ghetto, refused to abandon his children even though he had the opportunity to escape and led them, with order and dignity, to the deportation train that would transport them to their deaths. As such, he can represent the persecuted, "heroic" Jewish victim destroyed by Nazi perpetrators. In form, *Korczak* is multilayered and metatheatrical, a skillful experiment in both history and allegory, but it resists any diminution of the culpability of Nazi perpetrators in mass atrocity and murder. Since its premiere, the play has become an international success and remains popular to produce. "Sylvanus drives home his point about his contemporary [German] audience's refusal to explore its recent history and presents a clear rebuke to the Nazi mentality and system" (Skloot 1988, 98).

It fell to another historical figure, Kurt Gerstein, a central character in Rolf Hochhuth's *The Deputy* (1963), to take up the challenge of the "accepted" picture of the Nazi perpetrator. Hochhuth's play became an international sensation, excoriated by critics who attacked his leftist politics and negative treatment of Catholicism. In Hochhuth's telling, the stain of perpetration adhered to Pope Pius XII who becomes an affiliate perpetrator, complicit in the Jews' murder. His "opposite" is Gerstein who belongs to the criminal Nazi hierarchy and to the resistance to it, the "good Nazi" who seeks to alleviate the genocide by working "within the system." Saul Friedlander writes about Gerstein's exceptional heroism: "Yet how many of them [the German people] demonstrated their will to resist by committing acts which, had they been discovered, would have cost the perpetrators their lives? Kurt Gerstein was one of these people" (Friedlander 1969, 227). Taken together, the two characters display the porous nature of Hilberg's typology, which was created about the same year as the play's premiere.[7]

Throughout the 1960s, the increased "blending" of perpetrator and victim was, for many critics and observers, an unacceptable ethical development. Another emblematic case appears in Robert Shaw's *The Man in the Glass Booth* (1967), where "the provocative imagery and thematic ambiguity would not be taken lightly by theatre audiences" (Skloot 1988, 83). Shaw's play is a clever "whodunnit?" in the literal sense, since revealing the true identity of the play's protagonist becomes the central action of the play, action conveyed effectively with theater tricks and misleading plot devices. In *Glass Booth*, the "who" begins as the Jew Arthur Goldman until he is (gradually) revealed to be an Adolf Eichmann doppelgänger named Adolf Karl Dorff. The play concludes with a long and passionate hymn of praise to Hitler after which a surprise witness declares that Goldman and Dorff were cousins who were both imprisoned in a concentration camp. The final image, powerful and confusing, shows "Goldman, naked inside the glass booth, the consummate human specimen (Jew and Nazi, victim and victimizer), locked in an impenetrable silence" (Skloot 1988, 86). Thus, by the end of the decade, the inquiry "whose evil is this?" was established clearly and effectively concerning the theatrical life of perpetrators.[8]

George Tabori's *The Cannibals* (1968), a highly theatrical reenactment of the torment of Jews (and others) in the concentration camps, seeks through farce, role-playing, and aggressive, non-realistic theater techniques to reassess perpetration through a focus on the condemned men's desperate attempt to survive. The incident that provokes the terror of the play is the decision to cook and eat their dead comrade Puffi ("the second fattest man in Europe"); their survival depends on a punishing ethical dilemma: to eat or not to eat. The playwright, with characteristic mordant humor, dedicates the text to the memory of his father Cornelius Tabori (named Uncle in the play) who "perished in Auschwitz, a small eater" (Skloot 1982, 197).

There is no disputing Tabori's antipathy for the Nazi criminals whose genocidal mission came close to complete success. The Nazi "Angel of Death" who appears at the play's conclusion to order the prisoners to eat Puffi and live (at least temporarily) or to refuse and be gassed is beyond both mercy and redemption. But Tabori saves his concern for the two inmates who do partake of the human meal, Heltai and Hirschler, and whose survival makes possible (and performable) the story of the prisoners' desperate choice to stay alive. Had they not become cannibals, the lessons conveyed would be lost to both the world and the theater. Tabori is not giving the evil Nazi perpetrators a pass. But his troubled conscience and extraordinary humanity strive to maintain an uneasy ethical balance in the face of nearly indescribable ruin. Thus, he reveals another, subtler struggle to discern whose evil it is. "In Tabori's Holocaust kitchen, *The Cannibals* is his *piece de resistance*, at once tasteless and astonishingly succulent" (Skloot 2009, 253).

The Portage to San Cristobal of A.H. originated as a novella by the noted literary and cultural critic George Steiner in 1982. In Christopher Hampton's dramatization, it conceives the last days of Hitler (A.H.) as a fugitive in the Amazon jungle, an escapee from the collapse of the Third Reich. On the run from a search party of Israelis, his capture is followed by a trial in the jungle, a substitute for the one he eluded in his downfall. In the confrontation with his pursuers, who are themselves diminishing in numbers and health, he displays a physical vitality and rhetorical brilliance that contrasts with a final stage image of legal and theatrical paralysis: A.H. sits on a throne with his slave attendant next to him and his exhausted antagonists subordinate to him.

In the play's conclusion, Hitler is set free to unleash upon the confounded public, both his trackers and his audience, one last spasm of hatred and falsehood. The play ends with a twenty-five minute monologue, an "aria" of astonishing vituperation, as A.H., one of history's brilliant orators—though until this moment in the play he has spoken only five words—overturns both history and logic to blame the Jews' evil as the model for his own and the destroyer of the Aryan dream. A.H.'s final speech, mesmerizing in the performance of a great actor (Alec McCowan in the 1967 London premiere), receives no rebuttal in the play, and without it many critics were outraged that A.H., revived and triumphant, had "the last word." It is important to again point to the power of performance to shape the meaning of a play.

Portage is important as an example of how audiences advocate their preferences and understandings with fierce partisanship. Steiner deliberately provokes his audience in order to impugn the complacency and self-righteousness of post-Holocaust Jewry. Thus, while maintaining the perpetrator's status as agent of atrocity and mass death, Steiner, abetted by the dramatic skill of Hampton, rewrites the historical A.H. to alter the understanding we have of ourselves and of the legacy of his evil.

What Did and Didn't Come After

In the decades after the Holocaust, mass atrocity continues unabated, as do the numbers of plays devoted to exploring the origins and results of historical genocides. Each murderous conflict has (or will have) playwrights who bring to audiences the stories of the dead and those who murdered them, the victims together with and tied to the perpetrators. Like the Holocaust plays that preceded them and provided models for them, the stories are often complicated, proposing profound ethical and artistic problems, foremost among them the subject of evil. Whereas they differ from earlier plays and from each other by reflecting the culture (Cambodian dance and poetry, Native American ritual), language (Khmer, Kinyarwanda, and Arabic), and specific geography (Bosnia, Darfur) of the places they engage with, they are alike in their preoccupation with the intentional disruption of the simple binary of victim vs. perpetrator.[9]

As we might expect, the expansion of the catalog of plays of perpetration is largely due to interest in post-Holocaust genocides that seek understanding of the same issues already mentioned: the possibility of justice, the burden of responsibility, and the knowledge of whose evil it was that brought the world so much death. Two plays that represent the large number of "perpetrator plays" are Colleen Wagner's *The Monument* (1996) and Hanoch Levin's *Murder* (1997/2002). Both come at the end of the "century of genocide," and like the many other plays noted in this essay, the two dramas are preoccupied with the revelation of complicity with evil on the part of victims, and with the possibility, however fragile, for reconciliation and healing on the part of the perpetrators.[10]

Wagner sets her two-character play in a desolate, unnamed landscape that represents war-torn Bosnia. It begins with Stetko, strapped in an electric chair, recounting in great detail the many rapes and murders he committed, and enjoyed, during the war. He is "saved" from execution by Mejra, the mother of Ana, one of Stetko's victims. In revenge, she abandons her status as bystander in order to commit great violence on him, including using him as a slave to build a monument to her daughter and to all the unnamed women victims of the war. "We are going to let the mothers reclaim their daughters." she says. At the play's end, after Stetko is made to dig up the corpses of his victims and give each one a name, the two characters reach a point of equilibrium in their violent relationship. They are remarkably alike: abject, solitary, regretful, fearful and guilty.

Wagner raises enormous ethical, gendered questions about forgiveness and revenge, love and desolation, violence and victimhood and, of course, about perpetration. Within the barren end-of-the-world landscape, she leads her two characters to "a moment of possibilities" concerning human continuance. What is important is to accept how the perpetrator (Stetko) and his victim (Mejra) exchange places. Wagner proposes the idea that both hate and love can produce violence and offers the audience evidence that perpetrator and victim are contained in both of her wounded characters.

Levin places the "confusion" between perpetrators and victims at the heart of *Murder*. His great overarching theme, like Wagner's, is that human violence (from whatever cause) insures a world filled with a continuous cycle of revenge and slaughter. The location of Levin's play is Israel, and its action represents the horrors of the unending conflict between Jewish Israelis and Arab Palestinians about which Freddie Rokem writes: "This narrative device ['of threats and counterthreats'] has enabled Levin to confront his Israeli audiences with their own role, not only as victims of cruelty but also as perpetrators of the suffering of others" (Rokem 2003, xxvi).

The play's action begins with the murder and mutilation of an Arab boy by three Israeli soldiers and the discovery of the murder by the boy's father. The action of the second act takes place at a beach resort where a Jewish wedding is taking place. It is interrupted by the crazed Arab father who shoots the groom and rapes and kills the Jewish bride. The chain of atrocities leads to the third act where a Jewish boy is killed in a bombing and an innocent

Arab laborer is beaten to death and decapitated for the crime. Violence and madness has seized everyone, and atrocity is provoked by and follows upon atrocity. For Levin, there seems to be no possible end to the carnage. People are perpetrators and victims, bound together by mutual loathing, wounding, and fear where "both parties share the same murderous, merciless, and sadistic impulses that they direct against each other" (Brenner 2002, 167). By the 1990s, it would appear, from these plays (and others) that unfold within genocidal landscapes, that staging perpetration involves for many playwrights the conviction that we are all perpetrators and all victims.

It Will Always Be Complicated

Brief summaries can only hint at the complexity of the issues that have been taken up by many playwrights in many countries and languages concerning the perpetration of genocide. The point of this chapter has been to describe how their work for the theater over two generations often centers on the question of identifying the nature and actions of those who commit evil (as well as those who don't). The plays described, some well known and others less so, appear in many forms and reject the simple definition of purely evil (or mad) perpetrator. Unaccepting audiences, seeking unambiguous characters and simple justice, might turn to Primo Levi for wise counsel. In "The Gray Zone," the concentrationary space where morals are turned inside out, Levi notes that it "possesses an incredibly complicated internal structure and contains within itself enough to confuse our need to judge" (Levi 2017, 31).

One common explanation for the transgressing of rigid identities is that the "purity" of characters runs counter to the facts of human nature and behavior, and that dramatizing binary conflicts results only in "untruthful" melodrama. What is surprising is that this explanation contradicts the acceptance of Hilberg's triad rigidly understood that, as noted earlier, has been accepted and disseminated by most commentators on genocide since his categories were originated and that research in Perpetrator Studies has thoroughly critiqued.

This much is clear: playwrights and other theater artists have much to teach (and learn from) other fields (psychology, history, philosophy) involved with exploring and explaining the nature of perpetration and its complicated motivation and aftermath. The theater's ability to put us inside the arena of perpetration makes its effect so powerful and lasting.

Finally, there are other conditions that contribute to the ethical "flexibility" in images of perpetrators besides the ones noted earlier:

a) All people are capable of doing terrible things when the threat or reward (or both) is great enough, and if the cultural dynamic supports it, thus complicating the understanding of acts of perpetration
b) The complexity of ethical decisions leads to actions of terrible consequence that often are combined with or result from decisions intended to help or resist
c) The nature of "group culpability" for atrocities also diffuses responsibility
d) The individual's desire for reconciliation or forgiveness, the society's desire to reestablish social order, or the government's hope to diminish future atrocities through programs of "restorative justice" works to reduce the demand for "strict" justice in favor of something more practical, humane or, perhaps, just more likely.

That something, seen in the dramatization of perpetrators (and their victims), is found in Gerstein's struggle to save Jews, in the refusal to consume Puffi's body, and in the revenge of Mejra to honor her murdered daughter. From an altered way we can think about the terror of perpetration, Berel Lang advances the possibility of "expand[ing] the domain of the moral imagination" (Lang 2005, 30). In sum, "whose evil is this?" is a question with many answers depending on the playwright's understanding of evil and of how evil is understood to function in the world. The concern of this chapter has been to describe and assess how images of evil function in the theatricalized world of genocide. It seems that to find an accurate measure depends on accepting that we are capable of perpetrating evil as well as, less often, and sometimes less visibly, and perhaps at the same time, "perpetrating good."

Notes

1 I identified "perpetrator plays" in a 1994 essay "Stage Nazis: The Politics and Aesthetics of Memory" that touched on a number of the topics included in the current chapter. The plays discussed in the essay focus on the major Nazi figures of Hitler, Eichmann, Göring, Mengele, and Hess and "seek at least part of their impact through stark revision of historical 'content' and frequently by rejection of traditional form" (Skloot 1994, 61). Referring to an article by Yael Feldman titled similarly to mine: "Whose Story Is It, Anyway?" the essay discusses plays with characters who could be generally assumed to be perpetrators and then assesses how playwrights have dealt with them. The plays cited could be characterized as "canonical" in the decades in which they appeared. Note: the years mentioned for the plays are the dates of their theatrical premieres.

2 An example of this phenomenon is Rolf Hochhuth's play *The Deputy* (*Der Stellvertreter*), which is eight hours long and in performance has never used the same text (Hochhuth, *The Deputy*, 1964). The play utilizes something of a hybrid form having appended to it a voluminous number of documents Hochhuth collected under the heading "Sidelights on History." Documents and other texts appear within the play.

In the 1960s, especially in Europe, a number of playwrights created plays out of historical "texts" to establish the absolute and ruthless reality of the Jewish genocide. This unique theatrical form became known as "documentary theater." Perhaps the most notable and influential of these plays was Peter Weiss's *The Investigation* (*Die Ermittlung*), the "poetic condensation" of the 1964–65 court transcripts detailing the trial of perpetrators for the murders committed in Auschwitz. The play was produced simultaneously in sixteen German cities late in 1965. "Documentary theater does not invent; instead it presents authentic material on stage, ostensibly unchanged in content but now integrated in a different form. [...] The goal, then, is to make people think and ultimately to educate the audience" (Plunka, *Holocaust Drama: The Theatre of Atrocity*, 332). The English version of Weiss's play by Jon Swan and Ulu Grosbard contains this note: "The condensation should contain nothing but facts. Personal experience and confrontation must be steeped in anonymity" *The Investigation* (1966, 1). Another example is Richard Norton-Taylor's editing of the 1945–6 Nuremberg war crimes trials in the 1997 performance piece *Nuremberg*. A variation of the documentary form can be seen in Robert David MacDonald's 1994 stage adaptation *In Quest of Conscience* dramatizing the interviews between the journalist Gitta Sereny and Franz Stangl, the commandant of the Treblinka death camp. MacDonald's text is taken directly from Sereny's 1974 book *Into That Darkness* and not from "official" documents.

3 For further explication of the formal, characteristic differences between drama and theater, see Skloot (2013). It follows that if there is no fixed interpretation of the text in performance, there can be no fixed interpretation of the characters in the performance.

4 See for example, Alvin H. Rosenfeld, especially *The End of the Holocaust*. His wide-ranging work develops the most sustained argument for a "traditional" perspective. In practice, there is no single form that plays of perpetration take (Skloot 1990, 185–201; 1999, 51–58).

5 Hilberg's early analysis established the categories of "perpetrator" and "victim"; "bystander" appears somewhat later. In the "Preface" to *Perpetrators Victims Bystanders* he writes: "The Jewish catastrophe [...] was [...] an event that was experienced by a variety of perpetrators, a multitude of victims, and a host of bystanders. These three groups were distinct from one another and they did not dissolve in their lifetime. Each saw what happened from its own, special perspective, and each harbored a separate set of attitudes and reactions. [...] The reality [of keeping the groups separate and contained] was not always so uncomplicated" (Hilberg 1992, ix, xi). It needs to be said that plays about perpetrators required grounding in a specific genocide. It was the Holocaust that served that

purpose, and much of our later understanding of genocide and its representation was established through that historical event.

6 In the Introduction to *Representing the Holocaust: History, Theory, Trauma*, Dominick LaCapra adds his opinion to the merging of perpetrator and victim by insisting that the distinction between the two must be preserved "for even the most tentative moral and political judgments" (LaCapra 1994, 11). It is noteworthy that Brown's scrupulous judgments engage with writers, historians, and films, but he avoids theater preferring to cite Primo Levi: "that documentary evidence 'almost never has the power to give us the depths of a human being; for this purpose the dramatist or poet are more appropriate than the historian or psychologist'" (Brown 2013, 27). Christopher Bigsby quotes the same Levi passage in his deeply felt assessment of Hochhuth's play (Bigsby 2006, 148).

A number of "canonic" plays do focus on the Jewish victims, but from the perspective of Jews who held positions of responsibility within the administrative hierarchy of daily life under the Nazis. Heated controversy still trails many such historical characters who attempted to negotiate on behalf of the Jews with the Nazi perpetrators. Three are protagonists in important plays: Harold and Edith Lieberman's *Throne of Straw* (1980) focusing on Chaim Rumkowski of Lodz, Joshua Sobol's *Ghetto* (1984) retelling the terrible situation of Jacob Gens of Vilna, and Motti Lerner's *Kastner* (1985) whose protagonist Rudolf Kastner actually did save the lives of a large number of Hungarian Jews. Of the three figures, only Kastner survived the war and a later trial in Israel for his complicit actions. He was assassinated in 1957. All three plays had their supporters and detractors.

7 The German title of the play, *Der Stellvertreter*, is often translated as "The Representative." The Pope, the Doctor, Gerstein, and the priest Fontana are all "representatives," and asking "of what?" is not an unimportant detail in assessing the meaning of and reaction to the play. Tom Lawson incorporates Hilberg's triad but takes a different tack by calling Pius XII a bystander for not speaking out for the Jews (Lawson 2010, 86–124).

8 I discuss the form, theme, and reception of a number of perpetrator plays in *The Darkness We Carry: The Drama of the Holocaust*, 1988.

9 A number of other plays of genocide dating from the 1960s and 1970s focus on the destruction of indigenous populations at a great chronological distance from the twentieth century. They include Peter Schaffer's *The Royal Hunt of the Sun* (1967) [Incas], Arthur Kopit's *Indians* (1969) [Native Americans], and James W. Nichols's *Sainte-Marie among the Hurons* (1977) [indigenous First Nation people]. Some of these plays include the destruction of cultural rituals (ethnocide) as in Kopit's remarkable recreation of the Native Americans' Sun Dance. My brief analysis of a number of these plays can be found in a "Review Essay" dating from 2010. The plays discussed include: Roel Adams' play for children *On the Other Side* (2005) set during the destruction in the former Yugoslavia, J.T. Rogers' *The Overwhelming* (2006) about the violence in Rwanda, Winter Miller's *In Darfur* (2008), Dorcy Rugamba's 2007 restaging of Peter Weiss's documentary play *The Investigation* to refer to the Rwandan genocide, and Catherine Filloux's opera about Cambodia's genocide *Where Elephants Weep* (2008).

10 The two plays deal with "ordinary" people caught up in genocidal action, unlike other perpetrator plays that assess the historical events from the standpoint of people in authority. Todorov argues that doing evil does not permit categorizing people as pathological ("as monsters") since such action is "normal" and thus ordinary. "Those who took an active part in the perpetration of evil were ordinary people, and so are we: they are like us, and we are like them" (Todorov 1996, 121, 135). A list of plays about genocide in English appears in my 2008 anthology *The Theatre of Genocide*, 221. Three of the four plays in that collection deal directly with understanding perpetrators and their actions: Kitty Felde's *A Patch of Earth* (1999) [Bosnia], Catherine Filloux's *Silence of God* (2002) [Cambodia], and Erik Ehn's *Maria Kizito* (2004) [Rwanda]. All of the plays depart from normative realism, utilizing "unreal" characters, exchanges of identity, poetic language, fragmented time, and heightened symbolism to make their views known.

References

Bigsby, Christopher. 2006. *Remembering and Imagining the Holocaust: The Chain of Memory*. Cambridge: Cambridge University Press.

Brenner, Rachel Feldhay. 2002. "The Terror of Barbarism and the Return to History: Between the Text and the Performance of Murder by Hanoch Levin." *Hebrew Studies*, XLIII: 153–186.

Brown, Adam. 2013. *Judging "Privileged" Jews: Holocaust Ethics, Representation, and the "Grey Zone."* New York: Berghahn.

Friedlander, Saul. 1969. *Kurt Gerstein: The Ambiguity of Good.* New York: Alfred A. Knopf.

Hilberg, Raul. 1961. *The Destruction of the European Jews.* Chicago: Quadrangle Books.

Hilberg, Raul. 1992. *Perpetrators Victims Bystanders: The Jewish Catastrophe 1933–1945.* New York: HarperCollins.

Hilberg, Raul. 1996. *The Politics of Memory: The Journey of a Holocaust Historian.* Chicago: Ivan Dee.

Hochhuth, Rolf. 1964. *The Deputy.* Translated by Richard and Clara Winston. New York: Grove Press.

LaCapra, Dominick. 1994. *Representing the Holocaust. History, Theory, Trauma.* Ithaca: Cornell University Press.

Lang, Berel. 2005. *Post-Holocaust: Interpretation, Misinterpretation, and the Claims of History.* Bloomington: Indiana University Press.

Lawson, Tom. 2010. *Debates on the Holocaust.* Manchester: Manchester University Press.

Levi, Primo. [1986] 2017. *The Drowned and the Saved.* Translated by Raymond Rosenthal. New York: Simon & Schuster.

Levin, Hanoch. 1997/2002. "Murder: A Play in Three Acts and an Epilogue." Translated by Barbara Harshav. *Hebrew Studies* 43:4. 127–151.

Plunka, Gene A. 2009. *Holocaust Drama: The Theater of Atrocity.* Cambridge: Cambridge University Press.

Rokem, Freddie. 2003. *"Introduction" to The Labor of Life: Selected Plays of Hanoch Levin. i-xxxv.* Stanford, CA: Stanford University Press.

Rosenfeld, Alvin H. 2011. *The End of the Holocaust.* Bloomington: Indiana University Press.

Skloot, Robert, ed. 1982. *The Theatre of the Holocaust, Volume 1.* Madison: The University of Wisconsin Press.

Skloot, Robert. 1988. *The Darkness We Carry.* Madison, WI: The University of Wisconsin Press.

Skloot, Robert. 1990. "Theatrical Images of Genocide." *Human Rights Quarterly*, 12(2): 185–201.

Skloot, Robert. 1994. "Stage Nazis: The Politics and Aesthetics of Memory." *History & Memory*, 6(2): 57–87.

Skloot, Robert, ed. 1999. *The Theatre of the Holocaust, Volume 2.* Madison: The University of Wisconsin Press.

Skloot, Robert, ed. 2008. *The Theatre of Genocide: Four Plays about Mass Murder in Rwanda, Bosnia, Cambodia, and Armenia.* Madison: University of Wisconsin Press.

Skloot, Robert. 2009. "Staying Ungooselike: The Holocaust and the Theatre of Choice." In *Jewish Theatre: A Global View*, edited by Edna Nahshon, 241–255. Leiden: Brill.

Skloot, Robert. 2013. "The Theatre of the Holocaust: Its Past and Future." *Holocaust Studies*, 19(2): 25–42.

Todorov, Tzvetan. 1996. *Facing the Extreme: Moral life in the Concentration Camps.* Translated by Arthur Denner and Abigail Pollak. New York: Henry Holt.

Wagner, Colleen. 1996. *The Monument.* Toronto: Playwrights Canada Press.

27

Representing Infamous Others

Perpetrator Imagery in Visual Art

Diana I. Popescu

> We must not block out the memory of our perpetrators. Amnesia relegates images of evil into the land of fantasy. We may not recognize the evil once it arrives.
>
> (Uklański 2017, 5)

Introduction

At the Photographers' Gallery (London, 1998) and at the group exhibition *Mirroring Evil. Nazi Imagery/Recent Art* (New York, 2002) Polish artist Piotr Uklański presented *The Nazis*, an installation of 166 film stills displayed in a frieze-like form across the gallery's walls. The stills portray Hollywood stars impersonating male officers dressed in uniforms adorned with the military insignia of the regime. The men are defiant and commanding and create what one art critic has called, "a rogue's gallery of *Wehrmacht* and *Schutzstaffel* officers inhabited by a Who's Who of lionized leading men, from Marlon Brando to Michael Caine" (Welchman 2017). These beloved actors' charisma is transferred onto the Nazi characters they mimic. *The Nazis* exposes these acts of transfer and encourages viewers to reflect on the appeal Fascism exerts in the post-Holocaust world.

At the *documenta 14* in Kassel in 2017, Uklański presented a follow-up installation *The Real Nazis* showcasing over 200 archival photographs of this time real Nazi officers. Like the film stills, this collection depicted male officers, except for 5 women, including Leni Riefenstahl, the Third Reich's favorite filmmaker. If juxtaposed, the two installations reveal a striking resemblance between "the stagey, propagandistic imagery of the Third Reich and the mock-up Nazi iconography of Hollywood" (Edition Patrick Frey 2017). The very fact that Uklański's first installation *The Nazis* was purchased at a high cost on the art market is reason for concern (see webpage of Sotheby auction, 2017). What makes the art catalogue, currently out of print, a highly coveted asset? Is it the high value associated with this visual artist's prestige? Or does it signal a continuing fascination with Fascist images that the artist himself wished to expose? The fact that "glamorous impersonations of evil" captivate members of the public points to a distressing, albeit enduring, phenomenon (Edition Patrick Frey 2017).

This chapter will show how far visual art offers a productive platform to reflect on both aesthetic and ethical dilemmas relating to perpetrators of mass crimes, as raised by Uklański and others. Why are the perpetrators present in the works of visual artists from different artistic contexts and historical and national backgrounds? What imagery have artists chosen to depict the perpetrators? What meanings can be assigned to their imagery? The following is a succinct chronological narrative of perpetrator representation in a wide array of visual expressions produced before the onset of the exterminatory policies of Nazi Germany, during and after World War II and the Holocaust period well into the 1990s and the 2000s. Throughout this narrative, recurrent iconographies will be identified and their ethics problematized.

Why and How Do Artists Depict Perpetrators?

Perpetrator depictions appear in a wide range of art movements encompassing realist, modernist, and postmodernist avant-garde approaches. The media of expression are varied, from political caricature, to pencil drawing, oil painting, sculpture, photography, but also multimedia installations involving video and textual narrative and more recently, digital and virtual media. Despite differences in historical period and geography, artists are driven by a shared need to document and bear witness to the violence they suffered or witnessed, to resist and to shed light on historical injustice, to address uncomfortable truths about human nature, and to work through traumatic experiences. Temporal or spatial proximity to acts of aggression play a crucial role in how artists chose to depict perpetrators. For artists who suffered persecution, irrespective of the specifics of each historical case and artistic culture, visual expression represents an extraordinary act of spiritual resistance performed in conditions of extreme suffering and danger. A dominant characteristic of eyewitnesses' representations is an unambiguous depiction of aggressors as embodiments of evil, death, and destruction. Recorded is the aggression inflicted by perpetrators on their victims. Art is a means to testify to crimes and to act as evidence, to seek recognition and justice. The ethical dimension of art as historical evidence is captured tellingly in Holocaust survivor Karol Konieczny's statement, "my drawings ought not to be subjected to scrutiny and aesthetic artistic criticism … I wish them to be considered a living and shocking document of a world of horror and torment" (quoted in Blatter and Milton, 1981, 142). On the other hand, artists not directly affected by genocide tend to pay more attention to the mechanisms or motivations that led to acts of aggression.[1] Perpetrators are, in this case, subjected to a deeper degree of interrogation, which allows for more ambiguity and a potentially more open interpretation. The following account invokes artists depicting the perpetrators of the Holocaust and of other genocides who resort to a wide range of tropes and genres including realism, figurative art, expressionism, and surrealism, as well as pop, conceptual and installation art.

From Biblical Evils to Repelling Creatures

From the mid-1930s onward, Nazi perpetrators appear in European art as characters from the Bible; commonly as Cain, the murderer brother (e.g., George Grosz's *Cain*, 1944; Rico Lebrun's *Genesis* mural, 1959–60) or as Haman, the archenemy of the Jewish people from the Book of Esther (e.g., Leonard Baskin's *Haman*, 1955–56). Since these figures, standing for the human inclination to do evil, retained a level of humanity, they were replaced with replaced nonhuman, even god-like biblical characters. As Hitler's regime took hold over Germany and Europe, some artists felt that violence exceeded the agency of human beings and became a force of nature. Carl Zahraddnik's works (1941), for example, depict Hitler as Moloch, the god of the Amnonite people in the book of Leviticus under whose name children were sacrificed by being burnt to death in the furnace of its belly. As the regime took on a more visible aggressive turn, biblical images were replaced with animal imagery. Sinister half-human, half-animal figures start to appear in John Heartfield's political cartoons. Hitler is depicted as a hyena baring its teeth in a sign of aggression, wearing a World War I medal and standing on top of dead bodies (see photomontage *War and Corpses: The Last Hope of the Rich*, 1932). Hans Grundig chose wolves and wolf-like dogs to represent the Nazis (see *Brown terror*, 1935), and for Leonard Baskin, birds of prey symbolized "man's uglier nature ... [meant] to render acutely perceptible man's stupefying, intentful capacity for horror" (Baskin cited by Amishai Maisels 1993, 218). Marc Chagall's gouache *Apocalypse in Lilac, Capriccio* (1945) depicts a crucified Jewish Jesus wearing tefillin and a prayer shawl looking down in bewilderment at a wolf-like creature with a tail, wearing a black suit, a Hitler-like moustache, and a backwards swastika on his arm. As the collective realization of the enormity of the crimes deepened, terrifying animal figures were exchanged for unrecognizable monstrous creatures (see works by Jacob Steinhardt, Chaim Gross, and Hyman Bloom). Animal imagery depicting mankind's most primitive and brutal instincts appears in representations of other historical crimes, as in Albert Adams' monochrome drawings of ape-like figures sitting on the back of human figures, on a stack of skeletons or coffins, in reference to Darfur and Abu Ghraib (e.g., *Iraq: Abu Ghraib* and *Ape on standing man*, 2006). Alison Wilding's drawings of sinister bird-like silhouettes (e.g., *Drone 4*, 2012) symbolize manmade tools for destruction, such as drones, and remind of the mythical birds of prey associated with the Nazi perpetrators. Such animalized representations of perpetrators and their instruments of death effectively render the artists' and by proxy the viewers' shock and bewilderment in response to the gruesomeness of the crimes committed. While these depictions render the barbarity of the criminals, animal images have a defamiliarizing effect, as they reinforce the perception of perpetrators as nonhumans, as demons, and as evil. Such imagery is powerful, yet it detracts viewers from asking ethical questions about the capacity of most humans to be complicit in or to commit crimes. A contrast to such depictions is offered by representations of perpetrators in political cartoons.

Grotesque Human Aggressors

Perpetrator figures depicting enraged and violent men are recurrent in cartoons published in the European printed press.[2] In the pre-World War II period, John Heartfield's photomontages of the Nazi leader and his closest allies were, according to art critic Sabine Kriebel, amongst the "most effective visual language for political propaganda in the inflammatory context of Germany in 1932, its mode of psychological suture compelling and immediate" (2008, 101). *Mirror, mirror, who's the strongest of them all?* (AIZ, August 1933) depicts Hitler in semi profile, dressed in uniform, wearing the swastika band on this left arm and the iron cross military decoration. In the mirror facing him, a skeleton figure clutches his throat, making him gasp for air. Heartfield's satirical representations, exposing human evil through images of skeletons to represent death, find a more recent correspondent in the caricatures of military figures produced by Charlie Hebdo and Kjell Nilsson-Mäki in connection to the Bosnian war. The latter has portrayed war criminal Ratko Mladic against the background of human skulls stacked on top of one another; his arm protracted, holding a human skull. Irrespective of the historical context, in political cartoons the faces of leading perpetrators are under intense scrutiny and often are associated with skeleton imagery depicting death.

Furthermore, human ferociousness is unmasked and associated with authoritarianism, militarism, and inflammatory political rhetoric. Unlike the unworldly animalized representations of perpetrators, cartoons present us with unambiguous portrayals of human beings at their worst. These depictions have a clear moral message, designed as a wake-up call to the destructive force of human behavior, meant to mobilize societies and their political leaders to stop terror from taking its toll. In this case, cartoonists act as human rights activists who raise awareness of perpetrators as individual aggressors and urge viewers to oppose and defeat them.

The Perpetrator as Instrument of Violence, Effacing the Human Face

Like political cartoonists, victims of violence and torture choose a realist and figurative style to depict the aggressors. One common trope is the loss of humanity suggested in visual terms by the absence of facial expressions. In sketches by prisoners of concentration camps in Europe,[3] guards and Nazi officers of lower ranks are faceless, as they inflict violence on their victims (Toll 1998, 15, 19, 20). Foregrounded are the guards' uniforms and the weapons of violence. Nazi guards appear in small groups of two to three individuals, as ghostly apparitions wearing full uniforms, caps, holding clubs, whips, machine guns, and are accompanied accompanied by dogs that commit vicious attacks. In other historical contexts, too, perpetrators lack facial expressions. Vann Nath, a Cambodian survivor of mass crimes perpetuated by Khmer Rouge guards in the notorious killing camp S-21, depicts the guards as a collective wearing the same dark green-blue uniform, green caps, colored scarves, and sandals. Nath is interested to document the different methods used to torture prisoners. Instruments of torture, whips, and clubs are clearly visible. Here too, the perpetrators appear in groups that form the machinery of torture. In contrast, the victims are portrayed in more detail; their pained expressions contrasted with the numbed features of the guards.[4]

Perpetrators also appear in drawings by children survivors. Eva Weissberger, who survived Terezin, portrays a Nazi officer with a club in his hand (Volavkova 1994). Children survivors of the Rwandan genocide depict male figures holding machetes or machine guns as they commit brutal crimes (Salem 2000).[5] For the victims, the agents of aggression are individuals whose faces are effaced by the acts of violence they have committed. Their aggression is recorded as factual evidence to be used in the court of law and for the historical record. While the individual aggressors cannot be identified, the murderous nature of the political regime can be documented. The absence of the faces of perpetrators suggests to us something of the unbearable trauma inflicted on the prisoners. In contrast, postwar courtroom illustrations shed light on the identities and personalities of the leaders of murderous regimes, revealing that it is the ordinary man with a face who is responsible for atrocious crimes.

Ordinary Men

In the period immediately after the liberation of the concentration camps, Nazi perpetrators appear in the drawings and sketches of courtroom illustrators and war artists. The perpetrators do not possess monstrous features, as in earlier paintings and drawings, but are presented in a realist documentary style, as military officials.[6] Photographic materials of war criminals at trials in Rwanda and Bosnia depict the perpetrators in similar ways. If prior to 1945 evil was depicted as an external force that took possession of Nazi Germany, post-World War II artists approached evil as an inherent part of human nature. References to madness, pathology, and irrationality developed through animal and monster imagery could no longer hold true in the face of what Hannah Arendt termed "banality of evil." The monstrosity of the perpetrators' deeds was referenced using complex and often ambivalent images that conveyed an unsettling coexistence of evil with what appears to be commonplace. The trial of Adolf Eichmann in Jerusalem (1961) drew even closer attention to the human character of the perpetrators. Eichmann appeared as an authoritative and somewhat defiant figure in satirical cartoonist Roland Searle's drawings for *Life Magazine* (1961). Arendt famously argued that nothing in this perpetrator's appearance disclosed the heinous crimes he was responsible for organizing. On the contrary, he was deemed a "completely normal man, more normal, at any rate, than I am after examining him," noted an Israeli court psychiatrist. Arendt's observation about "the coexistence of normality and bottomless cruelty" (Arendt 1963) haunted the visual imagery of West German postwar artists who questioned whether their country had truly broken with its criminal past.[7] In America, Jewish artist Sid Chafez extended the notion of ordinariness of evil to the Nazi regime's accomplices in a series of 42 monotone lithographs *Perpetrators* (1992) including portraits of industrialists, businessmen, professionals, soldiers, churchmen, physicians, lawyers, and bureaucrats. In other contexts, the photographs of Rwandan survivors posing next to Hutu perpetrators produced by Pieter Hugo, 20 years after the genocide (e.g., *Portraits of Reconciliation*, 2014) reveal nothing of the atrocious nature of the deeds committed by these now remorseful-looking individuals. These criminals are ordinary men—an unnerving realization for the post-Eichmann global community of witnesses. Ronald Ophius's *Gacaca, 4 Hutu prisoners during their trial, Rwanda 2004* (2010) focused on the elusiveness of evil and the myriad ways it hides behind seemingly innocent human faces. This humanized representation withholds moralization, meant to shock viewers into awareness that, in the right circumstances, any human being is vulnerable to become a perpetrator. Zygmunt Bauman poignantly captured this in his statement "monstrosity does not need monsters," since "in the right circumstances no one is exempt from perpetrating crimes" (Bauman 2012). As perpetrators became ordinary people, they start to be associated with sexual violence or are portrayed using sexualized imagery.

Sexual Violence and Sexualized Perpetrators

It is worth noting that depictions of sexual violence in relation to Nazi perpetrators are largely missing in visual art. An early exception is Jerome Witkin's drawing in the sketchbook *The Beating Station* (Berlin, 1933) based on a newspaper story of a well-dressed Jewish woman who was dragged off the streets of Berlin in 1933 by Stormtroopers and raped. To this day, rape remains a taboo subject in visual depictions of the Holocaust. From the 1960s onwards, however, sexualized imagery of Nazi perpetrators starts to emerge especially in popular films produced in America. Prior to film, sexualized images of female and male camp guards appeared in popular men magazines of the 1950s and the 1960s in America, the same genre known as *Stalagim* in Israel.[8] In the context of visual art, critic Susan Sontag was the first to note pop art's use of sexualized images in Robert Morris's 1974 poster *Untitled,* which depicted the "artist, naked to the waist, wearing dark glasses, what appears to be a Nazi helmet, and a spiked steel collar, attached to which is a large chain which he holds in his manacled, uplifted hands" (Sontag 1975). Sontag questions the allure associated with this imagery. Some decades later in 1998, Uklański's *The Nazis* drew attention to the appeal associated with German officers in Western film and popular culture, calling on viewers to interrogate why the Nazis murderers are depicted as attractive.

In academic discourse, Saul Friedländer addresses this question eloquently in "Reflection of Nazism: An Essay on Kitsch and Death" (1984) when he draws attention to the moral responsibilities at stake when one engages with the so-called "frisson" offered by Nazi-centered imagery (in film and in literature) through what he terms "lavish aestheticism." Does the eroticized representation remind us of the psychological "phantasms" Nazism itself evoked in its supporters? Sontag and Friedländer address an ethical dilemma that endures to the present day: how can visual and popular arts avoid reproducing or propagating aesthetics and utopian ideals of beauty and purity endorsed by criminal regimes, and instead work to shed critical light upon the mechanics of violence?

Unlike Holocaust-centered art, brutal violence inflicted by male perpetrators on women appears in Peter Howson's unsettling figurative expressionist works relating to the Bosnian war, *In House Warming*, and *Croatian and Muslim* (1994–1995). The latter is "Howson's most brutal painting, depicting not only the cruel rape of a Muslim woman, but also the total humiliation associated with the act as well as defiling of home and family traditions" (Feinstein 1999, 233–255). Explicit imagery of rape also emerges in political cartoons in the Western press to raise awareness of the crimes in Bosnia. A political caricature from 1993 in the French magazine Charlie Hebdo depicts the grotesque figure of a deformed oversized male soldier naked from waist down surrounded by the bodies of half-naked women. The alarming image raises international attention to the mass rapes committed by members of the Serbian army, calling for intervention. In the Rwandan context, sexual violence is only hinted at. In Pieter Hugo's photography project *Portraits of Reconciliation*, mentioned earlier, Hutu male perpetrators and Tutsi women survivors let themselves be photographed side by side, indirectly invoking the history of sexual violence largely unaddressed in the public sphere. In Holocaust-centered art, glamorized and sexualized images of men aggressors make viewers complicit with sexualized violence, while explicit imagery of rape as in the case of the Bosnian war shock and alarm and raise awareness of the enduring presence of rape in conditions of war and of mass destruction.

A Defining Moment

This dilemma of what constitutes ethical representation becomes the main topic of the group exhibition *Mirroring Evil. Nazi Imagery/Recent Art* (2002), held at the Jewish Museum in New York and curated by Norman E. Kleeblatt, the museum's then chief curator for fine arts. This exhibition marks a key moment in contemporary art world's recognition of the need to interrogate in a critical manner the presence of Nazi images in contemporary societies and in visual art. It remains a groundbreaking endeavor, because of the intensity with which it confronted the American public with the question of evil and the legacies of the Nazi era. In this exhibition, the perpetrator figure served an ethical purpose "to mirror moral and ethical issues that resonate in contemporary society" (Kleeblatt 2002, 13). Despite these intentions and having been safely framed by a scholarly critical narrative, *Mirroring Evil* revealed the limits in contemporary art's ability to communicate this critical message to its audiences. Like Morris, the artists of *Mirroring Evil* demanded from their viewers a critical-reflective stance, which implied that they step out of their comfort zones. Their conceptual art was intent on exposing popular culture's glamorization of perpetrators and the public's acceptance and fascination with them. But, it also asked the public to reflect on its own latent potential to act out violence at the service of radical ideologies and under the influence of propaganda. In most of the exhibition's works the perpetrators became a metaphor (lacking historicity) and a visual tool to expose to the viewers the unethical ways in which, in the interest of entertainment and consumerism, historical aggressors are summoned to produce cheap thrills. *Mirroring Evil* is a singular event in contemporary art's engagement with the perpetrators, having proposed daring yet largely misunderstood imagery to criticize post-Holocaust societies' continuing flirtation, particularly with Nazi sexualized masculinities, as well as with the aesthetics and ideals of totalitarianism. Its artists artists playfully juxtaposed historical, art-historical, and commercial references and collectively made an uncommon case for how contemporary art can act as an effective social critique.

Given its daring subject matter, outrage and opposition among members of the New York Jewish communities were to be expected. Many works included in the exhibition were heavily criticized as provocative and sensationalist trivializations of the Holocaust and as reflecting what is commonly perceived as the meaninglessness of conceptual art in general.[9] Opening six months after the 9/11 attacks, it encouraged discussions about the nature of evil when New Yorkers were recovering from a state of crisis, when ideas of safety long associated with America were shaken to the core, and when responding to the the assault meant the start of the war against international terrorism. The exhibition touched on a sensitive chord as it encouraged viewers to look inwards. The term "mirroring" implied that evil was not external, but a phenomenon that existed within societies and individuals themselves. This self-reflective rhetoric was unpalatable to many Americans, both Jewish and non-Jewish.[10] This response is not surprising. Symbols and images of genocidal regimes are usually eradicated from public spaces; their central function is to memorialize the victims and recognize the suffering of survivors. Statues of former dictators are taken down in post-dictatorial countries, and memorials to their victims are often erected. The critiques surrounding *Mirroring Evil* hinted at these legacies and indicated that publics and artists alike are yet to find the means to eloquently face up to genocidal histories in unequivocal ethical ways.

To this day, no other exhibition tackling recent genocides has devoted a similar focus to the perpetrators. Similar art projects, but more limited in scope, were held in Israel. For instance, the group exhibition whose title references Hitler's biographical details, *1899 (Braunau, Austria)-1945 (Berlin, Germany)* at Tel Aviv's Rosenfeld Gallery (2005) incorporated representations of Fascist iconography (symbols such as the swastika, the colors red and black, Hitler's moustache) in allusive but provocative ways. Hitler-centered imagery haunts the visual art of younger generations of Israeli artists including Roee Rosen, Boaz Arad, and Tamy Ben Tor. The *Führer's* most iconic physical features: the moustache, voice, and haircut are referenced in playful and disturbing ways aimed to belittle, ridicule, and poke fun. Arad's video installation *An immense inner peace* (2001) shows the artist wearing a sinister mask of Hitler's face as he speaks about the dictator's failed career as an art student and symbolically evokes the disturbing connections between art's unethical use as propaganda under Fascism and the art world's tendencies to separate aesthetics from discussions of ethics (Sheffi 2005, 21). Arad's other film works *Safam* (1999), *Hebrew Lesson,* and *Marcel Marcel* (2000) also displayed at *Mirroring Evil*, manipulate archival audio-visual recordings of Hitler's voice and image to erase the figure's identity and recognizable features (e.g., moustache) and in this way to convey ridicule and symbolic castration. In Arad's work, the fear associated with Hitler's image is dismantled by means of comedy and satire. In doing so, this artist draws on pre-existing genres of political caricature developed in John Heartfield's 1930s anti-fascist photomontages (Willet 1997) and emergent in Charlie Chaplin's satirical film *The Great Dictator* (1940).

In contrast to Arad's instrumentalization of Hitler's voice and physical appearance, Ben Tor's video *Women talk about Hitler* (2005) and Rosen's installation *Live and Die as Eva Braun* (1997) address how Hitler might have been perceived from women's perspectives and allude to women's often underplayed roles as supporters and enablers of evil. Notably, female SS guards or female perpetrators are largely absent from visual art's engagement with genocide although they surface in Nazisploitation films such as the Canadian production *Ilsa—She Wolf of the SS* (1974) and in the earlier mentioned *Stalagim*, pornographic graphic novels that appeared clandestinely in Israel in the 1950s and 1960s, and which Rosen also references in his installation works. Arad's and Rosen's works, alongside other works displayed at the *Mirroring Evil* exhibition, problematize contemporary culture's prevailing fascination, even obsession with Hitler figures, and ask viewers to consider what Friedländer called the "frisson" they feel when presented with Nazi-centered imagery.

Conclusion—The Lingering Presence of Perpetrator Images in the Public Imagination

As evidenced by *Mirroring Evil* exhibition, images of perpetrators in public spaces continue to haunt, disturb, and trigger reactions. As shown by public debates before and after this exhibition, images of perpetrators fulfill a crucial function as reminders of the fact that non-engagement with difficult questions about human nature raised by perpetrators is not be acceptable.

If one looks closely enough, such reminders appear again and again in contemporary art. The swastika emerges in various postwar works as in for example, Mel Bochner's *Photographs and 12 diagrams* (1966). Bochner wonders if through repetitions and recontextualizations of the image, he can purge the symbol of its hateful Nazi past, whether new meanings could be given to this sign without making the viewers feel unease. The potency of this sign as a Nazi icon continues to startle (Godfrey 2007, 181–190; Jaskot 2012). More recently, images of Hitler surface in unexpected places, as garden gnomes with arms outstretched in a Hitler salute in German artist Ottmar Hoerl's installation *Dance with the devil* (Hall 2009; Jones 2012) or in the body of a harmless boy who takes an apologizing kneeling position in Maurizio Cattelan's sculpture *Him* (2001). This startling figure makes it difficult to look away. The fact that *Him* was sold in 2016 for the staggering amount of £12 million at London's Christie's is another reason to be startled (Christie's 2016, Shepherd 2016). Like Uklański's *The Nazis*, images of Nazi perpetrators sell well in the art world (Sotheby's 2017). This chapter is not the place for adventurous speculations about the impetus behind such exorbitant amounts. It does, however, invoke this example to remind readers that the art world's own unreflective commodification of images of perpetrators should be challenged in same way that the *Mirroring Evil* exhibition endeavored to do. More sustained interrogations of this subject are required in scholarly studies too. Although present to some extent in art historical accounts, in essays in art catalogues, and even in chapters of interdisciplinary studies on Holocaust representation, critical examinations of perpetrator representations in the diverse media of contemporary arts (including fine arts, conceptual and installation, and even performance and participatory arts) are not given the full critical attention they deserve.

This chapter has mapped the varied tropes associated with the figure of the perpetrator and conveyed how visual artists have, in their own ways, posed questions about the nature of aggressors and societies' changing perceptions of them. It has directed attention away from what in recent years has been discussed as "provocative art" (not to be taken seriously) to examples of visual art created under extreme conditions conveying and which conveyed the witnesses' experiences and views and their incredible acts of resistance. It has further conveyed that working with images of perpetrators provides a unique opportunity to look critically at one's own individual story and at one's own attitude towards past and present atrocities. Well-intended artists do not portray perpetrators for the sake of it or only to incite or gain popular acclaim; they do so to take the pulse of their own society, to gauge how far its members are willing to reflect critically about the legacies of violence and human nature. Artists have relentlessly employed visual imagery available to them to convey something about what appears to be the ever-elusive and familiar nature of evil. As this chapter makes clear, despite a healthy dose of mistrust in artistic representation's ability to inform about the full nature of evil, the many divergent visual lenses through which perpetrators are looked at convey something meaningful about the many and not so unfamiliar faces of the perpetrators.

Notes

1 This overview draws on several references including Ziva Amishai Maisels' comprehensive study of Holocaust depictions in art, *Depiction and Interpretation: The Influence of the Holocaust on Visual Arts*, pp. 161–165; 198–242 and pp. 325–366; Monica Bohm-Duchen's *Art and the Second World War*, chapters "Art of the Holocaust: Creativity in Extremis," pp. 191–211, and "Art under the Dictators: Nazi Art Reassessed," pp. 173–189; and Nelly Toll's *When Memory Speaks: The Holocaust in Art.*

2 Antifascist German and Polish Jewish artists such as George Grosz and Arthur Szyk produced highly persuasive responses to the rise of fascism in the mid-1930s, which placed their lives at great risk. Representations of evil as Satan appear in Arthur Szyk's *Anti-Christ* (1942) wherein Hitler's head is detached from his body as it floats above a scene of extreme violence. The figure's eyes are enlarged and have an intense paralyzing stare. The eyes are reddened in anger, and the pupils are replaced with human skulls. Hitler's head is framed by human sized skulls on one side and by SA and SS officers on the other (US Holocaust Memorial Museum 2017a and 2017b).

3 Among the most representative artists of this period are Leo Haas, Bedrich Fritta, Karel Fleischmann, Otto Ungar, and Felix Bloch in Terezin and David Olère (1989) and Alfred Kantor in Auschwitz. There are numerous art exhibitions of prisoner camp art displayed at Holocaust Memorial Museums in the USA, Poland, the Czech Republic, and Israel, as well as art catalogues published since the 1990s onwards which are accompanied by descriptive essays. Among the most notable art exhibition catalogues published by non-Holocaust art institutions are Stephen Feinstein's *Witness and Legacy. Contemporary Art about the Holocaust* (Minnesota Museum of Contemporary art, January-May 1995), *Burnt Whole: Contemporary Artists Reflect upon the Holocaust* (Washington: Washington Project for the Arts, 1994), *After Auschwitz: Responses to the Holocaust in Contemporary Art* (Sunderlad Tyne near Wear, England: Northern Centre for Contemporary Art, 1995), *Postcripts: End-Representations in Contemporary Israeli Art* (Tel Aviv: Genia Schreiber University Gallery of Art, 1992).

4 See Vann Nath's memoir *A Cambodian Prison Portrait: One Year in the Khmer Rouge's S-21.* Bangkok: White Lotus, 1998 and *Vann Nath Tribute* Phnom Penh: Friends of Vann Nath, 2013.

5 Drawings titled *Why am I being killed?*; *Where shall we flee to now?* depict instruments of genocide: spear, machete, guns, masu, and bow and arrows. *I Am Stabbing You with My Sword* shows a Hutu killer stabbing a Catholic nun.

6 These tropes appear in American illustrator Edward Vebell's sketches of Nazi high commanders (2017) and Laura Knight's *Nuremberg Trials*, 1946 showing Nazi male officers as a collective body with no identifiable facial features.

7 Amongst the most confrontational works are Anselm Kiefer's *Occupations* (1969, published in 1975) consisting of a series of photographs based on real-life performances and depicting the artist wearing his father's boots, riding pants, and military coat. The artist's father served as a military officer in the German army. Kiefer performed *Heil Hitler* salutes while standing before foreign monuments or European sites allegedly conquered by Nazi Germany and reported on an intergenerational symptom common to sons and daughters of the perpetrators (cf. Salzman 1999). Gerhard Richter's *Uncle Rudi* (1965) depicts the perpetrator as a smiling, approachable and loving family relative—the artist's uncle who poses happily in his army lieutenant's uniform. Similarly, French artist Christian Boltanski's *Sans souci* (1991) made visible the unnerving normality of family pictures depicting scenes of domestic bliss in which perpetrators appear as loving family men.

8 See recent research by Pascale Bos, for example her conference presentation "Pulping the Holocaust: Early Popular American Holocaust Memory and its Global Reach," at International Conference "Past (Im)Perfect Continuous," Sapienza University, Rome, June 26–28, 2018.

9 Art Spiegelman delivered a biting response in the form of a comic sketch entitled "Duchamp is our misfortune" portraying a neo-Nazi painting the swastika on a mural and then posing as an artist in front of the symbol, at the exhibition's opening reception.

10 The seeds of the controversy were planted by journalist Lisa Gubernick who wrote an article for the *Wall Street Journal*, in which she described *Mirroring Evil* to be the "next art-world Sensation"—a reference to *Sensation: Young British Artists* from the Saatchi Collection, held at the Brooklyn Museum of Art in 1999, which drew fierce criticism from New York's catholic community including Mayor Rudolph Giuliani. Her description of the exhibition as "unsettling and very disturbing," "out of bounds," and "repugnant" set the tone of the debate. James E. Young later explained that "with a little push" from the *Wall Street Journal*, the exhibition became a "journalistic sensation, as reporters from across New York City began showing a handful of the show's more provocative images to survivors and their children for reactions." See Lisa Gubernick's, "Coming Museum Show with Nazi Themes Stirs New York's Art World" *Wall Street Journal*, (January 10, 2002), James Young's "Demystifying Nazism, or Trivializing Its Victims?," *The Forward* (January 18, 2002). During the week following the publication of Gubernick's article, a series of reports were broadcast on TV channels: Fox 5, WB11, and Channel 2 and Radio stations WINS, WCBS, and NY1. Major American newspapers: *Daily News*, *New York Post*, *Newsday*, *New York Times* and Jewish press: *The Jewish Week* and *The Forward* carried reports. Approximately 200 media articles appeared between January 10 and March 17, 2002, the day of the exhibition's opening. For a detailed analysis of the public debates see Popescu, Diana I. (2012) *Perceptions of Holocaust Memory: A Comparative Study of Public Reactions to Art about the Holocaust at the Jewish Museum in New York and the Israel Museum in Jerusalem (1990s–2000s)*, University of Southampton, Faculty of Humanities, Doctoral Thesis, 317pp.

References

Amishai Maisels, Ziva. 1993. *Depiction and Interpretation: The Influence of the Holocaust on Visual Arts*. Tarrytown, NY: Pergamon Press.

Arendt, Hannah. 1963. "Eichmann in Jerusalem." *The New Yorker*, February 16.

Bauman, Zygmunt. 2012. "A Natural History of Evil." www.vwi.ac.at/index.php/en/events/simon-wiesenthal-lectures-en/icalrepeat.detail/2012/03/22/24/-/zygmunt-bauman-a-natural-history-of-the-evil.

Blatter, Janet & Sybil Milton. 1981. *Art of the Holocaust*. New York: Routledge Press.

Bohm-Duchen, Monica. 2013. *Art and the Second World War*. Princeton, NJ: Princeton University Press.

Christie's. 2016. "Maurizio Cattelan on the Nature of Evil." www.christies.com/features/Maurizio-Cattelan-on-the-nature-of-evil-7306-3.aspx.

Edition Patrick Frey. 2017. "Catalogue Description." www.editionpatrickfrey.com/en/books/real-nazis-piotr-Uklański.

Feinstein, C. Stephen. 1995. *Witness and Legacy: Contemporary Art about the Holocaust*. Minneapolis, MN: Minnesota Museum of American Art.

Feinstein, C. Stephen. 1999. "Art of the Holocaust and Genocide: Some Points of Convergence." *Journal of Genocide Research* 1(2): 233–255.

Friedländer, Saul. 1984. *Reflections of Nazism: An Essay on Kitsch and Death*. New York: Harper and Row.

Godfrey, Mark. 2007. *Abstraction and the Holocaust*. New Haven, CT: Yale University Press.

Hall, Alan. 2009. "Thousand Garden Gnomes giving Heil Hitler Salute invade German Town." *The Telegraph*, October 14. www.telegraph.co.uk/news/worldnews/europe/germany/6327858/Thousand-garden-gnomes-giving-Heil-Hitler-salute-invade-German-town.html

Hornstein, Shelley & Florence Jacobowitz. 2002. *Image and Remembrance. Representation and the Holocaust*. IN: Indiana University Press.

Imperial War Museum. 2017. "Searle, Ronald Jerusalem." (Collection Item). Accessed October 25, 2017. www.iwm.org.uk/collections/item/object/24528.

Jaskot, Paul B. 2012. *The Nazi Perpetrator: Postwar German Art and the Politics of the Right*. Minneapolis, MN: University of Minnesota Press.

Jones, Cass. 2012. "Controversy over Adolf Hitler Salute in Warsaw Ghetto." *The Guardian*, December 28, 2012.

Kleeblatt, L. Norman, ed. 2002. *Mirroring Evil. Nazi Imagery/Recent Art*. New York: Jewish Museum; New Brunswick, NJ: Rutgers University Press.

Kriebel, Sabine. 2008. "Photomontage in the Year 1932: John Heartfield and the National Socialists." *Oxford Art Journal* 31(1): 97–127.

Olere, David. 1989. *The Eyes of a Witness: David Olere - A Painter in the Sonderkommando at Auschwitz* (with a preface and foreword by Serge Klarsfeld). New York: Beate Klarsfeld Foundation.

Salem, Richard, A. (ed.) 2000. *Witness to Genocide: The Children of Rwanda, Drawings by Child Survivors of the Rwandan Genocide of 1994*. New York: Friendship Press.

Salzman, Lisa. 1999. *Anselm Kiefer and Art after Auschwitz*. Cambridge: Cambridge University Press.

Sheffi, Smadar. 2005. "Evil Is Everywhere." *Haaretz Guide*, November, 25.

Shepherd, Jack. 2016. "Hitler Stature by Maurizio Cattelan sells for £12 million at Christie's Auction House." *The Independent*, May 9.

Sontag, Susan. 1975. "Fascinating Fascism." *The New York Review of Books*, February 6. www.nybooks.com/articles/1975/02/06/fascinating-fascism/.

Sothebys. 2017. "Piotr Uklański. The Nazis." www.sothebys.com/en/auctions/ecatalogue/2017/contemporary-art-evening-auction-l17020/lot.52.html.

Toll, Nelly. 1998. *When Memory Speaks: The Holocaust in Art*. Westport, CT: Praeger.

Uklański, Piotr. 2017. *The Real Nazis*. Zurich: Edition Patrick Frey.

US Holocaust Memorial Museum. 2017a. "Anti-Christ (1942) - Arthur Szyk – Wartime Caricaturist." www.ushmm.org/exhibition/szyk/wartime/93866.htm.

US Holocaust Memorial Museum. 2017b. "Satan Leads the Ball (1942) - Arthur Szyk – Wartime caricaturist."

Vebell, Ed. 2017. *An Artist at War: The WWII Memories of Stars & Stripes*. Atglen: Schiffer Publishing.

Volavkova, Hana. (ed.) 1994. *I Never Saw Another Butterfly: Children's Drawings and Poems from Terezin Concentration Camp, 1942–1944*. New York: Schocken Books in association with the United States Holocaust Memorial Museum.

Welchman, C. John. 2017. "Piotr Uklański." Accessed October 25, 2017. www.documenta14.de/en/artists/13594/piotr-Uklański.

Willett, John. 1997. *Heartfield versus Hitler*. Paris: Editions Hazan.

28

Cultural Codes

Holocaust Resonances in Representations of Genocide Perpetrators

Rebecca Jinks

In the dusty heat, Mikael staggers along in a line of skeletal forced laborers who are constructing a railroad. As his team struggles to lift a heavy, cast-iron rail, one man stumbles, and the rail crashes onto his leg, breaking it. As he lies screaming on the ground, the officer overseeing the works shoves another man into his place with his baton. Mikael's team moves on as the officer turns around and beats the injured man. At the end of the day, Mikael's team passes by the man with the crushed leg lying on the ground; he begs them to help him. Mikael and the replacement worker pick him up and stagger on, supporting him between them. Behind them, the officer notices what is happening and slowly turns away from his discussion with his colleagues. A bullet cracks: the injured man falls to the ground, dead, his weight dragging the two horrified prisoners down with him. The officer saunters up to them as they lay on the ground, the dead man between them. "You should thank me: I eased your burden. Thank me." His eyes harden, and he points his pistol at them. "I said: *thank me.*"

The prisoners' exhaustion and terror, their knowledge that "they're going to kill us [all]," and the mocking, cold cruelty of the officer—the indifference with which he executed a human being "not fit to work"—all seem very familiar: the iconography and script of this scene are characteristic of Holocaust representations since the 1990s. And yet these scenes are not from a recent Holocaust film, but from Terry George's film *The Promise* (2017), a dramatic, emotion-laden portrayal of the Armenian genocide. Indeed, the film's sense of familiarity can only be heightened for viewers a few minutes later, when Mikael—who has managed to escape—hauls himself onto a moving freight train, only to discover that the carriages are packed with terrified Armenians being deported towards the Syrian desert.[1] The Armenian genocide is becoming more widely known in the West, and there are now hundreds of films and testimonies, memoirs, and novels that explore the process, impact, and legacies of the Armenian genocide in complex and sometimes unexpected forms (e.g., Shafak 2007; Çetin 2008; Khardalian & Holquist 2011). Nevertheless, it is telling that in this film—which was intended to reach a broad, mainstream audience[2]—the representation of the violence, and especially of the perpetrators, conforms to a very standard, recognizable cultural code. Especially in a context where denial of the genocide is still effective, it indicates the enduring usefulness of such cultural codes for filmmakers and writers who are seeking to represent these atrocities as genocides.

Scholarly interest in such resonances and transfers between representations of the Holocaust and other genocides and atrocities has increased in the last two decades. Initially, scholars tended to focus on genocide representations that made explicit comparisons and analogies with, or reference to, the Holocaust: some refer to an "Armenian holocaust," for example, or compare Slobodan Milošević to Hitler (Steinweis 2005; MacDonald 2008; Buettner 2011). Many scholars approached such representations as protagonists of the moralizing battles over the Holocaust's "uniqueness" in the 1990s and early 2000s, and sought to defend the Holocaust from being "appropriated" by other groups, whose comparisons to the Holocaust would, they argued, "devalue" its memory and significance. David B. MacDonald, for example, inventoried in his book *Identity Politics in the Age of Genocide* (2008) multiple examples of victimized groups explicitly "copying" the vocabulary and imagery of the Holocaust, arguing that it "trivialize[s] the Holocaust and the unique suffering of the group they represent" and that "each group must find its own vocabulary and imagery for what happened to *them*" (MacDonald 2008, 196, 3). More recently, however, a less moralizing and more genuinely comparative body of interdisciplinary scholarship has emerged, which explores the more subtle resonances and structural similarities between representations of the Holocaust and other genocides and atrocities—whether in literature, films, graphic novels, or other media (Eaglestone 2008; Rothberg 2009; Bangert, Gordon and Saxton 2013; Pettitt 2018). These works are less concerned with the "use and abuse" of Holocaust tropes and do not see memory as a "zero-sum game," as Michael Rothberg put it (2009, 11). Instead, they are interested in creative transfers, non-competitive interconnections, and structural echoes that can point to deeper, shared conceptions of violence and atrocity within societies. In my own work, *Representing Genocide: The Holocaust as Paradigm?* (2016), I explored the "script" to which many representations of genocide conform, which enables Western audiences to recognize the events depicted in film, literature, museums, and photography *as* genocide (Jinks 2016). This script, I argue, understands and depicts genocide as an aberrant and "inhuman" event, planned and perpetrated by "evil" men upon innocent victims. The script thus revolves around a particular portrayal of the perpetrators, victims, and the process of genocide. Adhering to this "plot," where the perpetrators are coded as planning and pursuing the total annihilation of an innocent victim group, is also what seems key in distinguishing the representation of genocide from the representation of other atrocities or tragedies—whether wars or mass murder.[3] The representation of the perpetrators and their actions is thus key in cementing the portrayal of genocide *as* genocide.

In this chapter, I explore how the cultural codes used to depict Holocaust perpetrators are re-deployed in literature and films like *The Promise* to portray the perpetrators of other genocides. I focus largely on what I have referred to as "mainstream" representations of genocide—those which aim to appeal to (and have appeal for) a wide popular audience—in order to show how these cultural codes have solidified into an accepted representational framework (see Jinks 2016, 22). I focus on film and literature here—a representative mix of documentaries and feature films, and a range of testimonies, memoirs, and novels—because they depict most clearly the planning and *process* of genocide, as well as the character of the perpetrators (since most conform to the standard narrative format). I draw on examples from the four cases of genocide that had become canonical by the end of the twentieth century—Armenia, Bosnia, Cambodia, and Rwanda—as well as genocides that came later and others generally less accepted by the public as genocide, including Darfur, Myanmar, and colonial genocides such as took place in Australia. I show that the redeployment of these cultural codes—whether intentionally or otherwise—demonstrates their power and also lays bare what is at stake if the codes are not (or cannot be) followed: recognition.

Across the landscape of Holocaust representations, the depiction of perpetrators is changing, as the chapter by Stephanie Bird in this volume demonstrates (see Brown 2011; Adams and Vice 2013). Nevertheless, in many mainstream Holocaust films and literature, the archetypes persist—of a dogmatic, driven Nazi leadership; of crisply uniformed, cold SS ideologues; and of brutal, thuggish Nazis. From *Schindler's List* (1993) to *Inglourious Basterds* (2009) to the novel and film *The Boy in the Striped Pajamas* (Boyne 2006; Herman 2008), audiences are presented with "stock characters" who are, as Scott Montgomery has argued, somehow "faceless" (1995, 81). Most popular Holocaust narratives operate in the genres of the "escape story," "rescue story," or story of loss and survival: each of these uses the stock narrative device of the "villain," who remains resolutely one-dimensional and "other" (see Picart and Frank 2006, 4). Thus, rarely are the motives and individual psychologies of the perpetrators portrayed in any real depth, and rarely do we see the sort of character development that might provoke audiences and readers to explore how "ordinary" individuals become radicalized, or acquiescent, in the state programs of social and political violence and genocidal exclusion.[4] Instead, we know Holocaust perpetrators only through their actions, as they drive the process of destruction forward. The complexities of the Holocaust's origins and process thus also tend to remain opaque: the Holocaust often appears as an inevitable progression through successive stages towards total annihilation, according to a preconceived plan—especially and understandably so when narrated through the experiences of a victim or witness. The Holocaust, thus, tends to be "explained" through reference to the Nazis' actions and their innate "evil"—whether implied or explicitly stated. In a circular fashion, this depiction of the perpetrators also removes the need for any deeper exploration of their motivations, precisely because their "evil" serves as an explanation: their role in the narrative is predetermined and also understood to be "incomprehensible." Holocaust perpetrators, then, are depicted in the most stereotypical terms, as one-dimensional monsters engaged in the fulfillment of a predetermined plan for genocide, resulting in the murder of millions. As such, they are thoroughly distanced from the readers and viewers of mainstream literature and films.

These are the cultural codes that are redeployed in mainstream representations of other genocides, and this coding cements their portrayal not just as murderers, but as *génocidaires*. Representations of genocides other than the Holocaust interact with cultural memories of the Holocaust (or rather, its representation) and (re)produce its genres and topoi: in Astrid Erll's terms, these representations are "premediated" by Holocaust representations (and, as the canon builds and solidifies, representations of other genocides too), and they "remediate" the cultural codes of genocide for their audiences (Erll 2009). Thus, although most mainstream representations of other genocides never make any explicit mention of the Nazis or the Holocaust, replicating the representational framework of mainstream Holocaust film and literature produces what Christoph Classen, in a related context, called an "atmosphere of familiarity" (2009, 91). Classen refers to Spielberg's use of stereotypical scenes and imagery in *Schindler's List* to trigger "effects of recognition" in viewers, "thus helping to stage those images of the film that could not be made available by documentary material that had been passed down" (2009, 91). As anthropologists Andrew Strathern and Pamela Stewart have suggested, representations can resonate with audiences "by appealing to, and conforming with, basic scenarios in people's minds, mental habitūs in the terms of Pierre Bourdieu, connected to cosmic schemes of 'good versus evil' and 'the lessons of history'" (2006, 2). Echoing the "basic scenario" associated with Holocaust perpetrators, then, helps the events to be recognized *as genocide*.

In the following section, I depict the ways in which mainstream representations of genocide use these cultural codes to echo the Holocaust's "basic scenario." First of all, in mainstream genocide films and literature, genocide perpetrators—just like Holocaust perpetrators—are seldom explored in any depth. A few mainstream documentaries and some literature focus on perpetrators (mostly political leaders) (e.g., LeBor 2002; Drakulić 2004; Dunlop 2005; Hatzfeld 2005). Beyond those, genocide perpetrators tend to appear only fleetingly in films and literature, generally in moments where they are needed to fulfill a particular role within the context of the narrative. Here, too, we do not meet the perpetrators in their "pre-genocide" lives—only at moments where they order deportation or killings, where they are patrolling or guarding the victims, or where they are performing brutal acts. As such, they remain distanced and underdeveloped, driving the genocidal process without our having an explanation of *why* or *how*; audiences and readers usually have to fall back onto those cosmic schemes of "good versus evil" or basic understandings of their political ideologies as "extremist" in order to explain the genocide to themselves.

When they do appear, the *génocidaires* are vilified and demonized, both visually and narratively. In a scene in Atom Egoyan's film about the Armenian genocide, *Ararat* (2002), for example, the governor of the city of Van sits at his desk, framed by the flickering light of his fireplace, as he orders one young Armenian boy to be taken away and tortured. In an exchange meant to make clear the "evil" behind the Turks' plans for genocide, he snarls at another Armenian boy, "What is about to happen to your people is your own fault." Similarly, Antonia Arslan, in her novel *Skylark Farm* (2008), adopts the role of omniscient narrator, and imagines a meeting at which Talaat Pasha issues his genocidal instructions—"the plan"—to complicit officials and ideologues, taking pleasure in the trap he has set for the empire's unsuspecting Armenian population (Arslan 2008, 73–5). In Terry George's *Hotel Rwanda* (2004), the figures of Georges Rutaganda and General Bizimungu—an *Interahamwe* leader and the army chief-of-staff respectively—are sly, cunning, and corrupt; Rutaganda's expression and tone are cold and hard when he tells the main protagonist, Paul Rusesabagina, that "Soon, all the Tutsis will be dead." "You do not honestly believe that you can kill them all?" asks Paul, a look of disbelief on his face. "And why not? Why not. We are halfway there already," says Rutaganda, with quiet menace. In literature and films about the wars in the former Yugoslavia, the political and military leaders—Slobodan Milošević, Radovan Karadžić, Ratko Mladić—most often appear at a remove, their words conveyed through TV screens or newspapers into the homes of their victims. Where we do encounter these leaders directly, though, their control of the process is made evident. Leslie Woodhead's 1999 documentary, *A Cry from the Grave*, uses original footage of Mladić and his soldiers entering the enclave of Srebrenica in July 1995—Mladić giving orders, strolling through the emptied streets, and making victory speeches; it is spliced with footage of the distraught refugees being separated from one another and huddling together, frightened, under the watch of the Bosnian Serb soldiers. In this documentary, as in the other films and texts, the leaders are cold and uncompromising, but most importantly, conspiratorial; their direction of and control over the carnage is clear.

Calmly doing the bidding of the genocidal leaders are the soldiers, officers, and political allies who appear in these films and literature as the impassive executioners of the genocidal plan. Like *The Promise*'s Turkish officer who coldly executes the injured prisoner for being a "burden," this archetype tends to act according to an inhuman, exterminatory logic, one that turns morality upside down for readers and viewers. In one of the best-known feature films about Cambodia, Roland Joffé's *The Killing Fields* (1984), the main protagonist (Dith Pran) is confronted by a band of Khmer Rouge children, their expressions taut and accusatory. Like automata, they rip up the small garden he has been growing in order to stave off hunger, and chain him to a tree as punishment for owning private property. In literature and films about Rwanda and Bosnia, often the actions of a neighbor-turned-génocidaire produce the same jolt of understanding—that a lifetime of proximity and friendship has been suddenly superseded by their calculating, dispassionate adherence to the new genocidal order. As Révérien Rurangwa writes in his testimony *Genocide: My Stolen Rwanda* (2009), none of the explanations he can think of—political, economic, or ethnic—

> explain why Simon Sibomana, the Mugina bartender who was well-liked by his clients, transformed himself into a merciless and dedicated killer of every Tutsi who fell into his hands and under his knife—and became the assassin of my family, and of me.
>
> *(Rurangwa 2009, 32)*

For the victims, and the readers or audience, these perpetrators serve to underscore the cruel, determined nature of the genocidal plan, and they also often anchor these "moments of epiphany" (Eaglestone 2008, 82)—the points at which the victims realize the existence and true extent of the plan.

Alternatively, the perpetrators appear in menacing crowds, like the gangs of drunk, whistle-blowing Hutu gathered around roadblocks or storming churches, machetes raised, in films such as *Hotel Rwanda* or Michael Caton-Jones' *Shooting Dogs* (2005). Likewise, almost every foreign correspondent's memoir about the wars in the former Yugoslavia, or feature film based around their experiences, depicts similar roadblocks around the former Yugoslavia, manned by menacing, gun-toting Serbs (e.g., Nicholson 1993, 109; Bell 1996, 101; Winterbottom 1997).[5] In *The Promise*, a Turkish mob rages around the streets of Istanbul, smashing and looting Armenian shops and beating up their owners. Armenian genocide survivors, in their testimonies of forced marches on foot towards the Syrian desert, frequently recount how the weary deportation columns were attacked by groups of Turks, Kurds, or Arabs who looted, killed, and carried off young women and children, while the Turkish gendarmes guarding the Armenian deportees looked on or took their cut (e.g., Panian 2015, 39). If the leaders and their functionaries are typically depicted as coldly detached and in control, these foot soldiers are the purveyors of intimate violence, and they solidify the image of genocide perpetrators as inhuman, evil, and guided by irrational hatreds.

Many films, testimonies, and memoirs explicitly refer to the perpetrators as "evil." "As for the Khmer Rouge soldiers," recounts Cambodian survivor Sokreaksa S. Himm, "we called them 'The Black Evils', because they all wore black clothes. We never saw them as human beings: it seemed to us that they were filled with evil spirits" (2003, 18). Indeed, some films and literature explicitly discuss the disconnect between the "inhuman" actions of the perpetrators, and the witnesses' knowledge that, of course, they *are* human. Roméo Dallaire, the French-Canadian UN General in charge of the peacekeeping mission in Rwanda, draws some of the above elements together in his memoir, *Shake Hands with the Devil.* He recounts his first meeting with the leaders of the *Interahamwe*, a Hutu paramilitary organization that played a key role in the genocide:

> I had made my way to the Diplomates, jostling through the ubiquitous roadblocks, drunken and downright mad militiamen, and hundreds of children jumping around, all excited among today's kills. These kids were being egged on to throw stones at our

> vehicles and yell at us as we stopped for the militiamen to open the gate … Arriving at the hotel, I took the bullets out of my pistol just in case the temptation to shoot them was too extreme, and went inside. The three young men Bagosora introduced me to had no particularly distinguishing features. I think I was expecting frothing at the mouth, but the meeting would be with humans.
>
> *(Dallaire 2004, 85)*

Dallaire's insistence on the contradictory binary of monster/human—which mirrors the common designation of some Holocaust perpetrators as "cultured demons" (Gradowski 1944/1985, 175)—can be read as the beginnings of an attempt to grapple (and ask readers to grapple) with the question of perpetratorhood. But the passage also seems to resonate with other problematic cultural codes, of "African barbarity" and "tribal hatreds"—just as, for example, European notions of the "uncivilized" Balkans often run through foreign correspondents' memoirs of the Yugoslav wars. The BBC correspondent Martin Bell, for example, discusses a litany of abuses perpetrated by the Bosnian Serbs, but nevertheless, "rather to my surprise, I found the Serbs quite easy to like, on a personal and social level, they could be warm-hearted and hospitable and even almost innocent" (Bell 1996, 103). These expressions of surprise, or perplexity, do not really demystify the perpetrators for readers and viewers; instead, they seem to reinforce existing cultural codes that maintain a distance between the perpetrators' mental makeups and our own. We are not usually encouraged to make this imaginative leap, and their motives remain oblique and inexplicable.

In addition to these visual and verbal framings of the perpetrators, the depiction of their acts of violence further distances them. Bosnian survivor Kemal Pervanić recalls, for example, how "the guards at Omarska very quickly turned into beasts, of two breeds": the first would immediately jump on and crush their victims, and the second would toy with and keep their victims alive until the next day (1999, 84). Survivors' testimonial descriptions of the sadistic tortures, cruel beatings, rapes, and indiscriminate killings are often excruciatingly detailed (e.g., Rurangwa 2009, 40–50). Feature films likewise often depict brutal violence, especially killing, as a narrative and emotional climax. Often, though, they conduct such violence off-screen (sometimes within ear-shot) or at a grainy distance—in much the same way as Holocaust films refuse to depict the victims' last moments in the gas chambers. In the aforementioned scene in *Ararat*, for example, the Armenian boy whom the Turkish governor has ordered to be tortured is dragged into another room; we hear only his screams, which punctuate the rest of the governor's hate-filled monologue. *Shooting Dogs*, for example, includes two extremely tense moments when killing occurs, once at a roadblock and once as a Tutsi woman tries to escape across a field. Both times, the white English volunteer schoolteacher Joe stares in horror but looks away at the last moment; instead, the visceral impact of the violence is created by the audio-track and the audience's imagination.

Those films that do not directly depict the killings and massacres instead confront their audiences with the brutal results—the aftermath of a massacre, with piles of bodies or skeletal remains—to demonstrate both the indiscriminate brutality of the genocide and its extent. In *The Promise*, for example, Mikael discovers his entire family and village, massacred together during their deportation, lying in a bloody heap by a river. In this way, audiences of mainstream films and literature tend to encounter perpetrators through their actions or the results of those actions. Most often, the vehicle is a victim or witness, which of course positions the viewer or reader's response. The perpetrators' motives remain incomprehensible, but their plan of mass murder is clear.

Thus, mainstream genocide representations, following Holocaust representations, usually portray the origins and perpetrators of genocide through what I have elsewhere called "closed narratives," which "explain" genocide by demonizing the perpetrators and their actions and occluding the broader social movements and international contexts that contribute to the causal chain of any genocide (Jinks 2016, 67–104). In representations of the Armenian genocide, for example, the crumbling Ottoman Empire, with all its attendant social and economic anxieties, the rise of Turkish exclusivist nationalism, and the crucial context of the First World War are largely absent. With Cambodia, the crucial Cold War context is often overlooked: few representations explain that the Khmer Rouge enjoyed widespread support amongst the Cambodian peasantry because of their anti-American, anti-imperial message, which resonated with those who survived the American carpet-bombing campaign along the Vietnamese border. Likewise, Khmer Rouge nationalism, its search for "organic purity" (Straus 2001), and its escalating military war with Vietnamese forces after 1977—which radicalized the Khmer Rouge's purges of suspected "traitors"—tend to be ignored as explanatory factors in mainstream representations. Representations of the wars in the former Yugoslavia too often rely on notions of "ethnic hatreds" rather than economic and political instability, competing ethnic nationalisms, and aggressive Serb expansionism at the end of the Cold War period. Finally, mainstream representations of Rwanda, too, peddle ideas of ethnic hatred between Hutu and Tutsi, instead of the interlocking broader context of the growing influence of exclusivist nationalist politics, economic and social tensions, the Rwandan Patriotic Front invasion of 1990, and the specter of power-sharing.

Within all of these contexts, most representations also simplify the actors into a clear binary of (powerful) perpetrator and (helpless) victim: representations of genocide in the former Yugoslavia tend to write the Croats out of the story and minimize Bosnian agency; the Rwandan Patriotic Front, the exiled Tutsi forces who invaded Rwanda in 1990 in the hope of forcing the right of return, are also often absent from much of the story, appearing only as they rescued the helpless Tutsi survivors at the end; representations of the Armenian genocide avoid depicting the existence of Armenian nationalist groups before the genocide, who the Turkish authorities feared as a disloyal "fifth column." This simplification avoids the events being understood as a "civil war" or a situation in which the victims could be said to have "provoked" the perpetrators.

Instead, the focus is on the perpetrators and their "plan." In each representation, genocide appears as an inevitable, inexorable event, with its roots in the perpetrators' extreme hatred and political ideologies. The use of foreshadowing—Arslan's description of "the plan" discussed above, for example, or Dallaire's discussion of his meeting with an informant who explains the plans for genocide in Rwanda to him, which are re-enacted in two feature films (Dallaire 2004, 79; George 2004; Spottiswoode 2007)—only heightens the sense of a genocidal blueprint and does nothing to encourage an understanding of the "stages of deliberation," the gradual processes of radicalization, which produce genocide and *génocidaires*. By embodying agency and responsibility in the genocidal leadership and their followers, and suggesting that genocide is the product of abnormal or extreme domestic politics or "ethnic hatreds," these representations distance genocide and *génocidaires* from "normal" society and are unable to show that genocide is the product of very ordinary structures of human society, in extraordinary combinations.

The Holocaust's "basic scenario," then, has proved to be a very potent representational structure for authors and filmmakers who seek to portray genocide—whether the events they depict took place in the Ottoman Empire more than a century ago, Rwanda a few decades ago, or indeed more recently. These cultural codes seem to have solidified over the

1990s and early 2000s—the period during which Holocaust memory "boomed," the genocides in Rwanda and Bosnia took place, and a significant number of representations of the Holocaust and other genocides were released (which deploy these codes). Later representations, including of more recent atrocities and genocides, also use this representational framework: certainly, it is evident in many of the activist literature and films about Darfur that were released in the mid-to-late 2000s, after the violence had reached its height. Each seeks, very explicitly, to have the violence against Darfuris recognized as a genocide, in the hope of galvanizing public attention and international action (Cheadle and Prendergast 2007; Steidle and Steidle Wallace 2007; Boll 2009).[6] Besides documenting the devastation of villages, and the impact upon the victims, these films and literature often portray the infamous Janjaweed and the Government of Sudan military forces in very familiar terms. In literature, such as Brian Steidle's memoir *The Devil Came on Horseback* (2007) or Uwe Boll's film *Darfur* (2009), the Janjaweed appear as a crowd of figures, wrapped in scarves, speeding on horseback, who descend upon villages and leave a trail of burning huts and dead bodies in their wake. The Government of Sudan officers, like other mid-level functionaries, are cold and obstructive and lie to journalists and peacekeeping forces about their movements and responsibility for attacks (e.g., Steidle and Steidle Wallace 2007, 73–4). Again, the broader historical context is often ignored and the state of civil war with the Sudan Liberation Army sidelined. But crucially, most literature and films about Darfur are careful to emphasize the coordinated, planned nature of the attacks and explicitly cite this—as well as the indiscriminate killings—as qualifying the attacks as genocide (Cheadle and Prendergast 2007, 3–6; Steidle and Steidle Wallace 2007, xvii). As Steidle, who was an African Union observer in Darfur, put it after describing the aftermath of an attack on an IDP camp: "I was convinced: this was ethnic cleansing. This was genocide. There was no other way to describe it." He continues:

> From the way the witnesses described it, the attack appeared to be a well-coordinated military offensive … this meant that the Janjaweed nomads had been well trained and were using a system of command and control in their attacks. These Arab militias appeared to enjoy a much deeper relationship with the GOS than I first realized.
>
> *(Steidle and Steidle Wallace 2007, 79)*

Thus, the representational framework for genocide perpetrators that has evolved out of Holocaust representations has been a powerful tool for those seeking to represent "the Darfur crisis" as genocide. Much the same could be said for the current atrocities against the Rohingya in Myanmar; the 2013 Al Jazeera documentary, *Myanmar: The Hidden Genocide*, likewise interweaves footage of the perpetrators burning, looting, pillaging, and killing and the inflammatory words of Myanmar's political and Buddhist leaders, with interviews with the victims, in order to make its case. The consolidation of this representational framework is clear, but it has serious consequences for those cases of genocides that do not "fit" this mold. The clearest examples are colonial genocides of indigenous peoples, which have usually taken place over decades or centuries (rather than concentrated periods of killing), often involving the assimilation (biological and/or cultural) of indigenous peoples, as well as their murder; states have often been able to cast themselves as pursuing benevolent or developmental goals, not destructive ones (see Moses 2004; Hitchcock and Koperski 2008; Bodley 2015). It is far more difficult to frame the perpetrators of these genocides as pursuing a plan for the destruction of a victim group. This is especially true in settler colonial cases like Australia and North America, where mainstream representations rarely question the legitimacy of the colonizing project itself, and representations of indigenous communities often presented them as living in a timeless (and futureless) past, outside their historical, geographical, and cultural context, and as a "dying race," where no perpetrator is needed to effect destruction (e.g., Buscombe 2006; Raheja 2011). Only a few films and literary works—such as Ralph Nelson's film *Soldier Blue* (1970)—focus on particular massacre *as a massacre* and attempt to call into question the settlers' treatment of, and relationship with, indigenous communities.

The chronologically later policies of the assimilation of children resonate even less with the mainstream representational framework of genocide. In Australia, for example, between the early 1900s and the 1970s, the government pursued a policy of the removal of Aboriginal and part-Aboriginal children from their families; they were sent to children's homes or adopted by white families in order to facilitate the biological and cultural absorption of Aboriginals into white settler society (Moses 2004). The insistence that this was done for "benevolent," "civilizing" reasons (rather than the forcible destruction of a group identity) and the lack of an outright policy of murder means that film and literature cannot meet the "basic scenario" outlined above. In Philip Noyce's film *Rabbit Proof Fence* (2002)—which traces the stories of three girls who were removed from their families in 1931 and escape and try to return home—the Chief Protector of Aborigines, A.O. Neville (played by Kenneth Branagh) certainly has some of the qualities of the cold, driven perpetrator and is unequivocally paternalistic and racist. But the policies he is doing his best to implement do not resonate with the "basic scenario" of genocide, and the film's core focus is—rightly—on the girls' stories of escape and dogged determination to return home.

Thus, the solidification of this "basic scenario" of genocide and genocide perpetrators—which rests upon the cultural codes used to represent Holocaust perpetrators—enables an "atmosphere of familiarity" to pervade representations of genocide. In reproducing its structures, perpetrators are cemented as perpetrators of *genocide* rather than atrocity. But these cultural codes also actively exclude other genocides, which cannot fit this mold, from being "familiar" and from being recognized as cases of genocide as easily. Equally problematic in these mainstream representations is the simplified, distortive portrayal of the perpetrators of genocide, who are cast as "abnormal" and utterly unlike "us." But perhaps mainstream representations of other genocides will begin to follow the lead of some more recent and striking representations of the Holocaust and of other genocides: those that focus in greater and revealing depth on the perpetrators, including their often strikingly unexceptional paths to becoming *génocidaires* (Dragojević 1996; Peck 2005; Sambath and Lemkin 2010; Bizot 2011; see Jinks 2016).

Notes

1 Most Armenians were killed in or near their homes or deported on foot to the desert. However, thousands of Armenians who lived in the vicinity of the Berlin-Baghdad railway were deported by train (Kaiser 1998). Terry George also directed *Hotel Rwanda* (2004), and critics noted certain (narrative) similarities to Steven Spielberg's *Schindler's List* (1993). Perhaps not unconnectedly, in *The Promise*, Mikael only notices that the carriages are full of Armenians when it begins raining, and they cry out for water, trying to catch it through the wooden slats. This scene bears more than a passing resemblance to Oskar Schindler cajoling Amon Goeth to "indulge me" in hosing the sides of a waiting cattle car full of Jews, who were crying out for water.

2 The film performed badly at the box office, but as the studio noted, the film's backers wanted to raise awareness of the Armenian genocide, not earn money. www.reuters.com/article/us-usa-boxoffice/fate-of-the-furious-stays-on-top-unforgettable-the-promise-bomb-idUSKBN17P0NZ

3 In this way, representations follow the UN Genocide Convention (1948) in emphasizing "intent," although they also emphasize *mass killing*, which is not a prerequisite: genocide involves the intent

to destroy a group, but this can also be achieved, for example, by causing serious bodily or mental harm to members of the group or forcibly transferring children to another group. I discuss the implication of the overwhelming focus on mass killing towards the end of this chapter.

4 The films *Good* (2008), dir. Vicente Amorim and *Amen* (2002), dir. Costa-Gavras, are interesting exceptions. Both depict the gradual transformation of "ordinary men" who become swept up in, and complicit with, the Nazi regime.

5 E.g., Martin Bell, *In Harm's Way: Reflections of a War-Zone Thug* (London: Penguin, 1996), p. 101; Martin Nicholson, *Natasha's Story* (London: Macmillan, 1993), p. 109. Michael Winterbottom's film *Welcome to Sarajevo* (1997) is based on Nicholson's *Natasha's Story*, and includes such stereotypical roadblock scenes.

6 For a critical perspective on activist responses to Darfur, see Lanz (2009).

References

Adams, Jenni & Sue Vice (eds.). 2013. *Representing Perpetrators in Holocaust Literature and Film*. Edgware: Vallentine Mitchell.

Al Jazeera. 2013. *Myanmar: The Hidden Genocide*. YouTube, 30 October. https://youtu.be/dSkZlgk76-E.

Arslan, Antonia. 2008. *Skylark Farm: A Novel*. London: Atlantic Books.

Bangert, Axel, Robert S. C. Gordon, & Libby Saxton, (eds.). 2013. *Holocaust Intersections: Genocide and Visual Culture at the New Millennium*. London: Legenda.

Bell, Martin. 1996. *In Harm's Way: Reflections of a War-Zone Thug*. London: Penguin.

Bizot, François. 2011. *Facing the Torturer: Inside the Mind of a War Criminal*. Translated by C. Mandell and A. Audouard. London: Rider.

Bodley, John. H. 2015. *Victims of Progress*. Lanham: Rowman & Littlefield.

Boll, Uwe. (Dir.). 2009. *Darfur*. DVD. Germany: VG Medienproduktions GmbH.

Boyne, John. 2006. *The Boy in the Striped Pajamas*. Oxford: David Fickling.

Brown, Adam. 2011. "Screening Women's Complicity in the Holocaust: The Problems of Judgement and Representation." *Holocaust Studies* 17(2-3): 75–98.

Buettner, Angi. 2011. *Holocaust Images and Picturing Catastrophe: The Cultural Politics of Seeing*. Farnham: Ashgate.

Buscombe, Edward. 2006. *'Injuns!': Native Americans in the Movies*. London: Reaktion Books.

Caton-Jones, Michael. (Dir.). 2005. *Shooting Dogs*. DVD. UK: BBC Films.

Çetin, Fethiye. 2008. *My Grandmother: A Memoir*. London: Verso.

Cheadle, Don & John Prendergast. 2007. *Not On Our Watch: The Mission to End Genocide in Darfur and Beyond*. New York: Hyperion.

Classen, Christoph. 2009. "Balanced Truth: Steven Spielberg's *Schindler's List* among History, Memory, and Popular Culture." *History and Theory* 48(2): 77–102.

Dallaire, Roméo. 2004. *Shake Hands with the Devil: The Failure of Humanity in Rwanda*. London: Arrow Books.

Dragojević, Srdjan. (Dir.). 1996. *Pretty Village, Pretty Flame*. DVD. Serbia: Cobra Films.

Drakulić, Slavenka. 2004. *They Would Never Hurt a Fly: War Criminals on Trial in the Hague*. London: Abacus.

Dunlop, Nic. 2005. *The Lost Executioner: A Story of the Khmer Rouge*. London: Bloomsbury.

Eaglestone, Robert. 2008. "'You Would Not Add to My Suffering If You Knew What I Had Seen': Holocaust Testimony and Contemporary African Trauma Literature." *Studies in the Novel* 40(1&2): 72–85.

Egoyan, Atom. (Dir.). 2002. *Ararat*. DVD. Canada: Serendipity Point Films.

Erll, Astrid. 2009. "Remembering across Time, Space, and Cultures: Premediation Remediation and the 'Indian Mutiny'." In *Mediation, Remediation, and the Dynamics of Cultural Memory*, edited by Astrid Erll and Ann Rigney, in collaboration with Laura Basu and Paulus Bijl, 109–138. Berlin/New York: Walter de Gruyter.

George, Terry. (Dir.). 2004. *Hotel Rwanda*. DVD. USA: Lionsgate.

George, Terry. (Dir.). 2017. *The Promise*. DVD. USA: Universal Pictures.

Gradowski, Zalman. 1985. *Scrolls of Auschwitz*, edited by Ber Mark. Tel Aviv: Am Oved.

Hatzfeld, Jean. 2005. *A Time for Machetes. The Rwandan Genocide: The Killers Speak*. In *Translated by Linda Coverdale*. London: Serpent's Tail.

Herman, Mark. (Dir.). 2008. *The Boy in the Striped Pajamas*. DVD. USA: Lionsgate.

Himm, Sokreaksa S. 2003. *The Tears of My Soul*. Oxford: Monarch Books.

Hitchcock, Robert K. & Thomas E. Koperski. 2008. "Genocides of Indigenous Peoples." In *The Historiography of Genocide*, edited by Dan Stone, 577–617. Basingstoke: Palgrave Macmillan.

Jinks, Rebecca. 2016. *Representing Genocide: The Holocaust as Paradigm?* London: Bloomsbury.

Joffé, Roland. 1984. *The Killing Fields*. DVD. Dir. Roland Joffé. USA: Optimum Releasing.

Kaiser, Hilmar. 1998. "The Baghdad Railway and the Armenian Genocide, 1915-1916." In *Remembrance and Denial: The Case of the Armenian Genocide*, edited by Richard G. Hovannisian, 67–112. Detroit: Wayne State University Press.

Khardalian, Suzanne & Per-Åke Holmquist. (Dir.). 2011. *Grandma's Tattoos*. DVD. USA: Cinema Guild.

Lanz, David. 2009. "Save Darfur: A Movement and its Discontents." *African Affairs* 108: 669–677.

LeBor, Adam. 2002. *Milosevic: A Biography*. London: Bloomsbury.

MacDonald, David B. 2008. *Identity Politics in the Age of Genocide: The Holocaust and Historical Representation*. Abingdon: Routledge.

Montgomery, Scott L. 1995. "What Kind of Memory? Reflections on Images of the Holocaust." *Contention* 5(1): 71–104.

Moses, A. Dirk. (ed.). 2004. *Genocide and Settler Society: Frontier Violence and Stolen Indigenous Children in Australian History*. New York: Berghahn.

Nelson, Ralph. (Dir.). 1970. *Soldier Blue*. DVD. USA: Universal Pictures.

Nicholson, Martin. 1993. *Natasha's Story*. London: Macmillan.

Noyce, Phillip. (Dir.). 2002. *Rabbit Proof Fence*. DVD. USA: Miramax.

Panian, Karnig. 2015. *Goodbye, Antoura: A Memoir of the Armenian Genocide*. Stanford: Stanford University Press.

Peck, Raoul. (Dir.). 2005. *Sometimes in April*. DVD. USA: HBO Films.

Pervanić, Kemal. 1999. *The Killing Days: My Journey through the Bosnian War*. London: Blake Publishing.

Pettitt, Joanne. 2018. "Memory and Genocide in Graphic Novels: The Holocaust as Paradigm." *Journal of Graphic Novels and Comics* 9(2): 173–186.

Picart, Caroline Joan (Kay) S. & David A. Frank. 2006. *Frames of Evil: The Holocaust as Horror in American Film*. Carbondale: Southern Illinois University Press.

Raheja, Michelle H. 2011. *Reservation Reelism: Redfacing, Visual Sovereignty, and Representations of Native Americans in Film*. Lincoln: University of Nebraska Press.

Rothberg, Michael. 2009. *Multidirectional Memory: Remembering the Holocaust in the Age of Decolonization*. Stanford: Stanford University Press.

Rurangwa, Révérien. 2009. *Genocide: My Stolen Rwanda*. Translated by Anna Brown. London: Reportage Press.

Sambath, Thet & Rob Lemkin. 2010. *Enemies of the People*. DVD. Dir. Thet Sambath and Rob Lemkin. UK: Old Street Films.

Shafak, Elif. 2007. *The Bastard of Istanbul: A Novel*. London: Penguin.

Spottiswoode, Roger. (Dir.). 2007. *Shake Hands with the Devil*. DVD. USA: Head Gear Films.

Steidle, Brian & Gretchen Steidle Wallace. 2007. *The Devil Came on Horseback: Bearing Witness to the Genocide in Darfur*. New York: PublicAffairs.

Steinweis, Alan E. 2005. "The Auschwitz Analogy: Holocaust Memory and American Debates over Intervention in Kosovo and Bosnia in the 1990s." *Holocaust and Genocide Studies* 19(2): 276–289.

Strathern, Andrew & Pamela J. Stewart. 2006. "Introduction: Terror, the Imagination, and Cosmology." In *Terror and Violence: Imagination and the Unimaginable*, edited by Andrew Strathern, Pamela J. Stewart, and Neil L. Whitehead, 1–39. London: Pluto.

Straus, Scott. 2001. "Organic Purity and the Role of Anthropology in Cambodia and Rwanda." *Patterns of Prejudice* 35(2): 47–62.

Winterbottom, Michael. (Dir.). 1997. *Welcome to Sarajevo*. DVD. UK: Miramax.

Woodhead, Leslie. (Dir.). 1999. *A Cry from the Grave*. DVD. UK: Antelope Productions.

29

Playing Perpetrators

Interrogating Evil in Videogames about Violent Conflicts

Holger Pötzsch and Emil Lundedal Hammar

Introduction

This contribution interrogates the figure of the perpetrator[1] as it emerges in narrative videogames. First, we provide a brief outlook on some key characteristics of videogames, before we discuss how the specific affordances of this "new" medium offer unprecedented ways of approaching and dealing with perpetrators and perpetration. Finally, we offer concrete examples from three games to illustrate different possible configurations of the player-perpetrator nexus—Yager Development's *Spec Ops: The Line* (2012), 11 Bit Studio's *This War of Mine* (2015), and Hangar 13's *Mafia III* (2016). In contrast to other media, games enable an active exploration of, and participation in, a variety of possible offenses. Rather than merely witnessing evil deeds, players are immersed in simulated environments that demand constant evaluations of complex settings and require decision-making under systemic limitations. This performative aspect of play makes games a unique medium for learning and teaching about the intricate logics and innate dynamics of perpetrations.

Videogames and Play: Some Basic Considerations

Compared to other media, videogames have a rather short history. Invented in the late 1960s with financial support from the military and quickly spreading throughout IT environments, especially at US universities and colleges, it gradually became clear that this technology had significant potential economic value as a new segment of the entertainment industry (Kline, Dyer-Witheford & de Peuter 2003, in particular Chapter 4; Egenfeldt-Nielsen, Smith & Pajares-Tosca 2013, in particular Chapter 4). The first commercially successful applications were developed from the 1970s onward. Today, this technology is one of the most important and profitable branches of an increasingly global entertainment sector (Kerr 2017). Blockbuster games, so-called AAA titles, require funding and resources equal to major Hollywood productions, and they reach equally broad audiences (Nieborg 2011). However, while a film is watched for the usual 90 to 180 minutes, videogames require the full dedication and concentration of players for tens if not hundreds of hours each. These differences in use and reception compared to other media have given rise to speculations about potential unprecedented impacts of games on individuals and society (Anderson, Barlett, & Swing 2009)[2] and have spawned hopes for improvements in education, work motivation, and more (McGonigal 2011).[3] Against this background, we will here briefly highlight what is new and what remains the same regarding a transition from film to games as the leading entertainment medium in what has been termed *the ludic century* (Zimmerman 2013).

Games tell stories. Similar to other media such as novels, films, or plays, videogames convey narratives. Every experience of play can be rendered in terms of a fundamental plot structure featuring such basic elements as protagonist, antagonist, challenge, and outcome, among others (Mukherjee 2015). However, in addition to this, games enable, and indeed require, actions and decisions—an active involvement of players who maneuver the various challenges and possibilities posed by the game space in a more or less conscious and reflected manner. Players directly configure the story told (Aarseth 1997; Murray 1997). Consequently, not only the digital devices through which a particular video game tells its—more or less sophisticated—story become crucial objects of inquiry in games research, but also the way player action and interaction with diegetic worlds, characters, and events is predisposed and limited are important areas of scrutiny (Aarseth 2001; Bogost 2007; Jørgensen 2012). Aarseth (1997) has therefore termed videogames *ergodic*—in contrast to literature or film, they require *non-trivial effort* via concrete player input and decisions.

This contribution deals with a specific genre of games, namely narrative historical games that play out in plausible and realistic diegetic worlds.[4] As such, our inquiry excludes merely skill-based games such as *Tetris* (Pajitnov and Pokhilko 1984) or *Pong* (Alcorn 1974) that almost exclusively center upon senso-motoric challenges and only present a very minimal narrative to frame game play. Our selection also excludes various types of historical strategy games, since these tend to focus on the simulation of large-scale processes in an accentuated top-down perspective, thereby directing attention away from situated individual historical experiences and responsibilities (Chapman 2016, 69). This is not to say that such games do not tell stories. Rudimentary as they might be, they of course do. Our interest, however, lies with games that convey complex narratives with a wide set of characters, a plausible world, and designed affordances allowing players to configure and partly determine the course of in-game events, including responses to ethical challenges, thus gradually forming the emergent narrative from the bottom-up. Within this topic, we focus on how a selection of narrative games frames possible player engagements with perpetrators and their deeds and how they can enable players to themselves step into the shoes of what appears to be an evildoer.

Being a significant cultural form, the ways videogames frame both imagined and actual perpetration and perpetrators matters. As Payne (2016) asserts, there is a dialectical relationship among games, players, and the social world, and the dominant meaning potentials offered by them provide important points of orientation, in particular for young people starting to maneuver through the complex terrains of contemporary politics and historical discourses. Mainstream culture, including games, offers a pervasive background of meaning that implicitly assigns plausibility to certain political or historical narratives and that de-legitimizes and marginalizes others (Artz 2015; Mukherjee 2018). As Pötzsch (2013, 2017) has shown, in delivering quickly applicable paradigm scenarios and schemata, mainstream films and games contribute to the formation and reproduction of cross-generic frames of war in the sense of Butler (2009) that abet the tacit justification of real-world violence and exclusion with reference to largely imagined or narrowly framed imageries of perpetrators and perpetration. Therefore, these cultural forms merit our continued critical attention.

Perpetrators in Videogames

The usual perpetrator of mainstream narrative games has the function of a one-dimensional antagonist in a dichotomous moral universe. Often, specific historical settings serve as mere props, as suitable backgrounds for conventional narratives to unfold, and as marketing ploys allowing for a commodification of history for Western audiences (Hammar 2017a). Similar to Hollywood story templates, the arch enemies of major digital game franchises are deployed with the objective of personifying evil and, thereby, enabling its ultimate demise by the hand of a benevolent main protagonist. To enable the moral disengagement of players—that, according to Hartmann and Vorderer (2010) is a condition for entertaining play—the main adversary is usually presented as directly responsible for some atrocious act that has been, or might be, carried out. The planned or actualized perpetration is of such a malignant quality that it implicitly justifies all the, usually grossly violent, means applied by the player-protagonist to stop it. By means of the structural trope of this evil deed, the story universe is disambiguated assigning clear roles of good and evil to the two factions involved in the conflict playing out on screen (in both film and games) (Pötzsch 2013; Hartmann et al. 2014).

To provide a few examples, the main adversary of the popular first-person shooter *Call of Duty: Black Ops* (Treyarch 2010) plans a devastating chemical attack on the US mainland, while the fifth entry in the highly popular organized crime series *Grand Theft Auto* depicts the antagonist as a ruthless corrupt FBI agent who forces the player-protagonists to kidnap, torture, and assassinate various characters for the ultimately benevolent objective of eradicating the main adversary and avoiding even greater evil. In both cases, the narrative frame justifies severely violent acts committed by the player-controlled main protagonist, including the eradication of the game's antagonist. Common to shooter games, key devices invite moral disengagement and transform non-player characters into virtual puppets without emotion or legitimate agency.[5]

Some games have successfully played with and somewhat expanded the genre conventions identified above by for instance enforcing a reversal of sides of player-directed characters suddenly making them realize that they have fought for the "wrong" side. This move, however, does not really re-ambiguate the dichotomous moral universe characteristic of most mainstream historical games since the new perpetrators retain the same structural qualities as their predecessors, as such making them fulfill the same overarching function in the narrative—moral disengagement as a condition for pleasurable violent play. Even forced to realize that a change of sides is required, players still retain moral superiority through the implicit framing of their struggle as doubtlessly benign and directed against a de-legitimized enemy posing an immediate and clearly defined threat.

A challenge for education in and through games is the wide dissemination of such disambiguated moral universes throughout virtually all the most popular titles of the medium. In constantly reiterating the benign qualities and ultimate necessity of grossly violent approaches to conflict resolution, and in putting players in control of usually white, male characters who resolve all contradictions and "save the day" by simply eradicating evil, most mainstream games neatly align with simplifying narratives dominating mainstream political discourse, in particular in the US. As such, the "cross-generic metascript" of war and action movies identified by Pötzsch (2013, 140) extends into the medium of digital games and increases its potential impact by pre-structuring not only the perceptions but also the actions and decisions of mass audiences.

Playing with, against, and as the Perpetrator

Things, however, can always be done differently. Surprisingly enough, some game titles that fundamentally challenged and discarded many conventions of the genre became relatively economically successful and culturally influential. Transgressing the frames of mainstream entertainment can, at times, be both profitable and aesthetically attractive even though the actual experience of play in these cases often is described as frustrating, difficult, or hurting or similar ranges of what Jørgensen (2016) refers to as "positive discomfort." The following sections will examine three such titles: Yager Development's *Spec Ops: The Line* (2012), 11 Bit Studio's *This War of Mine* (2015), and Hangar 13's *Mafia III* (2016). Particular attention will be directed to how these games, at the levels of narrative and game mechanics, invite play with and reflection about perpetrators and their potential roles in discourses about conflicts. By way of a conclusion, we will briefly outline possible potentials for applications of these titles in formal and informal education.

The Absent Perpetrator: Reconfiguring the Player–Hero Relation in *Spec Ops: The Line*

Spec Ops: *The Line* is a third-person tactical shooter videogame released by German developer Yager in 2012. It is the last in a series of nine games forming the Spec Ops franchise. From the outset, Yager's title seems to follow its predecessors and offers what appears to be a fairly conventional shooter experience. Brief cut scenes initiate and drive forward a narrative that is intersected by map-based fighting sequences where players have to shoot one-dimensional opponents. The narrative is tightly structured, leaving players with mainly battle-related tactical choices.

The story plays out in a fictitious, yet plausible, setting. The town of Dubai has been swallowed by a giant sand storm, and Colonel John Konrad's battalion is sent on a relief mission into the devastated city. When complications arise, Konrad defies orders from the US military to retreat and instead attempts to establish order with increasingly harsh measures that eventually cause an uprising among some of his soldiers. The CIA-facilitated attempt to topple Konrad apparently fails, and the only message penetrating the storm wall around Dubai is a repeated signal stating that Konrad's attempt to evacuate civilians ended in disaster. Players then take control of Captain Martin Walker, who leads a three-man spec ops team into the city to look for possible survivors and report.

From the beginning, players come under heavy fire from unidentified sources. Game mechanics make an exchange of bullets and other violent actions the only possible way to interact with diegetic environments. Dialogues and decision-making beyond mere tactical choices are largely scripted, limiting player freedom to determine the course of events. However, what from the outset appears like familiar shooter mechanics eventually evolves into a neat commentary on genre conventions and the role and responsibilities of players as political subjects (Keogh 2012, 2013; Heron and Belford 2014; Pötzsch 2017, 2019). This has led Keogh (2012, 4) to paraphrase the game as "a shooter about shooters." In *Spec Ops: The Line*, a lack of genuine player choice enables critical reflection on the player-perpetrator nexus.

As the game progresses, player character Martin Walker changes mission objectives and allegiances with increasing frequency and ease. What began as a mere recon mission gradually transforms into an operation with the aim of finding and eliminating what is presented as the main perpetrator of the game, John Konrad. To achieve this aim, Captain Walker and his players are forced to accept a series of negative consequences, unintended side-effects, and outright blow backs created by Walker's idiosyncratic leadership and decision-making style. The main protagonist appears increasingly wretched and worn, the relation to his companions strained, and his commands transforming from a calm conversational tone to aggressive barks. By such means, the game repeatedly signals a worsening condition of Walker and forces players to interrogate the meaningfulness of his decisions. However, players intent on completing the game have no option but to accept Walker's decisions and follow his lead.

As the narrative unfolds, *Spec Ops: The Line* gradually estranges players from both the player character and the events on screen. Chapter 8, titled *The Gate*, can be seen as a climax in this manner. Here, Walker decides against the will of his companions to use a drone to clear a town square guarded by US soldiers operating under Konrad. The drone fires white phosphorous, and the game map is cleared very quickly and with apparent ease. When passing through the gate, however, the game suddenly disables the running mechanic forcing players to walk slowly through the destruction they caused and to witness the horrible consequences of the weapon they used. At first, Walker and his players encounter burned and badly wounded US soldiers begging to be killed. Then, he learns that only about half of the dots identified through the drone sight were combatants with the entire rear area sheltering civilians. In particular, one image—the burned remains of a mother desperately trying to protect her child—invites very strong emotional responses from players who by then have to acknowledge their complicity in, if not outright responsibility for, the atrocity.

In the aftermath of *The Gate*, the game subtly changes. In deploying devices that directly address players, *Spec Ops: The Line* creates a Brechtian V-effect (Pötzsch 2019) to destroy the immersive illusion of the game, thereby directly connecting in-game actions and decisions to wider socio-political frames. When traversing into new areas, a complex game such as *Spec Ops: The Line* needs to load new data. On such occasions, a loading screen appears that usually offers advice on controller configurations or the game world with the objective of smoothing play and improving the immersive qualities of the experience. After the incidents at the gate, in *Spec Ops: The Line*, the quality of these messages changes. Now, the game directly addresses the player not as a ludic, but *as political subject* (Pötzsch 2019) and poses intrusive questions inviting, and increasingly demanding, critical introspection: *Do you feel like a hero, yet? The US military does not condone the killing of civilians, but why should you care? Nothing of this would have happened if you had just stopped.* The "you" in the sentences above refers to both the player character Walker and the players controlling his behavior in combat but otherwise blindly following his lead throughout the narrative. The decision to stop playing as such emerges as the only possible ethical choice enabled by the game. In Heron and Belford's (2014, 18) words, the loading screens "begin to deconstruct your relationship with the game and the extent to which you can declaim responsibility for the very act of playing." The game "deprives us [the players] of narrative or ludic justification" for our deeds (19). Or, as Keogh (2012, 7) puts it in his seminal work on Yager's title, even though the game does not allow for other than merely tactical choices, "the player is still responsible for these [Walker's] actions *because* of the one choice the player did make: to play the game in the first place" (emphasis in original).

In the end, Walker and his players learn the ultimate truth. What the game had consistently framed as the main adversary and supreme perpetrator of the story universe, John Konrad has been dead for a long time. His voice emanating from Walker's intercom is revealed as a mere hallucination caused by post-traumatic stress disorder. After this shocking discovery, a series of flashback sequences re-contextualizes past apparently heroic achievements and reframes them as the brutal actions of a massively violent character who gradually loses his mind. Players remain complicit in and, through their unwillingness to stop playing, ultimately responsible for these atrocious acts. This sudden turn of events enables critical reflections on the role of perpetrators in this game and in the discourse of popular cultural presentations of war and violent conflict more generally.

Who is the perpetrator in *Spec Ops: The Line*? Initially, the game elegantly lures players into accepting the received subject position of the apparently classical hero Walker as the moral center of the game universe and opposes him to a generic evil guy hiding out in some tower to be reached and wiped out. Gradually, however, this clear dichotomy is questioned and finally dissolves, but not to be replaced by a different configuration that is equally dichotomous. Rather, in subtly subverting established conventions of the shooter genre, the game makes precisely these conventions—both at the level of narrative and mechanics—its explicit theme and transforms the received subject positions implied by shooter games into an object of critical reflection.

Becoming Evil: Complicating Perpetration in *This War of Mine*

While *Spec Ops: The Line* critically interrogates genre conventions and a player-perpetrator nexus, the next game under scrutiny in this chapter enables an investigation into what perpetrations are and how they come about. Does war make everyone a (potential) perpetrator?

11 Bit Studios' *This War of Mine* is a simulation and resource-management game centering on the struggle of a group of civilians attempting to survive a violent conflict in a non-specific Eastern European urban setting. According to the developers, the game was inspired by an autobiography detailing childhood memories from the siege of Sarajevo in the mid-1990s but refrains from overtly connecting its setting to the Yugoslavian civil war (Smale, Kors, & Sandovar 2017). Even though difficult to play and frustrating, the game has been an economic success (Handrahan 2014) and has received praise by critics (Opencritic 2014). It is an outspoken anti-war game that issues a critical message on the devastating consequences of violent conflict (Kwiatkowski 2016).

Gameplay in *This War of Mine* is divided into day mode and night mode. During days, players can build items, produce or trade goods, and rest or heal the different characters they oversee. During the night, one character can be selected to scavenge nearby areas to acquire resources. The others can either sleep or guard the shelter. As the game progresses, weather becomes gradually worse and available resources quickly deplete. This forces players to take greater risks and requires increasingly difficult ethical decisions regarding challenges such as how to acquire vital goods or how to respond to other characters in danger or need. The areas open for scavenging that still hold resources become gradually more inaccessible and more dangerous to traverse. At the same time, temperatures drop, the shelter is raided, and characters become sick, depressed, or are wounded requiring expensive medical treatment. Exposed to such multiple strains, ethical and moral standards become increasingly difficult to uphold, and a quick raid of a defenseless old couple still retaining food and medicine suddenly appears a viable option to feed a starving character or keep the shelter safe and warm at night.

Through its complex choice-consequence architecture, the game articulates a systemic understanding of evil in war. This means that committed atrocities are not due to the malignant intentions of a particular individual who can be disposed of by a classical hero. Rather, evil acts are the inevitable result of war as a systemic pattern of supports and restraints that gradually reduces the paradigm of actions available to any subject involved until everyone, including the player character, can take only inherently unethical and immoral decisions with the simple objective to survive yet another bleak day. By these means, the game fundamentally undermines received conventions of the war genre that usually present violent conflict as an arena for heroism and bravery.

This subversion of the classic hero is strongly articulated in one nightly scavenging sequence in a derelict supermarket. Spying through a keyhole, the player character observes a scene playing out between a soldier and a young woman. Body language, gestures, and parts of dialogue clearly indicate that a rape is about to take place. The setting deliberately plays on players' received expectations of being able to heroically step in and save the girl. However, due to complicated combat mechanics and an incapability of most characters to fight (they are civilians), by far most attempts to save the girl will inevitably end in death or severe injury. War is thus brought to emerge as a bleak frame disabling heroism, mastery, and received fantasies of power and saviordom.

Regarding the figure of the perpetrator, *This War of Mine* articulates the simple but important fact that in times of war everybody gradually turns into a perpetrator. Once a lack of resources and the sufferings of one's own become dominant, the threshold of what are ethically and morally acceptable means to survive gradually moves, thus turning once-brave players into thieves, thugs, and cowards. Despite this grim realism, the game also enables genuine ethical decision-making where players can choose to help others. These deeds, however, are not rewarded by the mechanical system as such providing no new perks or goods, but always imply costs in terms of security, resources, or characters' work-time. Heroism is possible but implies severe risks and few material rewards.

With *This War of Mine,* 11 Bit Studios fundamentally reconfigures received pop-cultural frames turning war from a schematic arena for heroic exchanges of bullets between male combatants to a complex political economy in contingent ethical terrains. In this process, the game disperses the concept of the perpetrator and slowly extends it to potentially anyone attempting to survive the conditions of severe precarity inherent in any war situation. The decision by the developers to refrain from overtly referring to the Yugoslavian civil war strongly articulates this general outlook on the intricate logics of violent conflict. When seen from the vantage point of *This War of Mine,* war itself and by extension those responsible for it emerge as the ultimate perpetrator, somewhat alleviating the individual thug, thief, soldier, and murderer by pointing to the external conditions enforcing such actions for the sake of mere survival.

By these means, the game does not absolve individual characters and their players of responsibility for their decisions. Rather, it teaches how perpetrations come about and how they are motivated and justified. By these means, *This War of Mine* enables a critical interrogation of received mainstream notions positing the eradication of evil guys as the most salient solution to all kinds of conflicts. The game opens a problem space that forces players to actively maneuver complex socio-political settings and allows them to directly experience the consequences of their decisions under conditions of precarity—including inevitably failing attempts to precisely *play* the hero.

The Perpetrator as Liberal Hero? Narrative and Game Mechanics of Crime in *Mafia III*

Our last example is the historical action-game *Mafia III* that re-centers the figure of the perpetrator within a revenge-fantasy contextualized by US white supremacy in a fictional rendition of 1960s New Orleans. Developed by the California-based Hangar 13 studio in collaboration with the Czech studio 2K, *Mafia III* belongs to the so-called open-world action genre, where players find themselves in a limited but relatively open virtual space. Players control the main protagonist who can enter into dialogues with other characters, move around the game world, or engage in combat.

Mafia III puts players in control of Lincoln Clay, a black Vietnam veteran who returns from the war to help his surrogate crime family survive under harsh conditions. After a short tutorial, the narrative catapults players into violent action, when the local mafia turns on and brutally kills Clay's surrogate family—the ultimate evil deed of the game motivating subsequent player violence. *Mafia III* is an iteration of a classic organized crime narrative, in which the masculine protagonist is bereft of family and dignity to prepare the grounds for an enjoyable later revenge executed through extreme violence and domination. The Italian Mafia's evil deed constitutes a powerful moral disengagement device that alleviates moral concerns of players doling out violence on other characters for entertainment.

Unusual for a multi-million dollar production such as *Mafia III*, the game puts racism and racist practices at the forefront of its narrative and lets a black player character successfully take action against it. Already in the opening scenes of the game, the developers explicitly convey to players that they "felt that to not include this very real and shameful part of our past would have been offensive to the millions who faced—and still face—bigotry, discrimination, prejudice, and racism in all its forms" (Yin-Poole 2016). From the very beginning, Clay is verbally assaulted by white characters, he has to carry heavy money bags like a mule while his white partner walks unburdened, and his presence in white spaces is dismissed by white non-player characters with words such as "affirmative action [...] The whole country's spinning around the goddamn toilet. [...] Sad day when a God-fearing white man can't get a job, but any old n——who staggers in is hired on the spot." By such means, the game clearly signals early on that it will explicitly address the otherwise excluded memory politics of race.

Mafia III is part of the action crime genre and therefore akin to the highly popular *Grand Theft Auto* series (Rockstar North 1997 -). Hangar 13's game, however, uses key aspects of representation and mechanics to transcode the usually neutral virtual urban spaces found in such games into a representation of racial and economic stratifications dividing US society. For instance, predominantly black and immigrant neighborhoods are destitute and shoddy, while white districts are affluent and wealthy, white pedestrians yell racial slurs at Clay when he passes, and each area's racial and class structure determines how fast police authorities respond to a reported crime (Wawro 2017). Likewise, white characters are more likely to call the police if they notice Clay in their vicinity. By such means, racialized class dynamics are coded into the game at the level of mechanics and procedural rhetoric.

The two aspects of revenge crime tale and virtual representation of white supremacy go hand in hand when players seek racial justice and revenge without much moral concern about violence being the sole means of resolution. *Mafia III* deploys a plethora of ways to kill other characters—beating them, shooting them with a wide array of firearms, driving over them, stabbing them, or choking them are only a handful of available techniques. In addition, the reactions by enemies are animated and presented in high detail with large amounts of labor spent on visualizing the brutality enacted upon these virtual bodies. Ultimately, the game leaves open the question of whether such tactics are required to defeat and overcome racial and other injustices.

The narrative of *Mafia III* centers on the struggle of black people in the US and embeds this narrative in pastiche 1960s culture (music, art, and well-known historical events). The player-as-perpetrator and criminal here appears morally justified through his violent actions against implicit and explicit racism and white supremacy. As Russworm (SpawnOnMe 2016) states, the ultimate power fantasy in this game would have been to turn the weapons and abilities at Lincoln Clay's disposal against the systems and structures that uphold racist and otherwise unjust conditions. Unfortunately, the narrative and game design of *Mafia III* never afford such an opportunity to players. Instead, the game confines itself to the revenge genre, where Clay is more concerned with avenging the deaths of his surrogate family than facilitating black liberation. This way *Mafia III* follows a well-known pattern and re-articulates structural challenges and struggles from politics to the realm of the nuclear family. As such, the game begins and ends with the revenge-driven take-over of Mafia districts and illegal businesses by Clay and not with the dismantling of the legal and institutional structures upholding a racist system in the US, and players-as-liberal-perpetrators are deprived of the opportunity to enact a politically relevant form of empowerment and revenge—legitimate black liberation from white supremacy in the US.

In spite of these limitations in the overarching narrative, *Mafia III* still affords moments where players can enact what Hammar (2017b) calls "counter-hegemonic commemorative play." For example, throughout the city of New Bordeaux, players will repeatedly be exposed to anti-black racism. Whether in form of a pedestrian yelling a slur, Jim Crow laws segregating transport, shops, and bars, white protests against the de-segregation of schools, or Ku Klux Klan rallies. These instances offer players the opportunity to intervene with brute force. Testimonies by players highlight practices that deliberately explore such possibilities afforded by the game's open world environment. Videos of game play show Clay beating up by-passing white racists, shooting at KKK rallies, driving over corrupt racist judges, or throwing grenades into a crowd of segregationist protesters. These instances of gross violence reconfigure the role of the perpetrator within a cathartic space offered by the game and show how players can re-appropriate a simulated environment to act against racial oppression as liberal perpetrators.

Through its world, narrative, and mechanics, *Mafia III* re-contextualizes the hegemonic frames of the revenge-crime genre and redeploys it to launch an attack on racial oppression in the 1960s' US. Perpetrations of violence are rationalized and justified through the game's narrative, yet the game does not go as far as it might have in enabling and motivating revolutionary action. This neglect of collective approaches to liberation might hamper its critical role in contemporary US memory politics.

Conclusion: Perpetrators, Games, and Learning

The applicability of games in both formal and informal learning has been advocated and criticized. Summarizing the debate, it can be stated that games do afford learning at a variety of levels ranging from senso-motoric and cognitive abilities (Green and Bavelier 2006) to the acquisition of knowledge about complex processes and phenomena (Gee 2013; McCall 2016). However, using games to enhance learning requires a conscious and critical approach to this technology that takes heed of its commercial and affective nature, its multiple impacts and effects, and its possible unintended outcomes (Buckingham 2007, Chapter 6; Pötzsch 2014; Woodcock & Johnson 2018). Taking note of these perspectives, we will now briefly highlight what we perceive as potential benefits relating to learning about history and conflict dynamics in the games under scrutiny in the present chapter.

Through their mechanics and narratives, video games open up what McCall (2012) has termed "problem spaces" that afford a variety of potential player actions and interactions. Players can test and try alternative solutions to a series of challenges, ethical ones among them. As such, in the games discussed in the present chapter, players not only witness but also directly execute violence in various simulated settings. This performative dimension of play enables critical ethical reflection and learning at a level different from other media such as film or literature (Sicart 2009).

Spec Ops: *The Line* performatively enrolls players in the severely limited epistemological position implied by both the conventions of the shooter genre and the role of a soldier at war. In luring players to commit severe atrocities in the belief of following an implied moral trajectory, the game remorselessly exposes the detrimental consequences of violent actions and moral hubris—and makes players enact these. In forcing players to follow a staked path and endure the negative outcomes of their perpetrations or quit, Yager's title exposes the illusionary nature of choice in games, and by means of analogy, in the military. This invites learning both at the level of media literacy and genre conventions and conveys knowledge about perceptual regimes and the inevitable contingencies and insecurities of military interventions. *This War of Mine* shifts perspective to civilians and enables players to gradually explore the moral ambiguities of war as a socio-economic phenomenon. Players are forced to enact difficult moral choices and are remorselessly exposed to the often-detrimental consequences of their irreversible in-game decisions. This enables an understanding of the complexities of violent conflict and presents war as inherently fostering, rather than simply eradicating, perpetrators. As such, the game challenges received mainstream power fantasies positing violent conflict as an arena for heroism and mastery. Finally, *Mafia III* invites the adoption of a marginalized identity and enables players to experience the racism prevalent in the 1960s southern US. In playing a black perpetrator violently resisting oppression and fighting for his ascendance as a crime lord, the game makes possible a cathartic release in players. However, it also entails the problematic aspects of glorifying violence and of limiting the cathartic experience to the act of play. Still, by exposing players to everyday racism through the frames of the game, it makes a form of exclusion palpable that would otherwise probably remain unknown to many players in Western industrialized nations.

The three games discussed in the present chapter not only critically comment upon received discourses and scopic regimes of mainstream digital games, but also enable players to experience the responsibility of acting under the severe constraints posed by situations of violent conflict. This performative dimension of play makes games a medium of potentially high significance for the teaching and learning about perpetrators and perpetrations—and a suitable object of inquiry for the discipline of Perpetrator Studies.

Notes

1 For detailed introductions to the field of Perpetrator Studies, see Critchell et al. (2017).
2 For critiques of these positions, see Ferguson and Kilburn (2010).
3 For critiques of these positions, see Woodcock and Johnson (2018).
4 For an inquiry into realism in games, see for instance Galloway (2004) or Pötzsch (2017).
5 The perhaps most common form of moral disengagement can be found in games purportedly set in World War II. In games such as *Call of Duty* (Infinity Ward 2004), *Brothers in Arms: Road to Hill 30* (Gearbox Software 2005), *Company of Heroes* (Relic Entertainment 2006), and countless other WWII games, players usually adopt the position of Allied infantry who shoot waves of German soldiers. The moral disengagement is made relatively easy by virtue of the dominant conception of the Nazi soldier as the ultimate evil in mass culture. Yet, as Kansteiner (2017, 112) points out, even though set during World War II, these games usually avoid "the taboo subject matter of Holocaust gaming." Pfister (2018) aptly criticizes this form of historical erasure that omits "the crimes against humanity committed in the name of an inhuman ideology", a fact that clearly points to tacit "limits of play" identified by Chapman and Linderoth (2015). It would be interesting to further investigate such issues in a different contribution to the study of perpetrators and perpetrations in games.

References

11 Bit Studios. 2015. *This War of Mine*. Warsaw: 11 Bit Studios.

Aarseth, Espen. 1997. *Cybertext: Perspectives on Ergodic Literature*. Baltimore: Johns Hopkins University Press.

Aarseth, Espen. 2001. "Game Studies, Year One." *Game Studies* 1(1). www.gamestudies.org/0101/editorial.html.

Alcorn, Allan. 1974. *Pong*. Home Pong Console. Atari.

Anderson, Craig, Christopher Barlett, & Edward Swing. 2009. "Video Game Effects Confirmed, Suspected, and Speculative: A Review of the Evidence." *Simulation & Gaming* 40(3): 377–403.

Artz, Lee. 2015. *Global Entertainment Media: A Critical Introduction*. Oxford: Wiley Blackwell.

Bogost, Ian. 2007. *Persuasive Games: The Expressive Power of Videogames*. Cambridge: MIT Press.

Buckingham, David. 2007. *Beyond Technology: Children's Learning in the Age of Digital Culture*. Cambridge: Polity Press.

Butler, Judith. 2009. *Frames of War: When Is Life Grievable?* London: Verso.

Chapman, Adam. 2016. *Digital Games as History: How Videogames Represent the Past and Offer Access to Historical Practice*. New York: Routledge.

Chapman, Adam & Jonas Linderoth. 2015. "Exploring the Limits of Play." In *The Dark Side of Game Play: Controversial Issues in Playful Environments*, edited by Torill Mortensen, Jonas Linderoth, and Ashley M. L. Brown, 137–153. London: Routledge.

Critchell, Kara, Susanne C. Knittel, Emiliano Perra, & Ugur Ümit Üngör. 2017. "Editors' Introduction." *Journal of Perpetrator Research* 1(1): 1–27.

Egenfeldt-Nielsen, Simon, Jonas Heide Smith, & Susana Pajares-Tosca. 2013. *Understanding Videogames: The Essential Introduction*. London: Routledge.

Ferguson, Chris J. & John Kilburn. 2010. "Violent Video Game Effects on Aggression, Empathy, and Prosocial Behavior in Eastern and Western Countries: A Meta-Analytic Review." *Psychological Bulletin* 136(2): 174–178.

Galloway, Alexander. 2004. "Social Realism in Gaming." *Game Studies* 4(1), unpaginated. www.gamestudies.org/0401/galloway/.

Gearbox Software. 2005. *Brothers in Arms: Road to Hill 30*. PC. Montreuil: Ubisoft.

Gee, Paul J. 2013. *Good Video Games and Good Learning: Collected Essays on Video Games, Learning and Literacy*. New York: Peter Lang.

Green, C. Shawn & D. Bavelier. 2006. "Enumeration versus Multiple Object Tracking: The Case of Action Video Game Players." *Cognition* 101: 217–245.

Hammar, Emil Lundedal. 2017a. "The Political Economy of Historical Digital Games." *Media Development* LXIV(4): 25–29.

Hammar, Emil Lundedal. 2017b. "Counter-Hegemonic Commemorative Play: Marginalized Pasts and the Politics of Memory in the Digital Game Assassin's Creed: Freedom Cry." *Rethinking History* 21(3): 372–395. doi:10.1080/13642529.2016.1256622.

Handrahan, Matthew. 2014. "This War of Mine Covered Its Costs in Two Days." *GamesIndustry.Biz*. November 28. www.gamesindustry.biz/articles/2014-11-28-this-war-of-mine-covered-its-costs-in-two-days.

Hangar 13. 2016. *Mafia III*. Novato: 2K Games.

Hartmann, Tilo, K. Maja Krakowiak, & Mina Tsay-Vogel. 2014. "How Violent Video Games Communicate Violence: A Literature Review and Content Analysis of Moral Disengagement Factors." *Communication Monographs* 81(3): 310–332.

Hartmann, Tilo & Peter Vorderer. 2010. "It's Okay to Shoot a Character: Moral Disengagement in Violent Video Games." *Journal of Communication* 60(1): 94–119.

Heron, Michael James & Pauline Helen Belford. 2014. "'Do You Feel Like a Hero Yet?' Externalized Morality in Video Games." *Journal of Games Criticism* 1(2): 1–22. http://static.squarespace.com/static/51f9aac5e4b080ed4b441ba7/t/53b02ae2e4b0182daaf7f3c4/1404054242059/HeronBelford-1-2.pdf.

Infinity Ward. 2004. *Call of Duty 1*. PC. Santa Monica, CA: Activision.

Jørgensen, Kristine. 2012. "Players as Coresearchers: Expert Player Perspective as an Aid to Understanding Games." *Simulation & Gaming* 43(3): 374–390. doi:10.1177/1046878111422739.

Jørgensen, Kristine. 2016. "The Positive Discomfort of Spec Ops: The Line." *Game Studies* 16(2): unpaginated.

Kansteiner, Wulf. 2017. "The Holocaust in the 21st Century: Digital Anxiety, Transnational Cosmopolitanism, and Never Again Genocide without Memory. In *Digital Memory Studies*, edited by Andrew Hoskins, 122–152. London: Routledge.

Keogh, Brendan. 2012. *Killing Is Harmless: A Critical Reading of Spec Ops: The Line*. Marden: Stolen Projects.

Keogh, Brendan. 2013. "*Spec Ops: The Line*'s Conventional Subversion of the Military Shooter." In *Proceedings of DiGRA 2013: DeFragging Game Studies*, edited by Celia Pearce, Helen Kennedy & John Sharp, 1–17. www.digra.org/wp-content/uploads/digital-library/paper_55.pdf.

Kerr, Aphra. 2017. *Global Games: Production, Circulation, and Policy in the Networked Era*. London: Routledge.

Kline, Stephen, Nick Dyer-Witheford, & Greig de Peuter. 2003. *Digital Play: The Interaction of Technology, Culture, and Marketing*. Montreal & Kingston: McGill-Queen's University Press.

Kwiatkowski, Kacper. 2016. "Civilian Casualties: Shifting Perspective in This War of Mine. In *Zone of Control: Perspectives on Wargaming*, edited by Pat Harrigan and Matthew B. Kirschenbaum, 691–702. Cambridge: MIT Press.

McCall, Jeremiah. 2012. "Navigating the Problem Space: The Medium of Simulation Games in the Teaching of History." *The History Teacher* 46(1): 9–28.

McCall, Jeremiah. 2016. "Teaching History with Digital Historical Games: An Introduction to the Field and Best Practices." *Simulation & Gaming* 47(4): 517–542.

McGonigal, Jane. 2011. *Reality Is Broken: How Games Make Us Better and How They Can Change the World*. London: Penguin Press.

Mukherjee, Souvik. 2015. *Video Games and Storytelling: Reading Games and Playing Books*. London: Palgrave Macmillan.

Mukherjee, Souvik. 2018. "Playing Subaltern: Videogames and Postcolonialism." *Games & Culture* 13(5): 504–520.

Murray, Janet. 1997. *Hamlet on the Holodeck: The Future of Narrative in Cyberspace*. New York: The Free Press.

Nieborg, David. 2011. *Triple-A: The Political Economy of the Blockbuster Video Game*. Amsterdam: University of Amsterdam Press.

Opencritic. 2014. This War of Mine for PC Reviews. *OpenCritic*. November 14. https://opencritic.com/game/929/this-war-of-mine.

Pajitnov, Alexey & Vladimir Pokhilko. 1984. *Tetris*. Commodore 64. Alameda, CA: Spetrum HoloByte.

Payne, Matthew T. 2016. *Playing War: Military Video Games after 9/11*. New York: New York University Press.

Pfister, Eugen. 2018. "'Of Monsters and Men' – Shoah in Digital Games - Public History Weekly - The International Blogjournal." *Public History Weekly* (blog). June 21. https://public-history-weekly.degruyter.com/6-2018-23/shoah-in-digital-games/.

Pötzsch, Holger. 2013. "Ubiquitously Absent Enemies: Character Engagement in the Contemporary War Film." *Nordicom Review* 34(1): 125–144.

Pötzsch, Holger. 2014. "Games and Brains." *Dichtung Digital* 44 (December 29). www.dichtung-digital.de/journal/englische-artikel/?postID=2527.

Pötzsch, Holger. 2017. "Selective Realism: Filtering Experiences of War in the First- and Third-Person Shooter." *Games & Culture* 12(2): 156–178.

Pötzsch, Holger. Forthcoming. "Positioning Players as Political Subjects: Forms of Estrangement in and the Presentation of War in Spec Ops: The Line and This War of Mine." In *War Games: Memory, Militarism and the Subject of Play*, edited by Phil Hammond and Holger Pötzsch. New York: Bloomsbury.

Relic Entertainment. 2006. *Company of Heroes*. Agoura Hills, CA: THQ.

Rockstar North. 1997. *Grand Theft Auto Series*. PC. New York: Take Two Interactive.

Sicart, Miguel. 2009. *The Ethics of Computer Games*. Cambridge: MIT Press.

Smale, Stephanie de, Martijn J. L. Kors & Alyea M. Sandovar. 2017. "The Case of This War of Mine: A Production Studies Perspective on Moral Game Design." *Games and Culture*, August. doi:10.1177/1555412017725996.

SpawnOnMe. 2016. Spawn On Me MAFIA 3 Special, Part 1: The Panel of All Panels. http://spawnon.me/spawn-mafia-3-special-part-1-panel-panels/.

Treyarch. 2010. *Call of Duty: Black Ops*. Santa Monica: Activision.

Wawro, Alex. 2017. Writing Mafia 3: 'We Had a Lot of Very Uncomfortable Conversations.' February 28. /view/news/292663/Writing_Mafia_3_We_had_a_lot_of_very_uncomfortable_conversations.php.

Woodcock, Jamie & Mark R. Johnson. 2018. "Gamification: What It Is, and How to Fight It." *The Sociological Review* 66(3): 542–558.

Yager Development. 2012. *Spec Ops: The Line*. Novato: 2K Games.

Yin-Poole, Wesley. 2016. "Mafia 3's in-Game Statement on Its Depiction of Racism." *Eurogamer* (blog). October 7. www.eurogamer.net/articles/2016-10-07-mafia-3s-in-game-statement-on-its-depiction-of-racism.

Zimmerman, Eric. 2013. Manifesto for a Ludic Century. *Kotaku*, September 9, https://kotaku.com/manifesto-the-21st-century-will-be-defined-by-games-1275355204.

2.4 Teaching About Perpetrators

30

Playing Devil's Advocate

Classroom Encounters with Holocaust Perpetrators

Alasdair Richardson

What should educators tell children about the perpetrators of the Holocaust? There can be few more contentious questions in Holocaust Education. They must consider carefully how and when the perpetrator's voice might be educationally beneficial in their classroom, which perpetrators to introduce, and how to balance pastoral concerns with giving human and historical voice to the culprits of an event that "has come to symbolize the ultimate expression of evil" in human history (Short and Reed 2004, vii). This chapter puts forward a case for educators *playing devil's advocate* by placing the perpetrator at the center of Holocaust Education, in an effort to re-humanize perpetrators in the service of their victims and our pupils. It will consider the challenging educational issues around *why*, *when,* and *how* educators might address the complexity of the perpetrator and how teachers can provide their pupils with classroom encounters with the perpetrators that are both educative and safe.

Why Should We Tell Children about Perpetrators?

As teachers, we constantly remind our pupils that actions have consequences and that individuals have to acknowledge and accept responsibility for their actions. When teaching about the Holocaust, however, the enormity of the consequences can sometimes paralyze our ability to interrogate the causal actions. Pupils can be left with an over-simplified concept of perpetration, in which the perpetrator becomes a caricatured "bogey man." Such "comfortable explanations" (Salmons 2001, 35) enable pupils to uncomplicate the perpetrator. This sanitizes the complexity of the perpetrator, does a disservice to their victims, and enables the pupils in our classroom to avoid a nuanced, complex encounter with the perpetrator as an individual. Re-humanizing the perpetrators is an altogether more complicated business. Handing them back their agency suggests to pupils that perpetrators were no less human than they themselves, their friends, or their parents. This involves a multifaceted and challenging examination of the human condition. Teachers need to skillfully support their pupils through this potentially dislocating turn, whilst avoiding inadvertently exposing their pupils to an inappropriately sympathetic understanding of the perpetrator. The introduction of the perpetrator perspective is an essential facet of the complicated mosaic of the event, nonetheless, as its exclusion would present "a false version of history" (Supple 1998, 39).

When Should We Tell Children about Perpetrators?

Childhood is a special (and short) time, and educators have to consider their duty of care towards their pupils in deciding when they should learn about the Holocaust. The teacher/pupil relationship is key here in ensuring pupils are pastorally cared for. There is no international consensus about reference to the Holocaust in school curricula or the most appropriate age at which to teach it (see for example, Supple 1998, Totten 1999; UNESCO 2015). Teachers need to consider factors such as their pupils' emotional maturity, their understanding of the historical context, their socio-cultural setting, identity, etc. These are sensitivities that collectively represent the child's personal hinterland, influence their developing worldview, and in turn indicate their readiness to learn (and to begin to understand) about the Holocaust. Teaching might be necessarily very different in different contexts, both transnationally and within regional borders (see, for example, Rutland's work with Muslim and Jewish pupils in Australia (2010), or Nates's consideration of the complexities inherent in teaching about the Holocaust in post-apartheid South Africa (2010)). In Germany and other collaborative nations, the subject matter necessitates a careful consideration of the nature of collective responsibility within national memory (Kaiser 2014) whilst contextualizing the individual heritages of different pupils and modern events (such as migration). The (complicated) answer is that this might be at *different* ages for *different* children.

How Should We Tell Children about Perpetrators?

Teaching about the Holocaust is an exercise in complexity. Pupils can never *fully* understand the perpetrators' actions, but they can move *towards* a comprehension of their actions through a better understanding of the contexts within which they acted. But how can we introduce the perpetrator within our curriculum in a way that pupils can understand? Teachers might turn first to published textbooks, with their neatly packaged chapters on "the Holocaust." Such texts often offer the "comfortable explanations" noted above, making the teacher complicit in the over-simplification of the narrative for the pupils. Teachers need to approach textbooks with a critical eye—engaging with the content judiciously and analytically, to select activities that suit their schemes of work and *their* pupils, mediating between the text and the reader.

A key area of this mediation must be with the photographs plentifully populating the pages of most classroom textbooks. Teachers need to be aware that often these images are inappropriate—they present victims in humiliating situations or show images of graphic violence that are both dehumanizing for the victims and shocking for the viewer. Whilst these images tell us little about the victims, they do offer (perhaps inadvertently) an insight into the perpetrator. We should invite pupils to consider *who* the men and women behind the lens were and what they reveal of themselves through their gaze (Crane 2008). Teachers should encourage their pupils to look critically at photographs, giving them the tools to interrogate their provenance in an effort to hand back humanity to both the victim *and* the perpetrator. Pupils should ask *why* this photograph has been taken, *who* took it, what *purpose* it serves, and what it tells us about the perpetrator (whilst remaining vigilant of their responsibilities towards the victims depicted)? One key resource here should be *The Auschwitz Album*, which contains almost 200 photographs portraying the daily workings of the camp, while also providing a unique insight into the (invisible) intentions of the perpetrators behind the lens (online links to this and all other resources and individuals mentioned below can be found in order of appearance at the end of this chapter). Photographs collected by former

Auschwitz senior SS officer Karl-Friedrich Höcker offer a more personal perspective—showing various members of the Auschwitz camp staff "off duty" (particularly on visits to the SS resort at Solahütte). These albums present the perpetrators as complex figures—people who deceived, stole from, and murdered their victims, all the while enjoying time off with colleagues, taking day trips eating blueberries, etc. Collectively, they offer a version of the perpetrator that is inhuman, yet very human. By considering the perpetrator as a human being, historically literate pupils can begin to consider how this event was *humanly* possible.

Perpetrators *were* human beings, with pre-war lives that were for the most part unremarkable. Their lives epitomize Arendt's "banality of evil" (1965, xiv); her work can be explored further with older students. Teachers should engage pupils with individual stories to help them comprehend the complex nature of perpetration. They might study the life of Auschwitz commandant Rudolf Höss (whose family lived in a villa on the perimeter of the camp) or Adolf Eichmann (whose unremarkable school career led him to become a traveling salesman briefly before joining the Nazi Party). Similarly, Irma Grese (a notorious SS guard at several camps) was not educationally accomplished and her blind obedience might engage pupils in considering human vulnerability to extremism and the lure of Nazi ideology. In case these individuals leave pupils believing that perpetrators were *all* unintelligent, the academic achievements of Joseph Goebbels (who earned his PhD and was widely published in academia prior to the war) or Josef Mengele (who had earned both a medical degree and a PhD in physical anthropology) will challenge these misconceptions. The life and career of Amon Göth (commandant of the Kraków-Płaszów concentration camp) illustrates the cruelty victims suffered at the hands of the Nazis and their collaborators (he was Austrian). Testimony from survivors (such as Helen Jonas-Rosenzweig) attest to this, while his daughter (Monika Hertwig) and his granddaughter (Jennifer Teege) offer further perspectives on the legacy of a perpetrator's family (which might be relevant for pupils who are addressing their own difficult heritages). The trials and subsequent convictions of Sobibór guard John Demjanjuk and Oskar Gröning ("the bookkeeper of Auschwitz") raise further questions for pupils around culpability, post-war justice, and forgiveness.

Other narratives are more complex, perhaps blurring the lines of "perpetrator," "collaborator," and "rescuer." Wilhelm Hosenfeld was a captain in the German Army during the war who was also known to have assisted several Jews and Poles (most famously the pianist, Władysław Szpilman). Pupils might consider how his service as a Nazi officer made him culpable of complicity in war crimes, despite his actions as a rescuer. Similarly, a study of Oskar Schindler's life reveals the dichotomy of a Nazi Party member and profiteer, turned savior of 1100 Jews. Both illustrations enable a teacher to "play devil's advocate" in provoking discussion around the complexity of a character's flaws and virtues.

Playing Devil's Advocate—Some Reflections

Knowledge of the inhumanity of mankind cannot be ignored, nor can it be unlearned. Introducing the perpetrator in the classroom leaves pupils with two challenges: to understand *how* these people could act as they did, and to come to terms with *how they can live* in a world where such people exist. This will provoke complex discussions around choices, actions, and culpability. Teachers need expertise in their subject knowledge and their practice to be able to marshal these conversations, to provide answers, and to support pupils' learning. Working collaboratively, they can explore the Holocaust and its complexity through cross-curricular classes in literature, art, religion, or geography, for example.

Perpetration of the Holocaust did not happen in isolation, and neither should teaching (or learning) about it.

Exclusion of the perpetrator from a study of the Holocaust would be as significant an omission as it would be to ignore the diversity of pre-war Jewish life, Jewish resistance, or the history of antisemitism. Teaching about perpetrators is challenging pedagogically, morally, personally, and politically. Pupils need to understand the roots of perpetration and the conditions that give rise to its genesis in society. Only then can they comprehend the "banality" of perpetration not as an abhorrence, but as a consequence of indifference, ignorance, extremism, and prejudice. It is something to be confronted and challenged and to be exposed in the light of interrogation. It is only through playing "devil's advocate" that teachers can help their pupils towards this inoculating understanding.

Further Information:

The Auschwitz Album:
https://www.yadvashem.org/yv/en/exhibitions/album_auschwitz/index.asp?gclid=EAIaIQobChMI8qilytfJ3AIVqrvtCh3bZwyiEAAYASAAEgIpx_D_BwE

Karl-Friedrich Höcker's album:
https://www.ushmm.org/wlc/en/article.php?ModuleId=10007434

Rudolf Höss:
http://www.bbc.co.uk/history/worldwars/genocide/hoss_commandant_auschwitz_01.shtml

Adolf Eichmann:
https://www.ushmm.org/wlc/en/article.php?ModuleId=10007412

Irma Grese:
https://www.historytoday.com/lauren-willmott/real-beast-belsen-irma-grese-and-female-concentration-camp-guards

Joseph Goebbels:
https://www.britannica.com/biography/Joseph-Goebbels

Josef Mengele:
https://www.ushmm.org/wlc/en/article.php?ModuleId=10007060

Amon Göth:

- Interview with survivor Helen Jonas-Rosenzweig: https://www.ushmm.org/confront-antisemitism/antisemitism-podcast/helen-jonas
- Interview with Göth's daughter, Monika Hertwig: https://www.youtube.com/watch?v=SQrq4ljb48g
- Interview with Göth's granddaughter, Jennifer Teege: https://stmuhistorymedia.org/he-would-have-killed-me-the-story-of-jennifer-teege-granddaughter-of-nazi-commandant-amon-goeth/

Oskar Gröning:
https://www.bbc.co.uk/news/world-europe-43376105

John Demjanjuk:
https://www.ushmm.org/wlc/en/article.php?ModuleId=10007956

Wilhelm Hosenfeld:
https://www.yadvashem.org/righteous/stories/hosenfeld.html

Oskar Schindler:
https://www.yadvashem.org/righteous/stories/schindler.html?gclid=EAIaIQobChMI4cC84d3J3AIVrArTCh2KcgFgEAAYASAAEgIkbvD_BwE

References

Arendt, Hannah. 1965. *Eichmann in Jerusalem: A Report on the Banality of Evil.* New York: Viking Press.

Crane, Susan A. 2008. Choosing Not to Look: Representation, Repatriation, and Holocaust Atrocity Photography. *History and Theory* 47: 309–330.

Kaiser, Wolf. 2010. Nazi Perpetrators in Holocaust Education. *Teaching History* 141: 34–39.

Kaiser, Wolf. 2014. Teaching about Perpetrators of the Holocaust in Germany. In UNESCO (ed.) *Holocaust Education in a Global Context.* UNESCO.

Nates, Tali. 2010. 'But, Apartheid Was Also Genocide. What about our suffering?' Teaching the Holocaust in South Africa - Opportunities and Challenges. *Intercultural Education* 21(Supplement 1): S17–S26.

Rutland, Suzanne. 2010. Creating Effective Holocaust Education Programmes for Government Schools with Large Muslim Populations in Sydney. *Prospects: Quarterly Review of Comparative Education* 40(1): 75–91.

Salmons, Paul. 2001. Moral Dilemmas: History, Teaching and the Holocaust. *Teaching History* 104: 34–40.

Short, Geoffrey & Carol Ann Reed. 2004. *Issues in Holocaust Education.* Abingdon: Ashgate.

Short, Geoffrey, Carrie Supple & Katherine Klinger. 1998. *The Holocaust in the School Curriculum: A European Perspective.* Strasbourg: Council of Europe Publishing.

Totten, Samuel. 1999. Should There Be Holocaust Education for K-9 Students? The Answer is No. *Social Studies and the Young Learner* 12: 36–39.

UNESCO. 2015. *The International Status of Education About the Holocaust: A global mapping of textbooks and curricula.* Paris, France: UNESCO & The Georg Eckert Institute for International Textbook Research.

31

Teaching the perpetrator's perspective in Holocaust literature

Erin McGlothlin

In the last ten years, research into the representation of Holocaust perpetrators in literature and other cultural media has flourished, providing us with an increasingly sophisticated framework for how to analyze these depictions in terms of their formal properties, their historical context, and their reception by readers and viewers. Such work has been transformative for literary studies of the Holocaust, not only demonstrating the salience of the emerging cultural phenomenon of the figure of the Holocaust perpetrator but also arguing that this figure's perspective has been an important—if often covert and underexplored—component of the literature of the Holocaust from its inception. Less present in this recent scholarship has been an explicit focus on how to introduce and address ambivalent and troubling representations of perpetrators in the Holocaust literature classroom. While courses on Holocaust literature should rightly continue to put at their center the narratives of victims and survivors, without whose experiences and perspectives one cannot form any historically or ethically useful understanding of the events of the genocide and the challenges it poses to representation and commemoration, there are valid, salutary reasons for including at least a short unit that explores representations of perpetrators, not only historical texts that depict the perspectives of real-life perpetrators (such as primary documents, autobiographical writings, and postwar interviews) but also fictional explorations that attempt to render the inner life of the (mostly) men who conceived of, planned, and implemented the events of the Holocaust. First, such focused concentration on the diverse historical, sociological, and psychological features of perpetration and their representation in visual and textual narrative can help to impart more nuance to students' unidimensional images of perpetrators in general and "Nazis" in particular, reminding them that they were human actors who faced singular choices and behaved in distinct but diverse ways in particular contexts. Second, the focus on the figure of the perpetrator can illuminate the complex historical relationships between perpetrators and other actor groups (victims, survivors, other complicit parties, bystanders, rescuers, resisters, etc.) during the Holocaust. Third, the figure of the perpetrator can function as an excellent vehicle for exploring the ambivalent dynamics of Holocaust representation in particular and literary representation more generally, especially the deployment of reader empathy, identification, and perspective-taking, all of which are of course operative with texts that depict the experience of victims and survivors but which may be more obvious with regard to representations of perpetrators.

As Froma I. Zeitlin argues in her essay "Teaching about Perpetrators," while Holocaust perpetrators "are the core … of the entire catastrophe" (2004, 69), addressing perpetration in any comprehensive way in the Holocaust literature classroom "is to walk a tightrope between two unsatisfactory extremes: demonizing the perpetrators as the embodiment of absolute evil, on the one hand, and, on the other, insisting on the existence of 'the little Nazi' in all of us" (2004, 70). I have similarly found that the reactions of students tend to cluster along a binary; however, the opposition epitomized in my students' responses takes a slightly different trajectory. Particularly my undergraduate students in courses on Holocaust representation (a majority of whom identifies as Jewish) often come into the classroom with abstract but powerful images of perpetrators as unidimensional, almost superhumanly diabolical Others that they derive from popular representations of and public discourse on Nazis as the apotheosis of mystical maleficence. However, once confronted with literary or filmic texts—whether historical (such as Claude Lanzmann's interviews with perpetrators in his film *Shoah [1985]*) or fictional (such as Bernhard Schlink's depiction of a female perpetrator in *The Reader* [1995/1997])—that depict the experience or mentality of or otherwise attempt to humanize particular perpetrators, students increasingly experience a sudden volte-face in their position. In their earnest attempt to rethink and relinquish their stereotypes about "evil Nazis," they substitute their previous antipathy towards perpetrators with an overtly sympathetic attitude that decontextualizes the perpetrators' narratives, decouples them from their crimes, and delimits their experience to that of adversity and unfortunate circumstances. Students' reactions are thus not so much a matter of universalizing the character of the perpetrator or locating "'the little Nazi' in all of us" as they are one of individualizing and rehabilitating the perpetrator character by foregrounding the ways in which his complicity (voluntary or unwilling) has caused him distress and misfortune and by overlooking the suffering of the victims of his crimes. Students—especially younger students who are prone to dichotomous thinking and desire immutable, oversimplified paradigms and unambiguous conclusions—reflexively come to perceive the perpetrator as primarily a victim of circumstances, a victimhood that they tend to conflate (or quasi-equate) with the experiences of Jewish survivors and victims of genocide and victims from other groups. This phenomenon is especially germane to texts—whether fictional or historically referential—that either feature perpetrators as narrators or recount the events from their point of view. In such cases, students not only are inclined to assume the premises of the perpetrator's frequently self-serving narrative of his participation in violence (a dynamic that Leigh A. Payne, in her essay on methodological approaches to studying perpetrator testimony, ascribes to the "art of seduction" (2009, 243) frequently exercised by such narratives), they also seem to believe that the very exercise of humanizing him requires them to accept "his truth" uncritically. For that reason, they have a difficult time managing their impulses towards empathy and sympathy and reconciling them with a more circumspect approach that allows for critical distance. Their propulsion from one polar position (Nazis as evil) to its diametrical opposite (perpetrators as hapless casualties of their environment) is evidence of ambivalence about perpetrators of mass violence in the greater cultural imagination and an inability simultaneously to humanize and empathize with them and to hold them historically, legally and ethically accountable. My goal is to prod students into exercises in critical thinking that will help them reject trite and monolithic cultural stereotypes, that will stimulate a more self-conscious awareness of disquieting occasions in which they experience compassion and identification—particularly those moments of uncomfortable ambiguity that Dominick LaCapra terms "empathetic unsettlement" (2001, 102)—and that will encourage them to maintain a measure of analytical distance. The ideal result of such a pedagogical objective is students' rejection of dichotomous antitheses in favor of what LaCapra describes as "the middle area of undecidability [...] in which seeming opposites displace and internally mark each other" (2001, 20).

My chief strategy for introducing into the Holocaust literature classroom both accounts of historical perpetrators and fictional texts that feature Holocaust perpetrators as narrators is to situate such representations in a number of relevant contexts, whether on the level of referential discourse or that of concrete historical events. First, when at all possible, I present fictional representations of perpetrators of various types (such as Martin Amis's *Time's Arrow* [1991], Edgar Hilsenrath's *The Nazi and the Barber* [1971/1977], Marcel Beyer's *The Karnau Tapes* [1995/1997], and Laurent Binet's *HHhH* [2010/2012]) alongside non-fictional narrative and filmic depictions of actual historical agents (such as Rudolf Hoess's autobiography [1961], Lanzmann's filmed interviews in *Shoah*, and portraits of Adolf Eichmann by Hannah Arendt [1963], Harry Mulisch [1961/2005], and Haim Gouri [1962/2004]). Such juxtaposition of fictional texts with documentary or non-fictional representations allows the students to identify aspects and challenges shared by both types of discourse and divergent representational issues and approaches. What is more, by calling explicit attention to the relative dearth of first-person accounts by historical Holocaust perpetrators as compared to the recent proliferation of fictional narratives about perpetrators, I am able to highlight some of the historical conditions of and developments in post-Holocaust cultural representation. Second, like many instructors of Holocaust literature, I endeavor to present the disparate and often antithetical voices and viewpoints from participants from a range of subject positions, particularly but not exclusively those of victims and survivors. However, I also strive to localize and temporalize these perspectives as much as possible, allowing for a much more fruitful juxtaposition of experience, relative agency, and power dynamics. Such an approach involves balancing the testimony of real-life perpetrators with that of victims and survivors who are present at a particular point in space at roughly the same moment and with fictional texts that offer alternative viewpoints on the same set of events.

One of my most effective efforts in this regard is my pairing of Gitta Sereny's 1971 original article-length interview with Franz Stangl,[1] the former commandant of the Sobibór and Treblinka killing centers, with the testimony of Abraham Krzepicki [1979], who spent eighteen days in the summer of 1942 as an inmate in Treblinka before escaping and making his way back to the Warsaw Ghetto, where, after giving his testimony to Rokhl Auerbakh, he was killed in the Warsaw Ghetto Uprising in 1943. Krzepicki was present in Treblinka in early September 1942, when Stangl was transferred to the killing center as its new commandant in order to reorganize its operations during the height of the "Großaktion Warschau" deportations, in which a quarter of a million Jews from the Warsaw Ghetto were murdered. Prodded by Sereny's pointed questioning, Stangl appears to review earnestly—and at times with striking emotion—his experience at Treblinka; as Sereny claims, "he manifested an intense desire to seek and tell the truth" (2001, 120). However, in spite of Sereny's deliberate mode of skeptical criticism vis-à-vis Stangl's narrative and her explicit signaling of moments in the interview when she suspects him of dissembling, students are often inclined to take Stangl's frankness at face value, believing him to be fully forthcoming, self-reflective about his actions, and regretful. Yet, when juxtaposed alongside Krzepicki's breathless account of the traumatic frenzy experienced by the squads of Jewish men who were selected each day from the transports and forced to perform the grueling physical labor of receiving the deportees, helping direct them to the gas chambers, disposing of their corpses, and processing their material effects (activities during which the men were constantly beaten and themselves frequently killed by day's end), Stangl is revealed to be astonishingly silent about the concrete nature of the genocidal process at Treblinka and his own role in it. Demonstrating active self-justification and denial, he constructs a narrative in which he was an unwilling participant (and even a sort of victim) of the violence propagated there.

While a major objective of my pedagogical strategy is to facilitate my students' recognition of the challenges that Krzepicki's counter-narrative of Treblinka poses to Stangl's myopic and self-involved perspective, I do not end the exercise with this stark opposition. Rather, I introduce a third component by bringing into the dialogue a fictional text, in the case of this exercise the third chapter of Ian MacMillan's novel *Village of a Million Spirits: A Novel of the Treblinka Uprising* [1999]. Titled "Near Malkinia Station, Eastern Poland," the chapter introduces the reader to the world of Treblinka of roughly the same time period as that of Krzepicki's and Stangl's accounts. Utilizing the elastic narrative properties of fiction, MacMillan's text is narrated successively from the perspective of four characters in subject positions located on a spectrum of agency and complicity: a Jewish deportee from Warsaw who is killed upon arrival in the gas chamber, a Jewish prisoner performing forced labor in the camp, a Ukrainian SS auxiliary recruited from a German camp for Soviet prisoners of war, and a German SS guard. The chapter thus mobilizes an active network of interdependent relationships between characters from incommensurate circumstances in terms of agency and power; by extending its purview beyond the necessarily incomplete perspective of one actor group, it illuminates the dynamics of Treblinka as a joint encounter experienced discreetly by different participants. Moreover, by so doing, it is able to feature the perspectives of fully human perpetrators without seducing the reader into uncritical identification with them.

While the constellation I establish with the texts by Krzepicki, Sereny, and MacMillan offers a particularly precise example of the localization and temporalization of disparate Holocaust experiences (and moreover gives my students some knowledge of the conditions of the Operation Reinhard killing centers, at which over 1.5 million Jews were murdered), one could similarly triangulate other aspects of the Holocaust (geographical sites, time periods, national or local experiences, or participant groups) through non-fictional texts by victims or survivors and perpetrators (including diaries, documents, propaganda footage and photographs, wartime and postwar testimonies, documentary interviews, etc.) and fiction that represents the same set of events, particularly from the perspective of the perpetrator. By offering students the chance to engage with the depictions of perpetrators from a diversity of perspectives and in multiple types of texts in both fictional and non-fictional discourses, one thus can better encourage them to explore pertinent ethical issues regarding their representation, identify gray areas in their accounts (and in the accounts of victims and survivors who portray perpetrators), and recognize the difficulties and benefits involved in their remediation in fiction. The success of such a pedagogical goal would be measured by the extent to which the students are able to think past the binary that so dominantly structures our cultural imagination of the Holocaust perpetrator.

Note

1 Sereny interviewed Stangl in 1971 in the Düsseldorf prison in which he was serving a life sentence for joint responsibility for the murder of at least 900,000 people. She published an article based on that interview entitled "Colloquy with a Conscience" in *The Daily Telegraph Magazine* later that year; in 1974, her book-length account of the interview appeared under the title *Into that Darkness*. Although I have used both texts in the classroom, for the purposes described here I find the shorter text, which Sereny anthologized in her 2001 collection of writings, to be more useful.

References

Amis, Martin. 1991. *Time's Arrow or the Nature of the Offense.* New York: Vintage.
Arendt, Hannah. 1963. *Eichmann in Jerusalem: A Report on the Banality of Evil.* New York: Viking Penguin.
Beyer, Marcel. 1997. *The Karnau Tapes.* Translated John Brownjohn. London: Secker and Warburg.
Binet, Laurent. 2012. *HHhH.* Translated Sam Taylor. New York: Farrar, Straus and Giroux.
Gouri, Haim. 2004. *Facing the Glass Booth: The Jerusalem Trial of Adolf Eichmann.* Translated by Michael Swirsky. Detroit: Wayne State University Press.
Hilsenrath, Edgard. 1971. *The Nazi and the Barber.* Translated Andrew White. Garden City, NY: Doubleday.
Hoess, Rudolf. 1961. *Commandant of Auschwitz.* Translated by Constantine FitzGibbon. London: Pan Books.
Krzepicki, Abraham. 1979. "Eighteen Days in Treblinka." In *The Death Camp Treblinka: A Documentary,* edited by Alexander Donat, 77–145. New York: Holocaust Library.
LaCapra, Dominick. 2001. *Writing History, Writing Trauma.* Baltimore and London: Johns Hopkins University Press.
MacMillan, Ian. 1999. *Village of a Million Spirits: A Novel of the Treblinka Uprising.* South Royalton, VT: Steerforth Press.
Mulisch, Harry. 2005. *Criminal Case 40/61, The Trial of Adolf Eichmann: An Eyewitness Account.* Translated by Robert Naborn. Philadelphia: University of Pennsylvania Press.
Payne, Leigh A. 2009. "Confessional Performances: A Methodological Approach to Studying Perpetrators' Testimonies." In *Assessing the Impact of Transitional Justice: Challenges for Empirical Research,* edited by Hugo van der Merwe, Victoria Baxter, Audrey R. Chapman, 227–247. Washington, DC: United States Institute of Peace.
Schlink, Bernhard. 1997. *The Reader.* Translated by Carol Jane Janeway. New York: Vintage.
Sereny, Gitta. 1974. *Into that Darkness: An Examination of Conscience.* New York: Vintage Books.
Sereny, Gitta. 2001. "Colloquy with a Conscience." *The Healing Wound: Experiences and Reflections on Germany, 1938–2000,* 87–134. New York: WW. Norton.
Shoah. 1985. Dir. Claude Lanzmann. New Yorker Films. DVD.
Zeitlin, Froma I. 2004. "Teaching about Perpetrators." In *Teaching the Representation of the Holocaust,* edited by Marianne Hirsch and Irene Kacandes., 68-85. New York: Modern Language Association of America.

32

Teaching for/about Empathy in Peace Education

Michalinos Zembylas

Teaching for/about empathy is one of the pedagogical practices often advocated in the body of work known as peace education. Peace education is a field of social education that is concerned with war and violence in the world and has experienced considerable growth over the past four decades (Burns and Aspeslagh 1996; Salomon and Nevo 2002; McGlynn et al. 2009). At its most basic level, peace education is taken to be the process of promoting the knowledge, skills, attitudes, and values needed to bring about behavioral changes to prevent conflict and violence, both physical and structural; to resolve conflicts peacefully; and to create the conditions conducive to peace (Fountain 1999). As a value and pedagogical practice in peace education, empathy is advocated because it cultivates emotional connections between victims and perpetrators, thus promoting mutual understanding and facilitating the process of reconciliation, especially after traumatic experiences of war and conflict (Zembylas 2008). At the same time, work in peace education acknowledges that cultivating feelings of empathy with perpetrators is full of intellectual, emotional, political, and ethical challenges (Jansen 2009; Bekerman and Zembylas 2012; Zembylas 2015; Zembylas, Charalambous and Charalambous 2016).

The present chapter foregrounds the potential of teaching about/for empathy and asks what sort of pedagogies might encourage the cultivation of empathy in children and youth who grow up in conflict-affected societies and carry the burden of victims, perpetrators, or both. After providing a brief introduction to the notion of empathy, I discuss how *reconciliatory empathy* can be enacted in the context of peace education to then conclude with some thoughts on the need to enrich our understanding of how empathy is taught and negotiated in different conflict-affected societies.

The Notion of Empathy

Empathy is the subject of discussion in philosophical, psychological, anthropological, sociological, and theological literature. It is beyond the scope of this chapter to provide a review of the vast literature on this topic; however, it is sufficient to emphasize three important ideas: first, there are different understandings of empathy depending on the disciplinary field as well as the cultural and historical setting in which empathy is discussed (Hollan and

Throop 2008; Throop 2008, 2010); second, it is not always easy to define empathy, partly because it is often unclear how empathy differs from other related concepts such as sympathy and compassion; and, finally, empathy is generally understood as the imaginative understanding of others—both cognitive and affective—that "involves discerning aspects of a [person's] [...] experiences that might otherwise go unrecognized" (Halpern 2001, 94).

In other words, empathy is a *process* that unfolds over time; it is informed by the work of the emotions to learn more about the other's emotional states and perspectives. This process requires dialogue, imagination, and affective attunement; thus, one's emotional engagement with another through talk and storytelling helps to imagine how and why the other acts or feels the way she or he does (Halpern 2001). As Clifford Geertz (1984/1974) explains, one must delve into the symbols and conceptual systems that are used by others to express themselves. Geertz warns us about the dangers of projecting one's own feelings and experiences onto others. Although Geertz's warnings were addressed primarily to anthropologists who presumed to be empathic with their subjects of study, his idea of paying attention to people's meanings in the context in which they are embodied, felt, and experienced is pertinent not only in identifying empathy but also in teaching and learning about/for empathy. Therefore, it is important that empathy is understood in the context of particular political and cultural meanings, beliefs, practices, and values (Hollan and Throop 2008; Throop 2010).

Furthermore, Rosaldo (1993/1989) emphasizes that having homologous experiences to the experiences one attempts to understand is extremely helpful. For example, a student who is overwhelmed with grief about a family or community loss can ground his or her empathetic understanding of the other's grief in his or her own suffering. On the other hand, Wikan (1992) asserts that the greatest impediment to empathy is the lack of sufficient practical knowledge of and engagement with the other's life experience (Hollan 2008). For example, a student's ability to empathize with someone from an enemy community is often overestimated, because it may be grounded in limited practical knowledge of others' lives rather than on whether members from conflict-affected communities share common life experiences.

All in all, there seem to be many complexities and ambivalences in the process of empathy, and thus imagining the other's perspective is rarely, if ever, unambiguous or uncontested (Hollan and Throop 2008). What this suggests is that empathy may have variable consequences, depending on the context in which people gain knowledge of others. Gaining empathetic insight into the life of an enemy or a perpetrator (those not being necessarily the same) may not always be considered a positively valued practice by members of one's community (Halpern and Weinstein 2004). For instance, acknowledging and empathizing with the enemy's sufferings because the other has also suffered at the hands of my community may be considered politically dangerous or even treasonous. The politics of empathy and their relation to the broader historical and political context, then, can reinforce or undermine connectedness with others. This is one of the reasons Kirmayer (2008) argues that to maintain empathic openness in the face of all obstacles to understanding requires also an ethical stance, not only an emotional and intellectual one.

Cultivating Reconciliatory Empathy in Peace Education

Let me now turn to the pitfalls and possibilities of *reconciliatory empathy* in peace education. Reconciliatory empathy is defined as both the attitude and practice that draws victim and perpetrator into shared understanding of common humanity (Halpern and Weinstein 2004). This means that the enemy or perpetrator is re-humanized, rather than viewed perennially as the "monster" who has committed unspeakable atrocities against one's community. For example, the students in peace education efforts could be the children or grandchildren of perpetrators or victims, or they could even be part of victim and perpetrator communities. The major function of reconciliatory empathy is realizing that the other is a human being like me and that I should be engaged in a renewed relationship with him/her. Reconciliatory empathy is a mutual process in which the perpetrator acknowledges the injury he/she has inflicted on the other, while the victim and his/her community chooses to rebuild their relationship and move forward in life. To have a broad impact, reconciliatory empathy has to be nurtured at various levels of life—cultural, political, social, and religious to name a few; here, I focus on the role of peace education.

Re-humanizing the other in the context of peace education could happen when students who are part of victim and perpetrator communities are explicitly engaged in educational activities and projects that provide possibilities to handle critically the difficult emotional remains of their traumatic experiences. For example, this means that in cases where both communities suffered, students learn to recognize that the other has suffered too and that he/she is also a human being; also, to empathize with one's perpetrator involves struggling to get over resentment, anger, and hatred (Gobodo-Madikizela 2008).

Needless to say, pedagogical efforts to cultivate reconciliatory empathy in peace education are fraught with pitfalls and challenges. Here I want to highlight two pitfalls. The first is promoting passive rather than active empathy in efforts to see things from someone else's perspective, namely, a benign state of empathizing with the other from a safe distance (Boler 1999), which would amount to cultivating empty or "cheap sentimentality" (Arendt 1963). In practice, this means that students simply acknowledge some generic commonalities with their enemies or perpetrators at a very superficial level, while putting aside difficult ethical and emotional questions (e.g., what it means concretely to reconcile with the other who committed atrocities against my family or my community; what one would gain by empathizing with the enemy or a perpetrator; or what the limits of empathy are) (cf. Kirmayer 2008). As Boler notes, passive empathy is deeply problematic because "in and of itself may result in no measurable change or good to others or oneself" (1999, 178), as it leads to no political action for transforming animosity and hatred into mutual understanding (see also Arendt 1963; 2006).

The second pitfall is to end up with exactly the opposite result, namely, to exacerbate feelings of anger and resentment, because students might feel they are "forced into" reconciliatory empathy (Zembylas 2015). This is why some scholars argue that teachers need to teach about/for empathy in a strategic manner (Lindquist 2004). These strategies could include developing a supportive emotional atmosphere and a trusting, open relationship between teacher and students before the difficult issue of reconciliatory empathy is introduced; being sensitive to students' personal biographies and traumatic experiences; explicitly acknowledging how the teacher and students feel about what is gained and what might be lost from empathizing with the enemy or perpetrator; emphasizing the importance of teachers and students reflecting critically on their difficult emotions, including emotional ambivalence towards reconciliatory empathy; developing a step-wise process of working with less difficult issues and moving gradually to more difficult ones in which they are asked to explore the possibility of empathizing with an enemy or perpetrator; recognizing and examining multiple perspectives and interpretations, including those of the enemy or perpetrator; and finally, using familiar active approaches such as discussion, small groups, and independent learning as short-cuts into engagement with the difficult emotions involved in the process of reconciliatory empathy.

Conclusion

Reconciliatory empathy generates a number of provocative pedagogical questions for students and teachers to explore: What enables a student to imagine well and accurately the emotional perspective of another individual, especially someone from an enemy community (who could be a perpetrator or not)? Is it ethically and politically appropriate to teach students to empathize with others who may be deemed as perpetrators, particularly in a conflict-affected setting in which the roles of victims and perpetrators are interchangeable? How does the political, historical, and educational context shape the process of teaching about/for empathy at schools in a conflict-affected society? Does a student who gets to know about the enemy's life experiences necessarily empathize with him or her? It seems clear that complex personal, interpersonal, historical, and political influences are always at play in the process of deciding whether to cultivate reconciliatory empathy with enemies or perpetrators (cf. Zembylas 2013). Researching such complexities is a significant enterprise in peace education.

References

Arendt, Hannah. 1963. *Eichmann in Jerusalem: A Report on the Banality of Evil*. New York: Viking Press.

Arendt, Hannah. 2006. *On Revolution*. New York: Penguin Books.

Bekerman, Zvi & Michalinos Zembylas. 2012. *Teaching Contested Narratives: Identity, Memory and Reconciliation in Peace Education and Beyond*. Cambridge: Cambridge University Press.

Boler, Megan. 1999. *Feeling Power: Emotions and Education*. New York: Routledge.

Burns, Robin & Robert Aspeslagh. 1996. *Three Decades of Peace Education around the World: An Anthology*. New York: Garland.

Fountain, Susan. 1999. "Peace Education in UNICEF." Working Paper. New York: UNICEF. https://www.unicef.org/lifeskills/files/PeaceEducationUNICEF.pdf.

Geertz, Clifford. 1984/1974. "From the Native's Point of View: On the Nature of Anthropological Understanding." In *Culture Theory: Essays on Mind, Self, and Emotion*, edited by Richard Shweder and Robert LeVine, 123–136. Cambridge: Cambridge University Press.

Gobodo-Madikizela, Pumla. 2008. "Empathetic Repair after Mass Trauma: When Vengeance is Arrested." *European Journal of Social Theory* 11(3): 331–350.

Halpern, Jodi. 2001. *From Detached Concern to Empathy: Humanizing Medical Practice*. New York: Oxford University Press.

Halpern, Jodi & Harvey Weinstein. 2004. "Rehumanizing the Other: Empathy and Reconciliation." *Human Rights Quarterly* 26(3): 561–583.

Hollan, Douglas. 2008. "Being There: On the Imaginative Aspects of Understanding Others and Being Understood." Ethos 36(4): 475–489.

Hollan, Douglas & Jason Throop. 2008. "Whatever Happened to Empathy? Introduction." *Ethos* 36(4): 385–401.

Jansen, Jonathan. 2009. *Knowledge in the Blood: Confronting Race and the Apartheid Past*. Stanford, CA: Stanford University Press.

Kirmayer, Laurence. 2008. "Empathy and Alterity in Cultural Psychiatry." *Ethos* 36(4): 457–474.

Lindquist, Julie. 2004. "Class Affects, Classroom Affectations: Working Through the Paradoxes of Strategic Empathy." *College English* 67(2): 187–209.

McGlynn, Claire, Michalinos Zembylas, Zvi Bekerman & Tony Gallagher, eds. 2009. *Peace Education in Conflict and Post-conflict Societies: Comparative Perspectives*. New York: Palgrave, MacMillan.

Rosaldo, Renato. 1993/1989. "Introduction: Grief and a Headhunter's Rage." In *Culture and Truth: The Remaking of Social Analysis*, edited by Renato Rosalto, 1–21. Boston: Beacon.

Salomon, Gavriel & Baruch Nevo (eds.). 2002. *Peace Education: The Concept, Principles, and Practices around the World*. Mahwah, NJ: Lawrence Erlbaum Associates.

Throop, Jason. 2008. "On the Problem of Empathy: The Case of Yap, Federated States of Micronesia." *Ethos* 36(4): 402–426.

Throop, Jason. 2010. "Latitudes of Loss: On the Vicissitudes of Empathy." *American Ethnologist* 37(4): 771–782.

Wikan, Unni. 1992. "Beyond the Worlds: The Power of Resonance." *American Ethnologist* 19(3): 460–482.

Zembylas, Michalinos. 2008. *The Politics of Trauma in Education.* New York: Palgrave Macmillan.

Zembylas, Michalinos. 2013. "The Emotional Complexities of 'Our' and 'Their' Loss: The Vicissitudes of Teaching about/for Empathy in a Conflicting Society." *Anthropology & Education Quarterly* 44(1): 19–37.

Zembylas, Michalinos. 2015. *Emotion and Traumatic Conflict: Re-claiming Healing in Education.* Oxford: Oxford University Press.

Zembylas, Michalinos, Charalambous, Constadina & Panayiota Charalambous. 2016. *Peace Education in a Conflict-Troubled Society: An Ethnographic Journey.* Cambridge: Cambridge University Press.

33

Beyond Thinking Like a Lawyer

Providing a Space for Perpetrator Studies within the Legal Classroom

Brianne McGonigle Leyh

In general, the legal classroom approaches perpetrators of mass killings, political violence, and genocide from a formalized set of rules centered on a judicial process. Law students learn not only about establishing that a crime has occurred, but also about holding the wrongdoer criminally (or sometimes civilly) accountable. Principles of liability, or theories of perpetration, provide the ways through which a court of law can find a person responsible for the crimes committed. Law students will learn all about the formal categorizations, including, for instance, direct or indirect perpetration, aiding and abetting, and command responsibility. A law student will also learn about defenses available to an accused, defenses that provide grounds for excluding responsibility, such as mental incapacity, self-defense, or duress, as well as mitigating or aggravating factors that go towards sentencing and punishment. Students learn all of these concepts by delving into primary legal sources, including treaties, legislation, and case law. They may supplement these sources by studying legal scholarship, but very little room—if any—is allocated for non-legal texts. As a result, when teaching about perpetrators of mass crimes in a legal setting, reliance on interdisciplinary sources or delving into broader discussions about perpetrators are minimal. In this regard, the legal classroom has a lot to learn from the interdisciplinary field of Perpetrator Studies, and thankfully, important steps are being taken by educators who want to broaden the idea of what it means to "think like a lawyer."

"Thinking Like a Lawyer": Emotional Detachment

When students choose the study of law, they are often reminded that their studies are training them to "think like a lawyer" because of the underlying belief amongst law professors and law practitioners that lawyers somehow think differently than the average person. But what does "thinking like a lawyer" really mean? There are countless journal articles, editorials, and blogposts dedicated to this question (Vandervelde 1996; Rapoport 2002; Natt Gantt 2007). They are similar in that they almost all stress analytical rigor, logical reasoning, and the ability to recognize and draw distinctions. They also emphasize an ability to persuasively advocate various sides of an issue, whether or not one agrees with or believes in the position one is advancing. Very often:

> [t]o "think like a lawyer" means adopting an emotionally remote, morally neutral approach to human problems and social issues; distancing oneself from the feelings and suffering of others; avoiding emotional engagement with clients and their causes; and withholding moral judgment. To think like a lawyer one must be dispassionate in analyzing a client's legal problems and options, and in developing a legal strategy for achieving the client's goals.
>
> *(Wizner 1998: 587)*

Accordingly, what often happens in the traditional classroom is an emphasis on formalistic legal rules, legal sources, remaining "emotionally remote," and adopting a "neutral approach to human problems and social issues." When teaching about perpetrators of mass crimes or serious criminality, discussions that fall outside the formal legal setting, for instance about broader ethical questions or contextual structures of inequalities, get sidelined. Because motive (the motivation behind a criminal act) is immaterial to liability, questions of why perpetrators did what they did are usually only important for purposes of sentencing. Attempts to better understand the perpetrator's background, wider issues surrounding the crime, or structural societal factors are simply not the focus. Rather, the focus is on the intent, or the mental state, of the suspect, which, unlike motive, is an element of the crime. To help clarify: many people may have motive to commit a crime, but for the most part, only the individual who possesses the necessary mental state and carries out an action leading to the crime can be held legally responsible. Students, therefore, are rarely encouraged to view the criminal acts and the person who committed them holistically or from any other standpoint than one centered on liability.

In order to objectively study a case, students are encouraged to refrain from inward moral reflections on the higher values of the law or its tensions with morality and ethics. For example, students learn that a lawyer for a property owner may not want to seek the eviction of a single mother with young children but will need to do so in order to perform the duties falling under her lawyer-client relationship. Questions about why and how social structures facilitate social exclusion (and discrimination) of the tenant are usually not seen as relevant. Students will further learn that a defense lawyer may find her client's actions morally reprehensible but must nonetheless zealously advocate on his or her behalf because of the belief that all people deserve strong legal representation. The mental health of the accused, and lack of health care services, would only get addressed in the classroom to the extent that it would affect liability or punishment. When it comes to legal issues concerning serious crimes or perpetrators of mass violence, the reasoning and approach remain largely the same.

Because the emphasis is on formal legal characterizations, analysis of case law, and approaching fact patterns "neutrally," the legal classroom becomes an environment for delving into technical and sometimes minute legal issues and debates. This environment is important because understanding legal processes, legal decision-making, and legal developments is essential for a future in the legal profession. Yet, it may also do a disservice to young legal minds because they may become too detached or distanced from the individual accused of committing horrendous acts. They may also become too technically focused and therefore less creative in their thinking or lose sight of the bigger picture. Perhaps "thinking like a lawyer" should also mean something beyond good analytical skills and the ability to distance oneself emotionally.

"Thinking Like a Lawyer": Context Matters

Thankfully, more recently, law professors, myself included, have been expanding what it means to "think like a lawyer." According to Anne-Marie Slaughter, it requires the following:

> [T]hinking with care and precision, reading and speaking with attention to nuance and detail. It means paying attention to language, but also understanding that words can have myriad meanings and can often be manipulated. It thus also means *paying attention to context and contingency*. [...]
>
> Thinking like a lawyer means *combining realism with idealism*. It means believing in the possibility and the desirability of both order and justice, and in the capacity of the law to help us achieve them. But it also means *knowing the full range of human conduct*, and understanding that grand principles will remain paper principles unless they are implemented with an eye to human incentives.
>
> *(Slaughter 2002) [emphasis added]*

Along this line of thinking, the aim of "thinking like a lawyer" requires the law to be understood within a broader context and "knowing the full range of human conduct." If this is the case, then equipping law students to view perpetrators from disciplines other than law would benefit the learning process. But how easy is it to introduce greater context into the legal classroom?

Law students in Africa, Asia, Central and South America, and Europe generally start their Bachelor of Law (LLB) directly after their secondary education and then potentially follow up with a Master of Law (LLM) [or equivalent]. These students therefore have had little or no exposure to university-level coursework in fields other than law, and the same may be the case for their professors. The growing number of liberal arts colleges around the world whose students then do additional degrees in law are therefore a welcome development. For US legal classrooms, students will already be bringing in a wide array of disciplinary backgrounds since students must first complete a minimum of a Bachelor's degree in a field other than law before they can commence their graduate-level legal education for a Juris Doctorate (JD). American legal classrooms regularly have students with degrees in political science, social science, history, economics, engineering, mathematics, literature, international relations, philosophy, business, and psychology, amongst others. This diversity of background lends itself well to introducing more interdisciplinary concepts into class discussions. Moreover, since law professors in the US have educational backgrounds in disciplines other than law, they should, at least in theory, feel comfortable introducing linkages between disciplines in order to show how another field could potentially impact legal reasoning or legal developments.

Yet, even in the American legal classroom where arguably the students and professors have broader disciplinary backgrounds, with a few exceptions, progress has been slow. This reluctance on the part of legal educators to introduce more contextual background and interdisciplinarity may be due, in large part, to the fact that in many places legal classrooms are generally geared towards training students to enter the legal profession rather than focused on legal academics as such. It results in there being only limited space for broader academic debates, even if "thinking like a lawyer" requires more.

What the Field of Perpetrator Studies Can Offer

Despite the slow progress, undoubtedly, in the last few decades there has been a greater emphasis placed on interdisciplinarity in legal classrooms all over the world. In those legal classrooms that do delve into political violence, serious criminality, or mass victimization and perpetration, Perpetrator Studies has a lot to offer precisely because of its interdisciplinary emphasis. In my experience, exposure to scholarly work and concepts from other disciplines is invaluable to legal students in order to better understand and appreciate the role of the perpetrator within his or her social environment or the legal and political backdrop of a criminal process. For instance, legal educators could introduce philosophical texts, such as those by Hannah Arendt on the trial of Adolf Eichmann and concepts of evil and pair them together with an analysis of her work and its influence on theories of international criminal law (Luban 2011). This would allow students to view their discipline from another perspective and be encouraged to question the very categorizations and labeling that they have been applying in their studies. It would allow them to grapple with tensions between morally wrong actions and legally wrong actions and assess how well the law responds to these differences. Another option would be to bring in anthropological texts focusing on the ethnographic study of cultures and/or political violence or the failure of courts to take cultural traditions into account. Books such as those written by Tim Kelsall on culture and cross-examination apply an anthro-political perspective to the trials at the Special Court for Sierra Leone (Kelsall 2009). He highlighted how the court failed to understand local culture to its detriment, negatively impacting its ability to properly charge crimes or to find a convincing means for assessing the credibility of witnesses. Likewise, research into "cultural defenses" from anthropology are now gaining attention because of the decision by the International Criminal Court to prosecute Dominic Ongwen, who was himself a former abducted child soldier, for war crimes and crimes against humanity (Eltringham 2013; Wilson 2016).

Additionally, looking at documents that prosecutors and defense attorneys at the international criminal courts and tribunals introduce into trial may be a good starting point to show how non-legal fields have tremendous importance within legal settings. At the Extraordinary Chambers in the Courts of Cambodia, for example, entire books on the history of the Khmer Rouge were entered into evidence. One such author, Professor of History, David Chandler, was called as an expert witness in the first trial to testify about the day-to-day operations of the prison where the accused worked. Other expert witnesses included Dr. Chhim Sotheara to testify on the psychological impact of the Khmer Rouge regime on the general population and Stéphane Hessel, a former French diplomat and Holocaust survivor, was called to testify on the issue of forgiveness and about his opinion of historical processes and events such as the Nuremberg Trials of Nazi war criminals. Students should learn early on how such an array of perspectives lends itself to better understanding the crimes and the perpetrators.

Beyond scholarship, Perpetrator Studies opens up other avenues of learning, including through film and other media. Film scenes can offer a visual portrayal of abstract theories and concepts taught in the legal classroom (Champoux 1999). They can be used as case study examples as well as an introduction to different cultures and histories, and they tend to work well for increasing student engagement with the written material. Introducing law students to socio-psychological studies through the documentary film *Obedience* (1969), which focuses on the famous Milgram experiments, or *Quiet Rage: The Stanford Prison Study* (1992), which documents the well-known attempt to investigate the psychological effects of perceived power, may enhance law students' understanding of the complexities behind mass perpetration. Non-documentary films may also be useful. Films such as *Im Labyrinth des Schweigens* (Ricciarelli et al. 2016) [Labyrinth of Lies] can show some of the contextual and moral issues at play when domestic systems seek to pursue the accountability of perpetrators of mass violence years after the crimes have taken place. Film footage is also a useful tool for showing the variety of approaches (or lack thereof) to how trials around the world have taken place and how they have developed over time. Issues of agency and inclusion are very important for the students to understand and critique. For example, contrasting images from the Nuremberg trials where few women played prominent roles with modern proceedings before the International Criminal Court would allow the students to discuss and debate what changes, if any, have taken place over the last 70 years.

One of the main difficulties when teaching about perpetrators in law school is creating a space for more interdisciplinary readings, methods of teaching, and discussions in the classroom. This is certainly something that I have grappled with. As in most fields, within law, there is a limited timeframe in which to convey a great deal of information and material to the students. Moreover, depending on the institutional setting, teachers may face challenges when trying to introduce the above-mentioned non-legal material, due to administrative constraints. Yet, the benefits of drawing on a broader array of sources and methods are clear. As a first step, I suggest that legal educators experiment with new approaches to teaching that go beyond primary legal sources and legal scholarship. They can show how law operates through lived experiences, where it succeeds, and where it fails. By doing so, law students will learn to "think like a lawyer" in its broader sense, embracing a variety of human experiences and contexts. They will likely become more rigorous in their analytical reasoning and more creative in their argumentation. For both students of law and legal scholars, Perpetrator Studies, which is inherently interdisciplinary, opens up great possibilities for better understanding the roles, values, and limitations of law in societies around the world.

References

Champoux, Joseph E. 1999. "Film as a Teaching Resource." *Journal of Management Inquiry* 8(2): 240–251.

Elkins, James. 1996. "Thinking Like a Lawyer: Second Thoughts." *Mercer Law Review* 47: 511, 523.

Eltringham, Nigel. 2013. "Illuminating the Broader Context: Anthropological and Historical Knowledge at the International Criminal Tribunal for Rwanda." *Journal of Royal Anthropological Institute* 19(2): 338.

Kelsall, Tim. 2009. *Culture under Cross-Examination: International Justice and the Special Court for Sierra Leone*. Cambridge: Cambridge University Press.

Luban, David. 2011. "Hannah Arendt as a Theorist of International Criminal Law." *International Criminal Law Review* 11(3): 621–641.

Natt Gantt, Larry O. 2007. "Deconstructing Thinking Like a Lawyer: Analyzing the Cognitive Components of the Analytical Mind." *Campbell Law Review* 29(3): 413.

Rapoport, Nancy B. 2002. "Is 'Thinking Like a Lawyer' Really What we Want to Teach?" *Journal of the Association of Legal Writing Directors* 1: 91.

Slaughter, Anne-Marie. 2002. "On Thinking Like a Lawyer." First printed in *Harvard Law Today*. www.princeton.edu/~slaughtr/Commentary/On%20Thinking%20Like%20a%20Lawyer.pdf.

Vandervelde, Kenneth J. 1996. *Thinking Like a Lawyer: An Introduction to Legal Reasoning*. Boulder: Westview Press.

Wilson, Richard Ashby. 2016. "Expert Evidence on Trial: Social Researchers in the International Criminal Classroom." *American Ethnologist* 43(4): 730.

Wizner, Stephan. 1998. "Is Learning to 'Think Like a Lawyer' Enough?" *Yale Law & Policy Review* 17(1): 583, 587.

Films

Obedience, Stanley Milgram, Published by Penn State Audio-Visual Services (1969).

Im Labyrinth des Schweigens [Labyrinth of Lies], Giulio Ricciarelli, Elisabeth Bartel, Martin Langer, Roman Osin and Niki Reiser, Sony Pictures Home Entertainment (2016).

Quiet Rage: The Stanford Prison Study, Philip G. Zimbardo and Ken Musen, Stanford Instructional Television Network, Distributed by Insight Media (1992).

34

The Ethics of Discomfort

Critical Perpetrator Studies and/as Education after Auschwitz

Susanne C. Knittel

In his seminal 1966 essay "Education after Auschwitz," Theodor W. Adorno writes that "[t]he premier demand upon education is that Auschwitz not happen again" (2003, 19). This opening sentence has become something of a mantra in civic education, with Auschwitz serving as a metonym not just for the Holocaust, but also for other genocides and acts of mass violence. In the essay, Adorno characterizes genocide as "the expression of an extremely powerful societal tendency" (20), and thus the imperative that Auschwitz not happen again presupposes the acknowledgment that it was not a historical aberration without precedent or analog. He refers to the Armenian genocide as a precursor to the Holocaust and to the atomic bomb as belonging to the "same historical context as genocide" (20). In order to perceive the similarities between these acts of mass violence, Adorno argues, it is necessary to study the perpetrators rather than the victims. In this sense, then, Adorno's essay can be regarded as a foundational text for Perpetrator Studies. Talking about education after Auschwitz also means talking about education *before* Auschwitz, namely the education that the perpetrators received: "One must come to know the mechanisms that render people capable of such deeds, must reveal these mechanisms to them, and strive, by awakening a general awareness of those mechanisms, to prevent people from becoming so again" (21). Thus, he continues, "the only education that has any sense at all is an education toward critical self-reflection" (ibid.).

Adorno conceives of this cultivation of critical self-awareness in Kantian terms, emphasizing the need for "autonomy," which he defines as "the power of reflection, of self-determination, of not cooperating" (23). Later (1999), he will refer to this self-critical attitude as maturity or responsibility [*Mündigkeit*] in reference to Kant's famous definition of the Enlightenment as "man's emergence from his self-imposed immaturity" [*Unmündigkeit*] (Kant [1784] 1983, 41). Education after Auschwitz, then, is a continuation of the project of Enlightenment, or rather, a return to the fundamental principle of that project, namely critique. The lack of critical self-reflection, in Adorno's view, had made it possible for something like the Holocaust to occur. The only appropriate response to this failure of the Enlightenment project is to insist on more Enlightenment. This view is supported by Michel Foucault in his response to Kant's essay. Like Adorno, Foucault seeks to decouple the Enlightenment project from a narrative of progress and teleology and instead redefines it as an attitude, a "philosophical ethos that could be described as a permanent critique of our historical era," as a particular way of relating to one's own position in history and a specific configuration of power/knowledge (Foucault 2007, 109). "Critique is the movement by which the subject gives himself the right to question truth on its effects of power and question power on its discourses of truth." It is "the art of voluntary insubordination" (47). Critique for Foucault is thus analogous to what Adorno calls autonomy. Both are predicated on a rigorous self-questioning. This process is profoundly uncomfortable because it threatens to destabilize one's own subject position, which is why Foucault associates it with what he calls "desubjectivation" [*désassujettissement*] (47). If subjectivation [*assujettissement*] is the process whereby an individual becomes a subject within a given socio-historical context, which also means being subject to specific norms, obligations, and limits, desubjectivation is the process whereby the individual can attempt to resist or to push against the limits imposed by society. The cultivation of a critical attitude is thus bound up with the questioning of limits, it is, indeed a "*limit-attitude*" (113), which, moreover, is aligned with what Foucault calls an "ethics of discomfort" (121). This is first and foremost a willingness to tolerate ambiguity and uncertainty and to question one's own assumptions and the conceptual frameworks according to which one apprehends the world. Furthermore, it has to do with a recognition of the continuities between past atrocities and present-day structures of inequality and political violence and one's own implicatedness in them.[1] This recognition is doubly uncomfortable because it entails an awareness of a certain responsibility on one's own part to resist and be critical of power and at the same time an acknowledgment of the fact that there is often very little one can do as an individual to combat structural forms of violence and injustice. The discomfort, thus, pertains on the one hand to our critical instrumentarium and on the other to our positionality and embeddedness within regimes of power/knowledge. The ethics of discomfort implies a commitment to critique and dissent but also a form of modesty regarding what one can achieve.

The ethics of discomfort pinpoints the affective dimension of education after Auschwitz. Affect has of course been a powerful tool in Holocaust and genocide education. The dominant strategies for making past atrocities relevant to young people have sought to promote identification and empathy with the victims and to elicit shock at the scale and brutality of the crimes. This is often done with photographs or archival footage, survivor testimony in the form of memoirs or recordings, or artistic or literary representations. Other popular affective strategies include visiting sites of memory and immersive experiences designed to allow students and visitors to feel (at least some approximation of) what it was like to be a victim of these atrocities. Such approaches become infinitely more complex if we shift our focus from the victims to the perpetrators.[2] What is the educational value of prompting students to imagine what it was like to be a perpetrator? Clearly, such an approach requires a great deal of careful framing and contextualization in order to avoid the potentially enormous moral and ethical pitfalls. On the one hand, there is the problem of fascination and of fetishization of the perpetrator as a figure of transgression. Another concern is that understanding the motivations of the perpetrators might in some way lead to a justification of their actions, or even an exculpation, to thinking of them as victims of the times, the system, or the prevailing ideology. Yet another pitfall is approaching them through a moralistic framework or from a position of moral superiority with today's knowledge of how things ended, which is based in hindsight. Nevertheless, there is something to be gained from an affective engagement with the figure of the perpetrator, which has to do with the ethics of discomfort. Moreover, literature and art have a crucial role to play as they can both model and elicit a productive sense of discomfort.

In what follows, I will discuss two examples of creative and critical engagements with the figure of the perpetrator: a work of literary non-fiction, Helga Schubert's *Die Welt da drinnen* (2003), and Milo Rau's *Breivik's Statement* (2012), a performance piece.

I discuss these works in terms of the concepts of empathic unsettlement and affirmative critique, respectively.[3] My aim here is to show how they are each committed to a critical perpetrator pedagogy that is informed by an ethics of discomfort.

In her 2003 book *Die Welt da drinnen* [*The World in There*], psychologist and author Helga Schubert explores the history and memory of the Nazi euthanasia program. Drawing on medical records that became available after German reunification, Schubert reconstructs the biographies of the victims and perpetrators of the euthanasia killing center Bernburg in Saxony-Anhalt. The different biographies serve as a backdrop for a discussion of the treatment of people with disabilities and the biopolitical discourses on mercy killing, prenatal diagnostics, and genetic engineering in present-day Germany. In this way, the book draws attention to the continuities between discriminatory mechanisms of the past and the present. In the final chapter, Schubert documents a visit to a secondary school in Berlin. She recounts how she gave the students a copy of Hitler's infamous 1939 decree authorizing the mercy killing of the "incurably ill" and asked them to imagine themselves as Nazi doctors and health care officials who are now tasked with implementing this decree. At first, the students struggle with the document, puzzling over its wording, which is deliberately vague and obfuscating, and hence open to interpretation. One student says that he would simply refuse to comply. Schubert reminds him that he is a Nazi administrator, and so therefore he is probably predisposed to acquiesce to orders from the *Führer*, but that he does have the choice not to comply, though this may result in him being sent to the Eastern front. In this way, Schubert makes the students aware of the scope and the limits of their own agency in this situation. While some of the students continue to refuse to think along the lines of the perpetrators, preferring to identify with the victims, others begin to discuss criteria for selection and strategies for compliance that would be in some way justifiable. The students are obviously uncomfortable with putting themselves in the shoes of the perpetrators: "We decide who lives or dies. That's a dangerous feeling. I would rather not have to think about it anymore, it sucks you in. That was 1939. There is no reason to ponder such selection criteria today" (2003, 227, my translation). This statement by one of the students points to another avoidance strategy, namely the denial of continuity. Schubert recounts how the discussion then turns to the question of disability and mental illness and the question of what makes a life worth living and who gets to decide. Through this exercise, the students begin to question their preconceived notions of disability and what Foucault would call their own position in relation to the Nazi past and their historical present. In my book (Knittel 2015), I read this as an example of what I call the historical uncanny, namely the sudden feeling of a well-known history becoming strange and unfamiliar and at the same time much closer to home than one had previously imagined. The historical uncanny refers to a disruption in one's sense of belonging to an imagined community and hence in one's identity and relationship to a shared past. In this sense, it can trigger a process of desubjectivation in Foucault's sense.

In the end, Schubert counterbalances the perpetrators' perspective with the reconstructed biographies of some of the victims, thus confronting the students again with the incommensurability of the diagnosis and murder of these patients with the reality of their lives. In asking the students and the readers to put themselves in the perpetrators' place, Schubert employs a principle that Dominick LaCapra has called "empathic unsettlement" (2001, 41). For LaCapra, empathic unsettlement describes a responsiveness or openness to the "traumatic experience of others" that does not entail the "appropriation of their experience" (41). LaCapra is primarily concerned with the role of affect in historiography relating to trauma and victimhood. For him, the principle of empathic unsettlement is designed to work against the desire for closure, redemption, and it "places in jeopardy harmonizing or spiritually uplifting accounts of extreme events from which we attempt to derive reassurance" (41–42). LaCapra does discuss the issue of perpetrator trauma as an object of empathic unsettlement, but this may in fact be too narrow a definition. As the example of Schubert shows, an empathic engagement with perpetrators may be productively unsettling in precisely the ways LaCapra describes, regardless of whether the actual perpetrators were traumatized. Returning to the question of education after Auschwitz, we can see how empathic unsettlement can be a vehicle for the kind of critical self-reflection that Adorno calls for. What makes Schubert's approach so compelling is that she creates an environment in which the students can engage critically with the mechanisms of perpetration while avoiding the aforementioned pitfalls of fascination, exculpation, relativization, and condemnation. In this way, the students' discomfort can become productive and meaningful. The space in which critique takes place is not pre-given, but must be produced.

This brings me to my second example, Milo Rau's performance piece *Breivik's Statement*, a re-enactment of the speech Anders Breivik read out at his trial in Oslo in April 2012. The hour-long speech was not broadcast in its entirety at the time, though the text was soon available on the internet. Rau was concerned that the decision to censor Breivik's speech in this way ultimately served only to fetishize it as dangerous and auratic. He felt that it was important for the public to be confronted with the words of this perpetrator not because they were exceptional or particularly outrageous, but rather because the rhetoric Breivik employed was so familiar. Indeed, after Breivik's trial, spokespeople for several of Europe's right-wing populist parties, including Geert Wilders's Party for Freedom and Christoph Blocher's Swiss People's Party, responded to his self-justification by saying that they condemned his violent actions but shared his concerns about multiculturalism and immigrants. This is a distinction Rau will not accept; for him, the violence is already inherent in the words. The purpose of re-enacting this statement was thus to demythologize it and to draw attention to the dangerous proliferation and normalization of these views. In the years since, of course, this rhetoric has become increasingly prevalent and mainstream throughout Europe and the rest of the world. In the staging, Rau takes a number of steps to dissociate Breivik's words from his persona and self-presentation. The speech is read out by the Turkish-German actress Sasha Ö. Soydan, who stands behind a lectern wearing a tracksuit and chewing gum. She looks not at the audience, but rather into a camera, which relays her image to a large screen, which occupies center stage. Such layers of mediation are typical for Rau's style and serve to heighten the awareness that this is a representation, even as the live video-feed and the physical presence of the actress produce a sense of immediacy. Soydan reads the speech in a matter-of-fact style and does not comment on the text at any point. Nor does the staging provide any cues to the audience for how they are to interpret or respond to the speech. This absence of an unambiguous interpretative frame is deliberately uncomfortable. Two days before the piece was due to premiere at the German National Theater in Weimar, the theater abruptly canceled the performance, citing concerns that it might be misconstrued as an endorsement of Breivik's views. In this way, the theater demonstrated a remarkable unwillingness to be uncomfortable and a singular lack of confidence in the critical abilities of its audience. Rau's aesthetic program is built on the principle of what I refer to as affirmative critique (Knittel 2019). If negative critique entails judgment or evaluation of an object and grants a position of aloof superiority to the critic, affirmative critique, by contrast, entails an openness and a willingness to engage with the object on its own terms. This is not the same as taking it at face value or naively assenting to its premises and demands; it is rather a form of critical questioning that also puts the subject in question. Hence, affirmation is a fundamental prerequisite for critique as Foucault defines it. Critique cannot content itself with refuting or debunking views with which it disagrees, but rather must first understand how it was that these views came to be widely held in the first place. Though it is necessary to condemn Breivik, it is not sufficient, and it does not help us understand what it is about his views that made sense to him and others like him. Affirmative critique forms part of the ethics of discomfort. As the theater's reaction to Rau's re-enactment shows, it is profoundly uncomfortable and entails a risk, one that it was clearly not prepared to take. In fact, it is a twofold risk: on the one hand, there is the risk that the affirmation will not appear critical and that the performer and director have simply reproduced a hateful speech that fails to stimulate any critical self-reflection in the audience. In order for critical self-reflection to happen, the audience must consent to be made uncomfortable. They must step out of their comfort zone and listen to the perpetrator's words, in this setting and at this moment, and re-evaluate their own position in relation to them without being told what to think. This is precisely what Kant and Adorno and Foucault mean when they define the principle of Enlightenment as a form of maturity and responsibility for one's own opinions and ideas. Rau is committed to the institution of the public sphere and to theater as an educational space. *Breivik's Statement* has been performed in theaters and other venues in many European countries and at the European Parliament. After each performance, the audience is invited to participate in a discussion about the piece and the role of art in responding to and representing political violence. The emphasis on discussion and on participation is important here since this is a fundamental function of the theater. As Hans-Thies Lehmann writes, theater is the site of a "*real gathering*, a place where a unique intersection of aesthetically organized and everyday real life takes place" (2006, 17; original italics). The theater is thus not simply a medium for the transmission of content to a recipient but rather a forum, a place of assembly, in which something is produced communally.[4] Milo Rau's approach to political theater precisely emphasizes the collaborative and open-ended nature of this negotiation. In this regard, Rau is less an author than a facilitator of an encounter both on stage and off, between the audience and the perpetrator's words.

Through their interactive and confrontational staging of encounters with the figure of the perpetrator, Schubert and Rau foster critical self-reflection and a sense of discomfort with regard to the continuities between the past and the present and our own implicatedness in structures and processes of violence, discrimination, and exploitation. Furthermore, they demonstrate the important role that artistic and creative engagements with the figure of the perpetrator have to play in civic education and in critical Perpetrator Studies.

Notes

The research and writing of this chapter was made possible in part by a VENI research grant from the Dutch Research Council (NWO). I'd like to thank Kári Driscoll for his helpful comments and suggestions on this chapter.

1 For a theorization of implicatedness see Rothberg (2013, 2019), and for a discussion of Adorno's "Education after Auschwitz" in light of current global structures of inequality and violence see Snaza (2017).
2 For further reflections on the ethical implications of teaching about perpetrators, see van Alphen (2001); Zeitlin (2004); Totten (2004); Jelitzki and Wetzel (2010); Kaiser (2010); Jinks (2016); and Beorn (2015).
3 I discuss each of these at greater length elsewhere; see Knittel (2015, 125–133) and (2019).
4 I elaborate on this point in my article about Rau's Europe Trilogy (Knittel 2016).

References

Adorno, Theodor W. 2003. "Education after Auschwitz." Translated by Henry W. Pickford. In *Can One Live after Auschwitz? – A Philosophical Reader*, edited by Rolf Tiedemann, 19–33. Cultural Memory in the Present. Stanford, CA: Stanford University Press.

Adorno, Theodor W. & Hellmuth Becker. 1999. "Education for Maturity and Responsibility." Translated by Robert French, Jem Thomas, and Dorothee Weymann. *History of the Human Sciences* 12(3): 21–34.

Beorn, Waitman Wade. 2015. "Perpetrators, Presidents, and Profiteers: Teaching Genocide Prevention and Response through Classroom Simulation." *Politics and Governance* 3(4): 72–83.

Foucault, Michel. 2007. *The Politics of Truth*. Edited by Sylvère Lotringer. Translated by Lysa Hochroth and Catherine Porter. Los Angeles, CA: Semiotext(e).

Jelitzki, Jana & Mirko Wetzel. 2010. *Über Täter und Täterinnen sprechen. Nationalsozialistische Täterschaft in der pädagogischen Arbeit von KZ-Gedenkstätten*. Berlin: Metropol.

Jinks, Rebecca. 2016. *Representing Genocide: The Holocaust as Paradigm?* London: Bloomsbury.

Kaiser, Wolf. 2010. "Nazi Perpetrators in Holocaust Education." *Teaching History* 141: 34–39.

Kant, Immanuel. [1784] 1983. "An Answer to the Question: What Is Enlightenment?" In *Perpetual Peace and Other Essays on Politics, History, and Morals*, translated and with an introduction by Ted Humphrey, 41–48. Indianapolis: Hackett.

Knittel, Susanne C. 2015. *The Historical Uncanny: Disability, Ethnicity, and the Politics of Holocaust Memory*. New York: Fordham University Press.

Knittel, Susanne C. 2016. "The Ruins of Europe: Milo Rau's Europe Trilogy and the (Re)Mediation of the Real." *Frame: Journal of Literary Studies* 29(1): 41–59.

Knittel, Susanne C. 2019. "Memory and Repetition: Reenactment as an Affirmative Critical Practice." *New German Critique* 46(2): 171–195.

LaCapra, Dominick. 2001. *Writing History, Writing Trauma*. Baltimore, MD: Johns Hopkins University Press.

Lehmann, Hans-Thies. 2006. *Postdramatic Theatre*. New York: Routledge.

Rothberg, Michael. 2013. "Multidirectional Memory and the Implicated Subject: On Sebald and Kentridge." In *Performing Memory in Art and Popular Culture*, edited by Liedeke Plate and Anneke Smelik, 39–58. London: Routledge.

Rothberg, Michael. 2019. *The Implicated Subject: Beyond Victims and Perpetrators*. Stanford, CA: Stanford University Press.

Schubert, Helga. 2003. *Die Welt da drinnen. Eine deutsche Nervenklinik und der Wahn vom "unwerten Leben."* Frankfurt am Main: Fischer.

Snaza, Nathan. 2017. "Posthuman(ist) Education and the Banality of Violence." *Parallax* 23(4): 498–511.

Totten, Samuel. 2004. *Teaching about Genocide: Issues, Approaches, and Resources*. Greenwich: IAP.

van Alphen, Ernst. 2001. "Playing the Holocaust." In *Mirroring Evil: Nazi Imagery/Recent Art*, edited by Norman L. Kleeblatt, 65–83. New York: The Jewish Museum; New Brunswick, NJ: Rutgers University Press.

Zeitlin, Froma I. 2004. "Teaching about Perpetrators." In *Teaching the Representation of the Holocaust*, edited by Marianne Hirsch and Irene Kacandes, 68–85. New York: Modern Language Association of America.

Index

The Routledge International Handbook of Perpetrator Studies

For Product Safety Concerns and Information please contact our EU representative GPSR@taylorandfrancis.com
Taylor & Francis Verlag GmbH, Kaufingerstraße 24, 80331 München, Germany

www.ingramcontent.com/pod-product-compliance
Ingram Content Group UK Ltd.
Pitfield, Milton Keynes, MK11 3LW, UK
UKHW050753180926
475701UK00007B/1014

* 9 7 8 1 0 3 2 0 8 5 7 9 1 *